EUROPE AND ENGLAND
IN THE
SIXTEENTH CENTURY

'T.A. Morris has succeeded admirably in writing a clear, accessible, and up-to-date survey of sixteenth-century European history. The text itself is clearly written and makes comprehensible some extremely complex events and phenomena.'

Mark Konnert, University of Calgary

'*Europe and England in the Sixteenth Century* is informed by the most recent and best scholarship in the field . . . I especially liked the author's strategy of using significant source materials.'

Professor Roger Schlesinger, Washington State University

'A well-written and helpful text. The balance between historiographical debate and the provision of information is good . . . and the juxtaposition of European and English history provides a valuable aid to the understanding of sixteenth-century themes.'

John Ross, Hemel Hempstead School, London

'Coverage of early-modern European history is wide-ranging and comprehensive. Particularly valuable are the summaries of historical debates at the outset of each chapter and the many tables, maps and diagrams. The book is clearly written, sensibly organized and balanced in its judgements.'

Susan Doran, St Mary's University College, Surrey

This innovative textbook uniquely combines an integrated survey of European and English history in the sixteenth century. The book is structured in three parts: the Western European Environment, the Rise of the Great Monarchies and the Crisis of the Great Monarchies. It covers political, social, religious and economic history from the late Renaissance to the end of the reigns of Elizabeth I and Philip II. It recognises the amount of common belief and interest between the British Isles and Western Europe in the century of the Reformation and Counter-Reformation and indicates how events were linked.

Key features of the book are:

- Colourful and informative biographical sketches of major figures
- Clearly structured genealogical charts, chronologies and full glossaries
- Surveys of changing historiographical debates, including contemporary issues
- Documentary exercises related to examination questions
- Lavish illustrations including maps, tables, photographs and line drawings.

Terry Morris is Director of Studies at University College School in Hampstead, North London. He has taught history to A-Level for over 25 years. He is the author of *European History, 1848–1945* (1985).

EUROPE AND ENGLAND IN THE SIXTEENTH CENTURY

T.A. MORRIS

London and New York

First published 1998
by Routledge
11 New Fetter Lane, London EC4P 4EE

Simultaneously published in the USA and Canada
by Routledge
29 West 35th Street, New York, NY 10001

Designed and typeset in Garamond 3 by 🅣 Tek-Art, Croydon, Surrey
Printed and bound in Great Britain by The Bath Press

British Library Cataloguing in Publication Data

A catalogue record for this book is available from the British Library

Library of Congress Cataloging in Publication Data

Morris, T.A. (Terence Alan), 1947
Europe and England in the sixteenth century / T.A. Morris.
    p.   cm.
Includes bibliographical references (p.   ) and index.
1. Europe–History–1517–1648.   2. Great Britain–History–Modern period–1485–   I. Title.
        D228.M58   1998
        940.2'3–dc21   97–13192
                    CIP

ISBN 0–415–15041–8 (pbk)
ISBN 0–415–15040–X (hbk)

• CONTENTS •

PART II THE RISE OF THE GREAT MONARCHIES

PART III   THE CRISIS OF THE GREAT MONARCHIES

• ILLUSTRATIONS AND SUPPORTING MATERIAL •

• INTRODUCTION •

How To Use This Book

Traditionally, the histories of England and Europe in the sixteenth century are studied separately. While such an approach may make good sense in the study of later periods, when British history and that of many continental countries developed different priorities and preoccupations, it is less easy to justify in the era of the Renaissance, the Reformation and the Counter-Reformation. Then, a variety of intellectual, economic and dynastic themes linked the affairs of the British Isles closely with those of Western Europe. This book attempts to clarify those links, and to spare the student duplication and repetition, by associating the history of sixteenth-century England with that of its nearest continental neighbours.

The coverage of so much ground dictates that the material must be presented in a concise format. The opening section of the book, therefore, sets out to define and to explain the main features of the intellectual, social and economic context in which the political events of the sixteenth century were played out. Although this section is less directly related to familiar examination questions, a thorough understanding of its contents will ensure that the student gains maximum benefit from the subsequent, examination-orientated chapters. These chapters, in their turn, provide a clear and uncluttered introduction to the major political developments of the century. While the text outlines the principal themes, much more narrative, biographical, statistical and analytical material is presented in the tables, digests and maps that accompany the text. These should not be treated merely as illustrations; they are essential

means for conveying a greater amount of information without adding to the bulk of the book. Repetition within the text is also avoided by the separate explanation of issues which are important to more than one chapter. The provision of documentary exercises also serves a dual purpose. For some time such exercises have been a central element in examination papers. Apart from providing the student with the necessary experience of such questions, the author uses documentary material here to examine areas of each topic in greater depth and detail.

The book addresses the fact that ability ranges among A level and undergraduate students are now wider than ever before. While some students will be content to limit themselves to the present text, others will wish to use it as a springboard to more advanced study. To that end, the book provides an introduction to the historiographical debates that surround each topic, together with a select bibliography of readily available works that will further enhance the student's understanding of the period.

At the same time, the book recognises the unfamiliarity to the student of very many sixteenth-century concepts. Every attempt has been made, therefore, to define contemporary terminology and to anticipate areas of confusion. Unfamiliar terms are either defined in the text when they first occur, or are indicated in bold print and defined in a glossary attached to the chapter. As a further safeguard against misunderstanding, the index at the back of the book indicates the page upon which each unfamiliar term is defined.

— PART I —

THE WESTERN EUROPEAN ENVIRONMENT

• CHAPTER ONE •

The Sixteenth Century in Context

Western Europe as a unit

The political map of Western Europe

International relations

Population

Monarchy

The nobility

The commons

Patterns of trade and commerce

'Distance, the first enemy'

The fear of the Turk

KINGDOM
OF
SCOTLAND

IRELAND

*NORTH
SEA*

KINGDOM
OF
ENGLAND

HOLLAND
ZEALAND

FLANDERS

BRANDENBURG

See also
P. 209

POLAND

SAXONY

*ATLANTIC
OCEAN*

BRITTANY

LUXEMBOURG

LORRAINE

BOHEMIA

KINGDOM
OF
FRANCE

BURGUNDY

BAVARIA

AUSTRIA

HUNGARY

SWISS
CONFED

See also
P. 189

D. OF
SAVOY

D. OF
MILAN

GENOA

REPUBLIC
OF
VENICE

OTTOMAN
EMPIRE

KINGDOM
OF
PORTUGAL

KINGDOM
OF
CASTILE

KINGDOM
OF
ARAGON

ESTATES OF THE
CHURCH

FLORENCE

KINGDOM
OF
NAPLES

See also
P. 105

SARDINIA

*MEDITERRANEAN
SEA*

SICILY

Territories of the House of Habsburg

Territories of Ferdinand of Aragon

– · – · – Boundaries of the Holy Roman Empire

European state boundaries c.1500

WESTERN EUROPE AS A UNIT

Most histories of Europe in this period deal with the continent as a whole, suggesting a unity of history, culture and economic life that did not exist in the sixteenth century. At the same time, it has become the normal practice to deal separately with the British Isles which, in this period, certainly had many cultural, economic and political ties with the opposite side of the Channel. This study presents an integrated survey of Britain and Western Europe, that part of the Continent lying west of a line from the River Elbe in eastern Germany to the Adriatic and down the east coast of Italy. East of that line lay the Ottoman Empire, whose religion, politics and culture were alien and fearful to her western neighbours. Further north, the politics of Poland, Lithuania, Muscovy and Sweden only rarely came seriously into contact with the affairs of any Western European state. When Queen Elizabeth of England sought a husband in the latter part of the century, even those Englishmen most eager for a wedding felt that proposed matches with the King of Sweden or with the Tsar of Muscovy were far too exotic to be taken seriously.

This east–west line was not impregnable. In the south, the Mediterranean was criss-crossed with traditional trade routes and with common cultural traditions that extended back into classical times. In his greatest work the outstanding French historian Fernand Braudel (*The Mediterranean and the Mediterranean World in the Age of Philip II,* 1949), made a powerful case for treating the Mediterranean as an historical entity in its own right. Yet the expansion of the Ottoman Empire weakened this unity in the course of the fifteenth and sixteenth centuries, and one of the greatest European movements of these centuries, the European Reconnaissance, began as a deliberate and conscious attempt to bypass the traditional Mediterranean axes of trade and exchange.

THE POLITICAL MAP OF WESTERN EUROPE

France, Spain and England

Within this western part of Europe, by the end of the fifteenth century, an embryonic state system had developed. It was 'embryonic' in the sense that the present political divisions of Western Europe were only vaguely discernible within it, and also in the sense that modern forms of state government and administration were only partly developed. Indeed, contemporary Western Europe displayed a wide and complex variety of political systems.

Some of the political units of Western Europe showed features of modern statehood. France, for instance, was no longer the mass of conflicting feudal interests that had made the country prey to civil wars and invasion a century earlier. In terms of territory, population and other resources, France was by 1500 the greatest state of Western Europe. A succession of strong monarchs had established a centralised kingdom ruled by the House of Valois. Even so, diversity existed within her territories in law, in language and in social customs. Although the Valois kings busily added new territories to their realm, it is certain that the populations of those territories felt themselves to be primarily Breton, Burgundian or Provençal, rather than French.

The absence of a strong national identity was even more marked in Spain. Here too a central monarchy had been created, but only by the marriage of the monarchs of the two strongest kingdoms in the peninsula. In effect, the Iberian peninsula still consisted (after the conquest of Granada) of three separate kingdoms, each the product of the various stages of the *reconquista,* the long struggle against the Moors. Aragon and Castile preserved their separate laws, customs, representative institutions and privileges deep into the sixteenth century. The independent nature of Portuguese development, despite a brief period of annexation to the Spanish crown, helps us to appreciate how different the Iberian kingdoms were from one another at the beginning of the sixteenth century. The union of the crowns of Castile and Aragon illustrates how much the shape and nature of the early sixteenth-century state were determined by the persons and policies of its rulers, rather than by any considerations of cultural, national or linguistic identity.

In many political respects the British Isles resembled the Iberian peninsula. Here, too, one realm, England, had emerged as the most populous and powerful, and a dominant monarchy was establishing itself, more or less in partnership with the aristocracy. As in the case of Portugal, another kingdom, Scotland, maintained her separate political and cultural identity. Hard as England might try to absorb Scotland, the latter was still an independent political unit at the end of the sixteenth century. Another element also existed. Ireland displayed a mixture of political forces unique in Western Europe, feudal influences existing alongside more primitive, tribal forces, often largely unrestrained by any central authority.

Italy and the Habsburg Territories

Many areas of Western Europe lacked even this degree of political consolidation. In many regions, by 1500, the age of the city state and of the modest **feudal fief** was by no means over. Northern Italy was one such area, where Milan, Florence, Venice and other states flourished under the rule of great families, whose mercantile wealth, or whose success as soldiers of fortune, had enabled them to impose their authority upon the city and its surrounding territories. In all three states, and in many smaller ones, a high degree of civic development and of cultural achievement went hand in hand with serious political instability, sufficient to put the independence of the state at risk. South of Florence the Italian peninsula was divided between the feudal kingdom of Naples and the territories of the Church. From the year 321, when the papacy was first granted the right to own land by the Emperor Constantine, it had steadily accumulated territory across central Italy. There the Pope ruled much like any other European prince. After the trauma of the papacy's temporary exile to Avignon (1309–78), this '**temporal** power' became a question of particular importance, and was regarded as an essential guarantee of the political independence of the papacy.

Political fragmentation similar to that of northern Italy was also found in the Netherlands. In the early years of the sixteenth century we must understand the Netherlands as including, not only the modern states of Belgium and the Netherlands, but also substantial areas of what is now western Germany and northern France. Here, theoretically, a form of central, political authority existed that

had no parallel in Italy. Initially, this was the authority of the Dukes of Burgundy, but with the death of Charles the Bold in 1477 the remarriage of his widow took these lands into the hands of the Habsburg dynasty. Nevertheless, the individual privileges of cities and provinces remained even stronger in the Netherlands than in Italy. Indeed, they remained so fresh and strong that attempts to subordinate them to centralised authority in the second half of the sixteenth century led to the revolt which destroyed Habsburg control over half of the Netherlands.

Since 1440 the Habsburgs had also monopolised the elective office of Holy Roman Emperor. The political authority of the dynasty thus divided into two distinct categories. On the one hand they were direct feudal overlords of their own territorial possessions, notably in Austria, the Tyrol and parts of the Netherlands. Within the Holy Roman Empire, however, they were elective lords, sworn to respect the privileges and the rights of the many territorial rulers within its boundaries. Here their rights derived, not from God, but from the consent of other princes.

The Holy Roman Empire, then, was not a state, but rather a collection of many states, united only by the theoretical authority and protection of the Emperor. It embraced traditional principalities such as Saxony and Bavaria, smaller feudal duchies such as Württemberg, and many independent cities governed by *bourgeois* **oligarchs** (Strasbourg, Nuremberg or Frankfurt) or by princes of the Church (Cologne, Magdeburg or Mainz). The idea that one prince might exercise authority over all this owed something to medieval theories about the unity of Christendom, but such an idea was extremely old-fashioned by this time. The sixteenth-century identity of the Empire owed far more to the ambition of the Habsburg dynasty in the fifteenth century.

INTERNATIONAL RELATIONS

Diplomacy

The history of diplomacy in Europe was a long one. The Church had been its pioneer, with her archbishops and cardinals officially representing her interests in their native lands. In addition, legates were dispatched from Rome to foreign courts to conduct pieces of specific and urgent business. Throughout the middle ages European ambassadors operated very much like the legates of the Church. They might be great statesmen, trusted servants of their royal master, or eminent churchmen, whose mission was to travel to a foreign court for the conduct of a specific piece of business: the declaration of war, the negotiation or ratification of a treaty, or simply an exchange of honours and assurances of friendship.

Italian city states in the mid-fifteenth century, with their increasing needs for secure alliances, began to practise a different form of diplomacy. More frequently their ambassadors operated as permanent residents in distant states, with the dual role of providing a steady flow of news and information, and of permanently and sympathetically representing the interests and values of their own state. From Italy the 'new diplomacy' spread northwards and westwards. Ferdinand and Isabella had dispatched resident ambassadors from Spain to Rome by the 1480s, and to Venice and England by the end of the century. Most other states imitated the trend over the next decade or two.

'Resident' ambassadors did not necessarily mean permanent representation. Spain sent three ambassadors to the French court in the first fifteen years of the sixteenth century, each of whom stayed between one and three years. For nine years of this period there was no Spanish ambassador in France. Sixteenth-century ambassadors could be tactless and inefficient. Dr John Man, Queen Elizabeth's ambassador to Madrid in the 1560s, cannot have helped Anglo-Spanish relations by his habit of referring to the Pope as 'a canting little monk'. Many of Man's Spanish counterparts in London were guilty of listening to the wrong rumours, of hearing what they wanted to hear, and thus of misleading their masters. A system developed in the intimate context of northern Italian politics did not always translate easily to the wider European stage, where enormous problems of distance and communications often left ambassadors without news or instructions from home for months on end.

War

Writing of the years between 1450 and 1620, J.R. Hale concluded that 'there was probably no single year throughout the period in which there was neither war nor occurrences that looked and felt remarkably like it'. States fought one another over disputed territories; factions fought each other within states over power and precedence; the common people were moved by desperate circumstances to rebel against their rulers. Even in times of nominal peace, rulers issued licences, 'letters of marque', to their seafarers to authorise them to raid the shipping of their rivals, while on land substantial bodies of mercenary soldiers travelled the Continent to find a quarrel in which they might earn their living.

As the sixteenth century opened, Western Europe was witnessing changes in the nature of warfare which some writers have perceived as a 'military revolution'. 'Before 1494', J.R. Hale stated, 'wars in Western Europe were chiefly a matter of violent housekeeping.' The English Wars of the Roses, the French struggles against Burgundy and Brittany, and the conflict in Spain which eventually brought Ferdinand and Isabella to power were all wars to decide 'who were to be the supreme landlords of the realm'. In most cases a swift and lasting conclusion was reached, and where the issue took longer to resolve the fighting tended to be sporadic and localised.

The wars of the sixteenth century became more intense and of longer duration. In part this was due to the fact that the states that fought them were now bigger and had access to greater resources. No single battle could destroy the capability of Francis I or Charles V to continue their struggles. In part, it was because the wars of the sixteenth century came increasingly to be fought over religious ideology. Protestantism in the north and west of Europe, and the Islamic advance in the east and south, provided causes which for some men were more important than life itself, and for which they would fight on, whatever the fortunes of war. Instead of short, formalised confrontations in which the fate of a dynasty could be decided in an hour, vast armies now moved at a painfully slow pace over large distances, at a cost which frequently bankrupted their masters.

A further revolutionising factor was the spread of firearms. Developing rapidly from the largely symbolic role that cannon played in the mid-fifteenth century, artillery was effective enough a hundred years later to render obsolete all medieval concepts of fortification. The development of handguns also revolutionised the infantry tactics of sixteenth-century armies. In the mid-century Venice and France both assumed that 30 per cent of their infantrymen would carry guns. By 1600 the proportion had risen to 50 per cent in France, and to 60 per cent in Spain's armies. Firearms killed more effectively, and they wounded more dangerously, as the clean sword cut gave way to the bone-shattering impact of the musket ball. Contemporaries estimated that the use of artillery increased the cost of a campaign by between 30 and 50 per cent. Firearms also hastened the death of the **chivalric** element within warfare which, by the mid-century, would rarely be seen beyond the context of the joust. The superiority of the mounted nobleman in expensive armour meant little if his opponent could shoot him down at a range of 200 yards.

In general, armies grew in size in the sixteenth century. The French government estimated that it could call upon 20,000 soldiers in 1451, 50,000 in 1558 and 68,500 in 1610. The United Provinces of the Netherlands claimed a total of 51,000 soldiers in 1607, while Charles V calculated in 1552 that he could mobilise 150,000 men throughout his Empire. Yet such figures may be misleading. It was always easier to raise such a host for defensive purposes than it was for campaigns 'out of the realm', when it was unlikely that such forces could be kept together for any length of time. It was equally unlikely that any large proportion of them would be properly trained.

Where did the troops come from? By the end of the fifteenth century only three states, France, Burgundy and Venice, had anything that might be regarded as a standing army. In each case the force numbered about 8,000–9,000 men. In Castile, the Catholic Monarchs had a reasonable substitute in the form of the forces maintained by the *Santa Hermandad*. Only as increasing foreign commitments imposed the need for permanent garrisons did Spain undertake the expense of a permanent military establishment. In the early part of the century, and for certain wars, the feudal system still supplied a substantial proportion of most armies. Magnates assembled forces made up of their own feudal tenants and other clients to maintain their own honour and prestige and to maintain their favour with the king. The king in turn often found it advantageous to provide military employment for men who had the capacity otherwise to make nuisances of themselves at home. Such feudal armies, however, were unlikely to travel willingly to distant foreign wars.

The military history of the sixteenth century was thus dominated by the mercenary, the professional fighting man, moving from war to war as his only means of legal livelihood. Little changed in the 150 years that followed the first French agreement (1474) to retain a force of 6,000 Swiss pikemen. Even the wars that we think of as great national enterprises were substantially undertaken by foreign labour. Englishmen, Frenchmen, Germans and Flemings helped Ferdinand and Isabella to capture Granada, while Englishmen, Frenchmen and Germans predominated in the armies that fought for Dutch independence. By employing such men, kings and commanders raised the cost of warfare, and further lowered its moral tone, but they avoided the social risks of arming large numbers of their own native poor, and ensured an army that would not melt away at harvest time.

POPULATION

Most of the estimates made of the population of Western Europe in the sixteenth century are educated guesswork. They are based upon isolated bodies of recorded evidence that have chanced to survive to the present day. Nevertheless, there is broad agreement over general population trends during this period.

The century and a half that preceded the opening of the sixteenth century had witnessed a major **demographic** disaster, a period of stagnation, and at last a period of slow recovery and growth in population. The disaster struck in the form of the Black Death, an extremely virulent outbreak of bubonic plague, which first reached the west in 1347, spread rapidly along the trade routes, and killed perhaps one-third of Europe's population. The deaths of so many who would have been the parents of future generations meant that more than a century passed before the population of Western Europe could begin to recover. As these figures indicate, even in the middle of the sixteenth century the population of Western Europe was still way below levels pertaining before the Black Death.

	Population (millions)		
	1340	1550	1680
France	c. 24	17	21.9
England	6	3	4.9
Netherlands	4	1.2	1.9
Spain	14	9	8.5
Italy	15	11	12
Germany	17	12	12

Source: S.J. Watts, *A Social History of Western Europe 1450–1720*

The sixteenth century saw only a modest increase in population. In general the birth-rate could not outrun the death-rate sufficiently to maintain any widely sustained growth. The most widely accepted modern estimates have assumed an average annual birth-rate of thirty-eight per thousand, and an annual death-rate in normal years of about thirty to thirty-five per thousand. By modern standards the birth-rate was low, and the most widely accepted explanation for this is the comparatively late age at which people married in the sixteenth century, between 24.5 and 26.5 years for women and two or three years older for men.

A death-rate that was roughly equal to the birth-rate in 'normal' years would bound ahead of it in the many years which were not normal. At the best of times the rate of mortality among infants and younger children remained very high. C. Cipolla has estimated that, of every 1,000 children born in Western Europe at this time, between 150 and 350 would die within a year, depending upon local conditions. A further 100 to 200 would die before they reached ten years of age. All too often such 'normal mortality' would be overshadowed by one form or another of 'catastrophic mortality'. Famines were still regularly recorded during the century, and if people did not actually starve to death

malnutrition would leave them easy victims to disease. Although the disaster of the Black Death was not repeated, epidemics of plague were still likely to occur several times in any normal life-span. London suffered plague in twenty-six years between 1543 and 1593, and Barcelona experienced seventeen epidemics between 1457 and 1590. Even when the plague did not appear there were sufficient outbreaks of typhus, dysentery or influenza ('the sweating sickness') to take a heavy toll of the population. War was the third great killer, and not only in the obvious sense of casualties on the battlefield. The indirect impact of harvests spoiled by the march and the demands of armies, and of the disease which armies were notorious for spreading, contributed significantly to European mortality.

MONARCHY

For many centuries before 1500, monarchy was the standard form of government over a very large proportion of Western Europe. Kings ruled in France, Aragon, Portugal, Castile, England and Scotland. Princes, with equal power but less territory, ruled throughout Germany and in parts of Italy, many of them acknowledging the wider overlordship of the Holy Roman Emperor, the greatest of all the European monarchs.

The institution of monarchy rested upon a mixture of at least three political principles. The principle of primogeniture, the right of the eldest son to succeed the father, was universally acknowledged. England, France and Scotland all tolerated the rule of impotent boy-kings in the sixteenth century rather than go against a principle of inheritance which in other circumstances acted as a guarantee of stability. Boys at least might be expected to grow into men. Women, on the other hand, were not seriously considered at the beginning of the sixteenth century to be capable of exercising the coercive power demanded of a monarch. Not all states followed France in formulating a Salic Law, which forbade the accession of a woman to the throne. All others, however, gave precedence to a younger prince over an older princess, and all assumed that if fate forced a female monarch upon them, then she would have to rule, as Isabella of Castile did, in cooperation with a royal husband.

Most monarchs paid at least lip-service to the theory that they were freely accepted by their subjects. Acknowledgement by the representatives of the major **estates of the realm**, the Church, the nobility and the leading citizens of the great towns, was a ritual of great importance. The King of Castile graciously received the acknowledgement of the Cortes, and English constitutional theorists even went so far as to state that the king's power was never greater than when he sat in Parliament, surrounded by the estates of his realm.

Lastly, every Western European monarch claimed divine sanction for his royal authority. Some went so far as to claim that their dynasty was directly marked out by God with the 'divine right' to rule. The kings of England and of France proved their point in elaborate ceremonies in which they sought to cure sufferers from the skin disease scrofula ('the king's evil') by the power of their touch. Lesser princes did not claim such miraculous powers, but stressed an indirect link with God in that they were the guarantors of the peace and stability that He desired on Earth. One way or another, rebellion against the monarch was widely equated with rebellion against God, especially if the rebels were unsuccessful. Rebels were thus careful to protect themselves with euphemisms, claiming that they sought to protect the prince against evil and greedy ministers. Once defeated, however, they were punished with the same deterrent ferocity as was used against heretics or blasphemers. Where the English crown developed a taste for ritual disembowelling, the French traditionally preferred to break a traitor on the wheel, or to rip him apart between four wild horses. The message to the onlooker was the same in all cases, that here was a dreadful death to atone for a dreadful crime.

To a considerable extent the king was still a warlord. It remained a primary duty to conduct the defence of the realm, and to resist encroachments upon the territories and rights of his dynasty. It was widely expected throughout the century that he would do so in person, at the head of his army, and a king who did not do so effectively might expect to have slurs cast upon his manhood by his political

enemies. It remained so important for the king to demonstrate his warlike prowess that as late as 1559 the King of France could risk his life and the whole political stability of the realm rather than shirk the challenge of the joust. The king was also the protector and enforcer of the laws of the kingdom. Of course, he held a highly privileged position within the legal structure of the realm, but he was expected to act within it. In principle, the theory stated by the English medieval lawyer Bracton would have been accepted in most of the states of Western Europe: 'The king ought to have no equal in the realm, but he ought to be subject to God and the law, since law makes the king.' The concept of unjustifiable tyranny, the arbitrary rule of a king who refused to acknowledge such limitations upon his freedom of action, was well established by 1500, and was to prove irresistibly attractive to religious rebels who differed from their monarch over the interpretation of the laws of God.

Although the monarch was in principle the protector of all his subjects, his position in practice depended very largely upon his relationship with the nobility of the realm. He confirmed them in the possession of their privileges and wealth, and they in turn guaranteed in principle that the king's laws were enforced in the distant provinces of the realm. They also provided the king with the means to make war when the need arose. The king might adapt and modify this relationship, but he could never ignore it altogether. In Castile and in France, for example, the crown made a concerted effort to exclude leading magnates from the great administrative offices of state. In compensation for this, the great noble families were left secure in the tenure of the landed estates and provincial influence which made them the essential instruments of local administration.

Another complicating factor was local particularism. By this we mean the desire of the inhabitants of the remoter provinces in the realm to preserve traditional privileges and liberties, and thereby to protect their homeland from total domination by the national monarchy. Great as were the powers of the Spanish crown in the last decade of the sixteenth century, it still had not overcome the extensive privileges claimed by the people of Aragon. The rights and privileges claimed by many of the greatest cities of Europe provided a similar complication, although the cities usually had less physical power with which to back their claims.

The picture was further complicated by the overlapping of royal authorities. The classic example of this was to be the Spanish Habsburg monarchy in the second half of the sixteenth century. An absolute monarch in Castile and in his dominions in the New World, Philip II found himself subjected throughout his reign to irksome constitutional restrictions upon his powers in Aragon, in Sicily, and most notably in the Netherlands. This overlapping occurred in another form in cases where one monarch claimed that he was the feudal superior to another, and that the 'vassal' monarch was subject in some respects to his will. The King of England maintained such claims in respect of some of the territories of the King of France throughout the century, even if they were seldom taken very seriously by the French. A more substantial example of this kind of complication is evident in Germany, where the claim of the Holy Roman Emperor to be the feudal superior of the territorial princes provided a major factor in German politics throughout the sixteenth century.

THE NOBILITY

The monarch stood at the apex of a complicated social and political hierarchy. Immediately beneath him stood the nobility, a difficult concept to define, even in the fifteenth and sixteenth centuries. In France the definition was a relatively narrow one, and thus only 1 per cent of the population could be considered 'noble'. In Castile, with its more complex gradation of nobility, as much as 10 per cent of the population claimed *hidalgo* (noble) status, although the most eminent nobles, the 'grandees', consisted of only twenty families. Nor was it clear whether nobility was a distinction bestowed by the monarch, or an independent condition enjoyed by certain families by virtue of their ancient blood-lines, a condition only a little less elevated than royalty. One way or another, noble families surrounded themselves with an array of privileges denied to lesser men. In France, Spain and elsewhere, the nobility were immune from direct taxation. Lesser privileges, such as the right to wear clothing made of certain expensive fabrics, or to wear a hat in the presence of the monarch, marked out the special status of a privileged caste.

It is easier to define the role that the nobility played. 'War, land and jurisdiction', wrote Henry Kamen, 'were the three basic and traditional aspects of nobility.' The basis of European nobility in the fifteenth century was military, and this remained substantially true in the next century. War remained so central to the mentality of the French nobility that successive kings from Charles VIII to Henry II had to provide campaigns to supply their noblemen with the honours and material rewards that came from that source alone. If they could not do so, then they ran the risk of severe domestic instability, as the Wars of Religion were to demonstrate in the second half of the century. Even in times of peace, the military mentality of the French nobility manifested itself in jousting and duelling, so important in terms of honour and of status.

The other two elements cited by Dr Kamen were closely related to each other. In all of the major monarchies of Western Europe the great nobles were substantial landowners. In France, the Dukes of Guise owned and controlled vast tracts of Lorraine, while in Castile the estates of the Marquis of Villena covered an area of some 25,000 square kilometres. His tenants totalled 150,000 and his annual income from rents was estimated in 1470 at around 100,000 ducats. Invariably, such mighty landowners were also the governors and the law-enforcers in their localities and were indispensable to the smooth administration of the realm. On the other hand, the local, feudal patronage that they exercised was often seen as a threat to the central authority of the monarch. The relationship between these **clients** and the great magnates that they followed was indeed a smaller version of the relationship between the king and his subjects. In return for their obedience and service, the clients received favour and protection. It was no easy matter for a provincial client in the fifteenth or sixteenth century to distinguish between his obligations to the monarch and those that he owed to his direct, feudal lord.

It was a peculiarity of the English hierarchy that the nobility, distinguished by their formal titles, shared this local governmental role with another element, the gentry. This landowning class lacked the formal privileges and titles of the peerage, but shared its influence in local government, as well as some of its social prestige. 'The titular peerage and upper gentry', Perez Zagorin has concluded, 'formed a practically homogeneous social body by the later sixteenth century'. In parliamentary terms, the representatives of the gentry came together with the peers of the realm, and with prominent citizens of the leading towns, to form a political class whose support and cooperation were vital to the monarch if the affairs of the realm were to run smoothly.

The relationship between this local power and the central authority of the monarch is one of the great political themes of Western European history in the sixteenth century. Speaking of the Castilian grandees, Henry Kamen has concluded that 'together they could have overwhelmed the monarchy', yet 'they were more concerned to consolidate their estates, live as beloved patriarchs among their vassals, and flex their muscles against their neighbours'. Neither nobility nor monarchy conceived of a society in which the other did not exist. At the highest social levels sixteenth-century politics were dominated by the desire to balance the interests of crown and nobility. Prestigious chivalric orders, such as the Golden Fleece in the Low Countries and the Garter in England, represented what Zagorin has described as the 'symbiotic relationship' between these two elements.

This picture is complicated in the sixteenth century by the emergence of a 'new' nobility. Increasingly, men were raised to noble status in return for service to the state, not on the battlefield, but in the council chamber, in the law courts, or even in the field of finance. The French distinction between the 'Nobility of the Sword' (*noblesse d'épée*) and the 'Nobility of the Robe' (*noblesse de robe*) became valid in all European states in the course of the sixteenth century. Inevitably, tensions existed between the 'old' and the 'new' nobility, and these became greater as the great economic trends of the sixteenth century eroded the traditional economic bases of the nobility's power. In particular, the relationship between the nobility and the rising forces of commerce and finance

aroused enormous controversy. A nobleman of Ferrara, in central Italy, spoke for many of his caste when he remarked that 'inherited wealth is more honest than earned wealth, in view of the vile gain needed to obtain the latter'. In France the great noble families distanced themselves consistently from trade, as a stain on their honour. In Spain, this prejudice broke down more easily, and noblemen argued that their honour could remain intact if they traded on a grand scale, or if they did so in the dominant role. In England, crown and nobility alike embraced the temptations of commercial profit with relatively few qualms. Thus George Talbot, 9th Earl of Shrewsbury, could boast interests by the end of the century in shipping, coal-mining, and in the manufacture of iron, steel and glass.

Finally, we must note that the Church provided another variant of nobility. In England the use of the term 'Lords Spiritual' to describe the archbishops and bishops of the realm indicated that they shared many of the traditional attributes of the lay nobility, the 'Lords Temporal'. They too enjoyed great wealth and substantial local authority in return for the services that they rendered. As the sixteenth century progressed, they also functioned more and more as servants of the temporal state. Although, in theory, distinctions of family and breeding did not apply to high Church offices, a very high proportion of such appointments clearly were made with the social and dynastic status of the candidates in mind. In England, France and Spain it would be hard to draw a clear distinction between the political status of a high churchman and that of a 'nobleman of the robe'.

THE COMMONS

The Peasantry

Sixteenth-century society in Western Europe was essentially rural. Its economic mainstays were the food and the other natural resources that came from the land. At the basis, therefore, of all the social, political and economic structures of the age stood the peasants, those who worked on and lived in the countryside.

Few of the peasants of Western Europe were serfs. East of the river Elbe it was still quite usual to find peasants on a nobleman's estate who were his private, physical property. In the west, however, different economic and political circumstances had largely eradicated serfdom, although pockets of it remained in some parts of France and in southern Germany. 'Freedom', however, was a relative term for the peasants of Western Europe. Some were the freehold owners of the land they worked and could achieve a considerable degree of prosperity. Others, probably the majority, worked land which they held from their landlord in return for certain obligations, financial or otherwise. Others had no land of their own to work, or too little to make a living from, and stayed alive mainly by hiring themselves and their families to others as wage labourers.

In most cases, therefore, the peasant worked hard for the benefit of others. This was particularly true where feudal relationships between lord and peasant tenant remained strong, and where the peasant was likely to be subject to a wide and complex series of obligations to his social superiors. Research in northern France suggests that, once all taxes and costs had been paid, the average peasant might have left some 20 per cent of his harvest for his own purposes. It was also likely that the peasant would be subject to the authority of the manorial court, which still had an important role to play in disputes over tenancies, and in disputes between tenants. In principle, the peasant might expect in return the protection and assistance of his *seigneur* in financial or legal matters, by which means the lord ensured the loyalty of his tenants.

'Agrarian revolt', wrote Marc Bloch, 'seems as inseparable from the seigneurial regime as the strike is from large-scale capitalist industry.' Under such circumstances, this can hardly seem surprising. The real surprise to the modern mind is rather how patiently the peasant bore his lot, and that he did not revolt more frequently.

The Towns

The towns of Western Europe played an important role in many of the historical developments of the period. They contributed much of the wealth and expertise that princes needed in order to control their territories. On the other hand, the towns often nurtured and spread radical political and religious ideas. They sometimes produced alternative power structures to challenge those of the great land-owners, and they sometimes provided daunting physical obstacles to the policies of their princely rulers.

In the course of the sixteenth century urban populations as a whole grew substantially. Economic prosperity was an obvious magnet, and in many parts of Western Europe the towns offered security against the disruptions that occurred beyond their walls. In general, increases in urban population were always the result of immigration from the countryside. In London, for instance, as late as the first thirty-five years of the seventeenth century, burials consistently outnumbered baptisms, yet the population continued to grow.

The majority of town dwellers were poor people, artisans, small tradesmen, labourers, not to mention beggars and vagrants. It is an anachronism, however, to think of most of them as a separate social grouping, distinct from the peasantry that inhabited the countryside. Every rural village would contain artisans, such as blacksmiths and wheelwrights, who provided minor industrial services for the populace. Equally, the towns contained many who tilled the land, either within or without the city walls. 'The country', wrote Perez Zagorin, 'reached into the towns, which contained not only fields, gardens, orchards and livestock within their limits, but often resident peasants and rural labourers, who went out to work the surrounding fields.'

In some rare cases, all the same, as in London or Paris, this urban proletariat formed a distinct political and social entity. Its members were more vulnerable than their country cousins to the economic fluctuations of the period, and could more easily gather in numbers. They thus constituted a political force which princes and city fathers ignored at their peril. The population of Paris, in particular, was to play an explosive political role on at least two occasions in the sixteenth century.

If the urban poor made only fleeting appearances on the historical stage, the *bourgeoisie*, the urban elite, the substantial citizens of the great cities,

1.1 Urban populations

	Over 100,000	50,000 to 100,000	20,000 to 50,000
In 1500			
Italy	Venice Naples	Florence Milan Palermo Bologna Verona Rome	Brescia Perugia Cremona Lecce Vicenza Piacenza Ferrara Lucca Taranto Mantua Parma Padua
Low Countries		Ghent Antwerp Brussels Lille Bruges	Ypres Amsterdam Utrecht Valenciennes Arras Douai Leyden Groningen Maastricht
Germany			Nuremberg Lübeck Hamburg Augsburg Magdeburg
Spain/Portugal		Lisbon Granada Valencia Seville	Toledo Barcelona Valladolid Jaen Burgos Cordoba Segovia Salamanca Saragossa
France	Paris	Lyon Rouen	Mulhouse Marseilles
British Isles	London		
In 1600			
Italy	Naples (280,000) Venice (148,000) Palermo (104,000) Rome (100,000) Messina (100,000)	Florence Milan Genoa Bologna Verona	Cremona Lecce Vicenza Piacenza Padua Turin Brescia Ferrara Mantua Parma Perugia Lucca Taranto
Low Countries	Antwerp	Brussels Lille	Amsterdam Utrecht Leyden Groningen Haarlem Maastricht Ghent Bruges Douai Valenciennes Arras
Germany		Hamburg Nuremberg Vienna Augsburg	Cologne Bremen Lübeck Breslau Magdeburg
Spain/Portugal	Seville Lisbon	Granada Valencia Madrid	Toledo Barcelona Valladolid Segovia Jaen Salamanca Cordoba Burgos Saragossa
France	Paris	Lyon	Rouen Aix Tours Toulouse Nantes Marseilles Orléans Poitiers Bourges Dijon Bordeaux Rennes Amiens Montpellier Caen Reims
British Isles	London		

formed a consistently influential element in contemporary politics. Contemporaries and later historians alike have found it difficult to decide how the *bourgeoisie* can be fitted into the conventional class structures of sixteenth-century Europe. Marxist historians have tended to view them as a class apart, hostile alike to the peasantry and to the national monarchies, whose growing power increasingly invaded their local, urban privileges.

In general, however, as Perez Zagorin has concluded, 'it makes little sense to speak of a class struggle between aristocracy and *bourgeoisie* in the period we are discussing'. The great cities often played an important role in the operation of the national monarchies and there was less and less conflict between their interests. London, Paris, Brussels and Naples all contained major royal courts and benefited from the patronage that they provided. Only in the Dutch Republic, after it had thrown off the authority of the Spanish crown, did many of the towns retain the privileges and the degree of independence that they had enjoyed a century earlier. Some conservative noblemen, of course, continued to protest at the adulteration of the aristocracy by men who had more money than breeding. The *bourgeoises* themselves, however, eagerly sought to convert their wealth into noble status. They took part in 'the flight from *bourgeois* status' (R. Mandrou, *Classes et luttes de classes en France au début du XVIIe siècle*, 1965) by buying land or by investing in the state through such bonds as the *juros* in Spain and the *rentes* in France. As the century progressed it also became easier to acquire positions in both local and central administration as the crown created and sold offices as a further means of meeting its desperate need for money.

PATTERNS OF TRADE AND COMMERCE

Most economic activity in Western Europe at the opening of the sixteenth century consisted of small-scale and highly localised production. Alongside this, however, there existed complex patterns of national and international commerce. The scale of this trade was to increase considerably in the course of the century, and it was to generate some vast mercantile fortunes.

Textile production, particularly the production of woollen cloth, was by a very wide margin the most important industrial activity in Europe. England and Spain boasted the finest quality of woollen cloth, but major centres of production were dotted all over the Continent. The wool guild of Florence, the *Arte della Lana*, reputedly employed 30,000 workers, and Flanders remained an important centre until the mid-century. Other forms of textile production were more largely based upon local specialisation, Italian silk production providing a prime example.

Among heavier industries, mining was the most important and the most widespread. At the opening of the century the demand for precious metals in Western Europe was largely met by silver production in the Tyrol and in Carinthia. Other metal industries were scattered far and wide. Iron was mined in parts of England and France, or imported from Sweden. Tin was mined in Cornwall, zinc and mercury in parts of Spain. Coal production played only a small part in the mining industries of the sixteenth century, and only in England and in the regions around Liège in the Low Countries were significant quantities produced.

Technological limitations placed as many restrictions upon the distribution of goods as they did upon their production. Transport overland, in particular, was hampered by the scarcity of established roads and by the poor condition of those that existed. Few great trading centres developed as a result of their location upon important land routes, although Milan owed much of its commercial prosperity to its situation close to the great passes across the Alps.

Water played a much greater role in the definition of European trade routes. Great rivers such as the Rhine, the Seine and the Meuse were dotted with great trading centres. Quicker, safer and more reliable, river transport could nevertheless be costly as towns, feudal lords and monarchs set up toll stations at regular intervals to profit from the trade that passed through their territories. Thirty-five such tolls were payable on the river Elbe, and a startling 200 were recorded along the river Loire. Sea routes also played a major role in both local and international commerce. Smaller ships plied from port to port along the coast, while larger vessels followed international routes across the North Sea, the Channel and the Bay of Biscay, especially concerned with the cloth trade. Complex and ancient trade routes crossed the Mediterranean, where oared galleys and galleasses linked European markets with those of North Africa and the Levant. The oriental spice trade depended upon these routes, as did the trade in southern Italian grain which supplied much of the Mediterranean region.

Two other factors had greatly facilitated the expansion of international trade by the beginning of the sixteenth century. One was the number of trading fairs held at regular intervals in some of Europe's great commercial centres. Medina del

Campo hosted the greatest of Spain's fairs, while Lyon became increasingly important as a meeting-place for merchants from the north and from Italy. The greatest trading centre of all by 1500, however, was Antwerp in the Low Countries, her geographical location making her accessible to merchants from virtually every region of Western Europe.

Hand in hand with these fairs went the development of an international banking system, dominated by such Italian families as the Medici and the Bonvisi, or by their German equivalents, the Welzers and the Fuggers. Their bills of exchange, their loans and their system of payments by transfer all aided large-scale international commerce freed from the inconveniences of limited money supply or the risky transport of bullion.

1.2 Trade and commerce in Western Europe

'DISTANCE, THE FIRST ENEMY'

We will only have a very imperfect understanding of the political and economic life of Western Europe in the sixteenth century unless we grasp the pace at which such affairs were conducted. Anyone with business on an international or inter-provincial scale faced problems with which we are no longer familiar. The merchant or administrator could never feel confident over the length of time taken for news, money or supplies to cover any specified route. By land, business could at best be conducted at the pace of the fastest horse, and even then was likely to be further obstructed by natural obstacles and by local political conditions. If communications by sea were sometimes quicker,

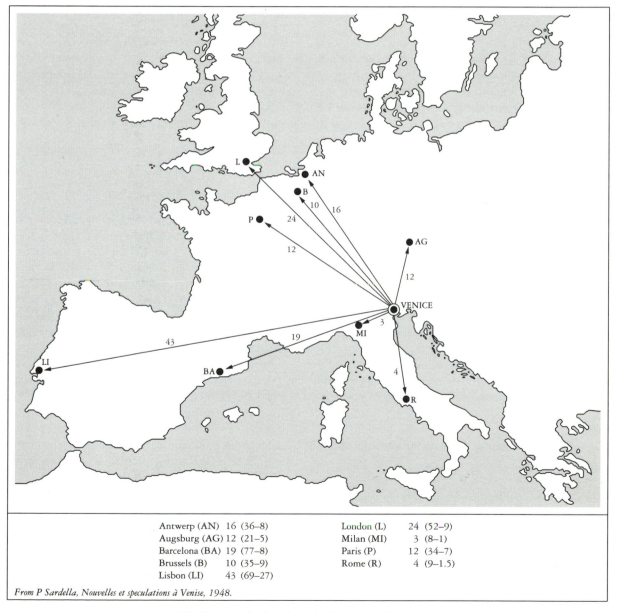

Antwerp (AN)	16 (36–8)	London (L)	24 (52–9)
Augsburg (AG)	12 (21–5)	Milan (MI)	3 (8–1)
Barcelona (BA)	19 (77–8)	Paris (P)	12 (34–7)
Brussels (B)	10 (35–9)	Rome (R)	4 (9–1.5)
Lisbon (LI)	43 (69–27)		

From P Sardella, Nouvelles et speculations à Venise, 1948.

1.3 Communication times in the sixteenth century

wind and weather made such routes even more unpredictable. On the one hand, contemporaries marvelled at the fact that Cardinal Cisneros, on a crusading campaign to North Africa in 1509, could cover the 200 kilometres from Spain in a single day's sailing. On the other, merchants and diplomats might wait for weeks on the shores of the English Channel because bad weather rendered the short passage impossible. As Fernand Braudel has written: 'In the sixteenth century all timetables were completely dependent on the weather. Irregularity was the rule.'

The map and table in illustration 1.3 are based upon the complex information network organised by the city of Venice in pursuit of its commercial interests. The first figure indicates the average number of days taken for letters to travel between a given city and Venice, while the figures in brackets show the time-span in days between the slowest and the fastest recorded journeys. Thus the long and complicated journey between Venice and Lisbon could be completed in as little as four weeks, although seven weeks was more normal, and a journey of very nearly ten weeks was not unknown.

The problems would clearly be much greater if armies, supplies or money with cumbersome escorts were in transit. This is well illustrated by the records relating to the forces regularly sent by Spain in the second half of the century from Italy, across the Alpine passes and up the Rhine valley to the Netherlands. These figures indicate no close correlation between the size of the force or the season of the year and the duration of the 680-mile journey. Unpredictability is once again the theme for these journeys.

1.4 The transit of Spanish troops to the Netherlands

Year	No. of men	Left Italy	Arrived Namur	Journey (days)
1567	10,000	20 June	15 Aug.	56
1573	5,000	4 May	15 June	42
1578	5,000	22 Feb.	27 March	32
1582	6,000	21 June	30 July	40
1584	5,000	26 April	18 June	54
1587	2,000	7 Oct.	7 Dec.	60
1591	3,000	1 Aug.	26 Sept.	57

Source: G. Parker, *The Army of Flanders and the Spanish Road*, 1972

To distance, to weather conditions, to inadequacies of transport must be added the slow pace of bureaucracy. A monarch who took his duties seriously, as Charles V did by travelling to all corners of his possessions, or as Philip II did by personally reading and replying to the bulk of official correspondence, made it inevitable that decision-making and administration would proceed at a snail's pace. The governor of the Netherlands complained (February 1575) that he had received no official communications from Spain for four months, and a viceroy of Naples joked that 'if death came from Spain I should live for ever'. Political decisions in the sixteenth century were slowly taken and slowly implemented. Very often the weighty arguments of blood, dynasty, religion and wealth were largely cancelled out by the banal considerations of distance and of time.

THE FEAR OF THE TURK

On 29 May 1453, forces of the Ottoman Turks seized Constantinople, the capital of the Byzantine Empire. The fact that a great Islamic Empire was now firmly established on the European side of the Bosporus initiated fears that would constitute part of the mental baggage of Western Europeans for at least a century and a half. In a Europe divided by issues of faith and dynasty, common hostility to and fear of the Ottoman Turks were rare unifying factors.

Inspired in part by the Islamic concept of *Jihad*, the holy war aimed at the conquest and conversion of the unbeliever, the Ottoman Turks posed the first serious threat in 600 years to the Christian integrity of Europe. Following the victories of his predecessors against the Bosnians and the Serbs, Mehmet II, 'The Conqueror', drove Ottoman power deep into European territory. Albania was conquered in 1468, and in 1479 the Venetian republic conceded control of the Balkans to the Ottomans. When Turkish forces captured Otranto, in southern Italy, in August 1480, causing the Pope himself to make preparations for flight, it must have seemed that there was no necessary limit to the Ottoman penetration of Christendom.

The respite granted by the death of Mehmet (1481) was only temporary. The accession of

Suleiman, 'The Magnificent' (1520–66), brought to power the last and greatest of the Ghazi sultans. Free from the constraints of disputed successions or domestic power struggles, Suleiman renewed the terrible prospect of Islamic conquest in Europe, capturing Belgrade in the first year of his reign, and the island fortress of Rhodes two years later. In 1526 the greatest Turkish victory since the fall of Constantinople, at the Battle of Mohacs, destroyed the independence of the Kingdom of Hungary. Vienna, the gateway to Germany and the Habsburg Empire, was first besieged by Suleiman in September 1529. By now, however, Ottoman lines of communication were stretched beyond realistic limits. Limited to a campaigning season of only a few months each year, Suleiman penetrated anew into central Europe in 1532, 1541, 1543 and 1544, but the high point of Ottoman power was passed by the time that he died on campaign in September 1566. Four generations of Europeans by this time had lived in fear of Turkish power and of the fanaticism of Islamic warriors, and the place of the 'cruel Turk' in the Western European mentality was assured.

The roots of this stereotype lay in religious differences. Centuries of crusading had firmly established Islam as the object of hatred for all good Christians. Now the Ottoman *Jihad* reversed the process and threatened to bring the rival religion to the very centre of Christendom. The division of Christendom in the course of the Reformation only aggravated the anti-Ottoman neuroses of the time. Protestant preachers with no great concern for the safety of Rome readily interpreted the Ottoman advance as the terrible judgement of God upon His corrupt servants. 'We must not be amazed', wrote one of Luther's associates, 'if God is now punishing the Christians through the Turks – for they are the rod and scourge and fury of God.'

There was also a strong element of what we would today call 'culture shock' in this fear of the Ottomans. Western European societies with shared notions of monarchy, nobility and feudal obligation received with disgust distorted reports of a society and a political hierarchy organised upon dramatically different lines. In a sense, for example, it was true that Ottoman power was based upon slavery. Under the practice of *devshirme* ('gathering'), specified numbers of boys were taken at intervals by the Ottoman authorities from the Christian regions of the empire. From these, the servants of the court, the elite Janissary troops, and the great ministers of state were raised up. For the *devshirme* boys this was very far from the 'horrible servitude' of which contemporary western writers spoke. For the sultans, this was a source of servants and subordinates who, unlike the nobles and churchmen who served western monarchs, owed all their authority and even their very lives to their royal master. The system made a fundamental contribution to the stability and the absoluteness of Ottoman power. It is not surprising, however, that it was viewed with horror by Europeans used to systems in which the ability to build dynasties upon the power and rewards of government was not limited to one family.

The meticulous and disciplined organisation of the Ottoman armies was similarly perverted into a vision of vicious barbarian hordes, ready to ravage and plunder Europe as earlier barbarians had done. Closer acquaintance with Ottoman administration did not necessarily diminish the sense of terror felt by westerners. The Austrian emissary, de Busbecq, for all his considerable experience of the Ottoman state, could still write of its power in a manner which would have been echoed by most Western Europeans at any time during the 150 years which followed the fall of Constantinople: 'The sultan stands before us with all the terror inspired by his own successes and those of his ancestors; he overruns the plains of Hungary with 200,000 horsemen; he threatens Austria; he menaces the rest of Germany. Like a thunderbolt, he smites, shatters and destroys whatever stands in his way. He roars like a lion along our frontier, seeking to break through, now here, now there.'

1.5 Glossary

Bourgeois. A French term initially indicating an inhabitant of a market town, or trading community. It has come to mean a member, usually a prosperous member, of the urban, mercantile middle classes.

Chivalry (adj. **chivalric**). The code of honour which governed the military conduct, and other aspects of courtly behaviour, of the nobility. In theory, it remained an important element in the relationship between the crown and the nobility that the former should provide the latter with the opportunity to gain honour and prestige on the battlefield ('exercising the chivalry of the realm'). In times of peace, such prestige might also be gained in formalised tournaments ('jousting'), which reproduced the challenges of the battlefield.

Client. An individual or family which has attached itself, for its own protection or benefit, to the service of a nobleman of higher rank. The political prestige and authority of a nobleman would be largely dependent upon the extent of his 'clientage'.

Demography (adj. **demographic**). The statistical study of human population.

Estates of the Realm. The major social and political interest groups within the kingdom. These had normally been formalised by the beginning of the sixteenth century into three: the Church, the nobility, and the 'Third Estate', technically the commoners, but in effect the wealthy, non-noble elements, such as the urban middle classes and the rural gentry.

Feudal. The medieval system of social and political organisation based upon the relationship between a lord and his tenants and 'vassals'. The latter usually owed military service and social allegiance to the former in return for the lord's protection. The feudal estate owned by a nobleman under this system was known as his **fief**.

Oligarchy. The form of government (e.g. within a city state) in which power is exercised by an elite group of individuals or families ('oligarchs').

Proletariat. The class(es) of society which have no other legal means of subsistence other than selling their labour. The working classes.

Seigneur. French term indicating a feudal lord, or a man's superior within the feudal system.

Temporal. (Latin: *tempus* – time). That which is subject to time and to change. In the sixteenth century the term was used to designate things of this world (e.g. political power), as opposed to spiritual things which, like God, are eternal.

Further reading

J.R. Hale. *War and Society in Renaissance Europe, 1450–1620.* Leicester, 1985.

H. Kamen. *European Society 1500-1700.* London, 1984.

H.A. Miskimin. *The Economy of Later Renaissance Europe, 1460–1600.* Cambridge, 1977.

S.J. Watts. *A Social History of Western Europe 1450–1720.* London, 1984.

P. Zagorin. *Rebels and Rulers, 1500–1600.* Cambridge, 1982.

• CHAPTER TWO •

The Intellectual Context of the Sixteenth Century

The religion of Western Europe

The Church

Themes of religious controversy

The Renaissance

Towards an Italian Renaissance

The political and intellectual impact of Humanism

The Northern Renaissance

*The crucifixion of Christ remained throughout the sixteenth century the
central intellectual and emotional image of Western European society.
A particularly harrowing example is presented in the Isenheim Altarpiece,
painted in Alsace by Matthias Grunewald between 1510 and 1515*

THE RELIGION OF WESTERN EUROPE

'The life of man', wrote the political philosopher Thomas Hobbes, 'is solitary, poor, nasty, brutish and short.' For the great majority of Western Europeans in the sixteenth century all or most of this description held good. In the midst of war, famine, plague, short life-expectancy and painful death, therefore, religion was a central fact and primary support of life.

On the face of it, Western Europe in 1500 was uniformly Christian, with the exceptions only of the Jewish colonies that survived in some cities and the last remnants of Islam in the south-eastern corner of Spain. Even before the coming of the Reformation, however, such a general truth concealed a wide range of practices. For the uneducated majority, religion probably consisted of a range of traditional, and often semi-pagan, beliefs and rituals. Keith Thomas (*Religion and the Decline of Magic*, 1971) showed in remarkable detail the role played in sixteenth- and seventeenth-century English society by astrology, witchcraft and allied beliefs, and argued that these had at least as great a hold upon the popular mind as had the orthodox teachings of the Church. On the other hand, John Bossy (*Christianity in the West, 1400–1700*, 1985) has argued that a genuine and sincere popular Christianity was widely in evidence in Western Europe during this period, and that this formed the basis for popular enthusiasm both for the Reformation and for the Counter-Reformation.

Long before 1500, the Church had developed a complex and sophisticated body of doctrine. At its centre lay the concepts of sin, forgiveness, salvation and damnation. As all humanity was descended from the original inhabitants of the Garden of Eden, Adam and Eve, so all inherited the sin that they had committed in disobeying their Creator by eating from the Tree of Knowledge. Unless one's sins were forgiven, one's inevitable fate was to be damned on the **Day of Judgement**, and condemned to the eternal torments of hell. The delights of heaven were reserved for those who died with their souls unburdened by sin. By the sixteenth century orthodox doctrine proclaimed that very few could expect to die in such a state of grace. Most would thus be obliged to purge their sin in the temporary torments of **purgatory**.

The enormous social and moral power of the Church derived from its claim to control the means of salvation. This it did partly through education, preaching and other forms of spiritual advice, but particularly through the administering of the sacraments. These may be defined as the channels by which God's grace is communicated to mortals, and according to the Catholic Church are seven in number. Four of the sacraments (baptism, confirmation, marriage and extreme unction for the dying) relate to the passage of the individual through the Christian community. The priest is so much set apart from the community of laymen that it requires a further sacrament, that of ordination, to mark his transition from laity to priesthood. The last two sacraments are directly concerned with the individual's relationship to God. Penance represents the sinner's admission of guilt and his or her atonement for it. The sacrament of the Eucharist, or the **Mass**, was probably the most holy of all. Catholic theology teaches that in the celebration of the Mass the bread and the wine become in substance, but not in form, the flesh and blood of Christ (transubstantiation). The claim that the priest had the power miraculously to reproduce the sacrifice of the crucifixion before their eyes provided one of the firmest bases for priestly authority, and such spiritual powers placed the Church in an unassailable position. In this light, we can appreciate that the claim, repeated, but not invented, by the Protestants in the course of the Reformation, that the Church did not in fact possess such extensive sacramental powers, was one of the most revolutionary claims ever postulated.

THE CHURCH

In 1500 the Pope was generally recognised as head of the Church. The fourteenth century, however, had provided two major crises of papal authority. The first had begun in 1309 when Clement V moved the seat of the Holy See from Rome to Avignon, on the borders of the territories of the King of France. For some seventy years successive Popes operated under the evident control of French monarchs, severely compromising the independent prestige of the papacy. This period became known

2.1 Erasmus and the Church

Source A It is commonly said that godliness depends on a style of clothes, a pattern of living, upon outward activities. These rituals may have come from a sense of religious zeal, but I think that serious harm has been done to Christian godliness by them. From their start they have mushroomed, and a million different types have appeared. Because of the leniency and indulgence of the popes the whole situation has been made worse. I doubt that anyone could identify Christ's image in any of these practices. It is more in keeping with Christ's ideals to consider all Christians to be of one family, one monastery, to treat everyone like a fellow canon or fellow brother, to hold baptism to be the most important religious profession. One should not dwell upon where one lives but how one lives.

From a letter from Erasmus to Servatus Roger, a friend of his youth, July 1514

Source B I strongly disagree with the people who do not want the Bible, after it has been translated into everyday language, to be read by the uneducated. Did Christ teach such complex doctrines that only a handful of theologians can understand them? Is Christianity strong in proportion to how ignorant men are of it? Royal secrets may well be best concealed, but Christ wants his mysteries told to as many as possible. I want the lowliest woman to read the Gospels and Paul's letters. I want them translated into every language so that, not only will the Scots and Irish be able to read them, but even the Turk and Saracen. I would like to hear a farmer sing scripture as he ploughs, a weaver keep time to his moving shuttle by humming the Bible.

Erasmus on the importance of translating the scriptures into the vernacular, 1516

Source C
PETER: Tell me now. Why did you attack Bologna? Was it heretical?
JULIUS: No.
PETER: Was Bentivoglio a tyrant?
JULIUS: No.
PETER: Why, then?
JULIUS: I needed the revenues.
PETER: Why did you harass Ferrara?
JULIUS: I needed it for my son.
PETER: What? Popes with wives and sons?
JULIUS: No. Sons, not wives.

as the 'Babylonian Captivity of the Church' and largely explains the neurotic concern of subsequent Popes for their freedom of political action. Even when the papacy returned to Rome (1378), some cardinals elected another 'pope' who continued to reside in Avignon. Only with the election of Martin V (1417) was this 'great schism' of the Church healed and an unchallenged papacy once more installed in Rome.

The Pope ruled over a complex hierarchy. His decrees, papal bulls, generally identified by the first few words of their Latin text, were the orders by which all major ecclesiastical decisions were made. They were also a major source of the canon law, the law of the Church which applied in spiritual matters throughout Western Europe. The closest advisers of the Pope were the **cardinals** who worked permanently in Rome in the *curia,* or papal civil service. Other cardinals represented papal interests and authority in their native states, and this combined body of cardinals performed the task of electing each Pope, usually from among their own number. Across the states of Western Europe, the Pope's authority was also delegated to archbishops and their subordinate bishops. The bishop took responsibility for the conduct of affairs in his diocese, and a number of dioceses were grouped together as an archbishop's province. The papacy claimed the right to make all such appointments, but in reality the claims of

PETER: Is it possible to get rid of a Pope, say for murder, patricide, fornication, incest, simony, sacrilege or blasphemy?

JULIUS: Add six hundred more and the answer is still 'no'. He can be deposed only for heresy, and he determines what is heresy.

PETER: [Saint] Paul did not speak of the cities he had stormed, the princes he had slaughtered, the kings he had incited to war. He spoke of shipwrecks, chains, dangers, plots. These are the glories of the Christian general.

St Peter interrogates Julius II at the gates of heaven. From *Julius Exclusus*, an anonymous satire on the papacy, attributed to Erasmus

Source D About these propositions of Luther's, to which they object. Luther has dared to cast doubts on indulgences, and others before him have made exceedingly rash statements about them. He has had the temerity to speak somewhat moderately about the power of the Roman pontiff. He has been so bold as to condemn the conclusions of St Thomas [Aquinas], which the Dominicans esteem almost more than the four Gospels. He has presumed to raise scruples about the matter of confession, a subject which the monks use perpetually for entangling the consciences of men.

From a letter from Erasmus to Albert of Brandenburg. October 1519

Source E I trust that your Holiness will not listen to the calumnies against me and Reuchlin. We are charged with being in confederacy with Luther. I have always protested against this. Neither of us has anything to do with Luther. I do not know him. I have not read his writings. I have barely glanced at a few pages.

From a letter from Erasmus to Pope Leo X, September 1520

QUESTIONS

a. Explain the following terms that appear in these documents: 'Paul's letters' (source B); 'Simony' (source C); 'Reuchlin' (source E).

b. In the light of sources C and E, summarise Erasmus's attitude towards the papacy.

c. To what extent do these documents support the view that Erasmus lacked the courage to be an effective religious reformer?

d. 'I laid a hen's egg, but Luther has hatched a bird of a very different feather.' To what extent do these sources suggest that there was, after all, common ground between Erasmus and the leading Protestant reformers?

emperors, kings and princes in this respect were often difficult to resist.

In addition to this 'secular' clergy, so called because it operated at large in the world (Latin: *seculus*) alongside the laity, there existed the 'regular' clergy, who obeyed a monastic rule (Latin: *regulus*). Monasticism involved a rejection of the values of this world, and a life of prayer and reflection, and its history was marked by a constant search for an ideal form. St Benedict (*c.*480–*c.*543), founder of the Benedictine order of monks, had laid down a strict rule embracing prayer, meditation and manual labour. A later burst of enthusiasm had produced such orders as the Carthusians (1084) and the Cistercians (1098). St Francis of Assisi founded

the Franciscan order (1209) to restress the fundamental principles of the monastic movement: poverty, prayer and preaching. Nevertheless, many monastic communities acquired lands, gifts of money and magnificent buildings, which tended to blur the original ideals of the monks' calling. Such worldliness was not only resented by laymen, but also drew persistent opposition from religious thinkers. In the century and a half before 1500, conventional monasticism was challenged by a movement known as the 'modern devotion' (*devotio moderna*). The greatest work of this movement, *The Imitation of Christ*, attributed to the German scholar Thomas à Kempis (*c.*1425), proclaimed afresh the need to follow closely the example of Christ himself by living simply, rejecting the temptations of the world, and doing good works among the needy.

Themes of religious controversy

The two most bitter arguments which split the Church in the centuries before the onset of Protestantism both centred upon the authority of the papacy. The traditional justification for the Pope's authority was the passage in St Matthew's Gospel in which Christ addressed St Peter: 'You are Peter and on this rock I will build my Church, and the powers of death shall not prevail against it. I will give you the keys to the kingdom of Heaven.' The claims of subsequent Popes to be the direct successors of St Peter were widely accepted, but the exact nature of papal authority had been the subject of much controversy.

Was the power of the Pope, for instance, purely concerned with spiritual matters, or did it also extend to temporal, political issues? While successive Popes argued that this was indeed the case, the political struggles of the fourteenth century produced a number of attacks upon this notion of the Pope's 'temporal power'. John of Paris (d.1306) and Marsilio of Padua (d.1343) both claimed that, as monarchs were ordained by God, their political authority had higher sanction than that claimed by the Pope. In *Defensor Pacis* (1324), Marsilio argued that political and spiritual authority should be strictly separated, the one left in the hands of kings and princes, and the other remaining with the Church. Taking its familiar title from a later, German advocate, Thomas Erastus, this principle of 'Erastianism' was to exercise enormous influence upon the events of the sixteenth century.

A further challenge to papal power came from within the Church itself. The 'great schism' had been resolved by a General Council of the Church, meeting at Constance; in establishing its authority, the Council issued a remarkable decree, *Sacrosancta* (1415). In it the Council claimed to be 'lawfully assembled in the Holy Spirit, representing the Catholic Church, and that therefore it has its authority immediately from Christ'. This 'conciliar theory', that in sufficiently grave circumstances the

combined wisdom of the cardinals, bishops and doctors of the Church was greater than the authority of the Pope, was an extremely radical claim. After fighting off such claims in the first half of the fifteenth century, the papacy entered the sixteenth century with a profound suspicion of such councils.

The actual teachings of the Church were also subject to controversy. These disputes too had some connection with the issue of papal authority, for a number of theologians were always ready to claim that the holy scriptures themselves were the only valid source of religious truth. Neither the Pope nor indeed a council had similar authority to define doctrine. In particular, the Church had been challenged on this score by the English theologian John Wyclif (c.1320–84), and by the Bohemian, Jan Hus (1369–1415), the latter being condemned for heresy and burned alive by the authority of the Council of Constance. Both denied that priests had an automatic power to absolve sin, and were critical of the sale of indulgences. Both disagreed with the practice whereby, in the celebration of the Mass, only the priest received both bread and wine ('Communion in both kinds'), while the laity, as evidence of their supposed spiritual inferiority, had to be content with the bread alone ('Communion in one kind'). As early as 1380, Wyclif had also attacked the doctrine of transubstantiation as a novelty without scriptural foundation. In this respect, as in many others, he anticipated the claims of Martin Luther by nearly a century and a half.

While such sophisticated doctrinal disputation was the preserve of the educated few, the Church was frequently unpopular with a larger proportion of laymen for its failure to live up to the high standards of morality and conduct which it preached to others. The sin of simony, the sale of offices within the Church, existed at all levels. An almost automatic consequence of simony was pluralism, whereby one man held a variety of offices, and was subsequently unable to take sufficient care of each of his spiritual responsibilities. Nepotism, the appointment of one's relatives to offices, was less lucrative than plain simony, but also damaged spiritual standards. Lay critics were also quick to demonstrate how the veneration of saints, and the contemporary passion for collecting and displaying relics, the bones or clothing of saints, were often motivated by the money that could be gained from such traffic. Erasmus remarked that there were enough pieces of the true cross, the cross on which Christ was crucified, for a ship to be built from them.

Finance was also at the heart of other Church practices greatly resented by the laity. Tithes, whereby each layman surrendered one-tenth of his produce or income for the support of the clergy, constituted only one of many ecclesiastical taxes. The Church courts intruded into many areas of social life, such as marriage and the making of wills. Many claimed that the clergy themselves were often in need of moral guidance. The Church's official insistence that the clergy should remain unmarried and should renounce all sexual activity proved too strict a discipline for many clerics. Complaints concerning the sexual conduct of the clergy were matched by those condemning the lack of education at the lower levels of the vocation. Priests who knew little or no Latin, who could not read the scriptures, and who were unable to preach to good effect had, by the time of Erasmus and Luther, become the main targets of anti-clerical propaganda in every country of Western Europe.

THE RENAISSANCE

The intellectual climate of the sixteenth century was a blend of these medieval currents and a great new impetus provided by the intellectual and artistic movement that had developed in Italy in the preceding 200 years. Although the word 'Renaissance' is of relatively recent origin, a small elite of remarkable contemporaries expressed the idea of a cultural reawakening or rebirth after a medieval 'dark age'. Petrarch wrote as early as the fourteenth century that he felt that he stood on the verge of a new age which would see the regeneration of cultural values and standards that had lain dormant since the fall of Rome.

The origins of the Italian Renaissance lie beyond the scope of this book. To understand the growth of the movement, however, it is important to remember the political division and weakness of contemporary Italy. The failures of successive Holy Roman Emperors to impose their authority in Italy, and the years of papal 'exile' in Avignon, caused political decentralisation and fragmentation on a scale unparalleled in Western Europe, with nearly fifty independent political units existing in Italy.

The related decline of military feudalism in Italy created in many parts of the peninsula a governing class that was no longer compelled to devote large sums of money to military expenditure. Nor did the men who governed many of Italy's city states have to maintain costly courts and lavish households. Their funds were diverted into building, and into furnishing these buildings with objects of beauty. Rather than growing out of political greatness, artistic patronage may rather have been the product of political insecurity, which led rulers to use impressive public projects as a substitute for any real security. Thus it was not in such dominant states as Milan and Naples that the greatest artistic achievements originated, but in less powerful states such as Florence and Urbino. This may have been allied to a strong sense of civic pride and local patriotism that existed in many parts of Italy. Thus many of the major cathedrals of the great Italian cities were constructed as civic projects, rather than being built solely by ecclesiastical authority as was usually the case elsewhere in Europe.

These factors coincided with the development of humanism, a movement which exercised an enormous influence upon the intellectual history of the next two centuries. Initially this term simply indicated a concern with *studia humanitatis*, human or liberal studies, as opposed to studies based upon theology. These included grammar, rhetoric, poetry, history and ethics. In the context of the Renaissance, however, humanism quickly took on a wider significance as scholars reached the conclusion that the classical world was different in its preconceptions, in its values, in its whole view of life, from the world of medieval feudalism and theocracy.

Humanism, in this sense, made its greatest progress through the work of Petrarch (Francesco Petrarca 1304–74), scholar, writer and assiduous collector of manuscripts, discovering on his travels many new works and texts, and using classical styles and techniques in both his Latin and his **vernacular** works. His contemporary Boccaccio (1313–75) also

2.2 Historical perceptions of the Renaissance

The modern perception of the Renaissance as an all-embracing intellectual movement is often attributed to the great nineteenth-century French historian Jules Michelet. Beyond its significance for art-lovers and scholars, he believed that the Renaissance 'in its full and legitimate extension, runs from Columbus to Copernicus, from Copernicus to Galileo, from the discovery of the earth to that of the heavens'. In his most famous phrase, the Renaissance was 'the discovery of the world, the discovery of man'. In short, Michelet turned what had once been viewed as a fashion in art and literature into an epoch in European history.

The Swiss historian Jacob Burckhardt (*The Civilisation of the Renaissance in Italy*, 1860) went further even than this. He made what his predecessors had seen as a renewal and a rebirth into something much more like a new departure. To Burckhardt, the Italian Renaissance was essentially the birth of the modern world. He stressed that, while art forms and architectural styles were undoubtedly borrowed from the classical past, man's new consciousness of his value as an individual was novel and radical. It produced new political organisations, a new desire to discover more of mankind's physical and geographical surroundings and, above all, a new realisation of the individualism of man.

Nevertheless, other lines of thought have emerged in more recent years which go directly against Burckhardt's vision. Some writers have refused to accept that the Renaissance constituted a clean break from the intellectual climate of the 'medieval' centuries. Etienne Gilson (*The Spirit of Medieval Philosophy*, 1936) claimed to find the Renaissance spirit of individualism in certain thinkers of the high Middle Ages, while the American scholar, C.H. Haskins (*The Renaissance of the Twelfth Century*, 1927), showed that an intimate knowledge of classical literature was to be found among scholars in medieval universities.

Recent writers have also been less willing to view history as being shaped by great currents of intellectual ideas. The prominent art historian Sir Ernst Gombrich (*In Search of Cultural History*, 1969) returned to the view that the artistic Renaissance was really little more than an artistic reaction against earlier styles. Much recent work has concentrated upon the social context of the Italian Renaissance, and especially upon the structures of patronage that provided the commissions for the great artists, writers and architects of the period. The essays collected and edited by F.W. Kent and P. Simons (*Patronage,*

Art and Society in Renaissance Italy, 1987) suggest that much of the work of Renaissance artists might be seen as a reflection of the traditional political and social needs of the great men or the cities which commissioned their work. Instead of being the incidental instruments by which the spirit of the Renaissance found the light, the Medici and the other great Italian patrons of the fifteenth and sixteenth centuries re-emerge in this research as the central figures in the story.

---

produced notable Latin works, but used classical themes in his more famous, Italian work, the *Decameron* (1348–53). Such works in the 'vulgar', native tongue set a precedent that would dominate the literature of subsequent centuries. Alongside the 'hunters' of manuscripts stood the great collectors. In later generations, many of the greatest patrons of the arts, such as Lorenzo de Medici and Pope Nicholas V, had large collections, as did a number of less illustrious Florentine citizens.

The next stage of the humanists' work was the criticism and analysis of these classical texts. Sometimes this took the form of translations from Greek, to make the texts more widely accessible to an educated public which still had little understanding of that language. Lorenzo Valla (1407–57), who translated Herodotus and Thucydides into Latin, was perhaps the most penetrating researcher, and his critical analysis of what purported to be classical documents sometimes had far-reaching effects. Valla showed that the *Donation of Constantine*, claimed to be a fourth-century document in which the Roman Emperor granted temporal powers to the papacy, could not have been written before the ninth century. Apart from its political implications, such a demonstration provided spectacular vindication of the analytical techniques routinely applied by leading humanist scholars.

TOWARDS AN ITALIAN RENAISSANCE

It was predominantly in the Tuscan city of Florence that the movement blossomed and reached maturity. The city's economy is often seen as the crucial factor in this development. The city had an unusually long traditional of mercantile prosperity, and by the middle of the thirteenth century the two mainstays of banking and trading in woollen cloth had become firmly established. As the fifteenth century progressed, the city's bankers embarked increasingly upon the profitable but risky business of making major loans to foreign princes.

Despite the absence of strong political authority in Florence, the growing influence of ruling capitalist groups, eager to emphasise their power and their benevolence towards the community, provided the conditions necessary for the city's remarkable artistic output. The Medici family dominated Florentine politics for much of the fifteenth century, Giovanni de Medici and his son Cosimo establishing their political ascendancy so successfully that Cosimo's grandson could win comparison with the great princes of Europe, and rule (1469–92) under the nickname of 'Lorenzo the Magnificent'. The guilds through which the industry and commerce of Florence were organised were also used to playing an active role in civic affairs. The Wool Guild, the Cloth Guild, the Banking Guild, and eighteen other groupings would frequently attempt to outdo each other in the erection or decoration of the cathedral and other civic institutions. The patronage of the arts thus served as an important means by which to proclaim one's arrival on the scene, or to advertise one's prominence. An outstanding example is provided by the Medici Chapel in the church of San Lorenzo. Commissioned by Lorenzo de Medici as a burial place for his family, it utilised the talents of the city's greatest architect, Brunelleschi, and of its greatest contemporary sculptor, Donatello. By the middle of the fifteenth century Florence had attained such heights of architectural and artistic magnificence as to claim the status of 'a second Rome'.

The first Italian rulers to import these Florentine styles were men whose origins were even less illustrious than those of the Medici. Sigismondo Malatesta, ruler of Rimini 1427–68, Lodovico Gonzaga, ruler of Mantua 1444–78, and Federigo da Montefeltro, ruler of Urbino 1444–82, were either *condottieri* (professional soldiers) or their close descendants. Such men had exactly the same need as the Florentines to astonish neighbours with the splendour of their cities and courts. In embracing the Renaissance in the middle of the fifteenth century, the papacy shared some of the political motives of these smaller states. The papal exile in Avignon was still a relatively fresh memory, and the prestige of the papacy had by no means recovered. Under Nicholas V (1447–55) Rome became a centre for the collection and analysis of ancient manuscripts, and a centre of architectural patronage. Of his successors on the papal throne, Sixtus IV (1471–84) undertook a series of building projects which earned him the reputation of *restaurator urbis,* the restorer of the city. Alexander VI (1492–1503) and Julius II (1503–13) presided over the richest days of the Roman Renaissance, culminating in Bramante's rebuilding of the basilica of St Peter and in the great works of Raphael and Michelangelo in the Vatican.

2.3 Artists of the Renaissance

DA VINCI, Leonardo (1452–1519). Painter and scientist. Born near Florence. Worked in Milan (1481–99), completing *The Last Supper* in S. Maria delle Grazie. Worked in Florence (1500–6), completing *Virgin and Child with S. Anne* and *Mona Lisa.* Worked in Milan (1506–13), Rome (1513–16) and in France, under the patronage of Francis I (1517–19). Also worked extensively on anatomical studies and on projects concerning bird flight, mathematics, weaponry, etc.

DONATELLO (1386–1466). Sculptor. Born Florence. Visits to Rome (1402–6 and 1431–3) excited his interest in classical forms, and he worked for twenty-five years on statuary for Florence's new cathedral. His bronze *David* (c.1434) was the first nude statue of the Renaissance, and established his reputation as the greatest fifteenth-century sculptor of the human figure. Worked in Padua (1443–53) where he executed the famous equestrian statue of the *condottiere* Gattamelata, based upon a classical Roman statue of Marcus Aurelius.

MICHELANGELO, Michelangelo Buonarroti (1475–1564). Sculptor, painter and architect. Born Caprese, Tuscany. One of the most versatile geniuses of the Renaissance. Worked as a sculptor in Rome and in Florence. His *Pietà* (1497–1500) in St Peter's and his *David* (1501–4) are widely regarded as the greatest sculptures of the 'high' Renaissance. His most famous works as a painter are the ceiling (1508–12) and the *Last Judgement* (1536–41) in the Sistine Chapel in the Vatican. As an architect, he worked substantially upon the design and rebuilding of St Peter's during the last thirty years of his life spent in Rome.

RAPHAEL, Raffaello Sanzio (1483–1520). Painter. Born Urbino. Produced much of his early work in Florence (1504–8). Worked in Rome under the patronage of Julius II from 1508, producing the famous series of frescoes in the papal apartments in the Vatican. Appointed chief architect of the new St Peter's (1514).

TITIAN, Tiziano Vecellio (1489–1576). Painter. His career centred upon Venice from *c.*1510–33. He then became court painter to Charles V (1533), producing notable portraits of the Emperor and of Philip II. Also worked in Rome (1545), producing the striking portrait *Paul III and His Grandchildren.*

The Art of the Renaissance

Although the emphasis of recent historical research has shifted, the Renaissance has often been viewed in the past primarily as an artistic movement. In this movement several generations of Italian painters and sculptors rediscovered the accuracy and sensitivity of classical art and made a succession of technical advances which raised the plastic arts to new levels of sophistication. As early as the 1540s, Giorgio Vasari distinguished distinct phases in this process: an 'early' Renaissance, represented by the lifetime of Giotto (1266–1337), a 'middle' Renaissance, best represented by Masaccio (1401–28), and a 'high' Renaissance, during which flourished Leonardo da Vinci (1452–1519), Raphael (1483–1520) and Michelangelo (1475–1564).

Modern art historians are more inclined to see Giotto's work as the 'high point in Italian Gothic art' (C.G. Nauert), and to see the work of Brunelleschi and Donatello, in architecture and in sculpture, as the true point of departure for the artistic styles that dominated sixteenth-century Europe. Giotto, nevertheless, displayed elements of the naturalism and realism universally associated with the art of the Renaissance. He was a pioneer of perspective, attempting to escape the two-dimensional flatness of medieval paintings by foreshortening, and thus portraying objects and figures as if they stood at differing distances from the viewer. Many years of research into mathematical principles lay ahead, however, before Brunelleschi could be regarded as having mastered perspective. In addition, Giotto and his contemporaries sought to convey the emotions and the humanity of their subjects. There is a world of difference between the stylised emotions of medieval saints and virgins, and the portrayal of pity, anger and fear that one sees in Giotto's frescoes in the Arena Chapel in Padua.

The fifteenth century saw extensive experimentation with these techniques of realism. The great battle scenes of Uccello (1396–1475) and the researches of the young Leonardo da Vinci into anatomy represent attempts to ensure that central figures and the spatial contexts into which they are set were wholly accurate and natural. Leonardo, in particular, left notebooks filled with his observations of nature, and a very large number of drawings and studies of the flight of birds, the formation of muscles and a host of other details for inclusion in his paintings.

The 'high' Renaissance period, from the last years of the fifteenth century, saw the development of this naturalism into what Vasari called 'the grand manner'. The figures often became larger, and it became more important that their poses, gestures, dress and composition should convey dignity, nobility and grandeur, rather than that they should be exactly true to nature. In Leonardo's *Last Supper* the gestures of the assembled disciples lead the eye to the calm figure of Christ. Michelangelo's *God Creating Adam,* on the ceiling of the Sistine Chapel, contains, in the touching index fingers of its two main figures, the most famous 'grand manner' gesture of them all. The work of such men represented the high point of Renaissance art, before it gave way to the 'mannerist' style in which self-conscious virtuosity, elegance and refinement often replaced the naturalism achieved by two centuries of Italian artists.

The distinction of being regarded as the first true Renaissance sculptor is disputed between Ghiberti (1378– 1455), famous for the remarkable bronze doors that he designed for the baptistry of Florence cathedral in 1401–25, and Donatello (1386–1466). Donatello, however, was undoubtedly the greatest fifteenth-century sculptor of the human figure. The classical influence upon Donatello is clearly seen in his equestrian statue of the Paduan *condottiere* Gattamelata, based upon that of the Roman emperor Marcus Aurelius. His *David* (*c.*1440), however, transcends the achievement of antiquity, drawing from Vasari the comment that 'the figure is so natural in its vivacity and its softness, that it is almost impossible for craftsmen to believe that it was not moulded on the living form'.

The sculpture of Donatello was only ever equalled by that of Michelangelo (1475–1564). Most of his greatest single sculptures, such as the *Pietà* in St Peter's (1498–9) and his *David* in Florence (1501–4), were completed in the early part of his career, but like Donatello he was never a slave to classical fashions. The *Pietà* is notable as a remarkable solution of novel compositional problems, while much of his later work displays a roughness of finish that has no parallel in classical sculpture.

The status of the artist developed over this period from that of an artisan, similar to any other skilled craftsman, to that of a cultural 'superstar', whose services were eagerly sought and richly rewarded by the greatest men in Europe. As Rudolf Wittkower wrote, 'it is an undeniable achievement of Renaissance artists that they raised art from the level of a mechanical to that of an intellectual occupation'. Michelangelo's close but stormy relationship with Pope Julius II has been the subject of many books and films. Leonardo da Vinci ended his days in a French château, in the service of Francis I, while Raphael married the niece of a cardinal.

Of all the visual arts of antiquity, architecture left the most visible remains to be studied and imitated. Similarly, no other art left such prestigious masterpieces to testify to the glory of the cities and dynasties which patronised the Renaissance. Both of the greatest Florentine architects of the fifteenth century, Filippo Brunelleschi (1377–1446) and Leone Battista Alberti (1404–72), owed a substantial debt to the study of classical prototypes. Brunelleschi visited Rome to study the construction of classical buildings. Upon his return to Florence, he produced the first truly neo-classical building of the Renaissance, the Ospidale degli Innocenti (1420), whose classical arcades exerted a major influence upon Florentine architecture for the next century. He also played a major role in the rebuilding of the city's cathedral, designing and constructing a dome for the building, inspired by the Pantheon in Rome, which spanned a greater space than had ever been achieved before. Alberti relied heavily on the work and experience of ancient architects, and he remained largely faithful to such Roman prototypes. In converting the church of San Francesco in Rimini into a 'Malatesta Temple' (*c.*1450), he created a façade based directly upon a Roman triumphal arch, and similar inspiration may be seen in his work at Santa Maria Novella in Florence (1458–60). In addition, Alberti was a radical theorist of architecture (*De Re Aedificatoria,* 1459). Believing that the concern of the architect should be less with individual buildings than with the creation and blending of the civic whole, he has been considered by some authorities as the first great advocate of town planning.

The last great departure in the architecture of the Italian Renaissance is represented by the work of Andrea Palladio (1518–80). He achieved his greatest fame by applying classical forms to domestic architecture. His Palazzo Chiericati in Vicenza (1550) and the nearby Villa Capra (begun in 1567) started a fashion for the application of Roman design features to domestic architecture, and particularly to country houses (the 'Palladian' villa), which was to sweep Western Europe over the next century.

In the more powerful states of Italy the Renaissance was much slower to make its impact. Venice, with its Doge elected from a rigidly defined mercantile elite, had little of the social or political fluidity of fifteenth-century Florence. Milan and Naples, one the possession of successful military adventurers and the other a feudal monarchy, lacked the range of patronage enjoyed in other states. Art, furthermore, had to wait in line while other priorities made their demands upon the resources of the ruler. Only after the usurpation of the Sforza dukes (1450) did Milan find a use for Renaissance scholarship and art. Then the *Sforziad* of Francesco Filelfo (*c.*1450) and the history of the city written by Bernardino Corio (1485) fitted neatly into the pattern of works commissioned for the greater glory of the patron. Under Ludovico Sforza (1452–1508), the state used the greater talents of Bramante and of Leonardo da Vinci. Only a generation later, with the work of Titian (1489–1576) and Tintoretto (1518–94), did the Venetian school rise to a leading position in Italian art.

THE POLITICAL AND INTELLECTUAL IMPACT OF HUMANISM

Humanism would not have excited such academic enthusiasm if it had limited itself to the collection of classical remains. Far more important was the humanists' application of what they read in classical texts to the life of their own age. Some of the greatest humanists of the fifteenth century were not only scholars, but also followed the active life of diplomats, secretaries and chancellors to the princes of Italy. Men such as the Florentine chancellors Salutati (1375–1406), Bruni (1427–44) and Bracciolini (1453–8) argued that Cicero had shown that it was the duty of the scholar and philosopher to immerse himself in the life and in the service of his state. In this 'civic humanism' they drew a further message from antiquity, arguing that the pursuit of wealth was not automatically to be condemned, for it had a valuable contribution to make to the life of the civic community. Such ideas departed some way

from the medieval Christian traditions of poverty, of the contemplative existence, and of renunciation of the world.

The greatest and most enduring political writer of the Italian Renaissance portrayed a political mentality very different from Florentine civic humanism. Niccolò Machiavelli (1469–1527) wrote at a time when brutal political reality was undermining the idealism of the Renaissance and when Italy was subjected to a succession of foreign invasions. In *The Prince* (written 1513) and *The Discourses* (published 1531), he wrote little that could properly be called political theory, but much that could serve as practical advice for rulers concerned with the continuation of their power. Machiavelli subscribed to the view that history moves in cycles. Popular, democratic government would inevitably degenerate into chaos, and to escape from this men would eventually look to a strong prince who could restore stability. In time, that prince would overreach himself, causing rebellion, and the cycle would begin over again. To maximise his tenure of power, the prince could trust only in his own authority, skill and good sense. Machiavelli therefore advised the prince to be bold in choosing his policy and to follow it ruthlessly, for attempts at compromise and conciliation lead to disaster. It is more effective for him to be feared by his subjects than loved by them. It is wise for the prince to avoid acts of tyranny, but only on the practical grounds that such acts may encourage rebellion. 'Reasons of state', a term first coined by the contemporary historian Guicciardini, replaced abstract principle as the guiding principle of the governors.

Humanism also did much to alter intellectual priorities. In imitation of such Roman writers as Plutarch and Quintilian, the greatest of the early Renaissance schoolmasters, Vittorino da Feltre (1378–1446), advocated a much broader educational syllabus, based upon Latin and Greek language and literature, music, mathematics, games, dancing and such social graces as deportment. In so doing he was preparing the way for the archetypal 'Renaissance Man', most clearly delineated by Baldassare Castiglione in his celebrated *Book of the Courtier* (1528). The spread of this humanist conception of education across Western Europe probably represents the widest cultural success achieved by the Renaissance. In the course of the late fifteenth and early sixteenth centuries a knowledge of Latin and Greek literature and philosophy became essential in the formation of public figures, rulers and administrators. Humanists were to populate the chancelleries and secretariats of every administration in Western Europe, and even women's education was to have its fervent advocates as a means of ensuring the upbringing of future generations endowed with humanist skills.

The scholars and patrons of the Renaissance attached great value to the achievements of great men. From this grew a renewed and expanded interest in the study of history. To the wealthy patron, the historian's work was of unrivalled value as proclaiming the greatness of the city to those who would never see its cathedral or other works of art. Such was the aim of Leonardo Bruni (1377–1444) whose *History of the Florentine People* was a classic example of Renaissance historiography. Such writing reached its highest level in the work of another Florentine, Francesco Guicciardini (1483–1540). His *History of Italy*, written between 1534 and 1540, was remarkable for the author's willingness to reject overtly patriotic and biased accounts by earlier writers, and to check, confirm or reject sources of historical information. The aim of his writing was to achieve factual accuracy and impartiality, in the best traditions of humanist, classical scholarship.

THE NORTHERN RENAISSANCE

Origins and Nature

By 1450 the Renaissance had barely left its Florentine cradle. Fifty years later, however, its influences were making themselves felt in most regions of Western Europe. The development of a 'Northern Renaissance' has been interpreted by historians in two conflicting ways. To Burckhardt, the Renaissance was so much an exclusively Italian phenomenon that the emergence of its characteristics elsewhere could only be explained in terms of Italian ideas being consciously imitated by less

fertile cultures. More recently, scholars have rejected this 'reception' theory. They have preferred to see northern contacts with Italy blending with native traditions of classical scholarship and with independent artistic currents to form a movement which, while clearly related to the Italian Renaissance, was not merely its direct offspring.

The spread of humanism beyond the Alps was a slow and uneven process, of which C.G. Nauert has described a complex 'model'. It involved

increasing penetration of the universities by humanists, but in subordinate positions and without significant curricular changes; the gradual rise of humanist scholars to influential positions as headmasters of Latin grammar schools; and the emergence of a number of outstanding individuals whose growing fame marks the transition of humanism from being an eccentricity to being a movement of well-placed scholars having significant influence on the cultures of the local elites.

To a limited extent, the royal and noble courts of northern Europe played a role in this process. The court of the dukes of Burgundy enjoyed a glittering period of cultural patronage in the middle of the fifteenth century. Significant roles were played elsewhere by such men as Jean de Montreuil (1354–1418), Chancellor of France, and by Humphrey, Duke of Gloucester (1391–1447), brother of Henry V of England, whose manuscript collection became the basis of that of Oxford University. All the same, Nauert stresses, such men must be seen as unusual figures in what was still an essentially medieval intellectual landscape.

There were ample contacts between Italy and northern Europe by the mid-fifteenth century to accelerate the dissemination of Italian fashions and influences. Humanist clerics travelled north to attend such councils as those at Constance (1414–18) and Basle (1431–49). Humanists also served as diplomats, as papal representatives, or simply pursued their cultural researches in the north. Thus Aeneas Sylvius served as secretary at the Habsburg court, and Polydore Vergil travelled to England to collect papal dues, and stayed to write an outstanding *History of England*. Great banking families, such as the Bardi and the Medici, established branches throughout Western Europe.

Traffic also moved freely in the opposite direction. Many northern churchmen were drawn by their duties to Rome, while an increasing number of northerners studied at the great academic centres of Bologna, Padua, Florence and Pavia. Of the first great generation of English humanist scholars, Linacre, Grocyn and Colet had all studied in Italy. The most powerful and prolific diffusers of the culture of the Renaissance were the kings of France who returned from their repeated invasions with a taste for Renaissance art and architecture, which they then disseminated in their own land.

Product

The art of the Northern Renaissance illustrates the way in which Italian influences blended with flourishing and sometimes resistant native traditions. The Netherlands in particular was the home of advanced artistic techniques which worked upon the problems of naturalism completely independently of the Italian painters of the mid-Renaissance. There, Jan van Eyck (c.1390–1441) so perfected the techniques of painting with oils that he was once believed to have invented the medium. With Roger van der Weyden (1399–1464), he provided the most powerful influence upon the greatest Dutch and Flemish artists of the High Renaissance period. Hieronymus Bosch (c.1450–1516) and Pieter Breughel (1528–69) remained faithful to the Gothic traditions of their homeland and produced work inspired by religious mysticism, medieval religious allegorical traditions and the peasant culture of the Low Countries. The outstanding German painter of the period, Albrecht Dürer (1471–1528), undertook a series of Italian tours with the specific intention of studying the work of the Italian masters and thereby enriching his own talents. Dürer became probably the greatest naturalistic artist to work north of the Alps in this period, and by maintaining the element of Gothic religious emotion in his work he emerged as a unique figure in the Renaissance as a whole.

Compared with the paintings of northern Europe, Italian architectural fashions made only slow and limited progress north of the Alps. In regions where there was little or no genuine classical architecture to study and imitate, Renaissance styles were usually only adopted by princely patrons who had visited Italy and wished to appear fashionable. Only in France, in the magnificent châteaux constructed by Francis I, may a distinct architectural style be said to have developed in northern Europe in the first half of the sixteenth century. The châteaux of Blois, Chambord and Fontainebleau in particular show the influence of Italian builders and decorators.

In one respect, however, the north led the way, and could indeed claim responsibility for the greatest single contribution of the Renaissance to modern civilisation. While printing was not actually invented in Europe at all, the innovations produced by Johann Gutenberg (c.1399–1468) in Mainz completely revolutionised the medium. The use of movable type, of metal letters instead of wooden blocks, of a new kind of ink which would adhere to metal, and of a new form of press modelled upon the winepresses of the Rhineland, were all the products of his fertile mind. From the time of the production of Gutenberg's great Bible (1452–6), the art of printing spread rapidly over Europe. Strasbourg (1460), Cologne (1464), Basle (1467) and Nuremberg (1470) all had presses by the end of the following decade. Beyond Germany, presses soon appeared in Venice (1469), Paris (1470), Utrecht (1470), Milan (1471), Lyon (1473), Valencia (1474), Louvain (1474) and London (1476). Hand-in-hand with printing, the publishing of books became a rapidly expanding industry.

Printers completed and complemented the work of earlier generations of humanists. It was now far easier to circulate a perfected and generally recognised text of some piece of classical literature, and over 1,000 copies of Plato's *Dialogues* could be printed in Florence in 1484–5, in roughly the time that it would have taken a scribe to write out one copy by hand. The range of titles thus made available also expanded astonishingly. The catalogue of books published in Florence by 1500 shows 775 titles, and Florence lagged far behind Milan (1,121 titles), Rome (2,000) and Venice (3,000) in this respect. Generally, the presses seem to have catered for a wider readership than that of humanist scholars, initially producing a preponderance of devotional works, vernacular histories and romances.

2.4 Humanists of Northern Europe

AGRICOLA, Rudolf (1444–85). Studied at Erfurt, Louvain and in Italy (1469–79). Lectured on classical literature at Heidelberg (1482). Author of *De inventione dialectica*, an attack upon scholastic philosophy in favour of humanism. A major transmitter of humanist ideas to Germany.

CELTIS, Conrad (1459–1508). Studied at Cologne and Heidelberg. Crowned poet laureate by Emperor Frederick III (1487). Visited Italy (1487–9). Professor of Poetry at Vienna (1497). Taught rhetoric at Nuremberg and Ingolstadt. Author of *Amores* (1502), a collection of Latin love poems, and enthusiast of German history. Published Tacitus' *Germania* and began a comprehensive history, *Germania illustrata*, which was incomplete at his death.

COLET, John (?1467–1519). Studied at Oxford and (1493–6) in Italy. Delivered notable lectures on St Paul's *Epistle to the Romans* (1496) in which he abandoned the traditional, scholastic interpretation of the text. Dean of St Paul's Cathedral (1505). Founder of St Paul's School (1509). Friend of More, Budé and Erasmus, he shared in their attacks upon corruption and ignorance in the Church.

MORE, Sir Thomas (1478–1535). Studied at Oxford and at Lincoln's Inn. Close personal friend of Erasmus from 1497. Author of the *Life of Richard III* (1513–18), an early masterpiece of English historiography, and of *Utopia* (1516), a social and political fantasy. In a brilliant political career, he was successively Master of Requests (1518), Speaker of the House of Commons (1523) and Lord Chancellor (1529). A consistent supporter of Catholic orthodoxy, he refused to support Henry VIII's claims to supremacy over the English Church, and was executed for treason. Canonised by the Catholic Church (1935).

REUCHLIN, Johann (1455–1522). Educated at Freiburg, Erfurt and Basle. Visited Italy (1482, 1490 and 1498). Taught at Ingolstadt and Tübingen. The foremost Hebrew scholar of his day, and author of *De rudimentis hebraicis* (1506) and *De arte cabbalistica* (1517). Subsequently involved in fierce controversy over the value and orthodoxy of Hebrew studies.

WIMPFELING, Jakob (1450–1528). Educated at Freiburg, Erfurt and Heidelberg. Rector of Heidelberg University (1481–4). Author of *Epitome rerum Germanicae* (1505), the first general history of Germany, *Isidoneus Germanicus*, a treatise on humanist education, and *Apologia pro republica Christiana*, an appeal for reform within the Church.

Humanism, Christian Humanism and Erasmus

By the first decade of the sixteenth century every major court of Western Europe had felt the impact of humanist scholarship. The imperial courts at Linz and Vienna were havens for such men, and a generation later the French humanist Jacques Amyot was to salute Francis I as 'the father of good

literature, of the study of the ancient languages, and of the neglected arts and sciences in France'. In Germany, humanists was less constrained by the requirements of court patronage. There, a fertile generation of humanists which included Rudolf Agricola, Conrad Celtis, Johann Reuchlin and Ulrich von Hutten was to develop a uniquely patriotic tone in their writings, and did much to prepare the intellectual soil of Germany for the advent of Martin Luther.

In particular, the north provided fertile soil for Christian humanism, wherein scholars applied their Latin and Greek expertise less to the study of bygone classical civilisation than to the study and correct understanding of the scriptures. Humanism, and Christian humanism in particular, provides the best example of northern Europe receiving an element of the Italian Renaissance, but then surpassing the Italian achievement. For the greatest humanist of all, and perhaps the outstanding European intellectual of the period, was a native of the Low Countries. Desiderius Erasmus (1466–1536) was born in Rotterdam, the illegitimate son of a priest. Educated in the best traditions of the *devotio moderna* by the Brethren of the Common Life, he entered the Augustinian order (1487) and the priesthood (1492). Finding little spiritual satisfaction in either calling, he sought it instead in the study of philosophy, theology and many branches of classical literature. In the twenty-seven years between leaving the monastic life (1494) and settling in Basle (1521), Erasmus lived the life of the wandering scholar, living, studying and teaching in Paris (1495–9), England (1499–1500, 1506 and 1509–14), Venice, Bologna, Brussels, Louvain and Basle. His career reads like a general synopsis of all humanist activity. He edited the works of a wide range of classical authors. He produced editions of the works of such Church Fathers as St Augustine and St Jerome. He was professor of Greek and Divinity at Cambridge, and there began his great and influential Greek edition of the New Testament, finally published in 1516. There, too, he became the friend and inspiration of a great generation of English humanists, led by John Colet and Sir Thomas More.

The list of Erasmus's own works is long and complex. He received great acclaim for his *Adages* (1500), a collection of ancient Latin proverbs chosen to display the beauties of Roman thought and of Latin style. Yet his most famous and influencial works were those inspired by his contempt for the intellectual poverty and sterility of thought that he saw around him in the teaching of the universities and of the Church. His most famous work of satire, *In Praise of Folly* (1511), is an attack upon rigidly scholastic teachers and ignorant priests and monks, who lack humanity, love and a true understanding of what they claim to impart to others.

His *Enchiridion Militis Christiani* (*Handbook of the Christian Soldier*, 1504) was equally influential. In it the author set out to explain the true nature of Christianity to ordinary men. The stress, therefore, was not upon the theoretical theology of the Church, but upon those spiritual elements at the heart of the religion, such as piety, faith and love. Erasmus was capable of striking more penetrating blows at an imperfect Church. In *Julius Exclusus*, a satire so biting that Erasmus long denied its authorship, he depicted the arrival of Pope Julius II at the gates of Heaven, and contrasted the warlike virtues proclaimed by the dead Pope with the Christian virtues demanded of him by St Peter.

Yet, if Erasmus was eager to expose error, corruption and false priorities wherever he found them, he was neither heretic nor revolutionary. He had no alternative system of ideas to propose, other than that which he believed had been available for 1500 years in the Gospels. He regarded the Church, even if corrupted in part, as one and indivisible, and held that a renewed schism would be a worse tragedy than the worst existing abuses. After presiding over the 'Indian summer' of academic humanism, he found himself out of place as the politics and the theology of the Reformation began to dominate northern European thought. Erasmus was left in the position of a conscientious objector between two warring armies. He was reviled by reformers for refusing to put his intellectual influence behind their cause, and abused by Catholics for having led the way in criticism of the Church. To the claim that 'Erasmus laid the egg that Luther hatched', he replied wearily: 'I laid a hen's egg, and Luther has hatched a bird of a very different feather.' When he died in Basle in 1536 the age of religious and ideological conflict had already replaced the age of Renaissance scholarship.

2.5 Glossary

Cardinals. Senior officials of the Catholic Church, ranking immediately below the Pope, and appointed by him to act as his senior advisers.

Day of Judgement. In Christian belief, the day on which the world ends, and on which the dead are resurrected, to be judged by God and assigned to heaven or to hell.

Mass (also **Holy Communion** or the **Eucharist**). The central rite of the Christian Church(es), celebrating Christ's sacrifice and the communion of the congregation with Him. The word 'Mass' took on particularly Catholic connotations, and was usually rejected by Protestants.

Purgatory. A place or state in which, according to Catholic doctrine, those souls which are not damned to hell are punished in order to make amends for their earthly sins. They are thus made fit to enter heaven.

Vernacular. The native language or dialect of a region or country, as opposed to a literary, learned or foreign language such as Latin or classical Greek.

Further reading

J. Bossy (1985) *Christianity in the West, 1400–1700*. Oxford.

A. Brown (1988) *The Renaissance*. London & New York.

F.W. Kent and P. Simons (eds) (1987) *Patronage, Art and Society in Renaissance Italy*. Oxford.

C.G. Nauert (1995) *Humanism and the Culture of Renaissance Europe*. Cambridge.

CHAPTER THREE

The European Reconnaissance

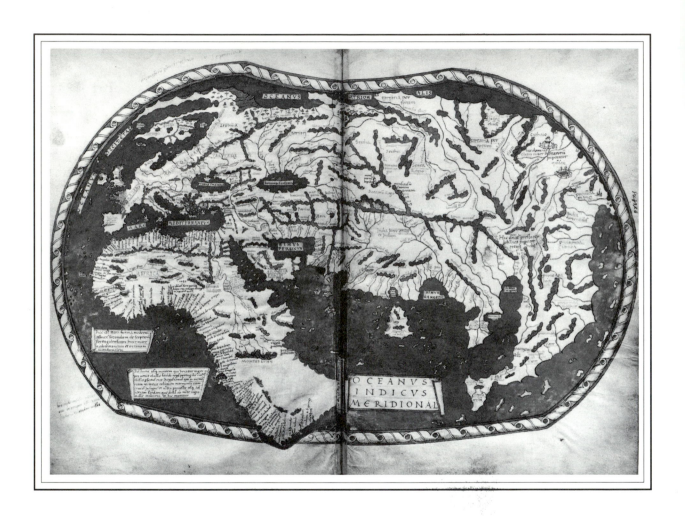

The world as Europeans believed it to be in 1500. This map, printed by Henricus Martellus about 1489, depicts Europe quite accurately, together with the west coast of Africa to its southern tip. Beyond the Cape of Good Hope, European knowledge was much less precise, and there is no sign at all of the American continent

THE HISTORICAL DEBATE

Traditionally the 'Age of Discovery' has been studied from a European angle. Contemporary accounts interpreted exploration and colonisation as expressions of European strength and supremacy. The pride with which Bernal Diaz wrote of his part in the conquest of Mexico (*History of the Conquest of New Spain*) was paralleled in Portuguese literature in *The Lusiads* (1572), in which Luiz Vas de Camoens celebrated the epic voyages of Da Gama. Richard Hakluyt (*Principal Navigations, Voyages and Discoveries of the English Nation,* 1598–1600) was equally certain that he was describing some of his countrymen's finest achievements. Such writers would all have echoed the contemporary judgement that 'the greatest event since the creation of the world (excluding the incarnation and death of Him who created it) is the discovery of the Indies'.

The long imperial histories of many European powers ensured that the European Reconnaissance continued for many centuries to be considered purely in a positive light. In many cases, the focus of the story was upon the daring deeds of the *conquistadores* themselves. They hold centre stage in the works of the great American pioneer in the field, W.H. Prescott (*History of the Conquest of Mexico,* 1843), and more recently F.A. Kirkpatrick (*The Spanish Conquistadores,* 1934) wrote with a similar emphasis. If the Reconnaissance was not viewed as the remarkable achievement of a few great individuals, then it was interpreted as a by-product of the collective greatness of contemporary European culture. It was the great nineteenth-century French historian Jules Michelet who first wrote of the Reconnaissance as a natural adjunct of the Renaissance, as 'the discovery of the world' to supplement 'the discovery of man'.

In a less confident and less imperialistic age, the Reconnaissance has often been viewed from different angles. J.H. Parry (*The Age of Reconnaissance,* 1963, and *The Spanish Seaborne Empire,* 1966) and C.R. Boxer (*The Portuguese Seaborne Empire, 1415–1825,* 1977) both wrote in the full realisation that European expansion had brought destruction and suffering, as well as profit and knowledge. In the last two or three decades, therefore, both American and European writers have paid a great deal of attention to the impact of the American discoveries upon the future development of Europe and upon those continents with which Europeans came into contact. From an American viewpoint, Walter Prescott Webb (*The Great Frontier,* 1964) has argued that the coming centuries of European greatness owed much to knowledge of the New World, to the 5,000 million hectares of land opened to European exploitation, and to the resources that could be derived from it. Since the pioneering work of E.J. Hamilton (*American Treasure and the Price Revolution in Spain,* 1934), historians have been keenly aware of the overall economic impact of the New World resources upon Europe. The primary authority in this area of research has probably been the French historian Pierre Chaunu (*European Expansion in the Later Middle Ages,* 1979), who has traced the effects of New World bullion as a stimulant not only to the policies of the Spanish government, but also to industry and commerce in western Europe as a whole.

The European Reconnaissance has been increasingly studied by non-European historians with a view to gauging its impact upon their own continents. A number of American writers have considered the fate of the aboriginal inhabitants of the continent, a line of research which has produced such classics as Lewis Hanke's *The Spanish Struggle for Justice in the Conquest of America* (1950). Asian historians, too, have begun to give their side of the story, which often sees the Reconnaissance as the beginning of an era of subjugation and exploitation. This growing school of interpretation may be represented by the work of K.M. Pannikar (*Asia and Western Dominance,* 1959), for whom the European Reconnaissance consisted primarily of 'the imposition of a commercial economy over communities whose economic life in the past had not been based upon international trade, [and] the domination of the peoples of Europe over the affairs of Asia'.

THE PORTUGUESE ACHIEVEMENT

Traditionally, European historians have dated the great 'Age of Discovery' from 1415, the year in which a Portuguese force captured the port of Ceuta on the northernmost tip of Africa. Just why this success should have sparked off the intercontinental expansion of one of Western Europe's poorest and weakest states is not clear. The traditional view, that the expansion reflected the enthusiasm of Dom Henrique, Prince Henry the Navigator, is now regarded as unsatisfactory, and many authorities have preferred to look to the increasing power and influence of the mercantile middle classes of Portugal in the late fourteenth century. These may have realised the opportunities presented by the capture of Ceuta, and consequently placed pressure upon their rulers to follow it up. It is certainly true that Ceuta was a terminus for the gold trade that crossed the Sahara, and Prince Henry proclaimed officially that one of his motives was to trace the sources of the gold supply in the African interior. Equally, he and his contemporaries claimed to be motivated by a strong crusading spirit. Above all, Henry hoped to establish contact with the fabled kingdom of Prester John, who was believed to rule a Christian kingdom in Africa, and who might have proved (had he existed) to be a valuable ally against Islam.

From his base at Sagres in the Algarve, Prince Henry dispatched regular expeditions from 1420. For a decade and a half progress was hampered by the belief that Cape Bojador was impassable. The success of Gil Eannes in rounding the cape (1434) had important consequences. A modest slave trade was established between Capes Bojador and Blanco by 1441, and in 1448 the first permanent trading post was established on the island of Arguim, in modern Senegal. Fernando Po explored the estuary of the Niger in 1471, gave his name to the large island at the river's mouth, and discovered that the African coast then turned south and ran far beyond the equator. Africa's southern extent remained a mystery until Bartholomew Dias became the first European to sail around the Cape of Good Hope (1488).

The dispatch of a fleet to India was now delayed for more than a decade, primarily because of the sensational claims of a Genoese captain that he had reached Asia by sailing westwards across the Atlantic. Once it became clear, however, that Columbus was mistaken, the Portuguese pressed home their advantages. Vasco da Gama's voyage of 1497–9 made him the first European to reach India, and opened an era of 450 years in which

Indian history was closely tied to that of Western Europe. Da Gama made navigational history in another sense. Learning from Dias that the winds and currents of the Cape made the traditional, coast-hugging form of sailing impossible, da Gama stood out into the Atlantic, accurately estimated when he would reach the latitude of the southern tip of Africa, and then cut eastward to enter the Indian Ocean. By doing so, he made a longer voyage out of sight of land than any European navigator before him.

By the end of the fifteenth century the Portuguese had built up a profitable commerce with the African territories in which they had established their bases. By 1457 the Lisbon mint was receiving sufficient bullion to produce a gold coinage for the first time in sixty years, and by the latter half of the century the fort of Elmina alone sent annual shipments to Lisbon to the value of 170,000 *dobras*. The slave trade, too, continued to flourish on these African coasts, and C.R. Boxer has estimated that some 150,000 Africans were shipped to Europe in the latter half of the fifteenth century.

THE ORIGINS OF SPANISH EXPANSION

No less surprising than the successes of Portugal is the fact that they were followed by those of Castile, which possessed few obvious qualifications for such ventures. Castile was embroiled in civil conflict until the 1470s, and had much less of a mercantile tradition than Aragon. On the other hand, southern Spain had developed a lively maritime tradition, fed by the steady immigration of seafarers from the north, from Galicia and from the Basque regions. The Canary Islands, in addition, had passed into Castilian hands by the Treaty of Alcaçovas, and were to prove to be an important staging post on a transatlantic route.

More important, Castile possessed a crusading tradition and a tradition of conquest far superior to those of Portugal. Between 1482 and 1492 the kingdom was locked in the struggle with Granada, and it cannot be purely coincidental that Queen Isabella finally agreed to Columbus's requests for financial support in the year in which the last

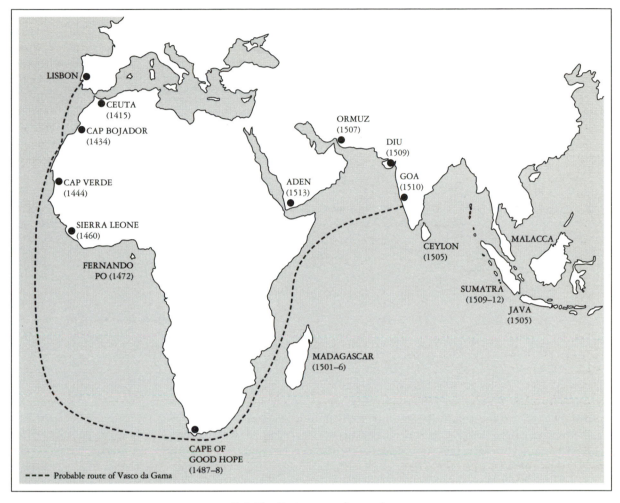

3.1 The Portuguese discoveries

Muslim stronghold in Spain finally fell. Columbus, indeed, framed his 'Enterprise of the Indies' very much in terms of a continuation of Castile's mission to spread the faith and to subjugate the infidel. In a very real sense, 'the long war against the infidel in the Peninsula was to continue against the gentile across the ocean' (F.A. Kirkpatrick). This 'Enterprise of the Indies' was based upon the assumption that the Indies could also be reached by a westward route which would not infringe any of the interests that the Portuguese had already established. Between 1492 and his death in 1506 Christopher Columbus made four voyages of exploration across the Atlantic Ocean. He struck land in the Bahamas (1492), assuming that he had landed off the mainland of Japan, and he died a disappointed man

as later, southward exploration (1498 and 1502) brought him into contact with the mainland of South America.

These disappointments were compounded by what seemed at the time to be a major diplomatic setback for Castile. Attempting to avoid an armed clash over their respective spheres of interest, Portugal and Castile concluded the Treaty of Tordesillas in 1494. Its terms broadly concurred with the papal ruling in the bull *Dudum Siquidem* (1493), whereby the respective spheres were separated by an imaginary line running north–south, 370 leagues west of the Azores. Not only did Portugal retain the monopoly of the 'true' route to the Indies, but exploration was shortly to prove that part of the South American continent also

3.2 The papacy and the New World

In the early years of the European Reconnaissance the papacy issued a succession of bulls granting privileges to the crowns of Portugal and of Castile in respect of their new territories.

Dum Diversas	1452	Granted to the crown of Portugal the lands, property and persons of all the unbelievers that they encountered on their voyages.
Romanus Pontifex	1455	Granted a monopoly to the crown of Portugal over all the lands, sea routes and trade in regions already explored or still to be discovered.
Inter Caetera	1456	Granted spiritual jurisdiction over all colonised territories to religious orders under the control of the crown of Portugal.
Dudum Sequidem	1493	Alexander VI proposed a division between Castilian and Portuguese spheres of interest based upon an imaginary line 370 leagues west of the Azores. Castile would enjoy rights in territories reached by sailing west or south of this 'line'.
Treaty of Tordesillas	1494	The papal proposals of the previous year were accepted by the crowns of Castile and Portugal. At this point, the settlement confirmed Portugal's monopoly of established routes to the Indies, while Castile gained rights in a largely unexplored region.
Eximiae Devotionis	1501	Alexander VI granted to the crown of Castile all tithes levied in her American territories.
Universalis Ecclesiae Regimini	1508	The crown of Castile was granted the right to make all ecclesiastical appointments in its possessions in the New World.

extended into the Portuguese sphere of influence. To this day, therefore, Brazil is the only part of Latin America whose heritage is Portuguese, rather than Hispanic. Although the picture was soon to change, Castile had to be content in 1494 with a few semi-explored islands inhabited by 'savages'.

EARLY SPANISH SETTLEMENT

The beginnings of Spanish colonisation in this new continent were also unpromising. The early settlers on the island of Hispaniola had given way to the temptation to plunder the local inhabitants rather than to provide for themselves, and had provoked both rebellion among the 'indians' and discord among themselves. By 1499 the crown was forced to send out professional administrators, and Columbus found himself shipped home in temporary disgrace.

The arrival of Francisco de Bobadilla (1499) and Nicholas de Ovando (1502) provided governors of greater social status, and showed that the Castilian crown was tackling the settlement of the Indies along lines already tried and tested in Granada. By the system of *repartimiento*, settlers had allocated to them a section of the tamed native population for their support by tribute and forced labour. These years also saw the slow development of an economy based largely upon cattle farming and some arable farming of cassava, yams and sugar. On the other hand, the harsh and novel systems that the settlers imposed upon the Indian populations disrupted native life and subjected aboriginal populations to burdens of which they had no previous experience. Native crops were often ruined by the settlers' cattle, and the Spaniards brought with them diseases to which the natives had no resistance. Smallpox and measles, in particular, killed a large proportion of the population, causing a serious labour shortage.

In the second decade of the century, two events confirmed that, instead of entering Asia by the back door, Spain was faced with the task of subjugating a different and unknown land mass. In 1513, Vasco Núñez de Balboa became the first European to look upon the Pacific Ocean. In 1519, Ferdinand Magellan, a Portuguese navigator in the service of Spain, embarked upon a westward voyage which ended in the first ever circumnavigation of the globe. The return of his expedition left nobody in any real doubt that Portugal had won what had been until then the main event. Fortified by papal bulls, by the Treaty of Tordesillas, and by the inescapable realities of geography, Portugal had won the race for the Indies. Before long, however, Castile's consolation prize began to appear very substantial indeed.

THE *CONQUISTADORES*

'If the first two decades of the sixteenth century may be called the age of the professional explorer, the next three decades from 1520 to 1550 were the age of the *conquistador* – the professional conqueror' (J.H. Parry). The Spanish *conquistador* emerged from the tradition of the Moorish wars, and

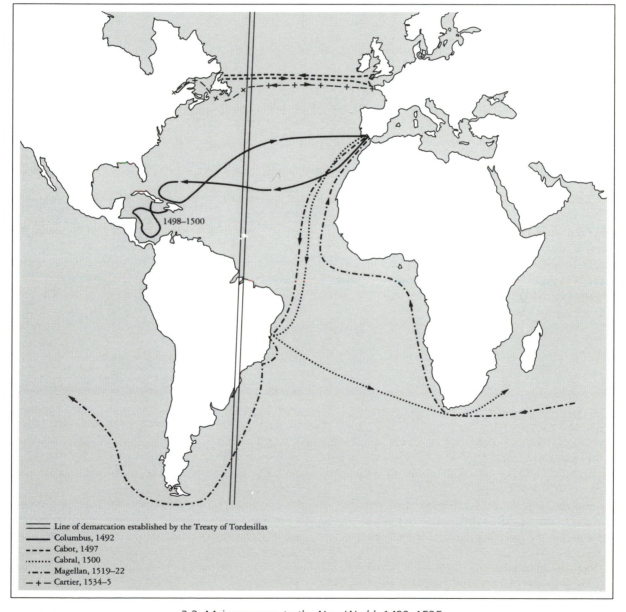

1498–1500

═══	Line of demarcation established by the Treaty of Tordesillas
────	Columbus, 1492
- - - -	Cabot, 1497
....	Cabral, 1500
·─··─·	Magellan, 1519–22
─ + ─	Cartier, 1534–5

3.3 Major voyages to the New World, 1492–1535

hundreds or thousands of his type were tempted to the Indies by the hope of quick profit or landed wealth such as were no longer available in Spain. All were broadly motivated by the ideas expressed by Bernal Diaz, one of their number, who sought 'to serve God and his Majesty, and to grow rich as all men desire to do'.

The high hopes of such men were sustained by two remarkable successes. The first of these was recorded in 1519–21 by an expedition of 600 men commanded by Hernán Cortés, and dispatched by the governor of Cuba to the Mexican mainland. There, acting upon information gained from the locals, Cortes located the Aztec civilisation, which had dominated central Mexico for nearly two centuries. Within two years, he had captured and destroyed its capital city, Tenochtitlan, and gained control of its substantial resources, human, mineral

Northward exploration:
Undertaken by Coronado (1540)

GUADALAJARA

MEXICO

GUATEMALA

New Granada:
Colony established by Belalcazar with capital at Bogotá (1540)

Guatemala:
Pedro de Alvarado conquered remnants of Maya civilisation (1513)

PANAMA

Amazon River:
Navigated by Francisco de Orellana in his unsuccessful search for 'El Dorado'–'the gilded king' (1539–42)

CARACAS

BOGOTA

QUITO

BRAZIL

LIMA

CUZCO

Peru:
Inca civilisation subjugated by Pizarro and Almagro (1532–3). Establishment of cities at Quito (1546) and Lima (1541)

POTOSI

Brazil:
Known from earlier Portuguese voyages, its colonisation was begun by Jão III. The crown founded 12 'captaincies', of which Pernambuco, São Vicente and Bahía (1549) became major centres

Chile:
After earlier reconnaissance by Almagro, the settlement of Santiago was founded by Pedro de Valdivia (1541)

SANTIAGO

Seat of bishop or archbishop
Cities underlined were also the seat of an Audiencia

3.4 The exploration of the New World

and territorial. Cortés owed his success to a remarkable combination of circumstances: to the political divisions within the empire, to the Aztec belief that he was a god, and to the technological and tactical superiority of his small force over a society still rooted in the stone age. His success, all the same, provides one of the great romances of the sixteenth century, and whetted the appetite of a generation of *conquistadores*.

Only one other expedition emulated the success of Cortés. In 1530 a business syndicate led by Francisco Pizarro and Diego de Almagro, with a tiny force of some 180 men, set out to explore the coast of Peru. In locating the Inca civilisation in the Peruvian highlands (1532) they again encountered a society wealthy and powerful enough to exert extensive control over a considerable area, yet unable to resist the impetus of the Spaniards. The capture of the Inca capital at Cuzco (1533), together with the capture and murder of the Inca leader Atahualpa, completed the military success of these *conquistadores*. Whereas the Aztec empire had been successfully divided into Spanish land-holdings, however, the capture of Cuzco was the prelude to a decade of jealousy and rivalry between the victors. Within eight years Almagro was dead, strangled on Pizarro's orders (1538), and Pizarro himself had been murdered by Almagro's surviving supporters (1541). The anarchy of post-conquest politics in Peru motivated the Spanish government to end the 'age of the *conquistador*'. Henceforth it insisted that Spain's new territories should come under the control of Spanish-trained, professional administrators sent from Europe for that specific purpose.

THE ADMINISTRATION OF SPANISH AMERICA

At the heart of these Spanish administrations lay two sets of institutions, one laid down by the conquerors themselves, and the other imposed upon them by the home government. At the centre of the system of long-term settlement and exploitation lay the *encomienda*. To replace the authority of former rulers, and to reward deserving veterans of the conquest, the recipient of the grant of *encomienda* (the *encomendero*) officially received the right to demand tribute, and sometimes labour, from the native population over a specified area. Cortés' own *encomienda* was enormous, probably comprising some 23,000 households. In the short term, this was a highly effective system which had a long and successful history both in Spain, in the case of lands captured from the Moors, and in the earlier settlement of islands in the Atlantic and in the Caribbean.

Equally important was the foundation of towns. If the *encomiendas* provided profit, it was the towns of Spanish America that were the focus of Spanish authority. No Spanish city had greater success than Mexico City, specifically built by Cortés on the site of Tenochtitlan to perpetuate the prestige of the Aztec capital. Elsewhere, Quito, Bogotà, Santiago and others all became thriving centres of Spanish government, commerce and culture. The government of these cities followed a common pattern. Initially it was the military commander who appointed a council (*cabildo*) of twelve *regidores*, which in turn oversaw the selection of the magistrates (*alcaldes*). Subsequently, the degree of democracy involved in municipal elections varied considerably. Although some cities, such as Havana, had open and direct elections, power usually circulated by prior arrangement among the leading families of the territory.

Oligarchy, however, was not what the Spanish crown had in mind for its new territories. It is probable that the Revolt of the Comuneros in the home country made the crown even keener to avoid a situation in which the distant towns and provinces developed liberties and a high degree of administrative independence. In Mexico and in South America royal governors were quickly appointed, and increasingly the office was held by a university-trained lawyer, a *letrado*. By the mid-century such governors had established a tight hold over the municipal administrations, and representative assemblies on the lines of the Cortes of metropolitan Spain were quite unknown in the American provinces. Instead, another Spanish institution, the *audiencia*, was transplanted to the New World. Ten such bodies were founded there in the course of the sixteenth century. Staffed entirely by Spanish lawyers, and serving as high courts of appeal and as advisory councils to the provincial governors, the *audiencias*

3.5 European attitudes towards the native populations

Source A On each altar was a giant figure, very tall and very fat. They said that the one on the right was Huichilobos, their war-god. He had a very broad face and huge, terrible eyes.

There were some smoking braziers of their incense, in which they were burning the hearts of the three Indians whom they had sacrificed that day; and all the walls of their shrine were so splashed and caked with blood that they and the floor too were black. Indeed, the whole place stank abominably.

A little apart from the temple stood another small tower, which was also an idol-house, or true hell, for one of its doors was in the shape of a terrible mouth, such as they paint to depict the jaws of hell. There were many great pots and jars in this house, for it was here that they cooked the flesh of the wretched Indians who were sacrificed and eaten by the priests. Near this place of sacrifice there were many large knives and chopping-blocks, like those with which men cut up meat in slaughterhouses. I always called that building Hell.

An eye-witness account of Cortés' arrival in the Aztec capital. From Bernal Diaz, *True History of the Conquest of New Spain*

Source B Some of the Indians, especially the old people and more often the women than the men, are of such simplicity and purity that they do not know how to sin. Our confessors search for some shred of sin by which they can grant them the benefits of absolution. The fact is, because of their simple and good nature, they do not know how to hold a grudge, to say an unkind thing to anyone else, or to forget one particle of the obligation that the Church had imposed upon them. And in this case I do not speak from hearsay, but from my own experience.

From Geronimo de Mendieta, a Spanish Franciscan monk, *Historia Ecclesiastica Indiana*, 1596

Source C The Indians are naturally lazy and vicious, melancholic, cowardly, and in general a lying shiftless people. Their marriages are not a sacrament but a sacrilege. They are idolatrous, lustful and commit sodomy. Their chief desire is to eat, drink, worship heathen idols, and commit bestial obscenities. What could one expect from a people whose skulls are so thick and hard that the Spaniards had to take care in fighting not to strike them on the head, lest their swords be blunted?

From Gonzalo Fernandez de Oviedo, Governor of Peru, *General and Natural History of the Indies,* a contemporary account

Source D Those who surpass the rest in prudence and intelligence, although not in physical strength, are by nature the masters. On the other hand, those who are dim-witted and mentally lazy, although they may be physically strong enough to fulfil all the necessary tasks, are by nature slaves. It is just and useful that it is this way. And so it is with the barbarous and inhumane [Indians] who have no civil life and peaceful customs. It will always be just and in conformity with natural law that such people submit to the rule of more cultured and humane princes and nations.

were the key institutions of Spanish colonial administration.

All of these institutions were directly linked to Castile through the Council of the Indies. Initially established in 1511, it became a formal element in the Castilian government in 1524, and formed at once the highest court of appeal in all matters pertaining to the colonies, the highest advisory body to the crown on all American matters, and the sole drafting body for all colonial legislation.

THE ECONOMY OF SPANISH AMERICA

The spread of arable farming to the South American mainland was a painfully slow process. The first major grape harvest seems only to have been gathered in Peru in 1551, and olive groves were only successfully established in the next decade. More rapid success was achieved in Mexico, especially in the production of sugar and of

These [Indians] possess neither science nor even an alphabet. In regard to their virtues, how much restraint or gentleness are you to expect from men who are devoted to all kinds of intemperate acts and abominable lewdness, including the eating of human flesh? These Indians are so cowardly and timid that they could scarcely resist the mere presence of our soldiers. Many times, thousands upon thousands of them scattered, fleeing like women before a very few Spaniards, who amounted to fewer than a hundred.

What is more appropriate and beneficial for these barbarians than to become subject to the rule of those whose wisdom, virtue and religion have converted them from barbarians into civilised men (in so far as they are capable of becoming so)?

From Juan Gines de Sepulveda, a Spanish humanist scholar, *Democrates alter de justi belli causis apud Indos,* written about 1547

Source E. The aim which Christ and the Pope seek and ought to seek in the Indies – and which the Christian Kings of Castile should likewise strive for – is that the natives of those regions should hear the faith preached in order that they may be saved. And the means to effect this end are not to rob, to scandalise, to capture or destroy them, or to lay waste their lands, for this would cause the infidels to abominate our religion.

From Bartholeme de Las Casas, *Collected Tracts,* 1552–3

Source F. The Devil could invent no worse pestilence to destroy [the Indies] and to kill all the people there than the *repartimiento* and *encomienda,* the institution used to distribute and entrust Indians to the Spaniards. This was like entrusting the Indians to a gang of devils or delivering herds of cattle to hungry wolves. The Indians were prevented from receiving the Christian faith and religion. The wretched and tyrannical Spanish *encomenderos* worked the Indians night and day in the mines and in other personal services. They collected unbelievable tributes. They persecuted and expelled from the Indian villages the preachers of the faith.

From Bartholeme de Las Casas, *Thirty Most Just Propositions,* 1552

QUESTIONS

a. The account by Bernal Diaz, from which source A is taken, was widely published in Europe. What evidence is there in the other sources that European attitudes to native Americans were influenced by such accounts?

b. Compare the grounds upon which European domination is justified in sources C and D.

c. In what ways are the approaches of Mendieta (source B) and Las Casas (sources E and F) to the problem of relations with native Americans

different from those taken by Oviedo (source C) and Sepulveda (source D)? What different priorities are evident in these attitudes?

d. 'In their approach to the natives of the New World, the only difference between one Spaniard and another was in the European prejudices which each applied to the problem.' How far do these extracts lead you to agree with this statement?

cochineal. Livestock rearing was a far more obvious agricultural pursuit for the retired *conquistador* and his descendants. If European crops took time to establish themselves, meat supplies quickly became plentiful, leather and cow hides became a principal export commodity, and, with the successful introduction of the merino sheep into Mexico in the 1530s, the wool industry also developed rapidly.

In the course of the 1540s, however, the economy of the Spanish Indies was transformed by

the growth of the mining industry. The great treasures seized by the *conquistadores* at Cuzco, and the persistent legends of other rich kingdoms, kept alive Spanish hopes of great mineral wealth in their new territories. Prospecting in the 1530s produced sufficient silver to constitute 40 per cent of the total value of goods shipped to Spain in 1540. This could not compare, however, with the spectacular discoveries of the next decade. In 1545 the first 'strikes' were made at Potosí in modern Bolivia.

With further discoveries of rich silver veins in Mexico, at Zacatecas and Guanajuato (1548), the whole economic configuration of the Spanish colonies came to be dominated by the mining industry. With one-fifth of its produce earmarked for the crown, a whole new civil service grew around the industry, testing and stamping the ingots, and ensuring the payment of bullion tax. An important industry developed at Huancavelica in Peru, concerned with the production of mercury, used in the most effective method of refining the silver ore. Considering the wider impact upon Europe of the flow of silver from the New World, J.H. Parry has judged that 'it is not a great exaggeration to say that the discovery of Potosí was one of the turning points in the history of the Western World'.

THE IMPACT UPON THE NATIVE POPULATION

The place of the native population in the colonial social structure was the subject of fierce debate for much of the first half of the sixteenth century (see documentary exercise 3.5). When an official Spanish policy towards native Americans emerged in the middle of the sixteenth century, it owed more to the views of Las Casas than to those of Sepulveda and his supporters. According to official theory, the Indians were the direct subjects of the Spanish crown, and should be rescued from their original, primitive state by a benevolent government. They could not be regarded as slaves, nor lose their property, except as punishment for a serious offence against Spanish law. Before that law, they were equal to Spaniards, and could take legal action against them. Conversion to Christianity was, of course, to be encouraged, but this was only to occur where the convert entered the faith without coercion. The theories of *limpieza de sangre* – purity of blood – which were applied so strictly to converted Jews and Muslims in metropolitan Spain, received no legal recognition in the American colonies.

In reality, aboriginal societies were transformed beyond recognition by their contact with the European conquerors. The degree of physical integration that took place between Europeans and natives differed greatly from one part of the Spanish

possessions to another. In Mexico, intermarriage and interbreeding were common. The offspring of such unions (*mestizos*) generally came to be regarded for social and financial purposes as Spaniards. In Peru, on the other hand, Indian communities preserved their traditions and social structures to a much larger extent. There, too, the attempts of royal officials to implement the official decrees concerning the treatment of the natives met with fierce resistance. Attempts to abolish the existing powers of the *encomenderos* in 1542 caused rebellion and led to the violent death of the viceroy. Only as the original *encomenderos* died could the crown revise the original grants to give real meaning to these 'New Laws'.

The papacy was quick to recognise that only the crown had the practical means to serve the interests of the Church in its distant dominions, and had subsequently bestowed upon it full authority over religious functions in the Indies. No branch of the Catholic Church was more independent of Rome than that in the New World. The crown put these powers to vigorous and positive use. The early missions were staffed mainly by the regenerated Observant orders, and the first Bishop of Mexico, Juan de Zumarraga (1527), was known to be an admirer of Erasmus. The influence of the great humanist was evident in the two works, the *Doctrina Breve* and the *Doctrina Christiana,* that he prepared for the instruction of the natives. The actual process of conversion seems to have been careful and thoughtful, and compares favourably with the approach taken to Moors and Jews in metropolitan Spain. Instruction and preaching were regarded as essential preliminaries to baptism, and some 270 churches were built in Mexico before the end of the century. Conversely, the Church was active in the destruction of the native religions, and of their trappings. By 1531, after only four years as bishop, Zumarraga claimed to have destroyed 500 temples and 20,000 idols in his diocese. In the long term, however, confrontation gave way to compromise, and missionaries found it desirable, or perhaps unavoidable, to allow the grafting of native tradition and practice on to Christian doctrine, to produce the distinctive hybrid religion that exists in much of South and Central America today.

The impact of the Spanish Church upon the natives was matched by the impact of the Spanish colonial economy. The spread of cattle farming involved a substantial degree of depopulation and did considerable damage to native arable farming. The great demand for labour sucked very large numbers of natives into such enterprises as the Potosí mines, and many more came together to form the artisan and servant classes of the great cities of the Spanish colonies. Worst of all, the Spaniards also brought with them diseases previously unknown in the New World, to which the natives had no immunity, and which brought about a demographic disaster. Recent work on population figures in Mexico has suggested that an Indian population in the region of 11 million in 1519 may have fallen to less than 6½ million within twenty years, and reached a low of 2½ million by the end of the century.

ATLANTIC COMMUNICATIONS

The establishment of Spanish dominance in the New World would have been impossible without efficient commerce and communication across the Atlantic. The major focus of this commerce in metropolitan Spain was Seville, the capital of the southern region of Andalucia. The first forty years of the century constituted a 'boom' period for Andalucia as its leather, textile, pottery, oil, wine and wheat production supplied the needs of the colonists. Founded in 1503, Seville's House of Trade (*Casa de la Contratacion de las Indias*) remained the monopolistic focus of all commercial and administrative activity concerning the Indies.

On the western shores of the Atlantic, Spanish commerce passed through three distinct phases. During the initial 'island phase', transatlantic trade was primarily concerned with the supply of necessities to the infant colonies of the Caribbean. By the beginning of the 1520s, a second phase was developing, focused upon Mexico. Coastal settlements such as Vera Cruz-San Juan de Ulua now found themselves the termini for the majority of the transatlantic voyagers. Incoming cargoes of cattle and settlers percolated into the Mexican interior, while the wealth of the New World found its way back to Spain. The political instability that followed the conquest of the Incas delayed the development of the 'Peruvian phase' until the 1540s, but by the middle years of that decade the ports that served the overland route to Peru were receiving nearly 40 per cent of all the ships which sailed from Spain. The cargoes they carried back to their homeland were increasingly dominated by the commodity most commonly associated with these transatlantic voyages – silver.

As the colonies produced more and more of their own foodstuffs, so the outward-bound vessels limited themselves more and more to the carriage of luxury goods, textiles, weapons, glass and books. The second half of the century also saw the development of the convoy system in an attempt to counteract those dangers experienced during the recent wars against France. From 1543 ships were forbidden to sail for the Indies unless in groups of ten or more, and from the mid–1560s all such voyages were undertaken under the protection of armed escorts. From that time onwards, the great transatlantic fleets operated according to a set pattern, the brainchild of a noted naval strategist, Pedro Menendez de Aviles. Each year two fleets left Spain, one in May bound for the Caribbean islands and Mexico, the other in August for Nombre de Dios and the Peruvian trade. March saw the rendezvous of ships from both fleets at Havana to ride the westerly winds homewards. The convoy system was thus slow, regimented, and expensive to protect. For the rest of the sixteenth century these great fleets, the *carrera de Indias*, were to provide the life-blood of Spain's European policies.

THE TECHNOLOGY OF RECONNAISSANCE

The successes of the earliest explorers provided the stimulus for a veritable technological revolution in the fields of navigation, shipbuilding and their related sciences. When the navigators of the fifteenth century sailed out of sight of land they sailed beyond the range of existing charts and navigational technology. Received academic ideas of the world beyond Europe were largely based upon the *Imago Mundi,* published by Pierre d'Ailly in 1410, and the *Geography* of the Greek scholar Ptolemy (*c.*AD90–*c.*168), recently rediscovered by Western scholars. Both relied greatly in their accounts of remote regions upon classical tradition, unsubstantiated reports and sheer guesswork. Only slowly were more accurate alternatives developed. The details of the coast of Africa were slowly filled in by the cartographers of the Portuguese court, and scale came to be standardised in the early years of the sixteenth century by reference to the meridian of Cape St Vincent. By 1508 the *Casa de la Contratacion* in Seville possessed a reference map (the *Padron Real*) which was regularly updated as further exploration progressed. Perhaps the greatest of all sixteenth-century contributions to map-making was that of the Fleming, Gerhard Kremer, known as Mercator. In 1569 he finally solved the problem of projecting the details of a spherical world on to the flat surface of a map. His version, Mercator's Projection, remains the basis for all maps and atlases today.

None of the classic ship designs of mid-fifteenth-century Europe was suited to the purposes of intercontinental travel. The Mediterranean was dominated by the galley, a large vessel widely used for commerce and for war, propelled by banks of oarsmen as well as by its sails. It maintained its effectiveness in the Mediterranean well beyond the close of the sixteenth century, but its rows of open oar ports made it quite unsuitable for the rougher seas of the Atlantic. The traffic of the Atlantic coast by the mid-fifteenth century was dominated instead by the *nau*. Its broad beam provided spacious holds for cargo, and it was defended by substantial superstructures fore and aft. Such a ship was well suited to the carrying of substantial cargoes, but it was heavy, slow and hard to handle in unpredictable winds. The caravel, on the other hand, was a smaller, lighter craft widely used by the Portuguese on their early explorations of the African coast. It performed excellently when speed and manoeuvrability were needed, but its small size rendered it unsuitable as a cargo-carrying craft for long-range commerce.

The period between the mid-fifteenth and the mid-sixteenth centuries witnessed two revolutionary ship designs to meet the demands of this new form of commerce. The first was the *caravela redonda*, the square-rigged caravel, which combined the power advantages of square sails on the foremast with the adaptability of lateen-rig on the main and mizen masts. The second was the galleon, which

began to appear in the mid-century on the Spanish routes to and from the New World. Galleons were fighting ships *par excellence*, designed to protect the vulnerable and tempting cargoes that now regularly crossed the Atlantic. Their design grafted the size and power of the Mediterranean galley on to an ocean-going ship. The result was a floating fortress, between 300 and 800 tons, capable of carrying bullion, but equally capable of housing heavy guns for the protection of its cargo.

THE PORTUGUESE IN THE EAST INDIES

In some respects the Portuguese achievement was as great as that of her more powerful neighbour. Apart from the geographical extent of their interests, the Portuguese in Asia found themselves surrounded by civilisations of great antiquity and of greater technological and cultural sophistication than those encountered by the *conquistadores*. To impose themselves upon these civilisations Portugal could draw on a total population of only some 1.25 million.

The title that the Portuguese crown assumed at this time, 'Lord of the Conquest, Navigation and Commerce of Ethiopia, India, Arabia and Persia', was a deliberate exaggeration, but reflected factors that genuinely explained Portugal's success. Portugal maintained an unchallengeable naval supremacy in Asian and African waters from 1509 until well into the second half of the century. The failure of native princes to challenge this supremacy owed much to the divided and enfeebled state of many Asian kingdoms at the beginning of the century. India itself, before the great Moghul invasion began in 1524, was a collection of native states divided by religious and political rivalry. The areas now covered by Malaysia and Indonesia, similarly, consisted of a multiplicity of modest sultanates.

The foundations of Portuguese supremacy in this region were laid by Francisco de Almeida and by Afonso de Albuquerque. By defeating a combined Egyptian–Gujarati fleet at Diu (February 1509) Almeida established Portugal's naval supremacy. This was then consolidated by the system of strategically positioned fortresses built by

Albuquerque to protect Portuguese interests. The key fortress was Goa, captured in November 1510, and the major Portuguese possession in the Indian sub-continent for nearly 450 years. Second only to Goa was the island of Hormuz, whose capture (1515) gave the Portuguese effective control of the Persian Gulf. Further east, the capture of Malacca (1511) had already established an important base for the trade in Indonesian spices. Albuquerque's only major failure was in his bid for possession of Aden, in order to control the entrance to the Red Sea. What he had achieved, nevertheless, was 'to change an entirely seaborne interloping commerce based on Lisbon, into a chain of permanent commercial and naval establishments covering the whole of the Middle East' (J.H. Parry).

Albuquerque appreciated the impossibility of imposing direct Portuguese rule upon local populations. Instead, consistent with Da Gama's original criteria of seeking 'spices and Christians', the bases were used only to aid commercial enterprise, providing havens for Portuguese shipping and bases for operations against commercial rivals.

3.6 Explorers and conquerors

ALBUQUERQUE, Afonso de (1452–1515). Captured Goa as a base for Portuguese interests in the Indies (1503). Appointed viceroy of Portuguese possessions (1509). Captured Ceylon (Sri Lanka), Malacca and Ormuz (1515).

CABOT, John (?1450–?1499). Anglicised version of Giovanni Caboto. Born Genoa. Involved in the spice trade, he went to England (c.1490) to work under the patronage of Henry VII, and was financed by the merchants of Bristol. On his second voyage (1497) explored the coastline of Newfoundland and Nova Scotia. Probably died on a third voyage (1499). His son Sebastian (?1470–1557) searched for a north-west passage (1508–9), and explored the east coast of North America. Chief Pilot to Charles of Spain (1518). Returned to England to become Governor of the Merchant Adventurers (1551).

CARTIER, Jacques (1494–?1554). Born St Malo. Made voyages under the patronage of Francis I to Newfoundland (1534) and down the St Lawrence River (1535). Established a French settlement in the region of modern Montreal (1541–2).

COLUMBUS, Christopher (1451–1506). In Spanish, Cristóbal Colón. Born Genoa. Made early voyages along African coast to Cape Verde Islands and Guinea (1474–7). Conceived the idea of sailing west to reach Asia (c.1474) and made four voyages with that intention under the patronage of Isabella of Castile. Landed in the Bahamas (October 1492) and explored Cuba and Hispaniola. Reached Dominica (1493). Reached Trinidad and explored South American coastline (1498–1500). Explored south coast of Gulf of Mexico (1502–4). Proved to be a poor administrator and recalled to Spain in semi-disgrace.

CORTÉS, Hernán (1485–1547). Born Estremadura, Spain, of minor nobility. Participated in the conquest of Cuba (1511). Sent to explore mainland of Mexico (1519), where he located and captured Tenochtitlan, the capital of the Aztec empire (1519–21). Appointed captain-general of New Spain (1530). Participated in Charles V's campaign against Algiers (1540).

GAMA, VASCO DA (?1469–1524). Commissioned by Manoel I of Portugal to follow up the voyage of Dias around the southern tip of Africa. His great voyage of 1497–9 took him out of sight of land for three months, and made him the first European to reach India (May 1498). On his second voyage (1502–3) he founded colonies on Mozambique and at Sofala. Emerged from a long retirement to serve as viceroy of Portuguese possessions in the Indies (1524).

MAGELLAN, Ferdinand (1480–1521). Anglicised version of Fernao de Magalhaes. Served in India under Almeida (1505). Entered Spanish service (1517). Undertook voyage to reach East Indies by sailing west (1519), during which he rounded the southern tip of America via the Magellan Straits (1520) and became the first European to cross the Pacific. After his death at the hands of natives in the Philippines, the survivors of his expedition completed the first circumnavigation of the globe on their return to Spain (1522).

PIZARRO, Francisco (?1475–1541). Illegitimate son of a military father, active in Spanish Indies from 1502. Mayor of Panama (1519–23). Led expeditions to explore coast of Peru (1524–5 and 1526–7). Located and conquered the Inca empire (1531–3). Founded Lima as capital of Spanish province (1535). Defeated rebellion by Almagro (1538), but was subsequently murdered by Almagro's son.

VESPUCCI, Amerigo (1452–1512). Born Florence. Originally involved in exploration as a contractor, he undertook two voyages of his own, exploring the coast of Venezuela (1499), and investigating the coastline of Brazil (1501–2). Chief pilot of Seville's 'House of Trade' (1505–12). A skilled and dishonest self-publicist, he claimed to have undertaken further voyages, with such success that his name was applied to the whole of the new continent, 'America'.

THE PORTUGUESE IN AFRICA AND IN BRAZIL

In the first decades of the sixteenth century, Portuguese possessions dotted along the Atlantic coasts of Africa and Brazil were largely limited to the role of staging posts *en route* to the riches of the Indies. By the mid-1530s, however, the Portuguese crown moved towards the more systematic settlement of Brazil by the granting of 'captaincies' along the settled coastline. This was done in part to ward off French interlopers, but was also due to the dramatic growth of sugar production in Brazil. Sixty-six sugar mills existed in Pernambuco alone by the 1580s, and forty ships sailed annually between Recife and Lisbon with this commodity. The grants of *donatario* made by the crown to the more substantial settlers conveyed the right to levy taxation and to license such enterprises as sugar mills. Some contemporary estimates placed the number of white settlers in Brazil by 1600 as high as 30,000.

The sugar industry also created the demand for a large and docile workforce. The answer for the Portuguese, as for the Spaniards in the Caribbean, was the import of large numbers of slaves, and the slave trade in West Africa became probably the greatest boom industry in the Portuguese colonies. Although the nature of the trade makes accurate figures hard to come by, C.R. Boxer's modern estimate is that between 10,000 and 15,000 Africans were being landed in Brazil each year in the last quarter of the sixteenth century.

THE PORTUGUESE EMPIRE IN DECLINE

In contrast to the Spanish hegemony in the New World, this Portuguese empire was in sharp decline by the end of the sixteenth century. In many respects, indeed, the empire always contained the seeds of its own decay. It was never possible for the Portuguese to man their empire as thoroughly as the Spaniards could. The population of the homeland was not more than 1.5 million in the sixteenth century, while that of Spain has been estimated at between seven and eight million. In addition, the journey to the Far East was long and dangerous compared to the passage of the Atlantic. The 2,400 Portuguese who, on average, left the homeland each year for the empire had to be spread widely among a range of colonies, most of them with climatic conditions highly dangerous to Europeans. Few Portuguese women made the voyage to the Indies, and the result was a high rate of interbreeding between Portuguese men and native women. No real tradition of Portuguese landownership and administration therefore developed in this empire. Probably the worst

consequence of this demographic trend seems to have been the decline in seamanship, as the Portuguese fleets came to rely more and more upon mariners of native origin or of mixed descent.

The Portuguese also made significant tactical errors in the administration of their possessions. They did very little to establish lasting alliances or understandings with native states. While generally recognising Muslim states as implacable enemies, little was done to establish lasting friendships with Hindu rulers. Instead, ruthless trading methods led to disputes with the Hindu rulers of Calicut and Cochin in the 1520s. The Counter-Reformation reached the Indies with the arrival of the first Jesuit mission in 1542. The teaching of St Francis Xavier established a minority Catholic community in India and Sri Lanka that still survives today. Subsequent missionaries in Portuguese India became increasingly heavy-handed, especially after the accession of Philip II to the throne of Portugal in 1580. Hindu temples in Goa were destroyed in 1540, and that policy was extended to all other Portuguese territories after 1567. In 1560 the Inquisition was established in the Indies for the first time, and in 1599 the Nestorian Christians, a native sect, were formally condemned as heretical.

The Portuguese empire in the Indies was increasingly subjected to external pressures. After the invasion of India begun in 1524 by Babur 'the Tiger', the Portuguese garrisons found themselves surrounded no longer by minor principalities, but by the outposts of the mighty Moghul empire. Thanks to Portugal's maritime supremacy, they were able to survive the threat, conducting a remarkable and heroic defence of Goa against Muslim attack in 1569. Further east, however, the advance of Islam placed greater pressure upon Portuguese commerce. Two powerful sultanates, Mataram and Bantam, emerged in Java, and successive sultans of Ternate severely pressurised Portuguese interests in the Moluccas.

These threats were partly alleviated by the union of the crowns of Portugal and Spain in 1580. Spanish interests in the Philippines gave them a strong motive for aiding Portuguese resistance to Muslim incursions further north. On the other hand, the union with Spain drew Portugal into the running fight between Spain and the Protestant states of northern Europe.

INTERLOPERS

Bypassing the Iberian empires

Inevitably the great wealth that filtered from Spain and Portugal into the wider economy of Western Europe acted as a magnet, drawing across the Atlantic and into the Indies those of other nations who desired a share. The earliest interlopers limited themselves to more northerly waters, and to a commodity that the Spanish had largely neglected. Although certain Portuguese seamen appreciated the value of Newfoundland and Labrador as sources of fish and of timber, they quickly encountered French and English competition. John Cabot had noted the potential of these waters in the reign of Henry VII, and vessels from Normandy and Brittany were fishing there regularly by about 1510.

While it remained too dangerous to confront Spanish and Portuguese interests directly, the second generation of interlopers challenged Portugal's spice monopoly by seeking alternative routes to the sources of this commodity. The long search for a 'north-west passage', skirting the north of the American continent to reach the Pacific, had begun early in the century. The Florentine Verrazano may have explored the Hudson River in 1523–4, and the great French navigator Jacques Cartier certainly explored the St Lawrence between 1535 and 1543. The English contribution to this vain quest began in 1576 with the first voyage of Martin Frobisher, who made three more voyages without success. John Davis (1585) explored the sea passages between Greenland and the Canadian mainland in the hope of finding a passable route through the ice-floes that blocked the route. The search for a 'north-east passage', around the northern coasts of Scandinavia and Russia, was led in the mid-century by English merchant adventurers, but it too was wholly unsuccessful.

Plundering the Iberian empires

Later interlopers sought to profit by direct involvement in the commerce of the Indies. The method chosen by Sir John Hawkins was that of semi-legitimate trade with the Spanish colonists.

He recognised that the monopoly claimed by Spain over the affairs of the New World colonies was unworkable, and that Spain simply could not supply many of the commodities required by the colonists. In particular, he aimed to satisfy the demand for labour by the transportation of African slaves carried in his famous 'triangular trade'. To understand Hawkins correctly it is important to appreciate that he belonged, not to the age of Drake, but to the age of Mary Tudor, when friendly relations between England and Spain seemed to raise the real possibility of an English share in New World wealth. His trade remained semi-legitimate because, while Spanish colonists were only too willing to accept goods that Spain could not supply, the central Spanish government bitterly resented any invasion of its monopolies. In the course of his third voyage (1567), therefore, Hawkins's fleet was attacked and severely damaged at San Juan de Ulua, an incident which ended peaceful participation in Spanish commerce.

The only alternative now for the adventurers of England, France and the Netherlands was outright piracy. Privateering, whereby individuals were authorised by their government to attack the shipping of a specified enemy, was a product of French hostility to Spain, and occurred inter-mittently throughout the reign of Charles V. In the twenty years that followed San Juan de Ulua, however, the greatest of the privateers was an Englishman, Francis Drake. His capture of substantial quantities of bullion at Nombre de Dios (1572) and his circumnavigation of the globe (1577–80) proved an inspiration to future generations of privateers, and an unparalleled drain upon Spanish resources. By the time of the official outbreak of war between England and Spain, the principle had become well established that Spain's weakest point was her lines of communication with the main source of her wealth. Interloping became overt government policy with the conclusion of the Treaty of the Hague in 1596. Thereby, the governments of England, France and the Netherlands allied with the aim of combining their seaborne operations to dismember the Spanish empire. The project faded as the contracting parties concluded their separate peace treaties with Spain, but the death-knell of Spain's monopoly had been clearly sounded.

Portuguese commerce, too, was now the object of English, French and Dutch hostility. With the union of the Spanish and Portuguese crowns in 1580, it became a legitimate and a much easier target. Furthermore, the disruption of Dutch trade caused by Spanish attempts to subjugate the Netherlands provided Dutch adventurers, such as van Linschoten and de Houtman, with a powerful motive for seeking new profits further afield. Houtman's treaty with the Sultan of Bantam (1596) was followed by similar commercial treaties with the rulers of Ternate, Banda and Amboina in the Moluccas.

This same decade saw the beginnings of English involvement in the East Indies. The East India Company received its charter from Queen Elizabeth in 1600, two years before the Dutch amalgamated a number of trading bodies to form a similar company. In between, in 1601, the relative naval strengths of the Dutch and the Portuguese had been put to the test in a major engagement off the coast of Bantam. The decisive victory won by the Dutch showed that in the East Indies, too, the first wave of European imperialism was about to give way to a new and more enduring era.

Further reading

C.R. Boxer (1977) *The Portuguese Seaborne Empire, 1415–1825.* London.

J.H. Elliott (1972) *The New World and the Old, 1492–1650.* Cambridge.

D. O'Sullivan (1984) *The Age of Discovery, 1400–1550.* London & New York.

J.H. Parry (1977) *The Spanish Seaborne Empire.* London.

CHAPTER FOUR

The First Generation of Religious Reform

The historical debate

German thought on the eve of the Reformation

Martin Luther

Theological influences upon Luther

The Indulgences Controversy, 1517-19

Luther and the printing press

A summary of Luther's theology

Luther's political conservatism

Condemnation by pope and emperor

The impact of Lutheranism

The condition of Switzerland

Huldrych Zwingli

The Reformation in Zurich

Zwinglianism and its impact

Religious civil war in Switzerland

Anabaptism

The spread and impact of Anabaptism

Popular prints, flattering one party or demonising the other, were essential weapons in the early stages of the Reformation. Here the two tactics are combined. Martin Luther, holding a copy of his German Bible, triumphs over his Catholic opponent, Thomas Murner. His opponent, typically, is portrayed as a monster in a monk's habit

THE HISTORICAL DEBATE

The historiography of sixteenth-century Europe is dominated by the Reformation. So vast has its literature become that historians can no longer treat the Reformation as a single phenomenon, but concentrate instead upon a variety of different reformations: the Genevan reformation, the 'radical' reformation, reformation within different national contexts, and even reformation within the Catholic Church.

For many years the historiography of the German Reformation centred upon the neurotic personality of Martin Luther himself. Some commentators, such as the **Dominican** monk Heinrich Denifle (*Luther and Lutheranism*, 1904), explained the Reformation, not in terms of any deep-seated weaknesses in the contemporary Catholic Church, but as a misguided revolt by Luther and a small group of heretics. To sympathetic authorities such as R.H. Bainton (*Here I Stand*, 1950) or E.G. Rupp (*Luther's Progress to the Diet of Worms*, 1951), Luther remained the admirable driving force behind an essentially spiritual movement. 'Neither philosophy, sociology, nationalism nor economics can explain Luther', Bainton wrote. 'Only religion can provide the explanation.'

The twentieth century, however, has sought largely to explain the success of Luther's revolt in non-religious, or at best semi-religious, terms. The century has produced many intellectual movements liable to reinterpret the Reformation by their own lights. The great German sociologist Max Weber preferred to view it as part of a great ethical and rational revolution which played a major role in the development of modern capitalist society. German nationalist writers concentrated upon Lutheranism as an expression of German self-assertion against the claims and pretensions of a foreign Church. All these interpretations have been criticised by writers who refuse to see anything 'modern' in Luther, regarding him as essentially medieval and conservative in all aspects of his thought, often standing in opposition to the truly radical social and political forces of his time.

Historians of the German Reformation over the last three decades have often concentrated on such forces in their attempt to establish 'whether men were stirred by [Luther's] religion, or merely by his revolt' (R.H. Bainton). Following the lead of Friedrich Engels (*The Peasants' War in Germany*, 1848), socialist historians concentrated upon the element of class conflict within German society. They were naturally attracted to the study of the Peasants' War in 1525, and tended to place Luther's theology in a relatively minor role against a background of peasant distress and commercial decline. More recently Peter Blickle has produced an influential interpretation of these events (*The Revolution of 1525*, 1981), seeing them as constituting a 'revolution of the common man', produced by an explosive mixture of acute socio-economic problems with political expectations raised by the reformers' references to Christian liberty. More conservative writers have preferred to stress the political structure at the peak of German society rather than the social structure at the bottom. For such writers as Gerhard Ritter (*The Reformation in Europe in the Sixteenth Century*, 1950) or Hajo Holborn (*History of Modern Germany: The Reformation*, 1965), the decisive factor in Lutheran success was the fragmented and decentralised political structures of princely Germany.

The most prolific research in recent years has centred on the impact of the Reformation upon the cities of Germany. The pioneering work of Bernd Moeller (*Imperial Cities and the Reformation*, 1962) portrayed this 'urban reformation' as a classic case of 'reformation from below', in which city authorities frequently gave way to popular enthusiasm for reform in order to preserve political stability and their own positions. Following this line of research, T.A. Brady (*Ruling Class, Regime and Reformation at Strasbourg, 1520–55*, 1978), R.W. Scribner (*The German Reformation*, 1986) and many others have closely linked the 'urban reformation' to the politics of the cities, stressing the role played by socio-economic tensions within the communities.

For many years, Anabaptism was treated by historians with the same suspicion as it encountered from contemporary conservatives. Recently, however, this most proletarian element in the Reformation has been widely studied, especially by American writers. One of these, G.H. Williams, coined the term 'Radical Reformation' to distinguish its intellectual revolt from the wider 'Magisterial Reformation', backed and controlled by state or ecclesiastical power. The concept of a 'radical' Reformation has been attacked on two fronts. A.G. Dickens considers that it overvalues a set of ideas which lacked cohesion and which achieved very little. Others have insisted that the Reformation was always essentially radical in its origins. H.-J. Goertz (*Thomas Müntzer, Apocalyptic Mystic and Revolutionary,* 1993) has argued that Luther and such radicals as Müntzer sprang from similar intellectual and socio-economic origins, but that their paths separated in the early 1520s when they chose different routes towards their goal.

GERMAN THOUGHT ON THE EVE OF THE REFORMATION

Luther's impact could not have been so great had not many of his themes been familiar to contemporary audiences. Germany, for instance, had been substantially affected by the *devotio moderna*, and the foundation of nine new German universities between 1456 and 1506 illustrates the educational priorities of this 'new devotion'. Closely linked to this was the Christian humanism that formed one of the major features of Renaissance thought in northern Europe. There was nothing directly hostile to the Church in the writings of such men as Erasmus, and Luther himself seemed initially to many observers to be part of this 'orthodox protest' (A.G. Dickens). Luther's revolt coincided with a notable conflict between German humanists and the Church authorities over the study of Hebrew texts. When such study was banned, as leading to heresy, and when Johannes Reuchlin, a leading humanist and scholar, objected on academic grounds, a major ecclesiastical conflict developed. The publication in 1515–17 by Rubeanus and Ulrich von Hutten of *Letters of Obscure Men* was an attack of unparalleled ferocity upon mediocre and reactionary clerics. It was in this charged intellectual atmosphere that Luther launched his theology.

At the same time, other German thinkers had begun to examine the history and nature of the Germans. The discovery and publication in the 1470s of the text of *Germania*, by the Roman historian Tacitus, showed how their land had avoided the influence and domination of classical Rome and had largely preserved its pre-Roman culture. Was this Germany now to bow unconditionally to the influence of Catholic Rome? Over the century before Luther's revolt, both intellectuals and popular writers looked to the institutions of the Holy Roman Empire for the restoration and maintenance of this German independence. Political theorists, such as Nicholas of Cusa (*Concordantia Catholica,* 1431–3), put forward the view that the Empire existed quite independently of papal power, and presented the Emperor as the independent temporal protector of the faith. Such expectations were especially high upon the accession of Maximilian I in 1493, and were then transferred at the time of Luther's revolt to Maximilian's young grandson. Different though Luther's motives undoubtedly were, his own anti-Roman theme ensured influential support at the moment of his greatest vulnerability.

MARTIN LUTHER

Martin Luther was born in 1483 at Eisleben in Saxony, into a family that had achieved a modest prosperity through the local mining industry. Originally destined for a legal career, he reached the apparently quite sudden decision to embrace the monastic life and, entering the priesthood in 1507, he built himself a considerable academic reputation in the universities of Erfurt and Wittenberg. By 1515, Luther had also become a figure of some significance in the **Augustinian** order, the supervisor of eleven monastic houses in the vicinity of Wittenberg.

Luther gained little satisfaction from these successes. He testified that his decision to join the priesthood was largely motivated by an overwhelming sense of guilt, of his own inadequacy in the face of the demands that God seemed to make of him: 'I wanted to escape hell by being a monk.' The years of academic success at Wittenberg were marked by recurring personal crises, centring upon the problem of how Luther, imperfect as he knew himself to be, could satisfy a perfect God, and thereby achieve salvation. 'However irreproachable my life as a monk,' he later wrote, 'I felt myself in the presence of God to be a sinner with a most unquiet conscience.' Only in 1513–15, when he was at work on a series of lectures on the Psalms, did he discover the key which set him on the path to personal serenity and also indirectly upon the road to theological revolt.

which hung about the sinner like a cloak about a naked man. From that point Luther's formula for salvation was contained in the simple Latin phrase, 'semper peccator, semper penitens, semper justus'. A man never ceased to be a sinner, but nevertheless would be constantly pardoned by God if he remained truly repentant, and truly trusted in the mercy of God to save him.

THEOLOGICAL INFLUENCES UPON LUTHER

Although Luther's terror of damnation was largely unintellectual, he was also a scholar of great learning. His teachings resulted from long study, and contained a number of themes which had recurred through two centuries of ecclesiastical debate. Luther was greatly influenced, for instance, by the work of the early fourteenth-century English theologian William of Occam, agreeing with him that attempts to gain a systematic view of the supernatural were useless, and concluding that mankind's only guide to things divine lay in the single revelation that God had granted in the Bible. Unlike Occam, however, Luther refused to believe that one had the freedom of will, or the power, to do the degree of good that God demanded.

Luther's view of human helplessness in this respect owed much to the writings of German mystics, such as Johann Tauler, in the previous century. Here he could read that all human effort to please God was doomed to failure and that, instead, the human will had to become completely passive as a means of receiving the divine will. Neither Occam nor Tauler, however, provided a satisfactory answer to the central questions of salvation and damnation. At some point between 1513 and 1515, Luther found his answer in the Epistles of St Paul. There he found confirmation of ideas that he had already noted in the works of St Augustine, that 'the just shall live by faith'. This confirmed his conviction that one could not be saved by making oneself acceptable to God through one's own efforts. Yet, said St Paul, God would extend mercy and salvation to all those who identified through faith with the only man who did satisfy His demands, His son Jesus Christ. The merits that saved a man were not his own, but those of Christ,

THE INDULGENCES CONTROVERSY, 1517–19

It is not surprising, therefore, that Luther eventually came into conflict with the Church over the issue of indulgences. This practice of promising and certifying forgiveness of sins in return for a cash payment had a long and complicated history, and many besides Luther were shocked and offended by the suggestion that a state of spiritual grace could be reached by such mercenary methods.

A new wave of indulgence selling was launched by Pope Julius II in 1507 to finance the rebuilding of St Peter's church in Rome, and the spread of these sales to Germany was facilitated by a bargain struck between Leo X and the Archbishop-Elector of Mainz, Albert of Brandenburg (1514). By the sale of these indulgences Albert was allowed to raise money to recoup the bribes distributed to acquire his archbishopric. In Brandenburg and the surrounding territories the chief salesman was a Dominican monk, Johann Tetzel, whose methods were vulgar even by the normal standards. An eyewitness protested that 'he said that if a Christian had slept with his mother, and placed the sum of money in the Pope's indulgence chest, the Pope had the power in heaven and earth to forgive the sin, and that if he forgave it, God must do so also'. As senior theologian at the University of Wittenberg, Luther could not ignore the implications of these indulgences. His famous action (31 October 1517) of publishing his Ninety-five Theses on the subject was, nevertheless, nothing more than the normal method of initiating academic debate.

Within a year, Luther's attack on indulgences had become a cause célèbre throughout Germany and even beyond the Alps. The Archbishop of Mainz and the Dominican order both played major roles in the escalation of the affair, the one eager not to lose money, the other to protect Tetzel. Both used the tactic of attacking Luther for denying the authority of the papacy. In a public disputation at Leipzig (June 1519) the Bavarian theologian Johann Eck drew parallels between Luther's writings and those of the Bohemian heretic Jan Hus. Instead of the embarrassed recantation that he expected, Eck got only a blunt admission from Luther that, if Hus's views were supported by the scriptures, then Hus was right, and the Pope was wrong. At Leipzig, therefore, the purely academic stage of the dispute came to an end, and Luther became a rebel in spite of himself. Although he believed that he was only restating a message that had lain half-hidden in the scriptures for 1500 years, he now found the Church denying that message and defending abuses in the interests of its political power.

That a mere Saxon monk survived the hostility of Rome was very largely due to the protection of his political overlord, the Elector Frederick of Saxony, who sought equally to protect the academic reputation of his university and to preserve his territories against external interference. It was also important that Frederick occupied a position of some significance in the delicate politics of Germany. Even before the death of the Emperor Maximilian (January 1519), it was clear that the Elector's vote would be vital if Maximilian were to secure the election of his young grandson, Charles. On the other hand, if Pope Leo hoped to break the Habsburg monopoly of imperial power, he would

4.1 The Indulgences Controversy

Source A The only-begotten Son of God deigned to come down from his Father's bosom into the womb of his mother. His purpose was in this way to redeem fallen humanity and make satisfaction for him to God the Father. What a great treasure, then, did God acquire therefrom for the Church militant. Now, this treasure He entrusted to be dispensed for the wellbeing of the faithful through blessed Peter, who bore the keys of Heaven, and Peter's successors as God's representatives on earth. The purposes served should be proper and reasonable: sometimes total, sometimes partial remission of punishment due for temporal sins; and for these ends the treasure should be applied in mercy to those who are truly penitent and have made their confession.
Part of the bull *Unigenitus,* issued by Pope Clement VI, 1343

Source B Our aim is that the salvation of souls may be secured above all at that time when they most need the intercession of others and are least able to help themselves. We wish by our Apostolic authority to draw on the treasure of the Church and to succour the souls in Purgatory who died united with Christ through love, and whose lives have merited that such intercessions should now be offered through an Indulgence of this kind.

In reliance upon the divine mercy and the fullness of our authority, we grant indulgence as follows: If any parents or other Christians are moved by obligations of piety towards these very souls who are exposed to the fire of purgatory, let them during the stated period of ten years give a fixed amount of money for the repair of the Church of Saints. It is then our will that full remission should avail by intercession for the said souls in purgatory, to win them relief from their punishments.
Part of the bull *Salvator Noster,* issued by Pope Sixtus V, 1476

Source C We do herewith proclaim that our most holy Lord Leo X has given and bestowed to all Christian believers of either sex who lend their helpful hand for the reconstruction of the cathedral church of St Peter in Rome complete indulgence as well as other graces and freedoms. Concerning the contribution to the chest, the confessors are to ask those making confession, after having explained the full forgiveness and privilege of the indulgence: How much money or other temporal goods they would conscientiously give for such full forgiveness? But those who do not have any money should supply their contribution with prayer. For the kingdom of Heaven should be open to the poor no less than to the rich.
Summary Instructions of Albert of Brandenburg for the sale of indulgences, 1517

need Frederick's vote and perhaps even his candidacy in the election. Neither Emperor nor Pope could afford to make an enemy of the Elector of Saxony.

LUTHER AND THE PRINTING PRESS

Three main factors transformed a personal crusade into a substantial reforming movement between 1519 and 1521. One was the particular set of political circumstances that existed in contemporary Germany. The second was the recent development of the printing press. Some 200 printing presses already existed in Germany in 1500. Nuremberg, Strasbourg and Basle were all major centres of printing deeply sympathetic to the Reformation, and another, Leipzig, showed divided loyalties. The output of the German presses was also increasing even before the religious tracts of the Reformation accelerated the process. While recent research can identify 150 different titles printed in Germany in 1518, the respective figures for 1520 and for 1524 are 570 titles and 990.

The third crucial factor was the ability of Martin Luther himself to exploit this medium. He possessed a remarkable talent for the blunt and forceful expression of his views in print, and he showed shrewd judgement in his decision to abandon heavy Latin scholarship in favour of the popular pamphlet. Ten to forty pages long, written

Source D You should know that all who confess and in penance put alms into the coffer will obtain complete remission for all their sins. Don't you hear the voices of your wailing dead parents and others who say, 'Have mercy upon me, because we are in severe punishment and pain. From this you could redeem us with small alms and yet you do not want to do so. You let us lie in flames so that we come only slowly to the promised glory.' You may have letters which let you have, in life and in the hour of death, full remission for the punishment which belongs to sin.

Sermon of Johann Tetzel, 1517

Source E
1. When our Lord and master, Jesus Christ, said 'Repent', he meant that the whole life of believers should be one of penitence.
5. The Pope has neither the will nor the power to remit any penalties beyond those he has imposed either at his own discretion or by canon law.
6. The Pope can remit no guilt, but only declare and confirm that it has been remitted by God; or, at most, he can remit it in cases reserved to his discretion.
20. Therefore the Pope, by his full remission of all penalties, does not mean 'all' in the absolute sense, but only those imposed by himself.
21. Hence those preachers of indulgences are wrong when they say that a man is absolved and saved from every penalty by the Pope's indulgence.
22. Rather, he cannot remit to souls in purgatory any penalty which canon law declares should have been paid in the present life.
49. Christians should be taught that the Pope's pardons are useful only if they do not rely on them, but most harmful if they lose the fear of God through them.

From the Ninety-five Theses of Martin Luther, 1517

QUESTIONS

a. Explain the following terms that occur in these sources: 'souls in purgatory', 'the reconstruction of the cathedral church of St Peter', 'canon law'.

b. According to Sources A, B and C, in what ways was the range and purpose of papal indulgences extended between 1343 and 1517?

c. How far does Tetzel, in Source D, depart from the spirit of the papal bulls quoted in sources A and B?

d. In what ways do the claims that Martin Luther makes in Source E challenge the powers and claims of the papacy?

4.2 The Reformation treatises

Of the twenty-four works that Luther wrote in 1520, three were of particular importance in the working out of his theology, and these have become known as the 'Reformation treatises'.

To the Nobility of the German Nation (August 1520). In the light of the failure of the Church to reform its faults, that duty falls upon the temporal princes of Germany. To the objection that laymen had no right to interfere in Church affairs, Luther replied with the doctrine of the 'priesthood of all believers'. As he found no scriptural authority for the sacrament of ordination, he concluded that faith, rather than a spurious rite, is the true sign of spiritual superiority. Every faithful Christian, therefore, is in effect a priest and thus able to act in the affairs of the Church. This claim, that the established priesthood had no necessary superiority over the laity, had enormous implications for the moral authority of the Church, and in other areas such as canon law.

A Prelude Concerning the Babylonish Captivity (October 1520). Luther attacked anew the ecclesiastical laws and traditions that had been developed by the Church, rather than appearing in the scriptures. He recognised scriptural authority for only three of the Church's seven sacraments (Eucharist, baptism and penance), he denounced the doctrine of transubstantiation, and he advocated that all worshippers, and not just the clergy, should receive communion 'in both kinds'.

The Liberty of the Christian Man (November 1520). This was one of the most difficult and misunderstood of Luther's works. He stressed that, because the Christian was saved 'by faith alone', he or she was free of any obligation to perform good works as a means of achieving salvation. He stressed, however, that the true Christian would still perform good works, not out of any self-interest, but out of the unselfish love that derived from true faith. A little earlier, in *A Sermon on Good Works* (May 1520), he had used the metaphor that good works were to faith as healthy limbs were to the body as a whole, the result rather than the cause of health. Luther certainly did not intend to suggest that the true Christian was free from the political and social obligations that bound all men.

Hajo Holborn has estimated that between 1517 and 1520 Luther may have distributed as many as 300,000 copies of his works. Many different social and political circumstances contributed to the success of the Reformation in Germany, yet one must not minimise the impact made by the reformer himself, by his conviction, by his fervour in the pulpit, and by his literary output. Philip Melanchthon claimed that 'Luther is everything, a miracle among men; what he speaks and writes grips the heart and leaves behind a wonderfully deep impression.'

A SUMMARY OF LUTHER'S THEOLOGY

By the end of 1520 the main body of Lutheran theology had emerged, dominated by two positive elements. The leading principle of all Protestant teaching was the belief in the supremacy of the scriptures as the source of all religious truth. There existed no legitimate need for any external agency, such as the Church, to stand between mankind and God as an interpreter. Second, the most important conclusion that Luther drew from the scriptures was that hell could only be avoided through faith. The forgiveness of sins, without which no person could enter heaven, was not a prize to be won by human endeavour, but a gift bestowed by the mercy of God.

From these positive elements emerged several negative ones. Some of the teachings of the Roman Church seemed to have no foundation in the scriptures. Thus the claim of the Church hierarchy that the Pope possessed full powers, bestowed directly by God, over all spiritual affairs was unacceptable. He also rejected, as a consequence of the doctrine of 'justification by faith', the notion that salvation was achieved through the Church, the sole custodian of the almost magical powers of the sacraments. He rejected four of the seven sacraments of the Roman Church, and rejected the Church's emphasis upon good works as a means to salvation. Such works he saw as merely a symptom of faith, and not in themselves a cause of salvation. In short, the very keynote of Lutheranism, and of the Protestant Reformation, was that salvation depended upon the individual's relationship with

in German, and published at a price within the reach of most literate men, such pamphlets constituted a revolution in popular communication.

God through faith, rather than upon the Church's mediation between humanity and God.

Luther struggled to reach a satisfactory definition of the most important of the sacraments, the Eucharist. He could find no scriptural justification for the Roman doctrine of transubstantiation, yet the scriptures did clearly state, in referring to the bread eaten at the Last Supper, '*hoc est corpus meum* – this is my body'. Luther was forced by the scriptural evidence to conclude that Christ must still in some way be really, physically present in the bread and in the wine during the service. This notion has sometimes been given the name 'consubstantiation'. By way of explanation, Luther drew a parallel with what happened in the blacksmith's forge: 'Iron and fire are two substances which mix together in red-hot iron in such a manner that every portion contains both iron and fire. Why cannot the glorified body of Christ be similarly found in every part of the substance of the bread?'

LUTHER'S POLITICAL CONSERVATISM

Should Luther be regarded as part of a sixteenth-century movement away from medieval authoritarianism and intellectual rigidity, or did he simply represent a new form of rigidity? The reformer's social and political ideas generally reflected the essential conservatism of a man who saw himself as restoring the purity of a lost past, and who regarded popes and indulgence-sellers as the true revolutionaries and rebels against scriptural truth. Luther had no time for those radicals who held that the true Christian was free from the worldly obligations which bound the ordinary man to his political superiors. Laws of secular obedience, he stressed, were decreed by God to impose order and obedience of His commandments, and it was therefore the Christian's duty not only to tolerate the secular power, but also to aid it in all ways.

Yet it would be wrong to accuse Luther merely of pandering to the princes in order to gain their protection. He clearly instructed his followers that, while they had a duty to obey, they also had an obligation to 'rebuke, and judge boldly and openly'

in cases of corrupt or evil government. On the other hand, they were strictly enjoined not to go beyond frank criticism, for open rebellion was among the greatest of sins, far more dangerous and evil than the corrupt government which it sought to correct or destroy.

CONDEMNATION BY POPE AND EMPEROR

In June 1520 the bull *Exsurge Domine* condemned forty-one of Luther's theses or subsequent statements. It took issue with Luther over penance, purgatory, indulgences, and especially on the key question of papal authority. Luther produced a sarcastic and satirical reply, *Against the Accursed Bull of Antichrist*, and presided over the burning of a copy of the bull. This gesture represented a rejection of the authority of the Church hierarchy which was almost unprecedented. From this point there could be no turning back, and Luther was formally excommunicated by the Roman church (January 1521) in the bull *Decet Romanum Pontificem*.

In that same month the young Emperor Charles V convened his first Imperial **Diet** at Worms. The Diet represented a moment of extreme danger for the reformer, but his chances of survival were greatly enhanced by the remarkable degree of popular support that he seemed to enjoy in the town and the surrounding region. Charles's verdict, all the same, was one of unqualified opposition to Luther's views. With Luther remaining character-istically intransigent, the Elector of Saxony found himself faced with the options of surrendering Luther, with the political humiliation that this would entail, or risking the combined opposition of the Pope, the Emperor and the more orthodox German princes.

Luther's continued career thus owed much, perhaps everything, to a great piece of political cunning by the Elector Frederick. On his return journey from Worms the reformer was kidnapped and moved secretly to the relative security of the Wartburg castle, near Eisenach. There he remained *incognito* for several months, writing copiously. At this time Luther executed the most important of all his works, his translation of the New Testament of the Bible into German. Its impact was immediate and enormous. Published in September 1522, the first edition was sold out within three months, and another 300 editions appeared in Luther's lifetime. It was a revolution in at least two senses. The Bible formed a momentous stage in the development of the modern German language. In the context of the German Reformation, Luther was now placing the all-important source of divine truth in the hands of the masses. The many who could not read it themselves merely had to find a literate person to do the job for them, and the Word of God was available to them in their own tongue. 'The mass sale of the vernacular scriptures', commented A.G. Dickens, 'proved the most irrevocable act of the Reformation.'

THE IMPACT OF LUTHERANISM

The intellectuals

Many of the great humanist scholars who dominated the intellectual life of contemporary Germany had already reached conclusions similar to Luther's on many of the issues that he had addressed. The great humanists of the previous generation, Conrad Celtis and Johannes Reuchlin, had frequently attacked superstition, corruption and the excessive influence of a foreign Pope over Germany. It is scarcely surprising, therefore, that many men trained in this humanist tradition were to be found among those whose pens supported the reforming cause. Prominent among them were Andreas Osiander, Justus Jonas and Martin Bucer. If some of these men were later to part company with Luther on key points of doctrine, others followed him at the outset for entirely misconceived motives. The great humanist writer and satirist Ulrich von Hutten, for instance, followed with great enthusiasm what he understood primarily as a struggle for national independence.

The greatest of the humanists, however, could not bring himself to join the ranks of Luther's admirers. Erasmus regretted that Luther had abandoned the path of gradual reform for that of rebellion. He regretted, too, that Luther laid so

4.3 Leading figures in the German Reformation

AGRICOLA, Johannes (1494–1566). Follower of Luther, but parted company with him in 1536 over the issue of repentance. Active in implementing reform in Wittenberg, Frankfurt and Eisleben. Later (1540) served as court preacher to Elector Joachim II of Brandenburg.

BUCER, Martin (1491–1551). Born Alsace. Entered Dominican order, but was won over to evangelism by the writings of Erasmus and the preaching of Luther (1518). Prime mover in the reform of Strasbourg from 1523. His moderation was evident in his cooperation with Luther (1536) and later with Calvin. Regius Professor of Divinity at Cambridge (1549).

BULLINGER, Heinrich (1504–75). Born Bremgarten, Switzerland. Studied at Cologne where he encountered the writings of Luther. Joined Zwingli in Zurich (1527) and succeeded him as the city's religious leader (1531). Active in the search for common ground among reformers, producing to that end the *Helvetic Confession* (1536), *Consensus Tigurinus* (with Calvin 1549) and the *Second Helvetic Confession* (1566).

CARLSTADT, Andreas (1480–1541). An orthodox teacher of Thomist philosophy, he was greatly disillusioned by a visit to Rome (1515). Anticipated some of Luther's views, and carried out radical reforms in Wittenberg in Luther's absence (1521). Left Wittenberg (1524), and collaborated with Zwingli in Zurich (1530). Professor of Theology at Basle (1534).

HUTTEN, Ulrich von (1488–1523). German humanist and Imperial knight. Travelled and studied in Italy, and befriended Erasmus. Crowned poet laureate by Maximilian I (1517). Major contributor to *Letters of Obscure Men* (1515–17). Supporter of Luther and prime mover in the Knights' War against the German princes (1522). Following defeat, he lived briefly in exile in Zurich.

JONAS, Justus (1493–1555). Educated at Erfurt and Wittenberg, and a close associate of Luther from 1521. Attended Colloquy of Marburg (1529), and published many of Luther's writings.

MELANCHTHON, Philip (1497–1560). Born Baden. Professor of Greek at Wittenberg (1518) where he became closely associated with Luther. Published *Loci Communes* (1522) to establish common ground between the evangelicals. Assisted Luther in his translation of the Bible and at Colloquy of Marburg (1529). Leading Protestant representative at Diet of Augsburg (1530). Leading advocate of moderate Protestantism in the 1530s and 1540s. Leader of Saxon Protestantism after the death of Luther (1546).

MÜNTZER, Thomas (?1490–1525). Priest and early convert to evangelical ideals. Preacher at Zwickau (1520), expelled for his radical views. Broke with Luther, regarding him as socially conservative, and led the peasants of Thuringia during the Peasants' War (1524–5). Captured, tortured and executed after the defeat of the rising.

OECOLAMPADIUS, Johann (1482–1531). Educated Bologna, Heidelberg and Tübingen. Preacher at Basle (1515) and helped to prepare Erasmus's Greek New Testament. Early supporter of Luther and prominent advocate of reform in Basle and Berne (1528). Supported Zwingli at Colloquy of Marburg (1529).

OSIANDER, Andreas (1498–1552). Convert to Lutheranism (1522) and leading figure in the reform of Nuremberg. Forced to leave Nuremberg, he became Professor of Theology at Königsberg (1549).

---

little stress upon human worth or upon the freedom of the human will in the decision to do good or evil. Luther, equally, had little time for Erasmus. He wrote as early as 1517 that 'I am now reading Erasmus and each day my estimate of him decreases. Human things carry more weight with him than divine things.' Luther had discovered a cause worth dying for, and he despised Erasmus's continuous pleas for moderation and compromise.

The German intellectuals who opposed Luther were certainly in a minority, yet two Catholic writers are worthy of note. Luther's old adversary, Johann Eck, was perhaps the most persistent and penetrative of his intellectual opponents. On the level of satire and more popular writing, the Catholic cause was also well served by Thomas Murner, whose satire *Of the Great Lutheran Fool* (1522) gave the Roman cause its closest parallel to the punchy and immensely popular work of Hutten or of Luther himself.

Social radicalism and revolution

By 1520–1, Luther had attacked both the doctrine and the structure of the Church, but had offered no alternative social or political visions. There were many in Germany eager to propose such alternatives, and the majority of such men were not bound by Luther's profound sense of social and political conservatism.

Some of the earliest signs of social instability were to be seen at Erfurt (June 1521) in an outburst of incoherent anti-clericalism known as the *pfaffensturm*, in which clerical property was destroyed and tithe records were burned. Even at Wittenberg there were signs that the reforming movement might be slipping out of Luther's hands during his enforced absence in the Wartburg. Under Luther's university colleague Andreas Carlstadt a new liturgy was introduced, partly in German,

monks and nuns were released from their vows, clerical marriage was permitted, even encouraged, and **iconoclasm** was widespread. Carlstadt also showed increasing sympathy for such visionary extremists as the band of former weavers who called themselves the 'Zwickau Prophets'. They preached a direct relationship with God through mysticism, denied that academic learning had any role to play in the understanding of religious truth, and sought a radical reform of a corrupt society. Luther's opposition to such views was total. He returned to Wittenberg in March 1522 and achieved one of his greatest practical successes in a week of concentrated preaching, persuading the citizens to turn their backs upon such radicalism. Wittenberg was saved, but Carlstadt continued to radicalise Luther's doctrines elsewhere, refusing to accept baptism as a sacrament, and adopting a purely symbolic interpretation of the Eucharist.

Thomas Müntzer posed an even greater threat. He, too, was deeply influenced by generations of German mystical writers and became more and more convinced of the need for social revolution. Although often portrayed by left-wing historians as an early advocate of class struggle, Müntzer's beliefs were primarily spiritual. The common man, he protested, could not attain spiritual enlightenment while he remained wholly preoccupied with the crushing burden of his poverty. Social change was, therefore, important to him as a precondition of spiritual change.

Despite the links that many historians have drawn between the doctrines of Luther and the revolt of the German peasants in 1525, it would be misleading to view this event as part of the German Reformation. Luther's reaction to the revolt was in keeping with his social conservatism. His *Admonition to Peace on the Twelve Articles* (April 1525) clearly placed the initial blame on the shoulders of the princes on account of their tyranny and greed. The peasants, on the other hand, were severely criticised for the sin of rebellion against legitimate authority, and taken to task for using the gospels as a cloak for worldly aims. There could be, he reminded them, no such thing as Christian rebellion, for true Christians 'are not so many that they can get together in mobs'.

Within a month, however, angered by the growing violence of the rebellion, Luther wrote his notorious tract *Against the Robbing and Murdering Hordes of Peasants* (May 1525). In his most violent language Luther asserted that 'there is nothing more obnoxious and devilish than a revolutionary man', and exhorted the authorities to strike down the rebels 'as one must kill a mad dog'. This tract has led to the condemnation of Luther by historians of the left as 'one of the great bootlickers of absolute monarchy' (F. Engels). It must be made clear, however, that the work was written at the height of peasant power, before the peasant defeat at Frankenhausen, and that it therefore illustrates Luther's conservatism rather than any more sinister motives.

With the failure of the peasants' rebellion, Luther's message could no longer be seen as part of an answer to the spiritual and social ills of society as a whole. Lutheranism became increasingly a creed of princes, controlled by those very powers that the peasants' leaders had sought to curb. Increasingly, the common man would have to look elsewhere to satisfy his spiritual hunger.

The cities

The most spectacular area of success for the reformed religion was in the cities. This success was also a crucial factor in the survival of Lutheranism as something more than a state-sponsored faith. This development also gave it a great range of advantages. The cities were compact, so the 'word' could be communicated to many in a short space of time. This very compactness made it easier for the urban populace to exert pressure upon their social superiors than it had been for their rural counterparts. Once converted, cities offered substantial means of defence to the reformers, and extraordinary strategic problems to any prince or commander who wished to re-establish the old religion.

Two main agents contributed to the protestantisation of the cities. One was the Lutheran, or sometimes Zwinglian, missionary preacher arriving in the city from areas already reformed. Such was the role of Osiander in Nuremberg, of Frosch and Oecolampadius in Augsburg, and of Zell, Bucer and Capito in Strasbourg. The other agent was often the mob of

local citizens demanding the reform of religion, or at least the toleration of reforming preachers. Their motives were complex and open to dispute. Socialist historians have placed a heavy emphasis upon social and economic tensions, and have noted that in such northern cities as Stralsund, Rostock and Wismar the arrival of the Reformation coincided with economic stagnation and depression. Other motives included widespread

---

4.4 The Reformation in the German cities

Augsburg. Refusal to obey Charles V's order for the expulsion of evangelical preachers (1530). Preachers petitioned city council to take action against Catholic worship (1533). Council decision for reform (1534).

Berne. Edict on scriptural preaching (1523). City council, controlled by reformist majority, authorised clerical marriage (1527). Mass abolished, altars and images removed (1528). Establishment of reformed structure for Church (1532).

Memmingen. Introduction of Communion 'in both kinds' and abolition of clerical privileges (1523–4). Mass abolished (1528). Reformed liturgy (1529). Orders for reformed structure of Church (1531–2).

Mühlhausen (Mulhouse). Reform of worship (1523). Reform of structure of Church (1528–9). Educational reform (1528). Mass abolished (1528–9)

Nuremberg. Instructions on scriptural preaching (1522). Baptismal service in German and reform of the Mass (1524). Suppression of monasteries (1525). Mass in German (1525). Articles on reformed doctrine (1528). Reformed catechism (1533).

Strasbourg. Edict on scriptural preaching (1523). Introduction of Communion 'in both kinds' (1524). Baptismal service and Mass in German (1524). Reformed catechism (1527). Mass abolished (1529). Monasteries closed (1529). New Church structure introduced (1531–4).

Ulm. Edicts on scriptural preaching (1522–4). Educational reform (1528). Introduction of reformed hymn book and psalter (1529). Reformed liturgy and system of clerical discipline (1531). Mass abolished (1531).

What patterns of reform, if any, can be deduced from these details?

anti-clericalism, unrest among university students as at Erfurt (1521), objection to church taxes as at Speyer (1525), and social unrest connected with the peasants' war as in Frankfurt (1524–5). Amid all these secular, or partly secular, motives, it is important not to overlook the fact that humble citizens could also be moved by purely religious considerations.

The effect of Lutheranism on the German cities was profound and lasting. According to Bernd Moeller, reforming theology affected fifty of the sixty-five imperial cities in Germany, half of that number becoming 'fully and finally Protestant'. Such considerations have also caused A.G. Dickens to conclude that 'relatively too much has been said about the godly prince and the formula *cuius regio eius religio*', leaving too little emphasis upon the crucial importance of the reformation that flourished within the protective walls of many of Germany's cities.

The princes

For some of the German princes, the overriding lesson of 1525 was that **evangelical** theology invariably carried with it the risk of social upheaval. By July 1525, therefore, a grouping of conservative princes had formed, including Duke George of Saxony, Albert of Mainz and Joachim of Brandenburg, sworn to resist and destroy the insidious influence of Luther. On the other hand, a significant number of princes continued to support Lutheranism. Albert of Hohenzollern, for example, Grand Master of the Teutonic Knights, dissolved his order, secularised its lands, and embraced the reformed faith. The following year Philip, Landgrave of Hesse, joined the cause, concluding an agreement with the Elector of Saxony to defend the gospel. By 1528 they had been joined by Brandenburg-Ansbach, Mansfeld, Schleswig and Brunswick.

The motives of such princes in taking so bold and dangerous a step were complex and varied. The desire to rid their territories of papal taxation and ecclesiastical law was widespread. The prospect of profit from the seizure of Church property has also been as widely stressed by

historians as it was by contemporaries. 'Under cover of the Gospel', wrote Philip Melanchthon, 'the princes were only intent on the plunder of the churches.' On many occasions, nevertheless, only a relatively small proportion of secularised property passed permanently into the hands of the princes. Philip of Hesse managed to retain 40 per cent of secularised Church lands, but the proportions in Württemberg and in Electoral Saxony were far smaller. Such evidence suggests that there was in some cases a genuine concern about ecclesiastical abuses. Lastly, the political context of the time must be taken into account. Even the Emperor seemed to accept that the best hope of maintaining religious unity in Germany was through a General Council of the Church, but with the sack of Rome in 1527 relations between the Emperor and the Pope slumped to a level that made such cooperation a remote possibility. If in 1525 the problems of the imperial knights and of the rebellious peasants had been solved by the princes themselves, without the aid of an absentee Emperor, was the time not ripe now for those same princes to take the issue of ecclesiastical reform into their own hands?

Luther's direct influence over the religious struggle in Germany declined steadily after 1530. Patriarchal figure though he was in Protestant circles for the rest of his life (*d.* February 1546), his movement passed into other hands. Philip Melanchthon, for instance, continued to move away from, and to soften the impact of, his master's teaching on several points. Successive editions of his *Loci Communes*, the accepted compendium of Lutheran teaching, sought a middle ground between Luther's view of the Eucharist and the views of Bucer and Calvin. Andreas Osiander also began to go his own way, reopening questions about the role of the episcopacy and the validity of clerical marriage. Nor was Luther able to bridge the gap between himself and those Protestant theologians who had never been part of Lutheranism. The so-called Wittenberg Concord (1536), a conciliatory conference between Luther and Bucer, achieved little real agreement on the nature of the Eucharist, and the gap between Luther and Zwingli, evident at their conference at Marburg, continued to yawn.

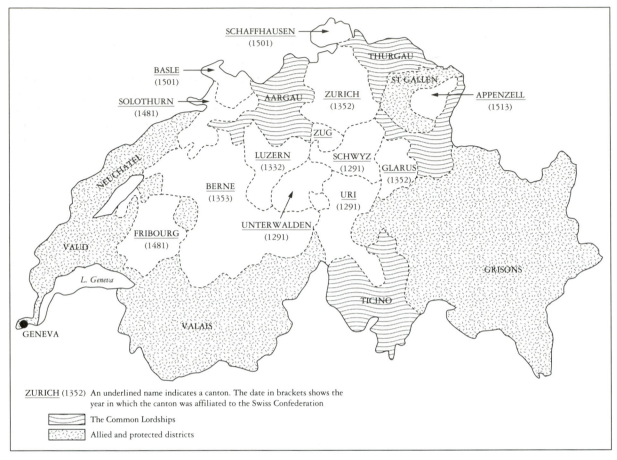

4.5 Switzerland at the time of the Reformation

THE CONDITION OF SWITZERLAND

Contemporary Switzerland was a region of great political diversity. The distinctive features of Swiss politics at the opening of the century were the jealous independence of each political unit, and their common desire to escape from the authority of the Habsburgs. Over the years state after state had broken free from the Empire and had sought security in membership of the Swiss Confederation which, by 1536, numbered thirteen member communities. Politically, this freedom was guaranteed by the Peace of Basle, concluded with the Emperor in 1499. Thereby, the Swiss gained exemption from all fiscal demands of the Empire, although their complete

political independence was not recognised until 1648.

A more realistic guarantee of independence was provided by the military qualities of the Swiss foot soldiers. The regular export of Swiss soldiers to fight as mercenaries in the armies of other Western European states was based upon economic necessity. Although the population of Switzerland in the middle of the sixteenth century was probably little more than 800,000, resources were so limited in many parts that even this amounted to over-population. Military manpower remained a major factor in the economies of the **cantons** until the disastrous defeat of the Swiss pikemen at Marignano in 1515.

Economically and socially these Swiss territories had relatively little in common. The leading towns of the Confederacy were a world apart from the rural cantons. Benefiting from their locations astride major north–south and east–west trade routes, Zurich, Berne and Basle swam 'on the flood-tide of wealth, self-confidence, military prowess and cultured living' (A.G. Dickens). In all three cities the government was dominated by rich merchants, whose trade guilds exercised great social and political influence. The population of the countryside, however, had rarely risen above the level of peasant farmers, their agriculture held back by the mountainous geography of the region, and often reduced to making a living by selling their services as mercenary soldiers. Relations between cities and countryside were distrustful. Unsurprisingly, therefore, this was a Confederation with no seat of government, no head of state, no shared legal code or currency. Its component parts seemed to agree only when they felt the need to defend themselves against an external threat.

The ecclesiastical structure of Switzerland had no greater unity than the political structure. The boundaries of the six Swiss sees (Constance, Basle, Chur, Lausanne, Sion and Geneva) did not correspond to the politicial boundaries, and the bishops struggled in vain to impose their will upon the political authorities or to stamp out the clerical abuses that flourished in the remote valleys. As in Germany, relations between the Church and the population at large were complicated by the political authority exercised by leading Swiss churchmen. The bishops of Basle and Geneva at the beginning of the sixteenth century were political lords in the same way that many German bishops were, while the substantial power and independence of such monastic landlords as St Gall or Engelberg provided further fuel for anti-clericalism.

HULDRYCH ZWINGLI

The Reformation in Switzerland was influenced by developments in other parts of Western Europe, yet it produced one native theologian and reformer worthy to stand alongside Luther and Calvin as a founder and shaper of Protestantism. Huldrych Zwingli was a native of Wildhaus in north-west Switzerland (*b.* 1484). He studied with distinction at the universities of Vienna (1498–1502) and Basle (1502–6), following the traditions of conservative scholasticism rather than the more fashionable Christian humanism. As a chaplain to Swiss mercenaries fighting for the pope against the French, receiving a papal pension for his pains, his career remained orthodox until some time between 1516 and 1518. He seems then to have suffered severe doubts about the morality of the trade in mercenaries, which he expressed in an early work, *The Tale of the Ox*. In it Switzerland is portrayed as the passive beast of burden, exploited and tormented by sharper, more ambitious animals.

There is no evidence that Zwingli read any of Luther's works before 1520, by which time his own conversion was well under way. Zwingli owed a clear debt, on the other hand, to Erasmus. Ten years earlier he had been inspired to learn Greek by his reading of Erasmus's works, and in 1516 he acquired a copy of the recently published New Testament, translated by Erasmus from the Greek. While the excitement of this access to the true word of God was still fresh, Zwingli accepted the appointment as priest at the Great Minster in Zurich (December 1518).

THE REFORMATION IN ZURICH

As in Saxony and Geneva, the Reformation established itself in Zurich through a combination of local political circumstances and the influence of an outstanding theologian. Politically, Zurich was among the most democratic of the Swiss cities. It was governed mainly by its guilds and by a body of electors which included perhaps a third of the city's 6,000 inhabitants. The magistrates of Zurich, who appointed Zwingli to his post in the Great Minster, were well used to dealing with ecclesiastical matters within their city, and would have seen little that was dangerous or radical in many of the ideas reaching Zurich from the north. Zwingli thus worked in a relatively liberal atmosphere.

Already affected by the evangelical spirit and eager to spread the true understanding of the scriptures that he felt he had acquired, Zwingli's first action was to undertake a series of sermons expounding the New Testament book by book. His increasing reformist sympathies can be seen in his renunciation of his papal pension (1520) and his stance in a local controversy over the eating of meat during Lent (1522). In the same year he rejected the laws of celibacy, and married. Zwingli had by this stage accepted the scriptures as the supreme authority in all such arguments. 'I came at length', he wrote at this time, 'to trust in no words so much as those which proceeded from the Bible. If I saw a teaching could bear the test, I accepted it; if not, I rejected it.'

By January 1523, when Zwingli presented to the city authority his Sixty-seven Conclusions on the subjects of salvation, the papacy, the Mass, the intercession of the saints, and the relative merits of faith and good works, Zurich had unequivocally embraced evangelical reform. In the course of 1524 the city council ordered that Zurich's churches be cleansed of images and pictures, and that the local monastic establishments be taken over by the city for charitable uses. In April 1525 the council voted by a small majority to discontinue the Roman Mass.

ZWINGLIANISM AND ITS IMPACT

By this greater concern with the external trappings of worship, Zwingli moved towards a more radical brand of reform than that of Luther. In placing greater emphasis upon the 'purification' of church buildings, upon the elimination of ornaments, music and other distractions, Zwingli foreshadowed the 'puritanism' of later decades. Zwingli also broke new ground in the reorganisation of the services and the social role of the Church. In place of the Roman liturgy he instituted two simple and functional forms of service. The Mass was replaced by a commemorative meal in which the bread and the wine were delivered from a table in the midst of the congregation, rather than from an altar with its suggestions of sacrifice. The other daily services were replaced by what Zwingli referred to as 'prophesyings', gatherings centred upon readings from the scriptures, accompanied by detailed commentaries. In short, Zwingli laid down in Zurich the bases of most modern forms of nonconformist Christian worship.

One major doctrinal difference existed between Zwingli and Luther. Although agreeing in their condemnation of transubstantiation, the two were unable to agree upon an alternative definition of the nature of the Eucharist. To Luther's interpretation, Zwingli objected that physical objects could not have spiritual properties. The bread and the wine in the Eucharist must thus remain merely bread and wine, and Christ's words at the Last Supper, 'This is my body; this is my blood', had to be read as meaning 'This signifies my body'. It is not quite true, however, to say that Zwingli preached a wholly symbolic interpretation of the Eucharist. He was willing to believe that Christ was indeed present in the bread and the wine, but only for the truly faithful. For others there was nothing present but ordinary food and drink.

Such theology had some appeal in Switzerland and in parts of southern Germany. Within Switzerland, Basle, Berne, Schaffhausen, Appenzell and Glarus had joined Zurich by 1529. Beyond Switzerland, Zwinglian communities were established at Ulm, Strasbourg, Augsburg, Memmingen, Frankfurt and Constance. It was far too radical, on the other hand, for the orthodox leaders of the Church in southern Germany, or for Luther himself. In an attempt to create a united front among the evangelicals Philip of Hesse brought Zwingli and Luther together at Marburg in May 1529. This Colloquy of Marburg produced agreement on fourteen articles of faith, but could find no common ground on the vexed issue of the Eucharist. Legend has it that Luther chalked the words '*Hoc est corpus meum*' on the table in front of him, and refused to depart from the literal meaning of the biblical text. The Marburg Colloquy guaranteed, in short, that Swiss-German Protestantism would enter the 1530s divided and at odds.

RELIGIOUS CIVIL WAR IN SWITZERLAND

With half of the Swiss cantons remaining faithful to the Catholic Church, open religious conflict was always a probability. In February 1529 the

Protestant cantons formed the Christian Civic Union (*Christliches Burgrecht*) to defend their faith, while the cantons of Uri, Schwyz, Unterwalden, Zug, Lucerne and Fribourg actively resisted evangelical preaching. Fearing a Protestant alliance with German Lutheran princes, they concluded an alliance of their own with the Habsburgs (April 1529). A short, bloodless conflict was concluded by the Peace of Kappel (June 1529), whereby the Catholics agreed to abandon their Habsburg alliance and to permit Protestant preaching in the so-called Common Lordships, Swiss territories outside the control of the cantons.

This was not enough for Zurich. The city's foreign policy seems to have aimed at nothing less than the evangelisation of the Confederation as a whole, and the Protestant territories continued to exert pressure upon their Catholic neighbours by means of an economic blockade. When war was renewed, Zurich suffered a military disaster. Poorly prepared and isolated from their allies, the city could muster only about 2,000 men to confront the Catholics near Kappel. Their force was overrun (11 October 1531), and Zwingli was among the 500 citizens of Zurich killed. The second Peace of Kappel left Zwingli's work in Zurich secure, for Protestantism was guaranteed there, as well as in Basle, Berne, St Gall and Schaffhausen. His hopes of a Protestant Switzerland were wrecked, however, and the Confederation left permanently split between the two creeds.

Like Luther and Calvin, Zwingli had achieved an enormous impact by his personality and by his power in the pulpit. Unlike them, he had failed in the political strategy with which he hoped to consolidate and extend his reformation. Zwingli has been criticised for an inflexibility of attitude which split the Protestant movement at a time when it badly needed to be united, and it was left to his successor in Zurich, Heinrich Bullinger, to achieve a much broader alliance with Calvinism than Zwingli ever achieved with Lutheranism.

ANABAPTISM

Luther and Zwingli both wished to combine scripturally sound theology with the strict maintenance of the existing social order and the continuing rule of the temporal authorities. Many of those who started as their followers wished to pursue the search for scriptural truth to its logical conclusion, even if that were as damaging to the hierarchy of the state as to the hierarchy of the Church. These more radical reformers were described even at this early stage by the blanket term 'Anabaptist'. The term derived from the sensation caused by Conrad Grebel, Felix Mantz and others when they claimed in Zurich (January 1525) that the Bible gave no authority for the baptism of infants, and that baptism should instead be administered to adults able, on their own responsibility, to embrace the word of God. Although several thousand people may have had themselves rebaptised in the region, the Zurich authorities prescribed the death penalty for all unrepentant Anabaptists, a penalty which Mantz suffered the following year.

It is hard to understand the ferocity of this official reaction unless one appreciates that the Anabaptist leaders were rejecting far more than infant baptism. It was these Anabaptists who truly broke with the old religious regime by rejecting altogether the authority of a governing hierarchy, and trying to free the individual to make his or her own peace with God. Applying the fundamental evangelical test of whether a practice was justified by scripture, the radicals also came to a variety of disturbing political and social conclusions. The first concerted manifesto of the Anabaptists was the Schleitheim Confession of 1527. The authors of the document considered it unjustifiable to use weapons or legal processes against one's fellows, and they rejected any form of oath as effectively taking the Lord's name in vain. Although Anabaptism was too diverse to be governed by one 'confession', it is generally true that the personal nature of this form of religious belief made it impossible for the believer to accept without question the demands and standards of any other social or political group. The authority of the princes, the doctrine of the Church, the payment of taxes and tithes, all seemed to be threatened. Fears that the very fabric of society was at risk soon seemed to find confirmation in the actions of some of the more extreme Anabaptists.

THE SPREAD AND IMPACT OF ANABAPTISM

The onslaught of the Zurich magistrates began a long process of persecution and dispersal for the Anabaptists. Balthasar Hubmaier carried his beliefs to Augsburg, and then on to Moravia, where the movement enjoyed its most notable successes. He attracted some 6,000 adherents in the region within a year, establishing so-called 'Hutterite' communities, which flourished until the 1620s. From there Anabaptism established its influence in Bohemia where, by the mid–1530s, eighty communities or more had been set up. The end product, however, was always persecution. Hubmaier and his wife were put to death in Vienna in 1528, while his successor Jakob Hutter died at the stake in 1536. Only in Strasbourg did Anabaptists briefly find the toleration that they preached and desired.

There was, however, another side to Anabaptism, for a few took the search for scriptural truth to extremes. The radical phase of Anabaptism can be dated from about 1529 with the rise to prominence of Melchior Hoffman (c.1500–43). Formerly sympathetic to both Luther and Zwingli, he had become a fierce critic of both, and his religion had moved towards fanaticism. He denied that Christ had ever become man, preached that academic learning had no value compared with divine inspiration, and prophesied that Strasbourg would become the 'New Jerusalem' from which the prophets of the new age would come forth. His last prophecy coincided with Strasbourg's acceptance of the moderate Augsburg Confession, and Hoffman spent his last years there as a prisoner.

Events elsewhere, however, were to haunt conservatives for the rest of the century. In 1533–4, in the aftermath of fanatical outbursts in several parts of the Low Countries, a group of Dutch and German extremists gained control of the city of Münster. Their leaders were Jan Matthys, a baker from Haarlem, and Jan Beukels, 'John of Leyden'. By February 1534 the city was besieged by its prince-bishop, and under the pressures of warfare the defenders established an extreme social and political regime. Property was declared to be held in common, the death penalty was imposed for such anti-social faults as adultery and malicious gossip,

and polygamy was introduced. There was no mercy for the defenders when the city was finally retaken in June 1535. Hundreds of them were slain and the leaders were slowly tortured to death, their remains left to rot, hanging from the church tower. 'God has opened the eyes of the governments by the revolt at Münster', declared Bullinger, 'and thereafter no one would trust even those Anabaptists who claimed to be innocent.' Certainly the Münster episode created great problems for Anabaptist communities elsewhere, and it has recently been claimed that 30,000 lives may have been lost in the subsequent backlash.

That Anabaptism survived the disaster of Münster was largely due to the emphasis placed by other Anabaptist leaders on the simple, inward-looking, pacifist faith of their early predecessors. The most notable of this next generation was the Dutch former priest Menno Simons (1496–1561). Converted in 1536, Simons spent the next years of his life wandering between communities in the Netherlands and northern Germany, preaching non-violence and providing guidance and encouragement to the threatened believers. His 'Mennonite' followers may be seen as the forerunners of the later Baptist churches. Other notable contributions were made by Henry Niclaes (1502–80), whose 'Family of Love' foreshadowed the Quaker movement, and such writers as Cellarius and Servetus, whose denials of the Holy Trinity paved the way for the later Unitarian Church.

4.6 Glossary

Augustinian. A monastic order, founded in 1256, and based upon the precepts of St Augustine of Hippo (354–430). The order was especially directed to undertake educational and missionary work, together with work within the parishes.

Cantons. The independent political units formed in Switzerland. Component parts of the Swiss Confederation.

Cuius regio eius religio (Latin: 'Whose principality, his religion'). Slogan representing the principle that the temporal ruler of a given territory had the authority, by virtue of his mandate from God, to determine the settlement of religion within his own territories.

Diet. A national or regional assembly. In this case the assembly of the principal estates of the Holy Roman Empire.

Dominican. A monastic order founded by St Dominic in 1215. The order came to be closely identified with the Church hierarchy and with the authority of the papacy.

Evangelical. Broadly used as an alternative term for Protestants. The term refers to the reliance of the reformers upon the gospels (Latin: *evangelium* – gospel).

Iconoclasm. The act of destroying religious images.

Further reading

E. Cameron (1991) *The European Reformation.* Oxford.

A.G. Dickens (1976) *The German Nation and Martin Luther.* London.

H.-J. Goertz (1994) *The Anabaptists.* London.

B.M.G. Reardon (1981) *Religious Thought in the Reformation.* London.

R.W. Scribner (1986) *The German Reformation.* London.

• CHAPTER FIVE•

Calvin and Calvinism

Jean Calvin

The Institutes of the Christian Religion

Calvin's theology

Calvin and the Reformation in Geneva

The *Ecclesiastical Ordinances*

Political opposition in Geneva

Religious opposition in Geneva

The international impact of Calvinism

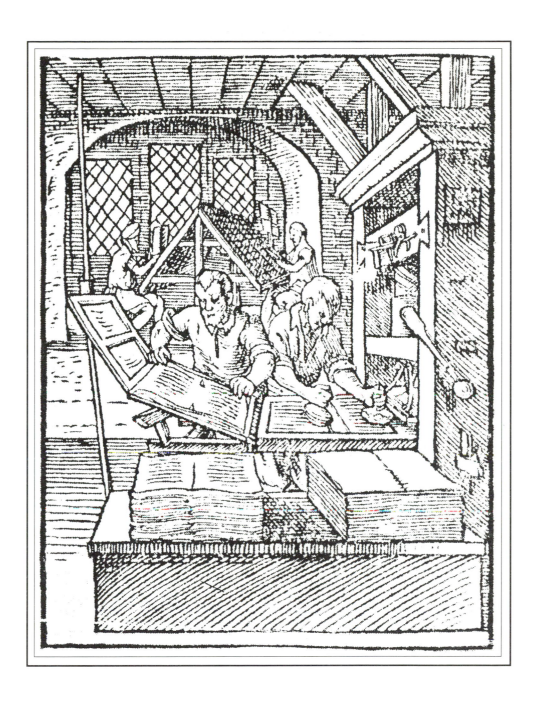

Contemporaries clearly recognised the central role played by the printing press in the spread of the Protestant Reformation. This portrayal of printers at work was engraved in the Netherlands by Jost Amman in 1559

JEAN CALVIN

The second generation of the Reformation was dominated by the theological and organisational genius of one man. Jean Calvin was born (July 1509) at Noyon, in northern France. A more retiring and introverted figure than either Luther or Zwingli, he left only scanty records of his early life, or of his intellectual and spiritual formation. Originally destined for the Church, Calvin changed direction in 1525 or 1526 to follow a familiar pattern of humanist studies. He studied law at Orléans and at Bourges, he acquired a knowledge of Greek, and he published his first work, a humanist commentary upon the Roman author Seneca (1532).

By this time, however, Calvin had come into contact with the doctrinal arguments of the German reformers. It has never been clear exactly when he embraced the reformed faith, but he was in contact by the late 1520s with men with Protestant connections. Pierre Robert, known as Olivetan, was one such, and Melchior Wolmar, a noted Greek scholar and teacher, introduced Calvin to the study of Greek. Different authorities have placed Calvin's actual conversion at a variety of dates between 1525 and 1534, but most probably in late 1529 or early 1530.

At this time France was becoming a dangerous place for Protestants. When Nicholas Cop, rector of the University of Paris, referred sympathetically to the works of Erasmus and Luther in an academic address (1531), he was forced to flee the country; and Calvin, who seems to have played a part in the preparation of the address, thought it wise to leave Paris for the provinces. The affair of the 'placards' in October 1534 , in which Zwinglian attacks upon the Mass were posted around Paris and other major French cities, caused a reaction which endangered all those sympathetic to reformed religion. With the formal outlawing of 'Lutherans' in January 1535, Calvin quit France and sought safety across the Swiss border in Basle.

THE INSTITUTES OF THE CHRISTIAN RELIGION

In Basle, Calvin completed (1536) his greatest theological work, *The Institutes of the Christian Religion (Institutio Religionis Christianae)*. The initial purpose of the *Institutes* was to provide Protestants with an authoritative statement of their doctrinal position. Melanchthon had already attempted to summarise the complex and diverse writings of Luther in his *Loci Communes* in 1522, and Guillaume Farel had undertaken a similar task in 1534, but Calvin now outstripped their efforts in clarity and conciseness. The work thus shows Calvin as a 'second-generation' reformer, able to survey the events of the last two decades and to judge the next necessary steps. The work also shows the importance of Calvin's legal education and training. Where Luther was forced to react, often with passion and emotion, to events that took place around him, Calvin now codified the essential beliefs of the Protestants, and argued their case. It was not their aim, he protested in a long preface addressed to Francis I, to create a new Church, but rather to guide men back to the paths prescribed by scripture and by the early Church. The *Institutes* grew and evolved throughout the rest of Calvin's life, the six chapters of 1536 growing to eighty by the time of the 1559 edition. The work was published in French in 1541 and in English twenty years later, becoming the most comprehensive theological compendium published in the sixteenth century, and the most important work produced by the Protestant Reformation.

CALVIN'S THEOLOGY

In what ways can one speak of 'Calvinism' as a teaching distinct from 'Lutheranism'? Throughout the *Institutes*, Calvin's debt to Luther is evident. With Luther he stressed the infallibility of the scriptures, and their total adequacy for the understanding of God's revealed truth. Like Luther, he accepted the need for careful teaching so that the words of the Bible might be fully understood. Doctrinally, both men by now accepted that only Baptism and the Eucharist could truly be accepted as sacraments with valid scriptural authority. Calvin also agreed wholeheartedly that the sinner was incapable of achieving any good by his own will and efforts, and that salvation was possible only through God's grace.

In two very important respects, however, Calvin placed his emphasis very differently from Luther. The writings of the two men were dominated by two very different conceptions of God. Luther's primary concern had always been with God the Redeemer, and the starting-point of his theology had been the specific problem of how one might achieve salvation. Uppermost in the mind of Calvin was the omnipotence of God and hence His complete mastery over all aspects of humanity. This view of God led logically to the doctrine of predestination. Luther had clearly indicated in his writings, based on St Augustine and St Paul, that one could not hope to influence the question of one's salvation or damnation, and could achieve nothing in this respect without the divine gift of faith. It followed from this that if an omnipotent God granted this gift of faith, then He decided who should be saved and, by denying the gift to others, condemned them to damnation. It also followed, given that God knows everything, that each person's fate must be known to God from the beginning of time. In short, one's eternal fate is decided by an almighty God even before one is born. The doctrine of predestination was to become a matter of fierce controversy, in large part because Calvin laid such stress upon the negative and less agreeable side of the doctrine, and concluded that God must create many humans simply for them to be damned at the end of their lives.

Calvin repeatedly stressed that God's purpose was totally hidden from mortals, and that it was impossible to distinguish the elect from the reprobate, yet this 'double predestination' was among the most radical ideas formulated in the sixteenth century. Consistently, men and women would be convinced that by leading them into the path of 'true' religion God was in fact giving them an unmistakable sign of their election to everlasting bliss. What need had anyone to fear the power of princes, if they were convinced that they were among the 'elect', among those whom God had chosen to be saved? Similarly, what became of the social pre-eminence of a ruler if in God's eyes he was one of the 'reprobate', one of those doomed to hell? Men such as the Dutch 'beggars' or the French Huguenots were imbued with a determination and self-confidence that had scarcely any parallel as a political force.

Calvin also modified earlier Protestant theology in one other important respect. While rejecting the doctrine of transubstantiation, Calvin also rejected Zwingli's claim that the Eucharist was only a symbol of Christ's sacrifice. He found Luther's desire to cling to the notion of a physical presence equally unconvincing. Calvin's own conclusion was that Christ, having ascended into heaven, could not be physically present in the earthly forms of bread and wine, but that the presence must be of a spiritual nature. Rather than feeding the Christian's body through earthly foodstuffs, Christ nourished the soul through His spiritual grace.

CALVIN AND THE REFORMATION IN GENEVA

Calvin was, in many respects, an unlikely revolutionary. He lacked Luther's passion and his common touch in communicating his ideas to a wide and often uneducated audience. He was by nature a scholar rather than a man of action, yet without Zwingli's sharpness of intellect and without his willingness to plunge into politics to achieve his aims. Yet he had other qualities. 'Will-power, discipline and order were Calvin's particular watchwords, and he put his powerful mental and moral gifts at the service of a single purpose: the erection of God's kingdom in this world' (G.R. Elton, *Reformation Europe, 1517–1559*, 1963).

Famous already by 1540 as the author of the *Institutes,* Calvin was to achieve even greater renown over the next twenty years as the founder and inspiration in the city of Geneva of what John Knox called 'the most perfect school of Christ that ever was on earth since the days of the Apostles'. Calvin first set foot in Geneva in August 1536, intending that it should be little more than an overnight stop on his way to Strasbourg.

Contemporary Geneva was in a state of political and religious flux. For two centuries the bishops of Geneva and the dukes of Savoy had disputed political control of the city, and for most of the fifteenth century Savoy had held the upper hand. By the beginning of the next century, this struggle had been superseded by another, as the Savoyard bishops contended with factions among the citizens of Geneva ('Patriots' or 'Confederates') who preferred to see the city linked to the Swiss cantons. Bishop de la Baume was eventually forced to flee the city in 1527, and Geneva established an alliance with the cantons of Berne and Fribourg. Subsequently, Geneva was a republic, governed by four 'Syndics', elected annually by the Commune, or general assembly of male citizens. For a decade from 1527 to 1536, Geneva suffered repeated attempts by Savoy and by the bishop to reassert their former authority.

Despite this new Swiss orientation, Geneva only slowly felt the influence of the Reformation. In the early 1530s the preaching of Guillaume Farel and Pierre Viret produced such popular enthusiasm that the city fathers could not resist. It was only a few months later that Calvin entered the city for the first time. Farel immediately saw in him a valuable ally in his work, and Calvin was eventually convinced that his arrival in Geneva at such a time was clear evidence of the will of God. He thus began a task for which he rarely felt any pleasure, but which he pursued with dedication for most of the rest of his life.

From the outset Calvin and Farel pursued a two-fold policy. They attempted to enforce scripturally sound doctrine in Geneva, and to impose a system of church organisation which would oversee all aspects of the city's religious, social and moral life. To that end they proposed to the governing councils in 1537 their Twenty-one Articles on doctrine, organisation and discipline. Overall the councils accepted the doctrinal proposals, but expressed some reservations over the organisational clauses. For instance, although it was accepted that participation in the Communion (Eucharist) service should be compulsory, the city government was unwilling to enforce attendance as frequently as the reformers desired.

Calvin and Farel faced greater problems with public opinion than they did with the city fathers. The two key elements in the revolt against Savoy were anti-clericalism and resentment of foreign influence. In both cases, many felt, two Frenchmen had substituted a new doctrine without removing the other problems. In 1538 the situation reached crisis point over the demand of the reformers that all citizens should sign a confession of faith. This caused a rupture between the secular and ecclesiastical authorities, and the leading reformers were expelled from the city. Calvin spent the next

5.1 Geneva: the chronology of an urban reformation	
1532 (Jan.)	First reformed preaching, by Antoine Fromment, under sponsorship of Berne.
1533 (May–July)	Riots in city. Loss of political control by Bishop of Geneva.
1534 (March)	Reformers granted use of a church.
1535 (April)	Farel and Viret settle in Geneva.
1535 (June)	Disputation between reformers and conservatives.
1535 (Aug.)	City authorities provisionally abolish Mass and confiscate monastic property.
1536 (May)	City authorities agree to live by the law of the Gospels.
1536 (Aug.)	Arrival of Calvin in Geneva.
1536–7	Calvin and Farel draft Church orders.
1537–8	Sympathetic city authorities attempt to enforce Calvin's *Confession of Faith*. Calvin and Farel propose Twenty-one Articles on doctrine and on the organisation of worship.
1538 (Feb.–March)	New Syndics withdraw support from Calvin and Farel. Calvin leaves for Strasbourg.
1540 (Feb.–Oct)	Shift of power in Geneva, with new Syndics sympathetic to Farel.
1541 (Sept.)	Calvin returns to Geneva.
1541	Proposal (Sept) to the city authorities, and acceptance (Nov.) of the *Ecclesiastical Ordinances*.
1542	Publication of new catechism and liturgy.
1559	Establishment of the Academy of Geneva.

three years as preacher and minister to the community of French exiles in Strasbourg, his work there dominated by the production of French and German editions of the *Institutes*.

THE *ECCLESIASTICAL ORDINANCES*

When further twists in local politics brought Calvin back to Geneva, his first task was to establish a system of teaching and authority along the lines that he had witnessed in Strasbourg. He requested that the Genevan magistrates allow him to formulate a proper constitution for their reformed Church, and successfully proposed to them the *Ecclesiastical Ordinances* (*Ordonnances ecclésiastiques*).

These were founded upon the principle that Church government, like Church doctrine, must take a form which has authority from the scriptures. The absence of any biblical reference to bishops, archbishops and Popes had from the start made reformers hostile to such forms of authority. Yet the scriptures made it clear that, although the true Church consisted of the 'elect' whom God had predestined to salvation, it was also God's will that mankind as a whole should obey the basic rules of social behaviour that were laid down in the Commandments. The 'invisible' Church, whose membership was known only to God, thus had to exist alongside a 'visible' Church, whose membership and activity were clear to all. It also appeared to Calvin that the scriptures and the organisation of the primitive Church set clear precedents for a 'godly' form of Church hierarchy.

Calvin created nothing in Geneva that was altogether original. He drew largely upon his experience with Bucer in Strasbourg, and similar institutions had been established in Basle by Oecolampadius. Nor did Calvin bring about any great political change in Geneva, where the traditional patrician families maintained their prominence, and the traditional civil authorities remained in control. It must be stressed that Calvin did not establish a theocracy, a government by the Church, in Geneva. Influential as the consistory, the weekly assembly of the pastors and the elders, was, it had no civil power, and Calvin and his colleagues frequently failed to get their own way. What was established in Geneva was not the dominance of Church authority over civil authority, but a remarkable degree of cooperation between the two. By establishing such a thoroughly developed system, and by maintaining it for so long against so

5.2 The system established by the *Ecclesiastical Ordinances*

The *Ordinances* proposed a system of four orders of officers who shared the work of the Church's teaching and administration:

The Pastors, whose task was 'to proclaim the Word of God, to teach, admonish, exhort and reprove publicly and privately, to administer the sacraments and to issue fraternal warnings'. In short, they were the ministers of the community. They were selected by the existing ministers, subject to the approval of the civil magistrates, and held office for as long as they satisfied the faithful in the performance of their duties.

The Doctors were the teachers of the community. They were 'to instruct the faithful in sound doctrine so that the purity of the gospel is not corrupted by ignorance or wrong opinion'. They were responsible for a full educational system, the aim of which was to prepare the young for a proper understanding of their religious and civic responsibilities.

The Elders were laymen, twelve in each parish, whose task was to oversee the moral discipline of the community. They held their office through the authority of the city council, indicating the cooperation that existed in Geneva between civil and ecclesiastical authorities. The Elders operated through their own 'friendly warnings', and might subsequently refer more difficult cases to the authority of the Pastors. The ultimate weapon of the community was excommunication, the expulsion of the individual from the social and religious life of the community. This penalty was prescribed 'for all idolaters, blasphemers, despisers of God, heretics, and all who form sects apart to break the unity of the Church,' and also for 'all who are seditious, mutinous, quarrelsome, injurious, all adulterers, fornicators, thieves, misers, ravishers of women, drunkards, gluttons, and all who lead a scandalous life'.

The Deacons were placed in charge of such social tasks as the collection and distribution of alms for the poor, and the provision and administration of hospital facilities for the sick.

In addition, the *Ordinances* provided guidance for the community on a wide range of social issues. These included marriage, divorce, provocative dancing, blasphemy, drunkenness; and even such apparently minor matters as the names that the citizens might give their children were subject to scrutiny. For example, names with a religious significance, such as Noel, Emmanuel and Baptiste, were forbidden.

many challenges, Calvin made Geneva the centre of attention for reformers in all parts of Western Europe. In Geneva, these observers saw a religious system which, through its cooperation with the local magistrates, was consistent with social order and stability, unlike the wild experiments of some of the Anabaptist cults. At the same time, however, it was independent of the will and influence of kings and princes. Thus a system that was not radical in the context of a small city republic might become radical when it was transplanted to England or to France, where it operated alongside the authority of a monarch. That such practical organisation had been achieved by a man whose reputation as a theologian was already so well established left many in little doubt that Jean Calvin was the greatest figure of the Protestant Reformation.

POLITICAL OPPOSITION IN GENEVA

By the mid-century, Geneva was one of the most powerful symbols in Europe. More than half of its population was made up of religious refugees, and the city became increasingly active as a centre for the printing and publishing of religious literature. To many Protestants it stood as the greatest achievement of the Reformation, as the example to be followed elsewhere. To the enemies of Protestantism, it was the focal point of a great heretical conspiracy, to which heretics flocked for shelter, and from which missionaries issued forth to subvert the Catholic religion all over Europe.

Unsurprisingly, there was much resentment within Geneva at the imposition of an all-embracing social and religious system, and at the favour frequently shown to foreign refugees. Jacques Gruet, a prominent member of an old Genevan family, fell foul of the ecclesiastical authorities in June 1547, after written threats had been made against Calvin and his fellow ministers. The civil authorities sentenced Gruet to death in July 1547. More serious opposition was provided by the 'Libertine' faction that gathered around Ami Perrin, commander of the city's militia. In 1553, indeed, he became one of the Syndics, and it seemed possible that the expulsion of 1538 might be repeated. Although it often manifested itself in a

frivolous emphasis upon exotic clothes, dancing, and other activities calculated to offend the consistory, there was a serious political point behind this opposition. Perrin and his supporters genuinely feared that if the influx of foreign refugees continued Geneva might attract the dangerous attentions of such conservative forces as the Emperor, putting the city's independence seriously at risk. This rivalry was for some years the central feature of Genevan politics, but the struggle began to turn in Calvin's favour in early 1555. Perrin's faction lost power in the municipal elections, and this defeat may have contributed to a foolish attempt at insurrection (May 1555) which ended in Perrin's flight from Geneva. Only now, seventeen years after his arrival in the city, could Calvin really claim that he had overcome local political opposition to his presence and to his work.

RELIGIOUS OPPOSITION IN GENEVA

Calvin also encountered opposition from religious thinkers, often more radical than himself, drawn to Geneva by the reformer's reputation. He even needed to win a number of battles with his own colleagues over doctrinal matters, such as the dispute with Sebastian Castellio, whom Calvin himself had appointed principal of the college in Geneva. Castellio's claim that the *Song of Songs* was not a valid book of the Bible, but rather a sensuous and obscene love poem, led to his expulsion from Geneva in 1544. A more serious doctrinal challenge was launched in 1551–2 by Jerome Bolsec and Jean Troillet against the doctrine of predestination. The refuting of Troillet's views provided an excellent example of solidarity between the Church authorities and those of the city. Faced with such a united front Troillet had the good sense to retire; and, defeated in public debate, Bolsec returned both to his native France and to Catholicism.

The most famous challenge to Calvin's doctrines was launched by Michael Servetus. A Spaniard by birth, Servetus was a scholar of great breadth and depth, and possessed a mind too inquisitive and original for his own good. He was a medical scholar of genius, but his contemporary notoriety depended upon his theological works. The Polyglot Bible which he produced in 1542 contained, for instance, some startlingly original and unorthodox views, many of them amplified in his major work, *The Restoration of Christianity* (*Christianismi Restitutio,* 1553). Here he denied the doctrine of justification by faith, and rejected infant baptism. Above all, Servetus maintained unorthodox views on the subject of the Trinity. He achieved the remarkable feat of being condemned as a heretic by every major sect in Europe. Having lived a double life for many years in France, it is hard to understand why Servetus visited Geneva, when Calvin had already condemned much of his teaching. But come he did, and was immediately recognised, arrested, tried and condemned to death (October 1553).

THE INTERNATIONAL IMPACT OF CALVINISM

Switzerland, Germany and France

To a greater extent than those of either Luther or Zwingli, Calvin's doctrines and concepts of Church organisation spread throughout Western Europe, exerting a complex and varied influence in the second half of the sixteenth century. In explaining this phenomenon, it has been argued that Calvinism was potentially international in its origins, that it was the artificial creation of a society of refugees, eager from the outset to return with their doctrines and organisation to their native lands. 'It never had the ethnic rootings in a single culture so evident in Germanic Lutheranism and in many forms of Germanic or Dutch religious radicalism' (R.M. Kingdon, 'International Calvinism', in *Handbook of European History*, ed. Brady, Oberman and Tracy, 1995).

In some areas of Europe, the spread of Genevan ideas was the direct result of the political policy of Calvin and his successors. In reaction to the political dangers of the time, Calvin appreciated the need to heal Protestantism's internal divisions, to resist the Catholic counter-attack. Within Switzerland, the impact of Calvinism upon another city often depended upon its political relations with Geneva. Thus, Berne and Basle were never greatly receptive to Calvin's ideas, but greater

5.3 Associates and followers of Calvin

BEZA, Theodore (1519–1605). Born Vézelay, France. Humanist student of Greek and Law, but converted to evangelical views (1548) and went to Geneva. Worked closely with Calvin as rector of the Genevan Theological Academy (1559) and as leader of Calvinist delegation to the Colloquy of Poissy (1561). Succeeded Calvin as head of the ecclesiastical organisation in Geneva (1564) and wrote first authoritative biography of the reformer.

FAREL, Guillaume (1489–1565). Born Gap, Savoy. A student of Lefèvre d'Étaples. Fled to Basle (1524) when accused of heresy. Expelled for criticism of Erasmus (1530). Settled in Geneva (1535) where he persuaded Calvin to assist him in the reformation of the city. Expelled from Geneva (1538) and subsequently worked in Neuchâtel.

KNOX, John (1513–72). Born Haddington, Scotland. Graduate of Glasgow University. Converted to evangelical principles by George Wishart (1546). Captured by French forces while preaching at St Andrews (1547). Active in England, collaborating in establishment of Protestant settlement under Edward VI (1549–52). Exiled during Mary's reign in Geneva and Frankfurt. Wrote *First Blast of the Trumpet against the Monstrous Regiment of Women* (1558) in protest against female, Catholic rulers. Returned to Scotland (1559) where he became the leading figure in the triumph of Protestantism. His *Confession of Faith*, *First Book of Discipline* and *Book of Common Order* provided the framework for Scottish Presbyterianism.

VIRET, Pierre (1511–71). Born Vaud, Switzerland. Studied in Paris. A leading figure in the reformation of Lausanne (1536), and a close associate of Farel in his work in Geneva and in Neuchâtel. Active in the Calvinist mission to France in the 1560s. His influencial *Instruction Chrétienne* (1564) advocated civil obedience, but stressed that disobedience might be justified on religious grounds.

progress was made in Neuchâtel, where Farel introduced them, and in Lausanne, where Viret spread the word. The greatest success in the search for Protestant unity was achieved in Zurich, where agreement was reached with Zwingli's successor, Heinrich Bullinger. Although the doctrine of predestination was at first the most contentious issue, both Calvin and Bullinger were sufficiently realistic to appreciate the security that compromise would bring. The result was the so-called Zurich Consensus (*Consensus Tigurinus*) concluded in 1549. Sometimes criticised for its vagueness on a number of important doctrinal matters, the Consensus proved how flexible Calvin could be when he felt that God's cause required it. By the end of the century the Consensus had been accepted by Basle, Berne and by the Vaud territories, representing a substantial degree of political unity between the different Protestant factions within Switzerland.

In Germany, on the other hand, Calvinism failed substantially to shake the supremacy of Lutheranism. Its one outstanding political success came in 1561 when Genevan principles were embraced by Frederick III, the Elector Palatine, and his capital city, Heidelberg, became a major centre of missionary work in Germany. The Heidelberg Catechism (1563) was one of the outstanding statements of Calvinist doctrine outside Switzerland. Calvinism also found support in some smaller states, especially along Germany's western frontiers. Emden, in the north-west, became a noted outpost of Calvinism, the 'Geneva of the North', but it owed this predominantly to the influx of refugees from the Netherlands, rather than to any deliberate initiative from Geneva. In seeking to explain why Calvinism made so much less impact in Germany than in Switzerland, historians have often concluded that xenophobia lay behind the phenomenon. German resentment at the pretensions of a foreign Church explains in part the impact of Luther, and only a minority of German Protestants were willing now to exchange Luther's teachings for those of a Frenchman.

Whether or not this 'nationalist' explanation is valid, it is certainly true that Calvin's native land provided fertile soil for his teachings. Geneva was the only major French-speaking refuge available for French Protestants during the periodic persecutions under Francis I and Henry II, and the influx of large numbers of these 'foreigners' into Geneva was a major source of concern for Calvin's local political opponents. A related line of argument has stressed the inconsistency of the persecutions under Francis I, a monarch whose religious policy was always strongly laced with political expediency. Thus, when temporary exiles returned to their homeland, it was the doctrines and organisation of Geneva that they took with them. Calvin himself took a lively interest in events in his native land, and his correspondence with the Huguenot churches scattered across France clearly illustrates his direct involvement in their struggle. The duration and the outcome of the religious wars in the second half of the century establish beyond doubt that Calvinism could achieve a profound effect upon even the strongest states in Europe.

The Netherlands and the British Isles

In other parts of Western Europe, the impact of Calvinism owed far less to the direct influence of Calvin and his successors. In the United Provinces of the Netherlands and in Scotland, for example, the spectacular successes of Calvinist doctrine and organisation have to be explained largely in terms of prevailing political circumstances over which Geneva had no control.

Although the Spanish authorities were eventually able to achieve the virtual eradication of reformed doctrines, the initial impact of Calvinism

---

5.4 Calvinism and capitalism

A major reappraisal of the impact of Calvinism was begun at the start of this century by the German sociologist Max Weber, in his work *The Protestant Ethic and the Spirit of Capitalism* (1904). Weber considered that Karl Marx had placed too much emphasis upon material factors in his classic explanation of the emergence of capitalist society. Protestant thought, he felt, was equally influential because, especially in its Calvinist form, it had released merchants and tradesmen from such restraints as the Church's condemnation of high rates of interest. In particular, he felt, the doctrine of predestination encouraged Calvin's followers to believe that material success in this world was a sign of God's elective favour in the next. This he regarded as 'a psychological revolution of the most profound importance'. R.H. Tawney (*Religion and the Rise of Capitalism*, 1926) followed a similar line. He believed that medieval Christianity imposed a series of restrictions upon commercial enterprise. It protected the poor, frowned upon money-lending, and supported the feudal authority of the crown and the aristocracy. Much of this conservatism lived on in Luther's teachings, but was not found in Calvinism, or in the other urban elements of the Reformation. To the Calvinist, productive and profitable work was a form of worship. Recent historians have criticised both Weber and Tawney as being more interested in the development of modern capitalism than they were in Calvinism, and for treating the sixteenth-century evidence in a selective fashion. 'Moral conviction', wrote A.G.Dickens more recently, 'is no substitute for historical evidence, and Tawney's evidence must be judged unimpressive in bulk, and outweighed by data to the contrary.'

in the southern Netherlands was considerable. In these areas it seems fair to explain the original spread of Calvinism in much the same way as in France. Much of the population was French-speaking, and the territories lay open to the influences of the German Protestant cities and of the Swiss cities further south. The persecutions attempted by the government before the 1550s were even less consistent and determined than those undertaken in France. In the north, the success of Calvinism was closely linked to the wider political history of the Dutch Revolt. The political opportunism of some of the leaders of the Dutch nobility and the refusal of Philip II to accept any form of religious compromise were factors which created an atmosphere of confrontation, to which the discipline of Calvinism was ideally suited. Few historians believe any longer that Calvinism was a major cause of the Dutch Revolt, or even that it played the decisive role in its success in the northern provinces. The fact remains that, even if they had been taken out of the hands of their Genevan authors, Genevan doctrines had, by 1600, come to occupy a place paralleled in only one other state in Western Europe.

In Scotland, too, local politics facilitated the triumph of Calvinism. The degree of noble factionalism in this remarkably unstable country was even greater than that encountered in France, and the marriage of the young Mary Queen of Scots to the French *dauphin* threatened the kingdom with foreign domination even more seriously than was the case in the Netherlands. To the south, a Protestant regime in England found in religion a perfect tool to separate the Scots from their traditional French allies. In December 1557 the Protestant lords of Scotland revolted against the French regent and adopted a 'Covenant' which bound them to labour for the triumph of the Gospel, and to support a prayer-book similar to that used in England. In addition, in such cities as Perth, Montrose and Dundee, Scotland experienced its own 'urban reformation' with the formation of local congregations along Calvinist lines. It was in this atmosphere that the most influential of all the Genevan missionaries, John Knox, returned to his native land from a spell of exile in Geneva. The personality and passion of Knox himself, combined with the political self-interest of the nobility, and

the potential of Calvinism as a weapon against a foreign oppressor, proved an irresistible mixture. Knox's preaching in Edinburgh (May 1559) was so forceful that the French regent was forced to flee her capital. Although the crown remained nominally with the Catholic Queen Mary, the estates of the realm enthusiastically accepted Knox's official confession of faith (*Confessio Scotica,* 1560), while the Assembly of the Kirk accepted a book of discipline heavily influenced by Geneva. Mary's refusal to accept the current of events led to her deposition and eventual exile (1567).

This was the greatest political success achieved by Calvinism in the sixteenth century. In Scotland, as in the independent Netherlands, Calvinism was established not just as the state religion, but as the major formative social force, whose influence is still very evident today. The price that Calvinism had to pay for it, however, was that the doctrines of Geneva would always from that point be viewed by conservatives as revolutionary and disruptive, even at a time when Calvin himself was trying hard to convey an image of reason and compromise in order to preserve and protect the reformed churches in France.

This negative aspect is seen very clearly in the failure of Calvinism to achieve similar political successes in England. Thanks very largely to the influence of refugees who had fled to Geneva during the reign of Mary Tudor, Calvinism acquired a considerable following in many regions of southern and eastern England. Yet Calvinists remained limited to the role of a pressure group, because they failed to gain the consistent support of the political establishment. With Elizabeth secure upon her throne, with the queen personally alienated from Calvinism by the radicalism of Knox in Scotland, and with the Anglican Church well able to play the role of a patriotic religion resisting the reimposition of a foreign creed, Calvinism had little chance to make the political impact that it had made in Scotland or in the Netherlands.

Indirectly, of course, this factor eventually forced many English Calvinists to the conclusion that they could only practise their faith adequately elsewhere. The export of Calvinist doctrine and organisation to the New World opened a new chapter in the impact of Calvinism, to be played out in a century and in a continent beyond the scope of this book.

Further reading

E. Cameron (1991) *The European Reformation.* Oxford.

A. McGrath (1990) *A Life of John Calvin.* Oxford.

T.H.L. Parker (1975) *John Calvin: A Biography.* London.

G.R. Potter and M. Greengrass (1978) *John Calvin* (a documentary collection) London.

• CHAPTER SIX•

The Catholic Counter-Reformation

A churchman in the image of the Catholic Reformation. This portrait of S. Carlo Borromeo (1538–84), Archbishop of Milan, was painted by Daniele Crespi in the mid-1660s. It emphasises the simplicity of his life and his devotion to learning

THE HISTORICAL DEBATE

The term 'counter-reformation' was the invention of the nineteenth-century German historian Leopold von Ranke. By this term, some historians have implied that the reforms within the Catholic Church were essentially a reaction to the challenge of the Protestant reformers, a deliberate and largely negative attempt to block their advance. The main features of the movement, therefore, were the Council of Trent and its preoccupation with the authority of the papacy.

Ranke, however, used the vivid image of Protestant and Catholic reform as two fresh springs, rising close together on a mountainside, and then flowing away on their separate courses. So was this movement rather a 'Catholic Reformation', a movement of loyal and orthodox Catholics working to regenerate their faith without damaging the unity and authority of their Church? For many years this interpretation was most popular among historians who commented from a committed Catholic angle, such as Pierre Janelle (*The Catholic Reformation*, 1963) and H. Jedin (*History of the Council of Trent*, 1957–61). To such writers it appeared that the events of the 1540s and of following decades derived directly from the attempts that Catholics had made for centuries, not always with the cooperation of their spiritual leaders, to maintain the purity and dynamism of their Church.

In recent years the view of the Catholic Counter-Reformation as a long process, with its roots in the *devotio moderna*, has gained wider acceptance. H.O. Evennett (*The Spirit of the Counter Reformation*, 1968) saw the movement as a relatively brief one, but refused to place his stress upon such great 'set pieces' as the Council of Trent. Instead, he accepted that the movement consisted as much of the spiritual struggles of many loyal Catholics working at a local level as it did of the political measures imposed from above by a hierarchical Church. This approach has since been developed by J. Bossy (*Christianity in the West, 1400–1700*, 1985), for whom the true significance of the Catholic Counter-Reformation lies in the regeneration of spiritual and pastoral values at episcopal and parochial levels. Wherever the origins of the movement

might lie, he feels, the Counter-Reformation has to be seen as a process that stretched, vital and continuous, deep into the seventeenth century.

While it is now easier to see the common origins of Lutheranism, Erasmianism and Catholic reform in the spiritual movements of the fifteenth century, it remains difficult to deny the element of negative resistance to Protestantism that shows through most clearly in the politics of the Council of Trent. Our starting-point, therefore, may be the judgement of A.G. Dickens: 'Counter Reformation or Catholic Reformation? Was it not quite obviously both?'

CATHOLIC REVIVAL BEFORE LUTHER

The Protestant Reformation arose from the conflict between a widespread desire for spiritual regeneration and the frustrating conservatism that reformers encountered in the Church hierarchy. It represented the decision of some reformers that pure forms of worship were more important than the maintenance of unity within a corrupt Church. In the decades before Luther's revolt, many reformers laboured with equal vigour for a purer form of Christianity, yet never took the awesome step towards schism.

The Rhineland and the Netherlands produced many such groups which rejected traditional monasticism, and devoted their labours to the benefit of the community at large. Most notable among these were the Brethren of the Common Life, who had founded houses by the beginning of the fifteenth century at Delft, Deventer and Zwolle. On the Rhine, the Friends of God established centres at Basle, Cologne and Strasbourg. To these men the ceremonies of the Church were far less important than practical works of charity and education. The most influential work of this movement was *The Imitation of Christ*, written by the German scholar Thomas à Kempis (*c.*1418). Its advocacy of a pattern of Christian life based upon the example of Christ himself has had such an effect over the centuries that it has been republished more often than any book other than the Bible.

The message of this 'modern devotion' was sometimes taken up within existing monastic orders. Within the Franciscan order, St Bernardino of Siena (*d.* 1444) inspired the emergence of a group known as the Observants, determined to return to the order's original values of poverty, charity and preaching. The Carthusian order had a remarkable reputation for maintaining its original standards of austerity and holiness, particularly in its houses in Cologne and in London. The Christian humanist scholars of northern Europe also played a role in orthodox religious revival. In Erasmus, in particular, the influence of the *devotio moderna* combined with that of the Renaissance to produce a perceptive critic of contemporary Catholicism who, nevertheless, shrank in horror from the schismatic steps taken by Luther.

The half-century or so before the Lutheran revolt also witnessed a remarkable expansion of university education. In Germany alone nine new universities were founded between 1450 and 1517, including Luther's own university at Wittenberg. Seven new universities were established in Spain, and a variety of colleges at Oxford and Cambridge were established over the same period. Such factors make it hard to claim the existence of a general malaise in the spiritual life of Western Europe.

RELIGIOUS REVIVAL AND THE STATE

Orthodox revival was not limited to isolated groups of intellectuals. Senior ecclesiastical figures in most Western European states remained political advisers and administrators rather than spiritual leaders, but some influenced spiritual revival at the highest political levels.

No man better illustrates this than the great Spanish churchman Ximenes de Cisneros. Highly reluctant in the first place to accept office and to abandon his life of contemplation and austerity, he eventually used the high office of Cardinal Archbishop of Toledo (1495) to launch a determined attack upon laxity in his own and other religious orders. Ximenes also provided an outstanding example of the resurgence of biblical scholarship within the Church, through his foundation of the University of Alcala, and his production of the great Polyglot Bible. Third, Ximenes was a crusader, participating in the conquest of Granada

and playing an energetic role in the conversion and cultural persecution of both Moors and Jews.

In France, the nearest to a Ximenes was the Cardinal Georges d'Amboise (*d.* 1510). Receiving legatine powers from Pope Alexander VI in 1501, he used them to attack abuses in some of the major monasteries of France, using force on several occasions against reluctant houses. In so doing, he acted in accordance with the consistent demand among the French educated and political classes for the reform of religious abuses and indiscipline. This manifested itself particularly in the group of humanist scholars who enjoyed the patronage of Marguerite de Navarre, sister of Francis I, in the so-called *Cercle de Meaux*.

The influence of Christian humanism was also felt in England. Although the humanist convictions of Cardinal Wolsey were probably genuine enough, they were largely submerged by his political preoccupations; and it was his successor as chancellor, Thomas More, who provided the link between the humanist movement and the Catholic Reformation. A close friend of Erasmus, his learned controversies, first with Luther (1523) and then with Tyndale (1528–9), show that he never departed from Catholic orthodoxy. At the same time, his *Treatise on the Passion* and *Dialogue of Comfort* rank among the leading works of religious instruction produced by the Christian humanists. A little further from the seat of power, John Colet, dean of St Paul's Cathedral, made his mark through a series of lectures delivered at Oxford (1496–7) on the epistles of St Paul and by his foundation of St Paul's School.

THE NEW ORDERS

Important steps were taken in Italy towards the redirection and regeneration of communal religious life. By the end of the fifteenth century, a movement was already evident there, in which devout Christians formed themselves into looser organisations for the purposes of perfecting their own lives and performing charitable works. Such bodies, or 'oratories', were the forerunners of the Oratory of the Divine Love formed in Rome in 1517. In the next decade, it counted among its members Gaspar Contarini, Jacopo Sadoleto, secretary to Pope Leo X, and Gianpietro Caraffa, later Pope Paul IV. The message of spiritual renewal was coming closer to the seat of ecclesiastical power.

This pattern was widely imitated in Italy in the next two decades. Founded in 1524, the Theatines took a vow of poverty, and refused to beg for alms, their funds deriving largely from the wealthy and aristocratic idealists whom they were able to attract into their ranks. The Franciscans produced another splinter group, the Capuchins (1529), whose main objective was to labour for the relief of the sick and the destitute and to win the poor to the Church by a mixture of preaching and charity. The narrow line that separated such orthodox enthusiasm from the more radical movements of northern Europe was demonstrated in 1541, when Bernardino Ochino, the vicar-general of the Capuchins, embraced Lutheranism. The movement also spread in the 1530s to female orders, and a direct female equivalent of the Capuchins, the Capuchines, was established in Naples. The most notable female order was that of the Ursulines, founded in 1535 by Angela Merici. Over sixty years old at the time, the foundress had already spent a lifetime tending the sick and teaching the poor in Brescia and in other parts of northern Italy.

THE FOUNDATION OF THE JESUITS

The most important and influential order of this kind was the Society of Jesus, founded by a Spaniard, Ignatius Loyola, and a group of companions in 1534. Loyola's background to the age of thirty was military rather than religious, and a military mentality remains evident in his later religious organisation. Unlike Luther and Calvin, his religious conversion did not deflect him from his belief in the legitimate authority of the Church. Between 1521 and 1535, Loyola was preoccupied with his own spiritual education, in Spain (1522–3), in the Holy Land (1523), at the universities of Alcala and Salamanca (1524–7), and in Paris (1528–35). The most prominent influences upon his thought seem to have been those of Thomas à Kempis, and of some of the leading Spanish mystics, such as Garcia de Cisneros. Loyola's second preoccupation was the composition

of the work that became the handbook of the Jesuit movement, begun in 1522 but still unpublished in 1534. *The Spiritual Exercises* is essentially a manual for meditation and spiritual reflection, arising from Loyola's fundamental conviction that man is a free agent and may 'find God where he will'. It provides a course of meditations that leads the reader from a starting-point of remorse and a rejection of sin towards a more positive state in which he or she is encouraged to understand more exactly what is implied by each act and lesson of Christ.

The impact of the Jesuit movement was largely due to the attitude that Loyola adopted to the authority of the Church. He firmly believed that private judgement should give way in all things to the will of God, and was equally convinced that the Divine Will could only be understood on earth through the Church. Unquestioning obedience to the head of the Church was therefore a prime principle of the Jesuit movement from its very beginnings. Indeed, Loyola stated in *The Spiritual Exercises* that 'we ought always be ready to believe that what seems to us white is black, if the hierarchical Church so defines it'.

The Society of Jesus was born in August 1534 when Loyola and nine companions in Paris took vows of chastity and poverty. Abandoning an original project for a missionary expedition to the Holy Land, they committed themselves to undertake whatever task the papacy might set them. Supported in Rome by Cardinal Contarini, the Jesuits obtained formal papal recognition in 1540.

THE ACHIEVEMENT OF THE JESUITS

The next major contribution of Ignatius Loyola, now the General of the Society, was its *Constitutions*, completed between 1544 and 1547. A member had to take a demanding series of vows, of chastity, poverty, the surrender of all private property, the severance of all family and personal relationships outside the order, and of total obedience to the commands of superiors within the order and within the Church at large. To guard against corruption, Loyola also forbade any member of the society to hold any benefice or office within the Church.

Aided by such high standards the society had recruited just under a thousand members by the early 1550s, and had established its reputation in three main areas of work: preaching, education and missionary activity. Its earliest educational establishments were for the training of members of the society, at Bologna (1546), Messina (1548), Palermo (1549) and the Collegium Romanum (1550). Within a decade of the society's formal recognition, seven colleges had been founded in Spain, while the establishment of the Collegium Germanicum (1552) provided a base for carrying the struggle into more hostile territory. At the end of the century the Habsburg Empire alone had 155 such colleges.

The missionary activity of the Jesuits was particularly concerned with carrying the word to the non-believer. In this respect, no figure in the Catholic Reformation achieved more than St Francis Xavier. Reaching Goa, the Portuguese settlement on the west coast of India (1542), he worked for the next ten years in Sri Lanka, in Travancore and in the Molucca Islands, and even penetrated in 1549 into Japan. Increasingly, however, the society worked to combat heresy within Europe. Le Jay and Bobadilla were active in Bavaria, and Loyola sought unsuccessfully to have a Jesuit mission accepted by the English government during the reconversion of that country under Mary Tudor.

English opposition to the proposed mission of 1555 illustrates that the absolute dedication of the Jesuits to the papacy often aroused the suspicions of monarchs who sought to protect their control over the Church within their own territories. This was particularly true in Spain, where the Jesuits met resistance from a formidable combination of monarchy, Church leadership and conservative monastic orders. In France, too, the Sorbonne and the Parlement of Paris resented the 'foreign' influence of the Jesuits, and limited their establishment within the realm for a number of years.

THE PAPACY AND REFORM, 1513–42

For the Catholic Reformation to be more than a collection of remarkable individuals rising above the spiritual mediocrity of the majority, its principles needed to be embraced in the highest echelons of the Church. The gradual realisation by the papacy that some substantial measure of reform was inevitable thus allowed the Catholic Counter-Reformation to emerge as a universal movement throughout the Church.

The sacking of Rome by imperial troops in May 1527 marked the bankruptcy of the papacy as a moral and political leader in Europe. Almost overnight, the familiar excuse that the authority and prestige of the Church would be damaged if it were to accept the criticisms of humbler souls lost all validity, for what authority and prestige had it left? Political leadership was now definitively beyond the Church's reach, and only by increased moral leadership could it recover any meaningful form of primacy. Such an argument was put strikingly into practice by Gian Matteo Giberti, Bishop of Verona, and Jacopo Sadoleto, Bishop of Carpentras. Both had followed the familiar pattern of non-residence in their dioceses, but now, accepting the popular explanation that the sack of Rome was God's judgement upon corruption, returned to their bishoprics to set glowing examples of how a bishop should fulfil his duties. Until his death in 1543, Giberti was the model bishop, touring his diocese to detect and correct clerical ignorance, immorality and absenteeism, and to promote such projects as hospitals, orphanages and almshouses.

This acute crisis in the affairs of the Church was inherited by Paul III (October 1534–November 1549), whose pontificate marked a transitional period of the greatest importance. Paul's early history provides a typical example of ecclesiastical careerism. Born in 1468, he was a bishop at the age of twenty, and a cardinal at twenty-five. Elected Pope in 1534, he distributed honours in corrupt fashion to his family, making two grandsons cardinals at the age of fifteen. Overall, however, his appointments to the College of Cardinals showed a greater concern for reform than had been shown by any of his recent predecessors. The Englishmen Fisher and Pole, the Frenchman Jean du Bellay, and the Italians Contarini, Sadoleto and Caraffa were all men of impeccable reputation, and all men who would voice the cause of orthodox reform in an otherwise highly conservative body.

Paul also showed a consistent, if cautious, commitment to the demand of the reformers for the summoning of a General Council of the Church. He summoned such a body in 1536, although it did not meet for another nine years. Also in1536 the Pope created a select committee of cardinals to investigate the most serious abuses within the Church and to recommend remedies. Contarini, Caraffa, Pole, Giberti and Sadoleto all sat on the investigating body. The report that the committee produced (March 1537) was an honest indictment of the worst ecclesiastical abuses. This *Consilium de Emendanda Ecclesia* severely criticised earlier Popes who had allowed Church offices to be bought and sold, the basic abuse 'from which, as from the Trojan horse, every abuse has erupted into the Church'. It also attacked most of the abuses that had been the traditional targets of Protestant reformers. Clerical appointments had too often been made without reference to the necessary standards of learning and morality. Absenteeism too often deprived congregations of proper leadership and instruction. The practice of selling indulgences had been grossly abused. The *Consilium* also advised a firm and clear stance on all disputed doctrinal issues, and deplored the easy and tolerant attitude to doctrinal detail which was to be found in the works of Erasmus and his followers. In doing so, the document set exactly the tone for papal policy that was to be followed throughout the long course of the Council of Trent.

THE POLITICS OF THE COUNCIL OF TRENT

The long delay between the publication of the *Consilium de Emendanda Ecclesia* and the first meeting of the General Council shows how enormously complex and delicate the task was which now faced Paul III and his successors. There was much resistance, both honest conservatism and cynical self-interest, within Rome. It was also essential that reform, and the promised General Council, should take place with the papacy in a position of strength, for there was little point in carrying out an orthodox reform which did as much damage to the hierarchical Church as the Protestant Reformation had done in the first place.

The international situation also remained highly complicated. In April 1541, Charles V opened formal negotiations at Regensburg between moderate theologians of the Protestant and Catholic camps. The possibility of a doctrinal settlement without the political risks of a General Council was a good enough reason to delay, yet by the end of 1542 all reasonable hope of a negotiated settlement was gone, the papacy steadfastly refusing the compromise policy of 'double justification', by which faith and good works were held to be equally important in achieving salvation. Meanwhile the Protestants were equally consistent in their refusal to acknowledge supreme papal authority.

In June 1542, Paul III finally summoned a General Council to assemble on neutral territory, at Trent in northern Italy. Even so, further warfare between Charles V and Francis I delayed the meeting for another three years, and obstructed the flow both of goodwill and of delegates. When the first General Council of the Church since 1447 finally opened in December 1545, the gathering was far less impressive than its title suggested. Of some 700 bishops eligible to attend, only thirty-one were present at the opening, and no more than 270 attended at any time during the Council's eighteen-year history. Of these, 187 were Italians. Only two German bishops ever attended, while England and most of the rest of northern Europe remained unrepresented throughout.

These limitations restricted the authority of the Council of Trent, but they served the immediate purposes of Paul III. Three further political decisions helped to ensure that the Council would be broadly amenable to papal authority. First, it was accepted that debate would be directed by a presiding panel of three cardinals, del Monte, Pole and Cervini, appointed of course by the Pope. Second, the Pope insisted that decisions should be reached by the bishops voting as individuals and in person. The fifteenth-century practice of voting *en bloc* by nations was abandoned, and the outlawing of proxy votes ensured that the decisions of the Council would always be determined by the numerical superiority of the Italian bishops. Lastly, Paul III insisted that doctrinal issues should be discussed first, knowing that this could only emphasise the differences between the parties. With an orthodox doctrinal position safely reaffirmed, the Church could proceed to the business of reform from a position of strength. The final decision, the result of considerable Spanish

6.1 The achievement of the Council of Trent

Duration
The Council sat in three sessions: March 1545–Winter 1547, when the decision to move the Council into papal territory at Bologna alienated some delegates; May 1551–May 1552, when the military success of the German Lutherans caused panic; April 1561–July 1563.

Doctrinal decrees
In the first session of the Council it was decreed:

1 that scripture and Church tradition have equal authority;
2 that the Church's authority was paramount in the matter of interpreting the scriptures;
3 that the Church's traditional affirmation of seven sacraments was correct;
4 that Protestant propositions on justification (i.e. salvation) were false. Good works were stated to play a central role in salvation, and participation in the sacraments of the Church was interpreted as an essential element of good works.

In the second session of the Council it was decreed:

5 that the doctrine of transubstantiation is a true interpretation of the nature of the Eucharist;
6 that, given the validity of the sacrament of ordination, there was no case for allowing the laity to take Communion 'in both kinds';
7 that marriage for members of the clergy was unacceptable.

In the third session of the Council it was decreed:

8 that the authority of bishops originated from their appointment by the Pope, and did not come directly from God, as some Spanish bishops had hoped to assert.

Disciplinary decrees
1 that bishops should reside in their dioceses, although a bishop might be absent for six months before he incurred any punishment;
2 that bishops enjoyed full rights to visit and inspect all parishes, monastic houses and other ecclesiastical institutions within their dioceses;
3 that all matters concerning the selection, education, ordination and discipline of priests lay in the hands of the bishops;
4 that preaching was the principal duty of the bishop. He should oversee the regularity and standard of preaching within his diocese. Parish priests should preach every Sunday, and no man should be allowed to preach without licence from the bishop;

5 that in all these matters the authority of the bishop is exercised subject to the authority of the Pope;
6 that no man shall in future be ordained before the age of twenty-five, or without appointment to a specific living;
7 that a seminary, or religious college, should be established in every diocese. The request of some delegates that the education at these seminaries should be based entirely upon the scriptures was rejected in favour of older academic traditions. This ran substantially against the ideas of the Christian humanists, and A.G. Dickens has concluded that 'at no stage did the spirit of Erasmus and Lefèvre suffer a more catastrophic defeat'.

---

pressure, that discipline and doctrine should be debated together, showed that the papacy still had some way to go to establish overall control. It nevertheless represented a substantial defeat for Charles V and for his hopes that the long-awaited General Council would bring together the warring factions in Germany and elsewhere in Christendom.

THE COUNCIL OF TRENT: CONCLUSIONS

Should the Council of Trent be regarded as a success? For the papacy, the Council brought many rewards. During its course, Paul III, Julius III and Pius IV confronted both Protestantism and the potential authority of the Council itself, and they ensured that neither would exert any future influence within the Catholic Church. Long-standing ambiguities in doctrine had been resolved, and the Church now stood in better moral and doctrinal shape to resist the encroachments of heresy than at any previous stage in the century. The hopes of the Emperors Charles and Ferdinand, and of the rulers of France, that the Council might create a basis for compromise and reconciliation in their domestic religious disputes were disappointed in every respect. Reconciliation was never seriously on the agenda at Trent, and the split between Catholic and Protestant became permanent. The future influence of Catholicism now depended upon the ability of the Church to put its new-found doctrinal certainty and moral health into practical form. At the same time as achieving its own regeneration, the

Church had irrevocably limited its own sphere of influence. Italian solidarity and support had enabled the popes to achieve most of their outstanding victories at Trent, and the price they paid for these successes was that in future the direct influence of the papacy would be largely limited to Italy. Nearly 400 years passed after the Council of Trent before the papacy passed again to a non-Italian.

6.2 The Counter-Reformation and the papacy

Pius IV (Dec. 1559–Dec. 1565). Gianangelo de Medici. Born Florence. Presided over the later sessions of the Council of Trent. Subsequently re-established the papal Index, and worked on the revision of the catechism, the breviary and the Vulgate version of the Bible along lines established at Trent. Foreign policy: he failed in his attempts to reconcile Elizabeth of England to the Catholic Church.

Pius V (Jan. 1566–May 1572). Antonio Ghislieri. Born Piedmont. Raised the tone of the papal court, ordering bishops to return to their dioceses, and halved expenditure. Abolished the sale of indulgences. Canonised St Thomas Aquinas, and was himself the last pope to be canonised. Foreign policy: published bull of excommunication against Elizabeth. Participated with Philip II in Holy League against the Turks.

Gregory XIII (May 1572–April 1585). Ugo Buoncompagno. Born Bologna. Endowed Jesuit colleges in Rome, and some twenty others elsewhere. Introduced the revised ('Gregorian') calendar.

Sixtus V (April 1585–Aug. 1590). Felice Peretti. Born Ancona. Undertook substantial political reform within the papal states. Created a system of fifteen 'congregations' or ministries, to oversee spiritual and political functions, and thereby consolidated papal authority and control. Established the first printing press within the Vatican. Carried out extensive reforms of sanitation, housing and communications within Rome. Foreign policy: gave substantial support to the Spanish Armada. Heavily involved in negotiations for the return of Henry IV of France to the Catholic Church.

Clement VIII (Jan. 1592–March 1605). Ippolito Aldobrandini. Born Florence. Continued the political reforms of Sixtus V, but was notable for generous grants to his kinsmen. Published the revised version of the Vulgate. Foreign policy: accepted Henry IV back into the Catholic Church, thereby renewing the possibility of a papal–French alliance against the influence of Spain, yet denounced the Edict of Nantes.

THE CATHOLIC REFORMATION IN ACTION

The Catholic monarchies

The decisions of the Council of Trent had a limited impact in Catholic Europe as a whole. There is ample evidence in the latter part of the century of further spiritual renewal in some of the Catholic monarchies, but it is hard to see Trent as the primary source of this regeneration.

In the 1520s and the 1530s, as in the age of Ximenes, the Spanish Church pursued a determined policy of reform and regeneration. It demonstrated many of the features associated with the Catholic Reformation, yet developed them directly from her own cultural and spiritual experience. The period between 1525 and 1533 saw an attack upon Erasmianism and upon the equally suspect Illuminists, which ended with the banning by the Inquisition of many of Erasmus's works and the removal of many of his admirers from university posts. In the years that followed Trent, Spain produced a fine crop of new and dynamic religious orders, notably the Discalced Carmelites founded by St Teresa of Avilà (1562) and the Hospitaller Brothers established by St John of God (1572). In one respect Spain resisted the impetus of the Council of Trent. The Tridentine decrees sought to reimpose the spiritual authority of the papacy, but when Philip II allowed their publication within Spain (1565) it was with the strict proviso that they should not operate in any way to the prejudice of royal authority. If the Spain of Philip II deserved its reputation as 'the strong right arm of the Counter Reformation', then it was earned by the country's independent contribution to Catholic renewal, and not by her willingness to follow the papal lead given at Trent.

The other leading Catholic monarchies of Western Europe present a mixed picture in their responses to the Catholic Reformation. Portugal shows a very direct debt to the movement, for it was in direct response to the work of the Jesuits in Italy that John III requested their assistance within his own realm in 1539–40. Under the leadership of Rodrigues de Azevedo, the Jesuits were subsequently prominent in the religious life of Portugal, and acquired a degree of influence over the actions of the monarch that was scarcely paralleled anywhere else in Europe. In France, on the other hand, the Catholic Reformation encountered a formidable variety of obstacles, ranging from bitter Protestant hostility during the Wars of Religion to a Catholic Church with strong traditions of Gallican independence. Charles IX refused to have the Tridentine decrees published in 1566, and rejected them once more in 1579. Yet reformed religious orders did make steady progress within France from about 1564, when the Jesuit Collège de Clermont was opened. At least fourteen other Jesuit institutions were founded in France in the course of the next thirty years, before an attempt on the life of Henry IV by a former student of the Collège de Clermont (1594) led to the expulsion of the order from France.

The decrees of the Council of Trent had done little to improve the overall state of the French Catholic clergy by the end of the sixteenth century. St Vincent de Paul (1576–1660) and St Francis de Sales (1567–1622) still had much work to do in the next century to regenerate a clergy who 'were seen but in the market or in some low artisan's shop; their tonsure was overgrown and they feared to wear their clerical dress, as providing matter for public railing'. To this, St Vincent de Paul added his own judgement that 'priests living in the manner most do today are the greatest enemies of God's Church'. His Congregation of the Mission, founded in 1625, worked for the education and spiritual improvement of the clergy, yet the fact that such extensive work remained to be undertaken deep into the seventeenth century illustrates both the timescale of the Catholic Reformation and the relative shallowness of its impact upon France during the sixteenth century.

Northern Europe

In northern Europe, similarly, missionaries such as the Jesuits achieved few successes unless they had the sympathy and support of the political authorities. In some cases such support was certainly forthcoming. In the Holy Roman Empire, the accession of Rudolf II (1576) brought to power a ruler thoroughly influenced by his Jesuit education and eager to revise the religious balance established in Germany by the Peace of Augsburg in 1555. His greatest successes against the further encroachment of Lutheranism came when he defeated the attempt of the Lutheran Prince Joachim Friedrich to assume the archbishopric of Magdeburg (1582), and when he deposed Gebhard Truchsess von Waldburg, Archbishop of Cologne,

who had announced in the same year his conversion to Lutheranism.

The Wittelsbach princes of Bavaria, Albert V (1550–79), Wilhelm V (1579–97) and Maximilian I (1597–1651), ensured that their realm remained the most rigidly Catholic territory in Germany. A Spiritual Council, established in 1570, oversaw education, organised visitations of the Bavarian bishoprics, and enforced the decrees of the Council of Trent. An Index was in operation from 1569, and compulsory attendance at Catholic services was gradually imposed, running parallel to the expulsion of Bavarian Protestants. Of the Jesuits who were so active in Bavaria, the greatest was St Peter Canisius. In half a century of work in Germany, between 1549 and his death in 1597, Canisius excelled as educator, administrator and preacher, and was a leading force in the establishment of the Jesuit colléges at Ingolstadt, Cologne, Innsbruck, Prague and Nymwegen.

Among the prince-bishops of Germany, the archbishopric of Trier, under the rule of Jacob von Eltz (1567–81), and that of Mainz under Adam von Bicken (1601–4) and Schweikard von Kronenberg (1604–20) provide examples of great energy in clerical education and the more rigid enforcement of orthodox doctrine. Yet in Germany the Catholic Reformation still had much to achieve after 1600. Above all, the accession of the Emperor Ferdinand II (1619) marked the beginning of a concerted attempt to dismantle the religious settlement of 1555. This policy was at the heart of the disastrous Thirty Years War which ravaged central and northern Europe between 1618 and 1648. In its course, Ferdinand's ambitious Edict of Restitution (1629) symbolised his desire to win back all those German lands lost to the Church since 1552.

Those southern provinces of the Netherlands that remained under Catholic control also witnessed a concerted policy of Catholic regeneration. Between 1596 and 1621, a series of regulations provided for compulsory attendance at Catholic services, and obliged parish clergy to report laxity among their congregations. Strict censorship was enforced, and a ban was laid upon all discussion of religious subjects by laymen. In these regions, too, the principal role in lay education and clerical training was played by members of the Society of Jesus.

The Catholic Reformation failed, on the other hand, to regain any of the ground lost to

Protestantism in the northern Netherlands in the course of the Dutch Revolt, and the renewal of religious conflict after 1618 saw even more determined efforts to exclude Catholics from office in Gelderland and Overyssel, where they had retained some influence. Political and religious opposition to all that Spain and the Catholic Reformation stood for remained immovable, and most commentators have confirmed the conclusion that although 'Roman Catholicism was never extinguished in the United Provinces, in reality the struggle was lost by 1609 and the Catholics of the north became passive and obscure' (G.W. Searle).

Much the same conclusion must serve in the case of England. Two major attempts were made at reconversion, under Queen Mary between 1553 and 1558, and by the Jesuit mission that entered England from 1574 onwards. This mission foundered on the twin obstacles of ruthless government action and the lukewarm response of the majority of English Catholics. Recognising such obstacles, Gregory XIII relieved the missionaries of any duty to win Englishmen away from their allegiance to the crown. He left them, in the phrase of Edmund Campion, 'to preach the gospel, to minister the sacraments, to instruct the simple, to reform sinners, [and] to confute errors'. In these respects, perhaps, the Jesuit mission to England enjoyed some success. It left behind a distinguished list of martyrs, and an honourable minority who maintained their faith in the teeth of bitter official hostility.

The wider world

The relative failure of Catholic missionaries in Protestant Europe was offset by some spectacular successes further afield, for the Catholic Reformation launched the great age of European missionary activity in other continents. Some historians of colonialism have seen Jesuits and Observant Franciscans primarily as cultural imperialists, foisting European religion upon unsuspecting natives. Against this it has been objected that the imperial adventures of the English and the Dutch were not accompanied by such spiritual missions, thus suggesting that such undertakings were predominantly a Catholic

concern. From this has arisen the 'compensation' theory, which suggests that in the latter part of the sixteenth century the Catholic Church was quite deliberately compensating with new believers for the legions of Europeans now lost to 'heresy'.

In the New World, of course, the propagation of the Catholic faith in the wake of the *conquistadores* pre-dated any significant measure of Catholic reform in Europe. Official sources already spoke of 5 million baptisms in the period 1524–36; 140 separate monasteries had been established in Mexico by 1570, and in their northward mission to the Apache tribe the Jesuits claimed over 80,000 baptisms by 1636. The Jesuits arrived in Peru in 1568, and had established five colleges there by 1582. Toribio de Mogrovejo claimed after fifteen years as Archbishop of Lima (1594) to have been responsible for the confirmation of half a million people, an achievement which won for him the reputation of 'the apostle of Peru' and subsequent canonisation. Whatever the methods used, and whatever the initial limitations of the faith learned by the native population, the net outcome of a century of missionary activity in South America was the catholicisation of a whole, vast continent.

The greatest of those who exported the Catholic faith to Asia was undoubtedly St Francis Xavier, but the following generations produced many outstanding men to continue his work. In India, Aquavivi carried the Gospel to the court of the Mogul Emperor in 1580, although he did not succeed in converting him. A third Jesuit, Robert de Nobili, also achieved outstanding results during a fifty-year ministry in the Madurai region. In China, Matteo Ricci achieved some of the success at the court of the Emperor that had evaded Aquavivi. Reaching Peking in 1600, he and his followers were able to win the respect of many influential Chinese by their advanced technical knowledge. Although this emperor, too, resisted conversion, converts were won at court, often by a clever fusing of Christianity with the more familiar precepts of Confucianism. By the time of Ricci's death in 1610, there were probably some 2,000 Chinese Christians, mainly concentrated in Shanghai, Chekiang and Hankow.

Most remarkable, perhaps, were the results achieved by Catholic missions in Japan. With the aid of a number of sympathetic rulers, the Jesuit,

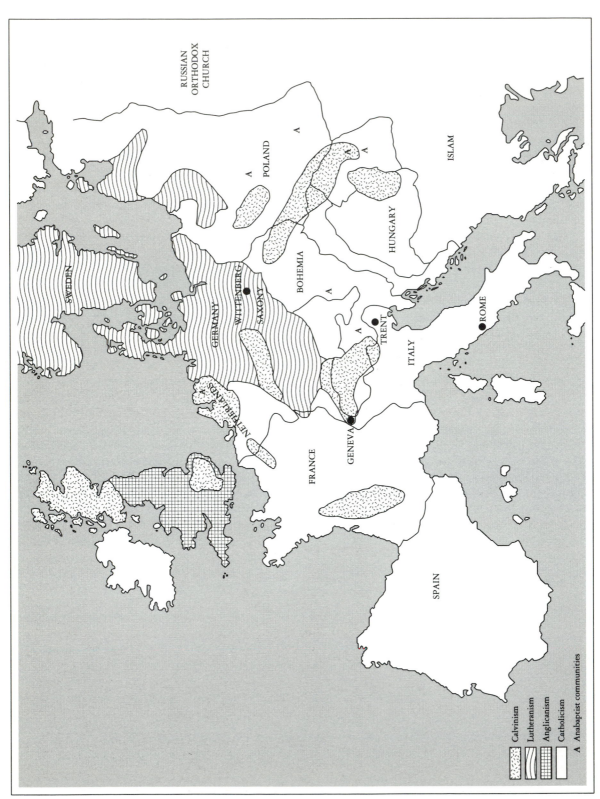

6.3(a) *The religious map of Europe, c.1560*

Calvinism

Lutheranism

Anglicanism

Catholicism

A Anabaptist communities

6.3(b) *The religious map of Europe, c.1600*

Official religions

- Calvinism
- Lutheranism
- Anglicanism
- Catholicism

Tolerated minority communities

- **L** Lutheranism
- **C** Calvinism
- **A** Anabaptist communities
- **R** Catholic communities

Augustinian and Dominican missions working there from the 1560s were able to claim some 200,000 Christian converts by 1582, rising to 600,000 by 1622. In 1610 and in 1624 violent persecution of these Catholic communities led to the deaths of some 30,000 Christians, most of them natives, and the Catholic missions to Japan were effectively ended.

THE CULTURE OF THE CATHOLIC REFORMATION

The great Italian historian Benedetto Croce had a low opinion of the cultural achievement of the Catholic Counter-Reformation, especially as it related to literature. 'No great book', he complained, 'that is one which reveals man more profoundly to man, was inspired by the Counter Reformation.' The architecture of the Catholic Reformation cannot, however, be dismissed so easily. The last decades of the sixteenth century saw the development of a more flamboyant and heavily decorated style of building. Regarding this style as an oddity, its critics referred to it by the term 'baroque'. Baroque architecture in many cases deliberately used elaborate decoration and magnificent furnishing to convey the glory of God and the glory of the hierarchical Church. In many respects a baroque church was a sort of splendid theatre in which the ceremonies of the Catholic faith could be played out in a setting of suitable grandeur. The style can be seen in its earliest stages in the Jesuit mother church in Rome, Il Gesu, begun by Vignola in 1568. It reached its maturity in Italy in the course of the seventeenth century in the work of Borromini and of Bernini. Perhaps the outstanding piece of baroque church-building in Italy is the Church of Sta Maria della Salute, built by Longhena in Venice between 1631 and 1685.

Sculpture and painting also felt the impact of the Counter-Reformation. Lorenzo Bernini's sculpted altarpiece in the Church of Sta Maria della Vittoria in Rome (1644–7), showing St Theresa receiving a heavenly vision, is perhaps the single most famous work of art directly attributable to the movement. In the emotion portrayed and in the theatrical framed setting above the altar, it departs significantly from any of its Renaissance forerunners. Such a work also makes it clear that, as the Counter-Reformation confronted the doctrines of Protestantism, so its churches deliberately countered the blank interiors of Protestant churches with unparalleled religious imagery aimed at conveying to the worshipper an impression of the religious experience and the eternal bliss to which the Church and its sacraments held the key.

Further reading

J. Bossy (1985) *Christianity in the West, 1400–1700*. Oxford.

A.G. Dickens (1968) *The Counter Reformation*. London.

M.A. Mullett (1984) *The Counter-Reformation and the Catholic Reformation in Early Modern Europe*. London.

G.W. Searle (1974) *The Counter Reformation*. London.

— PART II —

THE RISE OF THE GREAT MONARCHIES

• CHAPTER SEVEN •

Spain 1469–1555
From Unification to World Power

The impact of Islam and of the reconquista upon Spanish society. The cathedral of Cordoba was built in the eighth century as a mosque of a thriving Muslim city. Since the city's capture by Christian forces in 1236 the same building has served as a cathedral dedicated to the Blessed Virgin Mary

THE HISTORICAL DEBATE

The rise of Spain from obscurity to the position of Europe's greatest power is one of the central issues of Western European history in the sixteenth century. The reigns of Ferdinand and Isabella and of Charles have therefore been closely examined as the formative period of Spain's greatness. The classic view of Spanish historians is that expressed by R. Menendez Pidal (*Los Reyes Catolicos y otros estudios*, 1962), that the joint reign 'for all Spaniards represents a happy golden age, remembered nostalgically as incomparable by one and all'. Pidal questioned, nevertheless, whether the reign of the Catholic Monarchs was mainly notable as the prelude to a greater period of Spanish influence under Charles V, or whether it was supreme in its own right. Did it represent a 'golden age' of Spanish independence before the interests of Spain became inextricably confused with the wider interests of the Habsburg monarchy?

The image of a 'golden age' retained its appeal through the traumas of the nineteenth and twentieth centuries. As the government of General Franco sought to reinforce a sense of national identity after the civil war, such major Spanish writers as J. Vicens Vives re-stressed the importance of this period in the formation of the nation. The theme of a Spanish 'golden age' has also long been familiar outside Spain, and in the most influential English works of recent decades, R. Trevor Davies (*The Golden Century of Spain*, 1958) and J.H. Elliott (*Imperial Spain*, 1963) followed similar lines.

Recent writers have been less willing to accept such a positive view of the Spanish empire. In particular I.A.A. Thompson (*War and Government in Habsburg Spain, 1560–1620*, 1976) has shown that Spain had little claim to be considered a military power in her own right until the latter half of the sixteenth century. Previously, most authorities now agree, the Spanish crown relied heavily upon the accumulated inheritance of the Habsburg dynasty.

It is harder to deny that this period saw great advances in the political unification of Spanish government and witnessed the consolidation of an exclusively Catholic Spain. All the same, J.N. Hillgarth (*The Spanish Kingdoms, 1250–1516*, 1978) has stressed the survival of political diversity in 'united' Spain, despite the cosmetic unity of the crowns. He denies that Ferdinand and Isabella's reign marked the closing of the medieval period in Spanish history, and concludes that 'no date can be set for the end of medieval Spain. The tensions created by the past are still alive.' In Spain itself, the end of General Franco's dictatorship has coincided with the publication of a number of substantial regional histories, notably on the Asturias (1977), Andalucia (1980) and Granada (1986), which stress the survival of local political and social variety.

Undoubtedly, the first half of the sixteenth century saw unprecedented economic growth and prosperity in Spain. Pierre Chaunu's major work (*Séville et l'Atlantique, 1504–1650*, 1955–60) documented the flow of precious metals into Spain and the subsequent effects on prices and upon government policy. Other major economic works have confirmed a picture of population-growth and urban prosperity in the first half of the century. They have also established, however, that these unparalleled economic resources were used in such a way as to bring little long-term benefit to the Spanish economy and only temporary political benefits to the Spanish monarchy. If Ferdinand, Isabella and Charles raised the authority of the crown to new levels, they failed to create the preconditions for lasting national strength. H. Kamen (*Spain 1469–1714: A Society of Conflict*, 1983) represents the current historical consensus: 'Recent research leaves us with the unsurprising image of a poor country [which], although leader of a world monarchy, relied overwhelmingly on foreign money, foreign troops and foreign ships to sustain that leadership, an inverted situation to be found in no other empire in history.'

THE HISTORICAL BACKGROUND OF THE SPANISH KINGDOMS

Few observers in 1500 would have anticipated that in the course of the next century Spain would dominate the history of Western Europe. The resources of the peninsula were modest, and for the previous eight centuries its history had followed its own unique course, largely independent of events elsewhere in continental Europe. The central fact of Spain's medieval history was the power struggle between Islamic and Christian rulers. In the eighth century the Moors, Islamic warriors crossing from North Africa in the first flush of the Muslim religion, had established their authority in much of Spain and had pushed far north. Like this original conquest, the great Christian reconquest (*reconquista*) took over two centuries to accomplish, but by the end of the thirteenth century seven-eighths of the peninsula had been reclaimed by Christian rulers.

The only exception was the Islamic kingdom of Granada, extending along the south-eastern coast, facing Africa.

By 1450 the greatest of the Christian kingdoms was Castile, the major architect and beneficiary of the *reconquista*, stretching from the Asturias in the north to Cadiz in the south. The Mediterranean coastline of the peninsula was dominated by the smaller kingdom of Aragon. The survival within Aragon of separate customs, institutions and laws illustrated that this state was the result of a series of

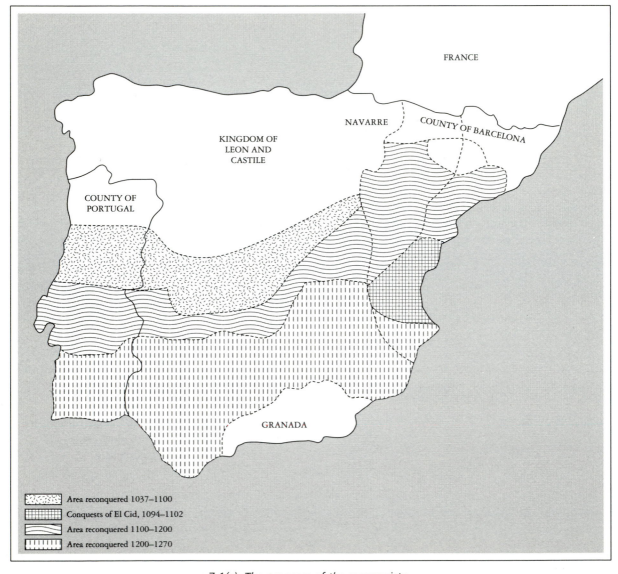

7.1(a) *The progress of the* reconquista

unions between lesser kingdoms. Although relatively small, Aragon's control of the Balearic Islands, Sicily, Sardinia and Naples gave it a prestigious international position, and made it a greater force in the western Mediterranean than within Spain itself. The third major kingdom was Portugal, extending along much of the Atlantic coastline and, like Aragon, exercising more international influence through her maritime interests than she could within the peninsula. All the same, it was only by the failure of the marriage

between King Afonso and Juana of Castile that the fate of Portugal was separated from that of the rest of the peninsula.

The Spanish kingdoms derived more from the *reconquista* than their territories and boundaries. The estates, wealth and influence of the nobility, especially in Castile, reflected the roles that their ancestors had played as crusading warlords. In particular this was reflected in the semi-religious Military Orders of Santiago, Calatrava and Alcantara. The Spanish Church, too, had derived lively

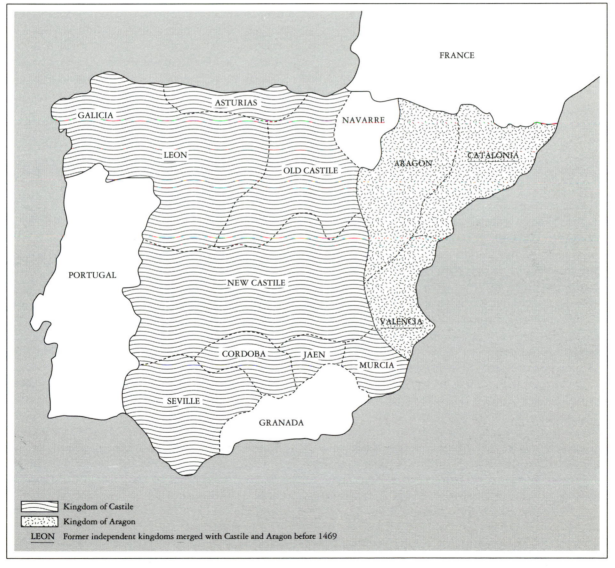

7.1(b) The political map of Spain in 1469

spiritual traditions from its long battle against the infidel. Lastly, the *reconquista* left Spain with a unique social and cultural legacy. Nowhere else in Western Europe was there such a mixture of racial and cultural elements. In many regions of Aragon and Castile, *Mudejar* peasants and artisans, the term applied to Moors living under Christian rule, lived and worked alongside their 'Old Christian' counterparts. A substantial Jewish population contributed further to a state of multicultural cohabitation known to contemporaries as *convivencia*.

ISABELLA, FERDINAND AND THE 'UNIFICATION' OF THE SPANISH CROWNS

In the mid-fifteenth century political chaos reigned in Castile. The usurpation of the crown by Henry of Trastamara (1369) had been paid for in substantial grants of land and local influence to the nobles who had backed him, and the reign of Henry IV ('the Impotent', 1454–74) provided many of the classic ingredients for civil war and the further decline of royal authority. A sensitive and allegedly effeminate king was unable to fulfil the role of warlord, and the absence of a male heir promised a disputed succession. At the centre of the dispute stood two young women. Supporters of Juana, Henry's daughter, sought to strengthen her position by marriage to Afonso V of Portugal; while Isabella, Henry's half-sister, made a daring and risky marriage alliance (October 1469) with Ferdinand, the seventeen-year-old heir to the kingdom of Aragon.

Upon Henry's death (December 1474), Isabella had many advantages in the struggle for power. She had been recognised as heir in 1468, and she had a strong husband to support her. It was a more difficult proposition, however, to impose her authority in such outlying provinces as Andalucia, Murcia and Galicia. Local nobles withheld their allegiance, and the conclusion of the marriage between Juana and Afonso (1475) provided them with a focus which ensured civil war. That war was decided by a substantial Castilian victory at the Battle of Toro (March 1476), supplemented by a series of deals struck with leading members of the nobility and by other favourable developments. The Pope's refusal to recognise the marriage of Juana and Afonso, and the birth of a son, Juan, to Ferdinand and Isabella, seemed to confirm that the future lay with them.

The personal union of the monarchs did not bring about the union of their kingdoms. Although each partner had equal rights and powers in the kingdom of the other, there was no guarantee that the union would survive the death of one partner. Aragon even maintained its laws against a female succession. The two kingdoms remained remarkably unequal and dissimilar. Castile was four times the size of Aragon and far richer. Castile was a unitary state, with one Cortes and a structure of taxation, coinage and administration common to the whole realm while in Aragon; each province jealously guarded its freedoms and privileges. The two kingdoms had developed diverse interests in foreign policy and in external commerce, Aragon remaining an essentially Mediterranean power, with a profound interest in the politics of Italy, while Castile had already begun to direct her interests and energies into the Atlantic.

THE GOVERNMENT OF CASTILE

Crown and aristocracy

The Castilian monarchy lacked the resources to break the power of the nobility in the provinces. Nor could it do without the vast military and feudal resources that the nobility commanded there. In the delicate atmosphere that prevailed after the civil war, no attempt was made to cancel the exemption of the nobility from taxation, nor to limit the military capacity of the loyal nobles. Even noblemen who had clearly been disloyal during the civil war were pardoned and left with substantial fortunes. The Castilian nobility was not 'tamed', but rather was 'taken into partnership with the crown and confirmed in their estates and private armies' (H. Kamen). There would be no doubt during the next century and a half that the Spanish crown governed through the medium of the great nobles. It was the achievement of Ferdinand and Isabella, however, that the monarchy would consistently prove to be the senior partner in this relationship. The independent power of the Military Orders was only slowly undermined. By 1500, however, the process had been greatly advanced by the nomination of Ferdinand himself as Master of the Orders of Calatrava (1485), Santiago (1492) and Alcantara (1494). A potential source of danger had thus been transformed into a royal asset. Meanwhile, by staffing the courts and councils with *letrado* 'new men', the crown sought to provide itself with a long-term alternative to the employment of the great noble families as political servants.

The great families derived ample compensation from their enormous landed wealth and their indestructible authority in the provinces. The Marquis of Villena commanded an immense fief of some 25,000 square kilometres, which gave him 150,000 vassals to command and an income of 100,000 ducats a year. Such resources were often strategically concentrated in particular regions of Castile. The house of Alva dominated the region of Salamanca, while Leon and Zamora constituted the heartlands of the houses of Luna and Benavente. Some of these men gained even greater prestige and rewards for their families by serving the crown in its foreign military adventures, or by achieving high office within the Castilian Church.

Institutions and royal authority

Illustration 7.2 indicates the slow development of centralised organs of government and administration during the reign of Ferdinand and Isabella. Yet many of the factors central to their success cannot be represented in this form. The power and influence of the monarchs depended essentially upon their personal energy and involvement in government. There existed few bureaucratic institutions to translate the decisions of central government into local action; and so, in stark contrast to the absentee Charles and the static Philip II, the Catholic Monarchs ranged about Castile making their authority a real and physical thing for their subjects. It was not unknown for Isabella to cover 2,000 kilometres in a year of **royal progresses**, to compensate with personal magnetism for what her monarchy lacked in formal, physical power. 'They had', H. Kamen has

stressed, 'none of the appurtenances of state power: no standing army, no bureaucracy, no reliable income, and certainly no theory of absolutism. Only gradually did institutions develop to take over the power they had created.'

Similarly, such a diagram cannot adequately convey the fact that the Castilian monarchy had to rely upon a solid basis of pragmatic support, such as that which it received through its partnership with the nobility. The crown also derived a large degree of support from the towns, which had often been vulnerable to the power and greed of the military nobility during the years of civil conflict. In peace, the urban patricians turned to the resurgent monarchy as their best protection against the feudal aristocracy. From this close but self-interested relationship developed three of the most prominent institutions of late medieval Spain: the Corregidores, the Santa Hermandad and the Cortes.

The Castilian Cortes is the most difficult of these institutions to assess. Its history stretched back to the end of the twelfth century, making it the oldest representative body in Western Europe. In Castile, by the beginning of the fifteenth century, it comprised representatives of three estates: Church, nobility and *bourgeoisie*. Yet this should not lead us to conclude that the monarchy of Ferdinand and Isabella was popular or consultative. Under their rule, the Cortes came increasingly to represent only the interests of the major towns, whose representatives (*procuradores*) often outnumbered the representatives of the other estates, and were sometimes the only persons present. Its main function was to vote financial subsidies (*servicios*) to the crown in time of particular need, and its legislative role was strictly limited. The crown alone had the power to make law, but increasingly it chose to perform this function in partnership with the Cortes. Certainly the Cortes met more often during the lifetimes of Ferdinand and Isabella than ever before, but the concentration of its meetings (four times between 1469 and 1481, and a dozen times between 1498 and 1516) suggests that the Cortes met when it suited the crown. It is true that the Catholic Monarchs 'consulted their towns more than any Spanish rulers of the next two centuries' (H. Kamen). It is also true, however, that this consultation masked increasing royal control over the Cortes. The number of towns represented

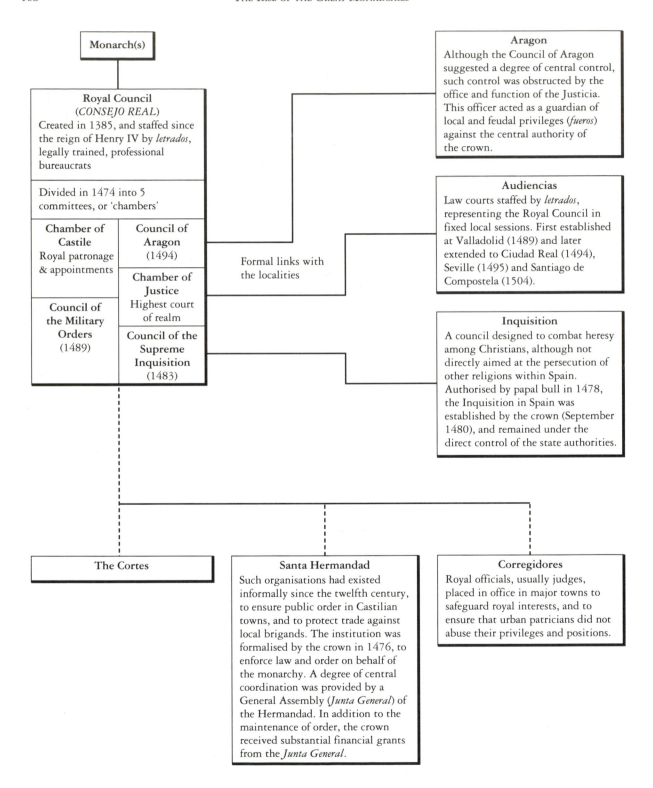

Monarch(s)

Royal Council
(*CONSEJO REAL*)
Created in 1385, and staffed since the reign of Henry IV by *letrados*, legally trained, professional bureaucrats

Divided in 1474 into 5 committees, or 'chambers'

Chamber of Castile
Royal patronage & appointments

Council of Aragon (1494)

Chamber of Justice
Highest court of realm

Council of the Military Orders (1489)

Council of the Supreme Inquisition (1483)

Formal links with the localities

Aragon
Although the Council of Aragon suggested a degree of central control, such control was obstructed by the office and function of the Justicia. This officer acted as a guardian of local and feudal privileges (*fueros*) against the central authority of the crown.

Audiencias
Law courts staffed by *letrados*, representing the Royal Council in fixed local sessions. First established at Valladolid (1489) and later extended to Ciudad Real (1494), Seville (1495) and Santiago de Compostela (1504).

Inquisition
A council designed to combat heresy among Christians, although not directly aimed at the persecution of other religions within Spain. Authorised by papal bull in 1478, the Inquisition in Spain was established by the crown (September 1480), and remained under the direct control of the state authorities.

The Cortes

Santa Hermandad
Such organisations had existed informally since the twelfth century, to ensure public order in Castilian towns, and to protect trade against local brigands. The institution was formalised by the crown in 1476, to enforce law and order on behalf of the monarchy. A degree of central coordination was provided by a General Assembly (*Junta General*) of the Hermandad. In addition to the maintenance of order, the crown received substantial financial grants from the *Junta General*.

Corregidores
Royal officials, usually judges, placed in office in major towns to safeguard royal interests, and to ensure that urban patricians did not abuse their privileges and positions.

7.2 The administrative system of the Catholic Monarchs

shrank from around fifty to eighteen, and the *procuradores* never successfully asserted any right to gain redress of their grievances before they voted funds to the crown.

THE CONQUEST OF GRANADA, 1482–92

Many contemporaries would have attached less importance to the union of the Spanish crowns under Ferdinand and Isabella than to their conquest of Granada, the last remnant of Islam in Western Europe. Few doubted that this conquest was the focal point of the reign of the Catholic Monarchs, or that it represented their finest achievement.

The advantages of war against Granada were so varied and obvious that the Castilian crown was likely to undertake such an enterprise as soon as it became politically possible. No doubt many believed that the war was a genuine crusade against the infidel, but there were also many more practical, political advantages to be gained by uniting the nobility of Castile against a common enemy and by acquiring new lands with which to reward loyal servants. Granada must also have appeared an easy target, for the emirate had been living on borrowed time. The small principality was crippled by internal political strife and isolated from potential allies elsewhere in the Islamic world. Since the death of Yusuf III (1417), rival claimants had disputed power more or less continuously, and relations with neighbouring Morocco were so bad that Moroccan wheat was actually sold in substantial quantities during the war to the Christian forces, rather than to those defending Granada. The survival of Granada depended upon the weakness and divisions of her Christian neighbours. Preoccupied with the establishment of their authority in Castile, Ferdinand and Isabella concluded three truces with Granada between 1475 and 1478, but the growth of stability in Castile sealed the fate of Granada. A Moorish raid on Zahara (December 1481) provided the perfect excuse for a full-scale war.

Yet this war lasted ten years. Castile's army increased steadily from some 6,000 in 1482 to some 50,000 nine years later, but this was of limited value in a war of sieges and scorched-earth campaigns. Only slowly did the Castilians gain the upper hand through their unparalleled efforts to supply provisions for this enormous army, and by their increasing use of artillery. An army that had only four artillerymen in its service in 1479 possessed 179 pieces of artillery by the end of the war. In the later stages of the conflict, reported the chronicler Bernaldez, towns fell 'within a month, the least of which in the past could have held out a year and could not have been taken except by hunger'. The very last stage of the war, the siege of Granada itself, lasted eight months (April 1491 to January 1492), before the emir Boabdil surrendered to the Catholic Monarchs. The extreme generosity of the surrender terms probably reflected the eagerness of an exhausted Castilian monarchy to bring the epic struggle to a close.

The financial cost of the war, 800 million *maravedis,* was enormous. Of this, the Church made by far the greatest contribution. The special taxes granted by Pope Innocent VIII amounted to about 500 million *maravedis,* while the Castilian Church probably contributed another 100 million. Although it had undoubtedly cost more than anticipated, the conquest of Granada was the single greatest achievement of the joint reign of Ferdinand and Isabella. It destroyed the last vestiges of independent Moorish power in the Iberian peninsula and enormously increased the prestige and charisma of the victorious monarchs. The title subsequently granted to Ferdinand and Isabella by the papacy, *Los Reyes Católicos,* was borne as a proud symbol of this achievement. The conquest did more than anything else to create the impression of a united and powerful Spain, and established Castile as a state of European stature.

THE END OF *CONVIVENCIA*

The campaign against Granada completed the long process of *reconquista,* but it also struck a mighty blow at one of the most distinctive elements in contemporary Spanish society, the concept of *convivencia.* The sequel to the conquest of Granada clearly indicated that the crown of Castile rejected such diversity of religion and culture.

Technically, the peace terms of 1492 maintained the principles of *convivencia,* and respected the

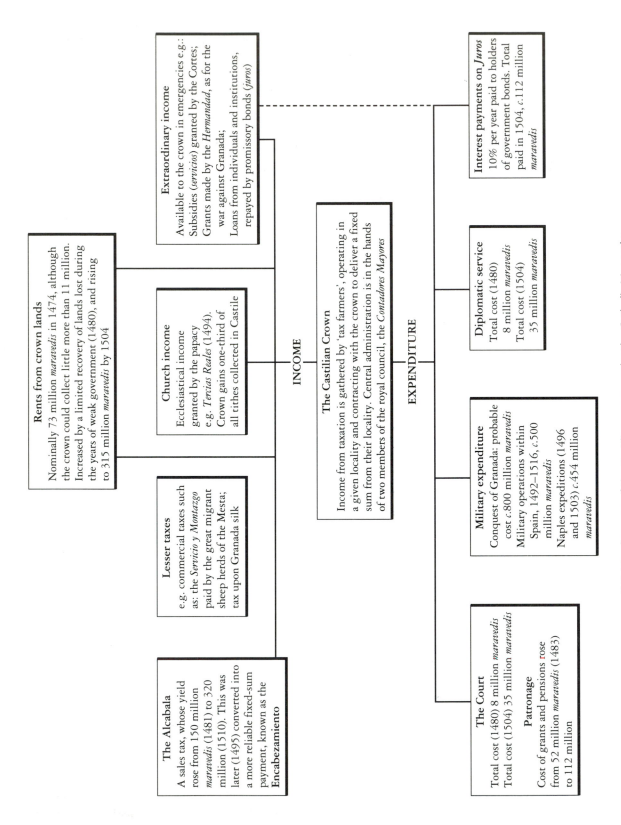

Rents from crown lands

Nominally 73 million *maravedis* in 1474, although the crown could collect little more than 11 million. Increased by a limited recovery of lands lost during the years of weak government (1480), and rising to 315 million *maravedis* by 1504

Extraordinary income

Available to the crown in emergencies e.g.: Subsidies (*servicios*) granted by the Cortes; Grants made by the *Hermandad*, as for the war against Granada; Loans from individuals and institutions, repayed by promissory bonds (*juros*)

The Alcabala

A sales tax, whose yield rose from 150 million *maravedis* (1481) to 320 million (1510). This was later (1495) converted into a more reliable fixed-sum payment, known as the **Encabezamiento**

Lesser taxes

e.g. commercial taxes such as: the *Servicio y Montazgo* paid by the great migrant sheep herds of the Mesta; tax upon Granada silk

Church income

Ecclesiastical income granted by the papacy e.g. *Tercias Reales* (1494). Crown gains one-third of all tithes collected in Castile

INCOME

The Castilian Crown

Income from taxation is gathered by 'tax farmers', operating in a given locality and contracting with the crown to deliver a fixed sum from their locality. Central administration is in the hands of two members of the royal council, the *Contadores Mayores*

EXPENDITURE

Interest payments on *Juros*

10% per year paid to holders of government bonds. Total paid in 1504, *c.*112 million *maravedis*

Diplomatic service

Total cost (1480) 8 million *maravedis*
Total cost (1504) 35 million *maravedis*

Military expenditure

Conquest of Granada: probable cost *c.*800 million *maravedis*
Military operations within Spain, 1492–1516, *c.*500 million *maravedis*
Naples expeditions (1496 and 1503) *c.*454 million *maravedis*

The Court

Total cost (1480) 8 million *maravedis*
Total cost (1504) 35 million *maravedis*

Patronage

Cost of grants and pensions rose from 52 million *maravedis* (1483) to 112 million

7.3 *The finances of the Castilian crown under the Catholic Monarchs*

property, customs and even the religion of the Moors who remained in Granada. By the end of the century, however, powerful forces were operating against the survival of an independent Islamic identity. Initially, the governor of the territory, the Marquis of Mondejar, worked to protect the Moors, while the newly appointed Archbishop of Granada, de Talavera, pursued an enlightened policy of teaching and persuasion to attract converts. Dissatisfied with the slow pace of such a policy, the primate of the Castilian Church, Cardinal Ximenes, replaced it by 1499 with a policy of bullying and compulsion. From 1501 it was officially assumed that the Muslim religion no longer existed in Granada. Moriscos (officially converted Moors) enjoyed equal legal rights with 'old' Christians, but could not carry arms; they also found their culture under attack, with the burning of Arabic books and the suppression of other aspects of Islamic learning. The following year the policy of conformity took a step further with the decree that all Moors in the rest of Castile should accept baptism or leave the realm.

The Jewish population also felt the impact of this changed mentality. The forced conversion of Jews dated back at least as far as the later fourteenth century, and had created a community of 'new' Christians (conversos). Their sincerity and orthodoxy were highly suspect, and they were widely viewed as a source of corruption within the Church. It was to counter this 'threat' of continued Jewish thought and belief that the Inquisition was established in Castile for the first time in November 1478. Its role was not to attack those Jews who openly retained their original faith, but to root out supposed heresy among the conversos. From 1483 the Castilian Inquisition was united with its Aragonese counterpart under the generalship of Tomas de Torquemada, and set about the task of eliminating Semitic cultural survivals. The impact of the Inquisition in areas of substantial converso settlement was dramatic. It is estimated that 4,000 converso families fled from Andalucia, while a contemporary account sets the number of conversos executed by the Inquisition between 1480 and 1498 at about 8,800.

Nevertheless, these campaigns were officially considered to be unsuccessful, and the conclusion was reached that Semitic influences could never be controlled while an openly Jewish population remained in Spain. Localised expulsions of Jews, in Andalucia (1484) and in parts of Aragon (1486), were followed in March 1492 by the great Edict of Expulsion. Within four months all Jews were to accept baptism or leave Spanish territories. It is possible that some 15,000 Jews left Castile, along with a further 10,000 from Aragon, seeking refuge in Portugal, North Africa, Italy or in Ottoman territories. About 50,000 Jews seem to have accepted baptism, thereby aggravating the problem of the converso communities which the Catholic Monarchs had originally set out to solve.

It does not seem that the Catholic Monarchs made any substantial profit from this policy. The sum gained from the confiscation of Jewish goods at the time of the expulsion (2,274,000 maravedis) pales into insignificance alongside the sums spent on the campaigns against Granada. One is forced to conclude either that the motives of the Castilian monarchy were indeed religious, or that the crown was responding to pressure from below for action against the Jews. 'To an extent', concludes J.N. Hillgarth, 'it is correct to see the Monarchs as taking over a popular movement against the conversos and the Jews. But they transformed it. They were too imbued with a sense of royal authority to allow riots against Jews or conversos.'

By the time of Isabella's death, the pluralist nature of Spanish society had been thoroughly undermined, and irreversible steps had been taken to fashion a society that was European and Catholic in all religious and cultural respects. In the sixteenth century it would become even more important for those who wished to pursue a successful career in Church or state to prove that they were untainted by descent from any of the 'new Christian' groups in Spanish society, and that they satisfied the strict criteria of 'purity of blood' (limpieza de sangre).

THE KINGDOM OF ARAGON

Throughout this period, the history of the kingdom of Aragon ran a largely separate course. Many of the most prominent themes of Castilian history are missing altogether from that of her neighbour.

There is, for instance, little evidence of a significant increase in royal authority in Aragon. Ferdinand was virtually an absentee monarch throughout his reign, spending a little less than seven years in Aragon during a thirty-seven-year reign. Even after Isabella's death in 1504, the political demands of Castile continued to distract him. Perhaps that is why, in the judgement of a recent Spanish historian, Aragon formed 'the great exception within Ferdinand's reforming policy, and his great failure'.

Certainly, Aragon made only a slight contribution to the major enterprises of the Catholic Monarchs, providing little more than 20 million *maravedis* towards the vast cost of the war against Granada. Aragon was an unpromising source of taxation, underpopulated, barely recovered from a lengthy period of economic decline, and protected by a complex system of local rights and privileges (*fueros*). Like Castile, Aragon had been afflicted by civil conflicts, notably in Catalonia (1462–72). Unlike Castile, however, these disorders did not encourage a trend towards greater royal authority. There was only localised enthusiasm for the revival of the Hermandad within Aragon, and by 1495 the organisation had been formally suppressed. The Cortes, at the same time, retained a high degree of independence from the crown. Even when the state was at war with France, the Cortes never granted subsidies to the crown without insisting at the same time upon the prompt redress of their grievances. Lastly, Ferdinand failed to impose royal control over the nobility, whose privileges were confirmed throughout his reign. The government of Aragon remained highly conservative and immobile, perhaps because Ferdinand had bigger fish to fry, but perhaps because the incentives for significant reform were missing.

Aragon played a greater role, however, in the foreign policy of the period. The concern of the Catholic Monarchs with the Mediterranean arose largely from Ferdinand's Aragonese interests. With this in mind, we can see that much of the foreign policy of the monarchy after the capture of Granada was motivated by factors that had relatively little to do with the interests of Castile. In the consolidation of its interests beyond the peninsula, the Aragonese monarchy showed evidence of greater ambition and energy.

THE SPANISH CHURCH IN THE AGE OF XIMENES

In an age when the Catholic Church was beset by similar problems throughout the greater part of Western Europe, the Church in the Spanish kingdoms, and in Castile in particular, was remarkable in several respects. First, while the Church in France, England or in the Low Countries had experienced at least five or six centuries of peace since the struggles of its foundation, the Spanish Church had been in the front line against the infidel throughout this period. The *reconquista* added to the material wealth of the Church as it did to that of the nobility. By 1500 the combined income of Castile's twenty-seven bishops and four archbishops was over 400,000 ducats a year, equal to the income of Castile's ten richest dukes. The total wealth of the Castilian Church has been estimated at some 6 million ducats.

Yet this wealthy and dynamic institution was subject to a remarkable degree of royal authority. Since 1478 it had acknowledged the right of the crown to make all ecclesiastical appointments within Castile and Aragon. The power to appoint all officers of the Inquisition acquired great significance ten years later when the religious orders in Spain were placed under the Inquisition's authority. In addition, the crown secured considerable access to the financial resources of the Church. The greatest step in this respect was the grant by Alexander VI of the *tercias reales* (1494), whereby the Monarchs had the right to take possession of one-third of all the tithes collected by the Church in Castile.

Equally remarkable was the extent to which the Castilian crown used such powers to reform and to strengthen the Church from above. The initial drive for reform seems to have come from Queen Isabella herself. She was responsible for major campaigns for reform of the religious orders in Galicia and Catalonia, and she used her influence to ensure the appointment of able and learned men to high ecclesiastical office. Hernando de Talavera, the first archbishop of the newly converted inhabitants of Granada, set an example of residence within his diocese, of personal preaching, and of ascetic living that would not be surpassed even by the reformed bishops of the Catholic Reformation.

Yet the greatest name in the history of the Spanish Church in this era is undoubtedly that of Francisco Ximenes de Cisneros, an Observant Franciscan who succeeded Talavera as the queen's confessor (1492). So effectively did he fill that place that he was appointed Archbishop of Toledo three years later. Apart from his reputation as an ascetic and statesman, Ximenes was a formidable reformer. In addition to his campaigns against heresy among converted Moors and Jews, he attacked laxity in his own Franciscan order with great vigour, and by the time of his death in 1517 the reformed 'Observants' had entirely supplanted their more decadent colleagues. Ximenes was also an outstanding scholar, founding the University of Alcala (1508), and compiling the great Polyglot Bible (published 1522). This work comprised, in six volumes, the texts of the scriptures printed in parallel columns in Latin, Greek and Hebrew. With extensive commentaries and grammatical notes, it was one of the major achievements of contemporary Christian humanism.

Of course, the Spanish Church continued to suffer at its 'grass-roots' from the problems and abuses that plagued sister Churches elsewhere in Western Europe. Many of the Franciscans attacked by Ximenes chose to live as Muslims in North Africa rather than give up their concubines; and Castile, alone in Western Europe, preserved a custom whereby the illegitimate son of a priest was allowed to inherit his father's property. The difference between Spain and its neighbours lay, not in the day-to-day standards of the clergy, but in the energy shown at the very head of the political and ecclesiastical hierarchy in the quelling of corruption and the maintenance of spiritual values.

THE FOREIGN POLICY OF THE CATHOLIC MONARCHS

In most respects the affairs of the Catholic Monarchs were dominated by the interests and concerns of Castile. Only in foreign policy were the interests of the crown of Aragon clearly reflected. Leaving aside the exploration of the Indies, which can hardly be said to have been directed by any coherent policy, and the long campaign against

Granada, the foreign policy of the Catholic Monarchs was concerned with traditional areas of Aragonese interest, in Italy, southern France and the western Mediterranean.

Ferdinand naturally played a dominant role in this policy, and his priorities have been interpreted in different ways. To Machiavelli, his was the archetypal pragmatic policy, seeking advantage and profit wherever they could be found. To more recent Spanish historians, Ferdinand attempted to pursue an idealistic policy of 'peace among Christians and war against the infidel', which anticipated the professed aims of Charles V. J.N. Hillgarth has struck a balance between these views: 'Ferdinand was a man preoccupied throughout his reign with two main threats to his Mediterranean policy, Islam and France. At certain times one, at others the other, predominated.'

The foreign policy of the Spanish states between 1474 and 1516 falls easily into two distinct eras, separated by the death of Isabella in 1504. Her death, for instance, transformed Ferdinand's relations with France. Rivalry with France now became a luxury that he could scarcely afford, given his dangerous international isolation. The death of Philip of Burgundy had ended the alliance with the Habsburg dynasty, but had not removed the threat of Habsburg domination of Spain in the long run. The alliance forged with England was similarly on the verge of collapse, owing to the death of Princess Catherine's young husband. The main result of these circumstances was Ferdinand's second marriage, to Germaine de Foix, concluded by the Treaty of Blois (October 1505) and celebrated the following year.

Ferdinand's other major area of activity after Isabella's death was in North Africa, which demonstrates a certain geographical logic to his foreign policy. Having neutralised France for the time being, having taken possession of Roussillon, Cerdagne and Navarre, and having established control over Naples, the crown of Aragon had established a large degree of control over the western half of the Mediterranean. The consolidation of influence in North Africa would 'close the Aragonese fence' around that sea. Given that this African expansion was carried out largely with Castilian resources, it is perhaps not surprising that Ferdinand paid substantial lip-

7.4 Major events in the foreign affairs of the Catholic Monarchs

Italian territories	Borders with France	Other
1489 – Treaty of Medina del Campo. Between Catholic Monarchs and Henry VII of England. Marriage and trade agreements linked crowns in anti–French alliance.		
1494 – Ferdinand formally claimed crown of Naples, as a means of protecting Sicily and Sardinia.	**1493 – Treaty of Barcelona.** Border territories of Rousillon and Cerdagne returned to Aragon by France. In return Ferdinand agreed not to oppose French claims to Naples.	**1497–** Expedition led by Duke of Medina Sidonia occupies **Melilla** on North African coast.
1500 – Treaty of Granada. Ferdinand agreed with Charles VIII of France upon joint action against Naples aimed at the partition of that kingdom.		
1503 – Battle of the Garigliano. Defeat of the French gives Ferdinand control of Naples.	**1505 – Treaty of Blois.** Ferdinand's marriage to Germaine de Foix reorientates his policy towards France.	**1505 –** Beginning of North African campaigns which lead to the capture of **Mers el Kebir** (1505), **Penon del Velez de la Gomera** (1508), **Bougie** and **Tripoli** (1510).
	1512 – Ferdinand exploits French preoccupation in Italy and the dynastic claims of his wife's family to attack Navarre and to annex its Spanish territories.	
	1515 – Navarre transferred to the crown of Castile.	

service to the crusading motives of his late wife. Several factors did indeed appear to link these later successes with the great Castilian campaign against Granada. Apart from Ferdinand's religious invective, there was the enthusiastic involvement of Cardinal Ximenes, and the involvement of many of those Andalucian noble families which had so distinguished themselves in Granada. On the other hand, it must be noted how careful Ferdinand was, during his last and unsuccessful preparations for a campaign against Tunis, to remind the papacy that all captured territories would henceforth belong to the kingdom of Aragon.

The diversion of Ferdinand's attentions in the last years of his life to the affairs of Italy confirmed that European politics remained his firm priority. The fact remains, however, that by 1510 he had established a greater dominance over North Africa than any European monarch was to enjoy for the next three centuries. There were good grounds, both in the domestic and the foreign context, for the claim that Ferdinand made in 1514: 'For over 700 years the crown of Spain has not been as great or as resplendent as it is now, both in the west and in the east, and all, after God, by my work and labour.'

CONSTITUTIONAL CRISIS AND REGENCY, 1504–17

Political stability in the first half of the sixteenth century depended upon human mortality, and as lives were so easily lost, so political stability was highly vulnerable. The years between 1497 and

1506 saw a remarkable sequence of royal deaths which seriously threatened to undermine the stability of the Castilian crown and the work of the Catholic Monarchs.

The death of Prince Juan (1497), the only male heir to the thrones, was followed by that of Queen Isabella herself (1504). The terms of his marriage treaty left Ferdinand with no rights to the throne of Castile, and the inheritance passed to his daughter Juana. It remained unclear, however, whether the woman known to history as *La Loca* – 'the mad' – was equal to the task. Certainly Isabella had changed her will and named Ferdinand as protector of Castile upon her death. Unfortunately for Ferdinand, there was another candidate for the job. In 1496, Juana had married Philip, lord of Flanders and of Burgundy, and Philip had at his disposal an array of resources that Ferdinand could not match. He was son and heir to the most powerful man in Europe, the Emperor Maximilian. He had the support of a motley collection of Castilian factions, the exiled remnants of all those groups defeated in the struggles of the last thirty years, which relished the chance to break the hold of the 'Old Catalan'. He also attracted the support of a nobility which realised the advantages of an absentee monarch. There was little guarantee that Philip, once in power, would govern in the best interests of Castile. In the last months of Isabella's life the future for Castile 'looked gloomy indeed. Her daughter and heiress, if not completely insane, was mentally unbalanced, her husband an undependable playboy led by the nose by advisers under the influence of Spain's major enemy' (J.N. Hillgarth).

The crisis was resolved by the same factor that had started it. In September 1506, Philip himself died suddenly and, due largely to the skill and tact of Ximenes, Ferdinand was accepted as Regent of Castile until Philip's son Charles (*b*. 1500) came of age. In general, those elements that had accepted and welcomed the rule of the Catholic Monarchs over the last thirty years now accepted the continuing rule of the surviving member of the partnership for another decade, until Ferdinand's death in 1516.

Domestic policy in this final phase of Ferdinand's political career contained few major innovations. It was dominated by the business of restoring order, and that task was considerable. 'Some', reported the chronicler Bernaldez, 'thought it was the end of the world and that the time of King Henry had returned. He who could take most did so, and each was king of his land and of what he could take from the crown.' By 1510 most of the nobility, particularly as they observed Juana's descent into madness, accepted Ferdinand's right to govern Castile until Charles reached the age of twenty-five.

Ferdinand's second marriage, to Germaine de Foix, niece of Louis XII of France (March 1506), constituted the major innovation of this period. Its purpose was in part to secure French friendship at a time when Ferdinand was politically isolated, and threatened by the ambitions of the Habsburgs. In large part, too, the marriage aimed to provide an heir to the throne of Aragon, and thus to prevent that crown, too, from falling into the hands of Charles of Habsburg. In 1506, after less than forty years of unity, the crowns of Castile and Aragon seemed likely to separate once more upon Ferdinand's death. Again, however, Ferdinand was cheated by the vagaries of nature. Germaine's only child, a son, died a few hours after his birth in 1509. Upon Ferdinand's death, therefore, there was no native alternative, in Castile or in Aragon, to the Habsburg claim.

THE INHERITANCE OF CHARLES OF HABSBURG

Since the premature death of Philip of Burgundy ten years earlier, the Habsburg claimant had been his son, Charles. He was heir to Aragon, Sicily, Sardinia and to the Aragonese claims in Italy and North Africa because Ferdinand's second marriage had been childless, and heir to Castile because of the insanity of his mother. There were many who favoured the accession of his younger brother, also named Ferdinand, who had the advantage of a Spanish upbringing. The laws of primogeniture, however, dictated that the crown pass to the elder child. At the same time, as grandson also of the Holy Roman Emperor, Maximilian, Charles was heir presumptive to the Habsburg estates in Austria, the Tyrol and parts of southern Germany. By the same token, he was also a strong candidate to succeed his grandfather in the elective office of Holy Roman Emperor.

The recipient of this vast legacy was an unprepossessing young man. His combination of typically Habsburg facial features left him, frankly, rather ugly, with a prominent jaw and teeth that did not quite meet when he chewed. More than one contemporary reported in secret that he looked like an idiot, yet he was not stupid. On the other hand, his intelligence was of a kind that made him throughout his life more likely to stick faithfully to received ideas than to seek perceptively for novel solutions to his problems. The two men primarily responsible for the received ideas of the young Charles were the humanist Adrian of Utrecht and the man who had served as his tutor from 1509, Guillaume de Croy, lord of Chièvres. While Adrian brought to Charles's moral and spiritual education all the classic precepts of the *devotio moderna*, Chièvres was a skilled and unscrupulous politician. If he may be credited with one consistent principle, however, it was his desire to ensure that Charles secured the power in Spain to which his father had aspired.

The reception of Charles in Spain

Far from heralding the opening of a 'golden age', Ferdinand's death seemed at first to threaten Spain with a return to political chaos. The confused situation and its uncertain outcome re-opened old feuds, between family and family and between towns and nobility. While Cardinal Ximenes maintained the government of Castile as he had done in 1506, and while some restated the claims of Charles's brother, a number of high-ranking Spaniards arrived at the Burgundian court to ingratiate themselves with the candidate they thought most likely to succeed. Charles took nearly two years to reach Spain. He spoke no Spanish, and had no Spaniards among his major advisers. The dominant figure was Chièvres; and, even before his departure from the Low Countries, Charles had begun the process of appointing Burgundians to important posts in his new kingdom. The presidency of the Cortes of Castile was bestowed upon the Burgundian chancellor, Jean de Sauvage, and one of Charles's first actions upon his arrival was to dismiss the regent of Castile, the great

Ximenes, the outstanding Spanish political figure of the last half-century.

The mistrust that many Spaniards felt for their new, foreign ruler was immediately evident when he met the Cortes of Castile at Valladolid (February 1518). Charles was reminded in no uncertain terms that he must respect the laws of Castile, and that he would be expected to learn its language and to reserve its chief offices for natives. Similar resistance was encountered from the Aragonese Cortes, which he met at Zaragoza (spring 1518), and from that of Catalonia.

Nevertheless, Charles's Burgundian followers did well in Spain. They secured lucrative grants of licences for the export of cloth, bullion and jewellery. The appointments of Chièvres as *Contador Major,* of Sauvage as Chancellor, of Chièvres' teenage nephew as Archbishop of Toledo, and of Adrian of Utrecht as Bishop of Tortosa and later as regent in the king's absence, would have been adequate in themselves to arouse mighty resentment. A.W. Lovett has recently maintained the traditional conclusion that 'the Habsburg entourage could not resist the natural temptation to regard the new domains as a source of limitless reward'.

On top of all this came the news in the early months of 1519 of the death of the Emperor Maximilian. Charles's haste to be gone from his Spanish kingdoms was unmistakable. Having secured his election as Emperor in June 1519, he summoned the Cortes to Santiago de Compostela (1520) and requested money to finance his voyage to a distant realm whose interests would doubtless be preferred to those of Castile. To most observers it seemed that the work of the Catholic Monarchs was about to be undone, and that Spain was doomed to become a province of an international empire with interests that transcended its own.

The Revolt of the Comuneros

Castilian resentment at the young king's treatment of his new kingdom was the major trigger of the Revolt of the Comuneros, the great rebellion of the Castilian towns which followed Charles's departure from Spain. The revolt, nevertheless, had deeper and more complex causes. It reflected the social and economic tensions that had accumulated in Castile in the troubled course of a decade or more. In the ranks of the 'Comuneros' could be found *hidalgos* and *caballeros,* lesser nobles favoured by Ferdinand of Aragon when he sought to reduce the influence of the greater nobility, but who were now in political decline once more. Alongside them were representatives of the textile producers whose protests against the excessive export of wool found favour with Ferdinand and with Ximenes, but not with those favourites of the new ruler who had the interests of the Low Countries closer to their hearts. The revolt also reflected the divisions between towns. Burgos, grown rich on foreign trade, took no part in the rebellion, yet her great rival, Toledo, was at its head. The attitude of the grandees, the greater nobility, was neutral in these early stages.

The Revolt of the Comuneros moved through two distinct phases. The first developed predominantly in the towns of Old Castile. Toledo expelled its *corregidor* in May 1520, and a number of town representatives gave solid form to the revolt by forming the Holy Council (*Santa Junta*) of the Comuneros at a meeting in Avilà. The threat to the monarch became more specific when rebels seized the town of Tordesillas and with it Juana – mad, but nevertheless widely regarded as the rightful Queen of Castile (September 1520).

The revolt has been interpreted over the years in different ways by historians with different perspectives on revolution. Some have seen the revolt mainly as a conservative one, undertaken by traditional forces guarding their interests against novel external threats. To others, the Comuneros were essentially the forerunners of later liberalism, furthering the interests of representative democracy against a growing autocracy. In general, the demands voiced by the Comuneros tend to support the former argument. Where they dealt with the Cortes, they did not claim for themselves any power of legislation, but rather attempted to preserve their ancient privileges. In addition, their demands included the reduction of taxation, restraints upon governmental corruption and government spending, and the independence of individual towns from direct royal or aristocratic control.

Only in its later stages did the revolt become unequivocally revolutionary. From September 1520 elements among the towns and the peasantry began specifically to aim their grievances at their direct social superiors, and to deny their allegiance to their feudal lords. This radical turn of events decided the stance of the greater nobles, and provided the distant king with the allies he needed to combat the revolt. He appointed two of the greatest Castilian grandees, the Constable Inigo de Velasco and the Admiral Fadrique Enriquez, to share the duties of regent with Adrian of Utrecht. Assured of the sympathy of the Castilian grandees, of loyal cities such as Burgos and of the King of Portugal, Charles was able to proceed with confidence against the rebels. Their collapse began with the recapture of Tordesillas and of Queen Juana in December 1520, and culminated in the rout of the Comunero forces at Villalar (23 April 1521).

Yet the Comuneros' revolt was not a sterile event. It demonstrated to Charles the limits of his freedom of action in Spain, and many of his subsequent moves conformed closely to the initial demands of the rebels. He did indeed learn Spanish, and henceforth governed the territories exclusively through Spanish institutions. His marriage to Isabella of Portugal (1526) produced a son and heir, Philip, so Spanish that he would rarely leave the peninsula after his accession to the throne. In the long run, however, the more serious fears of the Comuneros all proved to be well founded. Charles was to be largely an absentee monarch; his accession did fundamentally alter the orientation of Spanish policy without serving Spanish interests; this new policy was financed by the plundering of Spanish resources. In the narrower context of the government of Spain, the revolt created or revealed a community of interests between the Habsburg monarchy and the great nobles of Spain, which was to form the basis of Habsburg government throughout the 'Golden Age'.

Aragon, too, saw radical political unrest at this time. The collapse both of central authority and of local government, due to an outbreak of plague, assisted the revolt of the *Germanias*, the Christian brotherhoods, especially in Valencia and in Mallorca (1519). The objects of their wrath were the urban officials, the local aristocracy, and especially the Muslims, who were plundered and forcibly baptised. The Aragonese rebels made no significant contact with the Comuneros, and their military defeat in October 1521 was equally comprehensive.

CHARLES AND THE GOVERNMENT OF SPAIN

After the defeat of the Comuneros in his absence, Charles spent seven years in Spain, from July 1522 until July 1529, and in that period the governmental machinery was established that was to run Spain for the rest of the century. Historians have differed in their judgements upon that machinery, some seeing strong elements of modern government in it. 'No states', wrote J.H. Elliott, 'were more governed in the sixteenth century than those of the King of Spain, if government can be measured by the amount of discussion devoted to any individual problem.' Others, meanwhile, have stressed the continuation of medieval elements.

The complex conciliar system of Habsburg Spain owed much to the system of central government bequeathed by the Catholic Monarchs, but significant adaptations were dictated by the sheer extent of Charles's possessions. The councils divided into two main types. The 'advisory' councils existed to advise the king on all matters of policy, and were staffed by the highest ministers of the realm. In addition to those which dealt with purely Spanish matters, the Council of War coordinated military strategy and policy throughout the empire, while the major new creation of Charles's reign, the Council of Finance (*Consejo de Hacienda*), oversaw the increasing problems of financing the vast Habsburg *monarchia*. The second group consisted of the 'territorial' councils, responsible for the good government of the various component parts of Charles's realm, exercising administrative, judicial and ecclesiastical powers within their allotted territory.

If administration depended upon a complex bureaucracy, the actual decision-making processes of government were intensely personal. In theory, this meant that all aspects of government policy were determined by the king himself. 'The original purpose behind [the councils]', wrote J.H. Elliott, 'was to preserve the fiction central to the whole structure of the Spanish monarchy – that the King was personally present in each of his territories.' Hence the councils were not allowed to become the preserves of the great nobles, and these rarely served upon them. They were not decision-making bodies, but advisory ones, which communicated their views and recommendations to Charles in the form of a document known as a *consulta*, which he was under no obligation to act upon. Once the royal reply to the *consulta* had been received, the council took on the second of its roles, that of an executive body to enforce the king's decisions.

Given the long absences of Charles from Spain, the personal government of the territories had often to be left in other hands. The most prominent of these substitutes were Charles's viceroys, one for

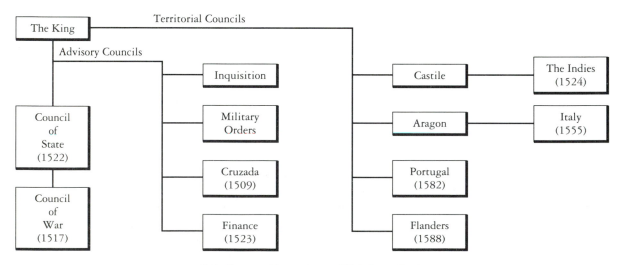

7.5 The conciliar system of Habsburg Spain

Note: Where no date of foundation is given, the institution dates from the time of the Catholic Monarchs

each of the territories of Aragon, Catalonia, Valencia, Navarre, Sardinia, Sicily, Naples, New Spain (Mexico) and Peru. Even so, these viceroys enjoyed only a limited freedom of action, and it was one of the principal roles of the territorial councils to keep a close check upon any abuse of the viceregal power. During his absences Charles left behind him an overall regent, someone close enough to him in terms of royal blood to be able credibly to exercise his authority. Initially this responsibility fell to his wife Isabella, then to his sister Mary, and later to his son and heir, Philip.

Less prominent than the powers of the viceroys and councils, but far more real, was the authority of the secretaries through whose hands most of the official correspondence passed. The 1520s and 1530s were dominated in particular by one man who elevated the post of Royal Secretary to a level that it had never reached before. Francisco de Los Cobos was an Andalucian of humble origins who threw in his lot with Charles before the king's arrival in Spain, and whose rapid rise was largely due to the patronage of Chièvres. A royal secretary by 1516, he became after 1523 the leading administrative figure on the new Council of Finance. The death of Chancellor Gattinara in 1530 left Los Cobos without a serious rival for the rest of his career (d.1547). The only man to attain comparable heights was Nicholas Perrenot, Lord of Granvelle, a Burgundian who had served his apprenticeship in the administration of the Netherlands. Partly as a direct result of this, Granvelle assumed responsibility after the death of Gattinara for the foreign affairs of the *monarchia,* leaving Los Cobos unchallenged in the domestic sphere.

THE REPRESENTATIVE INSTITUTIONS UNDER CHARLES

The Cortes of Castile continued to meet regularly in the early years of Charles's reign, but did not impose any realistic limitation upon the powers of the crown. Principally, it was now summoned to consent to taxation from which two of its three estates were exempt. Even the towns were usually represented by *hidalgos* who did not pay the taxes

that they voted. By 1544 the role of the Cortes had become so exclusively associated with the granting of taxation that the representatives who met in that year asked the king not to summon them more than once every three years in future 'on account of the great costs and expenses'.

Similarly, the various Cortes of Aragon met at regular intervals during Charles's reign, and the office of *Justicia* remained intact until the 1590s. Yet the survival of these institutions was evidence, not of their strengths, but of their weakness. In Aragon the institutions designed to protect regional liberties survived because there was so little material wealth in the kingdom. In Castile they were allowed to survive specifically because of their patent failure to keep the considerable wealth of the kingdom out of royal hands.

Charles was not an absolute monarch in Spain for the practical reason that he had no assured control over the nobility. This was further demonstrated when the Cortes was summoned in 1538 to sanction a new food tax, the *Sisa,* to be paid by all the estates. The nobility refused to allow their privilege of exemption to be overridden by the interests of the crown, and Charles had no choice but to abandon the project. Essentially, however, the system served the purposes of Charles. It provided a theoretical compromise between centralised authority and the wide range of liberties that were claimed by his various Spanish domains. It also made for quiet, but almost unchangeably conservative government. 'The government of Spain', wrote J.H. Elliott, 'ran so smoothly under the gentle guidance of Los Cobos that it almost seems as if for twenty or thirty years the country had no internal history.' This was due partly to the weaknesses of the representative institutions, and partly to those of the conciliar system. In practice, Charles was the only person who could get things done, and he was frequently absent. Finally, the work of the bureaucracy could only be as good as the men who ran it. The leadership of the bureaucracy became in time a vested interest in its own right, preserving its methods and machinery, not because they worked, but because only the bureaucrats understood them, thus guaranteeing their own continuation in power. By the end of his career, Los Cobos himself became the patron of a substantial body of ambitious bureaucrats, including

Molina, Idiaquez and Gonzalo Perez, whom he trained as his successors.

THE CASTILIAN ECONOMY UNDER THE CATHOLIC MONARCHS

The Castilian economy in the first decades of peace under the Catholic Monarchs had few features to suggest that it could support its future rulers at the pinnacle of international power. A fearsome array of natural obstacles stood in the way of economic prosperity. The climate tended to extremes, water was in short supply in many regions, the soil in many localities was poor, and communications were invariably difficult.

Wool dominated the Castilian economy, and by the middle of the fifteenth century the interests of the sheep farmers were firmly established and protected. Their greatest protection was provided by the *Mesta*, the great guild of the migratory sheep-owners, established two centuries earlier and exercising control over some 3.5 million sheep. The privileges of the guild were confirmed and extended by Ferdinand and Isabella. A decree of 1480 ordered that all pastures turned over to arable farming in the years of civil disorder should now be returned to their original use, the very reverse of the legislation so often passed in contemporary England. Another in 1489 confirmed the location and extent of the sheep-walks, the routes by which the herds had traditionally migrated. Such a degree of royal patronage is largely explained by the fact that the tax paid by the sheep farmers on their herds, the *servicio y montazgo,* was a major contribution to the Castilian treasury.

Such a policy also helped the crown's political relationship with the major towns of Castile. The privileges granted to the major wool centres served the dual purpose of increasing their prosperity and of ensuring their continued political support. In the greatest inland centre of the wool trade, Burgos, the *consulado* was created in 1494, a trading body which combined the functions of guild and mercantile court, and which was granted the highly valued monopoly of the wool trade with Flanders and the rest of northern Europe. The most notable product of this policy was the famous *casa de contratacion* –

the House of Trade – established in Seville in 1503 to regulate and to control trade with the New World.

This interventionist policy extended beyond the wool trade, for in the twenty-nine years of their joint reign the Catholic Monarchs issued 128 ordinances dealing with aspects of the Castilian economy, although none of these sought any degree of economic unity between Castile and Aragon. The creation of a guild of carters and wagoners, the *cabana real de carreteros* (1497), was an attempt to alleviate the dreadful difficulties in communications that dogged Castilian trade. By royal decree all Castilian peasants had the right to leave their lord and freely seek another (1480), and then to sell the produce of their land without any legal restriction (1486). The passage of grain in times of shortage was facilitated by a further decree that made it legal to transport grain anywhere, except into a Muslim territory. In practice, however, arable farming in Castile remained an uncertain and unprofitable pursuit. Too few of the great land-owners took an active interest in the exploitation of their land, and most were content with an income from the rents paid by their hard-pressed tenants. The years 1502–7 brought an unbroken run of bad harvests, during which the crown undertook price-fixing measures unlikely to help the producer. Over the reign of Ferdinand and Isabella as a whole, the years in which surplus grain was exported from Castile were far fewer than those in which grain had to be imported to compensate for a shortfall in domestic production.

SPAIN AND THE IMPACT OF EMPIRE

Finance

Castilians may have hoped, when their king assumed the crown of the Holy Roman Empire, that the governing principle of finance within the Empire would also be extended to Charles's Spanish possessions. In theory, taxes levied in one territory were to be spent exclusively on the affairs of that territory. Such an equitable principle was quickly rendered impracticable as the commitments of Charles V extended to campaigns against France, against the German princes and against the forces of Islam both in North Africa and in central Europe. By 1540, Charles could write to his brother Ferdinand, stating what had already been evident for some time: 'I cannot be sustained except by my realms of Spain.'

This development owed something to the resources that existed in Spain, but much more to the ease with which Charles could exploit them. Events in the Netherlands in 1539 showed that serious resistance was growing there to heavy taxation. Naples by 1540 had given most of what it could give, and Aragon had little to give in the first place. The failure of the Comuneros, on the other hand, left the tax-payers of Castile largely without the means to resist Charles's demands. The *alcabala* tax, a 10 per cent sales tax payable by all laymen, noble or otherwise, was a valuable and uncomplicated source of income, yielding a substantial sum, usually in the region of 1.25 million ducats a year. Customs duties, taxes on sheep and on silk, and the regular *servicios* voted by the compliant Cortes completed a sophisticated range of tax resources. In particular, the sums voted by the Cortes more than tripled in the course of the reign, from 130,000 ducats a year (1523) to 410,000 ducats by the end of the reign. Aragon, in contrast, provided Charles with the relatively modest sum of 3 million ducats over a period of thirty years between 1528 and 1557.

In addition, Charles gained further access to the wealth of the Castilian Church. In 1519 the papacy granted him the right to levy a charge known as the *subsidio*, representing a fixed proportion of Church income throughout Spain. By the 1530s, Charles also received about 146,000 ducats annually from his control of the Military Orders.

Increasingly, Charles also benefited from a new source of Castilian income, in the form of the precious metals imported from her new territories in the New World. Significant sums were not available from this source until after 1530, and Charles never derived the benefits from the New World that his son enjoyed. Nevertheless, he probably received some 11.9 million ducats as his legal share of American bullion between 1516 and the end of the reign, as well as occasionally seizing bullion that was not normally due to the crown.

Yet all these substantial figures do not begin to explain the true value of Spanish resources in the financing of Charles's imperial projects. The sums themselves remained largely inadequate for the Emperor's purposes, and there remained no alternative but to finance his campaigns by borrowing yet greater sums from the great banking centres of Europe. It was as collateral for these loans that the resources of Castile played their greatest role. By pledging the resources of Castile as security to German and Italian bankers, Charles had in the long term delivered large parts of the kingdom into the hands of foreign financiers. By the end of the reign Germans were permitted to purchase Spanish offices, Spanish lands and Spanish bonds as means of settling debts. In addition, the masterships of the three Military Orders passed from the crown into the hands of German bankers. Having been liberated from foreign princes and overmighty subjects, the crowns of Spain were now left by Charles very largely at the mercy of foreign capitalists.

The economy

One of the major features of Spain's economy in the first half of the sixteenth century was its high rate of inflation. In the region of Valladolid, for example, wheat prices rose by 44 per cent between 1511 and 1550, while rents in the same region rose dramatically, by more than 80 per cent between 1530 and 1555. The links between price inflation and the increase in the bullion supply were first made by Spanish analysts around the middle of the century. They received their most comprehensive restatement from the American historian Earl J. Hamilton (*American Treasure and the Price Revolution in Spain*, 1934), who produced evidence of bullion imports and of price inflation which established a close correlation between the two factors.

Critics of Hamilton have attacked him on several points. It has been argued that the sources he used to obtain his price figures, hospitals and charitable institutions, formed too narrow a basis for the figures safely to be considered typical, and a more genuine culprit may have been the credit which the bullion drew from bankers. Recent writers have pointed out that inflation rose more steeply in the earlier years of the century, when the quantities of bullion arriving in Spain were relatively small. This has led to the suggestion that rising population was also a powerful stimulus to inflation. It has been estimated overall that the population of Castile may have increased by some 50 per cent between 1530 and 1580, when it had reached about 8 million. While the larger population forced prices up by creating a greater demand for foodstuffs and goods whose supply remained relatively constant, further demand was created by the need to export goods to the colonies of the New World. This last factor had a particular effect upon Andalucia, in the region surrounding the great Atlantic port of Seville. The fact remains that bullion imports from the New World made a significant contribution to Spanish inflation, even if historians now tend to bracket it with other causes.

The increased supply of bullion in Spain also had another effect upon the economy. The availability of bullion proved a powerful magnet for foreign merchants, who preferred to exchange their goods for hard cash rather than for Spanish manufactures. 'Spain has become an Indies for the foreigner', complained a member of the Cortes in 1548, protesting at the manner in which the wealth of the Indies drained away into foreign hands without benefit to the Spanish economy. The Cortes petitioned the crown on twelve occasions between 1515 and 1551 on the subject of the exportation of bullion. Another detrimental effect of this mercantile activity was that foreign goods poured on to the Spanish market to compete with native manufactures.

with smaller landed resources and less ability to raise the rents paid by his tenants probably suffered the same fate as his equivalent in other parts of Western Europe. For other elements in society, inflation brought distinct benefits. Great mercantile fortunes were made and great trading dynasties were founded, especially by those engaged in the trade of Seville and the Americas. Juan Antonio Corzo, after a lifetime in that trade, left over 1.5 million ducats upon his death in 1597, and Spanish society raised no serious obstacles if such men sought to achieve noble status. Only in one respect were there major obstacles to social mobility in Spain, for it is certainly true that the principles of 'purity of blood' posed formidable obstacles to the social advancement of Moriscos or *conversos*.

Upward mobility was offset by socio-economic casualties. The lower classes of society were particularly vulnerable, and the problem of poverty was persistent and increasing. The research of the French historian B. Bennassar into the social structure of the city of Valladolid has shown that at the time of the 1561 census some 10 per cent of the city's 6,600 households were poverty-stricken to the extent of being sustained by public funds. Nor did employment necessarily protect the worker from poverty. A recent study of labourers' wages in Valencia has suggested that, whereas incomes generally met living costs comfortably in the first two decades of the century, they covered only half the labourer's normal costs by the mid-century, and little more than a third by about 1570.

Society

Despite the traditional, contemporary view of Spain as a rigid society, resistant to change and to social mobility, the effects there of such dramatic economic developments were only slightly different from those experienced in the rest of Western Europe. The greatest families of the Castilian nobility were undoubtedly cushioned from the effects of economic change by their enormous wealth and by the unusual degree of power that they exercised over their vast estates. Castilian grandees enjoyed the power to raise rents when necessary and to replace impoverished tenants with those better able to pay. The poorer *hidalgo,* on the other hand,

7.6 Glossary

Letrado. (lit.: one who is literate). Term applied to the educated, professional lawyers, used by the Spanish monarchs to staff their major administrative and legal bodies.

Monarchia. Term used to denote the collective territories of a ruler who, like Charles V or Philip II, was hereditary or elective monarch of a variety of separate kingdoms or principalities.

Royal Progress. Process whereby the monarch and the royal court toured the localities of the kingdom. The primary purposes were to display the monarch to his/her subjects and to facilitate the dispensation of personal justice.

Further reading

J.N. Hillgarth (1978) *The Spanish Kingdoms, 1250–1516.* Oxford.

H. Kamen (1983) *Spain, 1469–1714: A Society of Conflict.* London & New York.

A.W. Lovett (1986) *Early Habsburg Spain, 1517–1598.* Oxford.

M. Rady (1988) *The Emperor Charles V.* London & New York.

• CHAPTER EIGHT •

England in the Reign of Henry VII

The historical debate

The disputed succession

The Tudor seizure of power

The political inheritance

Consolidating the victory, 1485–6

Pretenders and conspiracies

Central government

Local government

Order in the distant localities

English foreign policy

Trade and the economy

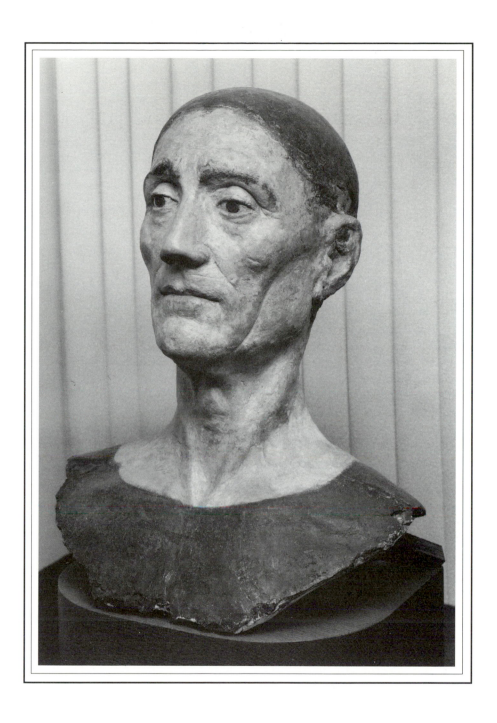

So important was it for artists in the sixteenth century to convey a propaganda message in their portraits of royal figures that it is unusual to find a simple portrayal of the individual behind the crown. This funeral effigy of Henry VII shows him as he was at the time of his death in 1509, and is now preserved in Westminster Abbey

THE HISTORICAL DEBATE

Until as recently as the Second World War, few topics in English history had provoked less 'historical debate' than the reign of Henry VII. While other 'turning points' were reinterpreted, the Battle of Bosworth in 1485 remained an undisputed landmark. Following the lines laid down by contemporary propaganda, and then by Shakespeare and by Francis Bacon, Bosworth was seen as a watershed between an age of feudal disorder and an era in which the re-establishment of royal authority prepared the way for peaceful and enduring development in all major areas of national life. Towards the end of the nineteenth century this view was elaborated by J.R. Green, who first used the phrase 'New Monarchy' to describe the constitutional developments of the late fifteenth century. He revised hitherto highly critical views of Edward IV, and saw both him and his Tudor successor as monarchs who brought about stability by novel and 'modern' means. The major elements in this 'New Monarchy' theory were the consolidation of royal control over the state, the introduction of such new machinery as the Court of Star Chamber and the thorough reorganisation of finances to establish invincible royal solvency. An important, slightly later addition to these theories was the claim that Henry also broke new ground in the appointment of his highest servants, countering the corrupt influence of the traditional nobility by favouring middle-class men of ability, with no feudal power base of their own. The notion of the 'Tudor New Man' was born.

The revision of such well-established theories was a slow process. Research at a local level undermined the traditional picture of the fifteenth century, and suggested that localised violence and disorder were not markedly greater than in the mid-sixteenth century. Work on the nobility, such as that of K.B. McFarlane (*The Nobility of Later Medieval England*, 1973), suggested that the relationship between lord and retainer was a stabilising one in local society, and that the disorder of the Wars of the Roses resulted less from this 'bastard feudalism' than from the simple collapse of royal authority under the weak-minded Henry VI. Research into the reign of Edward IV indicated that this king anticipated and practised all the main policies

followed by the first of the Tudors. Meanwhile, the work of B.P. Wolffe (*The Crown Lands, 1461–1536*, 1970) demonstrated the continuity of royal financial policy between the two reigns.

In recent standard works, such as those of S.B. Chrimes (*Henry VII*, 1972) and J.R. Lander (*Government and Community, 1450–1509*, 1980), Henry Tudor is less the founder of a new age than a talented and ruthless pragmatist whose initial inexperience forced him to adopt the methods which had served the most successful of his predecessors. The most convincing links are to be drawn between Henry and his predecessors, rather than between Henry and a subsequent 'modern age'.

THE DISPUTED SUCCESSION

The constitutional chaos of the fifteenth century has to be set against a complex background of declining feudal rents, economic depression and financial embarrassment at the end of the French wars. On a purely political level, however, the so-called 'Wars of the Roses' were triggered by a breakdown in the relationship between the monarch and the great feudal magnates, upon which the stable government of the realm depended. While adult kings of proven military ability, such as Henry IV (1399–1413), Henry V (1413–22) and Edward IV (1461–83), could maintain the delicate balance, the early death of such a monarch and the succession of an infant were potentially disastrous. The succession of the one-year-old Henry VI (1422) heralded a period of dynastic rivalry between several great English families, set against the background of English defeat in France. By 1471, Edward IV seemed to have resolved the issue of the succession in favour of his own House of York through decisive military victories and by the murder of the broken and deranged King Henry. Edward's own sudden death, however, undermined the prospects of York as that of Henry V had damaged the prospects of Lancaster. Edward, too, left his throne to a minor, the twelve-year-old Edward V. The usurpation of that throne (1483) by the late king's brother, Richard, Duke of Gloucester, may have been less sinister than Shakespeare suggested, and may well have been welcomed by many who feared the repercussions of

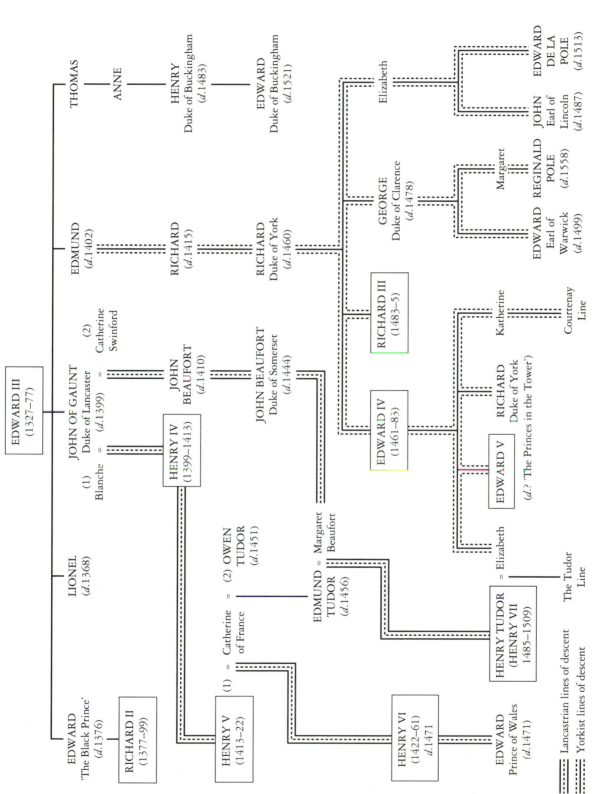

8.1 *Lancastrians and Yorkists*

a prolonged minority. Whether or not Richard killed the young Edward V and his brother, the 'Princes in the Tower', he eliminated them from the succession by declaring them illegitimate. In effect, therefore, the dynastic confusion of decades had boiled down by late 1483 into a confrontation between two principal contenders: Richard III of the House of York, and the obscure survivor of the House of Lancaster, Henry Tudor.

THE TUDOR SEIZURE OF POWER

Henry Tudor was not a formidable candidate. He had spent the previous fourteen years in exile in Brittany and in France, and his claim to the throne was not nearly so convincing as those of recent Yorkist contenders. His father, Edmund Tudor, was half-brother to Henry VI, but only by virtue of the outrageous remarriage of Henry V's widow, Queen Catherine, to one of her household officers, Owen Tudor. His claim through the pedigree of his mother, Margaret Beaufort, was more convincing, but any claim through the female line was always a relatively weak one. In reality, the issue was one of power politics, and Henry Tudor became a viable claimant to the throne because, with stronger candidates eliminated, he gained the support of men whose only alternatives were conspiracy or obscure poverty. His political prospects were transformed by the rebellion of the Duke of Buckingham against Richard III in October 1483. Failure cost Buckingham his life, and resulted in the flight to the Continent of a number of previously influential political figures. Men such as John Morton, Bishop of Ely, and John de Vere, Earl of Oxford, gravitated naturally to the one man whose claim to power might save them from permanent exile.

The Lancastrian expedition which left France to try its luck in England probably numbered less than 5,000 men, and its progress through Wales and the Midlands was notable for the indifference shown by the local gentry and nobility. When Henry's forces finally confronted those of Richard III near Market Bosworth in Leicestershire (22 August 1485), the battle was largely decided by treachery. Inaction and betrayal by prominent members of Richard's army were directly responsible for his death on the battlefield and for the acclamation there of the first Tudor monarch.

THE POLITICAL INHERITANCE

The material inheritance of the new king was not as unpromising as once it was painted. The impact of the Wars of the Roses upon English life as a whole can only have been slight compared with the effects of the conflicts that were to ravage France and the Netherlands in the later sixteenth century. The total period of military campaigning in the thirty-two years between the first Battle of St Albans (1455) and the Battle of Stoke (1487) amounted to twelve or thirteen weeks. Many of the battles were on a minor scale, and no English town suffered a sack during the wars.

On the other hand, the new king faced real problems of credibility and authority. In principle Henry VII took over a governmental system of some complexity, but in practice many parts of the system failed to perform their functions. In particular, the king lacked both the money and the manpower to ensure that decisions taken at the administrative centre of the state were enforced in the localities. Even at the centre of the administration, governmental and legal bodies were strikingly understaffed by modern standards. D.A.L. Morgan's estimate is that 'the staffs of those metropolitan offices of the crown – common pleas, king's bench, exchequer, chancery, privy seal – cannot have numbered more than 200' ('The King's affinity in the polity of Yorkist England', *Transactions of the Royal Historical Society*, 1973). In the localities, lack of manpower was complicated by a plague of corruption, bribery and intimidation, with the records of assize after assize providing evidence of high levels of violent crime, set against low levels of conviction.

CONSOLIDATING THE VICTORY, 1485–6

Bosworth made Henry king only in name. He was accepted without enthusiasm, and could feel confident that the next successful pretender to the throne would be accepted just as readily. His theoretical arguments of blood and descent impressed nobody. Having been totally detached from the sources of power and influence in recent English politics, Henry was forced to rely very heavily upon the small body of men who had recently joined him in exile, and whose fates were tied so closely to his own.

Survival depended upon securing many loose ends in a short time. The fifteen-year-old Earl of Warwick, who now had the best Yorkist claim to the throne, was secured and deposited in the Tower. Faithful followers were rewarded and established as pillars of the new hierarchy. Jasper Tudor, Henry's uncle, became Duke of Bedford; John de Vere was restored to his former dignity as Earl of Oxford; Lord Stanley became Earl of Derby and his son, Sir William Stanley, was established in a number of prominent positions in North Wales. By the end of the year Henry's most prominent ecclesiastical supporter, John Morton, had been appointed Archbishop of Canterbury. The parliament that met in November 1485 also had important business to transact. Henry required it to deal with a number of **Acts of Attainder**, reversing those against Henry and his followers and attainting Richard and twenty-eight of his followers.

At the launching of his expedition Henry had undertaken to marry Elizabeth of York, daughter of Edward IV, thereby ensuring that his offspring would embody both Lancastrian and Yorkist claims to the throne. Conversely, an unmarried Elizabeth would be a most tempting bride for other political aspirants, whose children would be able to claim Edward IV as their grandfather. Henry made it clear that it was his blood, rather than Elizabeth's, which determined the succession. He specified his right to marry again and to produce heirs by his second wife, should Elizabeth die childless. Nevertheless, the union of Lancaster and York achieved its first aim promptly, and Prince Arthur was born in September 1486.

8.2 Some early Tudor careers

BRAY, Sir Reginald (? –1503). Originally a lawyer in the service of Margaret Beaufort. Prominent in negotiation of Henry's marriage to Elizabeth of York. Chancellor of the Duchy of Lancaster (1485), in which capacity he took responsibility for financial administration, especially in respect of crown lands.

DUDLEY, Edmund (?1462–1510). Lawyer, employed in the implementation of Henry's financial policies. Speaker of the House of Commons (1504). President of the Council (1506). Accused of treason and executed by Henry VIII on grounds of financial extortions. Father of John, Duke of Northumberland. Grandfather of Robert, Earl of Leicester.

FOXE, Richard (?1448–1528). In service of Henry Tudor by 1484. Appointed Lord Privy Seal and Secretary of State after Bosworth. Bishop of Exeter (1487), Durham (1494) and Winchester (1501). Active as statesman and diplomat, especially in negotiation of Treaty of Étaples (1492), *Magnus Intercursus* (1496) and in marriage negotiations with Spain and Scotland. As patron of Thomas Wolsey his influence ran into Henry VIII's reign up to 1516. Humanist and scholar, founding Corpus Christi College, Oxford (1515–16).

LOVELL, Sir Thomas (1453–1524). Joined Buckingham's rebellion (1483) and subsequently fled to join Henry Tudor in France. Chancellor of the Exchequer (1485–1516). Treasurer of the Household (1485). Speaker of the House of Commons (1485). President of the Council (1502).

MORTON, John (?1420–1500). Initially a Lancastrian supporter, but was reconciled to Yorkists after Battle of Tewkesbury (1471). Served Edward IV as Master of the Rolls and Bishop of Ely. Chancellor and Archbishop of Canterbury (1486). Cardinal (1493). Active in the enforcement of Henry's policy of financial 'benevolences'.

PRETENDERS AND CONSPIRACIES

Henry had been on the throne for less than eighteen months when the first major Yorkist conspiracy broke out. In May 1487 the coronation took place in Dublin of a pretender claiming to be the Earl of Warwick. In reality the claimant was Lambert Simnel, the son of an Oxford joiner, recruited and trained for the part by a local priest of Yorkist sympathies. Apart from support in Ireland, the plot involved prominent English Yorkists, such as Viscount Lovel and John de la Pole, Earl of Lincoln, backed from the Continent by Edward IV's sister, Margaret of Burgundy. Although Burgundian money provided Simnel with 2,000 German mercenaries, he was defeated and captured at Stoke, near Newark (June 1487), in what has been termed 'the last battle of the Wars of the Roses'.

Its rapid defeat should not obscure the seriousness of the conspiracy. Henry could claim that it showed that there was no serious Yorkist faction in the country, but it was equally true that the events had revealed no serious degree of support

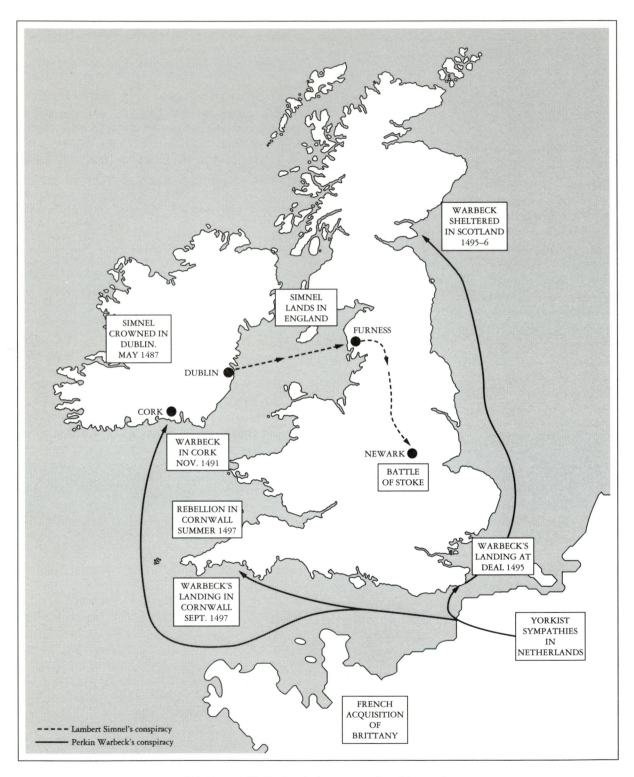

WARBECK
SHELTERED
IN SCOTLAND
1495–6

SIMNEL
LANDS IN
ENGLAND

SIMNEL
CROWNED IN
DUBLIN.
MAY 1487

FURNESS

DUBLIN

CORK

WARBECK
IN CORK
NOV. 1491

NEWARK

BATTLE
OF STOKE

REBELLION IN
CORNWALL
SUMMER 1497

WARBECK'S
LANDING AT
DEAL 1495

WARBECK'S
LANDING IN
CORNWALL
SEPT. 1497

YORKIST
SYMPATHIES
IN
NETHERLANDS

FRENCH
ACQUISITION
OF
BRITTANY

- - - - - Lambert Simnel's conspiracy
———— Perkin Warbeck's conspiracy

8.3 Henry VII's England: the geography of insecurity

for the Tudors either. Men everywhere appeared to be as wary of committing themselves as they had been at the time of Bosworth. There seems to be little reason to doubt that, had a fortuitous blow struck Henry down at Stoke, the Tudor dynasty would have fallen with him.

Simnel's conspiracy set the scene for a far more dangerous imposture. The central figure this time (1491) was Perkin Warbeck, apparently the son of a customs official from Tournai in Flanders. All the evidence indicates, however, that Henry was profoundly troubled by this new pretender, and he may even have feared that Warbeck really was who he claimed to be: Richard, Duke of York, the younger of the 'princes in the Tower'.

The real danger, however, lay in the interest shown in his cause in the early 1490s by James IV of Scotland, by the Archduke Philip and his father, the Emperor Maximilian, by Charles VIII of France, and of course by Margaret of Burgundy. Henry's reaction to the threat was vigorous. His foreign policy from 1492 to 1494 was largely dictated by the Warbeck threat, and his dynastic priorities were illustrated by the embargo that he placed upon English trade with the Netherlands, in response to the Habsburgs' patronage of Warbeck. At home the search for potential traitors brought down Sir William Stanley (February 1495), perhaps as a warning to half-hearted supporters. The danger also inspired the 'De Facto' Act, which spelled out the duty of the subject to obey the man who was in fact (*de facto*) king at the given moment, regardless of the justness of his claims to be king by right (*de jure*).

In the event, Warbeck found even less support in England than Simnel had enjoyed. His attempts to convert foreign sympathy into a political foothold in England developed into a pathetic odyssey embracing Kent, Ireland and Scotland, finally landing in Cornwall (September 1497). The West Country was unpromising ground for a second rising so soon after a rising against taxation earlier in the year, and within a month Warbeck's cause had collapsed and he was Henry's prisoner. His execution, along with that of the Earl of Warwick (1499), was the price demanded by Ferdinand of Aragon for the confirmation of his daughter's marriage to Prince Arthur. With the disappearance of both the true Yorkist claimant and the false one the Wars of the Roses were truly at an end.

CENTRAL GOVERNMENT

Finance

One of the clearest lessons to be learned from the Wars of the Roses was that the stability of the regime depended upon the state of its finances relative to those of its opponents.

In rebuilding royal finances, Henry remained faithful to the medieval principle that the king should 'live of his own', that he should meet the ordinary costs of government from his own resources. The greatest of these resources consisted of the crown lands, and the erosion or inefficient administration of these lands was recognised as a primary cause of the crown's financial embarrassment. Henry began his reign endowed with the lands of the Duchies of York, Lancaster and Cornwall, quite apart from the crown lands themselves. In addition, his two Acts of Resumption (1486 and 1487) re-established crown rights to lands alienated since 1455. Technically, the 138 Acts of Attainder passed during the reign also put the victims' lands at the crown's disposal, but the fact that one-third of these Acts were later revoked suggests that Henry saw attainders more as a threat, as a means of keeping untrustworthy subjects in line, than as a major source of royal income. In addition, the crown sought to maximise its income from feudal and prerogative sources, such as **wardship,** relief and the profits of justice. The fact that royal income from the potentially lucrative source of wardships totalled a mere £350 in 1487 indicated the extent of the problem that Henry faced.

Henry achieved considerable success in the regeneration of English crown finances. Receipts into the **Royal Chamber** between July 1487 and July 1489 totalled only £17,000 per year, of which £3,000 per year was derived from the crown lands. Between September 1489 and October 1495 the corresponding figures were £27,000 and £11,000 per year respectively, rising to £105,000 and £40,000 per year respectively (October 1502–October 1505). Over the reign as a whole, according to the estimates of B.P. Wolffe (*The Royal Demesne in English History*, 1971), income from crown lands rose by almost 45 per cent. Substantial as these increases were in the context of English government, it is important to remember that Henry remained a poor monarch by the standards of some of his European contemporaries. One only needs to set his income of £113,000 in 1509 against that of the Emperor (about £1,100,000) or that of the King of France (about £800,000) to appreciate that Henry achieved greatness only in the domestic context.

The achievement of Henry VII lay in the restoration of traditional elements in late medieval government, rather than in the foundation of any 'modern' administrative machinery. Where historians once saw the introduction of a new 'system' of financial administration, they are now inclined to accept that 'under Henry VII experiment and informality were the rule' (R. Lockyer). Given the choice between two main fiscal institutions, the **Exchequer** and the Royal Chamber, Henry seems to have made his decisions purely on grounds of political pragmatism. The predominant use of the Chamber between 1488 and 1493 was not a radical financial initiative so much as an emergency measure whereby Henry concentrated the most important financial business of the crown in his own hands and those of a few intimate collaborators.

What was unusual about Henry's financial administration was the personal day-to-day involvement of the king himself, and the extreme ruthlessness shown by the crown in the pursuit of financial recovery. The surviving Chamber accounts were apparently inspected daily or weekly by the monarch, whose signature appears on each page. With similar attention to detail, royal councillors met frequently in order to bring to account those who evaded debts or feudal obligations to the king. In particular, the methods of Richard Empson and Edmund Dudley were so successful that they achieved outstanding notoriety, which led the young Henry VIII to sacrifice them as a short route to popularity. If the novelty of Henry's administration consisted largely of the energetic implementation of traditional methods, we should not forget the role that fear and force played in the government of early modern England.

The King's Council

Throughout the sixteenth century the Royal Council remained the major advisory, coordinating and policy-making body of the realm. For many years, this institution also received much attention from 'New Monarchy' theorists, who claimed that a process of departmentalisation took place, subdividing the Council into a series of 'sub-councils', each with a specific area of responsibility. Much importance was attached to the statute of 1487 which delegated certain councillors to sit in the Star Chamber in the Palace of Westminster, to consider cases arising from 'unlawful maintenances, giving of liveries, untrue demeanings of sheriffs in making [jury] panels, and other untrue returns'.

It is now widely accepted that these bodies had no separate or permanent constitutional existence, and that they must simply be seen as groups of trusted royal servants, delegated temporarily by the king to fulfil specific tasks as the need arose. In Henry's reign the Council remained an informal body, whose meetings, agenda and composition all depended entirely upon the king's wishes. Most historians would now accept the judgement of S.B. Chrimes that 'the king's Council was simply the king's council; there was no Court of Star Chamber; there were no committees of the council; there was no "whole" council, no "privy" council, no "inner" council, no offshoots in the North or Wales'.

In analysing Henry's councillors by social class, S.B. Chrimes has identified forty-three peers, forty-five gentleman courtiers, sixty-one churchmen, twenty-seven lawyers and forty-nine civil servants. There is no ground here for maintaining the myth of the 'Tudor New Man', but only for concluding that 'loyalty and ability were the only criteria for service – mighty lord, bishop, or official, all were there, but only at the king's will' (J.R. Lander).

Parliament

Parliament remained in Henry VII's reign a secondary element in the government of the realm. In some respects, indeed, the reign marked a decline in parliamentary activity, for the body met for only sixty-nine weeks in a twenty-four-year reign, an average of eighteen days a year, where the annual average under the Yorkists had been twenty-four days. In the first half of the reign the active role of the Commons seems to have been minimal. Their direct advice was rarely sought, and their debates were controlled and monitored by a

8.4 Parliamentary grants in the reign of Henry VII

Year	Grant	Purpose
1485	Tunnage and Poundage	
1487	Two-fifteenths and two-tenths	Resistance to Lambert Simnel
1489	Extraordinary grant of £100,000	Intervention in Brittany
1491	A benevolence of two-fifteenths and two-tenths	For continuation of war against France
1495	Grant of £120,000, made theoretically as a loan	For precautions against an invasion from Scotland
1497	Two-fifteenths and two-tenths and an 'aid and subsidy of as great and large sums of money'	Resistance to Perkin Warbeck
1504	Subsidy of £30,000 and a feudal aid	For the knighting of Prince Arthur (who had been dead for two years) and for the marriage of Princess Margaret

Speaker who was invariably a royal nominee. Lovell, Empson and Dudley all served Henry in this capacity.

Nevertheless, Parliament performed two crucial functions, primarily as an important source of finance. A table of the grants made by Henry's parliaments indicates that every one of them was approached for money, and that each demand was satisfied, although a degree of opposition in 1504 left the king with a reduced total of £40,000. It also shows that taxation was usually sought only in cases of extreme urgency, and that Henry used this resource predominantly in the early, most insecure years of his reign. In the last fourteen years of the reign, Parliament might have seemed to be well on the way to obsolescence, sitting for only 123 days between 1495 and 1509.

Parliamentary taxation, however, entailed many disadvantages. Its collection was a slow and uncertain process, and it is unlikely, for instance, that much more than £18,000 of the enormous grant of 1489 was ever collected. It was also a gamble in terms of law and order. Resentment at being taxed for causes with which the tax-payers could not identify caused the riots in Yorkshire in which the Earl of Northumberland was murdered, and the more serious Cornish rebellion in 1497.

As regards law-making, their second crucial function, Henry's parliaments were prolific, but not profound. A total of 192 Acts was unusually high but showed little originality. Law and order were their main preoccupations, with thirty-five Acts of

Attainder, twenty or so Acts concerning the powers of the **Justices of the Peace,** and half a dozen modifying the laws of 'benefit of clergy'. Trade and fiscal matters also loomed large, with thirty-one Acts concerning prices and trade regulations. It is hard to see Henry's reign as a important era in parliamentary history, although it did see some significant developments. The growth of taxation by subsidy, and an increase in legislation initiated in the Commons, were modest matters in themselves, but were the precursors of greater things.

LOCAL GOVERNMENT

Much of the copious legislation for the maintenance of order in the localities aimed primarily to shore up the existing machinery of enforcement. Each parliament of the reign passed measures against the corruption of juries, and many more were passed to bolster the authority and efficiency of those mainstays of Tudor local administration, the Justices of the Peace. For all that, it remained unlikely throughout the reign that Justices could function independently of the local nobility, who so often threatened local law and order. The higher courts of the realm consistently heard complaints of the riotous disruption of local courts by the hired thugs of the local gentry and nobility. The king's frequent exhortations to the

Parliament and the frequency of Parliaments, 1485–1558

By 1485, Parliament was a well-established, though intermittent, feature of English government. It consisted of three elements, crown, lords and commons (in that order of priority throughout the sixteenth century) and thus assumed much importance as the coming together of the three great political 'estates' of the realm. The House of Lords comprised the chief officers of the Church as well as the nobility of the realm, while the House of Commons contained knights of the shires (representatives of the counties) and burgesses (representatives of those towns which had been granted the status of boroughs by the crown).

The monarch retained control over Parliament by his/her control of its duration and delibera-

tions. Parliament was summoned by royal writ, and was dissolved (brought to an end) or prorogued (its sitting adjourned to a later date) as the monarch desired. Debate within the Commons was controlled by the Speaker, invariably a royal nominee in the sixteenth century.

Although Parliament was still sometimes viewed in its medieval capacity as a 'Great Council' to advise the monarch, it served two other primary purposes in the sixteenth century. It passed statute law, the law enforced in the courts of the realm. It was thus increasingly important to the crown, as the Reformation Parliament showed under Henry VIII, that its policies should be enshrined in these Acts of Parliament.

Second, Parliament voted taxes, the crown's only source of extraordinary income, beyond its own landed and feudal resources. Increasingly in the sixteenth century this taxation was voted in the form of a subsidy (a fixed amount based upon the value of land or goods), rather than the more traditional 'tenths' and 'fifteenths' (based upon an estimated proportion of landed wealth). In addition, having granted the crown its taxation, Parliament would spend some time considering private bills, usually issues of local interest put forward by local representatives. The facility for proposing such legislation made it a matter of some local prestige to represent a locality in Parliament.

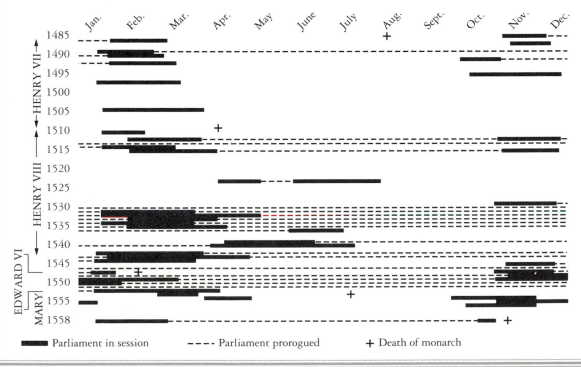

Parliament in session   ---- Parliament prorogued   + Death of monarch

Justices, and the frequency with which individuals were removed from office, all make it clear that some took the line of least resistance and worked with the local magnates rather than against them.

According to the statute book, Henry pursued a consistent policy of limiting the disruptive local influence of the nobility by forbidding the practice of livery and maintenance. By this practice a noble might enlist a man under feudal obligation to act as his armed servant, and thereby develop a private force with which to further his local ambitions. These dangers were addressed in four statutes between 1487 and 1504, while another (1488) prescribed punishments for royal servants or tenants who allowed themselves to be retained by another.

This repetition makes it clear that Henry was not succeeding in the elimination of livery and maintenance, but it is equally clear that he had no wish to eradicate the practices completely. The complete abolition of armed retainers would have left the king without the means to enforce his will in those localities controlled by his supporters, and almost without the means to defend the realm. Henry, in short, had to walk an indistinct line between stamping out such retaining as threatened his political security and tolerating and even encouraging that retaining which made him more secure. Thus only one nobleman, Lord Burgavenny in 1507, is known to have been prosecuted for retaining.

The king's preoccupation with livery and maintenance illustrates that the mentalities of civil war persisted at least until the beginning of the new century. Under such circumstances Henry was less likely to solve the problems of law and order by abstract legal theories than by the hard practicalities of force and fear. In his pursuit of this cruder form of public order, Henry's main weapons were the financial threats embodied in bonds and recognisances. By these, an individual entered into an agreement with the king, usually under the pressure of less subtle threats, whereby the individual acknowledged a debt to the crown of a specific sum of money. Such debts were rarely collected, and the point was rather to force that subject to choose between political conformity or financial ruin. In the contemporary phrase, the individual lived 'in the king's danger'. Thus, when

the loyalty of the Marquis of Dorset was in doubt in 1491, a total of fifty-five associates were bound to make him keep the peace in sums as high as £1,000. By the end of the reign forty-seven of the noble families in England had at one time or another been bound over in this fashion.

There is little to suggest that England was a more law-abiding or more peaceful realm in 1509 than in 1485. All that can realistically be claimed for Henry VII is that he took a firmer grip upon those who might disturb the security of his throne and did much to re-establish that fear of the crown that was an essential part of successful monarchy. He 'reduced lawlessness', in R.B. Wernham's phrase, 'from a political to a police problem' (*Before the Armada*, 1966).

ORDER IN THE DISTANT LOCALITIES

Distance was still a crippling handicap to the implementation of royal policy, when York was two or three days' march from London, and the Scottish border was up to a week away. Allied to this problem was that of feudal privilege and independence which was manifested in the dozens of semi-autonomous political units that existed in the distant corners of the realm. Durham, Cheshire and Lancashire were counties palatine, with extensive political liberties. Redesdale, Tynedale and Norhamshire, towards the Scottish border, were examples of smaller units with similar liberties. On the Welsh borders, over 130 **marcher lordships** survived from the days of the first English assaults upon the principality.

The problem was less complicated for Henry than for his predecessors. By the attainders of Buckingham, Stanley and others, and by the acquisition of Yorkist lands, some fifty of the Welsh marcher lordships came into royal hands between 1483 and 1500. Otherwise, Henry used traditional means to deal with such difficulties. Authority in these distant localities was placed in the hands of great men apparently worthy of his trust. In Wales, his uncle Jasper Tudor served as the main instrument of royal authority until the installation of Prince Arthur as Prince of Wales (1493) allowed the Council of the Marches to be resurrected in safer hands. In the north, Henry reverted to the practice of installing great noblemen as 'wardens' of these distant marches, suggesting that he was willing to settle for the appearance of conformity, knowing that the reality was beyond his grasp.

The most remote, most unruly and potentially most troublesome of the far-flung provinces was Ireland. Unlike the others, Ireland was not ruled by Henry as king but only as nominal 'Lord of Ireland'. Even that title meant little beyond the 'Pale', the area of English rule that extended some fifty miles beyond Dublin. Elsewhere, real power lay in the hands of the native Irish chieftains, or with the great Anglo-Irish magnate families, the earls of Ormond, Desmond and Kildare. Of these, the greatest influence was undoubtedly exercised by Gerald FitzGerald, Earl of Kildare, who had occupied the office of Lord Deputy since the latter years of Edward IV's reign, and who illustrated during the Lambert Simnel crisis that he enjoyed virtual freedom of action in Ireland.

Henry's aims were necessarily limited ones. He was once more predominantly concerned with the security of his crown, and aimed primarily 'to end the Wars of the Roses in Ireland as in England' (S.B. Chrimes). He dismissed Kildare as Lord Deputy (1491), pressurised him into giving recognisances, and dispatched a prominent royal servant, Sir Edward Poynings (September 1494), to carry out a comprehensive legislative programme. A number of Acts passed by the Irish Parliament at Drogheda (December 1494–April 1495) confirmed Ireland's legal subjugation to England. It was confirmed that all English laws relating to treason and to livery and maintenance applied with equal force in Ireland, and it was established, by a measure traditionally known as 'Poynings' Law', that no measures passed by Irish parliaments had legal force unless they were confirmed by the king.

Yet the system could not be enforced without Kildare, and whether or not Henry ever used the famous phrase that 'since all Ireland cannot rule this man, this man must rule all Ireland,' this was the principle by which he now operated. Kildare's conviction for treason was reversed (February 1496) and he was restored to the office of Lord Deputy (August 1496). He returned to Ireland and ruled with all his old energy, yet now he exercised his authority in the name of Henry VII. Warbeck's appearance at Cork in 1497 failed to tempt him, and when he summoned a parliament in 1498 it was in strict accordance with Poynings' Law. As in many other areas of his government, Henry had changed little in outward terms. What he had achieved was to bring an alternative source of authority under some degree of control.

8.5 Summary of English diplomatic agreements under Henry VII

Treaty of Redon (February 1489). Promised Brittany 6,000 men to fight in their defence, at Breton expense.

Treaty of Medina del Campo (March 1489). Broke Tudor isolation by a series of agreements with Castile and Aragon. Provided for the marriage of Prince Arthur to the Princess Catherine, and for an anti-French alliance, providing for English recovery of Normandy and Gascony and Spanish reoccupation of Cerdagne and Roussillon. Established trading privileges for both parties, and undertook to provide no shelter for rebels against either party.

Treaty of Étaples (November 1492). Henry agreed to withdraw from France in return for a substantial pension. Charles VIII undertook to give no further aid to Yorkist rebels.

Magnus Intercursus (February 1496). Henry and Philip of Burgundy concluded a trade treaty whereby English merchants enjoyed free trade within Philip's territories and equal status with his own subjects in courts of law. Both parties agreed to withdraw all support from those who rebelled against the other.

Treaty of Windsor (February 1506). Henry promised military support for Philip of Burgundy in return for Philip's renewed pledges to exclude Yorkist conspirators from his territories and to hand over the fugitive Edmund de la Pole. An agreement over English trade with the Low Countries (*Intercursus Malus*) was associated with the treaty.

ENGLISH FOREIGN POLICY

1485–92

For much of Henry's reign it is unhelpful to distinguish between domestic and foreign policies. Henry had one overall preoccupation: his personal and dynastic security. His priorities in his relations with foreign states were to protect himself against external assault, and to prevent aid coming from abroad to his domestic enemies. Abandoning the traditional Lancastrian policy of seeking possessions in France, his first diplomatic moves consisted of a series of truces, freeing his hands to cope with domestic crisis: with France for one year (October 1485), subsequently extended until 1489; with Scotland for three years (July 1486); with the Holy Roman Empire for one year (January 1487). When French designs threatened the independence of the Duchy of Brittany (1488), the king acted in typically pragmatic fashion. Equipped with an extraordinary parliamentary grant of £100,000 (January 1489), he prepared for military intervention. The impression of energy was deceptive, however. Henry's distaste for a long foreign campaign coincided neatly with Charles VIII's dreams of glory in Italy, and the campaign ended abruptly with the conclusion of the Treaty of Étaples (November 1492). Although the mission for the preservation of Breton independence had completely failed, and the future French threat to the English coastline had not been averted, the Treaty of Étaples was a triumph of realism. It sacrificed unattainable diplomatic and military dreams to the short-term considerations of domestic security.

1492–1503

The next decade witnessed the peak of Henry's diplomatic prestige and success. In its course he turned a position of vulnerability and isolation into one of security and respect among the princes of Western Europe.

Henry's diplomacy during this decade was dominated by the threat posed by the pretender Perkin Warbeck. On the face of it, the support that Warbeck received from James of Scotland, Philip of Burgundy, Charles of France and the Emperor Maximilian threatened Henry with diplomatic isolation. A coalition of these powers against Henry was never a serious possibility, however, primarily because of the fears generated by French successes in Italy. European diplomacy thus centred around attempts to form an alliance that might check Charles's progress. When the Holy League was

formed for that purpose in 1495, the interests of the member powers were better served by seeking the friendship of such a consistently anti-French nation as the English than by supporting Yorkist trouble-makers. Henry was admitted as an associate member in July 1496.

In the next few years, England was able to achieve a position of security virtually unparalleled in the fifteenth century. Friendship with the Spanish monarchies was confirmed along the lines established at Medina del Campo, the marriage between Prince Arthur and the Princess Catherine of Aragon being celebrated in May 1499. Ferdinand of Aragon may also have been instrumental in improving England's diplomatic relations with Philip of Burgundy. Philip's support for Perkin Warbeck had caused Henry to order all English merchants to quit the Low Countries (1493), and Philip's government responded with its own embargo in the following year. Now, however, the marriage of Philip to Ferdinand's daughter Juana (1496) and Henry's association in the Holy League with Philip's father, the Emperor Maximilian, placed relations upon a much better footing. In February 1496 the trade treaty known as the *Magnus Intercursus* brought a degree of cordiality to Anglo-Burgundian relations that had not existed since Henry's accession.

Although James IV of Scotland remained a loyal friend to Perkin Warbeck until the latter's career reached the point of hopelessness, Anglo-Scottish relations made significant progress thereafter. The sporadic truces between the states culminated in the Treaty of Ayton (February 1498), but it took another five years, and the execution of Warbeck, before the proposed marriage finally took place between James and Henry's daughter, Margaret. The marriage provided no permanent solution, for James was to die a decade later on the battlefield of Flodden, leading an invasion force into England. At the time, however, Henry could congratulate himself upon a significant addition to his overall international security.

1503–9

Yet in the last years of Henry's reign an extraordinary sequence of royal deaths brought his diplomatic structure close to disintegration. The death of Prince

Arthur, heir to the throne and bridegroom of Catherine of Aragon (April 1502) was closely followed by those of Elizabeth of York (February 1503) and Isabella of Castile (November 1504). Not only did these events leave both Henry and Ferdinand of Aragon free to remarry, with unforeseeable diplomatic consequences, but the death of Isabella threatened Ferdinand's power in Castile. There were strong grounds for assuming that his son-in-law, Philip of Burgundy, was a more attractive ally in the long term. Henry's secret agreement with Philip (1506) seemed to confirm that England's future lay with the Habsburgs. Such a move made good sense in terms of England's commercial interests in the Low Countries; and, with or without Castile, the power of the Habsburgs in northern Europe made them attractive allies against the French. Yet this happy position was also wrecked by the end of the year. By that point, Philip himself was dead, while Ferdinand had entered a French alliance through marriage to a niece of Louis XII. Despite Henry's attempts to confirm the Habsburg alliance in the last years of his life, he left England at his death in as great a state of diplomatic isolation as he had found it.

Yet the telling comparison is not between 1509 and 1503, but between 1509 and the desperately insecure opening years of the reign. Henry's aims, as R.B. Wernham wrote, 'remained essentially defensive, subordinated always to the overriding domestic purposes of making the monarchy rich and its subjects obedient' (*Before the Armada*, 1966) By 1509 he had brought England 'to the point at which her friendship had been courted by all the chief powers, who had learned to respect his financial power and his diplomatic skill, his shrewd judgement, and up to a point his reliability' (S.B. Chrimes).

TRADE AND THE ECONOMY

The traditional view of early Tudor England as a society enjoying a period of economic growth and prosperity still seems well founded. The opening of Henry VII's reign coincided in parts of the country with years of cheaper food and higher wages, and with boom conditions in the foreign trade in woollen cloth. Whereas export figures languished around

60,000 cloths per year in the mid-century, the figure for the period 1506–8 was an impressive 90,000 cloths per year. In the course of Henry's reign, the crown roughly doubled its income from the cloth trade. Indications of increased import trade may be gained from the rise during the reign in the crown's overall income from customs (68 per cent) and from wine imports (47 per cent).

Many parliamentary and diplomatic measures were taken in the interests of trade. Apart from the Treaty of Medina del Campo and the *Magnus Intercursus*, treaties with France (1492–5) removed obstacles to trade caused by the earlier crisis over Brittany, an agreement with Florence (1490) provided English cloth merchants with facilities in Pisa, and a treaty with Denmark in the same year extended trading rights to English merchants in Norway. There were also attempts to seek and develop new outlets for English trade, of which the most spectacular were the westward voyages of John and Sebastian Cabot from Bristol in 1497, 1498 and 1508–9. That city had its own Company of Adventurers to the New Found Lands by 1506, a testimony to the way in which Bristol had responded over the last two decades to the decay of its previous staple trading routes.

Significant though his reign was in terms of economic development, there is little in the process that could be directly attributed to Henry. It is hard now to support Francis Bacon's view of a king who 'could not abide trade to be sick'. The upward curve of England's foreign trade pre-dated Henry's reign by a dozen years, while the tensions of the Wars of the Roses, once supposed to have been so economically disruptive, persisted for at least a dozen years after 1485. Of the fifty parliamentary statutes of the reign that dealt with economic matters, the vast majority originated in merchants' petitions. The Act of 1486 declaring that no Gascon wines should be imported unless in English ships; the Act of 1489 prohibiting the export of bullion without royal licence; the Act of 1491 extending freer Continental trade to the Merchant Adventurers: all originated in this way.

What royal initiatives there were were primarily concerned with economic matters relevant to the political strength of the crown. Henry took extensive measures in 1485–9 to strengthen the currency, providing a new range of coinage and a clearly defined fiscal hierarchy. His dealings with foreign powers make it equally clear that trading interests were always secondary to political, and especially to dynastic, interests. When the two coincided, as they did in the alliance with Castile and Aragon, Henry was content to help his merchants to extensive privileges. When they did not, trade took a back seat. Thus, whatever gains English merchants may have derived from the *Magnus Intercursus,* they scarcely made up for the losses that they suffered when the sympathy of the Archduke Philip for Perkin Warbeck caused Henry to place an embargo upon trade with the Low Countries.

8.6 Glossary

Attainder. An Act of Parliament declaring an individual guilty of treason. The possessions and titles of the attainted individual passed automatically to the crown.

Exchequer. The financial office of the crown, responsible for the collection of revenue and for accounting. Staffed by professional civil servants, it was politically neutral in Henry's reign, but was less liable than the Royal Chamber to the personal supervision of the monarch and his trusted servants. The Court of Exchequer also served as a law court dealing with disputes over revenue.

Marcher Lordships. Areas of political jurisdiction in the 'marches', the border regions with Wales and Scotland. Originally placed in the hands of noblemen with the military means to pacify and control them, they were often resistant to the direct authority of the crown.

Justices of the Peace. Local magistrates, usually recruited from the gentry classes. They were responsible for the enforcement and implementation of statute law in the localities, operating through their Quarter Sessions. Their prestige derived from their direct appointment by the crown, and the office became one of considerable local importance. In the early sixteenth century, however, the JPs often found it impossible to resist the influence of the local nobility.

The Royal Chamber. The department of the royal household concerned with financial administration. Staffed by the direct servants of the king, it was more politically reliable than the Exchequer, and easier for the king to oversee directly. On the other hand, it lacked the capacity and the professional expertise of the Exchequer.

Wardship. A feudal institution, peculiar to England, whereby the orphaned child of a royal tenant was placed under the protection of the crown until he/she came of age. The crown stood to gain financially by the administration of the orphan's lands, and politically from its right to arrange the marriages of the wards before they came of age.

Further reading

S.B. Chrimes (1972) *Henry VII.* London.

J.R. Lander (1980) *Government and Community: England 1450–1509.* London.

R. Lockyer (1983) *Henry VII,* 2nd edn. London.

• CHAPTER NINE •

International Conflict

The Italian context

The campaigns of Charles VIII, 1494–6

The campaigns of Louis XII, 1498–1504

The League of Cambrai and the Holy League

Marignano

The ascendancy of Charles V, 1520–6

The League of Cognac, 1526–9

France on the defensive, 1530–47

The wars of Henry II

*The greatest land battle fought in Western Europe in the sixteenth century, the Battle of
Pavia, is portrayed here by an anonymous contemporary artist. The picture emphasises
the massed ranks of pikemen who dominated military strategies; the arms of
France and of the Habsburgs are clearly visible on the banners
carried by the two armies*

THE ITALIAN CONTEXT

Guicciardini wrote accurately that his native Italy abounded in 'inhabitants, merchandise and riches', and was 'renowned for the magnificence of her many princes, for the splendour of so many noble and beautiful cities, as the seat of majesty and religion'. Italy set standards of wealth and prosperity in the last years of the fifteenth century that were the envy of her neighbours.

Italy was, with the exception of the Low Countries, the most heavily populated region of Western Europe. Half the cities of Europe with a population above 50,000 were Italian. In the north, Florence and the Lombard towns of Milan, Como, Pavia, Brescia and Bergamo dominated a flourishing cloth industry. Venice was a commercial port without a rival in Western Europe, and with an income by 1500 which approached that of Castile. Italian families dominated every major banking centre of the Continent in the early sixteenth century. The Affaitadi family of Cremona operated from Antwerp, with branches in Spain, London and Lisbon, while the Bonvisi played the major role in Lyon. Sicily had long ago acquired a reputation as 'the granary of the Mediterranean'. Aided by ambitious irrigation projects, Lombardy and Venetia were notable not only for the quantity but also for the variety of crops that they produced.

Yet such prosperity was offset by a wide variety of political tensions. Milan, since the death of her last Visconti prince in 1447, had been controlled by the Sforza family, originally professional soldiers (*condottieri*) employed by the Visconti for their protection. Dubious in the first place, Sforza rule had been even harder to justify since 1480, when Ludovico Sforza had assumed a guardianship over the direct Sforza heir, his nephew Giangaleazzo. Milan's confident, public face hid a web of political disputes arising from the moral weakness of the Sforzas' position.

A republic rather than a duchy, Venice was free from dynastic complications, while her enormous commercial success ensured social stability. Civic patriotism was at a high level, and the relations between the city authorities and the *condottieri* that

they employed for their defence were generally stable. Venice, however, did not enjoy good relations with her neighbours. By deciding to expand her influence inland across the plains and cities of north-eastern Italy, Venice made herself the territorial rival of Milan, the Pope and the Emperor. At the same time her trade routes in the eastern Mediterranean were threatened by the Turks. On the other hand, the Venetians were 'buttressed by the one great advantage that they alone possessed over all their rivals: in so far as any city could ever be, theirs was impregnable' (John Julius Norwich, *History of Venice*, 1982).

Further south, the city republic of Florence also enjoyed great mercantile and artistic wealth. The rise of the Medici family had added stability and continuity to domestic administration, but Piero and Lorenzo de Medici lacked the skill of Cosimo in reconciling princely power with a republican constitution. In the last years of the fifteenth century the spectacular, puritanical preaching of the Dominican friar Girolamo Savonarola formed a focal point for popular opposition to the Medici style of government. Wholly lacking the military means to defend itself against any substantial enemy, the city relied for its security upon its commercial and financial importance.

The last two major Italian political units owed their influence to factors quite separate from the civic riches of the north. The states of the Church, spreading out from Rome, were ruled by the spiritual head of Christendom. The economic or strategic advantages which might be derived from the rest of Italy were as nothing compared to the political benefits that an invader might gain from influence over Rome. Papal policy was dominated by the abiding memory and fear of the 'Babylonish captivity' in Avignon, when the Pope's authority and independence had been so severely eroded by obvious subservience to the King of France. Successive Popes, therefore, sought to impose the political authority of Rome upon the outlying cities and territories of the States of the Church to form a bulwark against any future threat to their independence. Sixtus IV (1471–84) placed his Della Rovere nephews in ecclesiastical offices in order to consolidate control over the Romagna. Alexander VI (1492–1503) was even less subtle in

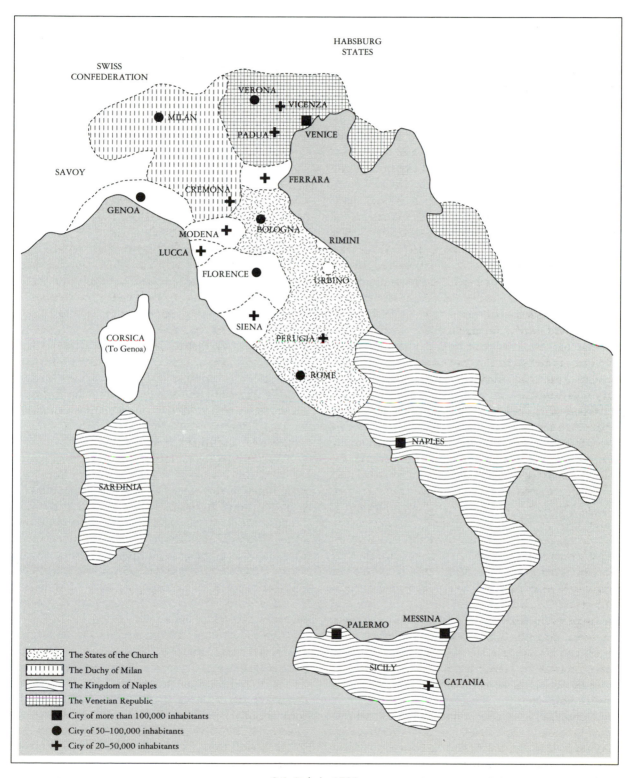

9.1 Italy in 1500

the military and political role that he allocated to his illegitimate son, Cesare Borgia.

Naples alone in Italy remained a feudal monarchy, governed by a branch of the royal house of Aragon. The fact that Ferdinand of Aragon, already secure in his control of Sicily, awaited his chance to impose his rule upon the mainland was only one of the elements which threatened the stability and security of the Neapolitan crown. In addition it had to contend with the claims of the French dukes of Anjou, with those of the Pope, who claimed feudal lordship over the kingdom, and with the widespread domestic unpopularity of the monarchy, which culminated in a major but unsuccessful rebellion in 1485.

A precarious balance was maintained by the Peace of Lodi, concluded in 1454 between Florence, Naples and Milan, but several factors combined to undermine this equilibrium in the 1490s. The first was the marriage of Giangaleazzo Sforza to Isabella of Naples, and his appeals to her father for support against the usurpation of Ludovico Sforza. To protect himself, Ludovico abandoned the principle of isolation from foreign powers, proposed a marriage alliance with the family of the Emperor Maximilian, and took the fateful step of appealing to the King of France to press his longstanding claims against their mutual enemies in Naples.

THE CAMPAIGNS OF CHARLES VIII, 1494–6

The direct, personal motives for Charles VIII's intervention in the quarrels of Italy will sound strange to modern ears. Wars in Italy made no sense in terms of national interest or of economic advantage. Furthermore, Charles's claims to be the rightful king of Naples carried little weight in neutral circles. In fact, Charles was about to embark upon one of the last great chivalric wars of the Middle Ages, in which the prize would be glory and honour for the king and his entourage. In addition, 'Italy exercised a kind of fascination upon him and his generation, and certain judicial pretensions gave substance to illusory dreams' (M. Mollat, 'La Réconstruction, 1440–1515', in *Histoire de la France*, ed. F. Duby, 1970).

Charles received encouragement from several factions with more realistic motives. Neapolitan supporters of the House of Anjou had been refugees at the French court since the rebellion of 1485, and were seconded by enemies of the recently elected Pope Alexander VI. For a complex variety of reasons, therefore, in July 1494, 60,000 men, including 8,000 Swiss mercenaries and the most modern artillery train yet seen in Europe, marched into Italy.

The French drive on Naples was less a military campaign than a triumphal progress. Genoa was seized by the Duke of Orléans, and Charles was welcomed into Florence by Savonarola and his followers as a man sent from God to purge the corruption of the city. By Christmas, Charles was in Rome, where the Pope had little option but to recognise him as King of Naples, and two months later he was installed in his new kingdom.

It was far easier, however, to win such victories than to exploit them. Men who had acquiesced in Charles's original plans now viewed with horror a triumph that threatened the whole shape and balance of Western European politics. Ferdinand of Aragon saw a likely end to his own ambitions in Naples, and a threat to his hold over Sicily. Venice and the Emperor Maximilian foresaw a serious threat to their interests in northern Italy. When these three powers formed the League of Venice (March 1495), they quickly received support from the Pope, haunted anew by the old spectre of a 'Babylonish captivity'. At the same time, the French position in Naples changed from triumph to disaster in a matter of months. Far from home, cut off by Aragonese naval power, and with enemies on two sides, they found themselves further harassed by local insurrections. An indecisive battle at Fornovo (July 1495) was enough to persuade Charles to head for home.

On the face of it, the League of Venice had achieved its purpose. It had reversed the misjudgement of Ludovico Sforza and had cleared Italy of the foreign 'barbarians'. Yet it had only done so in alliance with other foreigners. By drawing the Habsburgs and the Aragonese into the struggle, by destroying French armies but not French ambitions, the League had helped to ensure that Italy became the major international battleground for two generations to come.

THE CAMPAIGNS OF LOUIS XII, 1498–1504

The death of Charles VIII (April 1498) disrupted French plans to return to the offensive in Italy, but removed none of the motives for doing so. His successor, his nephew, had reasons of his own for intervention in Italy. Louis XII was of the House of Orléans, which claimed Milan as its own possession by virtue of their descent from the last Visconti duke. Within months of Louis's accession, the Pope had granted him an annulment of his marriage, and had given his blessing to a more advantageous match with Anne of Brittany. Cesare Borgia, the Pope's bastard son, was granted a prestigious marriage and the duchy of Valentinois. Florence, too, isolated since her failure to join the League of Venice, saw short-term advantage in throwing in her lot with the French. Venice's rivalry with Milan tempted her, too, into an alliance with the invader. Ludovico Sforza found himself completely isolated, and within three months (August–October 1499) had lost his duchy and his liberty to the King of France.

To succeed in Naples, where Charles VIII had failed, Louis had two options open to him. He could accept King Federigo's offer to acknowledge him as his feudal overlord, or he could attempt outright conquest. Choosing the more dangerous course, he agreed upon joint action with Ferdinand of Aragon, agreeing also to the subsequent partition of Naples between the two monarchs. By the spring of 1502, however, disputes had arisen over the unoccupied Capitana region which led the erstwhile allies to the brink of war with each other. More easily supplied and reinforced from Sicily, the Aragonese forces were better able to take the offensive. By the beginning of 1504 the second French occupation of Naples had ended and the future of that kingdom was decided. For logistical reasons France could never hope to be more than an occasional raider into southern Italy. Aragon's Mediterranean and Sicilian interests, on the other hand, made a permanent southern Italian foothold both necessary and viable. With this Aragonese triumph, foreign presence in Italy became a permanent feature.

THE LEAGUE OF CAMBRAI AND THE HOLY LEAGUE

Although Italy had largely lost control of its own destiny since 1494, the last round of warfare had produced one major change in the politics of the peninsula. The diplomacy of Alexander VI and the military leadership of his son had gone some way towards fulfilling the papal dream of full control over the territories and city states of central Italy. Their exploits set the tone for the policies of future Popes, especially of the warrior pontiff, Julius II (1503–13). Julius was willing to accept French help in order to complete the conquests of his predecessor, but he aimed in the longer term at the expulsion of the French as a means for ensuring papal security and supremacy within Italy.

In 1506, Pope Julius completed the first stage of his project by capturing the cities of Perugia and Bologna, and Italian politics now focused upon the city of Venice and her possessions. Venice began to feel the full force of the resentment stirred up by her inland expansion. The Pope himself laid claim to Ravenna, Rimini and Faenza, while the King of France eyed the Venetian cities on the borders of Milan. Ferdinand of Aragon claimed Brindisi, Otranto and other south-eastern ports occupied by Venice, while the Emperor Maximilian had recently lost Fiume and Trieste to the republic. Their League of Cambrai (December 1508) threatened to extinguish Venetian influence and prosperity. In the event, however, Venice was saved by her decision to withdraw from the mainland and to depend upon the Lagoon for defence, and by the collapse of relations between France and the papacy.

The year 1510 saw the collapse of the League of Cambrai and the opening of negotiations which culminated (October 1511) in the formation of the Holy League. The Pope, Ferdinand of Aragon and the republic of Venice spoke in their treaty of Church unity and the recovery of their rightful possessions, but the adherence of Henry VIII of England left no doubt that the League's primary purpose was anti-French. Led by outstanding commanders, such as Gaston de Foix, the French army fought well to preserve its recent northern

Italian gains. In an enormous and bloody engagement at Ravenna (11 April 1512), remarkable for its prolonged artillery bombardment, the French carried the day. Yet their casualties were so heavy that the pyrrhic victory left them ill-equipped to cope with the subsequent blows of their enemies.

The Emperor Maximilian now deserted his ally and adhered to the Holy League. Next, disputes with the Swiss cantons over trade and over the wages of their mercenary soldiers caused the Swiss leaders to offer their men to the Holy League. In their train came Massimiliano Sforza, son of Ludovico and claimant to the duchy of Milan. In 1513, French international fortunes were at their lowest ebb for twenty years. In Italy, the victory of Swiss forces at Novara confirmed that Milan could not be retained: and in July the King of England landed at Calais and achieved the greatest English successes on French soil for a century. With Ferdinand active in the disputed kingdom of Navarre, King Louis, exhausted and prematurely senile, sought to make peace as best he could. Peace, however, was unlikely to be prolonged. France had suffered losses and humiliations that a younger and more energetic ruler would find impossible to accept, while both Spain and the Holy Roman Emperor had assumed greater roles in Italian politics than ever before.

MARIGNANO

The death of Louis XII (1515) brought to the throne a new young monarch who would pursue traditional French ambitions in Italy with renewed passion and urgency. To the usual, outdated Visconti claims to Milan and Angevin claims to Naples, Francis I added a compelling desire for the personal and dynastic prestige that could only be found on the battlefield. On a less romantic level, a late medieval monarch could hardly have made a worse start to his reign than to ask his subjects, his soldiers and his nobility to accept the humiliations of 1513. 'Old commanders whose reputations had been tarnished and young noblemen who had yet to prove their valour looked to him for satisfaction'

(R.J. Knecht, *French Renaissance Monarchy*, 1984).

By August 1515, Francis was ready to lead the flower of the French nobility across the Alps. The army comprised 3,000 of the best cavalrymen in Europe, reinforced by some 23,000 German mercenaries (*Landsknechte*), and equipped with artillery of unparalleled quantity and quality. Having secured his northern frontiers by agreements with Charles of Burgundy and with the King of England, he found a ready Italian ally in Venice, eager to re-establish its position on the mainland. Against him stood the Pope, Milan, Naples, the Emperor, and those Swiss mercenaries who had routed French hopes two years earlier. By taking a remote and little-used route across the Alps, the French forced the main body of Swiss troops to give battle at Marignano (14 September 1515). The fighting raged through two days, with casualties amounting to some 16,500 dead, an enormous figure for the time. In the end, the Swiss were forced to retire, and Milan passed once more into French hands.

The battle of Marignano seemed to transform the international balance of power. It marked a turning-point, for instance, in Swiss history, shattering their military reputation and encouraging the cantons to retreat into a neutrality that has lasted until the present day. The conciliatory meeting between Francis I and Pope Leo X at Bologna (December 1515) produced the Concordat which dictated the shape of Church–state relations in France until the Revolution. Marignano also confirmed developments which had been taking place for some time in the political structure of Italy. The independence of Milan had now vanished as completely as that of Naples. With a Medici on the papal throne, Florence was virtually governed from Rome. Where five major Italian states had existed in 1490, only Venice and the States of the Church remained independent, with the rest of Italy partitioned between the crowns of France and Aragon. For the time being, however, circumstances prevented any clash between the two powers. The death of Ferdinand of Aragon (January 1516) brought his grandson, Charles of Burgundy, to the thrones of both Castile and Aragon, and the young kings of France and Spain concluded the Treaty of Noyon (August 1516), guaranteeing each other's possessions in Milan and Naples respectively.

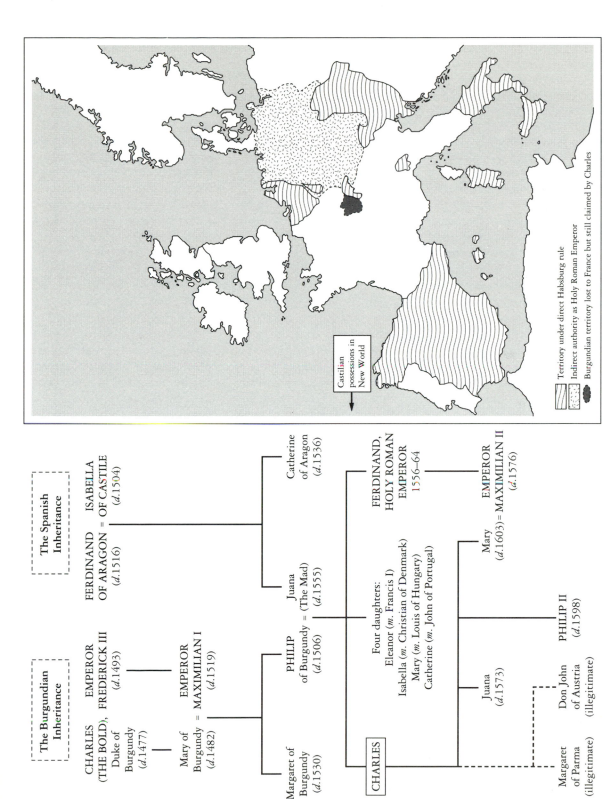

9.2 *The Habsburg inheritance*

Territory under direct Habsburg rule

Indirect authority as Holy Roman Emperor

Burgundian territory lost to France but still claimed by Charles

Castilian possessions in New World

The Imperial Election, 1519

The second decade of the sixteenth century saw the death of all the major political actors of the first decade. The death of Ferdinand of Aragon and of Louis XII did not fundamentally change the direction of their kingdoms' policies, but that of the Emperor Maximilian I (January 1519) was a far more important event. Whichever of the main candidates was chosen by the German electors to succeed him, the balance of power in Western Europe would be destroyed. Although Henry VIII of England announced his candidature, and although the Pope worked hard to produce a candidate from among the German princes who had no direct interest in Italy, the contest really lay between two men. Charles, King of Spain and ruler of the Low Countries, had the advantage of Habsburg blood, but he was young and inexperienced. He was physically unimpressive, and it was not yet clear whether he was touched by his mother's madness. The King of France was the man of the moment. His great victory at Marignano brought him prestige, admiration and considerable practical power. He had promises from the Elector Palatine

and from the Archbishop-Elector of Cologne, and had the support of other political elements in Germany. There can be no doubt that Francis wanted the imperial title badly, for not to win it would be to lose all the political benefits of Marignano and to be second once again in the European power game.

Why then did Francis lose? Financially, the King of Spain undoubtedly enjoyed a substantial advantage. Quite apart from the 600,000 ducats voted by the Cortes of Castile, he enjoyed the services of the Fugger bankers who at once forwarded huge loans to him, and refused to honour French bills of exchange. Charles was thus able to advance 103,000 florins to the Elector of Mainz and to his advisers, 139,000 to the Elector Palatine, and over 40,000 to the Archbishop-Elector of Cologne. The Fuggers alone put more than half a million florins at Charles's disposal, and his total 'bill' for the election seems to have come to about 850,000 florins. The limit of Francis's borrowing seems to have been about 360,000 florins. In addition, the celebrity and power of Francis may have served as handicaps, for the electors had no wish to be forced into

line by an overlord of character and power. Charles's preoccupations in Spain, Italy and the Netherlands would ensure that he would be an absentee Emperor. Yet, on the other hand, Habsburg territories in Austria would guarantee that he would respond to the Turkish threat to the east of the Empire if and when it arose. Charles really seemed to offer the best of both worlds. Perhaps, as R.J. Knecht has concluded (*French Renaissance Monarchy*, 1984), Francis was fighting a losing battle from the start: 'Francis failed to see that the German electors were interested less in his success than in promoting a contested election.' Such lucrative possibilities were unlikely to occur twice in a lifetime and they had to be exploited.

By May 1519, realising that Francis's cause was hopeless, Leo X began seriously to woo Frederick of Saxony to stand as a compromise candidate. Frederick, however, found the profits of bribery preferable to the costs of office, and his decision not to stand for election sealed the outcome. On 28 June 1519 the Habsburg candidate was unanimously elected as the Emperor Charles V.

THE ASCENDANCY OF CHARLES V, 1520–6

The international disputes of the previous thirty years had been contested by a host of greater and lesser powers, and France had prospered in them because its greater size and unity gave it access to resources that states such as Aragon, Castile,

Naples and even the papacy could not match. Now the international struggle had crystallised into a confrontation between two 'superpowers', the realm of Francis I and the personal *monarchia* of the new Emperor. The lesser states seemed to be left with the role of scavengers attached to one or other of the mighty predators.

There were also elements of medieval dynasticism and of personal antipathy involved. Charles remained convinced that Milan was rightly his, and that the French lands of the Duchy of Burgundy should be restored to his family, while Francis steadfastly refused to abandon Angevin claims to Naples. Francis's personal disappointment at his electoral defeat was later more than matched by Charles's disgust at a monarch who broke his word given in solemn treaties, and who made alliances with the prime enemy of Christendom, the Turk. On a more pragmatic level, the duchy of Milan was of crucial, practical importance to a monarch who ruled both Spain and Germany, and who was forced to rely for his communications between them upon a route via Genoa, northern Italy and the Alpine passes. For Francis, on the other hand, Milan represented the only possible breach in what would otherwise be a solid belt of Habsburg possessions encircling his own. At the worst, Habsburg claims to Burgundy and to other French provinces might threaten the very integrity and survival of the French state.

By the end of 1521, Charles had created a formidable anti-French coalition. In May, Leo X agreed to crown Charles as Emperor and to recognise his rights in Naples. Although Leo died in December, the election first of Adrian of Utrecht as Adrian VI (1521–3), and then of a well-disposed Medici cardinal as Clement VII seemed to confirm the Emperor's good relations with Rome. In August 1521 the King of England moved from ostentatious negotiations with Francis to conclude the Treaty of Bruges with the Emperor, agreeing to a marriage alliance and a combined attack on France.

Physically surrounded, diplomatically isolated and with her resources stretched to the limit, France lost in the course of four years all that she had striven for in northern Italy over the last thirty. The initial loss of Milan (November 1521) was reversed three years later, but Habsburg supremacy was emphatically confirmed early in 1525. The French advance into northern Italy was blocked by an imperial garrison at Pavia. After months of siege Francis chose to engage a relieving force. The French army relied once more upon Swiss mercenaries and upon the chivalric *élan* that had won so many past triumphs in Italy. The key to this battle, however, lay with the imperial gunmen who, using their arquebuses in concentrated numbers for the first time, wrought havoc among the French cavalry and won the day.

The scale of the imperial victory at the Battle of Pavia (24 February 1525) was staggering. Estimates of the number of French dead ranged from 10,000 to 14,000, while no estimate put the casualties on the Habsburg side above 1,500. The quality of the French losses was yet more striking. According to an English observer, not 400 out of 1,400 French 'soldiers of quality' escaped death or captivity. Worst of all, Francis himself became the prisoner of his great rival. The triumphs of Marignano became a mere memory, and the subsequent Treaty of Madrid appeared to confirm that the balance of power in Western Europe no longer existed, and that Charles V was now truly 'master of all'.

THE LEAGUE OF COGNAC, 1526–9

Yet how were the terms of the Treaty of Madrid to be enforced? Charles had defeated the French army but not the French state, and was wholly reliant for the implementation of the treaty upon the honour and cooperation of Francis. It meant little that the French monarch left behind his two sons as hostages upon his return to France, for it was unthinkable that Charles would harm princes of royal blood. Within weeks of his return to France, Francis had concluded a new alliance against Charles. The magnitude of Charles's victory at Pavia had brought it home to the princes of Western Europe that, alone, they could scarcely hope to succeed where the King of France had failed. The League of Cognac was signed (May 1526) by France, Venice, Florence and the papacy. Henry VIII of England expressed his full sympathy without actually joining the alliance, and informal contact was even made with the Turkish sultan. Indeed, this new challenge to Charles's interests coincided with the most serious manifestation of Ottoman power since he came to the imperial throne. In August 1526 the armies of the Sultan Suleiman routed the forces of the King of Hungary at Mohacs, destroying the independence of his kingdom.

9.3 Conflict in Italy, 1493–1529

Precipitants	Narrative	Outcome
1493–5. Pursuing dynastic claims to Naples, Charles VIII freed his hands by settling differences with the Emperor (Treaty of **Senlis**, 1493), Ferdinand of Aragon (Treaty of **Barcelona**, 1493) and Henry VII of England (Treaty of **Étaples**, 1493)	Charles occupied Genoa, Florence and Rome in the course of 1494, and entered Naples (Feb. 1495)	
1495–6. French success provoked formation of the **League of Venice** (March 1495) between Aragon, Venice and the Emperor	Extended French lines of communication threatened by Aragonese sea-power. Indecisive battle at **Fornovo** (July 1495) and Aragonese victory at **Atella** (1496) force French retreat	Failure of French designs on Naples.
1500–3. Louis XII put forward enhanced dynastic claims to Milan. Received support from Florence, Venice and the papacy	French victory over Ludovico Sforza at **Novara** (April 1500) leads to capture of Milan	Milan in French hands
Joint French–Aragonese action against Naples agreed by Treaty of **Granada** (Nov. 1500)	Naples captured (1501) and partitioned. Subsequent disputes between France and Aragon led to Battle of the **Garigliano** (1503)	French defeat led to abandonment of Naples. Naples now in Aragonese hands
1508–13. The League of **Cambrai** (Dec. 1508) links France with the Emperor, Aragon and the papacy against Venice	Major French victory over Venice at **Agnadello** (May 1509)	
Initial French success provokes formation of the **Holy League** (Oct. 1511), comprising Aragon, Venice, and the papacy. Adherence of the Emperor and Henry VIII makes this a full-blown anti-French alliance	Costly French victory at **Ravenna** (April 1512), together with defeat at **Novara** (1513), forces French withdrawal from Italy	French loss of Milan
1515–16. Accession of Francis I precipitated renewed French intervention in Italy. Francis secured his position by agreements with Charles of Burgundy and Henry VIII, and by a military alliance with Venice	French force defeated combined forces of the Emperor, the Pope, Milan and Naples at **Marignano** (Sept. 1515)	French regain Milan. **Concordat of Bologna** (Dec. 1515) in which papacy conceded to Francis substantial rights concerning the government of the Church in France. Treaty of **Noyon** (Aug. 1516) between Francis and Charles guaranteed French and Spanish possessions in Milan and Naples respectively
1521–6. Charles enhanced his position by closer relations with the papacy, especially with the election of Adrian VI (1522), and by the Treaty of **Bruges** (Aug. 1521) with Henry VIII	Milan and Genoa were seized by imperial forces (Nov. 1521 and May 1522), and a French counter-attack was defeated at **Bicocca** (April 1522)	
	French forces briefly reoccupied Milan (Oct. 1524), but then encountered complete military disaster at **Pavia** (Feb. 1525)	By the Treaty of **Madrid** (Jan. 1526) Francis surrendered his claims to Milan, Naples and Genoa. He also recognised Charles's rights to Flanders, Artois, Tournai and to the French lands of the Duchy of Burgundy

Precipitants	Narrative	Outcome
1526–9. Italian states now reacted to the dominance of Charles, and France was joined in the **League of Cognac** (May 1526) by Venice, Florence and the papacy	Charles aimed his main efforts at the papacy, but these plans misfired when imperial troops stormed and sacked Rome (May 1527), effectively ending the independent role of the papacy in European power politics	Charles and the Pope concluded peace by the Treaty of **Barcelona** (June 1529). Charles's possession of Naples was confirmed as was papal possession of territories recently acquired in central and northern Italy
	French ambitions in Italy were further undermined by defeat at **Landriano** (June 1529)	Charles and Francis made peace by the Treaty of **Cambrai** (Aug. 1529) which modified the Treaty of Madrid. Francis renounced all territorial claims in Flanders and Italy, while Charles abandoned his claims to the Burgundian lands within France.

In an attempt to undermine the opposition to him in Western Europe, Charles placed pressure upon the Pope. The Emperor's relatively subtle tactic of appealing to the College of Cardinals (May 1527) against the duplicity of Clement was quickly overtaken by spectacular catastrophe. An imperial army commanded by the renegade French nobleman Charles of Bourbon marched south from Milan, unpaid and uncontrolled, and took Rome by storm (6 May 1527). With Bourbon killed during the assault, his leaderless troops ravaged and pillaged Rome in one of the worst atrocities of the century, the more terrible because it was committed against the first city of Christendom.

The Sack of Rome was more remarkable for the sensation that it caused than for its immediate political consequences. Although it may be seen as playing an important role in the changing mentality of the papacy and in the development of the Counter-Reformation, the Sack failed to destroy the anti-Habsburg alliance. Instead, Henry VIII formally allied with France by the Treaty of Westminster (April 1527) to give that alliance a new dimension. If the League of Cognac could survive the Sack of Rome, however, it could not withstand the defection of one of its major Italian allies. In August 1528, Andrea Doria accepted a huge bribe from Charles, and took his Genoese fleet over to the Habsburgs. The French forces which had marched south to besiege Naples once more found themselves without vital Genoese naval support.

Largely deprived of the means to make an anti-Habsburg alliance work, Charles's main enemies moved towards peace in 1529. In June the Emperor and the Pope formally concluded peace by the Treaty of Barcelona. Only days before the treaty was signed, Francis had made one last attempt to regain the military initiative in Italy and had suffered another conclusive defeat, at Landriano (21 June 1529). For France, too, peace now seemed a more attractive prospect. The Peace of Cambrai (August 1529) modified the terms of the Treaty of Madrid in some important respects and was based upon military realities, rather than upon abstract dynastic ambitions. The new treaty granted Francis the territorial security which Madrid had denied, but recognised that Charles had gained an advantage in Italian affairs which could neither be denied nor reversed.

FRANCE ON THE DEFENSIVE, 1530–47

The events of 1525–9 altered the nature of Habsburg–Valois rivalry irreversibly. Charles V had established a superiority which could not be overcome. He had concluded two advantageous peace treaties, and had persuaded Pope Clement to crown him Emperor in Bologna in February 1530. The following year he secured the election of his brother, Ferdinand, as King of the Romans, so that the Imperial crown was safely in the possession of the Habsburgs for another generation at least. In Italy, too, the political situation was more favourable to Habsburg interests than at any time during the century.

Although Francis I could not effectively challenge this Habsburg ascendancy, the personal bitterness that existed between the two rulers made it impossible for the French king to accept the *status quo*. For the time being, all that he could do was to maintain diplomatic contacts with other enemies of the Emperor. French money, therefore, subsidised a political crisis in Württemberg in 1532, and by 1534 Francis had concluded formal alliances with both the Duke of Cleves and with Philip of Hesse. The annulment of Henry VIII's marriage to Catherine of Aragon severely strained Anglo-imperial relations, and in 1532 amicable conversations took place between Francis and the King of England. A year later, the marriage of the *dauphin* Henry to Catherine de Medici, niece to Pope Clement, improved Francis's relations with Italy. When, in 1534, Francis opened negotiations with Barbarossa, the Sultan's most dangerous agent in the western Mediterranean, it was clear that any enemy of Charles was eligible for French friendship.

The death of Francesco, the last Sforza Duke of Milan (1535), gave Francis the excuse to revive outdated and impracticable dynastic claims to the duchy. French forces occupied Savoy and Turin (1536), but received little Italian support. Charles retaliated by invading Provence (July 1536) with the aim of capturing Marseilles. There, persistent French resistance proved that Charles had badly underestimated the difficulties of his task, and some 8,000 men were lost through disease alone. From this stalemate, Pope Paul was eventually able to negotiate a Ten Years Truce at Nice (June 1538). Just as 1529 confirmed that Charles held the upper hand in Italy, 1538 confirmed that even the Emperor lacked the means to end French hostility once and for all.

The occasion for further trouble arose long before the expiry of the Ten Years Truce. The last round of largely personalised struggle between the two monarchs was fought on four fronts. In Italy, French forces failed to make any significant impact upon Milan. In the Pyrenees, too, they achieved little, the *dauphin* running into the same sort of resistance before Perpignan that Charles had encountered in Provence. Aided by the Duke of Cleves, the French had greater success in the north, causing extensive damage in the countryside around Antwerp and Louvain, but capturing neither city. Charles's rapid counter-attack against Cleves, on the other hand, drove the Duke out of the war, and opened a new phase in the conflict.

In this phase, Francis had to face the consequences of a major diplomatic miscalculation. His sensational decision to assist the Turkish fleet in its assault on Nice (August 1543), and then to allow Barbarossa to winter in the French port of Toulon, caused unanimous outrage in a Europe which saw the Turk as the greatest threat to their civilisation. German princes with little love for the Emperor now joined Charles against an enemy whose behaviour had passed beyond the accepted norms. At the same time, Charles renewed friendship with Henry VIII of England, and the two monarchs both declared war on France (June 1543). With the English operating in the region of Boulogne and the Emperor attacking from the east, Francis was probably closer to ultimate disaster than ever before. Imperial troops captured Saint Dizier, and were at Meaux, a mere forty miles or so from Paris, by the summer of 1544.

The proximity of disaster drove Francis to conclude his last peace treaty with his great rival. The Peace of Crépy (September 1544) revealed how, in Charles's mind, the struggle with Francis now took second place to the religious problems of Germany. Francis agreed to support Charles in his demand for the summoning of a General Council of the Church, and in return the Emperor showed himself willing to make a major territorial concession. A marriage alliance was planned between the Duke of Orléans and either the daughter or the niece of Charles, with either Milan or the Netherlands handed over as the bride's dowry. To Charles's huge relief, the death of Orléans (September 1545) released him from this disagreeable section of the treaty.

THE WARS OF HENRY II

To the siege of Metz, 1547–53

Within eighteen months, Francis's own death (March 1547) brought to the throne his son, Henry II. The new King of France bore a personal hatred towards Charles more bitter than his father's, rooted in fierce resentment at his three years' captivity as a hostage in Spain. 'Inheriting the Burgundian–Valois feud', writes F.J. Baumgartner (*Henry II, King of France, 1547–1559*, 1984), 'Henry added to them a personal antagonism toward Charles that went to the core of his being. Nothing motivated Henry quite as much as the thought that some action he could take might injure the Emperor.' Henry differed from his father, however, in his strategy. Less concerned with dynastic claims in Italy, he seems to have viewed the dispute with the Emperor as a power struggle, pure and simple, which needed to be prosecuted in those areas where his enemy was most vulnerable. Gradually, the focus of European great-power conflict moved away from Italy, to Germany and to the Netherlands.

Henry's great diplomatic breakthrough came in 1552. By the Treaty of Chambord (January 1552), he overcame his doctrinal hostility towards the German Protestant princes, and agreed to act as their protector and the guarantor of their liberties against Charles. In return the princes agreed that the French should take possession of the fortified cities of Metz, Toul and Verdun, within the imperial borders. Metz, in particular, was of great strategic significance, raising the possibility that the French might sever communications between Charles's Dutch possessions and southern Germany.

It was a threat that Charles could not ignore. He responded to the occupation of Metz by the Duke of Guise with one of the greatest military efforts of his career. His personal presence during much of the four-month siege, the expenditure of some 2 million ducats, and the deployment of 80,000 men, all bore witness to the importance that Charles attached to the undertaking. Yet all was in vain. By the opening of 1553 the siege had been abandoned, and its substantial consequences could be assessed. Guise and his royal master could claim that they had achieved more against the Habsburgs than

Francis had in a lifetime. The effect upon Charles was crushing, and many commentators have seen the great failure before Metz as a major factor in the breakdown which led to the Emperor's abdication.

To the treaty of Câteau-Cambrésis, 1553–9

Between October 1555 and September 1556, Charles abdicated his various offices and retired from public life. By inheriting his father's titles in Spain, in Italy and in the Low Countries, Philip II became the direct heir to the Habsburg–Valois feud. One of his earliest actions in this respect was to conclude the Truce of Vaucelles (February 1556) with France, a suspension of hostilities that was quickly undermined, especially by the resentment of Pope Paul IV at Spain's occupation of his Neapolitan homeland. When Spanish patience was exhausted and the Duke of Alva marched into the States of the Church, the Pope's appeal for French protection ended the truce.

The decisive battle of this last great Habsburg–Valois clash was fought in Flanders. At Saint-Quentin (7 August 1557) the French forces commanded by the Constable Montmorency were overwhelmed by the Spanish. Montmorency and a host of other French notables were captured. It was a disaster for French arms paralleled only by Pavia. It also spelled the end of French campaigns in Italy, as forces in the south were rushed north to head off any threat to the capital. The capture of Calais from the English, by the Duke of Guise, provided only a little consolation as Henry once more contemplated making peace with his enemy.

The Treaty of Câteau-Cambrésis (April 1559), nevertheless, represented a reasonable and viable compromise, reflecting the fact that, whatever the advantages of the Habsburgs during forty-five years of dynastic struggle, those struggles had proved that two 'superpowers' existed in Western Europe, neither able wholly to eradicate the other. The settlement endured because of the very different circumstances under which it was signed. There was not the personal hatred between Henry and Philip that existed between their fathers or between Henry and Charles. The division of the Empire upon Charles's abdication had lessened the direct threat of Habsburg power to France. The death of

Mary Tudor (November 1558), which entailed the collapse of the Anglo-Spanish marriage alliance, also improved France's diplomatic position considerably. Above all, neither France nor Spain could sustain the struggle as they had before, for both states had declared themselves bankrupt in 1557. Even so, we will never know whether the peace would have lasted had not Henry II met his death (July 1559) in a jousting accident during a tournament held to celebrate the peace. The removal of his authority, and the subsequent descent into civil war, left France for the rest of the century with greater preoccupations than the rivalry between her rulers and the Habsburgs.

• CHAPTER TEN •

Henry VIII:
The Ascendancy of Wolsey

The historical debate

The young king

The rise of Wolsey

The status of Wolsey

English foreign policy

Wolsey and the government of the realm

Wolsey and the Church

Wolsey and faction

The origins of the royal divorce

The struggle for the divorce

A late medieval image of monarchy: the king as chivalric champion.
Henry VIII jousts in the presence of Queen Catherine in a
tournament mounted in 1511 to celebrate the
birth of a baby son, who died shortly afterwards

THE HISTORICAL DEBATE

Writers investigating the reign of Henry VIII have focused consistently upon two elements. Henry's forceful and ruthless character impressed all observers, even if it horrified some, while the defeat of foreign ecclesiastical influence during his reign, and the foundation of the Church of England, gave Henry a special place in the affections of Anglicans and patriots.

Such a 'nationalistic' approach to the reign reached its peak in the early twentieth century in the work of A.F. Pollard. He accepted the 'New Monarchy' ideas, recently formulated with regard to the reign of Henry VII, and adapted them to highlight the development of the English nation state during the reign of his son. In this process the establishment of a national Church was paralleled by the resurrection of Parliament and by the king's nurturing of a middle-class, managerial caste in place of the old feudal aristocracy. Henry himself was acclaimed as the author and prime mover of the whole process. For Pollard, 'this self-willed tyrant was a man of cosmic genius' (J. Kenyon, *The History Men*, 1983).

Pollard's interpretations remained largely unchallenged until the 1950s. Since then, however, two outstanding historians have launched their own forms of revision. G.R. Elton published *The Tudor Revolution in Government* in 1953. It challenged the notion of the 'New Monarchy' under Edward IV and Henry VII by placing the great administrative transformation in the latter part of Henry VIII's reign. In addition, he firmly attributed it to a great minister, Thomas Cromwell, rather than to the king. Elton later modified these conclusions, but the essential notion of a decade of radical activity in English administration remained firmly established.

The second revisionist was J.J. Scarisbrick (*Henry VIII*, 1968). The king portrayed by Scarisbrick is forceful and impressive, but his personality is flawed by inconsistency, vainglory and a tendency to be swayed by the arguments of faction. He is the author of the broad lines of policy, but never the man to provide detail or to steer his policy through practical difficulties. For this he depended entirely upon his servants. As Elton

rehabilitated Cromwell, so Scarisbrick undermined Pollard's dismissal of Wolsey as a corrupt anachronism, a servant who put the interests of the papacy before those of his royal master. Scarisbrick's portrait of a sincere, if inconsistent humanist, of an immensely able diplomat working in the interests of peace and of his master's prestige, has been broadly confirmed by the work of Peter Gwyn (*The King's Cardinal*, 1990). In recent years David Starkey (*The Reign of Henry VIII: Personalities and Politics*, 1985) has also shed much new light upon Henry's reign. Concentrating upon the workings of the court and of the factions within it, he has added to the now widely accepted picture of Henry as a powerful personality, who was nevertheless not always in control of the intrigues that went on around him.

THE YOUNG KING

The extraordinary optimism that greeted the accession of the young Henry VIII (April 1509) was largely an expression of dissatisfaction with the governmental and financial methods of his father. The new king was an athlete, a musician of great enthusiasm and some talent, and a young man of considerable academic ability, if of limited academic appetite. Henry seemed to many contemporaries to represent the ideal of monarchy. In his prime, his size and strength and his enthusiasm for military sports made him the focus of his court, while his musical interests, his linguistic ability and his very respectable knowledge of theology made it impossible to dismiss him as a man with muscle in the place of brain.

The young king quickly took two steps which confirmed the clean break with the previous reign. The arrest of Richard Empson and Edmund Dudley, the two most unpopular financial agents of Henry VII, signalled the rejection of his father's unsavoury methods. At the same time, the decision to marry the Princess Catherine, the widow of his elder brother, directly reversed Henry VII's diplomatic policy.

Beyond these two events, what course would the new reign take? To a large extent the hopes of contemporary humanists were disappointed. Henry moved with far greater determination back into the medieval world of the warrior king than into that of the Renaissance 'philosopher prince'. Only rarely, and then in the latter part of his reign, did he show any serious interest in political reform. On the other hand, Henry quickly demonstrated that his natural enemy was the King of France, and that the road to follow was the one that led back to Crécy and to Agincourt. Henry was 'the last of the troubadours and the heir of Burgundian chivalry: a youth wholly absorbed in dance and song, courtly love and knight-errantry' (J.J. Scarisbrick).

THE RISE OF WOLSEY

At the beginning of his reign Henry VIII faced few of the problems that beset his father in 1485. He inherited a governmental system ruthlessly adapted to the specific purposes of the crown. His throne was relatively untroubled by pretenders or by dynastic rivals, and he inherited a council of experienced ministers of proven competence and loyalty. There were few new appointments at the highest level, and few people would have grasped the significance of the appointment (April 1509) of Thomas Wolsey, a protégé of Foxe, to the post of King's Almoner.

Wolsey entered the king's service at a relatively advanced age (b. c.1473). He had enjoyed a brilliant academic career in his youth, but had enjoyed mixed fortunes in his search for influential patrons, those leading court figures whose favour was essential if someone of more humble origins were to succeed in public life. Only in 1507 did his appointment as royal chaplain enable him to display his talents in the highest circles. At the opening of the new reign he appears to have come to the king's notice through the desire of such men as Foxe, Warham and Lovell to ease their administrative burdens while maintaining their political influence with the king.

Traditionally, Wolsey's subsequent rise has been explained in terms of Henry's style of kingship. Whereas Henry VII oversaw the detail of government to a remarkable degree, his son was bored by detail and routine, and was in the market for an industrious servant to bear such burdens. The years 1512–13 marked the decisive phase in

Wolsey's early career, as he demonstrated his immense administrative talents in directing the organisation of the wars with France. Such a view has been modified by writers who have seen Henry as more than a political dilettante. 'Where it is possible to follow the king at work over a period of time', Peter Gwyn has judged, 'what is striking is his close attention to business, and the strong feeling that he was very much in control of everything that was being done on his behalf.' In Gwyn's opinion, Henry saw in Wolsey a partner in administration rather than a substitute, and their long political relationship owed more to mutual respect than to the simple exploitation of Wolsey's talents by a lazy monarch.

THE STATUS OF WOLSEY

Wolsey quickly reaped the rewards of efficient service. He had a seat on the royal Council by 1511, and was appointed to a succession of ecclesiastical posts. The deanery of York (1513) was followed by the bishoprics of Tournai (1513–18), Lincoln (1514), Bath and Wells (1518–23), Durham (1523–9) and Winchester (1529–30). Wolsey became Archbishop of York in 1514, and was made a cardinal a year later. He never became Archbishop of Canterbury, because William Warham outlived him, but he came to outrank Warham by other means. Wolsey replaced him as Lord Chancellor, the highest political office in the land (1515), and effectively outranked him within the English Church once Pope Leo X had granted him the title of **Legate** *a Latere* (1518). Thereby Wolsey became the Pope's direct representative in England.

From the end of Henry's first French war until the end of the 1520s, there was only one royal minister who really mattered. Outwardly, contemporaries had every reason to believe that, at the height of his career, Wolsey was virtually, as the Venetian ambassador called him, *alter rex* ('the other king'). He displayed his authority lavishly, notably by the transformation of Hampton Court into a palace such as the king himself did not possess. Important as it was for a great servant of the state to display his power in this way, the notion that Wolsey was effectively usurping the authority of the monarch proved a popular line of attack among his contemporary enemies.

Yet Wolsey did not in any real sense usurp the king's power. He ruled the realm in the sense that all the details of government were ultimately in his hands. In administrative terms, in both Church and state, he held a monopoly of power that is unique in English experience. Yet, bored as he may have been with administrative detail, Henry never tired of the reality of political power. The key to Wolsey's position, therefore, lay not in his collection of offices, but in the trust felt and the power delegated by the only man in the realm who possessed real power. Wolsey gave substance and detail to broad lines of policy that he knew to be acceptable to the king. So far from poaching upon the king's **prerogative**, Wolsey rarely forgot that palaces and offices meant nothing if the royal trust were lost.

ENGLISH FOREIGN POLICY

Principles and early directions

English foreign policy in the first half of Henry's reign was unlike that in any other period of the sixteenth century. Relieved both of domestic anxieties and of Continental threats, the king had a unique opportunity to indulge himself in a search for glory and gain before more prosaic preoccupations reasserted themselves in the course of the 1520s. At the start of his reign Henry clearly considered it the primary aim of his monarchy to pursue an aggressive and prestigious foreign policy, based upon war with France in order to reassert traditional claims to the French throne and to such territories as Gascony, Guyenne and Normandy.

Acting in conjunction with Julius II's Holy League, English arms quickly achieved their greatest Continental successes of the sixteenth century, defeating an unimpressive French force at the 'Battle of the Spurs' (August 1513) and occupying Tournai and Thérouanne. A further victory, over France's Scottish allies at Flodden (September 1513), utterly destroyed the northern threat to Henry's kingdom.

Despite the successes of 1512–14, England did not fight on the Continent again for nine years.

One reason for this was the staggering cost of the wars, official expenditure totalling £111,455 in 1512, where £5,706 had sufficed the year before. A further reason lay in the fact that the detailed direction of foreign policy after 1514 lay in the hands of Thomas Wolsey. For many years historians accepted A.F. Pollard's thesis that the shifts and changes in Wolsey's foreign policy were dictated by the interests of the papacy. Wolsey, in short, sacrificed the king's interests in order to retain his legatine powers, and perhaps even to become Pope himself. J.J. Scarisbrick rejected this argument because he could find no other evidence that Wolsey sought to win favour or to build up support in Rome. He also found it unrealistic to imagine that Henry, so keen to pursue his own foreign policy in 1512–13, should abdicate direction and allow foreign policy to become a vehicle for the ambitions of his servant. In any case, as relatively minor states in a Europe dominated by France and the Empire, England and the papacy had very similar interests. Scarisbrick portrayed Wolsey instead as a loyal servant, horrified by the expense of war. He thus worked for a balance in European diplomacy that would ensure peace and the containment of France without the loss of Henry's prestige. If such a policy brought Wolsey personal prestige as 'the arbiter of Europe', so much the better. The king, however, remained the ultimate authority, and his demands for an active role in Continental affairs, combined with European developments that were quite beyond English control, meant that Wolsey was frequently forced anyway to commit England to renewed warfare on the European mainland.

1514–18: The search for European prestige

England ended her war with France (1514) because of its cost and because of her lack of allies. The treaty that ended the war collapsed within months, however, owing to the sudden death of Louis XII and the accession of Francis I, a king with little interest in peace.

In 1515, Wolsey was faced with the problem of maintaining Henry's high profile in a Europe potentially dominated by the young French king. Henry's attempts to construct an anti-French alliance by subsidising the campaigns of Spain and the Emperor were based upon an absurd overestimate of England's Continental influence. They failed in every respect. When Maximilian and his grandson Charles served their own interests by concluding peace with France, English foreign policy lay in ruins. Between 1517 and 1519, Wolsey rescued something from this wreck, only to be overtaken again by events beyond England's control. The conclusion of the Treaty of London (1518) must be seen as the high point of Wolsey's diplomacy. It also illustrates very clearly Wolsey's attempts to achieve his master's foreign aims by the cheaper means of diplomacy, and shows the limits of the cardinal's cooperation with the papacy. By 1517, England and Leo X were equally outgunned by France and equally convinced that they could only contain France by diplomatic means. When the Pope sought a respite, however, by the traditional means of summoning a crusade against the infidel, his peace initiative was effectively hijacked by Wolsey. Exploiting the visit of Cardinal Campeggio, he assembled the representatives of some twenty-five princes in London, and secured from them an agreement that their masters would condemn and resist any act of aggression on the Continent. At the same time, separate agreements for the return of Tournai to France, and for the marriage of Henry's daughter to the *dauphin*, greatly eased Anglo-French tensions.

This Treaty of London did not last, and thus it has often been dismissed as a mere exercise in egoism. It remains probable, however, that Wolsey was sincere, and he had temporarily outflanked the Pope in his role as European peacemaker. If the prominence and prestige of the crown were the primary aims of foreign policy, then that policy reached its highest point in the Treaty of London.

1519–29: From imperial alliance to international isolation

The Treaty of London, nevertheless, was wholly at the mercy of shifts in 'great power' politics over which England exercised no control. The momentous victory of Charles V in the imperial election (June 1519) caused the greatest of these shifts. It left Henry 'as no more than a petty potentate whom the might and range of this new empire must outdistance even more obviously than did the kingdom of France' (J.J. Scarisbrick). To make matters worse, Henry's own candidature in the election had been brushed aside as an irrelevance.

With Charles's success, confrontation became almost inevitable between the new Emperor and the King of France. The peace established by the Treaty of London was doomed, but on the other hand neither side could now ignore the advantages of England's friendship. The period 1520–1 saw some prolonged and spectacular diplomatic negotiations. The meeting between Henry and Francis outside Calais at 'The Field of the Cloth of Gold' was sumptuous but unproductive. The Emperor, meanwhile, met Henry at Canterbury (May) and Gravelines (July), and concluded the Treaty of Bruges in August 1521. Perhaps this agreement simply reflected Henry's overriding desire to be on the winning side in an anti-French coalition. Perhaps, as R.B. Wernham (*Before the Armada*, 1966) has argued, he was already concerned at this early date about the succession, for an agreement was reached that the Princess Mary would marry Charles V himself, a marriage that would guarantee her safe and peaceful accession.

The conflict that resulted from this diplomacy merely confirmed that England was out of her depth, diplomatically, militarily and financially. The Duke of Suffolk's offensive in northern France (1523–4) was an expensive fiasco, and when the French were routed by Charles at Pavia (1525) Wolsey's failure to raise sufficient funds through the **Amicable Grant** left Henry unable to afford a further offensive. Nor did it suit Charles to keep any of the major promises that he had made to the English. Having promised to support Henry's candidate, Wolsey, in the next papal elections, he first engineered the election of his former tutor as Adrian VI (1521), and subsequently sponsored the Medici candidate who succeeded as Clement VII (1523). The Emperor's marriage to Isabella of Portugal (1526), in order to protect his Iberian interests, was the final snub to Tudor ambitions.

Between 1525 and 1529 English foreign policy drifted at the mercy of the political winds prevailing upon the Continent. To add to the confusion, this policy was driven by two distinct and sometimes contradictory sets of priorities. For

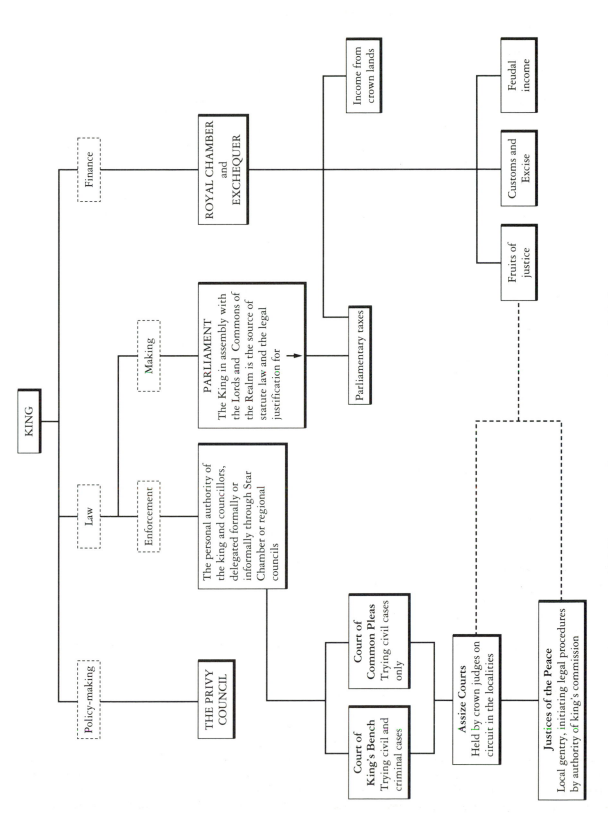

KING

Policy-making

Law

Making

Enforcement

Finance

THE PRIVY COUNCIL

PARLIAMENT
The King in assembly with the Lords and Commons of the Realm is the source of statute law and the legal justification for

ROYAL CHAMBER and EXCHEQUER

The personal authority of the king and councillors, delegated formally or informally through Star Chamber or regional councils

Court of King's Bench
Trying civil and criminal cases

Court of Common Pleas
Trying civil cases only

Assize Courts
Held by crown judges on circuit in the localities

Justices of the Peace
Local gentry, initiating legal procedures by authority of king's commission

Parliamentary taxes

Income from crown lands

Customs and Excise

Feudal income

Fruits of justice

10.1 The structure of government under the early Tudors

Wolsey, as for most European diplomats, the most important task was to undo the damage done by Charles's victory at Pavia. At the same time, Henry's direct intervention became more frequent as the matter of the queen's sterility, and the safe continuation of the dynasty, played increasingly upon his mind. The anti-imperial League of Cognac (1526) was supported only with fair words and a relatively small sum of money. Once that alliance had collapsed in the catastrophe of the Sack of Rome (1527), leaving the Pope in Charles's hands, Wolsey was forced into more direct action. He encountered significant rebuffs on two fronts. His audacious project of establishing himself in Avignon at the head of a papal government 'in exile', empowered to restore the peace of Europe and to satisfy Henry's marital requirements, met with absolutely no cooperation from other powers. Diplomacy proved equally unsuccessful. By agreeing (January 1529) to join France in the armed struggle against the Emperor, Wolsey effectively admitted the failure of his policy of peace and arbitration. The crumbling of the alliance a year later, in the Treaties of Cambrai and Barcelona, constituted the final defeat of his efforts to keep his master in the forefront of European decision-making. Even so, it makes less sense to see this as proof of the cardinal's misguidedness than to view it as the inevitable collapse of a policy forced upon him by the unreasoning ambition of his royal master. What is remarkable is that Wolsey was able to sustain the credibility of those ambitions for two decades.

WOLSEY AND THE GOVERNMENT OF THE REALM

Law

As Lord Chancellor from 1515, Wolsey was also responsible for those other great obsessions of Tudor monarchy: the application of the king's laws and the maintenance of good order. Historians have often contrasted his work in these respects with the fundamental reorganisation that was undertaken after his fall. To G.R. Elton, for instance, Wolsey was 'this superb amateur in government'. Yet contemporaries would have seen no reason why the essentially medieval machinery of Henry VII's reign should not have continued to fulfil its purposes if operated with sufficient energy.

Wolsey's greatest strength in domestic administration was indeed the enormous energy he brought to a system that still operated largely through personal charisma and authority. Here, too, his extraordinary capacity for work was his greatest recommendation. For six months of every year, the Lord Chancellor spent the greater part of every morning hearing cases in Westminster Hall. There seems little reason to doubt that Wolsey's main objective was to apply the king's law consistently to all the king's subjects. His main weapon was the committee of the Royal Council sitting at Westminster, in the Star Chamber. Research by J.A. Guy (*The Cardinal's Court*, 1977) has confirmed that Wolsey transformed an informal and loosely defined body into a settled institution of the realm. A body that had tried an average of thirteen cases a year under Henry VII heard 120 a year under Wolsey; and here, according to the chronicler Hall, 'he punished lords, knights and men of all sorts for riots, bearing and maintenance in their countries, so that poor men lived quietly'. Another body, which would develop into the Court of Requests, took this work further by hearing the complaints of poor men who were unlikely to get a fair hearing in the local courts. Such methods had one great weakness. They relied heavily upon Wolsey's personal authority and upon 'equity', that is upon his personal notion of justice, rather than upon the objective rule of law. Many historians have concluded that an important result of Wolsey's legal administration was that it caused tension between the cardinal and many of the common lawyers, whose mastery of objective law was the basis of their livelihood.

Wolsey's reliance upon energy and charisma is also evident in his attempts to curb **enclosures**. In 1514 and 1515, before he became Chancellor, new Acts forbidding unauthorised enclosure had been added to those of Henry VII's reign. Wolsey's proclamations of 1527 and 1528 suggest that these had been widely ignored, and that the cardinal could do little to improve the situation, other than to summon individual offenders before such courts as Star Chamber.

Finance

An equally important function of Wolsey's office was to provide the money that would pay for the king's policies. While war was an enormously expensive business, peace did not come cheaply either. The Emperor Maximilian was paid £80,000 in subsidies (1515–16) to favour English interests, while it cost £40,000 a year to defend the city of Tournai, all this at a time when the crown's revenue from its own resources produced only about £25,000 a year.

Wolsey's approach to the problem was imaginative and energetic. He produced unprecedented sums from traditional sources and exploited new sources, although by the end of his career he had done little to establish any long-term solution to the growing problem of heavy royal expenditure. Above all, Wolsey was a prodigious exploiter of parliamentary taxation, largely responsible for one innovation in national taxation, the subsidy. Five such subsidies (1513–15 and 1523) raised a total of £322,000, as well as £118,000 through the older method of tenths and fifteenths. In addition, some £240,000 was raised between 1515 and 1529 through taxation of the clergy. Traditional sources, however, could not meet the demand, and Wolsey was also compelled to use more devious means, raising £260,000 through a series of 'forced loans' (1522–3).

WOLSEY AND THE CHURCH

Wolsey's powers over the Church in England were even more comprehensive than those delegated to him by the king. His appointment as Legate *a Latere* in 1518, and the Pope's unusual step of renewing these legatine powers at regular intervals, left Wolsey effectively more powerful than Archbishop Warham. Faced only by 'an old and broken man, long inured to personal impotence' (A.G. Dickens), Wolsey exercised unqualified control over all Church functions and offices in England.

One of the most consistent charges against Wolsey is that he wasted a unique opportunity to right the many abuses and weaknesses within the English Church. Instead, his critics allege, he prepared the way for the royal assault upon the Church by lowering the morale of the clergy and by leaving it

alienated by its recent taste of indirect papal control. Similarly, his monopoly of ecclesiastical authority left the Church without the leadership to resist the king's will. The truth seems to be that, while Wolsey did not fully exploit his position for the benefit of the Church, he did not wholly abuse it either. His record on Church appointments, for instance, is ambiguous. There is much evidence that in making lesser appointments Wolsey showed genuine concern for the nomination of fitting and able candidates, even coming into open and successful opposition to the king in 1528 over his refusal to appoint a lady of doubtful reputation as Abbess of Wilton. On the other hand, he was not above using Church appointments to further his own or the king's political interests, as in the appointment of Italian bishops to English sees. Cardinal Campeggio became Bishop of Salisbury (1524) in the hope that his gratitude might serve English interests in Rome. In addition, his foundation of Cardinal College (now Christ Church) at Oxford (1527), with a grammar school at Ipswich, shows that Wolsey's professed interest in Christian humanism was more than mere fashionable posturing.

Yet it remains hard to acquit Wolsey of two charges. Despite his summons of the English clergy to Westminster (1519) to consider the reform of the Church, he achieved very little in that respect. His plans for the reorganisation of the English and Irish bishoprics were unfulfilled at the time of his fall. It is also hard to deny that, in his personal conduct, Wolsey set a poor example and presented a poor image of the Church. Instead he presented an object lesson in most of those classic ecclesiastical abuses, pluralism, simony and absenteeism, against which even the mildest reformers of the day protested.

WOLSEY AND FACTION

Wolsey could have achieved none of his successes in domestic politics had he not maintained the upper hand for so long in the factional struggles that were central to the political life of the Henrician court. Frequently absent from court, and unpopular with many courtiers on account of his birth, bearing or power, Wolsey was highly vulnerable to such intrigues, yet played the game with enormous skill

10.2 Cardinal Wolsey and his enemies

Source A Within the last few days, His Majesty has made a very great change in the court here, dismissing four of his chief lords-in-waiting, who enjoyed extreme authority in the kingdom. The French ambassador considers that this took place either from suspicion about the affairs of France, or at the instigation of Cardinal Wolsey, who, perceiving the aforesaid to be so intimate with the king that in the course of time they might have ousted him from the government, anticipated them, under pretence of their being youths of evil counsel, an opinion which I fully share. By this, the said Cardinal of York will secure the king entirely to himself, extremely to the displeasure of all the grandees of the kingdom.

Letter from the Venetian ambassador to the Venetian Senate, 1519

Source B

Ye are so puffed up with pride,
That no man may abide
Your high and lordly looks:
And virtue is forgotten;
For then ye will be wroken
Of every light quarrel,
And call a lord a iauell [i.e. a fool];
A knight a knave ye make;
Ye boast, ye face, ye crake,
And upon you ye take
To rule both king and kaiser.

Men say how ye appall [i.e. detest]
The noble blood royal
Therefore ye keep them base,
And mock them to their face:
This is a piteous case,
To you that over the weal
Great lords must crouch and kneel
And break their hose at the knee,
As daily men may see.

From 'Colin Clout', an anti-clerical satire by the poet John Skelton, 1522.
Skelton was a protégé of the Duke of Norfolk

Source C And for your realm, Our Lord be thanked, it was never in such peace or tranquillity: for all this summer I have had neither of riot, felony, nor forcible entry, but that your laws be in every place indifferently [i.e. fairly] ministered, without leaning [i.e. bias] in any manner. Albeit there hath lately been a fray between Pygot, your

and success until the great cataclysm of the royal divorce.

Throughout the 1520s Wolsey guarded his position by ensuring that the king was not surrounded by those who might poison the royal mind against him. He won a notable victory in 1519 by securing the expulsion from court of royal companions such as Nicholas Carew and William Carey. Contemporaries also saw the cardinal's hand in Henry's great assault upon the feudal aristocracy

which led to the execution of the Duke of Buckingham (1521). Wolsey's one major reform of the royal household may also be seen as a significant success in the factional struggle. The Ordinances of Eltham (January 1526) reviewed the size and the running of the household and of the Privy Chamber, but in the process excluded a number of individuals hostile to the cardinal.

By such means, and by close and careful attention to the king's political wishes, Wolsey

sergeant and Sir Andrew Windsor's servants, for the seizure of a ward whereto they both pretend titles, in the which fray one man was slain. I trust at the next term to teach them the law of Star Chamber, which, God willing, they shall have indifferently ministered to them according to their deserts.

Letter from Wolsey to the king, written 1517 or 1518

Source D But to tell you the number of people of the country that were assembled at the gates which lamented his [Wolsey's] departing was wondrous, which was about three thousand persons; who at the opening of the gates, after they had a sight of his person, cried all with a loud voice, 'God save your Grace! The foul evil take all them that hath thus taken you from us! We pray God that a very vengeance may light upon them!' Thus they ran crying after him through the town of Cawood, they loved him so well. For surely they had a great loss of him, both the poor and the rich: for the poor had of him great relief; and the rich lacked his counsel in any business that they had to do, which caused him to have such love among them in the country [i.e. locality].

George Cavendish, Wolsey's gentleman-usher, describing Wolsey's departure from Cawood, Yorkshire, after his arrest for treason, 1530

Source E Please it your most royal Majesty therefore of your excellent goodness towards the Weal [i.e. wellbeing] of this your Realm, to set such order and direction upon the said Lord Cardinal as may be to the terrible example of others to beware so to offend your Grace and your laws hereafter: And that he may be so provided for, that he never have any power, jurisdiction or authority, hereafter to trouble, vex and impoverish the commonwealth of your realm, as he hath done heretofore, to the great hurt and damage of every man almost, high and low.

From the speech of Lord Chancellor More, opening proceedings against Wolsey, 1530

QUESTIONS

a. Explain the meaning of the following phrases which occur in the extracts above: 'to rule both king and kaiser' (source B); 'for the seizure of a ward whereto they both pretend title' (source C); 'the law of Star Chamber' (source C); 'for the poor had of him great relief' (source D).

b. To what extent can the historian accept each or any of the documents above as an objective or unbiased record?

c. Sir Thomas More claims in source E that Wolsey had done 'great hurt and damage to every man almost, high and low'. To what extent do the other documents support this claim?

d. 'Wolsey was predominantly unpopular with the nobility, which he excluded from real influence in the government of the realm.' How far do these documents, and other evidence known to you, support this statement?

retained Henry's trust for a decade and a half. The next and fatal assault, however, came from quite a different quarter.

THE ORIGINS OF THE ROYAL DIVORCE

Between 1525 and 1529, Henry drifted into the decision to divorce his queen. A marriage that originally seemed warm and successful had run into a variety of problems. Above all, it had failed to provide Henry with a male heir. The king's fears for the future of his dynasty were sincere, and seemed to be becoming obsessive when he launched a bizarre project (1525) to legitimise his bastard son, Henry, Duke of Richmond. From 1525, furthermore, when Henry moved away from the Habsburg alliance, Catherine also represented a defunct diplomatic attachment.

The issue of the succession was transformed when Henry fell in love with another woman. Anne Boleyn was the daughter of a prominent courtier and the vivacious, sexy opposite of the pious, ageing Catherine. Henry's rapid infatuation confronted Wolsey with complex political problems, for Anne now stood in the way of the French marriage with which he hoped to redirect English diplomacy. More serious still, the Boleyns were a branch of the Howard family, and Anne herself was niece to Wolsey's great rival at court, the Duke of Norfolk. The fact that the Boleyn name was increasingly associated with ideas of religious reform further suggested that the reign was entering a new political phase which would test Wolsey's capabilities to the full.

The struggle for the divorce

On the face of it, Henry's prospects of gaining a divorce on the grounds of political convenience were bright. The papacy had set recent precedents, most notably in freeing Louis XII of France to marry Anne of Brittany. Henry also had a viable though inconclusive case in canon law, based upon the biblical text: 'Thou shalt not uncover the nakedness of thy brother's wife: it is thy brother's nakedness' (Leviticus 20.21). By Henry's interpretation, Catherine's barrenness was the direct result of God's anger. Unfortunately, the Book of Deuteronomy contained a contradictory command that actually instructed a man to marry the widow of a deceased brother. This theological wrangle occupied the first year of Henry's battle for his divorce, and increasingly it appeared to be a losing battle. By 1528 a number of the most learned theologians in Europe had given their opinion that Holy Scripture favoured Catherine.

In the midst of such abstract disputes, the issue was really decided by power politics. The fall of Rome to the forces of Charles V (1527) was a serious blow to Henry, compromising the Pope's freedom of action in the case. The Emperor, indeed, was a consistent opponent of the divorce, primarily because he assumed that Henry would use his liberty to construct a French alliance. While ambassadors pestered the Pope to comply with

Henry's requests, or to grant Wolsey the authority to act for him, Clement VII prevaricated. Cardinal Campeggio was indeed sent to England to try the case with Wolsey (September 1528), but was under orders to play for time. When, in mid-1529, Clement finally ordered that the case be referred to Rome, it became clear that Henry had little hope of success through papal channels.

That fact spelled the end for Wolsey. His legatine powers had achieved precisely nothing, the king's confidence in him was shaken, and he was now more vulnerable than ever to his enemies at court. Long-term hostilities were now compounded by the fact that Anne Boleyn herself was no friend to the cardinal, and was now closer to Henry than any other. By September 1529, Wolsey was sinking. Convicted on charges of *Praemunire,* the offence of diminishing the king's authority by procuring power and judgements from Rome, he was allowed to retire to York to attend at last to his duties as archbishop. Framed by the enemies who now surrounded the king at court, he was charged with treason (November 1530), but died of natural causes on his way to London to face trial.

10.3 Glossary

Amicable Grant. A ploy used by Wolsey in 1526 to secure taxation without parliamentary approval. In theory the money raised was a free gift granted by taxpayers to the crown. The project was abandoned after riots against it in East Anglia.

Enclosures. The fencing off of farmlands, usually undertaken either to consolidate personal land-holdings or to facilitate the conversion of the land from crop production to the grazing of livestock, usually sheep.

Forced loans. Another method of raising taxation without the permission of Parliament. In this case the grant was to be seen as a loan to the crown, liable in theory to be repaid from future income.

Legate (*Legatus a Latere*). A papal official entrusted with special ecclesiastical authority in order to carry out a specific mission (Latin: *legatus* = messenger) to a foreign court. 'Legatine' is the adjective from 'legate'.

Prerogative. Usually applied to a particular set of royal powers, necessary for the government of the realm and beyond the competence of Parliament. These included issues of foreign alliance, of war and peace and of marriage. After the Reformation, the monarch's powers as head of the Church were also regarded as prerogative powers.

Further reading

S.J. Gunn and P.G. Lindley (1991) *Cardinal Wolsey: Church, State and Art.* Cambridge.

Peter Gwyn (1990) *The King's Cardinal: The Rise and Fall of Thomas Wolsey.* London.

J.J. Scarisbrick (1968) *Henry VIII.* London.

David Starkey (1985) *The Reign of Henry VIII: Personalities and Politics.* London.

• CHAPTER ELEVEN •

The Henrician Reformation

The historical debate

The English Church –

– and its opponents: Lollardy and Lutheranism

Anti-clericalism

The royal divorce: the failure of a papal solution

Erastianism

Thomas Cromwell

The Reformation statutes

The dissolution of the monasteries

Resistance and the Pilgrimage of Grace

The Church of England

The Reformation in the localities

A revolution in government?

Royal authority in the distant localities

Social reform

Foreign policy and the Reformation, 1538–40

Foreign policy: France and Scotland, 1540–7

The final years: the rule of faction

A new image for the English monarchy: Henry VIII as the defender and champion of true religion. Enthroned, with Bible and sword of state, Henry triumphs over the Pope. The engraving identifies the crown's major servants in this enterprise, Cromwell and Cranmer

THE HISTORICAL DEBATE

Over the last half-century the debate over the nature of the English Reformation has produced four broad 'models' of the movement. Two of them view it as a movement 'from above', initiated by the leaders of the nation, and generally imposed upon the population as a whole. For G.R. Elton (*The Tudor Revolution in Government*, 1953) or for Peter Clark (*English Provincial Society from the Reformation to the Revolution*, 1977) the process was a relatively rapid and successful one, so that 'by 1553 England was almost certainly nearer to being a Protestant country than to anything else' (G.R. Elton). Other writers, such as Penry Williams (*The Tudor Regime*, 1979) and J.J. Scarisbrick (*The Reformation and the English People*, 1984), have accepted the concept of 'reformation from above', but have concluded that it was a far slower process. For them the Reformation had to overcome considerable popular resistance and indifference, and was not widely successful until twenty years or so into the reign of Elizabeth. Scarisbrick also challenges the traditional belief that the Catholic Church in England was essentially stagnant and ripe for change at the beginning of Henry's reign. This theme has been developed recently by Eamon Duffy (*The Stripping of the Altars: Traditional Religion in England, 1400–1580*, 1992), who argues that popular, orthodox religious traditions remained strong and vigorous up to the moment of the state's attack upon them.

The alternative thesis of 'reformation from below' is particularly evident in the work of A.G. Dickens (*The English Reformation*, 1964). He argued that the success of the movement owed as much to the survival of Lollardy in some localities, and to the enthusiastic local acceptance of Protestant ideas, as to government edicts. Support for this view may be found in the work of Claire Cross (*Church and People, 1450–1600*, 1976) or of J.F. Davis (*Heresy and Reformation in the South-east of England, 1520–59*, 1983). Such authors would agree with Elton, however, that the Reformation was a relatively rapid process. The last of these four 'schools', therefore, is that which accepts the importance of local evangelical enthusiasm, but which sees its effect as a slow one, often successful only in Elizabeth's reign. This view may be best represented by the work of Patrick Collinson (*The Religion of Protestants*, 1982). Meanwhile, in one of the most influential books on sixteenth-century mentalities, Keith Thomas (*Religion and the Decline of Magic*, 1971) has demonstrated how durable old ideas of ritual and magic were, and how well they resisted the hostility of Protestantism.

THE ENGLISH CHURCH –

At the centre of this debate lies the issue of the health of the English Church on the eve of its greatest danger. Traditionally, Protestant and liberal historians have portrayed a Church in spiritual decay, urgently needing the drastic surgery of the 1530s. Against this, Catholic writers have maintained a picture of a healthy institution overthrown only because the attack upon it came from the highest political level.

The English Church in 1530 was a powerful and wealthy institution. Recent estimates of its wealth range from £270,000 per year (A.G.R. Smith, *Emergence of a Nation State*, 1984) to £400,000 (W.G. Hoskins, *The Age of Plunder, 1500–1547*, 1976), and it is probable that the Church possessed one-third of the country's landed wealth and an annual income about three times that of the crown. The law of the Church, canon law, formed a system separate and parallel to the law of the state. In an age when the death penalty dominated the penal code, no death penalty existed within canon law, and no cleric could be handed over to secular punishment without ecclesiastical permission. This so-called 'benefit of clergy' was a privilege jealously preserved by the Church, and widely resented elsewhere.

As regards the state of the parish clergy, it is not hard to find evidence to support the main anti-clerical complaints. Lack of adequate learning or training was a common complaint from contemporary Christian humanists, and their concern was illustrated by their efforts to provide schools and colleges which might produce clergy of a higher calibre. The existing system supplied quantity, but not necessarily quality. In the province of York in 1510–11 alone, some 1,100 men were ordained, at a time when the country as a whole provided only a little more than 9,000 parishes for them to work in. Yet the proportion of university graduates among ordinands in the diocese of London (1522–30) was only 33 per cent, itself a higher figure than that in more remote areas.

This traditionally dismal picture of the parish clergy has usually been extended to their monastic counterparts. With their basic philosophy of retreat from the world undermined by the philosophies of humanism and the *devotio moderna*, the religious houses had often reached a stage where 'the shell had become too big for the oyster' (A.G. Dickens). Mighty medieval buildings often housed communities dwindling both in numbers and in purpose. Dealing only with the smaller houses dissolved in 1536, G.W.O. Woodward (*The Dissolution of the Monasteries*, 1966) estimated an average clerical population of about eight per monastery. As to the spiritual condition of these monasteries, the evidence is of stagnation rather than of outrageous abuse. The bishops' **visitations** in the years before the Reformation revealed a steady trickle of minor breaches of discipline, but few cases of gross misconduct. Certainly, with the growth of an educated laity, the monasteries were playing a smaller and smaller role in English education, yet the sympathy shown to dissolved monasteries in the Pilgrimage of Grace (1536) may suggest that the religious houses continued to play a more significant social role in the localities than government propaganda was prepared to admit.

Yet there were also strikingly healthy elements within the English Church. Three monastic orders, the Observant Franciscans, the Carthusians and the female order of the Bridgettines, reflected the influence of regenerated Continental Catholicism. Among its bishops, John Fisher of Rochester was 'a model pastoral bishop' (J.J. Scarisbrick), Bishop West of Ely was energetic in his struggle against Cambridge heresy, while Cuthbert Tunstall, successively bishop of London and of Durham, combined an active political career with evident concern for the spiritual demands of his offices. At the highest level, however, Thomas Wolsey was a pluralist of spectacular proportions, while the nominal head of the English Church, William Warham, was 'a typical civil service prelate', who 'patronised humanists without participating in their scholarship, [and] displayed no sense of urgency over Church reform at a stage when reform need not have entailed revolution' (A.G. Dickens).

– AND ITS OPPONENTS: LOLLARDY AND LUTHERANISM

Over the two decades before the Henrician Reformation, the major new religious ideas of the Continent had made their impact within England. Christian humanism had achieved as influential a following among the intellectual élite as it had in France or Germany, and Erasmus himself had lived and studied in Cambridge (1511–14). Among his English admirers, Thomas More consistently attacked moral shortcomings and ignorance among the clergy, while John Colet's work on St Paul led him to conclusions similar to those later reached by Luther.

At the same time England produced its first generation of openly Lutheran theologians. The focal point of English Protestantism was Cambridge University, and by 1520 the colleges that More, Colet and Erasmus had seen as producing enlightened humanists were producing scholars with more radical views. Barnes, Bilney, Coverdale, Cranmer, Frith, Latimer, Ridley and Tyndale were all to suffer martyrdom by the end of Mary's reign, while Matthew Parker was finally to lead the reformed English Church into its promised land. William Tyndale (1495–1536) also published the first English translation of the Bible (1526). It is hard to assess how far beyond Cambridge the influence of Lutheranism spread. There is evidence that Tyndale's New Testament circulated widely in London, the home counties and East Anglia. It is also clear that in those rural areas near the capital the influence of 'Lollardy', the reformist teachings of the theologian John Wyclif (*c.*1320–84), survived to a significant degree. Such localities, A.G. Dickens has argued, served as 'reception areas for Lutheranism', especially at social levels which may not have been normally susceptible to ideas imported from the Continent.

ANTI-CLERICALISM

The traditional 'model' of the English Reformation placed much emphasis upon popular hostility towards the clergy. It has usually been assumed that such feelings were widespread, inspired by higher standards of literacy and education among certain sectors of the laity. Such a thesis is supported by such *causes célèbres* as 'Hunne's Case' (1511–14). This centred upon the suspicious death of a London merchant, Richard Hunne, while in prison awaiting trial on charges brought by the Bishop of London. As the confrontation had originated with Hunne's refusal to pay **mortuary fees** upon the death of his son, the matter was seen by contemporaries and historians alike as a major 'test case' in the layman's struggle with canon law.

Recent research, however, has failed to confirm that such feelings were widespread. Christopher Haigh (in *The English Reformation Revisited*, 1987) has concluded that the records of local Church courts do not reflect any disproportionate concern with clerical standards or with financial demands. The thousand parishes within the diocese of Lincoln produced only twenty-five complaints about sexual misconduct between 1514 and 1521, while the diocese of Norwich produced only ten tithe cases from 1,148 parishes in 1524. J.J. Scarisbrick has also established from his study of wills in a dozen English counties, many of them in the supposedly radical south of the country, that 'up to the very moment when the traditional medieval religious institutions and practices were swept away, English layfolk were pouring money and gifts into them'. While it remains probable that discontent existed among the educated classes, who were more aware of Continental intellectual influences, there is little reason to doubt that popular piety, expressed in traditional ways, was as active on the eve of the Reformation as it had ever been.

THE ROYAL DIVORCE: THE FAILURE OF A PAPAL SOLUTION

At first the fall of Wolsey did not alter the assumption that the divorce could only be gained through Rome. The initial purpose of the Parliament that was summoned in November 1529 ('the Reformation Parliament') seems to have been to exert pressure upon Clement VII to that end. In its first year it gave an impressive demonstration of the apparent hostility of the merchant and gentry classes to the clergy. Anti-clericalism was manifested in a petition to the king against the tenure of secular offices by clergymen, and in bills against pluralism, non-residence and other abuses.

The law courts were also active. In 1530, after initial proceedings against fifteen clerics, eight of them bishops, the whole of the English clergy was charged with offences under the statute of *Praemunire*, arising from their acceptance of Wolsey's legatine authority. The confrontation was resolved (January 1531) by the decision of the two **Convocations** to buy Henry off with a grant of £118,000 and to recognise him as 'Protector and Supreme Head of the English Church and Clergy, as far as Christ's law allows'. Although these titles were very similar to those later assumed by Henry through Acts of Parliament, the king was as yet only flexing his muscles.

The two prongs of attack came together in the most outspoken example of parliamentary anti-clericalism. The Supplication Against the Ordinaries (March 1532) was a petition against the independent legal functions of the Church. Whether or not it was a 'put-up job', promoted in the Commons by royal agents as part of the royal campaign, Henry reacted with enthusiasm. Aware of the Church's vulnerability, the clergy ceased to resist, and in the Submission of the Clergy (May 1532) Convocation accepted Henry's royal authority and agreed that all existing canon law be subjected to examination by a royal commission, while all future ecclesiastical legislation would be subject to the approval of the crown. Such pressure won one concession from the papacy when, upon the death of William Warham (August 1532), Henry gained acceptance of his candidate, Thomas Cranmer, as Archbishop of Canterbury. This was merely a consolation prize, however, and by this time it seemed likely that Henry had chosen a different route to the main goal.

ERASTIANISM

In the form that it eventually took, the Henrician Reformation was an extensive exercise in Erastianism, in a political philosophy which advocated the complete separation of spiritual and temporal authority within the state, and which urged that the monarch should control all legal and political functions. By 1532, Henry had digested the idea that he might claim sufficient power within his own realm to decide his own case, and he began to play for higher stakes than the divorce alone. He now saw the prospect of extending his political powers to cover all the functions, and probably most of the property, of the Church in England. The dual principle of such Erastianism was that English law was sufficient to determine all English cases, and that the king exercised supreme authority under this law. It emerged as the cornerstone of the Henrician Reformation in the famous preamble to the Act in Restraint of Appeals: 'this realm of England is an **empire**, governed by one supreme head and king, unto whom a body politic be bounden and owe to bear next to God a natural and humble obedience'.

The process by which Henry accepted these theories is obscure. Without conclusive evidence, historians have linked the change in policy to the rise in the king's favour of two personalities. By tradition, it was Anne Boleyn who brought such principles to the royal attention in the form of William Tyndale's book, *Obedience of a Christian Man*. Certainly the hand that drafted the preamble to the Act of Appeals was that of Thomas Cromwell. The ultimate triumph of this new strategy remains closely linked with the career of this new royal minister.

THOMAS CROMWELL

Geoffrey Elton's work has placed Cromwell at the very centre of the processes that led to the development of the modern body politic. Yet in many respects Cromwell remains an obscure personality. It is possible to trace him with certainty from about 1512, when he began a legal career in London. He entered Parliament in 1523, and at some stage between 1520 and 1524 first undertook legal business for Cardinal Wolsey. It was as an increasingly prominent member of Wolsey's household that Cromwell entered the world of high politics, and through the fall of Wolsey that he passed into the service of the king. By the end of 1529, Cromwell was a member of the Reformation Parliament, sitting for the royal borough of Taunton. From that point his rise in the royal service was meteoric. He entered the king's Council early in 1531, and assumed the office of the king's Principal Secretary three years later. Whether he introduced Henry to the principles of Erastianism, or whether he rose because the king sought agents willing to implement his favoured policy, Cromwell became a key figure in the Henrician Reformation.

It is possible, although difficult to prove, that Cromwell held Protestant views. His religious views are hard to determine, yet Elton has produced a carefully balanced assessment of his position: 'Cromwell was speaking a cool truth when he said that in general he inclined to the Protestant side. However he was neither fanatic nor extremist. Thomas Cromwell was essentially an evangelical who found things to use in humanist thought.' It is probable, all the same, that his prime motives were political. He aimed to contribute towards the restructuring of the power, legal competence and financial dominance of the English monarchy in such a way that it would remain secure for the foreseeable future against the twin threats of foreign interference and domestic anarchy.

THE REFORMATION STATUTES

The years 1532–3 saw a dramatic change in the conduct of the 'King's Great Matter'. Royal policy crystallised sharply into one of the most important bodies of legislation in English history. The exact causes of the change are still not clear, but it coincided closely with the beginning of Anne Boleyn's pregnancy. If the issue of the divorce had lost some of its urgency after years of negotiation, Henry was now galvanised by the crucial requirement that the new royal child should be born legitimate.

By 1535 the legislative and constitutional revolution of the Henrician Reformation had been completed. Its implications, however, were complex and far-reaching. Much of the remainder of Henry's reign was occupied with the resolution of these implications in such fields as religious doctrine, foreign policy and domestic order.

11.1 The Reformation statutes

The Henrician Reformation was brought about in a series of statutes which reflect the various stages of Henry's ambitions. The first stage consisted of a series of measures aimed to put pressure upon the papacy. When this failed, the second phase of statutes brought about the legal separation of the English Church from the authority of Rome. Subsequently, a further series of statutes defined the political, ecclesiastical and financial details of the new religious settlement.

Act in Conditional Restraint of Annates (March 1532). Annual taxes paid by bishops to Rome were limited to 5 per cent of their income. Royal authority was declared to be adequate for the consecration of bishops. The Act remained inoperative until activated by future royal command.

Act in Restraint of Appeals (Feb. 1533). The authority of the crown and of English law was declared sufficient to deal with cases of canon law hitherto referred to Rome. The crown was now capable of acting on the matter of the divorce. On the strength of this statute, Cranmer declared Henry's marriage void in May 1533.

Act in Restraint of Annates (Jan. 1534). Activated the conditional legislation of 1532.

Dispensations Act (March 1534). Archbishop of Canterbury was declared to be the ultimate authority in English cases for the granting of religious dispensations. Peter's Pence and other papal taxes were abolished.

Act for Submission of the Clergy (March 1534). Gave statutory authority to the submission made in Convocation in 1532.

Act of Succession (March 1534). Established the right to the succession of those children who might be born of the Boleyn marriage.

Act of Supremacy (Nov. 1534). Declared the king to be 'Supreme Head on Earth of the Church of England', with statutory powers to conduct visitations, punish heresy and determine doctrine.

Treason Act (Dec. 1534). Extended existing treason laws to include denial of the Royal Supremacy.

Act Concerning First Fruits and Tenths (Dec. 1534). Diverted the payments formerly made to Rome into royal hands.

THE DISSOLUTION OF THE MONASTERIES

The Henrician Reformation was not just one revolution, but an interlocking series. There is little doubt, for instance, that Cromwell planned a financial revolution, aiming to set the crown above the constraints of parliamentary taxation, and to give it independent financial resources of the kind enjoyed by the crowns of France and Spain. The attack upon the monasteries was a substantially reduced version of a wider plan, devised by Cromwell in 1534, for the wholesale confiscation of ecclesiastical property. The abbeys were an easy target. Their wealth was substantial, the monastic vocation was generally in decline, and they had their critics not just among anti-clerical laymen, but among Christian humanists otherwise loyal to the Church.

Two very different tactics were used in the attack on the monasteries. The lesser monasteries, religious houses worth £200 per year or less, were dissolved by Act of Parliament in 1536. The measure was justified on the grounds that spiritual values had decayed in such houses, while in the larger houses, 'thanks be to God, religion is right well kept and observed'. In the course of 1536 nearly 250 of these houses were dissolved by royal officials, using the machinery provided by the new Court of Augmentations, which received and valued the monastic assets. Over the next two years the surviving, larger houses found themselves under relentless pressure to surrender 'voluntarily' to the agents whom Cromwell sent throughout England for this purpose. For those heads of houses who obeyed there were generous pensions or high offices elsewhere in the Church, while the only reward for resistance was death under the treason laws. The suppression of the greater monasteries, in short, was an act of naked political force, rather than of constitutional law. The Act passed in 1539 merely confirmed the king's title to what he had already seized.

Despite its smooth implementation, the dissolution of the monasteries has traditionally been regarded as a 'failed revolution'. The wealth initially derived from the monasteries probably increased the crown's income by about 75 per cent, yet within two decades the Tudor monarchy was reliant once more upon parliamentary grants. The wars with Scotland (1542) and with France (1543) forced Henry to raise money by selling lands, and as much as two-thirds of the former monastic lands passed to new owners between 1543 and 1547. The bulk of these lands went initially to well-established families, to civil servants connected with the Court of Augmentations, and to established families of local gentry. In the long term, therefore, the dissolution of the monasteries may be seen as a key factor in the survival of the Henrician Reformation. The acquisition of ex-monastic land and wealth by most of the leading figures in both local and national politics created an insuperable barrier to any future attempts to reverse Henry's attack upon the Church.

RESISTANCE AND THE PILGRIMAGE OF GRACE

Considering its radical nature, it is a remarkable feature of the Henrician Reformation that it was achieved with so little opposition. Within the Church itself, refusals to comply were rare. Much of the Reformation legislation was bitterly contested by the bishops and abbots in the Lords, yet, once it was passed, their respect for the king and their fear of the law left them ill-equipped to act as rebels. One bishop, John Fisher of Rochester, denied the Royal Supremacy, for which he was charged with treason and executed (June 1535). Reginald Pole chose exile. The dissolution of the monasteries was resisted by the abbots of Reading, Colchester and Glastonbury and by several monks of the London Charterhouse, all of whom paid with their lives.

Among the laity, the most famous victim was the great humanist scholar and former Lord Chancellor, Thomas More (July 1535). Yet More sought security for so long in his silence that it is easy to understand how lesser men accepted the Reformation without a murmur. Elizabeth Barton, the 'Holy Maid of Kent', was less cautious, and a stream of prophecies and curses condemning the royal divorce and the Boleyn marriage brought her and her associates to execution in April 1534.

These threats were slight compared to the risings that convulsed the north of England from the autumn of 1536, and which quickly acquired the collective title of the 'Pilgrimage of Grace'. The motives of the 'pilgrims' were complex, but the theme of conservative opposition to the government's religious policies recurs throughout their manifestos. The Pontefract Articles, framed by the York lawyer Robert Aske (December 1536), condemned the heresies of Luther and others, and rejected the Royal Supremacy in spiritual matters. On the other hand, they also attacked Cromwell and his agents, and drew attention to many local economic and social problems. The Pilgrimage may best be seen, therefore, as a broad protest 'against an unprecedented intrusion by the crown into local communities and traditional ways' (Penry Williams, *The Tudor Regime*, 1979).

Widespread and distant from the seat of his power, the Pilgrimage quickly became the most serious domestic challenge that Henry ever encountered. Occupying York, the rebels had an army of some 30,000 as far south as Doncaster by the end of October. There, however, facing the king's forces and persuaded by the king's promises, the rebels began to disperse, leaving their leaders exposed to the king's revenge. Lord D'Arcy, Sir Thomas Percy and Robert Aske were among some 180 victims of Henry's wrath.

11.2 Some Henrician bishops

BONNER, Edmund (?1500–1569). Chaplain to Wolsey (1529). Diplomat, active in the cause of the king's divorce (1532–43). Bishop of Hereford (1538). Bishop of London (1539), but deprived for conservative views under Edward VI. Restored to bishopric of London (1553) and active in Mary's policy of persecution. Deprived and imprisoned upon accession of Elizabeth (1558).

CRANMER, Thomas (1489–1556). Cambridge graduate and teacher. Defended royal divorce (1530). Archbishop of Canterbury (1533), and as such pronounced annulment of Henry's marriage. Author of Ten Articles of Religion (1536). Attacked unsuccessfully on heresy charges (1540–2). Promulgated Forty-two Articles (1552). Supported succession of Jane Grey (1553). Deprived by Mary, and tried and executed on charges of heresy.

FISHER, John (1469–1535). Professor of Divinity at Cambridge (1503). Bishop of Rochester (1504). Strongly opposed to Lutheranism and to Henry's divorce from Catherine of Aragon. Refused Oath of Supremacy (1534) and was executed for treason.

GARDINER, Stephen (?1497–1555). King's secretary (1529). Bishop of Winchester (1531). Supported royal supremacy but favoured conservative doctrinal settlement. Excluded from regency council (1547) and imprisoned during Edward's reign. Restored by Mary and appointed Lord Chancellor (1553).

TUNSTALL, Cuthbert (1474–1559). Humanist, educated at Oxford, Cambridge and Padua. Master of the Rolls (1516). Bishop of London (1522). Bishop of Durham (1530). Supporter of royal supremacy, but in favour of conservative doctrine. President of Council of the North (1537). Deprived of bishopric under Edward, restored by Mary, and deprived again for refusing Oath of Supremacy under Elizabeth (1559).

WARHAM, William (?1450–1532). Negotiated marriage between Arthur and Catherine (1496). Bishop of London (1502). Archbishop of Canterbury and Lord Chancellor (1506). Lost influence with the rise of Wolsey, and largely failed to defend the Church against Henry's attacks in the 1530s.

THE CHURCH OF ENGLAND

Although Henry VIII viewed and intended his Reformation as a political event, it was inevitable that the Church would subsequently be vulnerable to doctrinal and other changes. The completeness of the state's victory over the Church was made clear when the king immediately delegated his powers to a lesser layman. In January 1535, Thomas Cromwell was appointed Vicar-General, or Vicegerent in Matters Spiritual. Although this was essentially a further act of state, that is not to say that Cromwell had no interest in spiritual reform. Much of the ecclesiastical legislation of the years 1536–40 reflects the sympathies of the Vicegerent, and makes it clear, too, that Henry had moved some way from the solid orthodoxy of the 1520s.

The third important figure in the shaping of this new English Church was Thomas Cranmer, Archbishop of Canterbury since 1533. Although appointed for his political views, favourable to the Boleyn marriage and to the Royal Supremacy, Cranmer had probably moved further along the road to Protestantism by 1535 than Cromwell had. In two respects, these men were to make important contributions to the cause of reform in England. First, they presided over the official translation of the Bible into English, culminating in the so-called 'Great Bible' which appeared in 1539. Much was also done to improve standards of conduct and worship at parish level. Two sets of Royal Injunctions (1536 and 1538) contained instructions and guidance for the local conduct of religious life, clearly based upon humanist thinking. The importance of preaching and of clerical education was stressed, and each parish was ordered to acquire

a copy of the English Bible and to make it freely available to parishioners. As a symbol of the government's increasing desire for information about the localities, the Injunctions of 1538 ordered that each parish should register births, marriages and deaths within its jurisdiction.

The fiercest struggles were fought over the precise doctrine of the new Church of England. During what remained of Cromwell's lifetime, the tide ran in favour of the reformers. The Ten Articles, published in 1536, leaned towards Lutheran views. Only three of the seven Catholic sacraments were acknowledged, and no reference was made to transubstantiation. Cromwell and Cranmer, however, were advancing faster than Henry desired. By April 1539 he was content to see a major conservative triumph sealed by the passage through Parliament of the Act of Six Articles. The new statute was unequivocally conservative, reaffirming transubstantiation and the value of masses for the dead, declaring against Communion in both kinds and condemning clerical marriage. With the fall of Cromwell (June 1540) the future of the reformers was seriously in doubt. On the other hand, the very fact of Cranmer's survival in the face of bitter conservative hostility indicated that Henry was now aware of the value to the crown of a settlement based at least upon moderate Protestantism.

11.3 Politicians and courtiers

MORE. Sir Thomas (1478–1535). Lawyer and humanist scholar. Educated at Oxford and at Lincoln's Inn. Author of political treatise *Utopia* (1516). Entered royal service (1518). Knighted (1521). Under-Treasurer of England (1521). Speaker of House of Commons (1523). Published *Dialogue*, an attack on William Tyndale (1528). Lord Chancellor in succession to Wolsey (1529). Left office over opposition to Henry's marital and religious policies (1533). Eventually accused of treason for his views and executed. Canonised by the Catholic Church (1935).

NORFOLK. Thomas Howard, 3rd Duke of (1473–1554). Eldest son of Thomas, 2nd Duke of Norfolk. Fought at Flodden (1513). Lieutenant General of Ireland (1514–24). Warden General of the Scottish Marches (1522). Factional leader at court in opposition both to Wolsey and to Cromwell. Earl Marshal (1533). Suppressed Pilgrimage of Grace (1536). Implicated in his son's treason (1547), he was condemned to death, but saved by the death of the king.

RICH. Sir Richard (?1496–1567). Based upon legal service to the crown, his career was remarkable for his ability to survive the various political shifts of the period. MP for Colchester (1529) and for Essex (1536). Knighted and appointed Solicitor General (1533), he led the prosecutions of John Fisher and Thomas More. Speaker of the House of Commons (1536). Active with Cromwell in the dissolution of the monasteries (1536). Lord Chancellor (1548). Showed initial support for Jane Grey (1553), but was reconciled to Mary and played active role in the prosecution of Protestants.

SUFFOLK. Charles Brandon, Duke of (?1484–1545). Friend and favourite of the king, and husband (1515) of Henry's sister, Mary. Steward of the royal household. Commanded unsuccessful campaign against France (1523). Warden of the Scottish Marches (1542). Commander of the forces that captured Boulogne (1544).

THE REFORMATION IN THE LOCALITIES

The traditional view of the spread and acceptance of the Reformation is that London, the Home Counties and East Anglia received the reforms enthusiastically, while the north and the west of England remained more conservative. This now appears to be too simplistic. Recent local studies confirm some of the traditional assumptions but contradict others. Thus Kent appears as an area where official pressure led to wide acceptance of the new order; Cambridgeshire seems to have reflected the Protestant influence of its great university; Lancashire appears largely hostile to religious innovation. Yet, at the same time, A.G. Dickens has discovered centres of reform in Yorkshire. Even in the south of England, it has been shown how slow local parishes could be to comply with government requirements. The fact that 880 people were charged by Cromwell's agents with treason between 1532 and 1540, surely only the tip of a much greater iceberg of complaint and alehouse mutterings, further indicates the degree of individual non-cooperation that the government had to face.

This has led less to a new set of answers than to a redefinition of the problem. It now seems less reasonable to think in terms of broad religious divisions determined by factors of geography or of local economy than to see local religious opinion as bewilderingly complex, shaped mainly by the commitment of influential individuals. In short, Henry created a problem of local controversy and nonconformity that would barely be solved in the course of the sixteenth century.

A REVOLUTION IN GOVERNMENT?

A further controversy was triggered by the publication of G.R. Elton's first major work, *The Tudor Revolution in Government* (1953). In it he revised what had been the traditional view of Thomas Cromwell as a cynical and devious politician, and raised him to the status of 'the most remarkable revolutionary in English history'. In Elton's view Cromwell transformed central government from a personal process largely dependent upon the energy of the king and his leading ministers into one carried out by a centralised bureaucracy. At the centre of this process was Cromwell's novel use of statute law, and the most spectacular result was the extension of royal power over the English Church. Local liberties and franchises were widely abolished, and the extremities of the realm were governed by the same means as the areas closest to London. The functioning of central government was also enhanced by the formalisation of the Royal Council, by the development of the office of the king's Principal Secretary, and by the reorganisation of the revenue courts of the realm into a more comprehensive, bureaucratic system.

Such sweeping claims drew a variety of objections. Penry Williams and R.B. Wernham argued that Elton had exaggerated the novelty of much of Cromwell's work. Wolsey, for instance, had brought about significant changes through the Court of Requests and Star Chamber, and these bodies survived the 1530s unchanged. Historians studying the reigns of Edward VI and Mary argued that the factional intrigue of that period contradicted the notion of a Council with a clearly recognised constitutional role. Research also suggested that the structure of the Council under Mary was very different from the Cromwellian 'model'.

The current state of opinion is that government certainly underwent substantial development in the first half of the Tudor era. Nevertheless, as David Starkey has concluded, 'the new institutional structure did not spring fully armed from the head of one man; instead, much time and many factors were at work'. Significant changes in the administration of the royal household, for instance, occurred in the

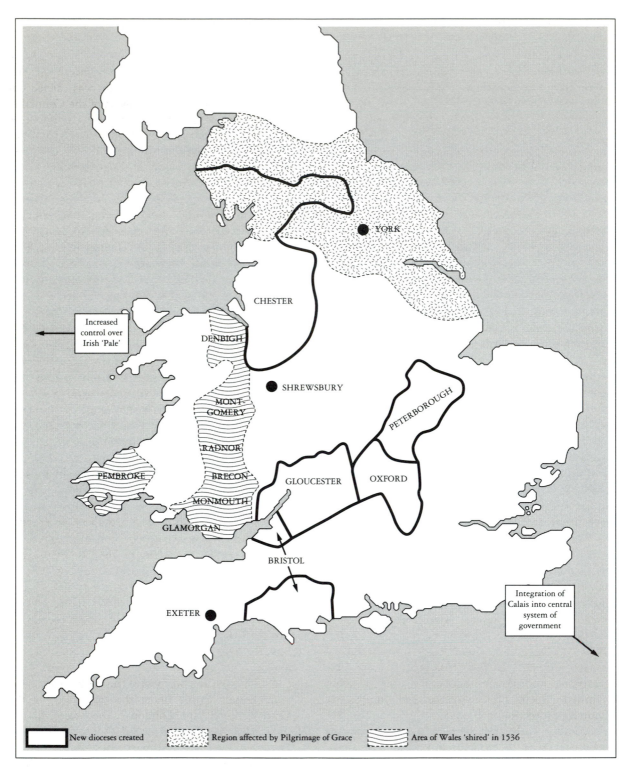

Increased control over Irish 'Pale'

YORK

CHESTER

DENBIGH

SHREWSBURY

MONT-GOMERY

PETERBOROUGH

RADNOR

OXFORD

PEMBROKE

BRECON

GLOUCESTER

MONMOUTH

GLAMORGAN

BRISTOL

Integration of Calais into central system of government

EXETER

New dioceses created   Region affected by Pilgrimage of Grace   Area of Wales 'shired' in 1536

11.4 Central government and the localities, 1536–47

reign of Henry VII and under Wolsey, while the reigns of Mary and of Elizabeth contain some important developments in financial administration.

Nevertheless, a very substantial body of administrative legislation was passed during Cromwell's tenure of office. Much of this was associated with the vast increase in royal income brought about by the Reformation, and especially by the dissolution of the monasteries. Thus the new Court of Augmentations was set up (1536) to handle the former monastic lands. The Court of Wards was established (1540) to deal with increased income from wardships; and the establishment of two new revenue courts very shortly after Cromwell's fall from power made it clear that his policies outlived him in this respect. The Court of First Fruits and Tenths (1540) provided more formalised administration of the income diverted from the Church to the crown five years earlier, while the Court of General Surveyors (1542) administered older crown lands.

ROYAL AUTHORITY IN THE DISTANT LOCALITIES

It thus remains clear that Cromwell's paramount concern was to extend and to consolidate the authority of the crown throughout the land, and to ensure that it was unhindered by rival claims or exemptions. Just as it was important to ensure that the ecclesiastical courts could not ignore the king's law, it was equally important that there should be no distant corner of the realm where feudal interests or traditional liberties limited royal authority. An Act of 1536, therefore, abolished all political and legal liberties within the realm and ensured that all legal officers would henceforth be appointed by the crown alone. Many of the abolished franchises were ecclesiastical ones. Similarly, an Act of 1540 greatly reduced the privileges of sanctuary, whereby criminals fleeing from justice had sought the Church's protection.

Cromwell also turned his attention to the periphery of the realm, where distance and vested interests had traditionally limited the impact of royal authority. The administration of Calais was brought into line with the rest of the realm by a far-reaching statute of 1536, whereby the direct rule of the Lord Deputy was restricted and Calais returned two MPs to the House of Commons. The process of integrating Wales and the Marches into the general administrative system of the realm was carried out initially by reinforcing the powers of the Council of the Marches. In addition to the firm rule of the Council's president, Bishop Rowland Lee (1534), an outstanding series of Acts in 1536 fully incorporated Wales into the English legal and political systems. Wales was divided into eleven counties and provided with Justices of the Peace on the English model. The principality received parliamentary representation for the first time, and the common law was imposed in place of traditional practice and feudal custom. Although it is often overshadowed by other aspects of his work, it is hard to disagree with A.G.R. Smith's verdict that the 'peaceful assimilation [of Wales] into the mainstream of English administrative and judicial life was one of Cromwell's most notable achievements'.

The case of Ireland has to be considered in the dual context of Cromwell's reforms and the traditional problems of enforcing royal authority there. The early 1530s marked a significant turning-point in the history of English government in Ireland, with the ending of the long ascendancy of the earls of Kildare. The death of the old earl (1534) and the defeat of the subsequent rebellion by his son, 'Silken Thomas', the Earl of Offaly (1535), destroyed the traditional poles of political authority. It was an apt moment for Cromwell to consider how Henry's authority might be imposed upon Ireland, too.

Rejecting the risky advice of those who wished to see a war of conquest over the whole of Ireland, Cromwell restricted himself to the establishment of good government within the Pale. In September 1537, a royal commission outlined reforms similar to those carried out in Wales and in Calais. The office of Deputy would henceforth be held by an Englishman, advised by reliable English or Anglo-Irish councillors, and the business of this Irish government would remain firmly under the supervision of the Privy Council in London. The Reformation legislation was implemented within the Pale, apparently with considerable enthusiasm on the part of the local gentry. All the same, Lord Grey, the Lord Deputy, could not resist the temptation to carry the fight to the Gaelic chiefs. He achieved much military

The Kingdom of Scotland, 1488–1542

The political history of Scotland in the first half of the sixteenth century comprises two reigns with very similar themes. Both James IV (1488–1513) and James V (1513–42) addressed the governmental and administrative problems of the kingdom with energy, and with some success within certain geographical limits. Both, however, were destroyed by the profound difficulties of Scottish foreign policy.

The imposition of order, especially in the border regions and the Highlands and the Isles, was a persistent problem, requiring the direct, military involvement of the monarch. James IV made a considerable impact in the south of his kingdom, cooperating effectively with English nobility in his 'Eskdale Raid' (1504) against the bandits ('reivers') who terrorised the border regions, and personally imposing a draconian form of justice in his assize at Jedburgh (1510), which passed into Scottish legend. Similarly, James V mounted expeditions against border 'reivers' in 1529 and 1530, and took energetic action against challenges to his central authority, notably from the Douglas family. Neither king could claim such success against the chieftains of the Isles, where geography and the clan system placed insuperable barriers in the path of central government. James IV undertook six campaigns in the region during 1493–9, while his son cruised the coasts of his realm with a powerful fleet in 1540, forcing local chieftains into temporary submission. In the long term, however, the kings of Scotland continued to use clan chieftains as their nominal agents, much as the King of England did in Ireland.

In similar vein, both reigns contributed to the development of governmental, and particularly of judicial, machinery in Scotland. Regular legal sessions were established in Edinburgh (1511), and James IV attempted to improve standards of local justice by ordering (1496) that every substantial landowner should educate his sons to university level. It is worthy of note that the foundation of King's College in Aberdeen (1495) provided Scotland with a third university, at a time when England had only two. The reign of James V was distinguished by an impressive body of legislation on currency, trade and the administration of justice. In particular, the reign saw the establishment by the

success in a series of campaigns between 1537 and 1540, but in the longer term succeeded only in renewing the fears and suspicions of the Irish chieftains as a whole. Their rebellious union in the 'Geraldine League' (1539) resulted in renewed violence and another expensive, if ultimately successful, military campaign. By the time of his fall, Cromwell may have strengthened the links between central government and the administration of the Pale, but he had done little to change the essential instability of Irish politics as a whole.

SOCIAL REFORM

Cromwell's ministry also coincided with a concerted effort to tackle the major socio-economic problems of the realm by means of statute law. Throughout this period there was much pressure in intellectual circles for 'commonwealth' measures, that is, measures that sought to provide social and economic justice for all the king's subjects. Cromwell seems to have sympathised with the 'commonwealth men' and to have promoted many of the bills that they presented to Parliament.

Acts of 1531 and 1532 sought to fix the prices of certain foodstuffs at a reasonable level, and a general Act of 1533 attempted to create machinery for determining fair food prices. Such Acts proved largely impossible to enforce, and the government effectively ignored them for some time before they were actually repealed in 1542. In common with most Tudor law-makers, the parliaments of the 1530s also attempted to limit the spread of pasturage at the expense of arable farming. Statutes

chancellor, Gavin Dunbar, Archbishop of Glasgow, of the 'College of Justice', a fully qualified body of judges, sometimes compared to the Parlement of Paris, financed by a substantial tax upon the clergy, authorised by Pope Clement VII.

Scottish foreign policy, meanwhile, was dominated by the traditional factors of suspicion of England and friendship, as very much the junior partner, with France. For much of his reign, given the domestic preoccupations of Henry VII and the French obsession with Italy, James IV enjoyed unaccustomed security. Although renewing the 'auld alliance' with France in 1491–2, he was able greatly to improve relations with England. By the marriage alliance of 1502, involving Henry VII's daughter Margaret, the two kingdoms were formally at peace for the first time since 1328. England's return to an expansionist policy under Henry VIII renewed Scottish insecurities. Tempted once more towards his traditional French allies, James led an army variously described as 'part feudal, part tribal' (J.D. Mackie, *A History of Scotland*, 1964) and 'the largest and most glorious army a king of Scotland ever led' (John Prebble, *The Lion in the North*, 1971) into England. He was routed and killed at Flodden (9 September 1513), with the additional loss of much of the Scottish nobility.

Despite being the grandson of Henry VII, and despite the pro-English influence of his mother Queen Margaret in the early part of his reign, James V also gravitated towards France in the course of the 1530s. His two marriages were French, to the Princess Madeleine (1537) and, upon her early death, to Mary of Guise (1538). This process, and Henry VIII's increasingly assertive attitude towards Scotland, led to war in 1542, and to a further disastrous defeat for the Scots at Solway Moss. James's death, a few days after the battle, deprived Scotland of effective leadership at a moment when the stability of the realm faced the dual threat of religious division and English domination. The Treaty of Greenwich, with its provision for marriage between Henry's heir and the infant Queen of Scots, represented England's determination to exploit Solway Moss more effectively than Flodden had been exploited.

(See also Chapter 19, p.328.)

---

of 1536 confirmed the existing laws against enclosure, while a more imaginative Sheep and Farm Act (1534) sought to impose limits upon the size of flocks. It is unlikely that this burst of agrarian legislation had any greater impact than that which had gone before.

The final traditional area of socio-economic legislation was poor relief. Legislation in this area was dominated by the Beggars Act of 1531, which attempted to restrict the social disruption caused by the severe economic depression that prevailed in the early 1530s. The act legalised begging by the old and the sick, the 'impotent poor', but provided fierce punishment for 'sturdy beggars': able-bodied men and women driven into vagabondage by poverty and unemployment. A more ambitious project envisaged the relief of the 'impotent' poor from parish funds and the establishment of a central 'council to avoid vagabonds', but it was undermined by the opposition of those who would have had to pay for such schemes. Nevertheless, it influenced the important Poor Law of 1536, which placed responsibility upon the parishes for collecting and distributing funds to the 'impotent poor', and thus established the parish as the main agency for poor relief. The more radical elements of the plan, however, perished without a trace.

The social legislation of the 1530s thus sought to tackle the three main issues which contemporaries perceived as lying at the root of the economic problems of the realm. The impact of the legislation was generally slight, thwarted in part by vested interests, but failing in many cases because the issues that it sought to tackle were far more complex than the 'commonwealth' legislators had imagined.

FOREIGN POLICY AND THE REFORMATION, 1538–40

English foreign policy was transformed by the repercussions of the Henrician Reformation, both real and imagined. Before 1529 that policy was characterised by a confident desire to cut a dash in the first rank of European powers. Much of Henry's last decade was dominated by fear of an anti-English coalition and a consequent preoccupation with the defence of the realm.

Theoretically Henry faced a significant threat from the Catholic princes of Europe. He was excommunicated by Pope Paul III in 1538, and the truce concluded in that year between Francis I and Charles V raised the possibility of concerted action against Henry in support of the papacy. In reality, of course, such an alliance was scarcely possible. Both rulers were financially exhausted by their earlier struggles, and neither had sufficient personal motive for intervention. Charles no longer had to fear an Anglo-French alliance, and the fall of Cromwell seemed to reduce the threat of English cooperation with the German Protestants.

Nevertheless, the English government reacted to the crisis of 1538–9 with great energy. A range of fortifications was built along the south coast at great expense, and the English navy was increased by as many as 150 ships. The crisis also set off a substantial political purge, as the government sought to eliminate the threat of potential traitors within the realm. The Pope was placed in the role of the 'orchestrator' of Yorkist rebellion, and Henry Courtenay, Marquis of Exeter, Sir Edward Neville, Geoffrey Pole, brother of Cardinal Pole, and their mother, Margaret, Countess of Salisbury, were all executed between 1538 and 1541.

The perceived danger also led to a fateful flirtation with the German princes. Negotiations took place in London (1538) in search of a doctrinal basis for such an alliance, and in October Henry reached agreement with the Duke of Cleves for his marriage to the Duke's daughter, Anne. Although not a Protestant alliance, for Cleves was not a member of the Schmalkaldic League, the marriage was possibly a hint to Charles of what the future might hold if Henry were placed under further pressure. The marriage was a disaster. Henry found Anne utterly unprepossessing, and no sooner had their union been celebrated (January 1540) than an improvement in relations between Charles V and the German princes rendered it politically pointless. Anne of Cleves was more accommodating than Catherine of Aragon had been, quickly accepting the annulment of her marriage and retiring from public life on a rich pension.

The domestic political implications of this German episode were far more serious. The flirtation with 'heresy' had proved unacceptable to Henry's more conservative ministers, and the Act of Six Articles (April 1539) was probably planned as a gesture of refusal, with its foreign impact very much in mind. The collapse of the Cleves marriage cemented the conservatives' success. It severely compromised Cromwell's position and ushered in a final period in Henry's reign in which the direction of policy by a well-established chief minister would give way to the selfish machinations of political factions.

FOREIGN POLICY: FRANCE AND SCOTLAND, 1540–7

From 1540, English foreign policy concentrated on issues nearer to home, and particularly upon the affairs of Scotland. Although Henry clothed his Scottish policy in expansionist rhetoric, his concerns remained primarily defensive. Scotland was traditionally the client of France, frequently playing a disruptive role in the north of England, and Henry's primary aim was to 'close that back door, and to seize the key to the British problem by drawing Scotland into England's orbit' (R.B. Wernham). Attempts to reach a negotiated agreement to this end collapsed in 1541, and relations degenerated to the extent that the countries were at war by October 1542.

Militarily, the war was a complete success. The Scots army was routed at Solway Moss (November 1542), and within three weeks the King of Scots had died of natural causes, leaving the throne to his six-day-old daughter, Mary. Scotland was defenceless, her nobility was divided, and with the pro-French party temporarily in eclipse English proposals for a marriage alliance between the infant

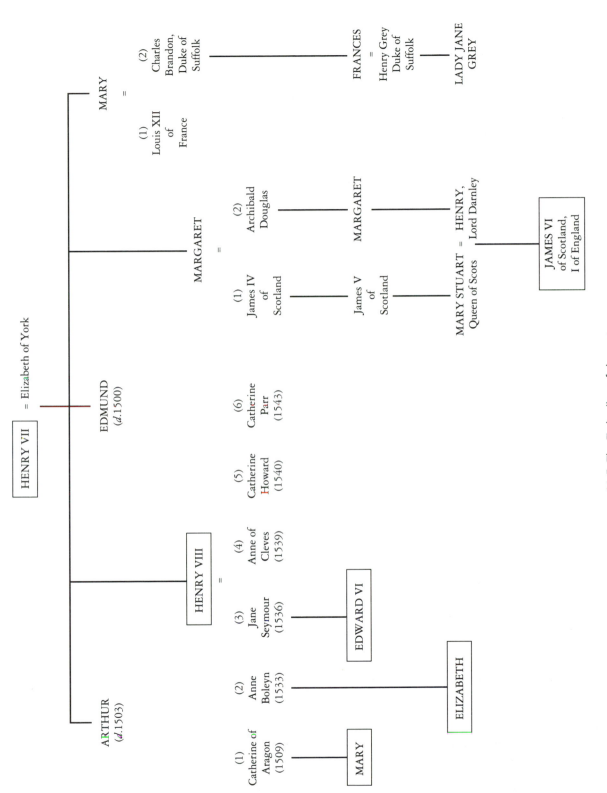

11.5 The Tudor line of descent

Queen of Scots and Prince Edward seemed to have a good chance of success. Yet Henry badly overplayed his hand. His rash declaration of his 'true and right title to the sovereignty of Scotland' put all Scots on their guard and ensured that, although they could scarcely refuse to sign the Treaty of Greenwich (July 1543), they never seriously intended to implement it. For the next five years the major concern of English policy was to force the Scots to do so. Punitive expeditions under the command of Edward Seymour attacked Edinburgh and Leith in 1544 and 1545, causing great damage to the surrounding countryside, but the effect of such 'rough wooing' was merely to deepen Scottish mistrust.

Yet, by the end of his reign, Henry's Scottish policy had achieved some results in the context of Continental politics. As the policy inevitably involved hostility towards France, Scotland's traditional ally, it provided a basis for improved relations with the Habsburgs. Anglo-imperial relations were better in the mid-1540s than they had been for twenty years, and England's involvement in Continental politics in the last years of the reign was reminiscent of the 1520s. A treaty for a combined invasion of France (1543) led to the capture of Boulogne by the English (September 1544) before the Emperor's decision to make peace left Henry isolated again. Briefly, England herself seemed in danger of invasion, but the logistics of a combined land–sea attack proved far too complicated for French resources. The peace concluded in June 1546 allowed England to retain Boulogne for eight years and granted Henry a 'perpetual' pension of 50,000 crowns.

Henry had survived, however, at a heavy cost. His diplomatic and military undertakings since 1538 had proved financially disastrous. The construction of coastal defences, the building of ships, the campaigns in France and in Scotland cost an extraordinary total of over £2.1 million. In addition to parliamentary grants and forced loans, Henry probably sold up to two-thirds of his ex-monastic property to meet these demands. Whatever may have been gained or avoided in diplomatic terms, therefore, the price that Henry paid was nothing less than the loss of the crown's independence over the decades to come.

THE FINAL YEARS: THE RULE OF FACTION

For most of the thirty years up to 1540 the impact of factional struggle upon English politics had been minimised by the authority of a great minister, secure in the king's confidence. Whereas Wolsey's loss of control had occurred gradually, Cromwell's ascendancy came to an abrupt end in June 1540, when he was arrested and executed on utterly false charges of treason.

Cromwell suffered the same fate as had Wolsey and Anne Boleyn before him, the victim of his conservative political opponents in the Council, led by Norfolk and Gardiner. Not only had Cromwell, like Wolsey, overshadowed Norfolk in the power politics of the reign but, unlike Wolsey, he had also used his power to push forward the Reformation in ways highly distasteful to the religious conservatives. It is hard to understand how the king allowed the overthrow of his minister unless we consider two sets of factors. In 1540, the failure of the Cleves marriage, the fear of foreign invasion, and Henry's own uncertainty about doctrinal developments, all left Cromwell in an exposed position and made Henry highly susceptible to conservative pressure. In addition, Henry was on the verge of a dramatic physical decline. Troubled for years by leg ulcers, he now found it increasingly difficult to ride or even to walk, and obesity set in at an alarming rate. He seems to have realised very quickly after Cromwell's death that he had been led into a very serious error, and this has led recent authorities to the conclusion that Henry was increasingly the dupe of court factions as his physical powers declined. The political history of his last seven years was marked by his conviction that he could rule without a chief minister, and by his patent failure to do so.

The conservative success in 1540 proved to be an illusion. Within weeks of Cromwell's fall they had consolidated their triumph by putting in Henry's path a young, vivacious niece of the Duke of Norfolk, Catherine Howard. Henry fell for her completely, but his fifth marriage (July 1540) was yet another disaster. Catherine was a poor choice as royal consort. She had led an adventurous sex-life before she met Henry and she lacked the common sense to curtail it once she was married. With clear evidence of her adultery presented to Henry by their political rivals, the conservative faction was undone by those very crimes for which they had 'framed' Anne Boleyn in 1536. Catherine was beheaded for treason in February 1542.

Although none of them was dragged down by the disaster in the way that members of the Boleyn faction had been, the influence of the conservatives was now on the wane. An attempt to arrest Cranmer on heresy charges in the spring of 1543 was blocked by Henry's unconditional support for his archbishop, and Cranmer was shortly to find a powerful new set of allies. Within weeks of this incident Henry had married for the sixth time. Catherine Parr, a middle-aged widow, was a lady of known evangelical views, who made her household a centre of patronage for those with advanced religious ideas. Equally important was Edward Seymour, Earl of Hertford, brother of Jane Seymour, and thus the uncle of the heir to the throne. He dominated the military affairs of the moment through his campaigns in Scotland, and he dominated the court through his office as Lord Chamberlain. His brother Thomas Seymour and John Dudley were also leading figures among a new generation of courtiers. To these were added some of the most important of Henry's professional officials: Sir William Paget, the king's secretary, and Sir Anthony Denny, chief gentleman of the Privy Chamber. By 1545 these officials deployed a key practical weapon in the form of the so-called 'dry stamp'. Instead of securing the king's personal signature for each document, the holder of the 'dry stamp' merely applied it to the document in question, making an impression of the royal signature, and inked in the lines to produce a perfect copy.

Norfolk's supporters could not match this, and suffered defeat after defeat. In particular, 1546 was a disastrous year for the conservatives. They failed spectacularly in an attempt to link Catherine Parr with the heresy charges brought against Anne Askew, wife of a Lincolnshire landowner. In November, Bishop Gardiner, a leading conservative, was dismissed from court and excluded by the king

from the list of those who would guide his son after his death. In December, treason charges were brought against Norfolk's son and heir, the Earl of Surrey. He was executed the following year and his father, implicated in his treason, was only saved by the king's own death (27 January 1547). These events effectively destroyed the factional balance that had existed within the court and left the Seymour faction in a dominant position at the moment of the king's death.

11.6 Glossary

Convocation. The assemblies of leading clerics which represented each province of the English Church, Canterbury and York.

Empire. In the English context, as used in the Act in Restraint of Appeals, 'empire' must be understood as a political unit which did not acknowledge the overlordship of any other.

Evangelical. Broadly used as an alternative term for 'Protestant'. Used to indicate the reliance of the reformers upon the authority of the gospels (Latin: *evangelium* = gospel).

Mortuary fees. A payment demanded by the clergy for the performance of funeral rites. One of several payments for routine clerical services to which anti-clerics objected.

Visitations. Inspections, carried out on the authority of bishops, of the condition of monastic and other establishments within their dioceses.

Further reading

A.G. Dickens (1989) *The English Reformation.* London.
M.A.R. Graves (1990) *Early Tudor Parliaments, 1485–1558.* London.
K. Randell (1991) *Henry VIII and the Government of England.* London, and (1993) *Henry VIII and the Reformation in England.* London.
J.J. Scarisbrick (1968) *Henry VIII.* London.
D. Starkey (1985) *The Reign of Henry VIII: Personalities and Politics.* London.

CHAPTER TWELVE

France in the Reigns of Francis I and Henry II

*Built between 1519 and 1540, the château of Chambord, in the Loire valley, is one of the
most ambitious of the many great building projects undertaken by Francis I.
Such palaces advertised the power and resources of the monarch, and
adapted the tastes and styles of the Renaissance for the
purposes of the French crown*

THE HISTORICAL DEBATE

The reign of Francis I has often been interpreted as the glorious flourish of French Renaissance monarchy before its virtual collapse during the Wars of Religion. In his reign a glamorous façade of châteaux-building and military campaigns barely concealed the decay and tensions that were eventually to lead to civil war. Perhaps for this very reason, the reputation of Francis has undergone violent fluctuations. Where some early commentators looked back sentimentally upon the image of *le grand roi François*, others were quick to focus upon the negative aspects of the reign. In the work of two of France's greatest nineteenth-century intellectuals, Victor Hugo and Jules Michelet, Francis emerges as a lecherous and devious king, unmoved by the finer considerations of Renaissance or Reformation thought; moved only, in Michelet's terse phrase, by 'war to please women'.

The most important works of recent decades have focused upon two wider issues. Some have concentrated upon the social history of the period, seeing it as a prelude to the civil disasters that followed. Others have studied the constitutional history of the period, and a lively controversy has centred around the claim that Francis I laid the foundations for the absolutism of later French monarchs. G. Pagès (*La Monarchie d'ancien régime en France*, 1946) interpreted the reign as a period of institutional centralisation following the territorial unification achieved in the fifteenth century, and concluded that 'it was at the beginning of the sixteenth century that the absolute monarchy triumphed'. An opposing school of thought accepted the king's absolutist aspirations, but stressed the practical limitations placed upon royal power by considerations of distance and resources. The American scholar J. Russell Major (*Representative Institutions in Renaissance France, 1421–1559*, 1960) placed his emphasis upon the local and provincial institutions of the realm, noting their practical freedom of action, and concluded that 'the popular, consultative nature of the monarchy continued unmodified for the first third of the period and was only mildly altered thereafter'.

Recent authorities have established a compromise between these positions. R.J. Knecht (*Renaissance Warrior and Patron: The Reign of Francis I*, 1994) has stressed the importance of Francis's reign as a stimulus to the constitutional, fiscal and cultural growth of the French state, but has acknowledged its contribution to the social and political crisis of the second half of the century. On the constitutional issue, he emphasises the king's essential lack of respect for provincial privileges, yet stresses his practical inability permanently and consistently to override them. Summarising wider research on the subject, David Potter (*A History of France, 1460–1560*, 1995) has chosen to compare this reign with its predecessors, rather than with those that followed. As a result, he has identified the growth of the power and institutions of the French monarchy as a much longer process, concluding that 'the rise of the modern state' is a process 'which should not be artificially allocated to any short period. There are elements of it present in the late thirteenth century and the process continued into the nineteenth.'

The reign of Francis's son, Henry II, has received less attention from historians. In some cases it has been treated as a virtual footnote to his father's reign, or as a period of political degeneration, leading into the dreadful years of the Wars of Religion. Only recently has an American scholar, F.J. Baumgartner (*Henry II, King of France 1547–1559*, 1988), attempted to provide a view of the reign as a distinct entity with significant features of its own. He notes that the extension of France's boundaries in Lorraine and in the Pas de Calais represented a more substantial success than Francis ever achieved after the mid-1520s. Meanwhile, administrative reforms, and the substantial development of Protestantism within France, gave the reign a significance of its own within French history.

THE KINGDOM OF FRANCE

At the outbreak of the Hundred Years War (*c.*1330) 'France' was a geographical rather than a political expression. The King of France was at best the greatest of many feudal lords and, at the lowest ebb of his fortunes, not even that. In the provinces, the authority of such great feudal princes as the dukes

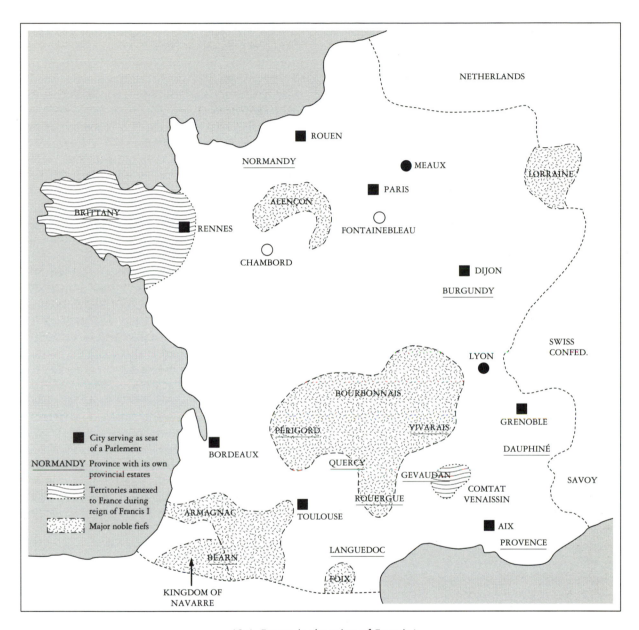

12.1 France in the reign of Francis I

of Anjou, Berry, Burgundy, Orléans and Angoulême far outweighed any authority emanating from Paris. The great political theme of the fifteenth century, however, was the steady erosion of this feudal independence; of eighty great feudal fiefs that had existed in 1480, half by 1530 were in abeyance or in the hands of the royal family. Charles VII (1429–61) finally ousted the English from Normandy and from Aquitaine. Louis XI

(1461–83) asserted French authority over Dauphiné and Viennois, and Guyenne reverted to the crown in 1472. The greatest triumph came in 1477, when the defeat of Charles the Bold, Duke of Burgundy, brought the French-speaking regions of his duchy under the control of the French crown.

It is by no means true, however, that modern France had been created by 1514. Many territorial anomalies survived. Brittany, though linked to the crown by marriage, remained technically independent until 1532. Lorraine remained divided between the French king and the Emperor. The 'kingdom' of Navarre, on the Spanish borders, survived as a great feudal fief, and Calais remained under English control until the middle of the century. On another level, the language of most of northern France, the *langue d'oïl*, still coexisted with the southern language, or *langue d'oc*, the latter dominant in Gascony and Provence. Other, quite distinct languages, such as Breton and Basque, still survive today. In terms of law, too, France was a patchwork of local customs and practices.

THE ECONOMIC CONTEXT

At the start of the century contemporaries regarded France, with much justification, as the most prosperous region in Western Europe. By the late fifteenth century, the great plagues that had first struck in 1348 and the ravages of the Hundred Years War were now far enough in the past to allow recovery. Most important was the recovery of population. Working from very incomplete figures, demographers have arrived at a total of about 18 million inhabitants by the early fourteenth century, a figure that was perhaps halved by natural and human disasters before 1450. After 1450, it has been estimated, the population increased in some areas by 10 per cent every ten years during the reigns of Francis I and Henry II, taking the French population back to its pre-plague levels by about 1560.

Agriculture also responded to the stimuli of peace and stability. On the one hand, agricultural recovery contributed to the growth of population. On the other, increased population stimulated demand for food and encouraged increased production. For all the increased demand, France suffered no major grain shortage between 1440 and 1520. The agricultural recovery had largely played itself out, however, by the accession of Francis, and crop production remained consistent in France from the latter years of the reign of Louis XII (*d.*1515) until the early years of the reign of Louis XIV (succeeded 1643).

The expansion of French commerce was of longer and more consistent duration. The populations of major towns appear to have expanded at a faster rate than the population-growth in general, and the realm of Francis I could eventually boast ten towns of more than 20,000 inhabitants and another thirty of more than 10,000. This background of urban growth enabled the reign to serve as the 'springtime of French trade' (P. Chaunu, *Histoire économique et sociale de la France, 1450–1660*, 1977). The expansion of the textile industry was perhaps the most spectacular case, in Normandy, Brittany and Champagne, while the silk industry was revived in Lyon and established in Toulouse. In Lyon, too, France developed a banking centre worthy of comparison with those of Italy, Germany and the Low Countries. Foreign trade also broke new ground. On or near the Atlantic seaboard, La Rochelle, Nantes, Rouen and Bordeaux all thrived as trade grew with the markets of Spain, Portugal, the Low Countries and even the Baltic. The foundation of the new port of Le Havre by Francis I provides further evidence of this trade boom.

Such prosperity, however, did not translate consistently into general social well-being, and these early decades witnessed the decline of 'boom' conditions for much of the population. For the French peasantry, some 85 per cent of the population, continued population-increases, linked to a levelling off of agricultural production, flooded the job markets and reduced wages. Such problems were aggravated by the return of grain famines in 1528–32, in 1538 and in 1543–5. Urban workers felt similar pressures as competition for jobs increased and as corn prices rose. The period witnessed some dangerous outbreaks of urban unrest, notably in the so-called *Grand Rebeine* riots in Lyon in 1529.

The twin pressures of rural economic stagnation and inflation had a serious effect upon the landed seigneurial classes. Many years ago, Marc Bloch (*Les Caractères originaux de l'histoire rurale français*, 1931) drew a classic picture of the noble *seigneur*, weighed down by the declining value of rents, eventually being forced to sell his lands to the urban merchant whose flexible prices allowed him to keep pace with inflation. The picture still commands wide respect, and the records of the land markets around Paris and Lyon show more and more former feudal estates falling into the hands of buyers from the cities.

THE MONARCH AND HIS AUTHORITY

'In the first half of the sixteenth century, the French monarchy was strong because it was in the hands of rulers who were adult, physically robust and reasonably long-lived' (R.J. Knecht, *French Renaissance Monarchy*, 1984). The dominant figure of this half-century was Francis I, King of France from 1515 to 1547. Like Henry VIII of England, he did more for the charisma of monarchy than for its substance, and it has become commonplace to regard him as the archetypal 'Prince of the Renaissance'. No contemporary better fulfilled the type of the multi-talented dilettante presented by Castiglione in *The Courtier* as the courtly Renaissance ideal. Francis was a lover and collector of books, but he limited himself largely to classical histories and to tales of heroism. He was a wit and a conversationalist, but he preferred to stick to such subjects as hunting and war. He was a fair poet, 'but he lacked the application necessary to scholarship' (R.J. Knecht). He was a soldier and a lover *par excellence*. The reign of Francis I did little to strengthen the French monarchy or France itself in the long term, yet it advanced the style with which France was governed to levels never before approached.

Francis ascended the throne at a time when it was becoming increasingly difficult to see the monarch as a feudal lord in the medieval style. The leading constitutional authorities of the day, patronised of course by the monarchy itself, consistently stressed the powers of the crown, while still disagreeing as to their exact nature and extent. Claude de Seyssel, churchman and jurist (*The Monarchy of France*, 1515), saw the king in the role of father, having 'all power and authority to command and do what he wishes', yet restrained by his voluntary acceptance of three 'bridles' upon his power: religion, justice and constitutional law. The greatest French humanist of the generation, Guillaume Budé (*The Institution of the Prince*, 1518), claimed that if the king shared his power with the nobility or the judges he merely granted them favours and privileges which he could easily and legally cancel. He did not thereby acknowledge that they had any legitimate right to share the political power that God had placed in his hands.

THE GOVERNMENT OF THE REALM

France was governed in the early sixteenth century along lines very similar to most other Western European states. At the heart of policy-making lay the royal council. In principle, the Council of State (*conseil d'état*) consisted of about twenty members drawn from a limited range of candidates, from princes of the blood, peers of the realm and great officers of state. In practice, more and more of the major decisions of state were taken by a more exclusive body, the *conseil des affaires*, its membership dependent purely upon royal trust, regardless of social status. The competence of the council was unlimited, but offshoots were formally established to deal with specialised areas of administration. The *Grand Conseil* (1497) dealt with specialised judicial matters, while the *Chambre des Comptes* and the *Cour des Aides* were staffed by financial specialists.

The decisions of the royal council were carried out by a relatively small body of permanent royal officials. Legal measures were formulated by the Chancery, headed by the Chancellor of France, and staffed by a little over 100 notaries and secretaries. As legal business increased, so more and more of the drafting and preparation fell into the hands of legal specialists known as Masters of Requests (*maîtres des requêtes*). Financial measures, by 1547, were the responsibility of four *secrétaires des finances*. The primary military office, that of Constable of France, lay vacant from 1488 until 1515, and then again from the time of Charles of Bourbon's revolt (1523) until 1538. Including local subordinates, Francis I had some 5,000 royal officials in his service at his accession, which illustrates the practical limitations upon absolute royal power at this time. The copious creation of offices in the course of the reign owed more to the king's desire to sell them for profit than to the search for more effective administration.

The question of Francis I's absolutism depends to a very large extent upon whether he possessed sufficient authority in the provinces of his realm to ensure the collection of taxation and the enforcement of his laws. The basic local unit of legal administration in France was the *bailliage* or *sénéchaussée*. The kingdom comprised one hundred

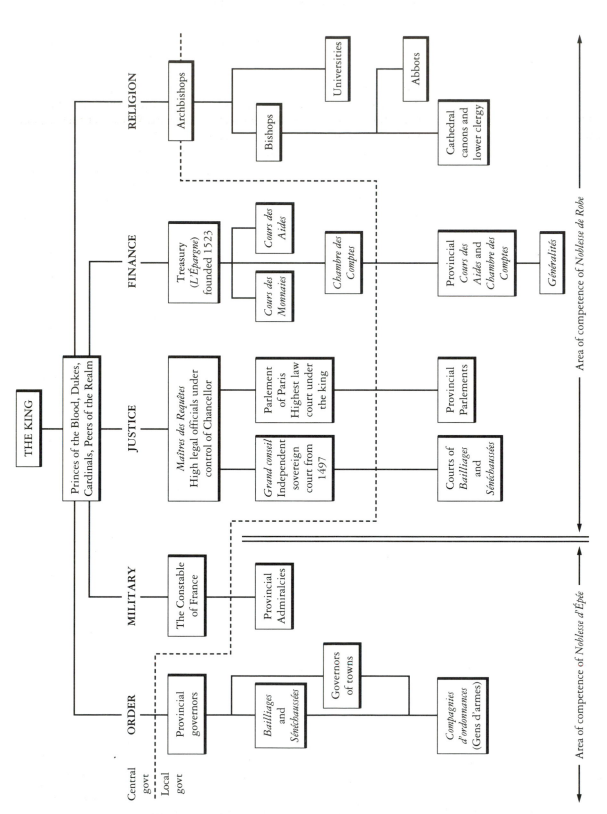

12.2 The government of France under Francis I and Henry II

of these units, whose powers ranged from the summoning of feudal military levies in time of crisis to hearing appeals from manorial courts. Their powers were more clearly defined by the royal edict of Crémieu (1536), but their effectiveness still depended upon the participation of the local nobility, who chose the major officials and who took primary responsibility for the enforcement of their judgements.

Above the *bailliages* stood the Parlements, the most powerful symbols and guarantees of provincial autonomy. Seven such bodies existed in 1515, sitting in Toulouse, Aix-en-Provence, Grenoble, Bordeaux, Dijon and Rouen, with the greatest of them based in Paris itself. In principle, each Parlement was a superior court of justice, with separate departments for criminal justice, requests and other forms of legal procedure. In practice, the role of the Parlements was under attack. While they claimed the right to decide upon the publication of royal ordinances in the localities, the king increasingly saw this as a duty which the Parlements should carry out automatically. In his view they were merely bodies for the administration of justice and were not to be seen as partners in the actual making of laws. In 1540, for instance, Francis suspended the Parlement of Rouen over its reluctance to register the Ordinance of Villers-Cotterêts. Francis could not claim, however, to have won this constitutional struggle by the end of his reign. As late as 1552, the Parlement of Paris refused three times to register certain legal reforms of Henry II because it felt that they invaded the rights of the Parlement itself.

The primary representative bodies of the realm were the Estates (*États*). In principle, these assemblies constituted a gathering of the representatives of the three main orders in French society: the nobility, the clergy and the *bourgeoisie*. They existed at two levels. Provincial estates represented Languedoc, Brittany, Burgundy, Auxonne, Normandy, Dauphiné and Provence, while the Estates General was the national version of these local assemblies, the French parliament in effect. The Estates General, however, were not summoned at any time during the reign, and although the provincial estates continued to meet attendance at them was irregular, and on several occasions local privileges were blatantly overridden by the king. Such was the case when the *gabelle* tax was extended to Languedoc (1537) and to Normandy (1546) despite their traditional exemption. In short, these bodies continued to function along traditional lines when no clash was involved with royal interests. Whenever such a clash occurred, however, Francis felt justified by his office in enforcing his will at the expense of local liberties.

The provincial governors played a far more direct role than these representative institutions. They were appointed by the crown from among the close relatives and favourites of the monarch, and were the direct local representatives of his central authority. The relations between the king and the governors were generally so close that the latter were in effect 'viceroys'. Even so, the governors' local authority and their contacts at court made them attractive patrons for lesser nobility and gentry in the provinces. This, and the fact that they were usually in control of local feudal military levies, gave them considerable local power in their own right.

As David Potter has concluded, 'the weight of government on the varied provinces of France undoubtedly increased over this period, but remained restrained in comparison with the developments of the seventeenth century'. Provincial and other sectional interests were represented in such a way that the king could not legally ignore them totally. In practice, however, Francis was perfectly willing to sweep such interests aside whenever he felt that they obstructed his path. Then, again, it was not always practicable, given problems of distance and resources, consistently to bypass such checks and balances. Jean Bodin undoubtedly spoke for Francis when he wrote thirty years later that 'the king has no companion in his sovereign power'. As R.J. Knecht has remarked, however, 'a monarchy whose effectiveness was subject to so many practical limitations cannot be called "absolute"'.

12.3 Key figures

BRIÇONNET, Guillaume (1472–1534). Bishop of Lodève (1504). Bishop of Meaux (1516). Active in conclusion of the Concordat of Bologna (1516). Under patronage of Marguerite of Angoulême, made Meaux a centre for Christian humanist studies. Although active in his diocese against Lutheranism (1523), he had to answer for 'advanced' views before the Parlement of Paris (1525).

MARGUERITE OF ANGOULÊME (1492–1549). Sister of Francis I. Married Henry d'Albret, King of Navarre (1527), and was thus grandmother of Henry IV. A fervent supporter of evangelical ideas, she acted as patron of Lefèvre d'Étaples, other Christian humanists, and some who leaned towards Protestantism.

MONTMORENCY, Anne de (1493–1567). Companion and favourite of Francis I. Fought with distinction at Ravenna (1512), Marignano (1515) and Bicocca (1522), before being captured at Pavia (1525). Governor of Languedoc. Defended Provence against Charles V (1536). Constable of France (1538). Disgraced (1541), but restored to favour by Henry II. Defeated and captured at Saint-Quentin (1557). Out of favour under Francis II, but a leading Catholic protagonist in the early years of the Wars of Religion. Killed in battle at Saint-Denis.

SEMBLANÇAY, Jacques de (1445–1527). Leading banker and financial administrator under Charles VIII, Louis XII and Francis I. Governor of Touraine (1517). *Surintendant des Finances* (1518). Accused of mismanagement and treason, and executed (Aug. 1527).

THE STYLE OF THE MONARCHY

More than any other contemporary European monarch, Francis I used the artistic styles of the Renaissance to advertise the extent of his political authority. First and foremost, Francis was a builder. The earliest years of his reign produced the magnificent works at Blois, where his new wing featured Italianate galleries and *loggias*, and at Chambord, where the major architect was probably the Italian Domenico da Cortona. Above all, Francis lavished money and attention throughout his reign upon the château of Fontainebleau, transforming a medieval hunting-box into one of the most admired palaces in Europe. In painting and sculpture, too, the king's patronage drew to France some of Italy's greatest talents, such as Andrea del Sarto and Benvenuto Cellini. Among native artists, Jean Clouet became 'one of the first artists in France to comprehend the principles of the Italian High Renaissance' (P. Mellen, *Jean Clouet*, 1971), and with his son François emerged as the leading portrait painter of the French court. As well as the artists themselves, royal patronage accumulated a magnificent collection of paintings and sculptures, making almost as great a contribution to the present-day collections in the Louvre as did the later adventures of Napoleon. Elsewhere, the greater nobility often imitated the king's tastes and palaces. The palaces of the Cardinal of Lorraine at Meudon and of Montmorency at Chantilly and at Écouen all showed the influences of Blois, of Chambord and of Fontainebleau.

There was much more to such projects than recreational patronage of the arts. Francis was acutely aware that such conspicuous display greatly enhanced the image and the prestige of the monarchy. Throughout this period, similarly, the crown consistently harnessed ritual and ceremony to advertise its authority. Both Francis and Henry developed and elaborated the coronation rites to emphasise the divine nature of the king's office, while Francis's funeral in 1547 represented new dimensions in royal ceremonial. Behind the complex ceremonies, as R. Giesey (*The Royal Funerary Ceremony in Renaissance France*, 1960) has explained, lay the important political message that, 'though the king may die, yet kingship is eternal'.

THE CROWN'S FINANCES

Whether at war or at peace, the king spent on an epic scale. His first, victorious campaign in Italy cost 1.8 million *livres*. After Pavia it cost at least 4 million *livres* to ransom his sons from imprisonment in Spain. Diplomacy, too, was enormously expensive. The settlement with Henry VIII for the return of Tournai to France (1518) cost Francis 1.2 million *livres*, and his attempt to secure the imperial election (1519) cost 800,000. Under such pressures the total deficit of the French crown in 1520 was only a little less than 4 million *livres*.

The financial system that struggled with such demands had changed little since the reign of Charles VII (1429–61). The crown's income fell into two broad categories: 'ordinary' income was derived from the royal estates, while 'extraordinary' income came from taxation. To a greater extent than anywhere else in Western Europe, the French crown had succeeded in securing a regular and largely uncontested income from taxation. In 1515 the king received only 300,000 *livres* per annum from his estates, against an unparalleled 4.5 million from taxation. Three well-established taxes accounted for most of this sum. The *taille* was a direct tax levied upon the value of land and yielded nearly half the total income from taxation, but the nobility were exempt from it. The *gabelle* was a tax upon salt, a crucial commodity for the preservation of meat, and one in which the crown held the monopoly. The *aides* consisted of a series of sales taxes levied on a wide range of commodities.

The first great financial crisis of the reign occurred between 1521 and 1523. Once aware of the problems that faced him, Francis's reactions were unimaginative. Existing forms of taxation were only increased by an average of 2.2 per cent per year over the rest of the reign. Instead, Francis resorted to the typical medieval expedient of tightening up the existing system and of exploiting dubious and short-sighted means of raising large sums at short notice. In 1521 alone he sold crown lands to the value of 200,000 *livres*, extorted a similar sum from the citizens of Paris, and seized plate and other treasures from the Church. To his credit, Francis resisted until 1545 the temptation to debase the currency. The only new tax to which he resorted was the *solde des 50,000 hommes*, which he imposed upon walled towns in the kingdom from 1543. On the other hand, his sale of over 150 noble titles and offices of state set a precedent for a practice that would undermine the efficiency of the French monarchy for years to come. He also practised the new financial vice of borrowing at high rates of interest. Loans of 720,000 *livres* from London, to finance his imperial election campaign, and of half a million from Lyon in 1520 set a pattern for the rest of the reign. At the time of his death, the king's debt to the bankers of Lyon was only a little below 7 million *livres*.

Francis also reacted to the crisis by examining the roles and activities of his leading financial officers, through a special body known as the *Commission de la Tour Carrée*. Several major officers suffered exile, while the Treasurer, Semblançay, (1527) and the *trésorier général* of Languedoc, Poncher (1535), were executed. This action had the effect of breaking the influence of the traditional financial oligarchs, and the system of financial administration became more centralised. Taxation income ceased to be regarded as 'extraordinary' and passed, along with the king's landed income, into the hands of a new central official, the *trésorier de l'épargne* (1523).

Despite such reforms, however, the overriding aim of financial policy remained the same: to find the means to fund an obsessive foreign policy. In this respect, Francis I continued throughout his reign to live from hand to mouth. The peace that lasted from 1529 to 1536 gave the king savings of 1.5 million *livres*, but a year of war in 1536 cost him 4.5 million. Similarly, the savings of four peaceful years between 1538 and 1542 were wiped out by four years of war (1542–6) which had a combined cost of 16 million *livres*. Whatever the constitutional significance of Francis's reforms, the struggle against bankruptcy remained the keynote of French financial policy for the rest of the century.

Humanism and heresy

Humanism

To make an accurate assessment of spiritual and intellectual developments in Francis's reign it is important to avoid treating contemporary events as part of an inevitable slide into religious civil war. It was once commonplace to see Francis as sympathetic and supportive towards 'heresy' until 1534, when the affair of the 'Placards' produced a reaction which made the king an orthodox persecutor of heretics for the rest of his life. It is only possible to maintain this view, however, by lumping together all the intellectual currents which were labelled indiscriminately as 'heresy' by French conservatives.

The dominant currents in French religious thought in the forty years before 1520 were not heretical, but humanist. They belonged less to the prehistory of the Reformation than to that of the Counter-Reformation. The ideas of the *devotio moderna* were imported into France by a Dutchman, Jan Standonck, under whose leadership the Collège de Montaigu in Paris became a great centre for such studies. French humanism found its first great native exponent in Guillaume Fichet, whose work paved the way for the greatest of the French humanists. Arguably, Jacques Lefèvre d'Étaples (c.1450–1536) stands second only to Erasmus among Christian humanists. Like Erasmus, he sought to instil new life into Christian theology by applying the lessons of classical study to the study of the scriptures. His work in this respect included a translation of St Paul's Epistles (1512) in which he defined the issue of justification by faith some years before Luther.

Lefèvre and his followers, however, remained within the bounds of doctrinal orthodoxy and of royal patronage. Lefèvre's closest associate was Guillaume Briçonnet, and when the latter became Bishop of Meaux in 1516 that diocese became a centre for the practical implementation of Christian humanist ideals. With absenteeism and clerical illiteracy rejected by the men who gathered around Briçonnet, and with great stress laid upon preaching, the so-called *Cercle de Meaux* became a magnet for leading French humanists and evangelicals.

The French court remained consistently well disposed towards such men and their teachings throughout the first decade and a half of Francis's reign. The king's personal secretary was the noted classical scholar Guillaume Budé, while his doctor (Cop) and his confessor (Petit) were also humanists. In 1516 he founded a classical college in Paris, later to become the Collège de France, and tried to tempt Erasmus to take charge of it. Throughout the 1520s he consistently intervened, even from prison in Madrid, to prevent Christian humanists from being treated as 'Lutherans' by the religious conservatives. The king's sister Marguerite wrote much religious literature in the same vein, and her palace at Nérac became an enduring centre for humanist studies.

Erasmus regarded France in 1517 as 'the purest and most prosperous part of Christendom', but others did not see it that way. In particular, the theological faculty of the University of Paris staunchly defended doctrinal conservatism. Its view was that 'Luther's errors have entered this kingdom more through the works of Erasmus and Lefèvre than any others'. Once the views of Luther had been formally condemned in France, humanists had to fight a constant rearguard action to avoid meeting the same fate as convicted heretics. A few, like Guillaume Farel, embraced Protestantism fully, but most of the other prominent members of the *Cercle de Meaux* remained orthodox in doctrinal terms. By 1526–7 the victory of conservatism over evangelical humanism seemed assured.

Heresy

The official attitude towards Lutheranism itself was clear by 1521. At that date the works of Luther had already been available in Paris for about two years, and the university responded to papal pressure by formally denouncing them. In June 1521 it became an offence to print or to sell any religious work without the sanction of the Sorbonne.

Where Francis differed from his more conservative theologians was not in his attitude to Lutheranism, but in his unwillingness to apply that term uncritically to all teachings that did not match up to the Sorbonne's rigid notion of orthodoxy. Thus when Catholic teaching was clearly under attack, as in the outbreak of iconoclasm in Paris in 1528, Francis was unreservedly conservative. On the other hand, when it was the Christian humanism of his court protégées that was under attack, the king resisted both the Sorbonne and the Parlement of Paris. A young aristocrat, Louis de Berquin, was twice saved from persecution by the direct intervention of Francis, but was eventually burned on the authority of the Parlement during the king's absence in 1528.

On 18 October 1534, posters appeared in Paris and in other major French cities, attacking the Catholic Mass and proposing a Zwinglian interpretation of the Eucharist. This 'Affair of the Placards' has frequently been seen as a turning-point at which the French state united unreservedly to launch a savage attack upon the ideas of the Reformation. Francis, despite the fact that his current policy demanded friendly relations with the German Lutherans, now had neither the grounds nor perhaps the inclination to restrain the conservatives any longer. Six Lutherans were burned in Paris in November 1534, and two months later the king suspended all printing of books until further notice. Although the tone of the next royal statement, the Edict of Coucy (July 1535), was conciliatory towards those who had renounced unorthodox views, Zwinglians were deliberately excluded from its terms. The Edict of Fontainebleau (June 1540), made when Francis was no longer reliant upon the German Protestant princes, was an uncompromising blueprint for persecution. The Parlements were made responsible for the enforcement of anti-heretical legislation, and royal judges were given much greater powers to override local and feudal privileges in their hunt for heretics. The Sorbonne, meanwhile, contributed its Twenty-five Articles (July 1543) to provide a theological framework for the definition of religious orthodoxy, and provided France with her first Index of Prohibited Books (1544).

A survey of the prosecutions for heresy in France in the last decade of Francis's reign reveals that the problem was widespread both in geographical and social terms. There were sixty arrests in Meaux in 1546, followed by fourteen executions; 118 in La Rochelle in the same year, involving twenty-five death sentences; 200 prosecutions in Languedoc during 1540–9. An analysis of 160 individuals prosecuted between 1547 and 1550 also shows a wide social diversity. They included fifty-five clergymen, six *seigneurs*, fourteen royal officials and sixty artisans or small shopkeepers. Not until 1555, however, did the decision of the Genevan authorities to undertake a coordinated mission to France give to French Protestantism a coherent form and local organisation sufficient to harness decades of religious dissent and discontent.

THE GALLICAN CHURCH

The campaigns of Francis I in northern Italy won prestige and international influence that were purely temporary. On the other hand, they brought the king important and enduring domestic advantages in the form of the Concordat of Bologna (1515). By this settlement, concluded after the French triumph at Marignano, the papacy recovered the right to exact annates from the French clergy, and secured the withdrawal of French support for a General Council. In return, the crown gained an extraordinary degree of control over all political aspects of the Church within France, including appointments and financial resources. In the years ahead it became common to refer to the French Church as the 'Gallican' Church, with the clear implication that, politically, it was independent of Rome, as Henry VIII's 'Anglican' variety would be.

Francis clearly regarded these powers as a valuable means of patronage, rather than as a tool

for the reform of the Church. The king's primary aim in making ecclesiastical appointments was to reward political service, and to attach the great noble families even more securely to the crown. Of the 129 men appointed as bishops by Francis, nearly 100 were the offspring of noble families. An eighteen-year-old was appointed Bishop of Poitiers and a fourteen-year-old was named as Bishop of Évreux. Charles of Guise, a member of one of the most powerful noble families, obtained the archbishopric of Reims at the tender age of nine years. The number of Italians appointed to French bishoprics also showed the king's willingness to use Church offices to reward those who supported his political ambitions outside France. At the same time the increase in the number of French cardinals, from five to seventeen in the course of the reign, illustrates the eagerness of successive Popes to cooperate in this abuse if it secured them a valuable ally against the Emperor.

At least in the 1520s such a picture was softened by the flourishing of the evangelical humanist movement and by the active patronage that it received from the royal family. By the 1530s, the triumph of conservatism was complete within the religious hierarchy. This ensured that the Gallican Church would not be supplied with enough fresh spiritual energy to enable it to resist more radical types of reformism. Ironically, therefore, one can argue that tight royal control and exploitation of the Church made a substantial contribution in the long run to the great crisis of royal authority in the second half of the century.

THE NEW REIGN: HENRY II AND HIS COURT

The death of Francis I (31 March 1547) brought to the throne his second son, Henry. Relations between father and son had been poor for some time, certainly since Henry's long years as a hostage in Spain. It is not surprising, therefore, that the new reign began with a 'palace revolution'. Within days of Francis's death the political careers of the Cardinal de Tournon and the Admiral Claude d'Annebault had been brought dramatically to a close, and the governors of Normandy, Provence and Bresse were all dismissed. The most spectacular gains were those of Anne of

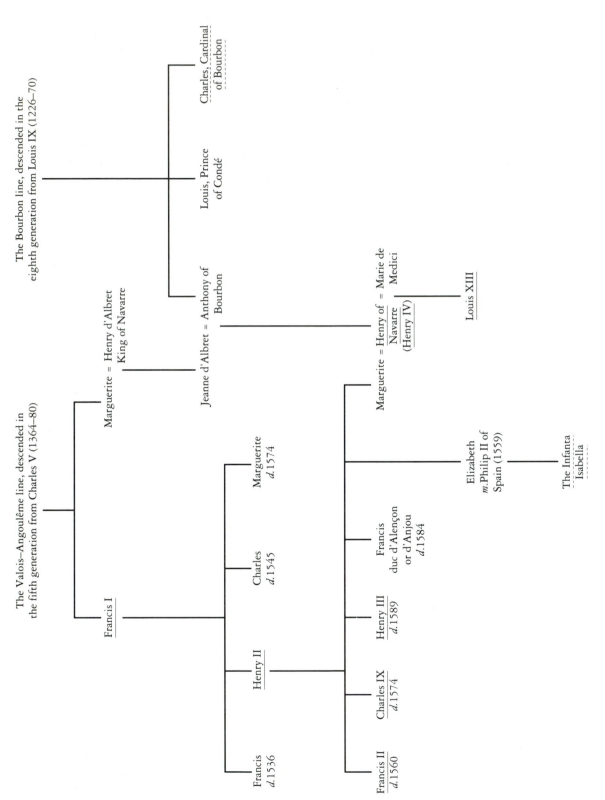

The Valois–Angoulême line, descended in the fifth generation from Charles V (1364–80)

The Bourbon line, descended in the eighth generation from Louis IX (1226–70)

Francis I

Henry II

Marguerite = Henry d'Albret King of Navarre

Francis d.1536

Charles IX d.1574

Henry III d.1589

Francis duc d'Alençon or d'Anjou d.1584

Marguerite d.1574

Charles d.1545

Francis II d.1560

Jeanne d'Albret = Anthony of Bourbon

Louis, Prince of Condé

Charles, Cardinal of Bourbon

Marguerite = Henry of Navarre (Henry IV) = Marie de Medici

Louis XIII

Elizabeth m.Philip II of Spain (1559)

The Infanta Isabella

12.4 The succession to the throne of France, 1515–1610

Note: The names of reigning kings are underlined. Those with broken underlining are unsuccessful claimants proposed by the Catholic League in opposition to Henry IV.

Montmorency, disgraced by Francis in 1541 but always greatly favoured by Henry. He resumed the dignity of Constable of France and was compensated for his earlier losses. Alongside the Montmorency family, the families of Guise and of Saint André also rose in the royal favour. Between them, these three families soon held six of the eleven governorships. With two more governorships controlled by the Bourbon family, the government of the state rested firmly upon a partnership between the king and the greatest magnates of his realm.

Older historians, such as Lucien Romier, have left us with the traditional view of Henry's court as a breeding ground for the factional disputes of the next generation. Family rivalries, however, were the norm in contemporary court politics, and could actually be a source of strength to the government if contained and controlled by the monarch. This is certainly the view that Baumgartner has more recently taken of Henry's court. For most of the reign, he concludes, 'the struggle for power was fairly evenly matched. The Guises' greater ability and youthfulness neatly balanced the great, almost filial reverence that Henry had for the Constable [Montmorency].'

For all the disagreements between Henry and his father, the two men were not very different in their styles of government. Henry, too, was essentially a muscular monarch, a soldier, as keen as Francis ever was to provide the wars from which the nobility might benefit. He was a sportsman, an enthusiastic huntsman, and so devoted to the martial sport of jousting that it would literally prove to be the death of him. 'The nobles', writes Baumgartner, 'were much taken with Henry since he was very much one of them.' Minor edicts, like that against poaching on noble estates (1555), and that which limited the wearing of silk to the nobility (1548), also showed the closeness of the king's mentality to that of the noble caste.

OLD PROBLEMS

Henry II and finance

Except in one respect, Henry II brought no new insights or new priorities to the finances of the French crown. Through the demands of his foreign policy, he subjected the fiscal system to the same pressures as Francis had done and he derived his income from much the same sources. Like his father before him, Henry's financial policy consisted largely of squeezing the maximum amounts from the traditional sources.

Henry's income from taxes in the first year of his reign was a massive 8.4 million *livres*, 25 per cent up on Francis's income upon his succession. Like his father, Henry was wary of social reaction against the introduction of novel taxes. This suspicion was probably heightened by major rebellions in the first year of his reign, in Saintonge and in the region of Bordeaux, mainly motivated by the extension of the *gabelle* to those areas. Henry was satisfied with only two new taxes, the *taillon* (1549), introduced to support military forces within France, and a new clerical tax (1552) which raised some 1.4 million *livres* per year.

More than ever, the French monarchy continued to rely upon the sale of offices and upon substantial banking loans to meet its commitments. To ensure an adequate income from these sources, Henry introduced the 'semester' system into many of the fiscal and administrative bodies of the realm. Two sets of officials now worked at one post, alternating in their duties every six months, and there were thus twice as many offices to be put up for sale. Similarly, the formation of a completely new Parlement at Rennes (1552) probably owed more to Henry's desire to sell offices than it did to the desire for administrative efficiency.

The king's greatest fiscal reform also brought ruin in the long run. Henry, too, relied heavily upon bankers' loans, borrowing nearly 1.2 million *livres* from Lyon bankers in 1552 and 1.7 million in the following year. It has even been suggested that he borrowed, not only to meet his own needs, but in order to draw from the bankers funds which might otherwise have been made available to his Habsburg rival. Such borrowing was made easier by the king's consistently good reputation as a prompt repayer of debts. It was in this spirit that Henry introduced (1555) the so-called *Grand Parti de Lyon*. This was an arrangement by which the crown consolidated the loans that it had previously negotiated with individual Lyon bankers, and made specific and generous arrangements for repayment. By its terms, the crown would repay 5 per cent of its debt at each of the banking fairs held in Lyon, and these were held four times per year. This was the first coherent scheme devised by any Western European government for the repayment of its debts, and the confidence of the bankers was stimulated to such an extent that Henry was able to negotiate loans of over 10 million *livres* in 1555–6. That confidence, however, was largely misplaced. Interest payments had already been suspended in 1558, before the king's accidental death (1559) put a stop to them altogether.

Henry II and heresy

The makings of religious conflict were evident throughout the reign, and the king proceeded in religious affairs without fully understanding the problems he faced. Henry applied the same guiding principles as his father, at a time when such principles were less and less suited to the problems in hand. Unswervingly Catholic as Henry undoubtedly was, he never ceased to regard religion as an adjunct of his political power. Throughout his reign, therefore, he remained consistently hostile to the two forces that he felt posed the greatest threat to his domestic authority: the influence of the papacy on the one hand, and that of grass-roots Protestantism on the other.

Henry's priorities in his relations with the papacy were to preserve the benefits of the Concordat of Bologna and to resist any extension of Habsburg influence over the policies of Rome. Such priorities ensured that relations between France and Rome were rarely cordial. After an apparent success in 1549, when French influence helped to defeat the imperial candidate in the papal election, Cardinal Pole, Henry was soon in dispute with the successful candidate. The dispute centred upon Julius III's attempt to nominate a candidate to the vacant bishopric of Marseilles (1550), and the Pope's decision to reconvene the Council of Trent. Fearing that the Council might reach an agreement on doctrinal questions that would ease the problems of Charles V in Germany, Henry plunged the French Church into direct confrontation with the papacy. While Henry threatened to convene a national Church council, at which French bishops would reach independent decisions on the issues at stake,

Julius responded with threats of excommunication. This 'Gallican crisis' only really subsided with the Pope's death and the election of a successor, Paul IV, whose anti-Spanish sympathies were much more in line with those of the King of France.

Henry was equally determined to defend the French Church against the challenge of heresy. One of the first acts of his reign was the establishment (October 1547) of the *Chambre ardente*, a new court within the Parlement of Paris with special powers for the detection and punishment of heresy. The new court successfully prosecuted over 500 cases in the next three years, yet the threat of heresy persisted. The Edict of Châteaubriand (June 1551) ordered public attendance at Mass and demanded proof of orthodoxy from those taking up public office. In 1557, Henry obtained permission from the papacy for the establishment of an Inquisition in France while, in the same year, the Edict of Compiègne imposed the death penalty upon all those who visited Geneva or who had books published there.

Yet Henry's assault upon Protestant heresy was riddled with inconsistencies. 'On one hand determined to eradicate heresy, on the other prepared to make allowances for high rank and the needs of diplomacy, Henry was not able to pursue the goal of religious conformity with single-minded intent' (F.J. Baumgartner). There can be little doubt that Henry saw Protestantism as a seditious lower-class conspiracy, and failed to appreciate that it could also take root among the political élite of the realm. 'The Protestants', he proclaimed, 'have no other aim and no other effect than to ruin the wealthiest personages.' Only six persons of noble origin were brought before the *Chambre ardente* during his reign and none of those was executed. Similarly, Henry experienced no difficulty in turning a blind eye to Protestantism when it served his diplomatic purposes, entering into an open alliance with German Protestant princes when it served his anti-Habsburg aims.

It is clear that Protestantism not only continued to find adherents in the lower classes of society but, more dangerously, also began to attract more recruits among the nobility and the upper middle classes. In 1555 alone 120 nobles fled to Geneva, and the powerful Prince of Condé openly visited the city. In 1558 there was a striking disturbance in

Paris, the so-called *Affaire du Pré-aux-Clercs*, during which several thousand people 'marched in dense battalions', singing psalms in French after the Genevan manner. This challenge to orthodoxy was made even more serious by the fact that one of the most powerful noblemen in the realm, Anthony of Bourbon, was involved.

Perhaps, in these last months of his reign, Henry was waking up to the seriousness of the problem. In June 1559, fearing that the Parlement itself was treating heresy too leniently, the king attended a session at which the views of each *parlementaire* were demanded, and arrested eight members who spoke in support of religious liberty. When one of these, Anne de Bourg, was burned in Paris (December 1559), he was by some way the most prominent Frenchmen so far to be executed for heresy. Henry did not live to see the execution. On 30 June, at a joust designed to celebrate the conclusion of the Peace of Câteau-Cambrésis, he suffered a serious accident and died in great pain some days later. The problems that he had only partially confronted would now have to be tackled by others with less charisma and less determination.

Further reading

F.J. Baumgartner (1988) *Henry II, King of France 1547–1559.* Durham, NC, and London.

R.J. Knecht (1984) *French Renaissance Monarchy: Francis I and Henry II.* London and New York.

——— (1994) *Renaissance Warrior and Patron: the Reign of Francis I.* London.

D.L. Potter (1995) *A History of France, 1460–1560.* London.

— PART III —

THE CRISIS OF THE GREAT MONARCHIES

• CHAPTER THIRTEEN •

Germany and the Holy Roman Empire in the Time of Charles V

Portrait of Charles V, painted by his court artist,
Titian, in the late 1540s. The sympathetic
treatment of the subject cannot conceal
the weariness of a ruler engaged in the
last great crisis of his political career

THE HISTORICAL DEBATE

As the dominant political figure of the early sixteenth century, Charles V has attracted apologists and detractors among historians in equal measure. Many of the former came from Spain, where Charles's successors reigned securely for centuries. They painted a picture of an age of titanic clashes between the crowned heads of Europe, in which one man struggled bravely against heresy, against the infidel, and against the duplicity of Christian rulers who should have been his allies against these greater enemies. Charles's eventual abdication, and his final years in the monastery of Yuste, were fitted neatly into this vision as the crowning act of the reign of a devout prince who thus stepped across the line from monarch to monk.

Such a heroic image has traditionally seemed less appropriate to German historians. Leopold von Ranke, writing in the nineteenth century against a background of contemporary German nationalism, saw the sixteenth-century Emperor, ruling the states of Germany on the same terms as a host of other foreign states, as an anachronism. Honourable and well-meaning as he may have been, Charles was a hangover from an earlier age, and his fatal error was to try to perpetuate medieval principles of government in a world that had begun to outgrow them.

Charles's image also suffered from the growing awareness that his private life and personality were not, in fact, those of a saint. From the English historian of sixteenth-century Spain, E. Armstrong (*The Emperor Charles V*, 1902), came the judgement that Charles was 'not quite a great man, nor quite a good man'. Even the greatest of Charles's modern biographers, Karl Brandi (*The Emperor Charles V*, 1939), saw him in an ambiguous light. Charles had a high sense of duty and he stuck doggedly to his tasks as he perceived them. On the other hand, he lacked imagination and approached his duties with nothing more than mediocre intelligence. In considering his final renunciation of his offices, such writers have been impressed more by the element of disillusion and perceived failure than by any element of sacrifice.

Charles has been defended against some of these charges in two ways. On the one hand, it has been stressed that much progress was made during his lifetime in some of his dominions towards administrative unity and centralisation. Thus some Belgian and Dutch writers have claimed that the Netherlands emerged more or less as a coherent political unit as a result of the consolidation that Charles carried out. Geoffrey Parker has also tentatively referred to a 'Habsburg revolution in government' in Castile.

Only relatively recently have historians of contemporary Germany begun to turn away from analyses of Charles, to concentrate instead upon the society and the economy against which he operated. Peter Blickle (*The Revolution of 1525*, 1981) has examined the trends and pressures which lay behind the great popular rising of that year, indicating the extent of the social and economic disruption that was taking place in the Germany of Luther and Charles. W.R. Hitchcock (*The Background of the Knights' Revolt, 1522–3*, 1958) has done the same for this earlier rising. Perhaps the leading authority on the wider social history of sixteenth-century Germany is Bernd Moeller (*Deutschland im Zeitalter der Reformation*, 1977). Such work certainly represents the future direction of research in this area, as historians become increasingly aware of the importance of the broader socio-economic elements which dictated or restricted the actions of the leading political figures of the time.

GERMANY: THE POLITICAL AND ECONOMIC CONTEXT

Politically, Germany appeared divided and fragmented at the opening of the sixteenth century. Apart from the substantial lands of the Habsburg dynasty, Germany was divided into some 390 political units, twenty-four of them ruled by temporal princes, fifty by prince-bishops, and 145 by counts or lesser lords. Such a list, however, hides the extent to which the greatest dynastic princes were increasing their power. By conquest, intermarriage and exchange of territories, the greatest princely families achieved a greater degree of territorial consolidation than ever before. The achievements of the Wittelsbach dynasty in Bavaria and in the Palatinate, and of the Hohenzollerns in Brandenburg, were imitated in Mecklenburg (1471), Baden (1488) and Hesse. Steadily, these leading princes also consolidated their political control within their territories. With the whittling away of tax exemptions and other traditional privileges, most of the major territorial princes enjoyed the sort of autonomous and reliable personal income that the Emperor himself never managed to establish. Most frequently these took the form of property taxes, excise duties and contributions for the upkeep of defences against the Turk.

If the princes emerge as the main 'winners' in this process, the list of 'losers' is more complicated. Attacks upon the autonomy of the Church in Germany, for instance, did not begin with the Reformation. In Bavaria and in the Palatinate, 'territorial' churches, dependent upon the laws and the patronage of the political ruler, were in existence years before the advent of Martin Luther. Also threatened were the so-called 'imperial knights', a feudal, military group which claimed to be independent of all authority other than that of the Emperor. This was a form of autonomy that could not easily be tolerated by the princes within whose territories the knights' lands and castles lay. The peasantry, of course, provided the taxes that supported the princes' administrations, and the local laws which had traditionally protected their rights to seek food and fuel in the forests and on common land could not withstand the centralising processes of the princely state.

The years 1460–1540 formed a boom period in the economies of Germany. The region experienced a sharp population-increase, and it is probable that the population of the Empire, excluding the Netherlands, stood at about 15 million in 1500. The pressures caused by this increase can be seen in the movement to cultivate new land, especially in the east of Germany. These same years saw a substantial boom in industry and commerce, especially in the south. Unprecedented capital investment led to growth in many heavy industries. In particular, mining industries thrived, producing copper, lead and zinc in Saxony, Bohemia, the Harz and the Tyrol. Mining for iron ore became a significant industry along the Rhine, in Thuringia and in the Upper Palatinate. Cloth production remained the other great staple of the German industrial economy, with major centres in the north at Danzig and in the south at Munich and Augsburg.

Contemporary Germany was highly urbanised. In 1520, some 3,000 places in Germany described themselves as towns or cities, although only twenty-five boasted a population above 10,000. Augsburg and Cologne, both with a population of 50,000–60,000, could claim to rank with the greater cities of Western Europe. The great banking families of Germany had their bases in the south, with Augsburg the greatest centre of all. This was the base of the Fugger family, the greatest banking dynasty of the early sixteenth century. Under the leadership of Jacob Fugger, 'Jacob the Rich' (1459–1525), the family extended its interests to most areas of European commerce, and became the greatest financial support of Habsburg policies.

THE HOLY ROMAN EMPIRE

Even though it had been largely restricted to the territories of Germany in the last two centuries, the form and nature of the Empire remained imprecise. Only as recently as 1356 had the election of the Emperor been formalised by the terms of the so-called Golden Bull. The privilege of election lay in the hands of seven German princes, four of them temporal and three ecclesiastical. These were the King of Bohemia, the princes ('Electors') of Saxony, Brandenburg and the Palatinate, and the archbishops of Mainz, Cologne and Trier. Once elected, therefore, the Emperor did not rule Germany by the will of God, but by the consent of an élite group of the German nobility. His position was strictly that of a feudal lord, with the power to nominate to certain Church offices, to raise an army to defend the territory, and to act as the supreme arbiter in internal disputes. Beyond these, the Emperor could claim no rights of direct intervention in the internal affairs of the states that made up the Empire.

There was scarcely any governmental machinery common to the Empire as a whole. There was no common law, and the Emperor had no form of independent income other than the revenues from his personal estates. The major institution of the

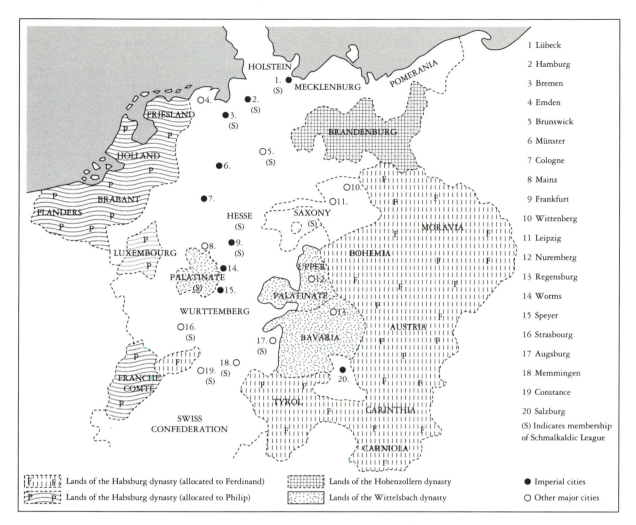

13.1 Germany and the Empire in the time of Charles V

Empire was the Imperial Diet (*Reichstag*), the great formal meeting between Emperor and princes, which was summoned by the Emperor to permit discussion of outstanding problems and issues among the principal members of the German political hierarchy. Membership consisted of the Electors, the rest of the temporal and ecclesiastical nobility, and the representatives of the eighty-five German towns which enjoyed the status of 'Imperial Cities'. The financial role of the Diet was also of major importance, and no lengthy period could be allowed to elapse without summoning the assembly. The other exception to the rule of diversity was that the Emperor had at his disposal

since 1488 the forces raised by the Swabian League, an alliance of princes, knights and cities dedicated to the maintenance of order in southern Germany. It was the only effective armed force within Germany until religious divisions caused its disintegration in 1534.

Stimulated in part by the advance of Ottoman power, a movement towards administrative reform reached its peak in the last decade of the century. The imperial chancellor, Berthold von Henneberg, proposed a programme (1495 and 1500) whereby the German princes would renounce the right to settle their own disputes. Instead, they would refer them to an Imperial Chamber of Justice

(*Reichskammergericht*), whose members would be nominated jointly by the Emperor and by the princes. The reforms also envisaged a regular form of taxation for the whole Empire, and the division of Germany into administrative 'circles' (*Kreise*). Within these ten units the laws of the Empire were to be enforced by the princes. This was probably the only reform which might claim any success, and the reason was one of the inescapable facts of German political life. The respective German territories could only be governed effectively by the prince with the local authority and power to carry out the task. Where the interests of prince and Emperor coincided, government would probably be effective. Where they diverged, the Emperor would invariably be hard-pressed to impose his will.

Recent emperors had displayed clear ideas as to how the Empire should develop. Frederick III (1440–93) and his son Maximilian I (1493–1519) were both members of the House of Habsburg. Originally 'a grubby little central European dynasty' (Gerhard Benecke, *Maximilian I: An Analytical Biography*, 1982) with lands in Switzerland and Alsace, the Habsburgs had by the mid-thirteenth century created an extensive power-base in Austria and in the Tyrol. Unmistakably, it was Frederick's intention that the various branches of the House of Habsburg should be welded together to form an international unit transcending territorial boundaries. His device based upon the five vowels (AEIOU – *Austriae est imperare orbi universo*: Austria is to govern the whole globe) may have been an outrageous claim when it was first used, but in the time of Charles V it could be regarded by many as a serious goal.

The primary weapon of the Habsburgs was dynastic marriage, and the greatest success was the union (1482) between Maximilian and Mary, daughter of Charles the Bold of Burgundy, and heir to his duchy. Maximilian was shrewder still, and the marriage of his son Philip to Juana of Castile (1496) was eventually to bring the Habsburgs to the thrones of Spain. Even after the election of Charles to the Empire, the process continued. His own marriage was to facilitate the acquisition of the throne of Portugal, while that of his brother Ferdinand (1526) was to bring Bohemia and part of Hungary within the Habsburg domains.

The election of Charles in succession to Maximilian (June 1519) may be seen as the crowning achievement of Habsburg policy. Three generations of the dynasty thus dominated the Empire for nearly 130 years. Yet the circumstances of that election also demonstrated that Habsburg expansion was approaching its practical limits. Foreign enemies had to be overcome, and German princes had to be attached to his cause. Even before his imperial career had begun, Charles already confronted the elements that would cause him most trouble over the next forty years: France, the papacy and the German princes.

THE POLITICAL PHILOSOPHY OF CHARLES V

To an age that did not believe in coincidences, the vast range of legacies that had fallen into Charles's hands by 1520 could only be explained as a megalomaniac conspiracy, or as a manifestation of the will of God. In the early years of Charles's ascendancy, two claims of this latter sort were put forward in his name. Bishop Mota of Badajoz told the Cortes of Castile when they met in 1520 that the aim of the young monarch was to use what God had given him for the benefit of the holy Catholic faith, and to continue the struggle against the infidel. In this, Mota was committing Charles to an essentially Spanish policy. An alternative view was provided shortly afterwards by the Imperial Chancellor, Mercurino Gattinara. In a memorandum to Charles (1523), he stated that it was clearly God's intention that Charles should proceed from this impressive basis to achieve a 'universal monarchy'. Gattinara's religious veneer barely concealed political and dynastic considerations that had much in common with the ruthless expansionism of Maximilian. Which of these views governed Charles's conduct over the next thirty-five years? On the one hand, Mota's aim may simply have been to convince Castilians that their new, foreign ruler would indeed follow traditional Spanish policies. On the other hand, Gattinara's vision did not survive his premature death in 1530, when Charles abolished his office and divided his functions between a Spaniard, Los Cobos, and a Burgundian, Granvelle.

The following seems to be a fair conclusion based upon the whole of Charles's career. He began his rule with an acute sense of his responsibilities, both to his ancestors and to God. Yet ten years' experience of the duplicity and complexity of European politics knocked out of him any romantic notions of a glorious 'new age'. By 1530 he was concerned primarily with the secure retention of those territories that were his inheritance. He could thus advise his son and heir in January 1548 to 'preserve peace and avoid war, unless you are forced to it for your own defence, for warfare is a heavy burden on our hereditary lands'. Then, again, Charles seems never to have lost sight altogether of his vision of the Emperor as the temporal protector of a united Christendom. His major political concessions in the 1520s and in the last years of his reign contrast starkly with his consistent struggle against Islam, and his consistent attempts to heal the rift within European Christianity. Here, as in the defence of his Habsburg legacy, Charles was essentially conservative, far keener to preserve the world into which he had been born than to create any form of 'brave new world'.

13.2 Key figures

HESSE, Philip, Landgrave of (1504–67). Succeeded as Landgrave of Hesse (1518). Led princely forces against Imperial Knights (1523) and against rebellious peasants (1525). Declared support for Luther (1524). Reformed Church within Hesse (1526). Founded first Protestant university at Marburg (1527). Attempted to establish common ground between Luther and Zwingli at Colloquy of Marburg (1529). Leading figure in formation of Schmalkaldic League (1530) and subsequently its major military leader. Imprisoned upon defeat of the League (1546–52).

GATTINARA, Mercurino (1465–1530). Born Piedmont. Entered service of Margaret of Austria as a lawyer (1501), playing a prominent role in the administration and the diplomacy of Burgundy. Leading councillor of Charles V, appointed Imperial Chancellor (1519). Appointed cardinal (1529).

MAURICE OF SAXONY (1521–53). Succeeded as Duke of Saxony (1541). Married the daughter of Philip of Hesse (1541), but sided with Charles V against the Schmalkaldic League (1546) in the hope of being nominated Elector of Saxony in place of his cousin, John Frederick. Having achieved that aim (1548), he deserted Charles, concluding a treaty with Henry II of France and forcing Charles to make important concessions to Protestant princes by Treaty of Passau (1552).

WORMS AND BRUSSELS, 1521–2

In January 1521, Charles met the Imperial Diet at Worms for the traditional purpose of regulating the outstanding problems of the Empire. Although the Diet has become so closely associated with Luther's revolt, Charles's major proclamations concerned the preservation of princely rights, the maintenance of political order in the Empire, and the revival of the imperial reform programme. At the heart of the issue of imperial reform lay the question of a Regency Council. This was a question of great delicacy, potentially a threat to Charles's prerogatives, yet clearly necessary for a ruler who was bound to be absent for long periods. As a compromise, a temporary council was set up to operate until the next time Charles attended a Diet, and then only when the Emperor was absent from Germany.

In the following year, Charles concluded an agreement which at the time appeared largely a dynastic affair, but which had far-reaching, long-term consequences for the Empire and for Germany. By the Compact of Brussels, Charles solved the problem of the role that would be played by his younger brother, Ferdinand. Dynastic links made it impossible to exclude so prominent a member of the family from a role in government, and the likelihood that Charles would be away from Germany for long periods made it essential to find a suitable regent to govern in his absence. In 1522, therefore, Ferdinand underwent the happy metamorphosis from a dispossessed younger brother into one of the greatest lords of Europe. Created Archduke, he assumed control of all the family lands in Germany, Austria and the Tyrol, and effectively became heir-apparent to his brother as Emperor. By the Compact of Brussels, Charles seemed to accept that his own political power-base lay in Spain and in the Netherlands, and traded the territories that had provided the traditional basis of Habsburg power for the security of a reliable regent in Germany. The subsequent division of Charles's vast inheritance into a German section under Ferdinand and a Spanish/Dutch section under Philip II has often been quoted as evidence of Charles's ultimate failure. Yet the lines of this division were established by this arrangement of 1522, and his achievement as Emperor must be judged in that light.

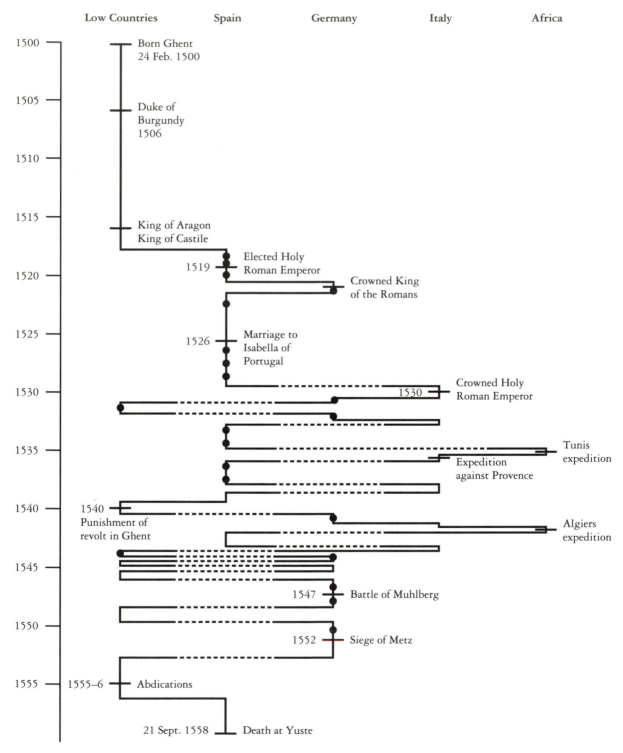

13.3 *The imperial roadshow: the logistics of personal monarchy in the first half of the sixteenth century. The line indicates Charles' movements between his various territories, a vertical line indicating his presence in given territory. A dot indicates his presence at a Cortes or Diet*

FERDINAND'S REGENCY AND THE KNIGHTS' WAR

Charles was absent from Germany between 1521 and 1530, during which time imperial authority lay in the hands of Ferdinand and the Council of Regency. This was a period of mixed fortunes for the Habsburgs. Ferdinand ensured that the Council of Regency never became an instrument of princely power, making it clear that he was unwilling to accord any real consultative role to the body. While he had prevented the princes from dictating to him, however, it was by no means clear whether he could dictate to the princes. Apart from the forces of the Swabian League, the Regent lacked any means to impose his will on Germany.

Only when the common interests of Germany's political élite were threatened could any concerted action be organised. This occurred twice during these early years of Ferdinand's regency. The first occasion was the revolt of the Imperial Knights in 1522, a genuinely conservative revolt, born out of the desperation of a dying class at the erosion of its influence. It arose from the initiative of the adventurer Franz von Sickingen, who saw in Lutheranism a fine opportunity to strike a blow at least at the ecclesiastical princes. Announcing his conversion, he fell upon the estates of the Archbishop-Elector of Trier in the Rhineland. Although the Regent lacked the means to combat Sickingen and his followers, the other princes were unwilling to tolerate such a challenge to their power. An army under the Landgrave of Hesse met Sickingen's forces at Landstuhl in 1523, and the latter's death brought the brief and desperate insurrection to a close.

THE PEASANTS' WAR

The Knights' revolt was closely followed by the great revolt of the south German peasantry. This began with risings in the region of Schaffhausen on the Swiss borders early in 1525 and spread rapidly through most of southern Germany. The exact nature and causes of the revolt have been debated by generations of historians. Many have treated it as part of the German Reformation. On the other hand, socialist historians have tried hard to minimise the connections with Lutheranism and have placed their stress upon the accumulated social and economic problems that faced the peasantry in many parts of Germany.

The revolt in southern Germany arose from a conjunction of several crises. The peasantry had suffered substantially from the increase in the power of the territorial princes. Their traditional freedoms and economic rights had come under great pressure, and the novel claims of their lords to forests, pastures and rivers threatened the peasants' ability to glean a living. The labour services that peasants owed their lords for the tenure of their land were liable to be increased in many places as long as the lord thought that he could get away with it. Such factors had already played a major role in the so-called *Bundschuh* rebellions that had disturbed the early years of the century. Other factors behind the explosion of 1525 include increased taxation, a run of bad harvests and an annual population-rise of a little under 1 per cent which placed considerable strain upon resources.

It was not only the peasants who rebelled. Peter Blickle has recently characterised the rebellion as 'a revolt of "the common man" in the towns and mining districts as well as on the land'. Alongside the peasants were to be found disaffected individuals and groups from all areas of society: remnants of the Imperial Knights, minor noblemen and even a few towns, such as Heilbronn and Rothenburg. The manifestos of 1525 showed the different priorities which prevailed in the various regions affected by the revolt. The most notable set of demands, the Twelve Articles of Memmingen (March 1525), were dominated by relatively conservative social and economic requests, with a number of articles which demonstrate the influence of Luther's ideas. In parts of the south-west, peasant demands reflected their desire to have no lord other than the Emperor. On the other hand, the so-called Tyrolean Constitution presented an altogether more revolutionary and Utopian system, in which all social distinctions and privileges vanished.

It remains impossible to deny that the revolt had some religious element. Martin Luther bears some direct responsibility in the sense that much of his publicity had deliberately been pitched, through crude and simple pamphlets, at a level which the peasantry could comprehend. They were like 'homemade gin: cheap, crude and effective' (R.W. Scribner, *The German Reformation*, 1986). Beyond Lutheranism, there existed a long history of peasant religious radicalism, in which lay the roots of Anabaptism, and the rallying cry of the *Bundschuh* rebels had been 'God's justice only'. It might also be argued that the princes themselves had set a worse example than Luther in their attacks upon the wealth and property of the Church. Perez Zagorin (*Rebels and Rulers, 1500–1600*, 1982) has pointed out that 'the Reformation plunged Germany into a great crisis of authority, bigger than it had ever known before'.

The most famous of the rebel leaders, Thomas Müntzer, had once followed Luther, before realising just how limited the social and economic targets of the reformer were. In 1525 he led the peasant cause in Thuringia with a vision of a new world for the peasant, organised on the basis of Christian equality. In his writings and speeches, Müntzer mixed the call for social justice with a wild and apocalyptic religious vision. He did the same disservice for the peasants' revolt as the Münster leaders did for Anabaptism. Even as some conservatives, such as Luther and the Elector of Saxony, reluctantly admitted that there was some justice in the rebels' demands, so Müntzer's extremism forced the landlord class to eradicate such dangerous views by the most drastic means available.

Confident that God would surely give them victory over the princes' army, the peasants gave battle at Frankenhausen in May 1525. Predictably, their ill-armed and ill-disciplined force was slaughtered by the troops of Philip of Hesse. At the same time the peasant rebels in Franconia were heavily defeated at Ingolstadt (June), while the overwhelming victory of the Duke of Lorraine at Zabern (May) left an estimated 18,000 peasants dead on the battlefield. The subsequent cost to the German peasantry was also enormous. 'Whole communities', writes Zagorin, 'were massacred and villages burned. Leaders and militants were tortured, beheaded, and roasted to death. Countless numbers were summarily executed. Fines and confiscations were a routine punishment.'

The events of 1523 and 1525 represented a total victory for the dominant social and political forces in Germany. The Emperor and his Regent were virtual spectators, and perhaps even emerged from these events in a weaker political position. The demonstration by the princes of their complete political and military domination over all other groups in German society made it clear that the Emperor could expect to find no adequate ally against them.

THE ESTABLISHMENT OF PRINCELY PROTESTANTISM, 1526–30

By the time the Imperial Diet was reconvened at Speyer in 1526, the issue of Martin Luther and his writings had become vastly more serious. Not only had the German Reformation passed beyond its original, academic stage, but also its teachings had threatened to become fearsome weapons in the hands of revolutionaries. The princes who attended the Diet divided into two clear 'camps'. Long traditions of loyalty to the Habsburgs and the pressing problems created by Turkish military successes to the east of the Empire created a powerful body of support for the Emperor and for religious orthodoxy. The Peasants' War also helped to encourage conservative sentiment. On the other hand, the events of the last five years confirmed that the Emperor was in no position to enforce his will, and that political and religious liberty for the princes was there for the taking. The decree of the Diet declared that the Emperor should convene a council to resolve the religious questions under dispute. In the meantime, the princes were responsible to God for the spiritual welfare of their subjects, and should be free to decide the doctrine of their state. This claim, summarised by the Latin slogan *Cuius regio eius religio*, was to dominate the future political development of the Reformation in Germany.

The Emperor's refusal to accept this principle was broadly ignored by the reforming princes. October 1526 saw the official ecclesiastical reformation of Hesse, carried out jointly by the Estates and by a Church synod summoned by the Landgrave Philip. Within two years, the policy of Hesse and of Electoral Saxony had been imitated in Schleswig, Holstein, Brunswick, Bremen, Goslar,

Flensburg, Strasbourg, Nuremberg and Ansbach.

When the Diet met once more at Speyer (March 1529), the Emperor seemed better-placed to impose his will. He was close to understandings with France and with the papacy, and the Turkish military advance had been checked. There seemed to be every prospect that Habsburg military resources might be concentrated at last upon Germany. With these advantages, Ferdinand demanded that all religious innovation should cease. The result was the famous Protestation of Speyer, in which a number of the Lutheran princes and cities restated their claims to religious autonomy and added that the resolutions of 1526, having been agreed in the Diet, could not be put aside at the whim of the Emperor, still less at the whim of the Regent. Their action added the word 'Protestant' to the vocabulary of the Reformation.

The Diet of Augsburg (1530) saw the last concerted and viable attempt to avert religious schism in Germany. While Charles remained eager to avoid conflict while so many other potential disputes existed in his territories, the Lutherans cannot have relished the political dangers which would inevitably result from their rejection and isolation. Philip Melanchthon thus sought to promote an understanding by presenting a coherent summary of the reformist position in deliberately mild terms. The Augsburg Confession was a splendidly diplomatic document, which steered clear of recognised areas of conflict, such as the doctrine of purgatory or the issue of papal supremacy. It was a clear attempt to distance the Lutherans from the more radical groups, from the Zwinglians and the Anabaptists, and might thus be seen as undermining the unity of Protestantism. The blank refusal of Catholic theologians to discuss doctrinal issues foreshadowed the uncompromising stance of the Council of Trent, and the indignant withdrawal of Philip of Hesse from the Diet opened a new era of religious confrontation in Germany.

THE SCHMALKALDIC LEAGUE

The events at Augsburg left the Protestants in a more exposed and dangerous position than ever. Their response to this danger was the League of Schmalkalden, or Schmalkaldic League, formed in February 1531. It was a uneasy alliance, for the interests of the towns, which formed the greater part of its membership, were not necessarily those of the princes who formed its political élite. Constitutionally, too, the position of the League was extremely uncertain. It clearly existed in direct opposition to the wishes and interests of the Emperor, and Luther was not the only person linked with the League who harboured severe doubts about the legality and morality of such opposition. The leadership of the Schmalkaldic League was shared between the greatest of its princely members, Philip of Hesse and the Elector of Saxony. In the long term, Philip must be seen as the outstanding figure on the Protestant side. A statesman of genuine ability, he played a mediating role of the first importance, not only between the princes and the towns within the Protestant camp, but also between Lutherans and Zwinglians.

For all the uncertainties of its beginnings, the League's position was considerably consolidated in the course of the decade. The 'triumph' enjoyed by Charles V in securing the election of Ferdinand (1531) as his designated successor was in reality a mixed success. The cost in bribes left both men with more prestige than resources, and the election so alienated the Duke of Bavaria that, despite his Catholic faith, he formed an alliance with the League. Meanwhile, the renewal of Turkish activity on the eastern borders of the Empire confirmed that, once again, the time was not ripe to seek a military solution to the problem of Protestantism. While the Emperor bought time through compromise agreements at Nuremberg (1532) and Frankfurt (1539), the League consolidated its international status as a symbol of resistance to Habsburg expansion. When it acted in 1534 against the extension of Habsburg influence in Württemberg, it did so with financial backing from Francis I; and agreements with the crowns of England and Denmark also indicated that the League had become a prominent factor in the international politics of Western Europe. Given that the purposes of the Schmalkaldic League were purely defensive, it achieved a very large degree of success in the course of the 1530s, and presented Charles with a substantial obstacle to his political authority within Germany.

13.4 The rise and fall of the Schmalkaldic League

1531		Formation of League at Schmalkalden (27 Feb.) as organisation for the defence of Protestant princes and cities against the declared hostility of Charles V
1532	**The Nuremberg Interim.** Charles accepted the temporary suspension of the Edict of Worms, which ordered princes to abandon religious innovations. Charles temporarily accepted the secularisation of Church lands and the need to call a General Council of the Church	
1534		League forces under Philip of Hesse struck a blow at Habsburg influence in south-west Germany, seizing Württemberg, ousting Habsburg agents and restoring Duke Ulrich
1536		**Concord of Wittenberg.** Achieved greater degree of doctrinal agreement between members of the League. Some Swabian towns accepted Lutheran position on the Eucharist
1539	**The Frankfurt Interim.** Charles agreed to a fifteen-month truce with the League on the condition that its members undertook no further seizures of Church lands. Made tentative arrangements for future discussions on Turkish problem and on religious settlement	
1542		League's position in northern Germany strengthened by forcible conversion of duchy of Brunswick-Wolfenbüttel to Protestantism
1544	Negotiations between Charles and the League at Worms failed to reach agreement on religious issues	
1546	**Diet of Regensburg** (June). Placed Philip of Hesse and others under the imperial ban, and Charles began military operations. By the end of the year Ulm, Frankfurt, Strasbourg and the Elector Palatine had surrendered to the Emperor	
1547	Defeat of the forces of the Schmalkaldic League at the **Battle of Mühlberg** (24 April)	

THE COLLOQUY OF REGENSBURG

Charles and Ferdinand did not cynically maintain peace in the 1530s merely because they lacked the means to fight. The years between 1539 and 1541 showed very clearly that Charles truly desired peace in Germany as a precondition for tackling the real responsibilities that God had given him. Frustrated by the failure of successive Popes to fulfil their promises of a General Council, Charles took matters into his own hands.

Attempts to reach a doctrinal compromise were launched in 1539 and received a considerable boost a year later, when the political and moral position of Philip of Hesse was severely undermined by a bigamous marriage. Protestant and Catholic theologians eventually met in Regensburg in January

1541. Had an agreement been reached, the Emperor might have defied papal authority by allowing a doctrinal compromise to exist in Germany without papal consent. Without an agreement, Charles faced the alternatives of acquiescence or war. Such theologians as the Catholic Gropper and the Protestants Bucer and Melanchthon seem to have worked at the Colloquy with a genuine desire to find a middle way, but their goodwill was not shared by others. Papal officials, doctrinal hard-liners on both sides, and even some of the princes, primarily concerned about issues of Habsburg authority, found the prospect of compromise less attractive.

Nevertheless, agreement was reached on several important issues, such as the marriage of priests and Communion in both kinds. On the other hand, no common ground could be found on the key issues of transubstantiation and papal authority. By July, with Charles eager to travel south to begin his campaign against Algiers, it was clear that no overall compromise would be reached, and the Colloquy broke up. Karl Brandi's summary of the situation would undoubtedly have received Charles's approval: 'The theologians at Regensburg, Luther at Wittenberg, the Pope in Rome, the Catholic and Protestant Estates of Germany, were unanimous in one thing – in repudiating Charles's policy of reconciliation. That Charles himself acted in good faith allows of no doubt.' A solution to the religious problems of Germany based upon consent would truly have freed his hands for greater undertakings, and would have brought him the credit for the preservation of Christian unity, where the papacy had failed. In the event, the Colloquy's failure marked a turning-point in imperial policy, leaving Charles with little alternative to imposing his authority through a war that he had sought for a decade to avoid.

Other factors in the early 1540s also made war an urgent necessity. Charles's political authority and the future prospects of his dynasty were now at greater risk than ever before. With the decision of Archbishop von Wied of Cologne to embrace Protestantism (1543), and with the conversion of the Elector Palatine to the reformed faith (1546), the Protestants actually had a four–three majority among the Electors, and were thus in a position to reject the Habsburg candidate in any future imperial election.

THE SCHMALKALDIC WAR, 1541–7

Military success –

The preparation of a campaign in Germany was such a complex undertaking that the Emperor had to proceed with care and with patience. Peace with France was an essential preliminary, and was finally achieved at Crépy (September 1544). The following year, a truce with the Turks brought Charles respite on his eastern front. Imperial diplomacy also sought to divide the German princes, and achieved its greatest successes by winning over Maurice of Saxony and the Duke of Bavaria to the imperial side. The one was bribed by the promise of the Electoral title once the Protestant Elector of Saxony had been defeated, while the other was offered a prestigious marriage alliance. Charles must have been still more gratified by the emergence of another ally. Quite apart from the summoning of the Council of Trent in 1544, Pope Paul III reacted enthusiastically to the suggestion of a military solution in Germany, and it seemed at last that the two heads of European Christendom would cooperate in the assault upon heresy. In reality, of course, Pope and Emperor were not fighting the same battle. While Charles still hoped that victory might enable him to force a compromise solution upon the Protestant princes, the Pope was in no mood for compromises.

The collection of adequate forces and finances for the German war was also a massive and time-consuming undertaking. For virtually the only time in his long reign, Charles was able to call upon the resources of all areas of his *monarchia*. In Germany itself 20,000 troops were raised, while further detachments arrived from the Low Countries and from the imperial garrisons in Milan and in Naples. As ever, Spain contributed men and large sums of money to this holy cause. Pope Paul contributed 12,000 troops and 200,000 ducats, along with permission to raise a further 900,000 ducats from the Spanish Church.

The members of the Schmalkaldic League began the war with three advantages. Their forces were greater: probably some 80,000 men compared to 56,000 against them; they were greatly superior in artillery; and they were well placed to prevent the junction of all the various elements of the Imperial army. On the other hand, they were handicapped, perhaps fatally, by serious psychological misgivings about the morality of war against the Emperor. The traditional divisions between towns and princes and the unstable state of the League's finances were serious additional handicaps.

Their failure to prevent the assembly of the imperial forces effectively cost the Protestants the war. This, together with the attack by Duke Maurice upon the lands of the Elector of Saxony, led to the forces of the Schmalkaldic League more or less abandoning the south of Germany to the Emperor by the end of 1546. The concluding blows were then struck in the early months of 1547. With Ferdinand and with Maurice of Saxony, Charles brought the Protestants to battle on the river Elbe at Mühlberg (24 April 1547). Outmanoeuvred and taken by surprise, the Protestant forces were routed, and the Elector John Frederick of Saxony was taken prisoner. The Schmalkaldic League quickly disintegrated, and with the exception of some strongholds in the north the whole of Germany was soon in Charles's hands. After nearly two decades of compromise, negotiation and frustration, Mühlberg seemed to represent Charles's finest moment.

– and political stalemate

To most contemporary observers, it seemed that this crushing military victory left Charles free to organise the future affairs of Germany as he wished. Such observers failed to grasp, however, that the size, power and consolidation of Western European states were now such that their fates could not be decided by the events of an hour or two on the battlefield.

In reality, Charles's victory had changed nothing of fundamental importance. The great truth of imperial German politics remained the same: that the Emperor could do nothing without the support of at least some of the princes. Some of his erstwhile German allies, such as Maurice of Saxony, were now uneasy at the extent of the military victory, and at the prospect of an all-conquering Emperor. Deprived of their support and cooperation, Charles would be impotent once more as he sought to achieve a lasting solution to the problems of Germany.

First, Charles still sought to achieve some degree of political unity within Germany. Realising that there was no further mileage in the Imperial reforms proposed at the start of his reign, he returned to the more traditional idea of a league which would bind together the principalities and towns of Germany under his authority. Such a proposal was put to the Imperial Diet at Augsburg in September 1547. It met with the same opposition and objections that had always greeted projects which promoted the authority of the Habsburgs. Charles's predicament was made clearer by the prominence of Catholic princes, such as the Duke of Bavaria, among his opponents, and by the opening months of 1548 plans for imperial reform were laid to rest for the last time.

Similarly, in religious matters, Charles's victory gained him no greater cooperation from the Protestants or from the papacy. The Pope's assistance against the Schmalkaldic League had been of short duration, and hopes that the Council of Trent might provide a solution also faded when the Council was adjourned in 1547. Unwilling to proceed on his own, and reluctant to grant further concessions from such a position of strength, Charles attempted a new form of compromise. The Augsburg Interim put forward a conservative doctrinal statement, but sweetened the pill for the Protestants by concessions on such 'external' issues as clerical marriage and Communion in both kinds. The issue of Church lands was not mentioned at all, and the whole plan was proposed upon the assumption that it served to fill the gap until the General Council was reconvened. Even then, the terms of the Augsburg Interim only really made any impact where Charles's military power was great enough to enforce it, and it was thus effectively ignored in large areas of northern Germany.

THE ISSUE OF THE IMPERIAL SUCCESSION

At the same time, Charles was faced with the collapse of the dynastic unity of the Habsburgs over the thorny question of the Imperial succession. He had recognised his brother Ferdinand as heir to the Imperial throne as long ago as 1519, yet there remained much uncertainty as to who would be Emperor after Ferdinand's own death. Charles's hope that his brother might be followed by his son Philip clashed with Ferdinand's ambitions for his own son, Maximilian. Charles, Ferdinand and their sister Mary met at Augsburg in 1550, where a tense and quarrelsome meeting produced one viable compromise: Philip would indeed succeed Ferdinand, on the condition that he accepted Maximilian as his own successor.

The apparent strength of this plan, that it maintained the links between the resources of Spain and the Empire, was probably its greatest weakness in German eyes. Philip was undoubtedly Spanish, while Ferdinand had achieved acceptance as a German prince over the years and Maximilian had effectively been born German. It was also natural that the Electors should object to a system which, by prearranging the imperial succession three generations in advance, deprived them and their own children of a major source of influence over the political affairs of Germany. Faced with growing evidence that the succession agreement could not be implemented, Charles seemed resigned by 1552 to the division of his inheritance. After seeking a Portuguese bride for Philip, Charles was negotiating the ill-fated marriage with Mary Tudor by 1554. The consolidation of Habsburg authority in the Netherlands, and the preparations for the transfer of power there to Philip, confirmed that Charles had accepted the fact that there would in future be two quite separate branches of the House of Habsburg.

DEFEAT AND ABDICATION

Within five years of his victory at Mühlberg, Charles was to suffer humiliations that finally convinced him that princely Germany was ungovernable. Their origins lay in the so-called Koenigsberg Alliance, a small confederation of undefeated Protestant princes in the north of Germany. Too small to pose a threat to the Emperor on their own, these princes soon found powerful friends. Maurice of Saxony, fearing that Charles might attempt to remove him from his recently acquired Electoral dignity, was joined by the

intensely anti-imperial King of France, Henry II. Claiming that he acted in defence of German liberties, Henry promised financial and military support for these malcontent princes by the Treaty of Chambord (July 1552).

Within two months of launching this revolt the conspirators had virtually destroyed all Charles's credibility as master of Germany. Having failed to anticipate the danger, and thus having failed to muster sufficient forces against it, Charles was driven south before Maurice's armies. With Franconia and Swabia falling to his enemies, Charles fled deeper into his Austrian possessions. Not for the first time, he was saved by the arrival of forces and funds from Spain, and a settlement was reached through Ferdinand's arbitration. The Peace of Passau (August 1552) represented little more than a truce, but at its base lay the mutual realisation that neither side had the power to dictate terms to the other. In that respect, the Peace of Passau should be seen as the basis for the later Peace of Augsburg. The year held one further humiliation for Charles. Concentrating his forces against the French, he set out to regain those border strongholds which the rebellious princes had granted to Henry II as the price of his assistance. The disastrous failure to recapture Metz represented the final disillusion of Charles's reign.

Much as contemporaries sought to romanticise the final acts of Charles's political life, it now seems clear that by 1553 he was in a state of physical and mental collapse. Although he did not officially cease to be Holy Roman Emperor until February 1558, and although the final agreement with the German princes was sealed in his name, the settlement of the German question lay once more in the hands of Ferdinand.

At the Diet of Augsburg in 1555 idealism gave way to realism, as both parties recognised the political realities demonstrated in Germany by the events of the past decade. After many years of attempting to find a doctrinal formula acceptable to both parties, the Emperor now accepted that the religious settlement within any given territory would be decided, not by imperial decree, but by the wishes of the territorial prince. The principle of *cuius regio eius religio*, that he who ruled the principality would decide its religion, lay at the heart of the Religious Peace of Augsburg. The princes undertook to support no missionary activity in the territories of another prince, and agreed that all ecclesiastical states ruled by Catholic bishops in 1552 were to remain Catholic. The settlement was a triumph not for toleration, but for political pragmatism. The Emperor lacked the power to impose a settlement upon the princes, and the princes lacked both the power and the consensus to coerce an Emperor with such resources as Charles possessed.

THE NETHERLANDS UNDER CHARLES V

The Netherlands were the only section of his hereditary lands in which Charles had the authority and scope to pursue a recognisable Habsburg policy of expansion and state-building. The acquisition of new territories was a significant part of Charles's achievement in the Low Countries. In 1521 the provinces of Flanders and Artois became integral provinces of the Netherlands, and their administrative links with France were severed. At the same time, Tournai was won from the French. In the years that followed, the Estates of Friesland (1523) and of Overijssel (1528) were persuaded that they had little to gain from continued independence, and the Bishop of Utrecht surrendered his territorial independence in 1527. Maastricht was transferred from imperial control, Groningen was purchased (1536), and Gelderland was secured from the Duke of Cleves (1543) as the price of his military defeat.

In the Netherlands, as in other Habsburg territories, Charles sought to achieve more efficient government at the expense of local and provincial authorities. His greatest project was the establishment in 1531 of three 'collateral' councils for the conduct of centralised administration. These were the Council of State, the main organ of Charles's central authority, a Council of Finance, and a Privy or Secret Council, for the centralisation of tax administration and of legal procedure. In 1548 the Low Countries were designated as the 'Burgundian Circle' of the Empire, and a year later a 'Pragmatic Sanction' ensured that these territories would pass to Charles's son as a single inheritance, regardless of any privileges claimed by individual provinces.

Such measures naturally provoked opposition. Proposals for a standing army for the provinces were dropped in 1534, as the provinces protested about the effects upon their liberties and upon their pockets. Rioters in 'sHertogenbosch (1525), Brussels (1532) and Ghent (1537) all voiced similar concerns about the cost, the effects upon trade, and the threats to local security that arose from Charles's wars with France, and such outbursts culminated in the full-scale rebellion that broke out in Ghent in 1539. Fearing a northern equivalent to the Comuneros' revolt, Charles reacted ruthlessly. The rapid suppression of the revolt, and the severe punishment meted out through the cancellation of Ghent's liberties, show just how effective Charles's political control in the Low Countries could be.

Nevertheless, Charles's greatest strength in the Netherlands, and the greatest contrast with his policy in Germany, was that he generally ruled in concert with the leading nobles. The *Stadtholders*, the governors who represented Charles's authority in the provinces, were drawn from their ranks. During his reign, the Council of State remained a genuinely consultative institution, and the dignity of the great chivalric order of the Golden Fleece was maintained. The greatest difference between Charles's methods and those of his son was that Charles extended to the Dutch nobility the same trust that he accorded to the grandees of Castile, while Philip seems to have seen in them the local equivalent of the treacherous German nobility.

Charles also sought to bring the Church in the Netherlands more closely under his control and extracted two important concessions from the papacy. The Pope conceded his right to nominate clergy to benefices within the Low Countries (1530), and accepted Charles's claim (1531) that papal Bulls should only be valid within the Low Countries if confirmed and reissued in the form of government edicts. Charles was frustrated, however, in his attempts to reorganise the bishoprics in the Netherlands so as to eliminate the influence of some French bishoprics within his territories, and this would remain one of the preoccupations of Philip II.

In part, at least, Charles desired this control for the purpose of protecting his territories from the threat of heresy. A series of edicts (placards) thus declared it to be a capital offence to bring Luther's works into the Netherlands, to print them or to read them there (1521). The following year, an Inquisition was introduced, under direct governmental rather than ecclesiastical control. The statistics for religious persecution in the Netherlands at this time are difficult to square with the picture painted by many historians of a relatively tolerant, humanist Emperor. In particular, fierce campaigns against Anabaptist communities in the late 1530s and the mid-1540s made a significant contribution to the estimated death-toll of about 2,000 Dutch 'heretics' during Charles's reign.

CHARLES V: CONCLUSIONS

Few rulers in the sixteenth century governed with so rigid and consistent a set of principles as Charles V. By his abdication, however, Charles indicated to contemporaries that he considered himself to have failed in the fulfilment of these principles.

It is undoubtedly true that Charles failed to achieve the daunting goals that he set himself: to maintain peace amongst the Christians of Europe, and to lead this united Christendom against the Turk. In the end no such European crusade materialised; and, for all Charles's efforts, the 1540s witnessed open warfare between the religious factions within the Empire. At the root of these failures lay Charles's inability to distinguish the political realities of Germany from the dynastic, imperial propaganda put about by his grandfather and great-grandfather; he misjudged the depth of the religious divisions that affected contemporary Europe; he was unable to appreciate the fear and apprehension that his vast personal inheritance inspired in others; he was perhaps naïve in underestimating the extent to which other men were motivated purely by their own political advantage. In these respects Charles was guilty of misconception rather than mismanagement and, given that his stated aims were unattainable from the outset, his consistent efforts to achieve the impossible deserve some respect.

If the Emperor is judged by more realistic criteria than his own, his reign may be seen as more

than a succession of gallant failures. On the contrary, he could be seen as having achieved remarkable feats of preservation. He had recognised as early as 1522 that his vast inheritance could only be governed effectively if the territories and responsibilities were shared by other members of the dynasty. If the details of the settlement reached in the 1550s did not reflect his personal wishes, the fact remains that the amount of territory in Habsburg hands in 1555 was significantly greater than that inherited by Charles nearly forty years earlier. Nor can Charles be accused of allowing the authority of the Emperor in Germany to be diminished. Strict constitutional limits existed upon the Emperor's powers; and, much as he attempted to influence the princes, he at no stage attempted to govern Germany other than through its territorial rulers. Indeed, one could justifiably claim that Germany never felt the impact of imperial authority more strongly than during Charles's reign. Finally, to the charge that Charles failed to check the growth of Protestantism within Germany, one might answer that the Emperor ensured the survival of Catholicism where once it was threatened with extinction.

THE EMPIRE AFTER CHARLES

The three Emperors who reigned between Charles's abdication and the end of the century all largely accepted the political realities that had painfully been made clear to their great predecessor. They abandoned the 'grand designs' of earlier Habsburgs and accepted both the religious divisions within the Empire and the practical limits that were set upon their personal political authority. Ferdinand I (1556–64) undoubtedly did so with some regrets. While honouring the terms of the Peace of Augsburg, he remained a faithful son of the Church, and continued to toy with projects for centralised government in his hereditary lands. In the end, however, he contributed to the further weakening of Habsburg rule by the division of these lands between his three sons. The eldest of them, Maximilian II (1564–76), showed a much more ambiguous attitude to religion and appeared much more sympathetic to Protestantism. He appointed Lutherans to influential offices within the imperial court, and pressed the Council of Trent for concessions on such issues as the marriage of priests and Communion in both kinds.

Rudolf II (1576–1612) presents a significantly different picture. Even if the letter of the Peace of Augsburg remained in force, it now clearly did so without the sympathy of the Emperor. Bit by bit, Maximilian's policy was reversed. and Rudolf's reign saw an extensive Catholic counterattack throughout the Habsburg lands. A bloody peasants' revolt (1594–7) allowed the government to dictate terms to frightened landlords of both religious persuasions, while military campaigns were fought in Bohemia and Hungary in this decade to combat the spread of Protestantism. Increasingly, however, in the last twenty years of his life, Rudolf became subject to prolonged bouts of depression which made him incapable of taking political decisions. In both its return to religious partisanship and his further loss of political authority, Rudolf's reign clearly prepared the ground for the disaster of the Thirty Years War.

In the second half of the century, the political authority of the Emperor scarcely extended beyond the boundaries of Germany, and no Emperor after Charles V was crowned by the Pope. Even within Germany, the role of the Emperor became increasingly limited by the charters of liberties (*Wahlkapitulation*) that each now granted at his election.

The greatest limit of all was that imposed by the Emperors' constant preoccupation with the Turkish threat. Peace was agreed by Ferdinand I in 1562, but only on disadvantageous terms. The Turks retained possession of much of their captured Hungarian territories, and the Emperor suffered the humiliation of paying an annual tribute. War began once more in 1566, and ended two years later with a similarly humiliating settlement. Indeed, it seemed that only the death of the great Sultan Suleiman had saved Austria itself from invasion. Constant border tension erupted into a further prolonged war between 1593 and 1606, before the Treaty of Zsitva-Torok heralded a half-century of peace. The Emperor derived no territorial benefit from the treaty but was rid at last of the humiliation of the annual tribute. For over fifty years this threat to the east of the Empire had

consumed the revenues of whole Austrian provinces, and had forced successive Emperors to humble themselves before the Diet in order to gain funds for the defence of their lands.

In many parts of Germany the stagnation of imperial power was aggravated by the continuing consolidation of the authority of the princes. Development of institutions and consolidation of territory varied from state to state, yet by the end of the century several of the leading princes had earned a place alongside the more influential rulers of Western Europe. Princely councils in the more advanced states, such as Saxony and Bavaria, were now staffed less by hereditary nobles than by professional jurists and administrators. Naturally, the Lutheran princes also exercised a strict political control over the Church within their territories, but the case of Bavaria showed that Catholic princes were not slow to exercise similar forms of control.

Several German principalities by the turn of the century had become strong enough to play a political role on a European scale. Electoral Saxony had maintained its territorial unity, and its mining industry continued to provide an enviable financial basis for the electors. By the end of the century, as heads of the so-called 'Torgau Alliance', they had emerged as the military leaders of the German Lutheran princes. The Dukes of Bavaria had firmly established themselves as the greatest princely champions of German Catholicism. Dukes Albrecht V (1550–79) and Wilhelm V (1579–97) consistently supported the principles of the Counter-Reformation, and worked to eliminate the influence of Lutheranism among the nobility and estates of their duchy. By the turn of the century, the Dukes of Bavaria ranked barely below the Habsburgs themselves as guardians of Catholicism in Germany. The Elector Palatine, with his territories spread between the middle Rhine (Lower Palatinate) and the western borders of Bohemia (Upper Palatinate), also deserves to be ranked among these leading princes. Lutheranism lost its hold on the Palatinate under the Elector Frederick III (1559–76), but here it had given way to the more radical creed of Calvinism. As the only significant Calvinist prince in Germany, Frederick challenged the terms of the Peace of Augsburg, which had recognised Lutheranism and Catholicism as the only legal alternatives for the princes. Further afield, he pursued perhaps the most adventurous foreign policy of any of the German princes by means of his involvement with the Calvinist rebels in both France and the Netherlands. His capital, Heidelberg, became one of the leading centres in Europe for the printing of Calvinist works and propaganda.

A wider and more persistent problem was the spread of Protestant influence and control among the independent bishoprics of Germany. The Peace of Augsburg had attempted to check the spread of Protestantism in this way by means of its 'ecclesiastical reservation' clause, which laid down that any Catholic bishop converting to Protestantism was legally bound to resign his bishopric. Subsequently, the Emperor had ruled it illegal for any Protestant prince to lay hands upon lands belonging to the Catholic Church. Yet it was not long before some of these princes, tempted by the wealth of these Church lands, found a convenient formula. A Protestant candidate for a bishopric could not expect to be accepted and consecrated by the Pope, but by styling himself an 'administrator' he might rule the episcopal territories without such papal blessing, and could still take full advantage of the funds of the territories. At an appropriate point the princely patron of the 'administrator' might step in and absorb the bishopric into his own territories without opposition. Magdeburg and Halberstadt were both absorbed in this way by the Elector of Brandenburg during the 1560s.

Attention centred during these years upon Cologne, where Archbishop Gebhardt took a wife and declared his toleration of Protestantism. The fact that the archbishop was an elector of future emperors made this a delicate matter on both an international and an imperial level, and the result was a full-scale war which only ended in 1589 with the defeat of Gebhardt's last supporters. This case had secular parallels at the turn of the century in the duchy of Cleves-Jülich and in the free city of Donauwörth. In Cleves-Jülich, the succession of a mad duke (1592) precipitated a long struggle for control which ended in success for the Catholic claimants. In Donauwörth, arguments between local Catholic interests and the predominantly Protestant town authorities were resolved by the intervention of the Duke of Bavaria (1607), who compensated himself for his trouble by annexing the town to his duchy. The reaction that the Donauwörth incident provoked in Protestant circles, and the role that it thus played in the formation of the defensive Evangelical Union under Frederick IV, the Elector Palatine, have caused many historians to give it a central place among the causes of the Thirty Years War.

Further reading

K. Brandi (1939) *The Emperor Charles V.* London.

H. Holborn (1965) *History of Modern Germany.* Vol. 1: *The Reformation.* London.

M. Rady (1988) *The Emperor Charles V.* London.

• CHAPTER FOURTEEN •

The Reigns of Edward and Mary: A Mid-Tudor Crisis?

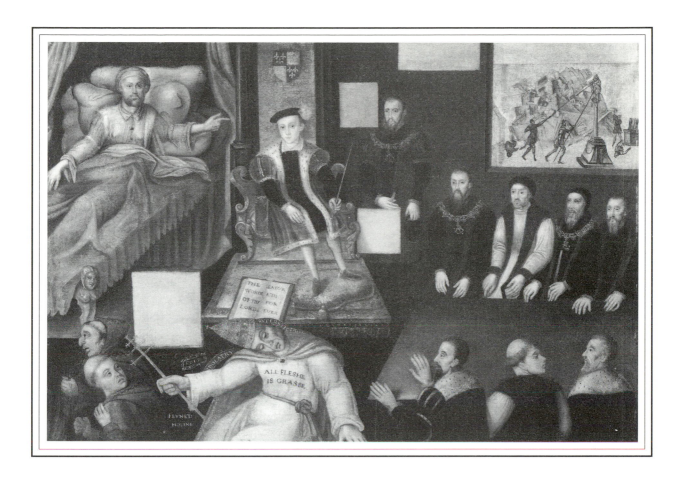

The succession to Henry VIII, represented in a painting which sets out to legitimise the coup carried out by the Seymour faction. Henry, on his deathbed, commends his young son to a group of councillors in which Edward Seymour and Thomas Cranmer are prominent. To the dismay of the other councillors, Edward discomforts the Pope, while in the background Catholic images are burned. The similarity between this scene and the engraving that opens Chapter Eleven is by no means coincidental

THE HISTORICAL DEBATE

For many years Edward VI and his half-sister Mary were treated as the 'poor relations' of the Tudor era. Short and troubled, their reigns suffered by comparison with the perceived glories of the reigns of Henry VIII and Elizabeth. On the reign of Edward VI, the work of A.F. Pollard at the turn of the century (*England under Protector Somerset*, 1900) established an orthodoxy that survived for some seventy years. For Pollard, Edward Seymour, Duke of Somerset was a remarkable figure. Socially enlightened and tolerant in religious matters, the 'good duke' sought social justice in an age of bigotry and greed. At the same time his policy towards Scotland represented a far-sighted bid to achieve the unity of the British Isles. Somerset fell from power because he could not convince lesser men of so lofty a philosophy. Consequently, the Duke of Northumberland, so influential in that fall, had to be seen as representative of all that was worst in sixteenth-century politics.

Such an interpretation was eventually overtaken by two major revisionist works. M.L. Bush (*The Government Policy of Protector Somerset*, 1975) portrayed Somerset as a more typical sixteenth-century politician, with more conventional objectives and priorities. By placing the Scottish war at the very centre of Somerset's policy, Bush also showed that all other aspects of policy could be explained in terms of the limitations imposed by the heavy commitment in Scotland. At the same time Dale Hoak (*The King's Council in the Reign of Edward VI*, 1976) concentrated upon the political environment in which Somerset operated, showing the extent to which he bypassed able colleagues who had supported his rise to power. In that light, Somerset's fall may be seen as resulting less from his policies than from his political ineptitude. As a result of this revision, Northumberland appears no more ruthless than any contemporary politician. Indeed, he emerges as a more realistic statesman than his predecessor, and one who genuinely exercised his authority through the constitutional channels of the council.

Queen Mary has suffered consistently at the hands of English commentators. The two policies closest to her heart, the Spanish alliance and the return of England to the Roman Church, have often been seen as unrealistic departures from the normal themes of Tudor policy. While Henry VIII and Elizabeth worked towards the development of the nation's identity and institutions, Mary sought unsuccessfully to return the country to such medieval concepts as a united Christendom. Such feelings found their most famous expression in Pollard's judgement that 'sterility was the conclusive note' of the reign.

Mary, too, has been the subject of renewed research in recent years. D.M. Loades (*Mary Tudor*, 1989) has placed the reign in the broader context of sixteenth-century English history, noting that the government maintained social order and effective administration under the most difficult social and economic conditions. He has also noted the extent to which the reforms of Elizabeth's reign were prepared in the reign of her predecessor. Researching into the role of the council during the reign, Anne Weikel ('The Marian Council Revisited', a chapter in *The Mid-Tudor Polity*, ed. J. Loach and R. Tittler, 1980) has concluded that it did not play the passive and sterile role ascribed to it by Pollard. Instead, it was an active and positive body of administrators, committed to the treatment of the many domestic problems that faced the government.

A number of recent writers have looked away from the issues of religion and of dynasty, and have surveyed the economic and administrative trends of the period as a whole. W.R.D. Jones (*The Mid-Tudor Crisis*, 1973) identified the years between 1539 and 1563 as embracing a 'mid-century crisis', an uncharacteristic period of instability in the Tudor century. It cannot be denied that these were years of rising prices, failing harvests and trade slumps. The associated idea that there was at the same time a crisis in Tudor government, a partial collapse of administration between the brilliant eras of Cromwell and Cecil, is not now so readily accepted.

THE ECONOMIC CONTEXT

England began to feel the impact of price inflation by the beginning of the 1540s. The price index in

Illustration 14.1 shows that the price of foodstuffs roughly doubled between the 1520s and the 1550s, while agricultural wages quite failed to keep pace. It also shows that these phenomena erupted upon a society lulled by decades of relative stability in prices and wages.

14.1 Prices and wages, 1491–1590

	Price of foodstuffs (1451–75 = 100)	Price of industrial products (1451–75 = 100)	Agricultural wages (1450–99 = 100)
1491–1500	100	97	101
1501–1510	106	98	101
1511–1520	116	102	101
1521–1530	159	110	106
1531–1540	161	110	110
1541–1550	217	127	118
1551–1560	315	186	160
1561–1570	298	218	177
1571–1580	341	223	207
1581–1590	389	230	203

Source: Extract from the Phelps Brown & Hopkins price index, quoted in D.M. Palliser, *The Age of Elizabeth: England under the Later Tudors, 1547–1603*, 1983

A society unused to such disruption could only guess at its causes. Many blamed the fencing of ploughland for easier conversion into pasture farming (enclosure), the buying up of smaller farms to create larger units (engrossing), or the raising of rents to meet the financial necessities of the landlords (rack-renting). Others stressed the debasement of the currency. Despite the increase in crown income in the latter half of his reign, Henry VIII had chosen since 1544 to produce extra coinage from a limited quantity of bullion by adding base metal to the precious metal that gave the currency its value in the eyes of the users. With the debased coinage easily recognisable, confidence in the currency slumped, and many would only accept it if handed over in larger quantities. The staple manufacturing industry of Tudor England went into a steep decline in these same years. After many decades of increasing prosperity, the export of woollen cloth suddenly dropped during 1550–2 back to the levels of the mid-1530s.

This crisis also coincided with an unusual run of poor harvests. The years between 1530 and 1548 had seen only two bad harvests, but five years out of seven between 1550 and 1556 produced harvests ranging from deficient to disastrous. Those of 1555 and 1556 became notorious as the worst of the century. A population weakened by food shortages was particularly vulnerable to disease, and as much as 20 per cent of the population may have died during the influenza epidemics of 1556–8. No other reigns in the Tudor era were played out against so dramatic a background of socio-economic distress and consequent political unrest.

THE POLITICAL CONTEXT: SOMERSET'S SEIZURE OF POWER

By passing the crown to a nine-year-old boy, the death of Henry VIII seemed to create the very situation that Tudor politicians had struggled to avoid. Yet the factional conflict between religious reformers and conservatives had been effectively won and lost in the last months of Henry's life, with power firmly in the hands of the faction that had formed around Edward Seymour. Within days of Henry's death, Seymour and his allies had subverted the king's last will, which had envisaged a council of regency of sixteen members, and had declared Seymour himself Protector of the realm.

Seymour's seizure of power undoubtedly had the support of leading members of the council, for he was in all respects the obvious candidate as Protector: 'His presence was handsome, his manner affable, his moral reputation good, his adherence to Reformation principles sincere' (A.G. Dickens, *The English Reformation*, 1964). As the new king's uncle, and as the leading military figure of Henry's Scottish wars, Seymour must have seemed eminently qualified to ensure political and social order. On the other hand, he was quick to enrich himself from his new office, establishing a particularly impressive land-holding in the south-west. As he set about the exercise of his office, the Protector showed himself to be 'self-willed, highminded, yet prone to *idées fixes*' (John Guy, *Tudor England*, 1988). Equally, it appears that he was autocratic and difficult to work with. He quickly established control over appointments to the council, and increasingly he conducted state

14.2 The search for a religious settlement, 1547–58

	Somerset's Protectorate	Northumberland as President of the Council	Queen Mary
The Episcopacy		Removal of 'Henrician' bishops, such as Heath, Day and Tunstall. Appointment of men with openly Protestant views, such as Ridley, Latimer and Hooper	Removal (1553) of leading Protestant bishops, such as Hooper, Ridley and Latimer, together with Archbishops Cranmer and Holgate. All except Holgate executed for heresy. Reginald Pole appointed to Canterbury (1556) by papal authority. Restoration of conservative bishops such as Bonner, White and Tunstall
Articles of Religion	Henry VIII's Six Articles abolished as part of a general Act of Repeal (1547)	Publication of 42 Articles (1553). These included unequivocally Protestant statements on the Eucharist, predestination, purgatory, the worship of saints, etc. These articles had not been passed as statute law by the time of Edward's death	The death of Edward VI saw the abandonment of the 42 Articles
The treatment of heretics	Abolition (1547) of the statute de Heretico Comburendo, which provided for the handing over of those judged guilty of heresy by the Church for execution by the civil authorities		Restoration of de Heretico Comburendo (Jan. 1555) restored the government's power to take action against those convicted of heresy
Royal authority over the Church	Abolition (1547) of the process of congé d'élire (leave to elect) removed the choice of bishops from the hands of cathedral chapters. Bishops were now appointed directly by the crown, by letters patent, like any other servant of the crown		Reginald Pole, as papal legate, absolved the realm (Nov. 1554) of its collective sin, and accepted in return the abolition of all

▶

business through the machinery of his private household.

THE WAR WITH SCOTLAND

The war with Scotland is now regarded as the main preoccupation of government policy under Somerset. A.F. Pollard saw this as part of a radical project of national unification, but M.L. Bush has explained the undertaking in more prosaic terms. War with Scotland had been a consistent feature of Henry's policy since 1541, the war was a major source of Somerset's public reputation, and the union of the crowns of the two kingdoms would be of obvious benefit to the Tudors.

The English invasion was launched in September 1547 and quickly achieved a crushing victory at Pinkie. Somerset now faced the problem of how to exploit his military success, and he proposed a novel solution. A series of garrisons would be placed in twenty-three fortified locations between Edinburgh and the border, which would hold the territory for the English and provide protection for those Scots who came over to the English side.

Two years after Pinkie the policy of garrisons had proved a thorough failure. In large part this was

	Somerset's Protectorate	Northumberland as President of the Council	Queen Mary
	Visitation of dioceses (1547) carried out by royal commissioners, rather than by the authority of the bishops		religious legislation passed since 1529. This clearly involved the abandonment of the royal supremacy
Prayer Book and conduct of worship	Publication of first Edwardian Prayer Book (Jan. 1549). Text exclusively in English. Deliberate ambiguity in wording of Communion service obscures the nature of the Eucharist. Prayers for the dead and commemoration of saints are retained. Communion 'in both kinds' is introduced	Publication of second Edwardian Prayer Book (1552). Communion table in place of altar stresses commemorative nature of the Eucharist. Use of vestments and music strictly limited. 'Black Rubric' stresses that, although kneeling is permitted, it does not imply worship of the host	Abolition of second Edwardian Act of Uniformity removes all authority for the Edwardian Prayer Book
	Act of Uniformity (1549) enforced exclusive use of the Prayer Book, but provided no penalty for non-attendance at church, and left no religious offence punishable by death	Act of Uniformity (1552) prescribes imprisonment for life for persistent refusal of Prayer Book	
Material state of the Church	Act of 1547 provided for the dissolution of chantry chapels, and for the transfer of their land and endowments to the crown. The Act was officially justified in terms of the irrelevance of prayers for the dead		Mary attempted to set an example by the voluntary abandonment of several Henrician gains. Crown's right to First Fruits and Tenths (1555). Monastic communities were refounded at Westminster and at several lesser houses
		Decree (March 1551) for confiscation of all Church plate and valuables, other than the minimum required for the conduct of services	

due to the response of the French, who could not allow so useful a diplomatic tool as the 'auld alliance' to lapse. A French army landed in Scotland in the summer of 1548, and a full-scale war was launched in the following year with an attack on Boulogne. English plans suffered a further blow when the young Queen of Scots was transported to the French court, beyond the reach of Somerset's matrimonial plans. Somerset compounded his problems by persisting with the policy of garrisons long after there had ceased to be any real prospect of its success. In little more than two years he spent £351,000 on his Scottish wars, whereas six years of warfare had cost Henry VIII £235,000.

RELIGION

A land safe for Protestants

In the traditional interpretation of Somerset's government, religious policy constituted a primary reason for viewing him as an enlightened thinker far in advance of his time. Not only was he remarkable as the first English ruler to embark upon a distinctly Protestant policy, but he also seemed to provide a rare example of tolerance in an intolerant age. The revision undertaken in recent years, however, has created a very different picture.

Protestantism certainly had many adherents at court in 1547. The upbringing of the young king was Protestant, Somerset himself had contacts with leading Protestant divines dating back to 1539, and Archbishop Cranmer was able at last, in the political atmosphere of 1547, to follow his conscience in doctrinal matters. Recent research has also suggested that a substantial minority of convinced Protestants, perhaps 20 per cent of the population, existed in London, Kent, Essex and Sussex.

This was too narrow a base, however, for a headlong plunge into Protestantism. Conservative views remained very strong, for instance, among the bishops. The debate in the House of Lords on the draft of the first Prayer Book of the reign (1548) showed seven bishops still supporting the Catholic doctrine of transubstantiation; and, as Anglo-French relations degenerated, it became less advisable to alienate Charles V. The priority of this initial phase of Edwardian religious policy, therefore, could be little more than to ensure that England was a country safe for Protestants to live in. The fact that no person was executed for heresy during the rule of Somerset may have owed more to political circumstances than to the Protector's enlightened thinking.

Initially Somerset's religious policy consisted of three main elements. The first was the removal of the weapons with which Protestants had hitherto been attacked: Henry VIII's additions to the treason laws, the restrictions placed upon preaching and printing the scriptures, and the statute *De Heretico Comburendo*. The second element was the energetic reaffirmation of royal control over the Church, especially important in response to conservative claims that a child could not exercise the Royal Supremacy. In doctrinal matters, meanwhile, the government followed a policy of studied ambiguity and compromise.

14.3 Victims and survivors of the 'crisis'

GRESHAM, Sir Thomas (1519–79). Son of a London banker, and himself Lord Mayor (1537). Served crown in Antwerp under Northumberland's patronage (1552). Close friend of William Cecil. Privy councillor (1558). Worked on rebasement of coinage (1559–61). Founded Royal Exchange (1566–70) and Gresham College (1575) in London.

LATIMER, Hugh (1485–1555). Converted to reformed religious views (c. 1525) and became a noted preacher. Royal chaplain (1530). Bishop of Winchester (1535). Resigned in opposition to the Act of Six Articles (1539) and subsequently preferred preaching to other ecclesiastical functions. Arrested upon the accession of Mary, condemned as a heretic and burned as one of the 'Oxford martyrs' (16 October 1555).

NORTHUMBERLAND, John Dudley, Duke of (1502–53). Son of Edmund Dudley, councillor to Henry VII. Deputy Governor of Calais (1542). Viscount Lisle (1542). Lord Admiral (1542–7). Governor of Boulogne after capturing that town from the French (1544–6). Earl of Warwick (1547). Saw military service against Scots and against Kett's rebels (1547–9). Duke of Northumberland (1551). Resisted the accession of Mary and was executed for treason. Father of Robert Dudley, one of the major courtiers of Elizabeth I.

PAGET, William (1505–63). Privy Councillor to Henry VIII (1541–7). Major supporter of Somerset in his establishment of the Protectorate. Sat briefly on Jane Grey's Privy Council, but supported the proclamation of Queen Mary (1553). Councillor and Lord Privy Seal (1556) under Mary. Left public life in 1558.

RIDLEY, Nicholas (?1503–55). Chaplain to Archbishop Cranmer (1537). Bishop of Rochester (1547). Bishop of London (1549). Denounced Mary and was deprived (1553). Convicted of heresy (1554) and burned as one of the 'Oxford martyrs' (16 October 1555).

SOMERSET, Edward Seymour, Duke of (?1506–52). In royal service from 1520s, and rose rapidly by virtue of his status as brother of Queen Jane Seymour. Privy Councillor and Earl of Hertford (1537). Lord High Admiral (1542). Prominent in Henry's campaigns against Scotland (1542–7). Lord Protector (1547). Deprived of that office (1549), imprisoned and executed on charges of conspiracy (1552).

WINCHESTER, Sir William Paulet, Marquess of (?1485–1572). Privy councillor to Henry VIII (1526). MP for Hampshire in the Reformation Parliament (1529–36). Lord President of the Council (1546). Keeper of the Great Seal under Somerset (1547), and Lord Treasurer under Northumberland (1550). Marquess of Winchester (1552). Supported Mary in 1553 and served her as Lord Privy Seal and Lord Treasurer. Retained office as Lord Treasurer under Elizabeth.

The dissolution of the chantries

Yet the parliamentary legislation of 1547 also contained an act for the dissolution of chantry chapels and other charitable institutions established for the repose of their founders' souls. Unlike the project put forward in the last years of Henry's reign, this measure was justified in wholly Protestant terms. Given that there existed no scriptural authority for the doctrine of purgatory and that salvation was no longer believed to depend

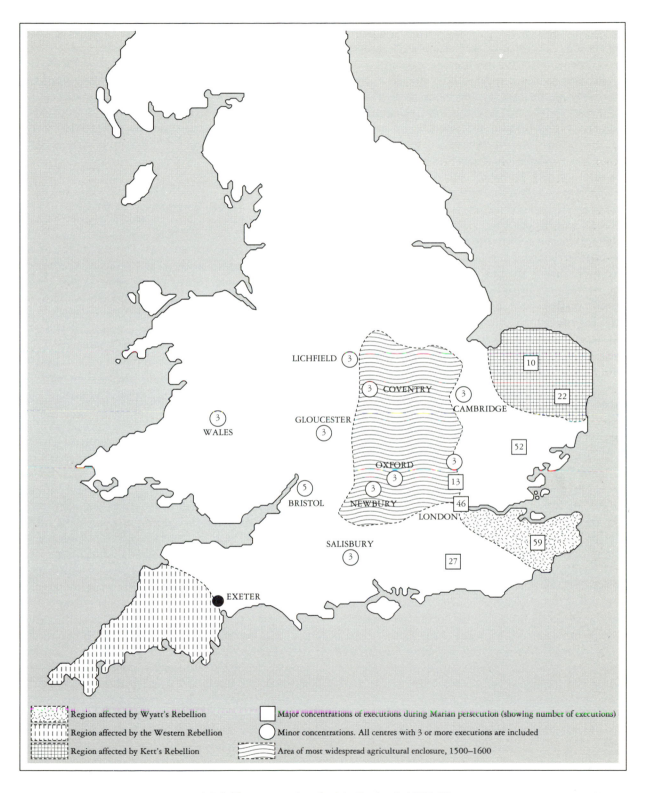

LICHFIELD ③

③ COVENTRY

③ WALES

GLOUCESTER
③

③ CAMBRIDGE

10

22

52

OXFORD
③

③

13

⑤

BRISTOL

NEWBURY

46

LONDON

59

SALISBURY
③

27

EXETER

Region affected by Wyatt's Rebellion

Region affected by the Western Rebellion

Region affected by Kett's Rebellion

☐ Major concentrations of executions during Marian persecution (showing number of executions)

◯ Minor concentrations. All centres with 3 or more executions are included

Area of most widespread agricultural enclosure, 1500–1600

14.4 *The geography of crisis: England, 1547–58*

upon good works, the prayers said in the chantries for the souls of the dead were at best useless, and at worst dangerously misleading.

Although the individual chantries were considerably smaller than the monasteries dissolved by Henry VIII, it is possible that the impact of Somerset's policy upon the popular mind was far greater. Chantries were widespread, and many were of recent foundation. There seem to be good grounds for A.G. Dickens's conclusion that 'if a man really believed that the ministrations of a chantry priest shortened the bitter years of purgatory for himself and his dearest departed relatives, then the dissolution gave him great spiritual offence and became a matter for his passionate concern'. However sincere the government may have been in its Protestant justifications for this policy, the profits of the dissolution were channelled straight into the financing of the Scottish war. In the minds of many, Protestantism would be further associated with the confiscation of property and the pursuit of purely political objectives.

SOCIAL POLICY, 1547–9

The Protector inherited formidable social and economic problems, and identified inflation and depopulation as the two major elements in the crisis. He was less clear-sighted, however, in his choice of remedies. Some of his advisers advocated the rapid restoration of the currency, ravaged by debasement. Debasement, however, and the extra coinage that it generated, remained essential if Somerset were to continue to finance his policies in Scotland. The alternative course, championed by a leading chancery official, John Hales, was a renewed assault upon the old problem of enclosures. Such a policy offered Somerset the attractive prospect of appearing to act with vigour on the social question while continuing to fight a war that was in itself proving economically disastrous.

Commissions nominated by Hales were active in the Midlands in mid-1548 investigating the legality of local enclosures, but they achieved little success. Somerset publicly ascribed this to the self-interest of the landlords, and once again made the mistake of persisting with an unworkable policy.

He introduced legislation for a tax on sheep and on woollen cloth, both designed to make the prospect of sheep farming less attractive. Although it was certainly not Somerset's real intention, it is easy to see how such policies took on the appearance of an attack upon the landed interest. Somerset's political fate was thus sealed by the extreme socio-political crisis that the governing classes now experienced.

THE RISINGS OF 1549

The spring and summer of 1549 saw the most widespread rural unrest that England experienced in the sixteenth century. In June the Western Rebellion convulsed Cornwall and Devon, and led to a prolonged siege of Exeter before the rebels were dispersed with heavy losses in August. In July the peasantry of Norfolk rose in what became known as Kett's Rebellion, and spent a month or so righting agrarian wrongs in East Anglia before they too were bloodily suppressed by the Earl of Warwick.

The Western Rebellion was to a large extent a reaction against the religious policy of the government. In demanding the restoration of the Act of Six Articles and of the Mass in Latin, together with the suppression of the English Bible and Prayer Book, the Cornishmen demonstrated what obstacles Protestantism still had to overcome in many parts of the realm. They also protested against the introduction of a sheep tax, showing that their movement, too, had links with current agrarian discontent.

The Norfolk rebels primarily attacked agrarian developments that threatened their livelihood, and expressed their hostility to the gentry class which they saw as responsible for them. As the rebels pulled down enclosure fences and slaughtered the deer that had been placed in newly created hunting reserves, Somerset shrewdly concluded that the rebels had 'conceived a wonderful hate against the gentlemen and taketh them all as their enemies'.

The risings of 1549 were suppressed as ruthlessly as any other lower-class rebellion of the sixteenth century, yet they were unique in that they played a major role in bringing down a government. There was little foundation for contemporary suspicions that Somerset sympathised with the rebels, but he had compromised himself by his policies, criticising those very enclosures against which the men of Norfolk had rebelled. He had delayed action against the rebels, probably because he could not spare troops from Scotland. Even this tenuous association with the risings was bound to be disastrous for a man who had entered office as the military champion of the landed élite.

THE FALL OF SOMERSET, 1549–50

By the autumn of 1549, that élite had supported the Protector in three lines of policy and had seen two of them, the Scottish war and the social programme, end in deadlock or worse. The events of 1549 had also brought forward a clear candidate to succeed in the role in which Somerset had failed. John Dudley, Earl of Warwick, already had a well-established military reputation at the end of Henry's reign, and had enhanced it by his role in the suppression of Kett's Rebellion.

Somerset's fall was protracted, beginning in October 1549, when he removed the king from London and appealed for support from the council, continuing through his formal loss of the protectorate a few days later, and culminating in his execution on spurious treason charges in January 1552. This power struggle, like the others in England in the late 1540s and 1550s, was remarkable for its relative lack of violence and its cold legalism. In part this was a testimony to the work of the two Henries, which had weakened the independent resources of the nobility and left a monopoly of political violence in the hands of the crown. The widespread desire for stability and respect for the rule of law helped to undo Somerset in 1549 as they undid Dudley four years later.

Dudley, created Duke of Northumberland (1551), never held the same degree of power that Somerset had enjoyed. He held the title of Lord President of the Council and governed by clever exploitation of the legitimate channels of conciliar government. He cemented his authority by appointing twelve new councillors and by ensuring that the Council functioned in a more regular and institutionalised fashion. Northumberland and his allies also made clever use of the king, creating the impression that Edward was increasingly involved in the business of government, while ensuring that the boy's opinions were carefully influenced.

NORTHUMBERLAND'S POLICY: CHANGE OR CONTINUITY?

As war had been the basic preoccupation of Somerset's administration, so peace was the necessary starting-point for Northumberland's. The Treaty of Boulogne with France (March 1550) was harshly dismissed by Pollard as 'the most ignominious signed by England during the century', yet it is hard to see what else the government could have done in this context of bankruptcy and domestic disturbance. By its terms, Boulogne was returned to France in return for a modest cash payment, and all hopes were abandoned of a marriage between Edward and Mary Stuart. Improved relations with France were confirmed by a further treaty concluded at Angers (July 1551) for the marriage of Edward to a daughter of Henry II. In the same year English garrisons withdrew from Scotland, and negotiations began for the clear definition of the borders between the two states.

Such developments represented the complete collapse of everything that English governments had sought in Scotland over the last decade. On the other hand, there was some logic in this new, pro-French orientation of policy considering the likely attitude of the Habsburgs towards England's increasingly Protestant religious policy. Most important of all, the achievement of peace left the English government free to address its crippling social and economic problems.

The domestic priorities of Northumberland's administration were the re-establishment of sound royal finances and the restoration of social stability. The years between 1549 and 1553 marked the first stage in the long consolidation of royal affairs which stretched on into the reign of Elizabeth. Income was maximised by the more efficient collection of debts owed to the crown, by economies in government expenditure and by a decree for the confiscation of Church plate and other valuables (March 1551). Over the next two years, royal commissioners stripped the parish churches as efficiently as their predecessors had stripped the monasteries. Meanwhile, government expenditure was greatly reduced by the work of Sir Thomas Gresham in manipulating and repaying some £240,000 of debts owed by the crown. Most fundamental of all, the government set out to restore the quality of the currency after its debasement, and by the end of 1551 the process of recoining in a purer form was in full swing.

At the earliest opportunity after Somerset's fall his sheep tax was repealed and the enclosure commissions were abandoned. Yet Northumberland's administration does not deserve its uncaring reputation. More prosecutions came to court for illegal, depopulating enclosure under Northumberland than under Somerset, and an Act of 1552 taxed all land withdrawn from tillage. The most significant measure of 1552 was a reform of the poor law, which took steps towards compelling local residents to contribute towards poor-relief funds. This government came no closer than its predecessors to solving such intractable social problems, yet it may be said that the worsening social crisis was confronted by Northumberland's regime with more realism and good sense than had been shown in previous years.

If the fall of Somerset led to the abandonment of his social and foreign policies, the Protestant elements in his religious policy were amplified. Between 1550 and 1553, England became for the first time a wholly Protestant state. Northumberland's own recantation of Protestantism on the scaffold in 1553 makes it hard to believe that he was sincerely committed to evangelical doctrines, and it is more probable that his motives were political. A Protestant policy was the price he had to pay for the support of Cranmer and others on the Council against both Somerset and more conservative elements.

It remains much more difficult to determine whether 'hearts and minds' were being won for Protestantism across the country as a whole. The official encouragement that was extended to prominent foreign theologians ensured that the highest academic posts in the land were held by reformers. Martin Bucer became Regius Professor of theology at Cambridge, while Knox, à Lasco and others were active in the country during these years. Nevertheless, the evidence from the country at large is inconclusive. On the one hand, Queen Mary was soon able to secure the wholesale repeal of all Edwardian religious legislation with only a limited degree of opposition. Bucer himself had noted that in so conservative an area as Lancashire the Edwardian legislation was only enforced 'by means of ordinances which the majority obey very grudgingly'. On the other hand, there is evidence that a firm minority support had been established, especially among the higher social classes. The eighty MPs who had the courage to oppose Mary in the House of Commons and some 800 'Marian exiles' who fled abroad during her reign have to be added to the more famous ranks of those who suffered death at that time for their beliefs.

THE ACCESSION OF MARY

The administration, a major religious experiment, and the power and influence of the Dudley dynasty all hung by the fragile thread of the young king's life, and Edward VI died on 6 July 1553. Northumberland and his supporters had taken two steps to preserve themselves and their interests. One was to replace the 1544 Act of Succession with a 'Device for the Succession', whereby the crown passed to Jane Grey, the teenage daughter of the Duke of Suffolk. The second step was the marriage (May 1553) of Northumberland's son, Lord Guildford Dudley, to Jane Grey, thus ensuring that the new Queen of England remained firmly under Northumberland's political control.

The rival heir, designated by the will of Henry VIII, was Edward's half-sister Mary. The Privy Council, still under the influence of Northumberland, initially rejected her claims to the throne, but was quickly overtaken by events outside the capital. Substantial support for Mary in the provinces may have been in part a manifestation of Catholic resentment at a Protestant usurpation, but probably had a wider basis of loyalty to the Tudor regime. When Northumberland left London to confront his rival, the Council took the opportunity to make their peace with Mary, forcing the Lord President to surrender.

MARY TUDOR

The formative years

Mary Tudor (*b.*February 1516) was the daughter of Henry VIII and Catherine of Aragon, and the collapse of her parents' marriage radically changed Mary's life. She was separated from her mother (July 1531), and lost her political status with the birth of Elizabeth (September 1533). With her acceptance of Henry's ecclesiastical supremacy and the birth of Prince Edward, Mary's position became regularised, and by the Act of Succession of 1544 she was restored to the line of succession directly behind her half-brother.

From these experiences Mary probably derived her unswerving commitment to her Habsburg family connections, and a bitter mistrust towards most English politicians. Her religiosity reflected a common trait on the Spanish side of her family, shared with her grandmother, Queen Isabella, as well as with Queen Catherine herself. From these sources and from her own unhappy experiences Mary derived a religion that was essentially traditional and conservative. As G.R. Elton (*Reform and Reformation*, 1977) has stated, 'humanism had passed her by as much as had Protestantism. If it is not clear whether she leant towards the new rigour of the rising Counter Reformation, this is mainly because she never gave any sign of a genuinely intellectual interest in the issues that confronted her. She depended upon the Mass because it gave her emotional satisfaction.'

Allies and problems

Like Henry VII, Mary came to the throne as the result of a successful rebellion against the *de facto* government. Yet Northumberland's regime had collapsed in so abject a fashion and the lack of sympathy for 'Queen Jane' was so clear that Mary seemed well placed to establish a strong and stable government. In addition to old friends and supporters, a number of very experienced royal servants had deserted Northumberland early enough to be welcome in Mary's camp. In prison and in forced retirement, there was a ready-made team of ecclesiastics, such as Tunstall, Heath and Gardiner, sympathetic to the religious priorities of the new monarch.

The weakness of Mary's government lay, not in its lack of able ministers, but in the lack of confidence that Mary showed in them. Nearly all the experienced administrators at her disposal were men who had served Henry VIII, and who had therefore had a hand in the initial attack upon the Church and in the humiliation of Mary and her mother. Mary could not see such men as kindred spirits in her 'mission'. As the Emperor Charles V had been Mary's major support in adversity, it is not surprising that she turned so readily to his ambassador in London, Simon Renard. Between 1553 and 1555, Renard was certainly the most important influence upon the queen, and it is probably to him that we owe the tradition of a faction-ridden Council upon which Mary could not rely. It is certain that the project for a Spanish marriage was fashioned by Mary and Renard and then presented to the Council as a *fait accompli*. That marriage, of course, provided her with a husband whom she saw as her most constant ally and support. With the return of Philip and Renard to Spain in 1555, Mary lost the only two guides that she trusted.

THE SPANISH MARRIAGE

The issue of marriage was an urgent one. The queen largely accepted the contemporary view of the place of women in government, and thus firmly believed that she would need a husband's help to carry the burden. Besides, she was thirty-seven years old at her accession and had few child-bearing years left to her. Without children, she would be succeeded by her half-sister Elizabeth, in whose hands the Catholic religion would be far from safe.

Although some councillors put forward the claims of Edward Courtenay, a great-grandson of Edward IV, Mary preferred a Habsburg marriage. Not only was the Emperor the queen's cousin, but he had also shown Mary much kindness during her times of trouble and was, of course, a prime representative of the Catholic religion. For Charles himself such an alliance would have the substantial advantage of drawing England conclusively into the Habsburg sphere of influence. Whatever the pragmatic advantages of such an alliance, there was little real enthusiasm for it on any side other than Mary's. Charles himself accepted that the English would 'dread having a foreigner, loathed as all foreigners are by all Englishmen, for their king', and Parliament reacted to the acceptance of the Spanish proposal (October 1553) by petitioning the queen to change her mind.

The terms of the marriage were finalised in January 1554. Although Philip received the title of 'king', it was understood that he should exercise none of the royal prerogatives. No English laws were to be changed and no foreigner was to be eligible for any English office. If the marriage produced no children, or if Mary died before her husband, then Philip and his descendants lost all rights within the realm. Any child of the marriage was to inherit England and the Netherlands, but would have no claim to Spain or to the Italian territories of the Spanish crown. In short, the marriage agreement did as good a job as possible of minimising the damage to English independence and interests. The marriage itself, however, with its implications of domestic unrest and declining relations with France, continues traditionally to be viewed as 'the first and fatal mistake of her reign from which she and it could not recover' (G.R. Elton).

WYATT'S REBELLION

The most dangerous reaction to the Spanish marriage was Wyatt's rebellion. The professed aim of Sir Thomas Wyatt, a substantial Kentish gentleman, was to marry the Princess Elizabeth to Edward Courtenay and to put her in her sister's place. Although Wyatt consistently claimed that his aim was 'only to defend us from overrunning by strangers', it is notable that the largest contingents of participants came from notably Protestant areas of Kent. Wyatt himself had benefited from the

sale of monastic lands, but had no clear Protestant links.

The plot was launched prematurely at the turn of the year 1553–4, and in all the planned locations except Kent the rising was a fiasco. There, however, Wyatt mustered a force of 2,000 men and marched on London. Mary had convinced the capital, however, that the revolt was the work of heretics and that 'the matter of the marriage seemed to be but a Spanish cloak to cover their pretended purpose against our religion'. Wyatt's attempts to enter the city were frustrated, and his advance turned into a rout. Wyatt himself was among seventy-five participants executed for treason.

It may be that 'Wyatt came nearer than any other Tudor rebel to toppling a monarch from the throne' (A. Fletcher, *Tudor Rebellions*, 1983), but his rebellion was the last of its kind. J.E. Neale (*Elizabeth I and Her Parliaments*, 1953), in particular, stressed that, in conjunction with the risings of 1549, this rebellion proved the uselessness of revolt as a means of influencing government policy. In future, he claimed, the gentry at least would prefer parliamentary means of airing their grievances.

FOREIGN POLICY

Along with her religious policy and its implementation, Mary's 'bad press' has always rested upon a foreign policy traditionally interpreted as surrendering national interests and independence to the interests of a foreign prince. The queen's marriage to Philip of Spain constituted the most binding foreign commitment undertaken by Tudor England. In theory, the marriage treaty guaranteed effective protection of English interests against an overwhelmingly senior partner, yet it is hard to see what England could do about it if Spain decided to ignore its terms. There were signs over the next two years that Spain intended to make few concessions to English commercial interests, maintaining its own monopoly in the New World and taking harsh action against English expeditions there (1556). English commerce was obstructed in other directions too. Expeditions to Africa were discouraged when they entered the Portuguese sphere of influence, and the privileges of the Hanseatic League were largely restored, to the disadvantage of the Merchant Adventurers of London.

Nevertheless, England did avoid involvement in the wars of the Habsburg dynasty until 1557. Then the uneasy peace established at Vaucelles (February 1556) broke down, largely as a result of the political machinations of that very papacy that Mary served so faithfully in her domestic policy. Lengthy debate within the Council about England's best response to renewed Continental tension ended abruptly when Thomas Stafford, with obvious French aid and collaboration, launched a hopeless assault on Scarborough (April 1557). Faced with a clear case of French provocation, England declared war in June.

Despite its eventual outcome, the conduct of the war was not without its merits. English troops performed creditably in the great Habsburg victory at Saint-Quentin (August 1557), and some researchers have argued that the military and naval organisation of this conflict formed the basis for the reforms of Elizabeth's reign. This was offset, however, by the disaster that befell English interests the following January. Seeking to redress the balance after Saint-Quentin, the French launched a surprise attack upon Calais. Within a week the town was in French hands. The material consequences of the loss of Calais were slight, but the impact upon English morale seems to have been enormous. The last trace of England's medieval Continental possessions was gone, and the tradition was instantly established that this was the result of pandering to foreign interests. Even today, it is still possible to dismiss the war of 1557–8 in words such as those of R. Tittler: 'It is hard to think of any subsequent English campaign which has resulted in less material gain and more loss of face.'

RELIGION

Reversing the Edwardian trend

Although Mary's earlier life had left no doubt as to her religious conservatism, it remained unclear at her succession whether she would be content to reverse the policies of Edward's reign or whether she would also attempt to erase her father's work. In fact, Mary was deeply convinced of the sinfulness of Henry's break from Rome and was passionately committed to its reversal. She believed that the changes of the last two decades were primarily the work of a small nucleus of desperate heretics, supported at court by an élite group of opportunists, and could thus easily be swept away. Reginald Pole, soon to become her Archbishop of Canterbury, shared this view, but he had the excuse of two decades of absence in a foreign land. The ecclesiastical hierarchy and the universities thus became prime targets for the government. Cranmer, Hooper, Ridley and Latimer were arrested, several other bishops were deprived, and foreign theologians at Oxford and Cambridge were expelled. Mary also ordered the removal of married priests from their livings, regardless of their doctrinal positions. The prospects of Catholic success, already bright, were further enhanced by the sensational recantation of heresy made by Northumberland on the scaffold.

The return to Rome

For all that, the legislation of Mary's first Parliament represented a compromise between the distinctly Henrician priorities of the assembly and Mary's desire to return England to the papal fold. Although some eighty MPs had the courage to resist, Parliament in general was willing to jettison the doctrinal legislation of the previous reign. It remained hostile, however, to any measure that restored lands recently confiscated from the Church, or which gave the Church greater powers in dealings with the laity. Gardiner struggled in his bid to restore the laws against heresy, and only when Cardinal Pole arrived from Rome (November 1554) with the Pope's assurance that he would not insist upon the surrender of former monastic lands did MPs relent and reintroduce the laws for the trial and execution of heretics, while repealing all doctrinal legislation passed since 1529. Most spectacularly, this involved the abandonment of the royal supremacy and the recognition once more of papal authority over the Church in England.

Pole was the key figure in the attempt to re-establish a thriving Catholic faith in England, equipped for the undertaking by his close involvement in the early stages of the Catholic Reformation on the Continent. He was not a profound theologian, but he possessed great pastoral gifts, having spent many years as 'guide, confessor and friend of the great' (D.M. Loades). He began the task of reversing twenty years of decay at the top. Finance and discipline were his priorities, and a major role was to be played by the bishops. They were ordered to be vigilant and thorough in their visitations and in the appointment and discipline of their clergy. To help them, Pole devised and enforced twelve decrees, mainly concerned with the discipline of the parish priest, a newly edited New Testament and a new Book of Homilies. In the interests of long-term education he demanded the regular visitation of Church schools, the establishment of seminaries in all dioceses and close supervision of the universities. Pole is most frequently criticised, however, for placing insufficient stress upon the regeneration of spiritual enthusiasm. Professor Tittler has argued that 'the version of Catholicism which the Marian regime attempted to reintroduce held little to capture the imagination of most Englishmen not already committed to it: no missionary zeal, no influx of money with which to create a "beauty of holiness"'. Despite their success elsewhere during the Counter-Reformation, Pole consistently refused the aid offered to him by the Jesuits.

Persecution

Active persecution began with the burning of the Protestant scholar John Rogers (February 1555), and in the course of the next three and a half years nearly 300 English men and women suffered similarly for their faith.

The burning of the Marian martyrs has always provided the focal point of the reign. In the view of contemporaries, responsibility for the policy seemed to lie variously with Gardiner, Bonner the Bishop of London, or King Philip, but such accusations now seem to be unjustified. Certainly, Philip was instrumental in the invitation to England of Dominican monks who had already distinguished themselves in the counterattack against Protestantism, and Juan de Villagarcia and Pedro de Soto were successively professors of divinity at Oxford. Yet most recent writers have been forced to conclude that the queen herself provided the main impetus behind the policy. Consistent with her view of Protestantism as the wicked conspiracy of a minority, the surviving records provide evidence of Mary's eagerness to see the policy carried through unstintingly.

The great Protestant publicist John Foxe commemorated 275 of Mary's victims in his hugely influential *Book of Martyrs*, published in the following reign, and regarded their sacrifices as the turning-point in the history of English Protestantism. The majority of the martyrs were men and women of humble origin, unable to afford the luxury of refuge abroad. Foxe records only nine gentlemen, twenty-two clerics and a handful of merchants in their ranks. The rest of the martyrs are described as weavers, husbandmen and the like. Fifty-five of the victims were women. Thus the policy of carrying out executions in the victims' locality meant that onlookers saw their neighbours and social equals die a horrible death for no reason other than their religious faith.

The death of that handful of public figures who did not escape abroad may have had an even greater impact upon the national consciousness. So far from repeating Northumberland's recantation, Bishop Hooper died bravely in his cathedral city of Gloucester (February 1555), as did Ridley and Latimer in Oxford (October 1555). The third of the 'Oxford Martyrs', the former Archbishop of Canterbury himself, was probably the most influential martyr of all. To all appearances the most flexible and opportunistic of Protestant churchmen, Cranmer too found the courage to withdraw his initial recantation and to die at the stake (March 1556).

These deaths in particular had exactly the opposite effect of that intended by the government. Instead of providing further evidence of the insincerity of Protestantism, they proved that many of the movement's political and intellectual leaders were men of firm spiritual beliefs. 'A discredited and ineffectual movement had become a cause that brave men would die for' (D.M. Loades). The prime responsibility for this spectacular failure appears to lie with Mary and with Pole, who made Protestantism what it had so far failed to become: a national and popular creed.

THE GOVERNMENT OF THE REALM

Substantial recent research has been unable to acquit Mary of the charge of failure in her religious and foreign policies. On the other hand, it no longer seems reasonable to decry the government and administration of the realm in general as incompetent and fruitless.

The familiar criticism of Mary's Privy Council, that it was impracticably large and paralysed by factional infighting, no longer seems valid. A. Weikel (in *The Mid-Tudor Polity*, c.1540–1560, ed. S.J. Loach and R. Tittler) has shown that the Council at its routine work usually consisted of a much more conventional number of ten to twenty members, and that these rarely included the 'Catholic backwoodsmen', as R. Tittler has described those elevated by Mary as a reward for past loyalty. Instead, the working Council consisted primarily of men such as Paget, Winchester, Gardiner and Heath, all with proven records of service to the Tudor regime. Of course there were disagreements among the councillors, and broad interest groups can be distinguished. That led by Paget sought to preserve what Henry VIII's reign had achieved for the crown, while Gardiner led a group dedicated to the restoration of the clerical influence lost at that time. The major weakness in the functioning of the Council seems, on the other hand, to have been Mary's own failure to use her councillors' debate profitably, to arbitrate, and to impose her authority positively on issues other than those linked to her personal enthusiasms.

It is unclear whether the reign should be regarded as a sterile period in parliamentary history. Successive parliaments took very firm stands on certain issues, yet with the notable exception of their vested interests in former Church lands there was little upon which the two Houses would not compromise. S.J. Loach and others have stressed the frequency with which Parliament met – five times in little more than five years – and have highlighted the degree of cooperation that existed

between government and Parliament over Mary's religious legislation, as well as over the government's substantial economic and social measures.

In many ways, Mary's government faced up to the severe social and economic pressures of the 1550s with imagination and initiative. Its attempts to encourage commercial enterprise to find alternative outlets for English wool were not generally successful, but a number of important measures were taken to maximise the crown's income from existing trade. A new Book of Rates (May 1558) represented a long-overdue revision of customs dues, with the result that the crown's income from these sources rose from £29,000 (1557) to £83,000 in the first year of Elizabeth's reign. Income from crown lands rose by £40,000 per year after the establishment of a committee of the Privy Council to adjust and revise rents. It is now appreciated that the great recoining of the national currency, undertaken by Elizabeth's government (1560–1) was largely prepared by Mary's ministers during 1556–8.

The government was also frequently willing to intervene with its own legislation to try to combat contemporary economic hardship. A Retail Trades Act (1554) and the Woollen Cloth Act (1557) show its efforts to protect traditional industries by strengthening the jurisdiction of guilds and urban authorities. The reign also saw the grant to many more towns of charters of incorporation, which gave their local authorities the power, among other things, to finance projects for poor relief and for public works.

Although such measures reflect greater credit upon Mary's government, there is little evidence to suggest that the queen herself played any positive role in such areas of policy. A.G.R. Smith (*Emergence of a Nation State*, 1984) has concluded that although 'Mary did not lack resolution when her vital personal concerns were involved, it was a different matter when it came to routine application to business, where her attention was patchy and uncertain'. Worse still, the outbreak of war in 1557 did much to undermine the good work of her senior councillors. The credit for such economic and administrative initiative seems largely to lie with an outstanding administrator, William Paulet, Marquis of Winchester. Instead, Mary's personal commitment was to foreign and religious policies which failed utterly and which are still often interpreted as unrealistic aberrations in the wider context of Tudor policy.

Further reading

M.L. Bush (1975) *The Government Policy of Protector Somerset*. London.

W.R.D. Jones (1973) *The Mid-Tudor Crisis, 1539–1563*. London.

D.M. Loades (1989) *Mary Tudor*. Oxford.

—— (1994) *Essays on the Reign of Edward VI*. Bangor.

R. Tittler (1983) *The Reign of Mary I*. London.

• CHAPTER FIFTEEN •

The French Wars of Religion

A contemporary print depicting the massacre of Huguenots carried out by the Duke of Guise at Vassy in 1562. Many features of the scene, such as the predominance of women and children in the congregation and the theft of the poor-box from the chapel door, reveal the sympathies of the artist

THE HISTORICAL DEBATE

In the first half of the sixteenth century France enjoyed a remarkable degree of prosperity, ruled by the most powerful national monarchy in Western Europe. Suddenly, in the second half of the century, all this appeared to fall apart in the most destructive set of civil wars experienced in contemporary Europe.

In this century, the French Wars of Religion have been studied exhaustively, but from two very different angles. Writers such as Lucien Romier (*Les Origines politiques des guerres de religion*, 1913–14) concentrated upon the French social élite, dwelling upon the development of noble factions at the royal court and the role that these played in the destruction of political stability. N.M. Sutherland (*The Massacre of St Bartholomew and the European Conflict, 1559–1572*, 1973) also studied the conflict

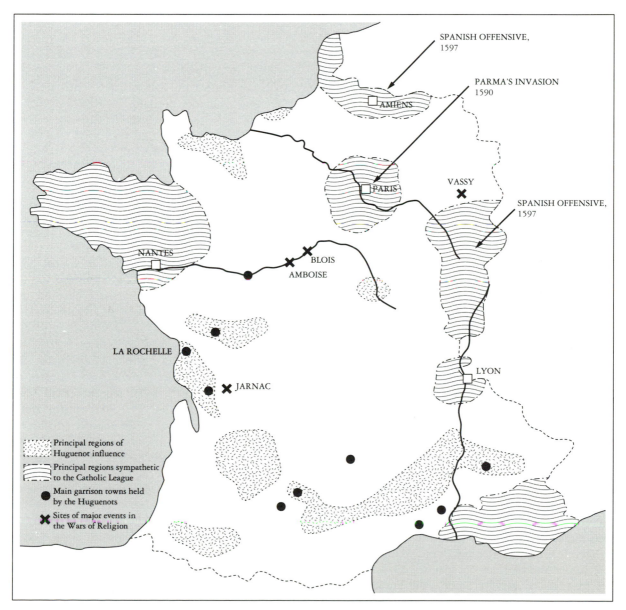

15.1 France during the Wars of Religion

at a rarefied political level, reassessing the roles of great political figures, such as Catherine de Medici.

Increasingly, however, studies have been reorientated towards detailed case-studies of religious and social developments in the localities. One of the pioneers of this movement was Lucien Febvre (*Une Question mal posée: les origines de la reforme française et le problème général des causes de la reforme*, 1929). His message was that historians would best understand the Reformation by studying its roots in the mental histories of individuals and of communities. His advice was followed by two generations of French historians, led most recently by Emmanuel Le Roy Ladurie (*Les Paysans de Languedoc*, 1966), and Janine Garrison-Estebe (*Les Protestants du Midi*, 1980). In English, the work of J.H.M. Salmon (*Society in Crisis: France in the Sixteenth Century*, 1975) provides the best study of the French civil wars as a crucial stage in the general reorientation of French society.

CALVINISM IN FRANCE

Until the early years of Henry II's reign, religious dissent in France had generally lacked the cohesion and direction that might have made it a major threat to the stability of the realm. This situation changed in the mid-1550s with the growth of a dynamic Calvinist movement within the country. From 1555 refugees were returning to France from Geneva, trained in the ministry and eager to spread the Word. Assessing their own strength on the eve of the war in 1562, Calvinist leaders estimated that some 2,150 separate communities existed in France.

The earliest Calvinist missions were deliberately aimed at the towns, and the initial impact of Calvinism appears to have been greater among the middle classes and among urban artisans than among labourers and the peasantry. Yet there were notable exceptions to such rules, and the peasant communities in the Cévennes contained strong Protestant enclaves for years to come. There is relatively little evidence of Calvinist influence among the upper middle classes or magistrates, but it seems to have spread rapidly among the lower levels of municipal and royal officers. The geographical distribution of Calvinism at this early stage can be traced with greater confidence. By 1561 there is evidence of substantial Calvinist communities in the towns of the Loire Valley (Tours, Blois, Angers, Orléans and Bourges), of Normandy (Rouen, Caen, Dieppe and Le Havre), of Saintonge (La Rochelle and Saintes) and of Languedoc (Nîmes, Montauban and Montpellier). Only Brittany, Burgundy, Champagne and Picardy seem to have been substantially immune from the influence of the mission.

Calvinism's political impact would not have been nearly so great, had it not attracted so much support among the great families of the realm. The House of Bourbon was most closely identified with the cause of the 'Huguenots', as the French Protestants came to be called. Anthony of Bourbon, King of Navarre, was never more than half-hearted in his religious convictions, but his brother, the Prince of Condé, was more consistent. He visited Geneva as early as 1555, announced his conversion in 1558, and for the rest of his life was the primary political leader and defender of the reformed cause. The House of Montmorency was divided on the issue of religion. The senior branch of the family, headed by the Constable Anne de Montmorency, never embraced the reformed faith, but three brothers of the junior branch, Coligny, Dandelot and Châtillon, were involved in the Calvinist mission from an early stage. Inevitably, the nature of feudal clientage ensured that the conversion of such mighty men would draw a host of dependent lesser nobles and their own client gentry in turn into the Calvinist ranks.

Historians have usually assumed that the motivation of such noble Calvinists was overwhelmingly political. Montaigne wrote at the time: 'Let us confess the truth; whoever should draw out from the armies those who take up arms out of pure zeal for religion could hardly make one complete company of *gens d'armes*.' This tradition has only recently been challenged. J.H.M. Salmon, for instance, has stressed the role played by some of the most prominent female members of the great noble families in generating reformist enthusiasm among their clans. The most notable of these was Jeanne d'Albret, wife of Anthony of Bourbon, and a far more dynamic promoter of Calvinism than her husband. With her could be linked Louise de Montmorency and Charlotte de Laval, the wife of Coligny. Indeed, there seems little reason to doubt the religious sincerity of the Coligny clan in general.

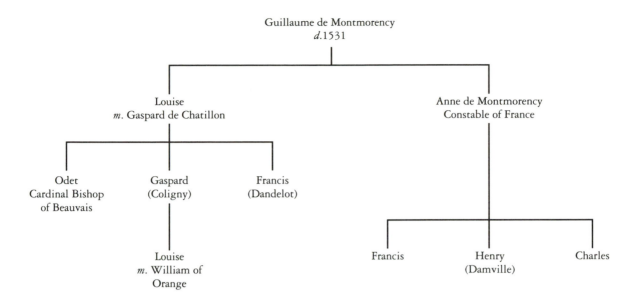

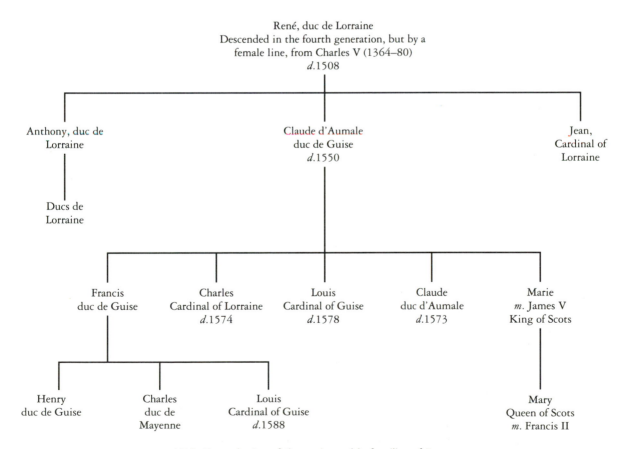

15.2 *Genealogies of the major noble families of France.*
Principal members of the Houses of Montmorency and of Guise

The crisis of the nobility

The wars which ended with the peace of Câteau-Cambrésis had a major impact upon the financial and political fortunes of the great families of the realm. They ended without a clear victor, and thus without major prizes to be distributed. The outbreak of peace thus created a crisis on at least two levels in the upper strata of French society.

On the first level the fortunes of war created a serious imbalance between the major feudal dynasties. Francis of Guise had had a 'good war'. He had defended Metz against Charles V and had commanded the French forces that captured Calais. The Guise family were already substantial feudal magnates with their greatest concentrations of land in Mayenne, in Normandy, in Picardy and in Flanders, as well as in the family's traditional heartland of Lorraine. Duke Francis was now at the peak of a brilliant court career, royal Chamberlain, godfather to the young Francis II, and peer of the realm despite his lack of royal blood. His brother Charles had made equally dazzling progress in the Church, being appointed Archbishop of Reims, with revenues of 300,000 *livres*, at the age of fourteen. The patronage of the Guise family was thus highly attractive to lesser mortals who sought profit and protection in return for their military services.

The House of Montmorency could match the Guises in terms of past glories and of feudal estates, but not in terms of present political fortune. Anne of Montmorency, Constable of France, had enjoyed great favour in the reign of Henry II, but had been less fortunate in the recent wars. He had suffered the humiliation of defeat at Saint-Quentin, and was abruptly excluded from office by the young king upon Henry's death. The head of the House of Bourbon, Anthony, enjoyed the title of King of Navarre by his marriage to Jeanne d'Albret, and thus claimed a degree of dignity second only to the King of France himself. His family had not completely recovered, however, from the humiliation and mistrust that followed the treason of Charles of Bourbon in 1523. Despite being a prince of the blood and a great feudal magnate, therefore, Anthony of Bourbon could expect nothing better from the ascendancy of the Guise family than long-term exclusion from political influence.

On a second level, this crisis embraced hundreds of lesser nobles, *seigneurs* and gentlemen. For these, the abrupt end to the wars and the disbanding of the armies by a king threatened with bankruptcy created a 'crisis of patronage' as a rich source of employment, pensions and political favours suddenly dried up. The situation contained great potential for local lawlessness as *seigneurs* returned to their mortgaged estates with no means of livelihood other than their prowess as soldiers. In so explosive a situation the need for strong and charismatic royal leadership was greater than at any time in the previous hundred years.

The road to war, 1560–2

Under such circumstances, the death of Henry II in a jousting accident (10 July 1559) was a disaster, leaving France with a fifteen-year-old king, Francis II. It was less the weakness of the new king that plunged the realm into civil disorder than the strength of his protectors. Francis was married to the young Mary Stuart, Queen of Scots and the niece of Francis, Duke of Guise. This Guise marriage alliance with the crown itself spelled political disaster for those factions which could now expect to be eclipsed. For those such as Condé, who had identified themselves with the reformed faith, the ultra-Catholicism of the Guise family provided another kind of threat.

This coincidence of political, religious and economic danger galvanised some of the Guises' many enemies into a desperate attempt to remove the young king from their control. The conspiracy or 'Tumult' of Amboise (March 1560) aimed to seize the king and arrest or murder the leading members of the Guise family. The conspiracy ended in disaster, and the number of those summarily executed ran into several hundreds. The Tumult of Amboise was virtually a declaration of war between the great feudal factions of the realm, and for the moment its failure seemed to leave Guise with all the advantages. In December 1560, however, the death of Francis II undermined years of careful preparation. It brought to the throne his brother, Charles IX, aged nine and in need of a regent. The first of the great political successes of the queen mother, Catherine de Medici, was to secure that regency for herself. The Guise faction was excluded from office, and a new chancellor, Michel de l'Hôpital, was appointed to work alongside Catherine.

The exclusion of the Guise faction was accompanied by the rejection of their strictly pro-Catholic policy. In seeking a new political and religious balance, the crown's obvious ally was the House of Bourbon. It also seemed likely that the summoning of the Estates General would provide the regent with a body of support which preferred peace and stability to the narrow factional interest of a handful of nobles. In response to this policy, the Guises formed an understanding with the aged Montmorency, who apparently considered religious orthodoxy more important than dynastic advantage. Another soldier of the old school, the *maréchal* Saint André, completed the so-called 'triumvirate'. By approaching Spain in search of assistance for their cause, these men began the tradition by which militant French Catholicism looked beyond national politics to identify itself with the mainstream of the Counter-Reformation.

Catherine's ideal course in 1561 seemed to be to establish a doctrinal compromise that would cut the theological ground from beneath the feet of all the rival factions. To that end, leading theologians met at the Colloquy of Poissy in September. The Colloquy had its successes, and moderates on both sides were able to establish some common ground. It was never likely, however, that Genevans and Jesuits would establish any working compromise in the long term. Poissy failed to eliminate the issue of heresy, and this left the government with the alternatives of renewed persecution or a policy of toleration. It opted for compromise, and in the Edict of January (1562) permitted public worship by Huguenots, as long as it did not take place within walled towns. It even accepted the principle of a national Huguenot synod, although royal authorisation was required for such a meeting. It was quite another matter to get such an edict accepted in the provinces. Such concessions persuaded many Protestants that the impetus of their movement, now enjoying the favour of kings and ministers, was irresistible, and that they would soon enjoy complete success. In their turn, many Catholics, equally impressed by the gathering

Protestant impetus, were bound to conclude that it must be resisted at all costs.

An uneasy peace lasted only until March 1562, when Guise discovered a Huguenot congregation within the walls of the town of Vassy. The confrontation that followed led to the death of a number of Huguenots, and ensured the demise of the Edict of January. Open warfare was only delayed by the need of both sides to prepare their ground. Toulouse was secured by the local Catholics at the cost of 4,000 Huguenot lives. In Grenoble and in Lyon it was the Protestants who carried the day, their triumph marked by orgies of image-breaking that produced an indelible impression upon Catholic opinion.

CATHERINE DE MEDICI

The death of Henry II and Francis II launched a political career that was to dominate French history for the next quarter of a century. As N.M. Sutherland has written, 'few great historical figures have come down to us so loaded with malediction as Catherine de Medici'. For two centuries, the 'legend of the wicked Italian queen' was only rarely questioned. As recent a writer as J.E. Neale (*The Age of Catherine de Medici*, 1963) could still portray Henry II's widow as a woman primarily motivated by ambition, for herself and for her children, and as one whose limited political understanding was complemented by an amoral mixture of deceit, conspiracy and assassination. Only recently have isolated voices been raised in defence of the queen mother. J. Héritier (*Catherine de Medici*, 1940) realistically concluded that those who accused Catherine were really only following the partisan views of contemporaries who, motivated by extreme religious convictions, could only condemn those who stood in the middle ground. N.M. Sutherland has further stressed the significance of the queen's Italian origins and of her gender. In the eyes of many contemporaries, being a foreigner and a woman were factors which wholly disqualified her from any influential role in French politics.

The fact that Catherine had remained a background figure, virtually a political nonentity, during her husband's lifetime does not square easily with the later legend of the power-hungry conspirator. A more realistic interpretation of Catherine's motives in her later years emphasises her concern for the French crown as an institution after the sudden death of Henry II. It can scarcely be said that the growing influence of the Guises put Catherine's power in jeopardy, for she had none. Francis was fifteen years old at the time of his father's death, no longer technically a minor, and therefore in no need of a regent. What was threatened by Guise influence was the integrity and status of the crown, and Catherine applied all her energies to counter this threat. One way or another, Catherine 'saw the whole period from 1559 to the outbreak of civil war in 1562 as a struggle against the Guises and all that they stood for' (N.M. Sutherland). In her hands the regency was to be a tool for the preservation of religious toleration at the highest levels of French society, and thus a means of preserving a delicate balance between noble factions too powerful to be dominated by the crown. 'She was dwelling on the past', Sutherland has concluded, 'and her intentions were always conservative: she strove to restore the previous state and order which had existed under Francis I and Henry II before her world collapsed.'

THE *POLITIQUES*

The political struggles that dominated the next three decades of French history were a three-cornered contest. Between the Catholic and Huguenot extremes the ground was held by a vague and shifting coalition known to contemporaries as the *politiques*. Outwardly, this coalition stood for the maintenance of good order, stability and government in opposition to the self-interest of the feudal factions. Its name, however, originated as a term of abuse. For the religious extremists, and especially for the Catholics, the coalition represented cynical, atheistic apathy, which put worldly interests above the defence of God's eternal truths. For others, and for many later commentators, the *politiques* were right-thinking, practical people, standing aloof from selfish factional interests.

In some cases, *politiques* do indeed seem to have been motivated by concern for the interests of the state and of the crown. Catherine de Medici herself and her chancellor Michel de l'Hôpital clearly fall into this category. Mark Greengrass has added that 'in a general sense, everyone in royal service was a *politique*'. Many others, however, joined the ranks of the *politiques* from less pure motives. Some, such as Henry of Damville-Montmorency, youngest son of the Constable, sought to promote their own dynastic interests at a time when the Guises dominated the patronage 'market'. The Duke of Alençon, youngest son of Henry II and Catherine, and unlikely therefore to succeed to the throne, sought elusive influence in the later stages of the wars by placing himself at the head of the *politiques*. The Huguenot leaders themselves often crossed the line into the *politique* camp, largely to forge a convenient alliance with the crown against a common enemy. The eventual conversion of Henry of Navarre to Catholicism was perhaps the classic *politique* gesture of the whole era.

The *politique* interpretation of France's problems is illustrated by the programme of judicial and administrative reform proposed by Michel de l'Hôpital during his chancellorship (1560–8). In the words of J.H.M. Salmon, 'he sought to replace the anarchic independence of the nobles with the rule of a loyal legal bureaucracy'. To these ends, the reforming Edict of Orléans (1561) called for the suppression of all offices created since the death of Louis XII, for the banning of pluralism in judicial offices, and for restrictions to be placed upon the number of such offices that could be held by members of one family. In the later Edict of Moulins (February 1566) he sought to check the proliferation of conflicting jurisdictions and the sale of offices. De l'Hôpital clearly envisaged a return to a traditional form of royal government in which the king alone made the laws, advised by his Estates, and in which the Parlements played the major role in local law enforcement.

De l'Hôpital's failure is explained by three main factors. Like many *politiques*, he refused to turn the resources of the state wholly against the Huguenots, and thus convinced many Catholics that he was secretly a Huguenot himself. In addition, his opposition to the sale of offices mobilised a powerful vested interest against him.

Finally, on a practical level, the crown could hardly do without its income from the sale of offices once civil war broke out anew in 1567. Indeed, the political developments of 1567, the renewal of hostilities, and the return of the Guises to a position of influence at court, largely undermined the position of de l'Hôpital, and within a year he had lost office.

THE BALANCE OF THE FORCES, 1562–70

The wars that were sparked off by the events at Amboise and at Vassy began a period of nearly forty years in which France enjoyed little lasting peace or stability. The duration of the struggle was largely due to the even balance that existed between the forces and resources of the two sides.

The most obvious advantage of the Catholic side was the extensive clientage of the Guise family and the substantial resources of manpower, finance and loyalty that they could thus muster. Before long, both Anthony of Bourbon and Anne of Montmorency were to reject the apparent social radicalism of Calvinism and, despite their traditional dynastic rivalry with the Guises, would place their own feudal resources at the disposal of the Catholic party. The proportion of the Catholic forces made up of Swiss, German and Italian mercenaries bears witness to the financial resources that they enjoyed at this stage in the conflict.

The Huguenots, however, enjoyed a quite separate set of advantages. At the outbreak of the civil wars they benefited from two distinct networks of influence. One was the clientage network of Condé. The other was the system of communications established between the Calvinist congregations dispersed across the country. Despite the fact that the two networks undoubtedly had different motives in the conflict, the latter placed themselves increasingly under the protection of the former. It was a political instrument such as few 'overmighty subjects' in the sixteenth century ever commanded.

Suspicious as Protestants increasingly were of a 'Catholic conspiracy' in Europe, there was a distinct element of international conspiracy about the Huguenot movement in France. Through the agency of Beza, the Genevan authorities provided arms for Condé's men. The financiers of Basle and Strasbourg provided loans, and foreign assistance was available at times from Germany, from the Netherlands and from England. In the early stages of the conflict, the religious fervour of the Protestant forces was remarkable, making possible a form of conscription among local Calvinist communities.

The limitations of the commanders on both sides also contributed to the indecisive nature of the conflict. Coligny scarcely won a battle in ten years, yet compensated by a strategy of rapid movement which made it impossible for the Catholic forces to strike a crushing blow at him. The Catholic commanders themselves, especially when in the direct pay of the crown, seemed reluctant finally to end a conflict that gave them such profitable employment.

In the middle ground between the two factions, Catherine had two main tactics for the pursuit of peace and stability. One was de l'Hôpital's programme of administrative reform. The other was the re-establishment of the mystique of the monarchy. To this end, the thirteen-year-old Charles IX was prematurely declared of age, and was paraded with his court around the realm in a sumptuous royal progress that lasted more than two years (January 1564–May 1566). Its aims were to consolidate the personal charisma of the monarch by showing him to his people, and to paper over the personal rivalries at court by a series of splendid entertainments and sumptuous court rituals. This illustrated once more Catherine's conviction that the political troubles of France could be understood best in terms of the nobility and of court factions.

ST BARTHOLOMEW –

After the Treaty of Saint-Germain (1570), Catherine de Medici continued to seek a balance between the rival court factions, in this case by inclining towards the more moderate Huguenots. As part of this policy Huguenot leaders returned to court, and the reconciliation was to be cemented by a marriage alliance between her daughter Marguerite and Henry of Navarre, now the most

15.3 Military narrative

	Cause of hostilities	Main events	Peace settlement
First War April 1562–March 1563		Battle of **Dreux** (Dec. 1562). Catholic victory, offset by death of St André. Capture of Condé and Montmorency. Death of Anthony of Bourbon at siege of Rouen. Assassination of Duke of Guise (Feb 1563).	**Edict of Amboise**. Protestant worship allowed on lands of sympathetic nobles, in cities where it was already established and in one town per *bailliage*.
Second War Sept. 1567–March 1568	Protestant attempt to seize king at **Meaux**, inspired by fears of Catholic contacts with the Duke of Alva. Protestant risings in several towns.	Montmorency killed in battle at **St Denis**.	**Peace of Longjumeau**. Largely repeated terms of Edict of Amboise. Extended further concessions to Protestants in the region of Paris.
Third War Oct. 1568–Aug. 1570	General failure of Peace of Longjumeau to restore order. Offensives by Coligny and Condé in region of La Rochelle.	Condé killed at Battle of **Jarnac** (March 1569). Protestant success at **Roche l'Abeille**. Catholic success at **Moncontour**.	**Peace of St Germain**. Restoration of Catholic worship where it had been prevented. Protestant worship allowed where it had existed in March 1570. Protestants to hold La Rochelle, Cognac, Montauban and La Charité as security.
Fourth War Sept. 1572–July 1573	Defensive mobilisation of Protestants in south and west after St Bartholomew massacre.	Catholics fail to capture La Rochelle despite a long siege.	**Edict of Boulogne**. Restoration of Catholic worship where it had been prevented. Protestant worship allowed only in Nîmes, Montauban and La Rochelle. Domestic rites permitted for Protestant nobility.
Fifth War Sept. 1574–May 1576	General failure of Edict of Boulogne. Court conspiracies centring upon Alençon.	Duke of Guise defeats Huguenot mercenaries at **Dormans** (Oct. 1575). Escape of Navarre from court to assume leadership of Huguenot cause. Alençon's alliance with Navarre created strong *politique*–Huguenot alliance.	**'Peace of Monsieur'**. Catholic worship restored where it had been prevented. Protestant worship allowed everywhere except within two leagues of Paris. All cases in Parlements involving Protestants to be tried by judges of both faiths. Protestants hold eight 'secure towns'.

	Cause of hostilities	Main events	Peace settlement
Sixth War April–Sept. 1577	Henry III's declaration that he is head of Catholic League compromised his neutrality and thus the credibility of the 'Peace of Monsieur'.		**Peace of Bergerac**. Restoration of Catholic worship where it had been prevented. Protestant worship allowed in all cities where it was practised in Sept. 1577, except within ten leagues of Paris and two leagues of the court. Special chambers appointed in Parlements to hear cases involving Protestants.
Seventh War April–Nov. 1580	Condé failed to enforce his authority as Governor of Picardy and tried to seize La Fère, near the borders with the Netherlands.		**Peace of Fleix**. Largely reiterated terms of Peace of Bergerac.
Wars of the League Aug. 1585–March 1598	Catholic League re-formed to forestall succession of Henry of Navarre. Assassinations of Guise and Henry III (1589) leave Navarre as king and leading military figure. He fought on in order to pacify his kingdom.	Guise victory over Huguenots and German mercenaries at **Auneau** (Nov. 1587). Royal forces defeated by Navarre at **Coutras** (Oct. 1587). Henry III expelled from Paris by citizens (1588). Henry of Navarre (Henry IV) victorious over League at **Arques** (Sept. 1589) and **Ivry** (March 1590). Spanish intervention on behalf of League (1591, 1592 and 1595). Conversion of Henry IV to Catholicism (1593) leads to his acceptance by Paris (1594). Henry defeated Spanish at **Fontaine–Française** in Burgundy (1595) and relieved **Amiens** (1597). War with Spain ended by **Treaty of Vervins** (May 1598).	**Edict of Nantes** (see Chapter 20).

prominent member of the Huguenot nobility. At the same time, national security was enhanced by a defensive alliance with England, sealed by the Treaty of Blois.

Some Huguenots, such as Coligny, believed fervently that the crown should heal the nation's wounds by more energetic means, by waging war against its traditional Spanish enemies in the Netherlands. The successes of the 'Sea Beggars' and of Louis of Nassau in April and May 1572 also caught the imagination of the king, and by the summer Charles IX was determined upon military glory in the Low Countries.

Such a policy was viewed with horror by the Guise faction, and for once Catherine shared their views. Not only could she see that French intervention in the Netherlands was bound to alienate her new-found English allies, but she also had a more realistic appreciation than her son of the possibility of failure. The annihilation at Saint-Ghislain (July 1572) of a French force advancing to aid Nassau confirmed that French intervention was folly. When Charles decided in the following month to commit another force to the Netherlands, his mother decided upon a desperate course. The assassination of Coligny would remove the leading advocate of intervention, and would be an act in which the Guise faction would certainly cooperate. The policy misfired horribly when, on 22 August, the assassin failed in his task. The Huguenots, gathered in Paris for the wedding of Navarre, howled for revenge and the inquest was sure to expose the part played by the queen mother. Catherine sought to rectify a bad decision with a worse one. The Guise faction was easily enlisted in a plan to wipe out the Huguenot leadership, and the king seems to have agreed, under the impression that this was the only way of forestalling a full-scale Huguenot rising against the crown.

Again, however, Catherine miscalculated. The planned purge of a hundred or so Huguenot leaders turned into a bloodbath engulfing the whole of the capital as the palace plot triggered off fanatical anti-Protestant feelings among the Paris mob. The morning of St Bartholomew's Day (24 August 1572) saw unbridled slaughter in the streets of Paris in which between 3,000 and 4,000 persons were butchered. Coligny was among the first to die, and of the leaders only Navarre and Henry of Condé

survived, saved by their royal blood and by their timely agreement to embrace the Catholic faith.

— AND ITS AFTERMATH

In the phrase of Jules Michelet, 'St Bartholomew was not a day, but a season'. As the news spread through the realm, the events were imitated on a smaller, localised scale: 1,200 Huguenots died in Orléans and some 600 at Meaux on the following day. In the south, in Bordeaux, Toulouse and Albi, the hunting and killing of local Huguenots continued until early October. As many as 8,000 may have lost their lives in the provinces.

Undoubtedly the St Bartholomew massacre was 'the greatest crisis the Huguenot movement had ever faced' (J.H.M. Salmon). It was deprived at a stroke of most of its national leadership. In some regions, such as Burgundy and Champagne, the movement now virtually ceased to exist. The massacre, however, was also to prove to be a disaster for the crown. As a direct result of her miscalculations, many of the elements in Catherine de Medici's policy were utterly destroyed. There was now little prospect of an anti-Spanish alliance with any Protestant state, and the balance of power in court politics was destroyed, with the influence of the Guise faction supreme once more. Worse still, the massacre transformed the Huguenot movement, making it impossible for the crown to control by means of compromises agreed within the ranks of the political élite. Inevitably, the massacre also signalled the resumption of civil war. Deprived of much of their noble leadership, the Huguenots in the provinces fell back upon other resources, the most important of which were the garrison towns that they held by the terms of earlier peace treaties.

This was also a new kind of civil war. 'To the Protestant communities of the south', Mark Greengrass has written, the massacre 'was a royal treason, a gigantic felony, perpetrated without warning'. Throughout the Midi region, Huguenot communities effectively renounced royal authority. In the latter part of 1573 elected representatives from each Huguenot community in the region gathered at Montauban (August) and at Millau (December). There they drew up a constitutional framework for a federal republic, independent of the French crown and possessing a remarkable degree of political liberty. Each town or province within the union was to elect its own governors and was to send representatives to an 'Estates General' representing the region of Languedoc as a whole. Many common features of royal government, such as plurality and venality of office, were specifically rejected, and laws were drafted whereby officials could be prosecuted for corruption. To finance the administration of this federation, taxes normally due to the crown, such as the *gabelle*, and revenues normally paid to the Church, were diverted and appropriated. The French state now faced the genuine threat of disintegration.

It was the French historian E. Haag (*La France protéstante*, 1846–58) who first described these southern provinces as the 'United Provinces of the Midi', highlighting the parallels that existed between this revolt and the contemporary revolt in the Netherlands. As in the case of the Netherlands, the elected representatives of the communities did not break free for long from the influence of the surviving Protestant nobility. The dangers of the time made it inevitable that military matters should be placed in the hands of the great nobles. The effective 'head of state' within the Protestant Midi was the 'Protector' nominated by the Estates General of the federation. The first Protector, Henry of Condé, was later replaced by Henry of Navarre, now escaped from court and returned to the Huguenot faith. Both men worked in alliance with another great magnate, Henry of Damville, governor of Languedoc and a leading figure among the *politique* faction. If such great families continued to play a prominent role, however, the constitution of the Protestant 'republic' made it very clear that they did so only by virtue of a 'contract' between them and the Huguenot communities they protected. Their authority depended wholly upon the effective fulfilment of their defensive role.

THE POLITICAL THEORIES OF THE WARS

The civil wars in France provided one of the greatest stimuli to political thought in the sixteenth century. The political theory of the Wars of Religion centred around two different interpretations of the nature of monarchy. One line of thought stressed its divine origins, and imbued it with a sacred aura which made any attack upon it an act of sacrilege. In reply, the rival 'school' quoted historical precedents to show that the power of the monarch was limited by the liberties and interests of his or her people. The monarchy, they claimed, forfeited both their obedience and their support if its actions damaged those interests. All sides in the struggle drifted from one theory to the other as it suited their circumstances at a given moment. In the early 1560s the former, 'legitimist' theories were largely the preserve of the *politique* monarchists and of the Huguenot nobles and gentry.

Such attitudes were totally transformed, however, by the St Bartholomew massacre. This blatant abuse of royal power caused Huguenot writers to lurch away from the defence of absolutism. Theodore Beza's *The Right of Magistrates over Their Subjects*, François Hotman's *Francogallia* and the anonymous *Reveille matin* (1573) all put forward the argument that rulers had a contractual relationship with their subjects, which they broke if they acted as tyrants. Beza provided a novel twist, however, by viewing power as a hierarchy running from the individual, through the lesser magistrates, to the monarch him- or herself. On this he based the conclusion that those lesser magistrates retained a degree of power and might use it to restrain the monarch from acting as a tyrant. In principle, he implied, this was what was being done by the Protestant magistrates of southern France.

Hotman believed the history of France proved that the monarchy had always been subject to the sovereign will of the people. As recent monarchs had usurped powers to which they had no historical claim, it was now within the rights of the people to depose them and to reclaim their powers.

The most famous justification of political resistance produced in the sixteenth century was the *Vindiciae Contra Tyrannos*, published (1579) under a false name, but probably the work of the Huguenot nobleman Philippe Duplessis-Mornay. It re-stressed the principle of the sovereignty of the people and the obligation upon monarchs to rule in the interests of their people. Following Beza, it laid down specific guidelines for opposition and resistance by other public magistrates, including the nobility, but refused to sanction rebellion by the individual, as leading to a state of anarchy that was an even greater curse than tyranny.

With the accelerating disintegration of royal authority in the 1570s, a growing fear of anarchy encouraged many *politique* theorists to produce renewed justifications of absolute monarchy. Louis le Roy's book *The Excellence of Royal Government* (1575) argued that the power of the monarch was limited only by the good laws and customs of the realm, which had been so subverted in recent years that many illicit limitations of royal authority had come into existence. Jean Bodin's *Six Books of the Commonwealth* (1576) departed much further from the main lines of monarchist thought. At the centre of his argument was the claim that monarchs possessed the fundamental right not only to enforce the laws of the realm, but also to legislate without the consent of the governed. The only constraints upon monarchical power were the fundamental principles of the succession and of divine law. At this stage, Bodin's claims constituted the classic statement of *politique* views, as they sought to re-establish royal authority as an antidote to social and political disintegration.

The following decade, in its turn, produced events that sent the theorists of all camps scurrying after philosophies they had once condemned. The death of Alençon in 1584 raised the prospect of a Huguenot, Henry of Navarre, as the next King of France. Huguenot writers suddenly found themselves back where they had been before 1572, with a vested interest in legitimate monarchy. The Catholic theorists were forced to undertake an equally remarkable turnabout, and it was they who now argued the case for the deposition of monarchs who acted against the true spiritual interests of their subjects.

1574–84

The three Henries

The premature death of Charles IX (30 May 1574) opened a new phase in the disintegration of the French state, in which a new generation of leading actors came to the fore. Of the old generation, Catherine de Medici was still present, and once again occupied the office of regent while the rightful heir made the long journey from the kingdom that he had recently acquired in Poland. Like his mother, Henry III has received a consistently bad 'press' from historians, but has perhaps deserved a better one. He was a man of considerable intelligence and political shrewdness. He alone, of all Catherine's sons, made a coherent attempt at reform of the rotten institutional structure of his realm. He also appears to have had a realistic and perceptive appreciation of the task that faced him. Even the little group of favourites that he constructed around him, his *mignons*, could be positively interpreted. Mark Greengrass has recently claimed that they should be seen as a group of able and ambitious young men, reliant upon the king alone, at a time when he could scarcely rely upon any of the factional leaders.

Unfortunately, however, there was another side to the king's character. He was inconsistent and unstable. His attention to affairs of state was sporadic, and his intense religious feelings manifested themselves in bouts of penitential humiliation which were viewed with distaste by many of his subjects. The king in sackcloth and ashes was not easily reconciled with the same king who, when his soul had been satisfied, encouraged the most spectacular acts of debauchery and immorality at his court. It was even rumoured, and widely believed, that the King of France appeared at court functions dressed as a woman. The *mignons*, similarly, were widely perceived as the king's partners in debauchery. Suspicions that they were his homosexual companions have never been substantiated but, as Mark Greengrass remarks, 'that the slander existed, is a sign of the gap between the court and the rest of France in this period'.

Henry, Duke of Guise, presented a public image as pure as that of the king was sullied. Now twenty-four years old, he was mature enough to succeed his murdered father as leader of the ultra-Catholic faction, but he was able to add to that role some decorations of his own. He had fought against the Turk at the age of sixteen, and was already a veteran of the battles of Jarnac and Moncontour.

His battle scars earned him the honourable nickname of *Le Balafré* – Scarface – and his personal reputation was such that it even earned him the grudging respect of the Huguenots.

The third Henry, Henry of Navarre, had not yet acquired the military and political reputation that would later strengthen his candidature for the French throne. Only twenty years old, he was effectively a prisoner at court until his escape in 1576, and his religious leanings remained unclear. Calvinist by upbringing, he had embraced Catholicism as the price of survival on St Bartholomew's day, and contemporaries found it hard to resist the conclusion that his return to Protestantism in 1576 was politically motivated. Nevertheless, he possessed a clear set of advantages over the Guises. He remained the first prince of the blood and, in 1574, stood third in order of precedence in the realm behind the king and Alençon, only a step away from the throne itself.

The social crisis

The reign of Charles IX had seen the factional struggles of the nobility degenerate into a deeper conflict liable to split the realm in two. That of Henry III was marked by an accumulation of social crises sufficient to threaten the very fabric of French society with disintegration.

For many French provinces the 1570s brought severe and enduring agricultural crisis. This was largely due to military activity, but was aggravated by two unusually wet summers in 1572 and 1573. The disastrously low grain harvests of those years set off a trend of high prices that lasted until 1577. By 1583 prices were rising once more, this time set off by drought. This crisis was paralleled by the decay of urban trade in France. Overseas trade, such as Marseilles' commerce with the Levant and that of La Rochelle over the Atlantic route, was not seriously disrupted by the internal unrest, but the trade of these and other ports with the French interior tells a very different story. In both cases commerce became limited to the port's immediate hinterland. Similarly, the 1570s witnessed a disastrous decline in the textile trade in the Paris region and a similar decline in the banking activities of Lyon. To a greater and greater extent,

French economic activity became regionalised and fragmented. David Parker (*The Making of French Absolutism*, 1983) has gone so far as to conclude that at this time 'there was no such thing as the French economy; rather there existed a number of regional economies – that of the eastern regions drawn into the orbit of Germany and the Rhine, that of the northern and western provinces increasingly dominated by the Dutch, and that of the Midi under the pull of the Mediterranean'.

The social and economic life of many regions of France was seriously threatened by military action, either by forces in the service of the great lords or by the bands of brigands that the war left in its wake. The regions of Brie and Champagne suffered terribly in 1576, first at the hands of the German cavalry that invaded to support the Huguenots, and then at the hands of the royal forces that repulsed them. In 1581, nominally a period of peace, the same regions were pillaged by units of Alençon's forces proceeding to the Netherlands.

The crown was now patently unable to enforce its laws or to protect its subjects, and this caused reactions potentially more dangerous to the integrity of the realm than the original lawlessness. From 1578 onwards more and more cases occurred in the provinces of the peasantry organising themselves for purposes of self-protection, and of resistance to the burdens that were being placed upon them. Frequently such organisations rebelled against their social superiors. At Cuers, near Toulon, a peasant force massacred 600 nobles and gentlemen commanded by the local representatives of the Catholic League (April 1579). At the same time, the Vivarais and Dauphiné regions saw a number of violent outbursts aimed at the châteaux of the local *seigneurs*. Another recurrent feature was the refusal to pay tithes or the *taille*, and the destruction of the relevant records. In some cases the risings produced viable political organisations. Thanks to the research of Le Roy Ladurie (*Carnival at Romans*, 1979), the best-known example of such activity is now the remarkable and radical political organisation set up at Romans by the cloth worker and former soldier Jean Serve in 1579–80. In such organisations religious differences were often submerged beneath the class interests involved.

As the authority and prestige of the central government declined, so local authority frequently increased to replace it. When Henry III tried to dismiss all existing provincial governors in 1576, his orders were ignored in many localities, and rival governors disputed control of the regions. In many areas of the south, the 'protector' of the Huguenot 'republic' simply commandeered royal taxation for the benefit of the Huguenot cause. During the lifetime of the Catholic League, taxes levied in Dijon, Rennes, Rouen and other Catholic strongholds were diverted directly into the hands of the Duke of Guise.

This disintegration of central authority also facilitated the resurrection of local representative institutions. In some areas the provincial estates met with unprecedented frequency, as in Guyenne, where they assembled forty-six times between 1561 and 1581. With greater frequency, too, they rejected royal requests for taxation, as in Brittany in 1573, in Burgundy in 1578 and in Normandy in 1579. A number of scholars have seen this period as a crossroads at which France could have turned permanently in the direction of representative government.

The further failure of reform

In response to economic crisis, political instability and social disintegration, the representative bodies of the realm persistently petitioned for institutional and financial reform. In 1575 the inhabitants of Champagne petitioned the king to take measures to prevent the depopulation and decay of their towns. A year later the Estates General assembled at Blois were so persistent in their criticism of royal financial policy and of the administration of justice that the king was forced to dismiss them despite his desperate need for taxation. In 1578 the provincial estates of both Burgundy and Normandy refused any financial grant to the king 'before the reformation of the kingdom be attended to'.

Until the end of the decade royal reforms concentrated mainly upon financial issues. An attempt was made in 1577–8 to stabilise the currency by linking its value to a new gold coin, and substantial confiscations of Church property were made in 1574 and 1576 to boost the resources of the crown. A coherent programme of institutional reform was at last undertaken in

1582–3, and proposals were formulated at an assembly of notables which met at Saint-Germain-en-Laye in December 1583. These included measures to reduce the number of royal officials, to outlaw the future mass repurchase of offices, and assurances that some offices would be allowed to lapse after the death of their present occupants.

To succeed, however, these reforms required a large degree of goodwill within the administration and in the provinces. Effective reform was also dependent upon an extended peace; and as the assembly of notables completed its deliberations France was less than a year away from the most prolonged and bitter phase of her civil conflict.

The formation of the Catholic League

The wars that emanated from the St Bartholomew massacres ended (May 1576) in the most advantageous treaty that the Huguenots had so far achieved. The 'Peace of Monsieur' granted freedom of worship to Huguenots in every city in the realm except Paris; and Navarre, Condé and Damville were all confirmed in their various provincial governorships.

Yet this peace lost the king his only likely ally. Outraged at this surrender to heresy and to the factional interests of his Bourbon and Montmorency rivals, Henry of Guise responded by the formation of a Catholic League for the defence of true religion against all its enemies. Socially conservative, this first version of the League was declared to comprise 'princes, *seigneurs* and Catholic gentlemen' and kept the towns well in the background. Its attitude to the monarchy was highly ambiguous. Its manifesto placed great stress upon the rights of the provincial estates and of the Parlements, and its members swore an oath to obey the authority of the League's leader, and no other.

In view of this last factor, it was a shrewd move by the king to declare himself head of the League (January 1577) in an attempt to forestall the emergence of yet another rival authority within his realm. At first this move seemed to be successful, for the League declared itself dissolved rather than serve the purpose of an unreliable monarch. By doing this, however, Henry III had clearly abandoned the principles of the 'Peace of

Monsieur'. Now that he had clearly identified himself with the Catholic side, his attempted compromise with the Protestants was a dead letter, which may have been a prime objective of the Guise faction in the first place.

The failure of the 'Peace of Monsieur' demonstrated for the last time that such compromises could not be maintained by a relatively small faction against the hostility of so much of the country. The League, brief though its first incarnation had been, had gained considerable support and popularity. This demonstrated, as clearly as the events of St Bartholomew's day had done, the conservative Catholicism of the majority of Frenchmen, particularly in the strategically important regions of northern, eastern and central France.

THE LEAGUE AND THE TOWNS

The early 1580s were a period of delicate political balance in French politics. It was preserved by factors similar to those that had maintained the uneasy peace of 1570–2. Once again, the French court adopted an anti-Spanish policy as a convenient distraction from domestic rivalries, but now Alençon played the role previously played by Coligny. In August 1579 he was in England proposing marriage to Queen Elizabeth, and in February 1582 he formally accepted sovereignty over the rebellious Netherlands. For a time the influence of the Guise family, with their traditionally pro-Spanish leanings and their vested interests in the cause of Elizabeth's rival, Mary Stuart, seemed to be at a low ebb.

In June 1584 the balance was utterly disrupted by Alençon's sudden death. The king himself was now the last-surviving male Valois, and the virtual certainty that he would now produce no heir presented French Catholics with an intolerable prospect: before long they would have the Protestant Henry of Navarre as their ruler. This led to the resurrection of the Catholic League. The revived League of 1584 consisted of two quite distinct elements. One was the aristocratic Catholic opposition, which once more looked to Spain for assistance, and received it in the form of the Treaty

of Joinville between the League and the Spanish crown. By its terms, Spain recognised as heir to the throne the elderly Cardinal of Bourbon, an uncle of Henry of Navarre. Furthermore, Spain pledged 50,000 ducats a month to subsidise the struggle against heresy in France, so vital to the outcome of her own struggle in the Netherlands. Philip II 'had thus achieved what his father had always vainly striven for: alliance with a Catholic France under the leadership of Spain' (H.G. Koenigsberger, in *Cambridge Modern History*, vol. III, 1968). In that respect, the Treaty of Joinville helped to clear the way for his dispatch of the Armada against England.

The second element within the Catholic League originated in the towns that remained faithful to the Catholic cause. In Paris there arose a conspiratorial and shadowy administration, led by lawyers, officials and clerics, and based upon the administrative quarters of the city, with a directing committee known as the 'Sixteen'. The prospect of a Huguenot succession was undoubtedly one of the motives behind the formation of the 'Sixteen', but a variety of economic grievances were also voiced by the Parisian leaders. These included the burden of taxation, the devalued currency, and the overall disruption of trade caused by the wars. Parisians also complained bitterly against the extravagance of the court and against the scandalous excesses of the royal favourites. The popular Catholicism of the city that had been so evident on St Bartholomew's day now served once more to stir up religious enthusiasm. The preachers of the city's churches, the members of its substantial printing industry and the theologians of its traditionally conservative university were all prominent in the outcry against heresy and public immorality.

The conspiratorial nature of the 'Sixteen' posed an even greater threat to the king's authority than did the influence of the Guises. The prospect of popular revolt in Paris was even more serious than that posed by the Huguenot administration in Languedoc, because it was that much closer to the seat of power. There were signs, too, that similar dangers existed in other towns. Sens, Troyes and Auxerre quickly established similar organisations, and the crisis of early 1589 was to cause the proliferation of such bodies throughout the Catholic cities of France.

15.4 Challenges to royal authority in France

Source A. These openly tyrannical practices, the setting aside of the princes and great lords, the contempt for the Estates of the realm, the corruption of the principal judges and their devotion to [the Guises]; in short, their violent and most unlawful government aroused great hatred of them and caused several noblemen to waken as from a deep sleep. Jurists and eminent persons in France and Germany were consulted as well as the most learned theologians, and it was established that one could lawfully oppose the government usurped by the Guises and even take up arms if necessary. To approach the king and his council would have been tantamount to warning the enemy, for the king had become their slave. Thus it was necessary to seize his person by any means and then to call the Estates so as to force them to account for their administration. Once this course of action had been decided by common consent, three kinds of people took the matter in hand: the first were moved by zeal to serve God, their prince and fatherland; the second by ambition and desire for change; and the third was spurred on by a thirst for vengeance for the outrages committed by the Guises against themselves, their kinsmen and their allies.

> An account of the planning of the Tumult of Amboise (1560), printed in *The Ecclesiastical History of the Reformed Churches in France* by Theodore Beza, published in 1580

Source B. 1 Until such time as it pleases God (who rules the hearts of kings) to change that of the King and restore the State of France to good order, or to arrange for a neighbouring prince of proven virtue to liberate the poor afflicted people: they will, after swearing an oath, elect by a public vote in their town or city a leader, or 'major', who shall command the army for their defence and run the civil administration.

2 For each of the said majors they will elect a council of twenty-four men who, like the major, will be chosen without regard to status from among the nobles or commoners of the town or surrounding countryside who are known for their public spirit.

11 The leaders and councils will elect a commander-in-chief in the manner of a Roman dictator, who will command in the countryside and whom the inhabitants of the towns and cities will obey.

35 When negotiating, the leaders should bear in mind the following rules: never trust those who have so often and so treacherously broken faith and the public peace; never disarm as long as the enemy continues to oppose the true faith and those who profess it; and sign no peace treaties that can be used to start massacres.

> Rules for the establishment of Huguenot assemblies and military commands in Languedoc, published in the *Reveille-matin des françaises*, 1573

Source C. It is thus apparent that there is a mutual obligation between the king and the officers of the kingdom; that the government of the realm is not in the hands of the king in its entirety but only in the sovereign degree; and that there are definite conditions on either side. If these conditions are not observed by

THE LEAGUE AND THE CROWN

The renewal of the League and the unparalleled popular enthusiasm for it in northern France placed the crown in a worse position than it had occupied for a decade. Henry III now exercised authority over a far smaller proportion of the French population than either Henry of Guise or Henry of Navarre. In July 1585 he reached an agreement with the League at Nemours, which entailed the revocation of all earlier compromises with the Huguenots, the dismissal of all Huguenot office-holders, and the acceptance of the League's army by the king as his main weapon against heresy. Faced with such a threat there was little that the Huguenots could do but resort once more to war. The treaty thus triggered off the newest phase in the civil wars, appropriately dubbed by contemporaries as 'The War of the Three Henries'.

the inferior officers, it is the part of the sovereign to dismiss and punish them. If the king, hereditary or elective, clearly goes back on the conditions without which he would not have been recognised or acknowledged, can there be any doubt that the lesser magistrates of the kingdom are free of their oath, at least to the extent that they are free to resist flagrant oppression of the realm which they swore to protect and defend?

From *The Right of Magistrates*, by Theodore Beza, 1574

Source D. We have all solemnly sworn and promised to use force and to take up arms to the end that the Holy Church of God may be restored to its dignity and to the True and Holy Catholic religion; that the nobility may enjoy the perfect freedom to which they are entitled; that the people may be relieved by the abolition of new taxes; that the Parlements may be left in the freedom of their conscience and entire liberty of judgement; and that all true subjects in the kingdom may be maintained in their governments, places and offices.

From the manifesto of the Catholic League, 1585

Source E. The king thus hoped to arrest a number of the Parisian bourgeois, Leaguers and followers of the Duke of Guise, and to execute them as an example to the Duke's other followers. But the king's plan misfired, for the people began to stir and, taking to the streets, stretched chains across them and erected barricades at the crossroads. Workmen left their tools, merchants their businesses, lawyers their briefs. One could only hear dreadful shouts and seditious words aimed at exciting and alarming the people.

[The Duke of Guise] stood at the window of the Hôtel de Guise until 4.00 p.m., when he left. As he emerged, some louts who had gathered to see him shouted 'Take Cardinal of Bourbon to Reims.' As the Duke walked along the streets the people vied with each other as to who would shout 'Long live Guise' the loudest. He pretended to dislike this and, doffing his large hat (no one could tell if he was laughing behind it), he told them repeatedly: 'That's enough, my friends. This is too much, gentlemen. You must shout "Long live the King"'.

Account of the Day of the Barricades (12 May 1588). From Pierre de l'Estoile,
Journal of the Reign of Henry III

QUESTIONS

a. Explain the following phrases that occur in the sources: 'the government usurped by the Guises' (source A); 'the Parlements' (source D); 'take the Cardinal of Bourbon to Reims' (source E).

b. In what ways do sources A and B differ in their attitudes towards established political authority? What events helped to bring about such a change?

c. Summarise the justifications given in source C for opposition to royal authority. In what ways do they represent a more radical position than those taken in sources A and B?

d. 'Religious conviction was the primary cause of opposition to the monarchy during the French Wars of Religion.' How far do these documents lead you to agree with this claim?

Events abroad added to the pressure upon the king. The execution of Mary Queen of Scots (February 1587) fuelled Catholic fervour in Paris with lurid stories of the fate of English Catholics. This, the propagandists claimed, was a foretaste of the fate that orthodox Frenchmen could expect if a Protestant succeeded to their throne. Emboldened, the nobility of the League drew up at Nancy (January 1588) a series of articles demanding that the king dismiss his *mignons*, accept the guidance of

Guise in the fight against heresy, and unreservedly accept the decrees of the Council of Trent.

Within four months the crown had suffered its greatest humiliation at the hands of the League. In April, Henry attempted to reassert his position by formally forbidding Guise to enter Paris. In open defiance of the royal order the 'Sixteen' invited the Duke to enter the capital, which he did on 9 May. The king ordered units of the royal guard to occupy strategic positions around the city, but the coup was frustrated by the populace, directed by the 'Sixteen'. Isolating and surrounding the royal guards by means of a series of barricades, they forced their surrender. On the following day the King of France fled his capital.

15.5 Key figures

ALENÇON, Francis Duke of (1554–84). Youngest son of Henry II and Catherine de Medici. With little prospect of succession to the throne, he featured prominently in the *politique* faction largely through motives of self-interest. Accepted title of 'protector' of the Dutch rebels (1578). Sought marriage to Elizabeth of England (1579–81). Offered sovereignty over the Netherlands as Duke of Brabant (1582), but lost Dutch sympathy through an attempted seizure of Antwerp (1583).

ANTHONY OF BOURBON (1518–62). King of Navarre (1550) by virtue of his marriage to Jeanne d'Albret (1548). Fluctuated between Protestantism and Catholicism, according to political advantage. Sought regency of France upon death of Francis II (1561). Lieutenant-General of France (1561). Died of wounds at siege of Rouen. Father of Henry IV.

COLIGNY, Gaspard de (1519–72). Military leader in wars against Spain (1542–4). Admiral of France (1552). Influenced by Calvin's theology, he played a leading role in demanding toleration for French Protestants and took joint command of Huguenot forces upon outbreak of civil war. Principal leader after 1569. Advocate of French intervention in the Netherlands (1569–72). Murdered in course of St Bartholomew massacre.

CONDÉ, Louis, Prince of (1530–69). Influenced by Protestantism at the court of Navarre. Successful military leader in wars against Spain (1551–7), but alienated by lack of recognition from Henry II. Sponsored the 'Tumult' of Amboise (1560) and assumed joint command of Huguenot forces. Killed at Battle of Jarnac.

CONDÉ, Henry, Prince of (1552–88). Son of Louis and cousin of Henry of Navarre. Forcibly converted to Catholicism after St Bartholomew massacre (1572). Escaped from court to fight in Huguenot cause. Governor of Picardy (1577). Died from wounds received in battle.

D'ALBRET, Jeanne (1528–72). Daughter of Francis I's sister, Marguerite of Angoulême. Queen of Navarre. Wife of Anthony of Bourbon and mother of Henry IV. After the death of Anthony she remained a major force for the independence of Navarre and a major influence within the Huguenot movement.

DAMVILLE, Henry of Montmorency, Count of (1534–1614). Son of Anne of Montmorency. Governor of Languedoc (1563). Marshal of France (1567). A leading *politique,* he revolted against the crown in support of Henry of Navarre in 1575 and 1585. Constable of France (1593) under Henry IV.

DE L'HÔPITAL, Michel (1503–73). Served papal court and Charles V before returning to his native France (1534). Chancellor of Berry (1548). *Maître des requêtes. Surintendant des finances.* Chancellor of France (1560). Proposed Colloquy of Poissy (1561) and Edict of January (1562) in search of a religious compromise. Resigned under pressure from Catholic enthusiasts (1568).

GUISE, Francis, Duke of (1519–63). Successful military commander, winning Calais from the English (1558). Leading figure at court under Francis II, but eclipsed during the regency of Catherine de Medici. Principal Catholic leader, his massacre of Huguenots at Vassy (1562) helped to trigger Wars of Religion. Assassinated, possibly at the instigation of Coligny.

GUISE, Henry, Duke of (1550–88). Son of Francis and his successor at head of Catholic cause during Wars of Religion. Won major victories at Dormans (1575) and Auneau (1587). Largely responsible for assassination of Coligny (1572) and for the expulsion of Henry III from Paris (1588). In response to this event, he was assassinated at the instigation of the king.

For many years this 'Day of the Barricades' was seen by historians as one of the great triumphs of the 'overmighty subject' over the crown. Recent writers have tended, however, to move Guise from the centre of the stage, leaving the rebellious Parisians in the place of honour. 'The Day of the Barricades', wrote Perez Zagorin (*Rebels and Rulers, 1500–1660*, 1982), 'was a great urban revolt, one of the biggest of the era.' Whatever its precise nature, it reduced the authority and prestige of the French crown to its lowest ebb for a century and a half.

For a while the king seemed to accept the humiliation. In July he accepted the so-called Edict of Union, in which he surrendered to all the major demands of the League. The Cardinal of Bourbon was recognised as his heir, all concessions to the Huguenots were once more cancelled, and prominent Leaguers were installed in strategic governorships throughout the country. Guise himself was made Lieutenant-General of the realm. In reality, however, the king had reached breaking-point and had decided to resolve his difficulties by a desperate act. Two days before Christmas he had the unsuspecting Guise murdered in his presence at Blois and his brother, the Cardinal de Lorraine, killed the following day. Like many contemporary commentators, Henry had assumed that Guise was the inspiration, as well as the central figure, of the Catholic League.

The main result of the assassination, however, was that the veiled hostility of the king's Catholic subjects was converted into open revolt. In Paris, the 'Sixteen' quickly directed an open political coup, replacing the city's governor, driving the *politiques* out of the Parlement, and forming a council to replace the royal government. The Sorbonne pronounced Henry deposed and at war with his subjects. Rouen, Blois, Amiens, Reims, Dijon, Orléans, Toulouse and Marseilles all followed the example of the capital. In the provinces royal government frequently collapsed in the face of alternative administrations directed by the League. Provincial councils of the League were established in twelve main centres across France, representing 'a new concept of participatory government created by the revolutionary situation' (J.H.M. Salmon).

The crown and its remaining *politique* supporters were thrown back into alliance with the Huguenots, reaching agreement with Navarre in April 1589. Against this alliance the League stood in an ambiguous position. In part it remained an organ of aristocratic faction, now headed by Guise's surviving brother, Mayenne. Yet to a greater extent than ever it was now a revolutionary association of towns as radical in its political theories as any movement of the sixteenth century.

All the same, the military skill of Navarre seemed likely to be the decisive factor in this new round of hostilities. By late July 1589 the army of the two Henries had pushed towards Paris and begun a siege that threatened to bring the capital to its knees. On the last day of that month, however, the city was afforded some respite by a young Jacobin monk, Jacques Clément. Entering the royal camp at Saint-Cloud on the pretext of seeking an interview, he stabbed to death the last Valois king of France.

Further reading

M. Greengrass (1987) *The French Reformation.* Oxford.

M.P. Holt (1995) *The French Wars of Religion, 1562–1629.* Cambridge.

R.J. Knecht (1989) *The French Wars of Religion, 1559–1598.* London.

J.H.M. Salmon (1975) *Society in Crisis: France in the Sixteenth Century.* London.

N.M. Sutherland (1984) *Princes, Politics and Religion, 1547–1589.* London.

• CHAPTER SIXTEEN •

The Revolt of the Netherlands

THE HISTORICAL DEBATE

The revolt of the Netherlands against Spanish rule was the central event of the second half of the sixteenth century. It produced a new nation, and it demonstrated the viability of a new kind of state, based upon mercantile prosperity and freedom of enterprise rather than upon the privileges and landed wealth of the nobility. The revolt was a central factor in the ruin of the dominant state of the century, Spain, and represented one of the greatest triumphs of the Protestant cause.

For a century the historiography of the Dutch revolt was dominated by the work of the American Presbyterian, John Lothrop Motley (*Rise of the Dutch Republic*, 1856). 'To Motley', as Pieter Geyl explained, 'this upheaval was nothing but an illustration of the eternal struggle between right and wrong. To him Catholicism and Absolutism were Powers of Darkness, while Protestantism was one with Liberty, Democracy and Light.' To the modern historian, however, it must appear that his interpretation of the Dutch revolt exaggerated the role of Protestantism, and largely misconstrued the motives of such leaders as William of Orange.

Geyl was the leading Dutch historian of the revolt (*The Revolt of the Netherlands*, 1931). For him its central, heroic element was not Protestantism nor the genius of a great leader, but the national identity and the desire for liberty of the Dutch people. Seeking an explanation for the division that took place between the northern and southern provinces, Geyl found it in geography. For him, the great rivers that cut through the centre of the Netherlands provided the defensive barrier behind which the northerners safely developed their state and economy. While Geyl believed that this division had maimed the cultural identity of the Netherlands, the great Belgian historian Henri Pirenne claimed in his monumental *Histoire de Belgique* (1900–32) that a specific and separate Belgian cultural identity existed in the southern provinces even before the revolt and the Spanish reconquest.

A standard work for over thirty years, Geyl's masterpiece is now liable to criticism from two angles. J.W. Smit (*The Present Position of Studies Regarding the Revolt of the Netherlands*, 1960) suggested that it is misleading to see the events in the Netherlands as a single revolt. Instead they should be seen as 'a number of revolts representing the interests and the ideals of various social, economic and ideological groups'. Meanwhile, the work of Geoffrey Parker (*The Dutch Revolt*, 1977, and *Spain and the Netherlands 1559–1659*, 1979) has moved in a new direction by giving full consideration to the Spanish viewpoint. In particular, his first major work on the subject, *The Army of Flanders and the Spanish Road* (1972), shed important new light on the logistics of the Spanish campaigns and helped to show that Spanish failings were as important in the outcome as Dutch achievements.

THE NETHERLANDS

The social context

The Netherlands were socially and economically diverse. The provinces of Flanders, Brabant, Hainault and Artois constituted their prosperous 'heartland'. To the north, across rivers and dykes, Friesland, Holland, Zealand and Utrecht shared much of this prosperity. In the east, the provinces of Limburg, Luxembourg, Gelderland, Overijssel, Drenthe and Groningen were altogether poorer and more sparsely populated.

The region encompassing Holland, Zealand, Flanders, Hainault and Brabant was the most densely populated in Europe. Where the British Isles had four towns of more than 10,000 inhabitants, the Netherlands had nineteen. Antwerp had a population of about 80,000, while Ghent, Brussels, Lille, Valenciennes and Amsterdam all had over 30,000. Disastrous shortages and crippling poverty were regular features of Dutch urban life, although the urbanised and mercantile nature of the society contributed to an unusual degree of literacy among the population. Many Dutch towns boasted a surprising number of schools. Antwerp alone had 150, and Ghent had forty, including twelve grammar schools.

A further distinctive feature of the Netherlands was their relationship with the sea. Most of the farmland north of Antwerp had been reclaimed from the sea, and the sea occasionally took it back

Dutch provinces
1 Flanders
2 Brabant
3 Limburg
4 Zealand
5 Holland
6 Utrecht
7 Gelderland
8 Overijssel
9 Drenthe
10 Friesland
11 Groningen

French speaking provinces

16.1 The Netherlands in 1555

again. The complex of lakes, bogs and waterways made the traditional sixteenth-century difficulties of communications especially severe in the northern and central Netherlands.

Central to the social and economic life of the Netherlands was the great trading wealth of Antwerp. A contemporary estimated that some 2,500 ships per week used the port, while 10,000 cartloads of goods left every week by land routes for other parts of the Continent. The great specialities of Antwerp were textiles and finance, while the city's virtual monopoly of the English cloth trade dated from the *Magnus Intercursus* trade treaty of 1496. All the same, Antwerp's greatness was past its peak. Much of the Portuguese trading colony departed in 1548, and from 1560 onwards, for religious, political and economic reasons, relations with the English worsened. The iconoclastic riots of 1566 signalled the beginnings of Antwerp's deep and damaging involvement in the Dutch revolt itself.

The political context

The political unity of the Netherlands, which Philip II was to try so hard to consolidate, was a very recent innovation. Not only had Charles V added substantially to his original Burgundian inheritance, but by the Augsburg Transaction in 1548 he had removed the collected provinces of the Netherlands from imperial jurisdiction to form a separate political unit. By the Pragmatic Sanction (November 1549) the estates of each province agreed that upon his death they would recognise Philip of Spain as their sole ruler.

Dynastic unity was offset by provincial diversity. Each province had its own estates, an assembly of representatives of the local nobility, clergy and towns. Such assemblies were about three centuries old by the mid-sixteenth century, and claimed the right to scrutinise the decisions and orders of the Habsburg government in Brussels. Since the 1420s it had been the custom for the local estates to send representatives to the States-General to deliberate on questions of common concern, most frequently about taxation. Some 700 different legal codes existed throughout the Netherlands. Holland and Brabant both forbade any but their own natives to hold local offices, while the principality of Liège

remained wholly free from Habsburg authority throughout this period.

Two generations of Habsburg rule had imposed some dynastic authority upon this mass of diverse political interests. Charles V expelled French influence from the Netherlands, the price that Francis I had to pay for his defeats there and elsewhere. The Dutch nobility had been recruited in support of Habsburg hegemony by the creation of the prestigious chivalric order, the Order of the Golden Fleece, a symbol of the trust that the Habsburgs placed in the nobility as their leading councillors. Finally, for the substantial and prosperous citizens of the leading towns, Habsburg rule offered security and stability after the inter-provincial feuds of the fifteenth century and the more recent wars with France.

The religious context

Dutch society was profoundly influenced by the religious innovations and currents of the early sixteenth century. The *devotio moderna* had its origins in the Netherlands, and the Netherlands provided the Christian humanist movement with its greatest exponent. The rigorous religious policy upon which the Habsburgs determined in the mid-century was bound to 'meet with endless difficulties', concluded Pieter Geyl, 'in a country where both officials and magistrates were impregnated with the spirit of Erasmus'. Nor could a region so much at the crossroads of Western European communications expect to avoid the traffic in heresy. Lutheranism was first condemned in the Netherlands by government edict in 1520, Charles V instituted a religious inquisition in the Netherlands in 1522, and by the end of the decade some thirty works by Luther had been translated into Dutch.

The most peculiarly Dutch form of heresy was Anabaptism. The Dutch Anabaptists in general represented the best side of the movement, with its gentle and rancourless rejection of the world's corruptions, and with its private and peaceful search for God's path. Unfortunately, Dutch extremists such as Jan Matthys and Jan Beukels were prominent in the great Anabaptist attempt to found a 'New Jerusalem' in Münster in 1534. The extremism of the few and the gentleness of the many combined to ensure that Anabaptism would never serve as a rallying-point for a national revolt. Instead, some 1,400 died for their beliefs during Charles's reign.

Calvinism, a late arrival upon the scene, provided the sort of dynamism and political direction that Anabaptism lacked. In 1545 the works of Calvin did not feature in an index of prohibited authors prepared by the Bishop of Liège; and in 1561, when there were reckoned to be 760 Calvinist communities in France, there were no more than twenty in the Netherlands. The great Calvinist 'boom' began in 1562, when the Massacre of Vassy and its aftermath in France unleashed a flood of refugees seeking an environment more healthy for Protestantism.

THE ADMINISTRATION OF PHILIP II, 1555–64

Philip II faced two outstanding problems in the first decade of his rule over the Netherlands. First, he inherited substantial financial difficulties. Wars with France (1521–9, 1536–7, and 1542–4), with the Turks (1521–38) and with the German Protestants (1546–7) had made huge taxation demands on all Habsburg territories, and the prosperity of the Netherlands had made them a particularly tempting source of revenue. Taxation within the Netherlands increased twelvefold between 1463 and 1535 alone, and the trend continued as the Emperor's deficit rose from 2 million florins in 1544 to 7 million in 1556. The first constitutional confrontations with the Dutch thus arose in 1557, when Philip sought to revoke a Brussels charter which allowed citizens' representatives to block new taxation proposals. In 1559 the States-General agreed to a substantial emergency subsidy, the Nine Years Aid, but fought successfully to ensure that its collection and administration would remain in their hands.

Even after the conclusion of peace at Câteau-Cambrésis (April 1559), it remained necessary to guard the borders with France, while the ambiguous attitude of the Queen of England added to Philip's uncertainties in northern Europe. Therefore 3,000 Spanish troops remained to garrison the strategic towns of the southern frontier, and the first great clash over Philip's royal powers centred upon the demand of the provincial estates that these garrisons should be withdrawn before any funds from the Nine Years Aid were released. In January 1561 they got their way.

The second clash between Dutch interests and royal authority centred around Philip's projected ecclesiastical reforms. With only four bishops to serve a Dutch population of some 3 million, Philip's plan to create fourteen new bishoprics was both logical and overdue. It was also of the first importance to Philip that foreign influences, such as those of Cologne and Reims, should be excluded from his domains, and that the Church in his territories should be equipped to combat the threat of heresy. Little objection could be raised on purely ecclesiastical grounds, but political suspicions were quickly aroused. Cardinal Granvelle, Philip's foremost adviser in the Netherlands, was to be Archbishop of Mechelen, in overall control of the Dutch Church under the new scheme, and it appeared to many that Philip's priority was to undermine the privileges and autonomy of the Dutch ruling classes.

PERSONALITIES

The development of events from this point depended in part upon the principal political figures involved. Philip's regent in his absence was his illegitimate half-sister, Margaret of Parma. Shy and inexperienced, she coped badly with challenges to her authority, and tended to tell Philip what she thought he wanted to hear. More influential than Margaret, therefore, were Philip's appointees on the Council of State, the Council of Finance and the Privy Council. Most prominent of these was Antoine Perrenot, Cardinal Granvelle. Granvelle had been bred and educated for his post, his father having performed similar tasks at the court of Charles V. Against this, he was personally unpopular, due largely to his own arrogance and domineering manner. To the Dutch nobility he was an outsider who stood in a position that they felt should be theirs by right.

This native nobility consisted in the early 1560s of some 4,000 members. Some were politically impotent, a declining class resenting royal power as an agent of further and faster decline. The greater families, however, exercised considerable political influence either as provincial governors or as leaders of the noble militia that formed the standard means of enforcing government decisions. The inception of the Order of the Golden Fleece had also given them an important role in central government. They were often interrelated, and many of them had strong political connections beyond the Netherlands. Philip, Count of Hoorn, was related to the great French house of Montmorency, while William of Orange took his title from French possessions and had powerful connections with Germany, especially after his marriage to the daughter of Maurice of Saxony (August 1561).

16.2 Spanish leaders

ALVA, Fernando Alvarez de Toledo, Duke of (1508–82). Knight of the Golden Fleece (1526). Spanish councillor of state (1545). Military commander against Schmalkaldic League (1547) and in Italy. Viceroy of Naples (1556). Suppressed early stages of Dutch Revolt and served as Governor (1567). Relieved of office (1573). Temporarily in disgrace, he later commanded Spanish forces in Portugal (1581).

DON JOHN OF AUSTRIA (1545–78). Illegitimate son of Charles V. Led Spanish forces against Algiers (1568) and against Moriscos (1569). Commander of the Holy League's forces at Lepanto (1571). Captured Tunis (1573). Governor of Netherlands (1576). Victor of Gembloux (1578).

GRANVELLE, Antoine Perrenot de (1517–86). Of Flemish descent, he succeeded his father as statesman and administrator in the service of the Spanish crown. Bishop of Arras (1538). Archbishop of Mechelen (1560). Councillor to Margaret of Parma (1560–4), until removed by pressure from Dutch nobility. Cardinal (1561). Viceroy of Naples (1571–5). Royal councillor in Spain until 1579.

MARGARET OF PARMA (1522–86). Illegitimate daughter of Charles V. Married to Alessandro de Medici (1533) and to Ottavio Farnese, Duke of Parma (1542). Regent of Netherlands (1559), until her resignation (1567) after the first revolt. Mother of Alessandro Farnese.

PARMA, Alessandro Farnese, Duke of (1545–92). Served at Lepanto (1571) and in Netherlands under Don John. Succeeded Don John as Governor (1578). Achieved notable military successes in Netherlands (1583–5) and against Henry IV in France (1589–91). Regarded as one of the great military commanders of the century.

REQUESENS, Luis de (1528–76). Governor of Milan, posted to Netherlands to replace Alva (1573). Victor over Louis of Nassau at Mook Heide (1574).

The young William pursued a successful courtly career, being appointed a Councillor of State at the age of twenty-three and being admitted to the Order of the Golden Fleece. So substantial was his role in the Dutch revolt that it is important to understand properly his personality and motives. To Motley he was one of the major Protestant leaders of the Reformation era. To his major English biographer, C.V. Wedgwood (*William the Silent*, 1944), Orange was a genuine *pater patriae* motivated by 'his deep and genuine interest in the people he ruled, his faith in their development, his toleration, his convinced belief in government by consent'. Yet we shall understand Orange best if we compare him with two groups of contemporaries. He was as much a *politique* as Henry IV of France or as Elizabeth of England, flexible both in political and religious ideologies as they served his main purposes. Orange's opposition to the central authority of Spain resembled the resistance of the German Protestant princes to the wider power of Charles V. For all his ideological flexibility there was, as K.W. Swart (*William the Silent and the Revolt of the Netherlands*, 1978) states, 'one cause which he embraced with grim determination and to which he remained wholeheartedly committed until the end of his life: the struggle against the king of Spain in order to ensure that justice be done to himself and other victims of Spanish tyranny'.

16.3 Dutch leaders

EGMONT, Lamoral, Count of (1522–68). Favoured by Charles V, he commanded imperial troops at St-Quentin (1558). Governor of Flanders and Artois (1559). Opposed extension of direct Spanish authority, and conspired successfully against Cardinal Granvelle (1564). Although distancing himself from rebels in 1566, he was arrested by Alva on treason charges and executed.

HOORN, Philip of Montmorency, Count of (1518–68). Administrator and military leader under Charles V. Member of Order of Golden Fleece. Opposed Granvelle and helped to bring about his dismissal (1564). Arrested and executed by Alva on charges of treason.

LOUIS OF NASSAU (1538–74). Younger brother of William of Orange. Active in presentation of noble grievances to Margaret of Parma (1566). Invaded Friesland in opposition to Alva (1567). Fought with Huguenot forces in France (1568–70). Led rebel forces against Alva in southern Netherlands (1572). Killed at Battle of Mook Heide.

MAURICE OF NASSAU (1567–1625). Second son of William of Orange. *Stadtholder* of Holland and Zealand (1584), and subsequently of Gelderland, Overijssel and Utrecht (1590–1). Commander-in-chief of the armies of the United Provinces (1588). Conquered Gelderland and other western provinces (1591–2). Opposed truce in 1612. With his political and personal victory over Oldenbarneveldt (1619) he was effectively sole ruler of the United Provinces.

OLDENBARNEVELDT, Johan van (1547–1619). Statesman with legal training, and a devoted follower of William of Orange. Town clerk of Rotterdam (1576), and member of the States of Holland. Negotiated Union of Utrecht (1579) and Treaty of Nonsuch (1585), and nominated Maurice of Nassau as *Stadtholder* (1584). Keen supporter of the truce of 1612, but this caused rift with Maurice of Nassau. Subsequent differences over religious matters caused Maurice to engineer his arrest and execution.

WILLIAM OF ORANGE (1533–84). Of German origin, he inherited substantial estates in the Netherlands in 1544 and entered the service of Charles V. Commander of imperial armies against France, member of Council of State and of the Order of the Golden Fleece (1555). Governor of northern provinces of Netherlands (1559). Joined noble conspiracy against Granvelle (1563), opposed Calvinist disorder, but retired to Germany upon arrival of Alva's troops (1567). Defeated in attempt to liberate southern provinces (1568), he established himself in Holland and Zealand (1572) to continue his opposition as *Stadtholder* of those provinces and of Utrecht. Joined Calvinist Church (1573). Influential in drafting Pacification of Ghent (1576), but reluctantly forced to accept division of Netherlands through Union of Utrecht (1579). Assassinated at Delft by Catholic fanatic.

This political crisis coincided with an economic crisis of the first magnitude. The temporary transference of English trade to Emden (December 1563–January 1565), the outbreak of war between Denmark, Sweden and the Hanseatic towns, and the fact that the winter of 1564–5 was the coldest of the century, all combined to disrupt Dutch commerce and cause widespread hunger. The riots and disturbances which attended these disasters often mingled with the third factor in the crisis, that of growing religious tension.

The years 1564–5 saw the spread of heresy in the Low Countries. The Inquisition noted religious incidents in Ostend, Ypres and elsewhere in Flanders, and riots occurred at the executions of Protestants in Valenciennes (1562) and Antwerp (1564). The Brussels government sought to secure royal permission for a softer line on heresy, and believed that they had received Philip's permission for such a step. In October 1565, however, in the so-called 'Segovia Letters', Philip totally dismissed the advice of the local nobility and ordered the unconditional enforcement of the existing anti-heresy laws.

THE TRIPLE CRISES OF 1563–5

Three crises rocked the Habsburg administration of the Netherlands in the middle of the decade. The first was the confrontation between Granvelle and the powerful nobles whose political influence he had largely eclipsed. Motivated primarily by personal ambition, the three greatest representatives of the Dutch nobility, Orange, Egmont and Hoorn, presented an ultimatum to Philip, threatening to resign from the Council of State unless Granvelle was dismissed. Philip's refusal to countenance this 'Solemn League' against Granvelle duly led to the resignation of the Dutch nobles, but Granvelle fell from office in any case (1564), brought down by opponents within the Habsburg regime. Subsequently, the increased influence of Margaret of Parma led to substantial modifications of government policies, and the impression was created that the affair had been, at base, a triumph for the privileges and influence of the Dutch nobility.

THE OUTBREAK OF THE FIRST REVOLT, 1565–8

The Segovia Letters precipitated confrontation between Philip and his subjects on two levels. The first opposition came from 400 nobles who, united as the League of the Nobility, signed a document known as the Compromise (December 1565), requesting that the heresy laws be moderated. The greater nobles made protests of their own. Orange resigned his governorships, and Egmont and Mansfelt informed the Regent that they would be unable to enforce the edicts. In April the greater and lesser nobility combined to set the Request before Margaret. Its demands were relatively moderate, but its direct demand that the king's wishes should be set aside made it the most overt act of rebellion in the Netherlands so far. The nobles thus formed the first coherent opposition party, adopting the name thrown at them as an insult by a royal minister, the 'Beggars' (*gueux*).

Margaret's conciliatory reply, the Moderation, was a realistic response to these local events and pressures.

Two groups, however, wanted more. Orange, Egmont and Hoorn all demanded greater influence over governmental decisions and threatened once more to withdraw from the Council of State if they did not get their way. The other element that would not be bought off with mere compromise was the hard core of Calvinist enthusiasts who now formed the central element in religious opposition. In the summer of 1566 their illegal public services spread throughout the southern and western Netherlands. Margaret pessimistically reported to the king that she thought one in two Dutchmen was a heretic, but modern writers have drawn a connection between the severe economic crisis and the large attendances at these 'hedge sermons'. Later in the summer, outbursts of image-breaking occurred in Flanders, and by the end of September these had spread throughout the provinces.

During these months the initiative had passed altogether out of the hands of the usual authorities. Margaret's desperate attempt to preserve social order by granting a greater degree of religious toleration in the Accord (August 1566) marked effective surrender to grass-roots pressure. Returning to their local governorships, the great nobles openly accepted the public meeting and worship of Calvinists and Lutherans, although Anabaptists remained beyond the pale.

ALVA AND HIS GOVERNMENT

Faced both with heresy and with treason among his leading Dutch subjects, it is easy to see why Philip decided upon the use of force. Fearing that failure to impose authority in the Low Countries would encourage disobedience elsewhere, the Spanish Council of State decided that a force of 10,000 men should be assembled in northern Italy and led north by the Duke of Alva. 'Philip II's fateful decision to send the Duke of Alva to the Netherlands', concludes Geoffrey Parker (*The Dutch Revolt*, 1977), 'was a turning point in European history. It was a threshold which, once crossed, transformed the political situation in northern Europe and, with it, the prospects of Habsburg hegemony there.'

Alva did not need to defeat the rebels militarily, for that had already been achieved by Margaret of Parma before he arrived, at Wattrelos and Lannoy (December 1566). It only remained for Alva to discredit the leaders of the nobility. Egmont had already changed sides; but Orange, after an initial flight into Germany, had made a desperate attempt to continue the fight. Despite an initial victory at Heiligerlee (May 1568), his forces were overwhelmed and the revolt appeared to be at an end. The religious and noble elements in this first revolt had remained isolated from each other, and they had paid the price for it.

Instead, Alva's main task was the administration of the Netherlands in the aftermath of revolt. The fearsome 'Council of Troubles' was established in September 1567 with the primary aim of punishing rebels. Egmont and Hoorn were among the first arrested, and both were executed for treason in June 1568. It is difficult to overestimate the impact that must have been made by this destruction of two members of the Order of the Golden Fleece, the apparently inviolable leaders of the nation and of Dutch society. In all, some 12,000 were tried for their part in the disturbances of 1566–7, of whom about 9,000 were found guilty and about 1,000 executed. It was a formidable act of justice which effectively broke the power of the greater nobility. In this respect, Alva brought about a change in constitutional structures probably more radical than any other attempted in Western Europe in this century.

Unexpectedly, however, the resignation of Margaret of Parma (December 1567) obliged Alva to govern the provinces himself for an unspecified period, instead of retiring to Spain once his soldierly tasks were completed. As Philip's other commitments left him unable to fund the government of the Netherlands, Alva also had to finance his own administration. To do this he proposed three taxes to the States-General; the Hundredth Penny (a one-off tax of 1 per cent on all capital), the Twentieth Penny (a permanent tax on land sales), and the Tenth Penny (a permanent 10 per cent tax on all other sales). The taxes were not to be farmed out to Dutch agents, but would be collected centrally by government officials. With such proposals, Alva risked the alienation of classes which had always been sympathetic to peace and good order, and which had remained loyal during the recent troubles.

Alva's administration ensured the implementation of the new bishoprics project, and did much good work on the codification and unification of Dutch law. On the other hand, the Spanish troops under his command became more and more unpopular. There were instances of unrest and attacks on the populace wherever they were billeted, and foolishly they were often billeted in towns which had remained loyal throughout the disturbances. The last straw came in July 1571, when Alva declared that he was ready to collect the new taxes without the consent of the States-General, contrary to all the constitutional liberties of the Netherlands. A flexible *politique* had been replaced at the head of the government by an inflexible soldier, and this had created a new confrontation by the beginning of 1572. This time the Spanish authorities faced the hostility of substantial and normally conservative citizens.

THE REVOLT IN HOLLAND AND ZEALAND

The roots of the second phase of the Dutch revolt were primarily constitutional and economic. In addition to Alva's financial policies, early 1572 brought renewed economic hardships. Trade was disrupted by the determination of some merchants never to pay the Tenth Penny, by the activities of the Sea Beggars, and by the impact upon the cloth trade of Queen Elizabeth's seizure of Alva's Genoese loan in December 1568. An unusually severe winter in 1571–2 disrupted communications, and successive harvest failures in the Baltic meant that little grain arrived from that quarter.

The trigger for renewed crisis was the capture of the port of The Brill by the Sea Beggars, sea-going rebels who had been sheltering in English ports. The collapse of the earlier revolt had sent a wave of refugees into foreign exile. By 1572, there were some 4,000 Dutch refugees in Norwich and some 3,500 in London. In Germany, 10,000 found their way to Wesel and Emden. In all, it is probable that about 60,000 Dutch refugees were driven out by Alva's administration. The Brill served at once as a base for the Sea Beggars' operations on their native soil and a bridgehead through which the most

committed of the Calvinist refugees could return to the struggle. Within two weeks, the provinces of Holland and Zealand had become the seat of renewed rebellion.

The Calvinist initiative naturally stimulated the hopes of William of Orange and of his French allies for a decisive blow against Spanish interests in the Netherlands. Such hopes were soon frustrated. Repeating the strategy of 1568, Orange's attack from the south and from the east won some initial successes, but Alva's forces were once more equal to their task. The St Bartholomew massacre (August 1572), by destroying Huguenot influence at the French court, ensured that no further aid would come from the south. In the months that followed, Alva steadily recaptured rebellious towns in Flanders and Brabant, encouraging others to surrender by means of savage reprisals which, though effective in the short term, had the opposite effect in the long run. In particular, the horrific massacre of the population of Naarden in December 1572, after the town had admitted Spanish troops without a siege, helped to create in Dutchmen of all religious persuasions a powerful and general antipathy to Spanish rule.

There was only one consolation for the rebels in the events of 1572. The campaigns had forced the withdrawal of most of Alva's forces from Holland and Zealand, and it was to Holland that Orange decided to withdraw 'to maintain my affairs here as well as may be, having decided to make that province my tomb'. In the years that followed a new order, wholly independent of the Spanish authorities, developed in the provinces under Orange's control. Their government was shaped by a series of decisions taken by the States of Holland. First (July 1572), Orange was recognised as the provincial governor (*stadtholder*) of Holland, Zealand and Utrecht, nominally still acting on behalf of King Philip. Having initially agreed to the free exercise of all religious creeds within the province, the States soon forbade (February 1573) public worship by Catholics as prejudicial to public order. In 1575, the political situation was also radicalised. In June, a formal act of union was signed with Zealand. The following October, the authority of Spain was formally renounced, and sovereignty was offered to Elizabeth of England, who refused it.

THE SUCCESS OF THE SECOND REVOLT

Between 1573 and 1576, Spanish forces, for all their successes elsewhere, made little significant headway against the two rebellious provinces. In explaining Dutch success, historians have traditionally stressed geographical and religious factors. Two great complexes of lakes existed in Holland, the southern one between Amsterdam and Haarlem almost dividing the province in half. Zealand itself was split into a mass of islands by the great estuary of the Maas. The two provinces seemed to be, as an English visitor remarked in the following century, 'the great bog of Europe, the buttock of the world, full of veins and blood, but no bones in it'. Naval power would always be a vital factor in the control of these regions, and in this the Dutch always maintained superiority. This was extremely difficult country in which to conduct siege operations, as was demonstrated when the defenders of Alkmaar and of Leyden (1573–4) deliberately flooded the surrounding countryside to force the enemy's withdrawal. The motivation of the defenders was also important, and Alva committed serious errors in this respect. When (July 1573) he promised amnesty to the defenders of Haarlem, and then executed 2,000 of them, he went beyond the normal rules of war and showed that any future garrison accepting his terms of surrender ran the risk of betrayal. After Haarlem, no other Dutch town ever surrendered to the Spaniards without resistance.

The Calvinist Church also played a very substantial role in the Dutch success. The great strength of the Calvinists was their organisation, and the characteristic structures of consistory, *classis* and synod soon appeared at parish and at provincial level. Yet its influence arose, not from force of numbers, but from the dynamism generated by a group of determined people believing themselves chosen to fulfil a divine mission. Estimates have put the proportion of Calvinists among the total Dutch population at no more than 10 per cent as late as 1587. In Dordrecht (population 13,000), in the early 1570s the reformed congregation numbered 368, while in Delft (population 14,000) the Calvinist congregation was only 200 strong. Geoffrey Parker has concluded that 'there can be no doubt that Calvinism alone did not and could not provide a broad enough base to unite the Dutch', but that 'the reformed faith was crucial in providing an ideology for the exiles in their hours of defeat and in sustaining them in times of trouble after 1572'.

THE SPANISH ARMY OF FLANDERS

Other important factors need to be considered which governed Spain's conduct of the struggle. In the Netherlands, Philip undertook a war of greater duration, greater expense and greater organisational complexity than any undertaken hitherto by any European state. He did so because he firmly believed that to give way to the Dutch would really be to surrender the upper hand in the greater struggle with the French. 'The surest means that we have of keeping the French in check', argued Granvelle, 'is to maintain strong forces in Flanders.' Similarly, it was argued that any major success for the Dutch rebels would be a mighty encouragement to all others who had an interest in the disintegration of Spanish power: Italians, Catalans, Moriscos, and the pirates that preyed upon the wealth of the Indies. For King Philip himself, the maintenance of true religion, of dynastic integrity and of his own *reputación* were also at stake, and such stakes were far too high for any sixteenth-century monarch to abandon the game.

Yet the rules of the game were changing, and were very different from those by which Charles V or Francis I had operated. The new shape of warfare was determined by the highly urbanised nature of the Netherlands and by the wide diffusion there of new defensive technology. In place of high but relatively thin medieval walls, there had appeared the *trace italienne*. Lower, but thicker, modern defensive walls were less easily penetrated by cannon fire, and were equipped with flanks, bastions and other projections from which defensive fire could be poured upon attackers. An English contemporary observed that 'one good town well defended sufficeth to ruin a mighty army', and the Netherlands had dozens of such towns. Cavalry was useless under such conditions, and the wars in the Netherlands came to depend upon the maintenance of unprecedented quantities of infantry, employed for unprecedented periods. The employment of 67,000 troops in the Netherlands in September 1572 and 86,000 two years later represented a new concept in military strategy.

At first, Alva was remarkably successful in his efforts to finance his administration from local resources. While Spain sent 3½ million florins in 1567, virtually nothing was needed in 1571. Unfortunately for Philip, these benefits were swept away in the military and political upheaval of 1572, and Spain had to send over 7 million florins in 1574. After 1574 the loyal Netherlands would never again pay more than a third of the Spanish expenses, and the burden had to be borne by the Spanish economy for the rest of the war. Between July 1580 and April 1585, Spain sent 14.95 million florins to the Netherlands, rising to 37.87 million (August 1590–March 1595). Spain's total contribution amounted to over 101 million florins in less than thirty years.

Getting troops to the Netherlands was almost as impressive an achievement as paying for them. The 'Spanish Road' remained the focal point of all communications – a complex network of roads, tracks and mountain passes that stretched through Savoy, the Franche-Comté, Lorraine and Luxembourg. Quite apart from distance, overcoming natural obstacles and securing adequate food and lodging for so many men posed complex problems for Spanish administrators and commanders. Well might Geoffrey Parker conclude that 'it is indeed a marvel that any Spanish troops ever reached the Netherlands'.

Nevertheless, Spain set herself tasks in the Netherlands that she could not fulfil. A mutiny at Valenciennes over pay (October 1570) was copied dozens of times throughout the period of the revolts. A wave of mutinies coincided with the crisis in royal finances during 1573–6, and thirty-four were recorded within the period 1589–1607, when the financial difficulties of the Spanish crown coincided with a long period of bad harvests and high prices in the Netherlands. At the very least these mutinies represented an unforeseen obstacle to projected military operations. At worst they resulted in the aborting of offensives vital to the war effort or in the ruin of relations between the Spanish forces and the loyal communities which should have been their allies in the fight against heresy and rebellion.

THE THIRD REVOLT

The next stage in the Dutch revolt was precipitated by just this kind of paralysis in Spanish policy. Coherent action against the rebels in Holland and Zealand was obstructed by the sudden death of Don Luis de Requesens, Alva's successor as Governor (March 1576), by Philip's own mixture of concession and inflexibility, and by a new decree of bankruptcy which severely limited his financial resources.

This bankruptcy in turn contributed to the collapse of discipline among much of the Spanish army in the 'loyal' Netherlands. Mutinies of unpaid troops occurred every year between 1573 and 1576, but reached intolerable proportions when Aalst, a town with no involvement in the rebellion, was viciously sacked (July 1576). Even that atrocity was soon overshadowed by the disaster (4 November 1576) of the 'Spanish Fury' in Antwerp. Mutinous Spanish troops burst into the city and carried out a brutal sack that constituted Western Europe's worst atrocity of the century. One-third of the city was destroyed, some 8,000 citizens slain and the credibility of Spain's 'protective' role was utterly undermined.

These events created the backdrop for a concerted rebellion, not by Calvinist radicals, but by the traditional representatives of the Dutch body politic. The sack of Aalst immediately provoked anti-Spanish riots in Brussels, and in September 1576 the States-General of the Netherlands overrode the authority of the Council of State; they assembled in Brussels without royal authority and began to make their own arrangements for the safety of the Netherlands. Having taken their illegal action, the States-General opened peace negotiations with William of Orange and concluded the Pacification of Ghent (November 1576). By its terms all fighting between Dutch provinces was to cease, Spanish forces were to leave the Netherlands, and only then would a decision be made on the future religious settlement of the territory.

At first, Philip's new Governor, Don John of Austria, appeared to accept that his position was untenable. A ceasefire was concluded in December, and in January 1577 he published the Perpetual Edict, which unconditionally accepted the Pacification of Ghent. Within two months a substantial proportion of the Spanish forces had set off towards Italy. In return, Don John was accepted as Governor by all except the Orangists of Holland and Zealand. Don John, however, was merely playing for time; for, like other governors, he was under strict instructions not to compromise on matters of religion or of sovereignty. His political circumstances were transformed in mid-1577 by the arrival from the New World of substantial silver supplies. He abandoned Brussels, recalled Spanish troops and confronted the States-General. They now found themselves in direct opposition to the Governor and utterly reliant upon the military power of the Prince of Orange. Still unable to match the Spanish troops, the forces of the States-General were thrashed at Gembloux (January 1578), and Orange sought safety again in Holland.

THE NETHERLANDS AND FOREIGN POWERS

At no stage did Dutch leaders expect the rebellion to succeed on its own. As early as 1572, William of Orange wrote to his brother that two years was the longest period that the revolt could survive without assistance from some foreign power. The Dutch could consider a number of potential allies; England, Sweden and several of the German princes all had a vested interest in the restriction of Habsburg power in northern Europe, but Orange was justified in his claim that 'all our hopes lie with France'. Family links bound many Dutch nobles to the great dynasties of France, there was close contact between Dutch Protestants and French Huguenots, and French policy was traditionally anti-Spanish. The first significant degree of French intervention occurred as early as 1572, but the project was thwarted by military defeat at Saint-Ghislain, followed by the domestic catastrophe of the St Bartholomew massacre.

When the States of Holland and Zealand formally repudiated the authority of Philip (October 1575),

the nature of foreign involvement changed significantly. It was no longer primarily a question of financial or military aid, but a wider matter of finding an eminent foreigner to add legitimacy to the Dutch cause. Although Alençon, youngest son of Henry II of France, turned down the offers of sovereignty made to him (1575–6), he remained a central figure in this question of foreign involvement. By an agreement of 1578 he accepted the title of 'Defender of the Liberty of the Netherlands', and a further pact (January 1581) named him 'prince and lord' of the Netherlands. The arrangement, however, was haunted by mutual suspicions. The States-General took the radical step of reserving sovereignty to themselves, leaving Alençon in the role of hired war-lord, and one provincial assembly after another refused the funds to finance his involvement. Infuriated by this impossible position, he blundered into an attempted *coup d'état* (January 1583) in Antwerp; and, although the attempt failed, Alençon's acceptability to the Dutch was damaged beyond repair.

French involvement in the Netherlands helped to renew the interest shown by the Queen of England. Whereas Alençon's success might have converted the Netherlands into a French satellite, his failure raised the equally distressing prospect of a complete Spanish triumph. The problem came to a head in June–July 1584, when the death of Alençon and Orange within a month of one another seemed to render the Dutch leaderless. At last, therefore, in 1585 a foreign monarch signed a formal treaty with the Dutch. The Treaty of Nonsuch (August 1585) provided for an English force of some 7,000 men under the command of the Earl of Leicester. In return, the English garrisoned Flushing, Rammekens and The Brill as guarantees of the repayment of their expenses. In direct terms, Leicester's forces achieved little. Their leader became deeply involved in local political machinations, and his men performed without distinction. Indirectly, however, this was a development of the greatest significance. In Philip II's eyes it was nothing less than a declaration of war on Spain, and from this point the desire to punish England through the medium of the 'Invincible Armada' was inseparable from Philip's attempts to subdue the Dutch. The diversion of vast financial and military resources to the 'Enterprise of

England' and the eventual disaster that befell the Armada were of the greatest significance in the eventual outcome of the Dutch revolt.

RELIGIOUS DIVISIONS AMONGST THE REBELS

The decline in Dutch fortunes in 1578–9 was partly due to the new lease of life granted to the Spanish economy, and partly to the continued superiority of the Spanish armed forces. It owed much, however, to splits within the Dutch ranks. These arose from mistrust of the political and personal ambitions of Orange and from widespread revulsion at the attitudes of his Calvinist followers. These widely rejected the religious *status quo* laid down in the Pacification of Ghent, and in Holland and Zealand Dutch forces attempted to starve into submission Catholic strongholds such as Haarlem and Amsterdam. At Kortrijk, Bruges and Ypres there were outbreaks of iconoclasm. By the end of the year open hostility was evident in the rebel ranks between Catholics and Calvinists, and by October the States of Hainault and Artois were negotiating a union to resist any attack upon the Catholic religion.

In the last months of 1578 the unity of the States-General began to disintegrate, as Flanders, Hainault and Artois refused to contribute men or money to the war against Spain. Holland and Zealand led the Protestant response, opening negotiations with their northern neighbours, the provinces of Utrecht, Friesland and Gelderland. In January 1579 they concluded the Union of Utrecht whereby they agreed to act as a single province on issues concerning the war against Spain. For the first time the term 'United Provinces' was used, by which the northern provinces were to be designated for the next two centuries. To a greater extent than any other agreement of the sixteenth century, the Union of Utrecht created a new state, ignoring the claims of Philip II and asserting the revolutionary principles of the Sea Beggars over the conciliatory terms of the Pacification of Ghent.

In the same month, the foundations of modern Belgium were also laid. Thoroughly alarmed at the increasing radicalism of politics and religion in the north, Flanders, Hainault and Artois concluded their own Union of Arras. These provinces opened

negotiations with the Spanish commander, and fully recognised the authority of Philip of Spain by the Treaty of Arras (May 1579). Philip's prospects of success now looked brighter than at any time since the start of the troubles, and it was his intransigence on the issues of religion and of royal authority that undermined peace negotiations at Cologne (May–November 1579). When the negotiations inevitably broke down, the States-General of the Netherlands, shorn of the southern provinces, formally rejected the authority of the King of Spain by the Act of Abjuration (July 1581).

THE CAMPAIGNS OF PARMA AND NASSAU, 1583–94

These events divided the Netherlands along lines very similar to those applied in the truce of 1609. In the intervening thirty years, however, both sides enjoyed periods of military success which gave them hope of eventual total victory. It was in the years immediately after the Peace of Arras that Spain came closest to overall military success. In the five years beginning in 1583 it had better troops at its disposal, many of them veterans of the recent campaigns in Portugal. They were commanded by the most able general to serve the Spanish crown in the second half of the sixteenth century, and that general brought to bear probably the most coherent and sensible strategy that the Spanish forces ever applied in the Dutch theatre of war.

The Duke of Parma aimed to establish control over the Flemish coastline and thus to cut the economic lifelines of the major industrial centres of Brabant and Flanders, forcing them into surrender. Great progress was made towards this objective in the latter half of 1583, while a secondary campaign in the north linked Friesland with the Spanish-controlled territory in the south. By the end of 1585, Parma had regained control of most of that territory which constitutes modern Belgium, and his success suggested that the destruction of Dutch independence in the northern provinces was now only a matter of time.

That this did not happen was primarily due to the fact that the disasters of 1584–5 finally persuaded Elizabeth of England to offer direct aid to the Dutch. It was not so much that Parma was thwarted by England's direct military intervention, for the achievement of the Earl of Leicester's forces was limited and in some cases negative. Having accepted the office of Governor-General (January 1586), Leicester tried consistently to override the influence of the provincial estates, and alienated important interests by proposing the cessation of all trade with Spain and with the provinces that it controlled. The real significance of the Anglo-Dutch treaty was that it provoked Philip into the disastrous decision to divert his forces to a punitive expedition against England. The Armada campaign itself confined Parma's forces to the Flanders coast, awaiting the fleet that would protect their crossing to England. Then, once it was clear that no conjunction could be made between the sea and land forces, Parma had to deal with the psychological consequences of the Armada's failure. 'The defeat of the Spanish Armada marked a turning point in the Dutch Revolt. It fatally weakened the prestige of Philip II and it put an end to Parma's impressive string of victories' (Geoffrey Parker). His failure to capture the town of Bergen op Zoom later in the year or to secure control of the island of Bommel in 1589 clearly showed that the mighty impetus of 1583–5 was exhausted.

By 1589, Parma had even greater distractions to worry about. The assassination of the Duke of Guise and of Henry III brought about the succession of the Protestant leader, Henry of Navarre, to the French throne. It was a development that Philip considered potentially fatal to his aims in the Netherlands, and for a second time Parma's efforts were diverted to another theatre of war. Between 1588 and 1595, some 4.5 million florins were also diverted to the struggle against Henry of Navarre. Parma's great successes in relieving the sieges of Rouen and of Paris meant, indeed, that an outright Protestant victory was delayed, but also that the civil war was prolonged and its demands upon Spanish resources were continued. If the 'Enterprise of England' had some logic and some reasonable expectation of success, Philip's intervention in the French wars can only be seen as an expensive and ill-conceived error.

The Dutch rebel leaders failed to exploit Parma's absence in 1590, but when he left once more for France in 1591 the Dutch forces at last took the offensive. Under the command of Count Maurice of Nassau, the army of the States-General was a better-organised body, better-disciplined, and more attuned to modern techniques, such as the effective use of artillery. In the next two years his successes in Gelderland and Overijssel greatly extended the control of the States-General and broke the Spanish stranglehold upon the rebellious provinces by opening communications with the Protestant princes of Germany.

In the midst of such military reverses, the death of Parma (December 1592) plunged the southern Netherlands, and the Spanish cause, into political chaos. With command now disputed between Parma's former deputy, the aged Count Mansfeld, and Philip's nominee Fuentes, the command structure was paralysed for much of the next two years. By then, with a further state bankruptcy imminent, the Spanish army was confronted once more with the spectres of hunger and mutiny.

STALEMATE AND TRUCE, 1595–1609

Yet Spain was still able to find the resources and energy to carry the fight back to the Dutch. The formal outbreak of war between France and Spain (January 1595) made the southern Netherlands an obvious theatre of war, and forced Spain into renewed efforts to protect those parts of the Low Countries that remained loyal to them. Dutch efforts to capture Liège, and thus to provide a corridor between their own territory and France, were frustrated by Fuentes, while Spain captured Cambrai (September 1595), Calais, Ardres and Hulst (all 1596). On the other hand, by the end of 1599, Philip III was faced with the familiar pattern of discontent and mutiny among his hungry soldiers. In addition, the Spanish war effort was seriously undermined by the disastrous outbreak of bubonic plague within Spain itself which killed perhaps 10 per cent of the population.

The last resurgence of Spanish fortunes coincided with the appointment of Ambrogio Spinola, the last of the great Spanish commanders in the Low Countries. The son of a Genoese banker, he was a millionaire with no military experience, but he possessed great financial and organisational ability.

Arriving in Flanders with his own military force in 1602, he assured his military reputation by capturing Ostend, the last foothold of the States-General in the southern provinces (1604). With the advantage of peace with England (August 1604), Spinola went on to the offensive, carrying the war for the first time in many years into Dutch territory to the north of the great rivers.

Although even Spinola lacked the resources to force a decisive victory in the north, his campaigns

were the crucial element in the peace that was achieved in 1609. Since the death of Philip II, Spanish policy had tended towards compromise with the northern provinces. The king's will had involved a major change in the constitutional standing of the southern provinces, bequeathing them to the Princess Isabella as her dowry upon her marriage to her cousin, the Archduke Albert, Governor-General of those provinces since 1595. Upon their marriage (April 1599), Albert and

---

16.4 The first and second revolts, 1565–74

December 1565. The League of the Nobility presented Margaret of Parma with **The Compromise,** requesting the moderation of the anti-heresy laws.

April 1566. Margaret granted **The Moderation,** requiring magistrates to proceed leniently in religious cases.

June–September 1566. Escalation of religious extremism. **Hedge sermons,** Calvinist meetings, illegal under The Moderation, were held in much of the western and southern Netherlands, in the countryside to escape the jurisdiction of the civic authorities. These were supplemented by the **Iconoclastic Fury,** in which churches were attacked and images smashed.

August 1566. Margaret conceded further religious toleration in **The Accord.** Calvinist preaching could continue where it already existed, but should not spread nor be accompanied by the bearing of arms.

December 1566. Margaret took the offensive against Calvinism, winning major victories over Calvinist forces at **Wattrelos** and **Lannoy.**

August 1567. Arrival of the Duke of Alva with substantial Spanish forces. Further victories over Orange at **Dalheim** (April 1568) and **Jemmingen** (July 1568) confirmed the defeat of the first revolt.

September 1567. Establishment by Alva of the **Council of Troubles.**

April 1572. Capture of **The Brill** by **Sea Beggars.**

April–May 1572. Flushing and other towns in Holland and Zealand declared for the Sea Beggars. **Mons** and **Zutphen** captured by Orangist forces with French support.

July 1572. Alva defeated French interventionist force at **St Ghislain. St Bartholomew Massacre** ensured withdrawal of French support. Alva

captured **Mons** (September) and sacked **Mechelen** (October) to end second revolt in the southern provinces.

July 1572. Orange appointed **Stadtholder of Holland, Zealand and Utrecht.**

Oct 1573–April 1574. Spanish land victory over Louis of Nassau at **Mook Heide** (April) offset by naval engagements on the **Zuider Zee** (October) and on the **Scheldt** (January) and the capture of **Middleburg** (February) which left the rebels in command of coasts and major waterways.

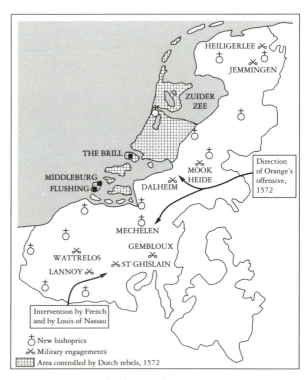

16.4 The first and second revolts

16.5 1580–8

March 1580. Defection to Habsburgs of **Count Rennenberg**, Stadtholder of **Groningen** and **Drenthe**, led to Spanish occupation of those provinces.

October 1581. Parma restored to office of Governor, nominally at the request of the estates of the southern provinces. Capture of **Enschede**.

February 1582. Southern provinces requested the return of Spanish troops to their territory. Capture of **Steenwyk**.

1583. Capture of **Dunkirk**, **Nieuwpoort** and **Diksmuide** gave Parma control of south-west coastline and most of the Scheldt estuary, and a base from which to attack the major cities of Flanders and Brabant. Capture of **Zutphen**.

1584. Capture of **Ypres** (April), **Bruges** (May) and **Ghent** (June) by Parma. **Assassination of William of Orange** (July).

1585. Surrender of **Brussels** (February) and **Antwerp** (August) left Parma in control of Flanders and Brabant. Conclusion of **Treaty of Nonsuch** (August) between England and the United Provinces.

1586–7. English forces lost several of the strongholds entrusted to them under the Treaty of Nonsuch. **Deventer** and **Geertruidenberg** were betrayed by their English commanders, and Leicester failed to prevent the surrender of the port of **Sluis** to the Spaniards.

1588. Armada campaign. Parma's forces confined to Flanders coast to cooperate with Armada.

16.5 Parma's reconquest, 1580–9

Isabella were effectively joint rulers of the southern Netherlands. Only the crucial power to decide on peace or war remained dependent upon the agreement of the Spanish crown.

In 1599 the major obstacle to peace was the conviction on the part of many prominent Dutchmen that a decisive victory could still be won in the south. Such hopes were diminished after 1600, by the decision of the English to make peace with Spain (1604), by the loss of Ostend and by Spinola's successes. A further Spanish bankruptcy in 1607 made that an apt time for serious negotiations, and in March an eight-month ceasefire finally interrupted thirty years of warfare. No agreement could be reached over the toleration of Catholics in the northern provinces nor over the question of Dutch commercial activity in the Spanish colonies. The arbitration of England and France, however, led to the proposal of a lengthy

truce instead of a definitive peace, and thus it was that the two sides signed the Twelve Years Truce at Antwerp (9 April 1609). In principle, the state of war persisted until the end of another great conflict, the Thirty Years War, in 1648; 1609 merely represented the realisation by both Dutch and Spanish that no overall victory could be gained.

THE DEVELOPMENT OF THE DUTCH STATE

The Dutch state that emerged from the truce of 1609 was by no means the natural and inevitable expression of deep-rooted Dutch national feeling. It was a pragmatic response to threats to the interests of the most influential Dutchmen, taking shape only when all other means of protecting those interests had failed.

The formation of a Dutch state also resolved the acute crisis of leadership that had afflicted the northern provinces since the early 1580s. They had lost William of Orange to an assassin's bullet (1584), and had been more or less betrayed by Alençon and by Leicester. The crisis was resolved in particular by Maurice of Nassau, William's second son, and by a man of more humble origins, Johan van Oldenbarneveldt. The latter played a leading role in the negotiation of the Treaty of Nonsuch and in the defeat of Leicester's subsequent bid for power, and had the decisive voice in persuading Gelderland, Overijssel and Utrecht to accept Nassau as their common *stadtholder*.

Neither Nassau nor Oldenbarneveldt, however, was in any position to dictate the constitutional shape of the new state. This was dictated instead by the whole logic of the Dutch revolt. As Geoffrey Parker has written, 'the provinces of the Netherlands had rebelled in 1572 against the tyranny of the Duke of Alva and again in 1576–77 against the tyranny of Don John of Austria and his Spanish troops. The nobles and patricians of each province had not staked everything in this defiance simply to surrender their lives and property to another absolute lord. They did not want an effective ruler.' Sovereignty in the Dutch state, therefore, lay neither with Nassau nor with the Dutch people. 'The sovereignty of the country', the lawyer François Vranck stated categorically, 'resides with the States: the States are now no less sovereign than under the rule of the former princes.'

In the States-General sat the representatives of the seven United Provinces, governing in the interests of the 'regent class', that is of those families who dominated the provincial states and virtually monopolised the seats therein. At a local level such men nominated members of the town councils (*vroedschappen*) and acted as local magistrates. In most provinces, these town councils then cast their votes for elections to the provincial states. Inevitably, the 'regent class' monopolised the offices of provincial 'advocates' to the States-General. That body, in its turn, acted consistently to preserve its monopoly of power. 'Here, indeed, was a world made safe for oligarchs. It was a world for which the leaders of the revolt, in Holland at least, had been fighting since 1572' (Geoffrey Parker).

16.6 1590–1606

1590. Beginning of offensives of **Maurice of Nassau**. Capture of **Breda**.

1591. Capture of **Zutphen**, **Deventer** and **Nymwegen**.

1592–4. Capture of **Steenwyk** (1592) and **Groningen** (1594) established Dutch control of provinces of **Groningen, Drenthe** and **Overijssel**. This extended territories of the United Provinces to the German borders and facilitated contacts with the German Protestant princes.

Sept 1604. Surrender of **Ostend** to **Spinola**.

1605. Spinola launched campaign against **Overijssel**, capturing **Oldenzaal** and **Grol**.

March 1607. Conclusion of an armistice between the United Provinces and the Archdukes.

April 1609. Conclusion of a **Twelve Year Truce** between the two sides at Antwerp.

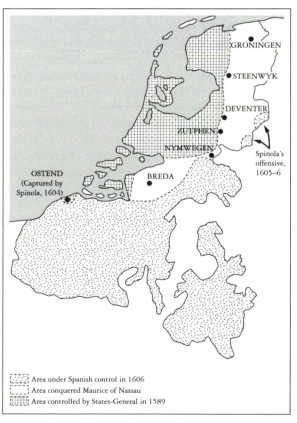

16.6 Campaigns of Maurice of Nassau and of Spinola, 1590–1606

THE DEVELOPMENT OF THE DUTCH ECONOMY

The Dutch state was founded upon the prosperity that had developed in the last decades of the sixteenth century behind the defensive barrier of the great rivers. Both contemporaries and subsequent writers have agreed that this prosperity had a firm basis in Dutch demography. Many contemporaries were as impressed as Samuel Pepys was in his famous exclamation: 'By God, I think the Devil shits Dutchmen.' The explanation, however, was simpler than that, and lay in the substantial migrations of the Netherlands population in the late sixteenth century from the troubled southern provinces towards the north. In the 1560s and 1570s it was more common to find emigrant communities in southern England or in the Rhineland than in the northern provinces of the Netherlands, but the increasing success and stability of those provinces made them increasingly attractive to displaced southerners. The flow of refugees from Antwerp reduced the city's population from 83,700 to 42,000 between 1582 and 1589, while most of the major trading centres of the north received substantial numbers of immigrants during a similar period. The province of Holland experienced a dramatic population-increase, far outrunning the increase in the birth-rate, from 273,000 in 1514 to 670,000 in 1622. These immigrants brought talent and expertise, particularly in the cloth trade. In Leyden, cloth production soared from an average of 500 pieces a year in the 1570s to 35,000 in the 1580s and on to over 66,000 in the 1620s. On a smaller scale, the influence of men trained in the ceramic industry of Antwerp can be seen in the development of similar industries in the north, most notably at Delft.

The immigrants also added significantly to the wealth available for investment in the north. These years saw the blossoming of the commercial enterprise which had already established Dutch supremacy in the Baltic trade. Surviving records of the ships that passed through the Danish straits show that as early as the 1560s Dutch ships conveyed 66 per cent of all the salt, 76 per cent of all the herring and 70 per cent of all the wheat that left the Baltic. Such a trade area, completely sheltered from Spanish naval activity, was naturally of great value to the Dutch war effort.

In the last decades of the sixteenth century important new areas of trade were opened. Herring fisheries operated increasingly from such ports as Rotterdam and Schiedam as the seas around Holland became safer from Spanish ships. The total annual catch was reckoned by 1630 to be in the region of 240,000 barrels. Despite the objections of some religious purists, Dutch ships also began to dominate the lucrative trade between northern Europe and Spain and the Mediterranean. In return for grain, timber and salt, the Dutch ships transported Spanish wool to the Low Countries, and in many instances sold back to Spain the textiles that they had manufactured from that same wool. Without doubt, the most important new departure was the trade links that the Dutch began to establish with India and the East Indies. The first circumnavigation of the globe by a Dutchman took place in 1598–9, and in 1602 the Dutch East India Company was born, with a monopoly of Dutch trade with India, Sri Lanka, the Moluccas and the Philippines. It is a remarkable testament to the amount of capital by now available in the northern provinces that the 6.5 million florins which formed the original capital of the East India Company was raised within the space of a single month.

On the other hand, the United Provinces in 1600 still carried the burden of a crippling war effort. Where the province of Holland had contributed 960,000 florins in 1579, her contribution had risen to nearly 5.4 million twenty years later, and to nearly 9 million in 1607. Levels of taxation in the United Provinces at the end of the century were far higher than those that Alva had sought to impose in the 1560s. Nor can one ignore the evidence of stagnation and decline in the eastern provinces, similar in many respects to that in the south. Certainly, the foundations of Dutch prosperity are clearly visible in the Dutch economy of the 1590s and 1600s, but they were as yet no more than foundations, and the future of the edifice remained uncertain.

THE SOUTHERN NETHERLANDS

The picture in the south was very different. Constitutionally, the southern Netherlands after 1598 formed an independent unit under the joint rule of Isabella and Albert, collectively known as 'The Archdukes'. From 1598 until the end of their reign in 1621, the government remained largely dependent upon Spain for money and for troops, and was increasingly directed by Spanish influences. The influence of Flemish noblemen was overridden by that of the 'Spanish ministry', the Spanish advisers who controlled the policies of the government, and it was remarked by a contemporary that Albert 'imitates the government of Philip II as closely as possible, and conforms in everything to the usages of the Spanish court'.

The economy of the southern Netherlands in 1600 presented a prospect of decay and devastation in contrast to the increasing dynamism and prosperity of the north. These provinces had suffered severely from being the location of two or three decades of fierce and constant warfare. Demographically, the period seems to have been disastrous. The regions around Ypres and Bruges, for instance, lost nearly 60 per cent of their population.

Industrially, Ypres claimed an income of 400 florins in 1584, compared to 20,000 florins around 1575. A rate of taxation that multiplied by nearly thirty times in the course of the century in some southern regions completed a miserable picture. Although economic recovery was substantial in the course of the seventeenth century, the wars had ensured that 'the southern provinces never fulfilled the promising destiny which seemed to beckon during the reign of Charles V' (Geoffrey Parker).

Further reading

P. Limm (1989) *The Dutch Revolt, 1559–1648*. London and New York.

G. Parker (1977) *The Dutch Revolt*. London.

—— (1979) *Spain and the Netherlands, 1559–1659: Ten Studies*. London.

M. Rady (1987) *The Netherlands: Revolt and Independence, 1550–1650*. London.

CHAPTER SEVENTEEN

Spain under Philip II

A contemporary painting, probably by a South German artist, of the Battle of Lepanto, fought in October 1571. The victory of the Holy League's fleet over the Turkish fleet was perhaps the greatest victory in which Spain participated during the reign of Philip II. The painting clearly shows the oared galleys which dominated the Mediterranean through the sixteenth century

THE HISTORICAL DEBATE

It is little wonder that, for centuries, judgements upon Philip II were intensely polarised, so central was he to the history of the Reformation, the Counter-Reformation, and to all the main issues of contemporary power politics.

On the one hand, we have inherited the image of Philip as *el rey prudente*, the 'prudent king', guided by the interests of his Spanish kingdom and of the Catholic Church. Such an image remains popular today, and not only with Spanish historians. The Philip portrayed by Gregorio Maranon (*Antonio Perez*, 1954) is a limited and insecure king, but essentially motivated by the same priorities. The image was confirmed by major English works, such as that of the American R.B. Merriman (*The Rise of the Spanish Empire in the Old World and the New*, vol. IV: *Philip the Prudent*, 1934). Merriman saw Philip as a man engaged for much of his life in an unequal struggle that he knew he could not win, yet the overall conclusion echoes that of contemporary Spaniards: 'From first to last, he was the "Prudent King".'

The major alternative view was based upon the 'Black Legend' fostered by Philip's contemporary opponents who were threatened by the power of Spain. This portrays Philip as an evil tyrant, motivated by religious bigotry and a desire for personal power. The most striking statement of this view was penned by another American, John Lothrop Motley (*The Rise of the Dutch Republic*, 1855): 'If Philip possessed a single virtue it has eluded the conscientious research of the writer of these pages. If there are vices from which he was exempt, it is because it is not permitted to human nature to attain perfection even in evil.' This tradition was only eroded very slowly, and when R. Trevor Davies attempted a more balanced approach to this period (*The Golden Century of Spain*, 1937) he still encountered fierce criticism from writers in America and northern Europe.

In the last fifty years most standard works on the subject have freed themselves from religious and moral preconceptions. Such writers as John Lynch (*Spain under the Habsburgs*, 1963–9), J.H. Elliott (*Imperial Spain*, 1963) and Geoffrey Parker (*Philip II*, 1979) have been more concerned with Philip's success or failure within the context of the aims that he set himself. The most widely accepted orthodoxy is that which sees the reign as an unsuccessful attempt to deal with the many problems which beset Philip's *monarchia*, and as a preparation for Spain's decline in the seventeenth century.

Other historians have sought to analyse contemporary Spain without concentrating upon the character of the monarch. The doyen of this 'school' has been the great French historian Fernand Braudel (*The Mediterranean and the Mediterranean World in the Time of Philip II*, 1972–3). In this classic work, Spanish policy is placed in the context of the great natural, economic and demographic forces which dictated the currents of events far more decisively than either king or councillors. Another Frenchman, Pierre Chaunu (*Séville et l'Atlantique*, 1969), has shown the crucial importance to Spanish policies of the money supply from the New World. The coming decades will see Spanish history written more and more in terms of the impersonal forces with which the monarch struggled with varying degrees of success.

FORMATIVE INFLUENCES ON THE REIGN

Philip came to the thrones of Spain as a mature and experienced prince, and the style of his reign was determined by the preconceptions that he had formed. He differed from his father at the same stage of his career in two important respects. In contrast to the cosmopolitan education of Charles, Philip's upbringing was unequivocally Spanish, dominated by the religious, racial and social assumptions of the Castilian governing classes. While the father came close to losing his Spanish territories in 1520 because he was too Burgundian, the son was eventually to lose half of his inheritance in the Low Countries because he was too Spanish.

On the other hand, where Charles had been raw and naïve upon his accession, Philip had extensive administrative experience, having served his father as regent and adviser for some time before Charles's abdication. Philip drew important conclusions from this experience. He had learned to see

Protestantism as a source of rebellion and sedition, and that only devious hostility could be expected from the French. In religious terms, a generation of bitter experience separated Philip from the tolerant humanism that his father had brought to Spain in 1517. Similarly, the self-interest of the German princes, which had robbed him of the imperial inheritance, left Philip extremely ill-disposed and suspicious towards their Dutch counterparts.

This experience, perhaps, was not accompanied by any great degree of intelligence or imagination. The famous 'prudence' which contemporaries saw as the reason behind long delays over policy decisions has more recently been interpreted as simple indecision on the part of a king frequently confused by the arguments put to him. A.W. Lovett has also portrayed Philip as a seriously deficient mathematician. 'Barely numerate,' he writes, 'Philip had difficulty with all but the simplest calculations; he never mastered the intricacies of public finance, and shuddered at the mysteries of borrowing in its various forms.'

Philip governed through an unswerving adherence to those principles which he could understand, to his sacred duty as a monarch, and through a lifelong devotion to the preservation of the Catholic faith within his territories. To understand the actions of Philip II it is necessary to appreciate that he believed that God had imposed two sets of duties upon him: those dynastic duties inherited from his earthly father, and those higher responsibilities imposed by his heavenly Father. It was a simple formula, requiring no great mental agility but placing awesome demands upon Philip's industry. It was a challenge ideally suited to a man variously characterised as 'devoted to virtue and justice' (de los Cobos), or as 'simple, slow and childlike' (A.W. Lovett).

THE ADMINISTRATION OF SPAIN

Philip II was the personification of static, centralised authority. He rejected his father's peripatetic methods of government, advising his own son in turn that 'travelling about one's kingdoms is neither useful nor decent'. He enclosed himself in the great palace of the Escorial and 'ruled his empire sitting at his desk, receiving the endless correspondence from all parts of the world, reading, annotating, replying, and insisting always on seeing everything himself' (John Lynch). Nevertheless, such an image requires some explanation and modification. Henry Kamen has argued that this static form of government was forced upon Philip by tragic necessity. Philip lost one wife (Maria Manuela of Portugal) in 1545, another (Elizabeth of Valois) in 1568, and witnessed the decline and death of his son between 1562 and 1568. His eventual successor, Philip III, was not born until 1578, so that, for the greater part of his reign, the king could not leave behind him a regent of sufficient royal authority.

There was little new, however, about the administrative machinery of Philip II. Only three significant elements were added to the network of councils that Charles left behind. The Council of Italy was separated from its 'parent' Council of Aragon (1555), while subsequent political developments caused the Councils of Portugal (1582) and of Flanders (1588) to spring from the Council of State. With the king rarely in attendance, these remained purely consultative bodies. Ministers might debate, but they could only communicate their opinions for the king's ultimate consideration through the traditional medium of the *consulta*, the documents containing ministerial recommendations over which Philip pored during his long working hours.

Traditionally, this distance between Philip and his ministers has been seen as a deliberate ploy, as one of his greatest claims to be considered 'the perfect master in the art of ruling'. Was he not deliberately encouraging argument among his ministers in order to hear all sides of the question before deciding his course of action? Historians have seen in the deliberations of the Council of State in the 1560s a distinct 'peace party' headed by Ruy Gomez da Silva and a 'war party' led by the Duke of Alva. Modern writers, however, have ascribed a much greater role to family ambition and faction within Spanish government. The scandal surrounding Antonio Perez, one of Philip's principal secretaries, has been taken to show that factional interest penetrated to the very heart of Philip's administration.

17.1 Administrative crisis: the cases of Don Carlos and Antonio Perez

The administrative stability of Philip's reign was all the more remarkable for the fact that it survived two great crises.

Don Carlos. The first of these crises centred around the descent into madness of Philip's son and heir. Born in 1545, Don Carlos seems to have embodied all that was worst in Habsburg heredity. Even by Habsburg standards he was an ugly child, with an oversized head and a fearful stammer. He was frequently ill, and from 1562 it became clear that his illness was not purely physical. Further degeneration over the next six years ensured that Don Carlos could no longer expect prestigious political employment or an advantageous marriage. He responded by a series of conspiracies which threatened the security of the state. He was arrested (January 1568) and died within six months. Although legends immediately arose, adding the 'murder' of Don Carlos to the other 'crimes' charged to Philip's account by the 'Black Legend', there is no evidence to suggest that Don Carlos suffered anything other than a natural death.

Antonio Perez. As secretary to the Council of State, with particular responsibility for affairs relating to northern Europe, Perez occupied a position of unprecedented influence in the royal administration from 1568 until his sensational fall eleven years later. At the height of his career, it was claimed, 'His majesty would not do anything save what Antonio Perez marked out for him'. With the death of his patron, Ruy Gomez, and the temporary disgrace of the Duke of Alva (1572), Perez became an important factional leader as well as a crucial element in the administration. It was, indeed, factional rivalry that brought about his downfall. Perez persuaded Philip to acquiesce in the murder of Juan de Escobedo, secretary to Don John of Austria (March 1578), on the grounds that he was perverting Spanish policy in the Low Countries. His factional motives were exposed, however, when Don John's own death brought his papers into the king's hands. Perez was stripped of his offices and imprisoned, although his escape in 1590 was to provide a new twist to his story. His career to 1579 illustrates two aspects of Philip's administration. On the one hand, it becomes clear that the king's absolutist principles could not prevent factional interests from penetrating the highest political levels. Equally, we can learn from it that these factions gained their influence only by acting as parasites upon the royal power and that, once isolated from the court and from the administration, a faction became utterly impotent.

One hundred and fifty years ago the great German historian Leopold von Ranke distinguished two distinct phases in Philip's administration, which he referred to as his 'first' and 'second' ministries. It is certainly true that by 1579 most of the leaders of the factional struggles of the past two decades were dead or in disgrace. Ruy Gomez died in 1573, Los Velez and Don John of Austria both died in 1578, and the Duke of Alva, in disgrace in the 1570s, was dead by 1582. After 1586 the 'second ministry' centred increasingly upon the principal secretaries, Juan de Idiaquez and Cristóbal de Moura. These years also witnessed an increasing degree of delegation in the administration of the state, especially to the committee known as the 'Junta of the Night', consisting of Idiaquez, de Moura and the Count of Chinchon. Similarly, in the last decade of the reign, a *Junta Grande* of eight to ten members was established, playing a substantial role in the 1590s in the affairs of Aragon, in the organisation of communications with the New World, and in the distribution of royal patronage. Belatedly, Spain seemed to be in the process of developing something like a genuine conciliar government.

THE FINANCES OF THE SPANISH STATE

The partitioning of Charles V's European empire made a profound impact upon Castile. A mere province of the Habsburg *monarchia* now became the centre of a *monarchia* in its own right, with all the obligations and costs that this entailed. The money derived from Naples, Sicily and Milan barely sufficed for the defence of those regions, and the Low Countries, once a prime contributor to the Habsburg treasury, were becoming the major drain upon it. Until the mid-1560s, the combined annual expenditure of the Castilian treasury on the affairs of Spain, the Mediterranean and the Low Countries never exceeded 2 million ducats for any one year, yet by the end of Philip's reign the annual figure averaged 10 million ducats. The Armada alone accounted for a similar sum. Such burdens were borne by a treasury whose income in 1550 had been a mere 1.25 million ducats.

How could such vast demands be met? The New World, of course, provided a rich source of income, and many contemporaries assumed that Philip's ability to sustain great military efforts was due to the flow of treasure from the Indies. More recently, Pierre Chaunu has shown the coincidence between the supply of South American silver and the periods of Spain's greatest military activity in Europe. As the mines at Potosí, Zacatecas and Guanajuato were more fully developed, the royal share in their output rose to a level of about 2 million ducats a year by the early 1590s. The crown also stood to benefit by increased tax income from the expansion of colonial trade; and in emergencies, as in 1566, 1583 and 1587, it might also lay hands on the privately owned bullion that entered Spain.

Nevertheless, the wealth of the Indies never constituted more than 20 per cent of Philip's income, and the greatest part of the burden of his imperial undertakings was borne by the taxpayers of Castile. With the Cortes ill-equipped to resist, Philip tripled his income from such traditional sources as the *encabezamiento* tax between his accession and the end of the 1570s. The levelling off of his income after that date suggests that such sources had been exploited to their limits. Only one new tax was introduced. In the aftermath of the Armada disaster, the Cortes was persuaded to introduce (1590) the *millones*, a levy on meat and certain other foodstuffs, extraordinary in that it was to be paid by all classes, including those otherwise exempted from taxation. Henry Kamen has estimated that the bill of the unprivileged Castilian taxpayer increased during the reign by 430 per cent, while his wages rose by 80 per cent.

The contribution of the Spanish Church to the royal coffers was roughly equal to that of the New World. The *subsidio* tax was transformed from an occasional to a regular payment (1561), while a new tax on Church property, the *excusado*, was granted by the papacy in 1567. The face value of ecclesiastical taxes was four times as high in the 1590s as it had been at the beginning of the reign.

Yet even this was insufficient, and the Spanish crown would never have been able to implement its policies but for the massive loans that it obtained from major banking houses, and especially from the Genoese. Throughout the reign, the *asientos*, the bills whereby such bankers supplied coin for the payment of Philip's forces, were an indispensable part of the state's financial structure. The income of the New World and of Castile, therefore, was primarily important as collateral whereby even greater sums could be borrowed. Other Spanish resources were also mortgaged to meet the bankers' demands. By the middle of the reign, the Fuggers controlled the silver mines of Guadalcanal and the sources of mercury at Almaden. Large parts of the territories of the Military Orders, with all their peasant dues and food production, together with the anticipated production of the South American mines, also passed into the hands of foreign capitalists.

Inflation continued to complicate Spanish finances, undermining the true value of the king's income. In addition, the traditional raising of loans through the issue of *juros* bonds meant that a substantial proportion of Castilian income was mortgaged in advance, earmarked for the repayment of earlier borrowing. The bankruptcies declared by Philip's government in 1557, 1576 and 1596 confirmed the state's failure to cope with its financial commitments. They failed, however, to bring about any break in the spiral of state debt. Interest payments that stood at 349,000 ducats per year at the accession of King Charles accounted for 4.6 million ducats in the year of Philip's death. The record of Spanish military success in the second half of the sixteenth century was largely offset, therefore, by a consistent history of financial chaos.

THE COUNTER-REFORMATION IN SPAIN

No European monarch exercised greater control over the Church within his territories than Philip II. The extensive powers enjoyed by his predecessors were enhanced in October 1572 by a royal decree which forbade any foreign jurisdiction over Spaniards in ecclesiastical matters.

In general, Philip used these powers most positively. The early years of his reign coincided with a new hardening of religious attitudes in Spain and with a new phase in the activities of the Inquisition. Under the leadership of Hernando de Valdes, Inquisitor General from 1547, and Melchior Cano, a leading Dominican and spiritual adviser to the king, the Church renewed its assault upon what it saw as threatening and heretical influences. Alarmed by the discovery of so-called 'Protestant' groups in Seville and Valladolid in 1557–8, the Inquisition tried some 800 persons, of whom thirty or so died in spectacular *autos-da-fé* in the two cities. If there ever was a truly Protestant movement within Spain, it did not survive these fires.

Recent writers, such as Henry Kamen, have rejected the traditional image of the Inquisition as a harsh and pervasive body engaged in an ideological holocaust. The primary task of the Inquisition was not so much to attack open heresy as to eliminate error within native Catholicism. In this respect, it launched a determined attack upon what conservatives saw as unacceptable tendencies in Spanish academic life, armed, after 1559, with a new weapon. Initially a relatively limited list, the Spanish Index underwent a radical extension in 1583 under the guidance of a new Inquisitor General, Gaspar de Quiroga. Alongside the list of forbidden books was also published (1584) an 'Expurgatory Index' listing books that could be published and read, provided doubtful or dangerous passages in them were deleted. The list featured the works of many Spanish Catholic authors, including St Juan de Avila and St Francis Borja, whose writings, it was felt, might be misunderstood or misused in the wrong hands.

Although Philip showed severe reservations about those decrees of the Council of Trent which concerned the international authority of the papacy, Spain saw many reforms that were fully in line with the Council's disciplinary decrees. The famous reorganisation of the Dutch bishoprics had a parallel within Spain itself. Burgos was designated an archbishopric in 1572, while six new bishoprics were created in Aragon and one (Valladolid) in Castile. It became the normal practice, if not a universal rule, for bishops to reside in their sees, and diocesan synods were held at regular intervals. In addition, the foundation between 1562 and 1582 of a new observant order known as the Discalced Carmelites was part of a remarkable wave of Spanish mysticism in the second half of the sixteenth century. St Teresa of Avilà and St John of the Cross were leading representatives of this movement.

On the other hand, Church reform at parish level was a long and difficult process. Throughout Philip's reign the authority of the king, the Inquisition and other leading churchmen whittled away at centuries of local superstititon, religious diversity and vested interests. Henry Kamen has gone so far as to decribe this as a period in which Spain was effectively 'reconverted' to an orthodox and consistent form of Catholicism. 'A worshipper in post-Tridentine Spain', he wrote, 'would experience whitewashed walls in churches, paintings purged of sensuality, a pulpit if there had been none before, a confessional to separate priest from penitent, sermons and a new liturgy.'

DOMESTIC CONSOLIDATION

The revolt of the Moriscos

A revolt of the Morisco population of the Alpujarra region was hardly an unexpected event. The bigger surprise was that it was delayed until the late 1560s. The hostility of Christian Spain towards survivals of Moorish society had led in the past to a stream of edicts forbidding, for instance, the use of the Arabic language, Moorish dress, and many customs that had their origins in the Islamic faith. Owing to the practical difficulties of enforcement, however, and to Charles's constant preoccupation with events elsewhere in his empire, the leaders of the Morisco community had been able to purchase a forty-year suspension of these edicts (1527).

Many factors combined to destroy this precarious balance. At court, the 1550s saw the decline of the influence of the Mondejar family, Captains-General of Andalucia and consistently tolerant towards the Moriscos. In their place rose the Fajardo family, headed by the Marquis de los Velez. At the same time, the Moriscos' primary industry was badly hit by an edict forbidding the export of woven silk (1552) and by the imposition of much heavier taxation upon the silk industry from 1557. A new Archbishop of Granada, Pedro Guerrero, appointed in 1546, brought from the Council of Trent a determination to ensure that the conversion of the Moors was more than a convenient fiction. The activities of the Inquisition were so intensified that 368 Moriscos were condemned in Granada between 1563 and 1569, whereas only three had suffered during 1520–9. The final straw was a government pragmatic, published on the first day of 1567, ordering the enforcement of all the anti-Muslim edicts of earlier reigns.

The revolt began with the attempted seizure of Granada by Morisco forces in December 1568, and quickly spread to the hills and valleys of the Alpujarra region. Failure to capture Granada or to secure aid from the Turks doomed the Moriscos to defeat from the outset, yet the struggle dragged on until the end of 1571. The Spanish forces suffered the disadvantages of fighting an enemy who enjoyed the support of most of the local population, and massacres and religious fanaticism on both sides created a vicious circle of hatred and revenge.

Once a military solution had been ground out, the government implemented a complex plan to disperse the Morisco communities all over Spain, where they would constitute a minority in any given area and where their presence would be less of a threat. In addition to the estimated 21,000 Moriscos who perished in the fighting, 80,000 were now forcibly displaced between late 1570 and early 1572. Perhaps 20 per cent of all the deported Moriscos died *en route* – as many as 15,000 victims.

A project that would have been beyond the means of any other government in Western Europe was only partially successful. In their new locations the Moriscos remained reluctant subjects. In Catalonia they were popularly associated with banditry, and suspected of treasonable contacts with the French Protestants. They were received in their new homelands with distrust and hostility, and the economy of their former homelands was ruined beyond repair. In 1582 and 1592, Philip rejected petitions for their total expulsion, but Philip III was finally to resort to that dramatic measure (1609) as the ultimate solution to the Morisco problem.

The annexation of Portugal

Philip made two other important contributions to the further unification of the peninsula. The first of these was his acquisition of the kingdom of Portugal. At the root of the Portuguese question lay the disastrous military campaign led by the young King Sebastian to re-establish his territorial claims in Morocco. He died with much of his army at Alcazarquivir (August 1578), leaving Portugal virtually defenceless. The throne passed to the aged Cardinal Henry who, sixty-six years old and under a vow of celibacy, was ill-placed to continue the line of succession. Upon his death (January 1580) there were few strong native candidates. Catalina, Duchess of Braganza, was handicapped by gender and illegitimacy, while Dom Antonio, the prior of Crato, had to combat rumours of Jewish ancestry. The strongest claim, albeit through a female line, was that of Philip of Spain, who also had the means to enforce it.

In general, Philip had the support within Portugal of the nobility and of the Church, although the Jesuits stood out against him. Dom Antonio, on the other hand, appealed to those interest groups which seemed, from the experience of their Spanish counterparts, to have most to lose by Philip's succession: the Lisbon *conversos*, the lower clergy and those communes which feared for their traditional liberties. When Dom Antonio seized the treasury in Lisbon and had himself proclaimed king by the commons, Spanish military intervention was certain.

Philip's army of over 37,000 men arrived in June 1580 under the command of the Dukes of Alva and Medina Sidonia. Because it enjoyed the support of influencial native élites, its rapid campaign was in stark contrast to the stalemate achieved in the Netherlands. By the end of October, Spanish forces had sacked Lisbon, Setubal and other towns, and Dom Antonio was a fugitive on his way to France. The political settlement was also unlike any offered to the Dutch. With no issues of heresy involved, Philip promised the Portuguese Cortes at Thomar (April 1581) that the administration of their state would remain in the hands of natives and that Portuguese trading monopolies would be respected.

The annexation of Portugal marked the real unification of Spain in the eyes of contemporaries. Only now did Philip begin to style himself 'King of Spain'. Yet the annexation brought far greater benefits to Spain than to Portugal. It brought her the trade and wealth of the Portuguese colonial empire, complete control of the peninsula's Atlantic coastline and, perhaps most important of all, control of the Portuguese fleet, both mercantile and military. Without such acquisitions, such an undertaking as the Armada would never have been possible. For Portugal the future was less bright. She would become increasingly embroiled in Spanish quarrels, and from now on her shipping would be increasingly liable to attack from the English and, more seriously, from the Dutch.

The question of Aragon

Until the 1590s, the *fueros*, or liberties, of Aragon remained an obstacle to the administration of royal justice and to royal control. In principle the king retained the power to summon the Aragonese Cortes, to nominate most higher officials and to decide issues of war and peace. On the other hand, long-standing tradition dictated that he could not overrule the court of the *Justicia*, the highest legal officer of Aragon. The kingdom also retained a far stronger feudal system than any other part of the peninsula, with lords retaining the legal right to dispose of the property and even the lives of their vassals as they wished. These liberties survived as much through Castilian indifference as through Aragonese conservatism. With little to hope for from Aragon in military or financial terms, Philip saw no reason even to visit the kingdom between 1563 and 1585.

Conflict with the *fueros* of Aragon began on a modest scale in 1582 when a landing of Muslim corsairs near Valencia caused Philip to send substantial infantry forces into Aragon without consulting the Cortes. Seven years later, another Spanish force intervened to ensure that the county of Ribagorza, on the northern borders, was not infiltrated by the French. The issue of Aragonese privileges was eventually resolved, however, as the final stage in the political career of Antonio Perez. In April 1590, Perez escaped from house arrest in Madrid and fled to Aragon, where he claimed immunity from Philip's direct jurisdiction. Attempts to bring him to trial by the Inquisition, whose courts had equal jurisdiction in Castile and in Aragon, provoked open rioting in Saragossa (1591) and the violent death of the king's representative. With both national security and his personal authority at stake, Philip marched on Saragossa (November 1591) and met with little opposition.

Meeting the Aragonese Cortes at Tarazona (June 1592), the king dictated significant changes in their constitutional position. The office of the *Justicia* survived, but henceforth it was held at the king's pleasure. Decisions in the Cortes henceforth would be carried by a majority and no longer by unanimity. In Aragon, as in Portugal, Philip had increased his central authority by relatively moderate means, and had avoided visionary political systems such as had caused him so much difficulty in the Netherlands. In the words of Peter Pierson (*Philip II of Spain*, 1975), he had 'realised the dreams of his ancestors of recreating Visigothic *Hispania*; he had changed the constitution of Aragon with the ideals of justice and common defence in mind'.

SPANISH MILITARY RESOURCES

Quite apart from the unequal financial burden that it bore, Castile undertook its central role in Spanish affairs with a military establishment that was quite inadequate for the task. By the beginning of the 1570s, when the lengthy resistance of the Moriscos had embarrassed the government, it became clear just how ill-equipped Spain was, even for her own domestic protection.

In quantitative terms, the achievement of the next thirty years was striking. The number of soldiers recruited in Spain averaged 9,000 per year, and that number doubled in years of particular emergency. In 1580, while nearly 50,000 men were in service in the Netherlands, an army of 37,000 could be sent into Portugal. Great progress was also made in the construction of a Spanish navy. Charles had barely had a navy at all, but by contrast Philip built 300 new galleys between 1560 and 1574, at a cost of some 3.5 million ducats. With the acquisition of Portugal, Spain had at her disposal a fleet of over 100 ships suitable for service in the Atlantic. Even after the disaster of the Armada campaign, the rate of naval growth was such that 136 ships could sail in the Armadas of 1596 and 1597.

Yet these resources were inadequate for the pacification and protection of Philip's empire. In the Netherlands, Spaniards never formed more than a small proportion of Philip's forces: 10,000 out of 67,000 in 1572. Remarkable as the sustained military effort was, raiders such as Drake and Essex were easily able to attack objectives on the Spanish mainland. Englishmen, Frenchmen and Dutchmen all found even easier targets in the distant colonies. The truth is that Spain only maintained her primacy by buying the military resources of others. Where military operations in Spain, Flanders and the Mediterranean cost less than 2 million ducats per year in the mid-1560s, these costs had risen beyond 10 million per year by the mid-1590s. By the end of Philip's reign, 80 million ducats of state revenue had been spent on the affairs of the Netherlands. This was an outpouring of Spanish resources upon non-Spanish interests that would

have staggered even the most apprehensive protestors of the Cortes and the Comuneros in 1519–20.

FOREIGN POLICY

Themes and aims

The Venetian ambassador remarked in 1559 that Philip's aim was 'not to wage war so that he can add to his kingdoms, but to wage peace so that he can keep the lands that he has'. Yet the next forty years

The Armada Campaign

The apparent settlement of Anglo-Spanish differences in 1573 proved to be little more than an uneasy truce. Within a decade, further interference in Dutch affairs had produced proposals for a naval campaign against England. This 'Enterprise of England' was then triggered by a series of events in the Netherlands and by the reaction of the Queen of England to them. In July 1584, William of Orange was assassinated by a religious enthusiast, and a little over a year later Antwerp surrendered to the Duke of Parma (August 1585). Faced with the definitive triumph of Spanish interests in the Netherlands, Elizabeth signed the Treaty of Nonsuch in direct support of the Dutch rebels. It was an unmistakable act of war, and by the middle of 1586 Philip had consented to the plans of Santa Cruz for a mighty 'Armada' to sail against England.

The two-year delay in the dispatch of this force is explained by

the logistical and diplomatic preparations that the undertaking demanded. Assembling 130 ships, with 22,000 men and 2,500 cannon, was a remarkable achievement in itself. Meanwhile, the conclusion of the Treaty of Joinville with the leaders of the Catholic League helped to ensure that England would stand alone and that France would not take advantage of this opportunity to interfere in the Netherlands.

The object of the campaign was to rendezvous with the forces of the Duke of Parma and to escort and protect them as they mounted an invasion of England. A combined naval and land strategy, difficult at the outset, was utterly frustrated by a combination of English tactics and adverse weather conditions. After safely negotiating the English Channel in a defensive formation, the fleet was prevented from making its rendezvous with Parma by the attack of English fireships and by the subsequent

engagement off Gravelines. The rest was done by the weather. Driven north by the prevailing winds and skirting the north and west of the British Isles, the scattered fleet lost many of its ships on the rocky and hostile shores of Scotland and Ireland. By considerable feats of seamanship the majority reached their home ports, but it has been estimated that little more than twenty of the warships which left Spain returned in a fit state for future service.

Although subsequent armadas were sent in the wake of this one in 1596 and 1597, the defeat of 1588 was decisive. These events sealed the fate of Spanish foreign policy in all that it had sought to achieve in the 1580s. 'If any one year', wrote J.H. Elliott (*Imperial Spain, 1469–1716*, 1963), 'marks the division between the triumphant Spain of the first two Habsburgs, and the defeatist, disillusioned Spain of their successors, that year is 1588.'

17.2 The European commitments of Philip II

	Domestic disruption	The Netherlands	France & England	The Mediterranean
1556				
	1557 First state bankruptcy		1557 Victory at St-Quentin	
			1559 Peace with France at Câteau-Cambrésis.	
1560	1560 Second state bankruptcy			1560 Expedition against Tripoli
				1563 Defeat of Barbary Corsairs at Oran
				1564 Capture of Penon de la Gomera
1565		1565 First Dutch Revolt		1565 Defence of Malta against the Turks
		1567 Arrival of Alva in Netherlands		
	1568–70 Revolt of the Moriscos	1568 Revolt of the Prince of Orange	1568 Seizure of Genoese bullion by Elizabeth	
1570	↓			1571 Formation of Holy League. Victory at Lepanto
		1572 Second Dutch Revolt	1572 First French intervention in the Netherlands	
		↓	1573 Convention of Nymwegen settles disputes with England	1573 Temporary capture of Tunis
1575				
	1576 Third state bankruptcy	1576 Third Revolt; Pacification of Ghent.		
		1576–7 Repudiation of Pacification by Don John		1577 Truce with Sultan

would bring open warfare with both France and England, primarily over events in the Netherlands. In reality, Spanish foreign policy in Western Europe revolved around issues that were not foreign at all in Philip's perception. The crisis in the Netherlands involved two issues upon which he could not compromise: the element of heresy and the issue of Habsburg dynastic rights which the Dutch rebels came increasingly to challenge. Philip had little concern for the religious opinions of the English or the French, for they were not part of his God-given

mandate. Instead, his attitude to those states was entirely dictated by the role they played, or appeared to play, in the affairs of the Netherlands.

The initial phase of Philip's foreign policy after Câteau-Cambrésis was pro-English. He had only just ceased to be King-Consort of England, and entertained some hopes of continuing that role by marriage to Queen Elizabeth. England and Spain had recently fought in alliance against France, and the ascendancy in that country of the Guise family posed considerable threats to Habsburg interests.

	Domestic disruption	The Netherlands	France & England	The Mediterranean
1580				
	1581 Dispute over succession to the throne of Portugal	1581–3 Intervention of the Duc d'Alençon in the Dutch Revolt		
		1583–5 Parma's successful campaigns in the southern Netherlands		
1585		1585–6 Treaty of Nonsuch leads to direct English intervention in the Netherlands		
			1586 Treaty of Joinville with French Catholics. Decision to launch Armada against England	
			1588 Defeat of the Armada.	
1590			1590 Parma's first campaign in France	
	1591 Revolt in Aragon	1591–4 Significant Dutch successes in northern provinces	1592 Parma's second campaign in France	
1595			1595 War with France	
	1596 Fourth state bankruptcy		↓	
			1598 Peace with France through the Treaty of Vervins	

Their kinswoman, Mary Stuart, was Queen of Scots and Queen of France and, as heir-apparent to the throne of England, personified the prospect of a dynastic conglomeration that might threaten the Netherlands from two sides.

Yet Anglo-Spanish relations degenerated steadily in the course of the 1560s, largely because of English interference in Philip's legitimate spheres of interest. Elizabeth sought to obstruct Alva's work in the Netherlands, the Dutch 'Sea Beggars' openly sheltered in English ports, and Philip was forced to take strong measures against English interlopers in the New World. In general, however, far from pursuing aggressive policies towards England, Philip showed remarkable restraint in the face of English provocation. Blocking papal projects for the excommunication of Elizabeth in 1561 and 1563, he forbade publication of the Bull in Spain when it was finally issued in 1570. By the Convention of Nymwegen (March 1573), all tensions over property seizures in England, Spain and the Netherlands over the previous five years were apparently resolved.

The direction of French politics, meanwhile, was more consistently acceptable to Spanish interests. The early death of Francis II (December 1560) widowed Mary Stuart, and Catherine de Medici subsequently worked to limit Guise influence over French policy. The disturbing growth of Protestant influence at the French court was also dramatically reversed by the massacre of Huguenots on St Bartholomew's day in 1572. This seemed to eliminate any immediate possibility that the Dutch rebels would receive aid from their co-religionists in France.

After the Armada

The loss of the great Armada was not the only disaster to befall Spanish foreign policy in 1588–9. In France, the murder of Guise and the succession of Henry of Navarre to the French throne dealt savage blows to the Catholic cause. To a greater extent than ever before, the Netherlands were encircled by forces sympathetic to the Protestant rebels. For the rest of Philip's reign, therefore, France provided the focus for Spanish foreign policy.

At first, Philip clung to the hope that the Catholic League, even without the Duke of Guise, could prevent Henry IV from establishing himself on the throne. To that end Parma and his forces were again diverted from the Low Countries where they had been so close to victory. They relieved the siege of Paris (1590) and broke that of Rouen (1591–2) before their impetus was destroyed by Parma's death (December 1592). The official conversion of Henry IV to Catholicism ended both Philip's hopes of cooperation with the Catholic League and Spanish influence over French policy. There was a note of desperation about his attempts to propose his daughter Isabella, a grand-daughter of Henry II, as an alternative candidate for the throne. Even before Henry's conversion it was never likely that the Estates-General would accept the succession of a Spanish monarch.

The war which occupied the last three years of the reign served French interests far better than it served Philip's. Spanish forces seized Calais (October 1595) and held Amiens for over six months in 1597, yet in November 1596 Philip was forced to declare his administration bankrupt for the fourth time. By the Treaty of Vervins (May 1598) Spain evacuated all occupied positions in northern and western France, and, apart from freeing troops for further expensive employment in the Netherlands, gained nothing in return. At the time of his death (September 1598), Philip had an unsatisfactory peace with France to set alongside a war with England, which was to drag on until 1604.

Italy and the Mediterranean

The Treaty of Câteau-Cambrésis in 1559 freed Philip's hands for what at that time seemed the most pressing of his foreign problems. He could now attempt to reverse Charles's failures in the Mediterranean and establish a barrier across the central Mediterranean to exclude Turkish influence from its western end. In Philip's view, Christendom's front line ran from his possessions in southern Italy, via the island of Malta, to La Goleta in North Africa. Initial attempts to strengthen this defensive line by capturing Tripoli and Bougie ended in disaster when the fleet of the Duke of Medinaceli was destroyed off the island of Djerba (July 1560), and for a decade afterwards Philip resisted the projects of successive Popes for grand crusading initiatives.

The Turkish question erupted in a more dangerous form when in 1570 the Ottomans seized Tunis and attacked the Venetian-held island of Cyprus. This prepared the way for the formation of a Holy League, comprising Venice, Spain and the papacy. Philip's decision to join this alliance, contributing half the manpower and bearing half the cost, represented the temporary triumph of Spanish considerations over Burgundian priorities, and seemed at first to have been blessed with remarkable success. In October 1571, the fleet of the Holy League won a victory of unusual proportions at Lepanto, off the coast of Greece. With only thirty-five Turkish ships out of 230 escaping, it was a victory to rank with Pavia and Mohacs as the most complete of the sixteenth century. Yet, like Pavia, its long-term consequences were negligible. The Turks still completed the conquest of Cyprus, and the following year they had a fleet in the Aegean almost as large as that which had fought at Lepanto.

Consequently, Spain made very limited gains in the western Mediterranean. In 1573, Don John and the Genoese admiral Gianandrea Doria captured Tunis. A year later, however, renewed Turkish efforts not only recaptured that port but took the Spanish garrison town of La Goleta. Over the next three years bankruptcy, allied with a deteriorating situation in the Netherlands, forced Philip to accept a truce with his arch-enemy. The relaxation of Turkish pressure on the western end of the Mediterranean was mainly due to unrest in Persia, which distracted Turkish attention and resources to the eastern extremities of their empire.

17.3 Key figures

EBOLI, Ruy Gomez de Silva, Prince of (1516–73). Councillor of State and *contador mayor* (1556). Subsequently leader of a powerful faction at the Spanish court, hostile to the Duke of Alva, and patron of Antonio Perez. Duke of Estremadura and grandee of Spain (1568).

IDIAQUEZ, Juan de (1540–1614). Ambassador to Genoa (1573–6), and to Venice (1576–8). Secretary of State for Italy (1579–85). Councillor of state and war (1585). President of the Council of Military Orders (1598).

MEDINA SIDONIA, Alonso Perez de Guzman, Duke of (1549–1615). Grandee of Spain, Knight of the Golden Fleece and Captain-General of the Coast of Andalucia (1588). Appointed Captain-General of the Ocean-Sea (1588), and placed in command of the Armada. Subsequently councillor of state and war (1598).

MOURA, Cristóbal de (1538–1613). Of Portuguese origins, appointed ambassador to Portugal (1578–80). Councillor of state and war (1585). Commander of the Order of Alcantara (1589). Viceroy of Portugal (1598–1613).

SANTA CRUZ, Alvaro de Bazan, Marquis of (1526–88). Leading naval commander. Captain-General of galleys of Naples (1566–78) and galleys of Spain (1578). Captain-General of the Ocean-Sea (1583) and of Portugal (1584). In these capacities he was responsible for the preparation of the Armada against England, but died before its dispatch.

ECONOMIC TRENDS

In most respects the reign of Philip II does not represent a distinct phase in the economic history of Spain. The boom conditions that prevailed in the last years of Charles's reign persisted, as rising prices and increasing population continued to create all the symptoms of agricultural and industrial prosperity. In Castile, in particular, the population continued to rise steadily until the last years of the century, from just under 4 million inhabitants in 1541, according to Fernand Braudel, to just under 6 million in 1591.

This increase in population stimulated the expansion of arable farming, as the demand for food came to outweigh the traditional privileges of the sheep farmers. It is also easy to find individual examples of continued industrial prosperity. Wool production continued to flourish in many of the traditional locations, and the shipbuilding industry in Biscay reached new levels of production to meet the demands of royal and mercantile policies. In 1583 alone, over 15,000 tons of shipping was under construction there. In the south, Seville continued to expand and to flourish, the number of vessels using the port on the Indies route increasing by 176 per cent between 1562 and 1608.

The greatest weakness of the Spanish economy was that the prosperity of the mid-century merely satisfied temporary demand, without any long-term changes in the structures of production. By the end of Philip's reign the boom was weakening in three respects. The decline in the supply of precious metals from the New World coincided with the decline in the New World demand for Spanish goods. At the same time, Spain reached the end of her demographic expansion, as earlier epidemics were eclipsed by the so-called 'Atlantic Plague', spreading from the northern provinces of the country in 1598–9.

The policies of the crown also had a detrimental impact upon the overall health of the economy. The classic example of this was the irreparable damage done to the silk industry of south-eastern Spain by the dispersal of the Morisco communities which were the main producers. Similarly, commercial relations with France and England were severely disrupted during the worst stages of Spain's conflicts with those states.

The economy also suffered from two fundamental structural weaknesses. The first was a permanent balance-of-payments deficit. The exports of Castile continued to be dominated by wool. Not only was this a relatively cheap commodity in its raw state, but it was also subjected after 1558 to export duties in the interests of royal finances. Against this, Castile imported relatively expensive finished goods and

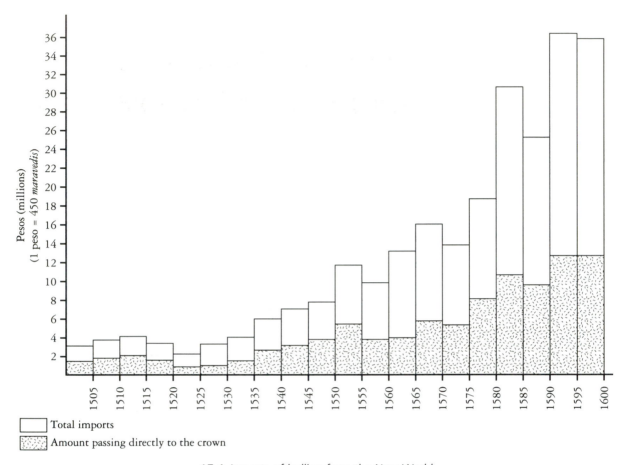

17.4 Imports of bullion from the New World
Source: P. Chaunu, *L'Espagne de Charles Quint* (Paris, 1973)

foodstuffs, such as cloth and tapestries (often produced from that very wool which Castile had exported in the first place) from the Low Countries, or metal and timber from Germany and Scandinavia. In addition, Spain's New World wealth, rather than leading to the development of powerful native capitalism, made her prey to an increasing army of foreign capitalists. After 1566, when the government permitted foreign financiers to export bullion, Spain was a particularly tempting source of gain for foreign merchants and bankers. Thus German merchants gained greater and greater stakes in Spanish mining and milling industries, while the Genoese played an increasing role in shipping and in financial services. At the same time, the bankruptcies declared by the Spanish crown undermined the native banking industry that had previously flourished at such centres as Medina del Campo.

Henry Kamen provided the epitaph of the sixteenth-century Spanish economy when he wrote that the course of Philip's reign 'changed Spain from a country that might have become rich through its imperial connections and its absolute control over America, into a nation whose economic fate was dictated by international capitalism'.

Further reading

H. Kamen (1983) *Spain, 1469–1714: A Society of Conflict.* London and New York.

A.W. Lovett (1986) *Early Habsburg Spain, 1517–1598.* Oxford.

G. Parker (1979) *Philip II.* London.

G. Woodward (1992) *Philip II.* London and New York.

CHAPTER EIGHTEEN

The England of Elizabeth: State, Church and Society

The political and social career of an English gentleman in the reign of Elizabeth. This
'narrative portrait' of Sir Henry Unton was painted shortly after his death in 1596.
Sir Henry served the crown as a soldier and a diplomat, and the various scenes
which accompany his portrait show him studying at Oxford, travelling on
various diplomatic and military missions (including his service with
Leicester in the Netherlands), and various episodes in his
domestic life in Oxfordshire. Taken together, the
portrait encapsulated the desired public
image of the Elizabethan gentleman

THE HISTORICAL DEBATE

No European monarch in the sixteenth century has received so consistently favourable a 'press' as Elizabeth. Three and a half centuries of English historiography have produced a remarkable consensus of interpretation only very recently subjected to serious modification. The instability of her successors' reigns made it tempting to view the period of Elizabeth's rule as a 'golden age' in which, as the eighteenth-century Tory, Bolingbroke, wrote: 'the sense of the court, the sense of Parliament and the sense of the people were the same, and she exerted the whole strength of the nation'. This English 'nationalist' tradition merged neatly with a wider 'Protestant' tradition, and the appeal of that combination is clearly visible in the greatest biography of the Queen written in this century, Sir John Neale's *Queen Elizabeth* (1934). It is largely uncritical of Elizabeth, and takes an evident pride in its picture of the queen triumphing over the dangers of a divided nation and over the threats posed by a divided Europe. Neale's Elizabeth has been characterised as 'a lonely, embattled ruler of a tiny island, heroically uniting the nation against military aggression backed by an alien ideology' (J.P. Kenyon, *The History Men*, 1983).

To a limited extent, these traditions were offset by historians with different priorities. The Protestant 'school' was countered by a Catholic 'school', whose writers see in the religious policy of the reign only the use of violence and hypocrisy in the pursuit of political power. The most notable Catholic interpretation of the English Reformation has been that of Father Philip Hughes (*The Reformation in England*, 1963), who viewed Elizabeth's settlement as 'an aggression, introduced to the ordinary man's notice not by sweet reasoning, or evangelical preaching, but by acts of state, commanding obedient acceptance under threats against life itself'.

Other writers have ascribed less importance to Elizabeth's will and personality in forming the events of the era. The great nineteenth-century writer J.A. Froude portrayed the queen rather as an indecisive and mediocre *politique*, reliant upon the genius of outstanding ministers such as Burghley.

The work of Wallace MacCaffrey (*The Shaping of the Elizabethan Regime*, 1968) and Conyers Read (*Mr Secretary Cecil and Queen Elizabeth*, 1955, and *Lord Burghley and Queen Elizabeth*, 1960), while less critical, have also drawn greater attention to the wider context within which the monarch operated.

Such works set a precedent for the massive re-examination of Elizabeth's reign which has been in progress for the last forty years. On most political and social issues, historians have reached conclusions that have modified traditional perceptions of the reign. As regards religious policy, the relative autonomy of the localities from the decisions of the central authorities has been stressed by such writers as Claire Cross (*The Royal Supremacy in the Elizabethan Church*, 1969) and Patrick Collinson (*The Religion of Protestants: The Church and English Society, 1559–1625*, 1982). Neale's view of Elizabethan Parliaments as the breeding-ground for the ideas that precipitated political revolution in the next century has been challenged by such writers as M.A.R. Graves (*The Tudor Parliaments: Crown, Lords and Commons, 1485–1603*, 1985). A vast new area of understanding has begun to be opened up by studies of mentalities, of which those of Keith Thomas (*Religion and the Decline of Magic*, 1971) and Lawrence Stone (*The Family, Sex and Marriage in England, 1500–1800*, 1977) are perhaps the most remarkable. Although new orthodoxies are far from being established, in the words of Christopher Haigh (*Reign of Elizabeth I*, 1984), 'a field that has been fallow for some years [is being] ploughed up before new planting can take place'.

THE GOVERNMENT OF THE REALM

The queen and her ministers

The young queen had been thoroughly schooled in adversity. Before her third birthday her mother had been disgraced and executed, and Elizabeth had been declared illegitimate. She lived in real danger during Mary's reign, often in the thoughts of such Protestant conspirators as Thomas Wyatt, and needing all her discretion to save herself from sharing their fate. Elizabeth thus came to the throne as a self-sufficient political survivor. What was new about the government of England in 1558 was not that the country now had a queen, but that it had a queen who wished to exercise her full powers without depending upon the support of a powerful husband. She clearly resembled her father in that she regarded the initiative and final decision in all matters as hers alone. It was a role that she cherished all the more because, being a woman, many considered her unworthy of it. Like her father, too, she could be an awesome proposition for any minister who forgot his place, yet she also had a supreme talent for public relations, for tying individuals to her by bonds of personal loyalty and affection.

One of the most remarkable features of the reign is that, despite the severe misgivings of the political nation, the prestige of the monarch was raised to new heights. In part this resulted from a triumph of propaganda and image-making. Unable to exploit the usual themes of military, masculine authority, the propagandists of the day achieved unprecedented success in their creation of a feminine mystique. The image of the 'Virgin Queen', sacrificing her private desires to the wellbeing of the nation, became so highly developed as to invite confusion with the cult of another Virgin, who Protestant Englishmen could no longer openly venerate.

Once established on the throne, Elizabeth's political instincts were unyieldingly conservative, aiming always, as Cecil observed, 'to win time, wherein many accidents may ensue'. Perhaps, as Wallace MacCaffrey (*The Shaping of the Elizabethan Regime*, 1969) has suggested, she sought by inaction to keep matters in her own hands, when action necessarily meant delegation to male agents far beyond the reach of the court. One sees her caution in the fact that direct intervention in the Netherlands was resisted for more than a decade before 1585, despite the enthusiasm of Leicester and Walsingham for such a policy, and in the long delay over addressing the dangers posed by the presence of the Queen of Scots on English soil.

Elizabeth's brand of cautious pragmatism was broadly reflected in the councillors she chose. Noblemen such as Arundel, Pembroke and Shrewsbury continued nominally to serve so that their influence in the shires would be exercised in the royal interest. Winchester, Gresham and others remained in office because they were administrators of proven ability. The last category of councillor was the most important: men excluded from office in the previous reign, to whom Elizabeth now turned because she valued them and because their views were broadly in accord with hers. By far the most important appointment was that of Sir William Cecil as Secretary of State. He was a practical politician and political survivor *par excellence*, a thorough conservative like the queen, yet without her tendency to take conservatism to the extent of paralysis. On at least two occasions, the military expedition to Scotland (1561) and the execution of the Queen of Scots (1587), he supplied the initiative that transformed royal indecision into positive and successful action.

Robert Dudley, fifth son of the late Duke of Northumberland, was another powerful influence upon the reign. As a companion of the queen from youth, as a soldier and a courtier in the best Renaissance traditions, he had all the qualifications to become a royal favourite. Before the end of 1559 rumour linked him with Elizabeth romantically, and although the queen refused to commit herself there was probably substance to the rumour. Dudley's court career moved rapidly, culminating in a place on the Privy Council (1562) and elevation to the earldom of Leicester (1564). For a further quarter of a century Leicester was to be an influence second only to Cecil, and at times second to none. In general, he was the mouthpiece of the 'party of action', urging positive measures against Spain, against Catholic France, or in support of the Dutch, while Cecil sought to impose restraint and caution.

The conduct of central government

Such men dominated a system of central government that remained a pragmatic mixture of formal and informal elements. The Privy Council became to a greater and greater extent a stable body of professional administrators. By the end of the reign it was usual for the Council to work a full week, where three meetings a week had sufficed in the 1560s. The office of Secretary of State (William Cecil, 1558–72; Walsingham, 1573–90; and Robert Cecil, 1596 onwards) resumed the importance that it had held under Thomas Cromwell, and the omni-competence of the office was conveyed by Robert Cecil when he wrote at the end of the reign that 'all officers and councillors of princes have a prescribed authority by patent, custom or by oath, the secretary only excepted'.

On the other hand, the management of the crown's finances remained conservative and unchanged. Income was still derived from the traditional sources, namely customs dues, feudal revenues, profits of justice and the rents from royal lands, with the occasional supplement of a parliamentary subsidy. Income from the first four sources seems to have increased by about 50 per cent in the course of the reign, to about £300,000 per year; Elizabeth, in contrast to many of her Continental contemporaries, seems to have accumulated a substantial surplus by saving about £100,000 per year from this ordinary income.

Yet careful housekeeping was probably the only virtue of Elizabethan financial administration. The government made little effort to ensure a realistic level of income from its traditional sources, and although Elizabeth benefited from the revision of customs duties undertaken at the end of Mary's reign she did little over the next forty-five years to encourage further revision. Thus an income from customs of £83,000 in 1558 rose only to an annual average of £96,000 in the late 1590s. Similarly, while income from crown lands increased in the reign from £66,000 to £88,000 per year, it is clear that Elizabeth's administration failed to keep crown rents at a realistic level, some royal lands yielding as little as a quarter of their true value.

In the short term the system met the needs of the crown, despite the severe strains imposed by the long war with Spain, which consumed the earlier surplus together with a succession of parliamentary subsidies. It was no mean achievement that, after eighteen years of warfare, Elizabeth died only £350,000 in debt, when a much shorter war in the mid-century had left Mary with a deficit of £300,000. On the other hand, the crown had to compromise its own political future by selling off large tracts of crown lands to raise ready cash. In the long term, the real burden was borne by Elizabeth's successors, who inherited a bankrupt and under-funded throne, and who had to run the political risks of pushing an outdated system to its limits.

The court

Political power still lay as much in the informal dealings of the royal court as in the formal machinery of the state. A contemporary courtier reported that the Queen 'ruled much by faction and parties which herself both made, upheld and weakened, as her own great judgement advised'. Yet it would be a mistake to think of Elizabeth's court as resembling the fluctuating and faction-ridden court of her father. Instead, the essential stability of Elizabeth's court formed an important basis for the political stability of her realm.

Because this was the court of a queen rather than of a king, there was far less opportunity for faction to penetrate the intimate environment of the monarch's Privy Chamber. Here the monarch's intimates were her chosen ladies-in-waiting, rather than the great and influential nobles with whom a king might hunt or joust. Another factor in the political stability of the court was the fact that the queen relied heavily upon men with a record of service to her and to her mother, upon what contemporaries referred to as 'the old flock of Hatfield'. A host of her closest servants, such as Sir Thomas Parry (Treasurer of the Household), Sir Thomas Benger (Master of the Revels) and John Ashley (Master of the Jewels), all fell into this category, as well as William Cecil, Leicester and Parker. The queen and her chief ministers were also able to maintain control by the distribution of a vast amount of patronage, far in excess of that at the disposal of provincial magnates. Wallace MacCaffrey has estimated that some 40 per cent of the politically active class in England, a class which he numbered at about 2,500, held offices in the crown's gift. From this he concluded that the crown used its patronage to secure 'not the adherence of a party or faction, but the goodwill of a whole class'.

There were certainly disputes within the highest political circles. Leicester and Sussex fell out over the issue of intervention in the Netherlands in the 1570s, and Leicester and Walsingham led a 'party of action' against the cautious Burghley in the next decade. These, however, were disputes over policy rather than over factional advantage. There were only two major exceptions to this rule, for genuine factional rivalry was involved in the rising of the Northern Earls in 1569 and in the reckless conspiracy of the Earl of Essex in 1601. For thirty years between these events, however, the pragmatism of a level-headed monarch, the influence of a great minister and the pressures of prolonged international crisis combined to create an atmosphere of unparalleled common interest in the politics of the court.

Local government

By the end of the reign the role of the Lord Lieutenant had become a major element in the crown's bid to ensure stability and obedience at a local level. First established on any significant scale by Northumberland, but rarely used under Mary, the office now became an essential link between central and local government. The fact that Lords Lieutenant were appointed for most English counties between 1585 and 1587, at the time of the Armada crisis, indicates that the office had much to do with the continuing Tudor obsession with order and security in the localities. Indeed, its development marked a significant stage in the imposition of central authority in the localities, for the men appointed were great officers of state rather than local magnates, and the office was not hereditary. Burghley, for instance, was simultaneously Lord Lieutenant of Essex, Hertfordshire and Lincolnshire between 1588 and 1598.

At a more humble level, the office of Justice of the Peace retained its importance, and there was a steady increase in the number of JPs appointed. The thirty who sufficed for Wiltshire in 1562 had increased to fifty-two by 1600, while in Norfolk and in Kent the numbers rose from thirty-four to sixty-one (1562–1602) and from fifty-six to ninety-six (1562–98) respectively. The workload carried by such local officials increased dramatically. The substantial religious legislation of the reign stood alongside an unprecedented body of social and economic legislation, all of which had in theory to be enforced by the local magistrates. William Lambard's contemporary work on the office of the JP, *Eirenarcha*, noted 306 statutes that needed to be enforced, 116 of which had become law since 1547, and seventy-five of which had been passed in Elizabeth's reign. The later advent of a long war, with its implications for taxation and for the raising of troops, ensured that between 1585 and 1603 the counties and their magistrates were carrying an enormous responsibility towards central government.

In general, it seems that local government ran smoothly when central and local interests overlapped. When these interests were at odds, central government still found it very hard to get its way. The government constantly failed, for instance, in its attempts to prevent local officers from making false tax assessments. Once a subsidy had been granted in Parliament, it was the task of local subsidy commissioners, often JPs, to assess the sums that had to be paid by the local gentry. The evidence is overwhelming that they often underestimated to an outrageous extent. In the enforcement of law and order, on the other hand, court and country had exactly the same interests. It is certainly true that, despite the religious divisions of the reign, the strains imposed by the war with Spain and mounting economic hardship in the last decade of the reign, Elizabethan England saw nothing resembling the serious popular disturbances of the 'mid-Tudor crisis'. Rebellious outbreaks in Oxfordshire and in Kent in 1596, and the food riots that occurred in the south and in East Anglia in 1596–7 were of a minor nature compared to the events of 1549.

THE RELIGIOUS SETTLEMENT: FORMATIVE INFLUENCES

The religious settlement was the most delicate issue facing the new queen, fraught with consequences both for domestic stability and for foreign relations. Historians have fluctuated between two interpretations of Elizabeth's motives. A.F. Pollard followed the view of many contemporaries in seeing the eventual settlement as a triumph of moderate Protestantism, consistently pursued by a Protestant queen, yet obstructed temporarily by a Marian rearguard in the House of Lords. This interpretation was radically revised by Sir John Neale, in whose view Elizabeth's ambitions were limited to the recovery of the royal supremacy. Doctrinally, he believed, she inclined towards her father's Anglo-Catholicism, but was forced into something more radical by her need to rely upon a vociferous Protestant minority in the Commons in order to defeat the Marian bishops. More recently still, the research of N.L. Jones (*Faith by Statute*, 1982) has placed the emphasis once again upon the House of Lords. Finding little evidence of what Neale called the puritan 'choir' in the Commons, Dr Jones has concluded once more that the government's priority was to force both a doctrinal package and the royal supremacy through a hostile upper house.

The puzzling search for Elizabeth's religious beliefs revolves around two sets of clues. In two respects she was distinctly conservative, showing consistent hostility to clerical marriage and a consistent liking for pomp and display in her domestic religious services. On the other hand, she had a clear vested interest in moderate Protestantism, for Catholicism denied her supremacy over the Church and thus diminished her political powers. Calvinism, however, not only rejected so great a degree of political control over the Church, but also seemed to question the right of any woman to govern either Church or state. Elizabeth thus had much to gain in 1559 from a settlement that embraced Protestantism without accepting the radical elements of Genevan doctrine.

The Elizabethan settlement was only achieved after the first great domestic crisis of the reign. In February 1559 three religious bills, concerning the supremacy, uniformity and the suppression of the anti-heresy laws, passed the Commons but were rejected in the Lords. There the balance of power still lay with the surviving Marian bishops, along with the Abbot of Westminster and some Catholic lay peers. The situation was saved by a combination of subtlety and political muscle. The arrests of Bishops White and Watson further weakened a bench of bishops already reduced by natural deaths, while a second version of the supremacy bill sought to sweeten the pill (for both Catholics and Calvinists perhaps) by substituting the title of 'Supreme Governor' for that of 'Supreme Head'. This amended supremacy bill squeezed through the House of Lords, although it took the unexplained absence of Abbot Feckenham to ensure that the uniformity bill negotiated the same passage.

18.1 The Elizabethan religious settlement: a Protestant settlement?

The Act of Supremacy (April 1559). Elizabeth was recognised as 'Supreme Governor' (rather than 'Supreme Head') of the Church of England, with the same powers and prerogatives as her father had enjoyed. All clergymen, civil servants and academics were required to take the Oath of Supremacy. Refusal to do so resulted in loss of offices; a third refusal was punishable as treason.

The Act of Uniformity (April 1559). Attendance at Anglican services was made compulsory. The fine for non-attendance was set at one shilling per offence. Priests refusing to use the Prayer Book were liable to a fine upon the first offence and life imprisonment for a third refusal.

Repeal (April 1559) of those Acts of Mary's reign which had re-established the papal supremacy and reintroduced heresy laws. All religious Acts repealed by Mary's parliaments were duly reinstated.

Royal Injunctions required that images not be honoured, that sermons be preached frequently and that clergy actively preach the royal supremacy, that the English Bible be freely available, and that priests be free to marry.

The Bishops. The government hoped to reach agreement with surviving Marian bishops, but only one (Bishop Kitchen of Llandaff) accepted the Oath of Supremacy. Of the bishops who had to be appointed to replace the Marian dissidents, thirteen had sufficiently Protestant views to have spent Mary's reign in exile.

The Prayer Book. A modified restatement of the 1552 Prayer Book. The wording of the Communion service was deliberately ambiguous, combining the formats of 1549 and 1552, and leaving unresolved the question of transubstantiation. The controversial 'Black Rubric' was withdrawn and an 'Ornaments Rubric' was inserted, prescribing clerical vestments and church decoration.

The Courts of High Commission. Prerogative courts established in the provinces of York and Canterbury, in which civil and ecclesiastical officers, appointed by the crown, ensured that the clergy obeyed royal decisions on ecclesiastical matters.

The Thirty-nine Articles (1562). A revised version of the Forty-two Articles which had been prepared by Northumberland's government before its fall. They preserved the Protestant flavour of the original in many respects: 'We are accounted righteous before God by Faith and not through our own works' (Article XI); 'Predestination to Life is the everlasting purpose of God' (Article XVII). Drawn up in Convocation, the Articles of Religion were embodied in statute law by the Subscription Act of 1571.

CROWN AND PARLIAMENT: COOPERATION OR CONFRONTATION?

Whatever the dynamics behind the phenomenon, the Commons grew in size. Thirty-one new boroughs gained the privilege of returning MPs during Elizabeth's reign, and the House accommodated 462 members by the end of the century. Substantially, the pressure for new parliamentary seats came from the boroughs' noble patrons at court, so the new MPs represented primarily the creation or expansion of governmental or courtly pressure groups. Generally, the MPs sought local rather than national political influence. M.A.R. Graves has confirmed this by emphasising the high degree of absenteeism that marred most parliamentary sessions. Once elected, it seems, many MPs found the business and the pleasures of the capital more attractive than the tedious routine of legislation.

It is hard now to sustain the notion of consistent confrontation between crown and Parliament, for Elizabeth was never in danger of anything more serious than frustration or annoyance at the hands of the House of Commons. On no occasion did the will of that House deflect her from her chosen policy. It could hardly have been otherwise when the Oath of Supremacy excluded from Parliament all serious opponents of the regime, and when she had at her disposal so formidable a range of controls. The House only sat when the Queen wanted or needed it to do so. Apart from the Parliaments of 1559 (which had crucial legal work to do to establish the succession) and of 1572 (specifically summoned to consider the fate of the Queen of Scots), all Elizabethan Parliaments owed their existence to the government's chronic need for money. Even so, Parliament was only in session for 140 weeks in a reign of forty-five years. The crown and its ministers could exert considerable influence over elections to the Commons, and the forty-four members whom Neale perceived as a puritan 'choir' would have been substantially outnumbered by those MPs who owed their places to the court. Once the Commons were elected and sitting, the government still exercised considerable powers over the choice of business and the conduct of debate. Apart from the 'rumours and messages' of royal wishes or displeasure, of which Wentworth complained, the presence of royal ministers in the chamber largely ensured the smooth pursuit of royal aims.

18.2 Elizabeth and her Parliaments: the historical debate

Sir John Neale was for many years the leading authority on the development of Parliament during the reign of Elizabeth. His monumental work *Elizabeth and Her Parliaments* appeared between 1953 and 1957, following his earlier work, *The Elizabethan House of Commons* (1949). The theme of Neale's work, initiated by the work of Wallace Notestein (*The Winning of the Initiative by the House of Commons,* 1924), was that the reign saw the emergence of the Commons as the senior partner in the parliamentary relationship with the crown and the House of Lords. The period also saw the growth of those habits of independence and opposition to the policies of the crown which were to culminate in the civil conflict of the next century. In the puritan 'choir', a concerted party of religious radicals, and in the vociferous claims of such as the Wentworth brothers for the maintenance of the privileges of the House, Neale believed that he saw the forerunners of Pym and of Hampden.

In recent years, however, a new generation of historians has revised this view of Elizabethan parliaments. N.L. Jones (*Faith by Statute: Parliament and the Settlement of Religion, 1559,* 1982) has cast doubt upon the notion of any coordinated puritan opposition group within the Commons. To his work may be added that of M.A.R. Graves (*The Tudor Parliaments: Crown, Lords and Commons,* 1985) and of G.R. Elton (*The Parliaments of England, 1559–1581,* 1986). Their view is that, by writing of Elizabeth's reign with one eye fixed upon the crisis of the next century, Neale had seen opposition where none really existed. When Elizabeth came under pressure, it was not from an increasingly hostile parliamentary middle class, but from a loyal and united governing class which sought to pressurise an indecisive queen into positive action for their mutual benefit and protection. The attempts to find a decisive solution to the problem of the Queen of Scots provide a perfect example of just such a situation.

Concentrating now on the whole range of parliamentary legislation instead of those items which provide links with the seventeenth-century crisis, and upon the whole membership of the Commons instead of a vociferous minority, historians prefer to see a picture of cooperation and community of interest.

One of the most important elements of revision brought about by recent research has been the reappraisal of the significance of the House of Lords during this period. It now seems that the upper chamber continued to play a positive and active role, with between one-third and one-half of all parliamentary legislation between 1571 and 1593 initiated in the Lords. From 1571, the greatest minister of the realm sat in the upper house as Lord Burghley, and from that position he continued his work of managing and directing parliamentary procedure in the royal interest.

The issue of parliamentary privileges, central to the thesis of growing parliamentary independence, is not now regarded as a major element in the history of Elizabeth's parliaments. Such privileges had their origins in a grant from the crown, made so that the business of government should proceed efficiently. Instances such as Paul Wentworth's demand to be allowed to initiate debate on the succession (1566), or his brother Peter's protest at the 'rumours and messages' circulated by the government to encourage or to intimidate MPs (1576), were seen by Neale as essential blows in the battle to maintain the privilege of freedom of speech. To more recent writers, such issues appear rather to have been 'tactless outbursts [by] loners without support' (M.A.R. Graves). Neither initiative came close to success, and it was the Commons themselves who committed Paul Wentworth to prison for his unorthodox views. It is true that, in Smalley's Case (1576), the House upheld the privilege of freedom from arrest by confirming the right of an MP to protect his servant from arrest during a session of Parliament. On the other hand, the House acknowledged in Strickland's Case (1571) and in Fitzherbert's Case (1593) that an MP had no immunity from arrest if the lawsuit were brought by the crown itself.

Nevertheless, one genuine clash of interests arose between Elizabeth and her subjects in Parliament. The controversy that arose in the sessions of 1597 and 1601 over the crown's practice of granting trading monopolies to favoured courtiers in return for large cash sums was, in John Guy's words, 'the ugliest in Parliament during the Tudor period'. It arose purely from the economic damage that these grants did to the trading interests of so many members. Elizabeth met such a barrage of opposition in 1601, from the most troublesome Parliament of

her reign, that she was forced to promise that some monopolies 'should be presently repealed, and none put into execution but such as should first have a trial according to the law for the good of her people'.

PURITANISM: A DEFINITION

The role of puritanism in the parliamentary and religious history of the reign and its links with the revolutionary events of the next century have ensured that it has served as another major focus for historians.

The term 'puritan' seems to have appeared in the mid-1560s as a blanket term of abuse applied to many different groups. Not all puritans were Calvinists, and many of Elizabeth's bishops, including so reliable a servant as Whitgift, were Calvinists without ever being branded as 'puritans'. In the 1560s it was not easy to go beyond the broad definition of a puritan as 'the hotter sort of Protestant'. Yet much common ground existed between the various forms of puritanism that appeared during the reign. Puritans consistently stressed the importance of preaching, thereby emphasising the supreme doctrinal authority of the scriptures. They disapproved of the remnants of Catholic practice and trappings that survived within the Elizabethan Church. The common ideal of the movement was to achieve 'a literate, Bible-reading laity who led godly lives under the direction of a learned ministry purged of popish remnants' (A.G.R. Smith, *Emergence of a Nation State*, 1984).

Was the puritan movement in any real sense in opposition to Queen Elizabeth and her Church? It is easy to find men who were sympathetic to puritanism and yet had the closest links with the government. Among churchmen, Edmund Grindal provides an example, while at the highest levels of government Leicester and Walsingham both acted at court as energetic champions of puritanism. On the other hand, the returning Marian exiles included many who refused to compromise their principles. Coverdale, Foxe and Sampson all refused office because of the 'impurities' they perceived within the Church.

Once the outline of Anglican doctrine had been established, puritan misgivings usually centred

18.3 Elizabeth's Parliaments: A digest of statistics and chart of parliamentary sittings

Year Parliament summoned	Total no. of seats	New boroughs created	% of MPs who sat in previous Parliament	No. of MPs holding govt office	MPs elected through influence of 'great man'	Privy Councillors sitting as MPs	% of MPs with some recorded activity	MPs known to have been in exile during Mary's reign
1559	402	4	27	76	92	Cave, Cecil, Dudley, Knollys, Mason, Parry, Petre, Rogers, Sackville, Sadler (10)	7	19
1563	420	7	31	100	130	Cave, Cecil, Knollys, Mason, Mildmay, Petre, Rogers, Sackville, Sadler (9)	23	27
1571	438	9	28	88	124	Croft, Knollys, Mildmay, Sadler, Smith (5)	32	17
1572	440	1	40	136	139	Croft, Hatton, Knollys, Mildmay, Sadler, Smith, Walsingham, Wilson, Sidney (9)	51	20
1584	460	10	28	89	131	Croft, Hatton, Knollys, Mildmay, Sadler, Walsingham (6)	38	9
1586	462	1	52	90	113	Croft, Davison, Hatton, Knollys, Mildmay, Sadler, Walsingham, Wolley (8)	31	6
1589	462	—	42	93	129	Croft, Fortescue, Heneage, Knollys, Mildmay, Perrot, Walsingham, Wolley (8)	32	6
1593	462	—	37	91	131	R. Cecil, Fortescue, Heneage, Knollys, Wolley (5)	59	3
1597	462	—	32	76	122	R. Cecil, Fortescue, Knollys (3)	58	—
1601	462	—	36	109	129	R. Cecil, Fortescue, Herbert, Knollys, Stanhope (5)	49	—

Source: P.W. Hasler, *History of Parliament: The Commons, 1558–1603*, London, 1981

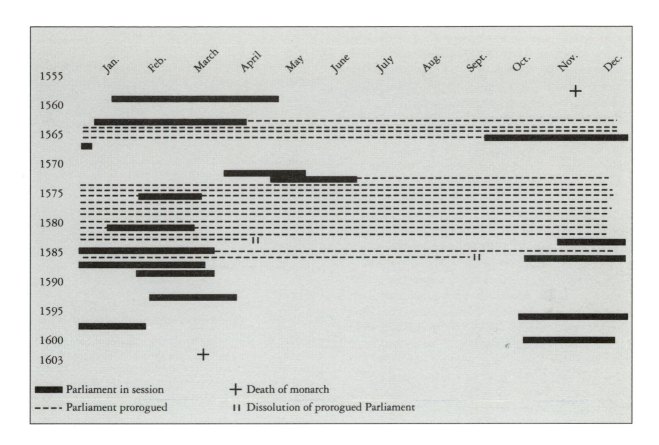

	Jan.	Feb.	March	April	May	June	July	Aug.	Sept.	Oct.	Nov.	Dec.

Parliament in session ▬▬▬   + Death of monarch
Parliament prorogued - - - -   ‖ Dissolution of prorogued Parliament

upon issues of Church government. Throughout her reign, Elizabeth successfully resisted any attempt to invade her royal prerogative in such matters, and viewed those who challenged her ecclesiastical authority with as much hostility as she viewed more overtly political enemies. A hierarchically minded monarch consistently mistrusted the puritans' freedom of mind. Elizabeth was in full agreement with her Bishop of Lichfield, who told a puritan arraigned before him in 1570 that 'the papists are afraid to stir or say anything, but you are wonderful presumptuous and bold, and fear no man, and you disquiet us and the whole state more than papists'.

THE CHURCH AND PURITANISM

The Vestiarian phase

By 1563 the form of the Anglican Church was still sufficiently vague to hold out hope for the returning exiles. Indeed, so great was the threat to Protestantism from its Roman enemies that the wisest course for those who wished to see further reform seemed to be to 'tarry for the magistrate'. They advocated patience and tact until the existing political authorities saw fit to proceed further towards 'godly' reformation. The first onward steps were taken within the Church hierarchy. At its session of 1563, as well as ensuring the acceptance of the Articles of Religion, puritans in the southern Convocation put forward Six Articles which summarised their disciplinary programme. They sought to ensure that the number of holy days should be reduced, and that only Sundays and the principal feasts of the Church should be observed; that priests should conduct the services clearly; that the sign of the cross should be discontinued in the baptism service; that kneeling at Communion should not be compulsory; that priests should not be compelled to wear the prescribed Anglican vestments; that music should not be used in services. It was a relatively moderate manifesto, but to Elizabeth and some of her bishops its moderation was irrelevant. The very fact of 'grass-roots' interference with a settlement which belonged properly to the royal prerogative was outrageous in the queen's eyes. The proposals were narrowly defeated, very largely by the votes of those connected with the royal interest.

Puritan controversy over the next few years centred ostensibly around the question of what vestments a priest should wear during the performance of his duties – the vestiarian controversy. To both parties, however, there was a great deal more at stake than vestments. Elizabeth demanded conformity as a matter of political principle, and the government's main weapon was the set of Advertisements issued by Archbishop Parker in 1566. They required all newly ordained priests 'to observe such order and uniformity in all external policy, rites and ceremonies of the Church, as by the laws and orders are already well provided and established'. Nevertheless, the issue raged for two or three years, especially in London and at the universities. There was also some evidence that some were no longer disposed to 'tarry for the magistrate', for in 1567 about one hundred people were brought before the High Commission for worshipping privately after the Genevan fashion at Plumbers' Hall in London.

The challenge of presbyterianism

The government's campaign for conformity had a dual effect. It frightened some of the faint-hearted into obedience, but demonstrated at the same time that, whatever their earlier connections with Geneva or Zurich, the bishops were now primarily the agents of the queen's religious settlement.

Cambridge University provided the stage for the next development. In a sensational series of lectures on the Acts of the Apostles, the Professor of Divinity, Thomas Cartwright, systematically criticised the constitution of the Anglican Church, advocating Genevan alternatives. Bishops should be deprived of all political roles and should be restricted to purely spiritual duties; Church government should be placed in the hands of a local presbytery, a body of local ministers and elders; ministers should be appointed by the congregation; the system should be overseen by a provincial assembly or 'classis', composed of representatives of the local congregations.

18.4 Elizabethan churchmen and their opponents

Bishops

BANCROFT, Richard (1544–1610). Cambridge graduate and noted preacher. Treasurer of St Paul's (1585). Bishop of London (1588). Major support of the ageing Whitgift and his successor as Archbishop of Canterbury (1604). Active opponent of puritanism and presbyterianism.

COX, Richard (1500–81). Headmaster of Eton, and tutor to Prince/King Edward (1544–50). Imprisoned by Mary (1553) and subsequently in exile in Frankfurt (1554–8). Bishop of Norwich (1559) and of Ely (1559–80).

GRINDAL, Edmund (?1519–83). Chaplain to Nicholas Ridley and to Edward VI. In exile during Mary's reign in Strasbourg and Germany. Bishop of London (1558). Archbishop of York (1570). Archbishop of Canterbury (1576). Suspended (1577–83) for refusing Elizabeth's orders to suppress 'prophesyings'.

JEWEL, John (1522–71). Oxford graduate. In exile in Mary's reign in Strasbourg and Zurich. Bishop of Salisbury (1559). A major publicist for the Elizabethan Church, notably in *Apologia Ecclesiae Anglicanae* (1562).

PARKER, Matthew (1504–75). Graduate of Cambridge, where he developed Lutheran sympathies. Chaplain to Anne Boleyn and later to Henry VIII. Vice-chancellor of Cambridge University (1545), but deprived by Mary. Archbishop of Canterbury (1559) and leading architect of Elizabeth's religious settlement.

WHITGIFT, John (?1530–1604). Master of Trinity College, Cambridge, and Regius Professor of Divinity. Bishop of Worcester (1577). Vice-president of the Council of the Welsh Marches (1577–80) and active in Courts of High Commission. Archbishop of Canterbury (1583). Privy Councillor (1587). Author of Lambeth Articles on religious uniformity (1595).

Puritan Critics of the Settlement

CARTWRIGHT, Thomas (1535–1603). Lady Margaret Professor of Divinity at Cambridge (1569). Deprived for preaching against role of bishops in Anglican Church (1570). In exile (1571–6, 1580–5, 1595–8). Returned under patronage of Leicester, but imprisoned (1590–2).

FIELD, John (?1545–88). Assisted Foxe in his research for *Book of Martyrs*. Convenor, with Thomas Wilcox, of the London conference of ministers (1570s and 1580s) which sought reorganisation of the Church on presbyterian lines. Co-author of Admonition to Parliament (1572).

FOXE, John (1517–87). In exile in Geneva (1554), Strasbourg (1554) and Basle (1555). Upon return to England he published *Acts and Monuments* (otherwise known as Foxe's *Book of Martyrs*) in Latin (1559), then in English (1563), with a revised, enlarged and illustrated edition (1570).

Catholic Critics of the Settlement

ALLEN, William (1532–94). Oxford graduate, later ordained as Catholic priest. In exile in Low Countries (1561 and 1565). Active among Catholics in Lancashire (1562–5). Founded college for English missionary priests at Douai (1568) and was thus active in Catholic missions to Elizabethan England. Cardinal (1587).

CAMPION, Edmund (1540–81). Ordained in Anglican Church (1569), but joined Allen in Douai (1571). Entered Society of Jesus (1573). Missionary priest in Lancashire (1580). Author of *Ten Reasons*, justifying Catholic doctrine (1581). Betrayed and executed (1 December 1581).

PARSONS, Robert (1546–1610). Jesuit. Arrived in England with Campion (1580) and worked extensively in Northamptonshire, Derbyshire, Worcestershire and Gloucestershire. Fled to France upon Campion's capture (1581). Rector of English College in Rome (1588 and 1596 onwards).

Cartwright was duly deprived of his professorship, but his intervention had placed the question of Church government at centre stage, and had indicated no place in his system for the royal supremacy. Another forty years were to pass before James I drew his simple equation, 'No bishops, no king,' but so subtle a politician as Elizabeth needed no prompting to see that the threat to the ecclesiastical hierarchy only thinly veiled a threat to its political equivalent.

This 'presbyterian' theme was taken up in the third and fourth Parliaments of Elizabeth's reign. In 1571, the MP for Scarborough, William Strickland, was suspended from the Commons for proposing a reform of the Prayer Book which the government interpreted as 'a bill against the prerogative of the queen'. The government ordered that no further religious bills should be presented to the House without the prior approval of the Church authorities. Thwarted in their attempts at legislation, the puritan leaders turned instead to a public appeal through the medium of Parliament. An Admonition to the Parliament (June 1572), probably the work of John Field and Thomas Wilcox, sparked off a period of fierce controversy through the pulpit and the printing press. Yet, with the memory of the rising of the Northern Earls still fresh and with the papal bull of excommunication resurrecting fears of a Catholic conspiracy, this was not a good time to risk accusations of disloyalty to the queen, or to open divisions in the ranks of 'besieged' Protestantism. Even veterans of vestiarianism distanced themselves from this new bout of puritan pressure.

Prophesying, classicalism and decline

Church–state relations from the mid-1570s to the early 1580s were dominated by an issue which well illustrates the ambiguous nature of the government's attitude towards puritanism. 'Prophesyings' were meetings of the lower clergy within a district, called for the purpose of scriptural discussion. The primary aim was clerical education, but such were the attractions of religious disputation that substantial crowds of laymen were known to travel some distance to attend. In some cases the Prayer Book and the organisation of the established Church came under fire.

This, of course, was something that the Supreme Governor could not tolerate. She instructed Parker (1574) and his successor, Edmund Grindal, to suppress such meetings. Convinced of the need for a more learned clergy, Grindal resisted the queen's demand, and his bold opposition stands out as the last major attempt by the Anglican hierarchy to resist the Erastian authority of the temporal Head. Yet the state maintained the upper hand. Grindal was suspended from all his administrative functions (June 1577) and remained so until his death in 1583. Although the bishops of the southern Convocation were instructed to suppress 'prophesyings' in their own dioceses, their continuation in the north further demonstrated the practical limitations upon the powers of the Supreme Governor.

Grindal's own successor, John Whitgift, had left the Cambridge puritanism of his youth behind him and was now completely loyal to the Church hierarchy and to the royal supremacy. In particular, he had been closely associated since 1572 with the Court of High Commission. Whitgift's first set of Articles (1583) had two aims, making moderate concessions to reform while seeking to impose conformity. The clergy were required to acknowledge the royal supremacy, accept the exclusive use of the existing Prayer Book, and accept the Thirty-nine Articles of Faith. Nearly 400 clergymen initially refused the articles, and puritan sympathisers on the Council forced the archbishop to produce a modified version of his requirements. Similarly, Whitgift produced his Twenty-four Questions (1584) to be put to suspect clergymen by the High Commission.

This new show of force by the authorities may have been one reason for a renewed burst of puritan activity. The 1584 Parliament received petitions against clergymen whose 'drunkenness, filthiness of life, gaming at cards, haunting of alehouses, and

18.5 The controversy over prophesyings

Source A. It is judged meet [i.e. fitting] by the brethren that the Prophecy be kept every Monday in Christ's Church in Norwich, at nine of the clock in the morning till eleven, if there be speakers to fill that time. Let all the speakers be careful to keep them to the text; abstaining from annoying allegations of profane histories [and] having always care to show the sense of the Holy Ghost.

As it shall be free for any godly-learned brother to lay forth any fruitful matter revealed unto him out of the text, so it is most requisite that they do it not rashly, disorderly, but soberly and reverently as in the presence of God. Let none be suffered [i.e. allowed] to speak in the prophecy except [i.e. unless] he will submit himself to the orders that are or shall be set down hereafter by the consent of the brethren.

From The Orders to Be Observed in This Exercise of Prophesying, published in Norwich, 1575

Source B. These orders of exercise [i.e. an alternative name for prophesyings] offered to me by the learned of the clergy of Hertfordshire I think true and godly, and greatly making to the furtherance of true doctrine and the increase of godly knowledge in them that are not as yet able to preach. Therefore I earnestly exhort and require all such as will not show themselves to be backward in religion and hinderers of the truth, diligently to observe the same and resort unto the exercise.

Nevertheless, I require that you admit not any to be president or moderator in that exercise but that I, upon particular trial, shall allow the same. Nor shall you permit any stranger to speak among you but such as you know will stay himself within the compass of these orders, and not break them to the defaming of the present state of the Church of England.

Grant of permission for the conduct of prophesyings by Thomas Cooper, Bishop of Lincoln, 1574

Source C. We hear to our great grief that in sundry parts of our realm there be no small number of persons, presuming to be teachers and preachers of the Church, which, contrary to our laws established for the public divine service of Almighty God, do daily devise and put in execution sundry new rites and forms in the Church, as well by their preaching, reading and ministering the sacraments, as by procuring unlawful assemblies of a great number of our people to be hearers of their disputations and new devised opinions upon points of divinity far and unmeet [i.e. unsuitable] for unlearned people, which manner of invasions they in some places call prophesying and in other places exercises.

And furthermore considering for the great abuses that have been in sundry places of our realm by reason of the foresaid assemblies, we will and straitly [i.e. strictly] charge the same forthwith to cease and not to be used.

From Queen's Elizabeth's letter suppressing prophesyings, May 1577

Source D. And so to come to the present case. I cannot marvel enough how this strange opinion should once enter into your mind that it should be good for the Church to have few preachers. Alas, Madam, is the scripture any more plain in any one thing than that the Gospel of Christ should be plentifully preached?

such like' made them a shame to the Church, while Turner's 'Bill and Book' advocated the replacement of the 1559 Prayer Book by another on Genevan lines. This, and a similar proposal by Sir Anthony Cope (February 1585), was obviously far too advanced an idea to stand any chance of success.

This renewed parliamentary activity would have been impossible, however, without substantial organisation in the localities. These early days of Whitgift's archiepiscopate were notable for the flourishing in London, Essex and some of the midland counties of what became known as the 'classis' movement. A 'classis' was a meeting of the puritan clergy of a given district. The first such meetings seem to have been held in the mid-1570s, and they probably had their roots in the 'prophesyings' of that period. Above these 'classes' stood provincial synods attended by delegates from the local units, and on at least two occasions a national synod was held, in London (1586) and in

Now for the second point, which is concerning the learned exercise and conference among the ministers of the Church: I have consulted with diverse of my brethren the bishops by letters, who think the same as I do: a thing most profitable to the Church, and therefore expedient to be continued.

And now being sorry that I have been so long and tedious to your Majesty, I will draw to an end, most humbly praying the same well to consider these two short petitions following.

The first is that you will refer all these ecclesiastical matters which toucheth religion, or the doctrine or discipline of the Church, to the bishops and divines of your realm. The second petition that I have to make to your Majesty is this: that when you deal in matters of faith and religion, you would not use to pronounce so resolutely and peremptorily, as from authority, but always remember that in God's causes the will of God, and not the will of any earthly creature, is to take place. It is the antichristian voice of the pope, 'So I will have it; so I command; let my will stand for a reason.' Remember, Madam, that you are a mortal creature.

From Archbishop Grindal's letter to Queen Elizabeth, December 1576

Source E. That none be permitted to preach, read, catechize, minister the sacraments, or execute any other ecclesiastical function, unless he consent and subscribe to these Articles following:

1. That her Majesty, under God, hath, and ought to have, the sovereignty and rule over all manner of persons born within her realms, either ecclesiastical or temporal.
2. That the Book of Common Prayer, and of ordering [i.e. ordaining] bishops, priests and deacons, containeth in it nothing contrary to the word of God, and that he himself will use the said book prescribed in public prayer and administration of the sacraments, and none other.
3. That he alloweth the book of [39] Articles, agreed upon by the archbishops and bishops of both provinces, and the whole clergy in the Convocation holden in London in the year of our Lord God 1562, and that he believeth all the Articles therein contained to be agreeable to the word of God.

The Three Articles of Archbishop Whitgift, 1583

QUESTIONS

a. What different attitudes are shown in these documents to the importance of preaching in the services of the Church? How would you explain these differences of opinions?

b. To what extent do sources A and B support Elizabeth's claims in source C that prophesyings were subversive?

c. On the strength of sources D and E, compare the priorities of Grindal and Whitgift as Archbishops of Canterbury.

d. On the strength of these documents, what do you think the controversy over prophesyings was really about?

Cambridge (1587). Certainly this was a 'church within a church', and Claire Cross's judgement is that 'for a few years something approaching a Presbyterian alternative to the established Church existed in embryo'.

The classis movement seems to have been at its peak about 1586–8, but the next five years were to witness an abrupt decline in the puritan cause. In part this was due to the coincidental deaths of many of the leading actors in the drama. John Field, who had coordinated and directed the 'classes' in London, died in 1588. The death between 1588 and 1591 of Leicester, Walsingham and Mildmay also removed some of the puritans' leading sympathisers on the Privy Council, leaving Whitgift in a commanding position.

Tactical errors also served to blunt the impact of puritanism during this period. In 1588–9 there appeared a new outburst of scurrilous and satirical tracts attacking the bishops and the government of the Church. Of these, the tracts bearing the *nom de plume* 'Martin Marprelate' were the most biting. They not only provoked a hostile government response, but also divided puritans by their violence. At the same time, more radical movements appeared to the left of puritanism. The 1580s saw the development of true Separatism, or Congregationalism, whose leaders, such as Robert Browne, Henry Barrow and John Greenwood, rejected the whole principle of a national Church in which compulsion drew in non-believers alongside the truly godly. In its place they advocated godly communities, 'gathered together' out of the world, bound to one another by covenant, and taught and guided by their own elected ministers. Browne seems to have established the first such community in Norwich in 1580 or 1581, and in 1582 he published his *Treatise of Reformation without Tarrying for Any*. The first executions of separatists were carried out in 1583, and the execution ten years later of Greenwood and Barrow effectively ended the Separatist movement in England, driving survivors to seek safety in the Netherlands and eventually in the New World.

THE SOCIETY AND ECONOMY OF ELIZABETHAN ENGLAND

Prices and population

Traditionally the second half of the sixteenth century has been associated by English historians with economic expansion and social dynamism. Recent research confirms that the Elizabethan age was one, first, of great economic upheaval and, second, of considerable adaptation and initiative to counter its effects.

At the basis of such upheaval lay a steady increase in England's population after a period of stagnation. The country continued to suffer from those factors which traditionally limited population-growth. The reign saw major outbreaks of plague in London (1563), Norwich (1579, 1584, 1589–92), Bristol (1565, 1575) and other cities, and further sickness and bad harvests in the latter part of the 1580s brought the death-rate in many parts of the country roughly level with the birth-

rate. Overall, however, the average mortality-rate between 1566 and 1586 was lower than for any subsequent period until the beginning of the nineteenth century. The consequent increase in population was not uniform, and modern methods of calculating it remain imperfect, yet the most widely accepted figures are probably those produced by E.A. Wrigley and R.S. Schofield and included in Illustration 18.6.

While England's population-boom was unusual, the great price inflation which accompanied it was a European phenomenon. The precise causes of English inflation remain unclear. While some bullion from the New World was diverted by state and by private activity into the English economy, it has not been satisfactorily demonstrated that the quantities were sufficient to have so dramatic an impact. On the other hand, pressure was certainly placed upon English food resources by increased population and by fluctuations in the harvests. In addition, debasement in the 1540s increased the money supply in England, perhaps from about £1.23 million of coin in early 1544 to about £2.66 million in mid-1551, before the Elizabethan rebasement reduced the supply once more. It is hard to go further at present than to accept a complex package of causes 'which includes war expenditure, land sales, debasement and bad harvests, features of the period of most rapid price increases in the 1540s, 1550s and 1590s' (R.B. Outhwaite, *Inflation in Tudor and Stuart England*, 1969).

The legislative response

The government's response to these pressures was characteristically conservative, an attempt to steer society and its economy back to familiar ground. Most successful in the long term were the measures to rebase and revalue the currency. The queen's ministers stuck closely to the example set in the two previous reigns, but their achievement was of the first importance. Debased silver coinage was called in over a period of some months in 1560–1 and reissued at the same standard as in 1544. Camden's claim that this was Elizabeth's 'greatest glory', while exaggerated, at least illustrates the importance that contemporaries attached to the revaluation.

18.6 The Elizabethan economy: a digest of statistics

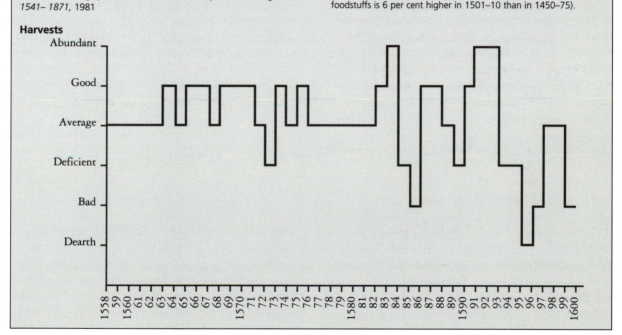

Population

Year	Population (millions)	% increase/decrease
1541	2.77	
1546	2.85	2.9
1551	3.01	5.5
1556	3.16	4.9
1561	2.98	−5.5
1566	3.13	4.8
1571	3.27	4.6
1576	3.41	5.4
1581	3.59	5.4
1586	3.81	5.7
1591	3.89	2.4
1596	4.01	2.9
1601	4.11	2.4
1606	4.25	3.5
1611	4.41	3.8

Source: E.A. Wrigley and R.S. Schofield, *The Population of England, 1541– 1871*, 1981

Prices and wages index (1450–75 = 100)

Period	Foodstuffs	Industrial goods	Wages
1491–1500	100	97	101
1501–10	106	98	101
1511–20	116	102	101
1521–30	159	110	106
1531–40	161	110	110
1541–50	217	127	118
1551–60	315	186	160
1561–70	298	218	177
1571–80	341	223	207
1581–90	389	230	203
1591–1600	530	238	219
1601–10	527	256	219

Source: E.H. Phelps-Brown and S.V. Hopkins.
Note: Changes are indicated by comparison with prices and wages in 1450–75, which are indicated as 100. (e.g. the price of basic foodstuffs is 6 per cent higher in 1501–10 than in 1450–75).

Harvests

The Parliaments of the reign also produced a steady flow of social and economic legislation aimed to alleviate the social dislocation caused by these problems. This legislation forms the basis for the traditionally paternalist reputation enjoyed by the Elizabethan regime, and was particularly prolific in the last two decades of the century. Thirteen bills were introduced into Parliament between 1576 and 1601 on the subject of drunkenness alone, while seventeen bills in the session of 1597–8 dealt with one aspect or another of poverty.

Perhaps, however, the Elizabethan state does not quite deserve its paternalist reputation. Apart from the measures listed in illustration 18.7, much of the initiative in poor relief seems to have come from the localities. Compulsory poor rates existed in London,

18.7 Elizabethan social and economic legislation

1563 **Act Regarding Tillage.** Sought to prevent depopulation by ordering that all land under tillage for four years since 1528 must remain so. Allowed no further conversion from tillage to pasture.

Alms Act. Any person refusing his bishop's exhortation to give alms might be prosecuted before a JP and imprisoned. This was the first attempt to apply compulsion in English poor relief.

Statute of Artificers. Major body of legislation on the regulation of industry and agriculture. Guild apprenticeship system was applied throughout the realm, with seven-year apprenticeships compulsory in urban crafts. Instructed JPs to fix wage rates in line with prices (subject to the approval of the Privy Council) and established maximum wage levels.

1571 **Act Sanctioning Usury.** Repealed 1552 legislation against moneylending, and established maximum interest rate at 10 per cent.

1572 **Poor Relief Act.** Sought to check vagabondage by imposing severe penalties. JPs were to register local paupers and to raise a local poor rate for the housing and care of crippled and aged paupers.

1576 **Act for the Relief of the Poor.** Town authorities were to provide materials for the productive employment of the able-bodied poor. Houses of correction were to be established for the punishment of those who refused to work.

1597–8 **Act for Repairing Houses of Husbandry.** Provided for the repair of rural dwellings which had fallen into decay, and where agriculture had ceased to be practised.

Act for the Relief of the Poor. Ordered JPs to appoint Overseers of the Poor in each parish, who were to provide work for the able-bodied poor and relief for the infirm. Funds were provided by a compulsory poor rate paid by members of the parish. This act was in force until 1834.

Act for the Punishment of Rogues. JPs authorised to establish houses of correction for vagabonds and for other able-bodied paupers who refused to work.

Act Regarding Cloth. Regulated cloth manufacture north of the Trent.

(A total of seventeen bills in this session addressed issues of poverty and disorder.)

Ipswich and York from the 1540s, with a particularly sophisticated system in Norwich. Many local workhouses also existed before the act of 1576. The parliamentary legislation itself also owed much to the zeal of private members. Besides, Elizabethan legislation was not necessarily very widely implemented, and research at a local level reveals that it was sidestepped or ignored as local circumstances dictated. Paul Slack (*Vagrants and Vagrancy in Tudor England*, 1974) has dismissed the impact of compulsory poor rates as slight, while W.K. Jordan (*Philanthropy in England, 1480–1660*, 1959) has shown that private charitable endowments continued well beyond the Reformation, probably raising much more substantial sums than were raised by the Poor Laws. Such evidence leads to the conclusion stated by Peter Ramsey that, in this respect, 'the statute book is a record of pious hopes rather than of actual achievement'.

Agriculture

Despite the increasing demand for food, real famine remained a rarity in Elizabethan England, as agriculture responded to meet the increased demand. Once more, enclosures were a feature of agricultural adjustment, especially in ten midland counties. Led by Lawrence Stone, recent historians have tended to see these enclosures as a positive reaction to population pressure, rather than as a manifestation of landlords' greed. After the hectic repetition of old anti-enclosure legislation in the first half of the century, no new laws on the subject were passed between 1565 and 1593, which suggests that contemporaries were coming to appreciate the benefits of the process. The modern consensus is that 'enclosures of open fields were after 1550 increasingly enclosures for more efficient arable farming than for pasture, were increasingly by agreement between farmers, and produced little friction outside the inner Midlands' (D.M. Palliser).

Other major innovations of these years included enhancing the productivity of existing ploughlands by liming – a method of treating acid soils – and marling – treating the soil with clay. In the 1590s the practice spread of 'floating' water meadows, allowing the temporary flooding of pasture land to improve subsequent yields of grass and hay. Moorland in Cumbria and Wales and drained fenland in East Anglia also came into agricultural use for the first time.

TRADE AND INDUSTRY

In the 1930s the American economic historian J.U. Nef (*Rise of the British Coal Industry*, 1932), went so far as to claim that the industrial development of this period in England constituted a veritable 'industrial revolution'. His claim was based largely upon figures for the increase in coal production and upon the stimulating effect of this fuel supply on the iron industry. The debate that such claims provoked has levelled out into the sort of compromise expressed by D.M. Palliser: 'If a Tudor industrial revolution is an exaggerated concept, at least one can discern the slow beginnings of a long-term prelude to the revolution of the eighteenth century.'

The Elizabethan domestic economy was indeed subject to a range of stimuli. The mining industry was stimulated by the legal decision (1568) that minerals found beneath the ground, other than gold and silver, belonged by right to the owners of the soil, and the industry came to be dominated for generations by noblemen and other landowners. Political events in the Low Countries drove many Protestant weavers into exile in England, where they helped to inject new life into the domestic textile trades. Probably the most important general stimulus, however, was the increase in population, which in some regions created a workforce too large to be absorbed by traditional agricultural employment.

Textile manufacturing maintained its status as the mainstay both of domestic production and of the export trade. With the export of raw wool to the Continent increasingly replaced in the first half of the sixteenth century by the export of semi-finished cloth, the industry was England's largest industrial employer in the latter part of the century. The industry also underwent a process of diversification in these years. The so-called 'new draperies' resulted largely from the settlement of Protestant refugees in such towns as Norwich and Canterbury in the 1560s and 1570s. They added many new varieties, often cheaper, lighter and more colourful, to the staple fare of English woollens. Stimulated by the introduction of the knitting frame by William Lee in about 1590, the stocking knitting industry was estimated to employ as many as 100,000 workers in the early years of the seventeenth century. Exports increased by some 600 per cent between the 1450s and the 1640s, and it is probable that domestic consumption increased substantially at the same time.

Against this element of continuity, a range of novel developments took place. In particular, J.U. Nef estimated that, although only 33,000 tons of coal were shipped from the Tyne in 1563–4, the quantity had risen by 1597–8 to 163,000 tons. Throughout the country as a whole, coal production had risen from 170,000 tons per year in the 1550s to roughly 2.5 million tons by the 1680s. Recent research has also indicated significant increases in the amount of iron ore mined in England and Wales and in the mining of lead.

Another 'school' of historians has argued, however, that it is misleading to study the economic history of Elizabethan England primarily in terms of industries which acquired their greatest importance over 200 years later. They have drawn attention instead to a range of other industries established in the second half of the century, often stimulated by the expertise of foreign craftsmen bringing their skills to England. These include the mining of copper and the manufacture of brass in the Lake District and the growth of paper production in Kent. Chester, York and Nottingham became important centres of leather production, and it was in this period that Sheffield established its reputation for the manufacture of cutlery and other metal goods.

Despite the emphasis placed by many writers earlier in this century upon the intercontinental

NEWCASTLE
COAL

SALT

YORK
WOOLLEN
CLOTH

METALWARE

SALT
COAL

CHESTER

YARMOUTH

LYNN
NORWICH

IRON
SHREWSBURY

WOOLLEN
CLOTH

METALWARE
COVENTRY

GLASS

SILK
COLCHESTER

COAL
IRON
OXFORD

WOOLLEN
CLOTH

COAL

BRISTOL

LONDON

CANTERBURY

IRON
COAL
GLASS

LACE

WOOLLEN
CLOTH
EXETER

LACE

TIN
PLYMOUTH

COAL Regions of specialised industrial production   ■ Towns with a population of more than 5,000   ⸛⸛⸛ Area producing the best-quality wool

18.8 *The English domestic economy in the second half of the sixteenth century*

exploits of English seamen and explorers, England's foreign trade in the latter part of the sixteenth century continued to be dominated by the export of woollen textiles, and the vast bulk of those textiles continued to be sold to markets relatively close at hand on the European mainland. Even when the political turmoil in the Netherlands made Antwerp and other ports less secure and less attractive to English merchants, the search for alternative markets led most English traders the short distance to the ports of northern Germany, or to such French ports as Rouen or La Rochelle. At the turn of the century nearly 90 per cent of English exports went to destinations in Europe, while twenty years into the new century London still derived as little as 6 per cent of her imports from Asia or America. Even the more spectacular overseas enterprises were conceived largely in terms of this traditional trade in textiles. Hakluyt's great work of propaganda for England's overseas expansion (*Principal Navigations*, 1589) admitted that the prime motives of English voyages of discovery were initially 'to find out ample vent of our woollen cloth'.

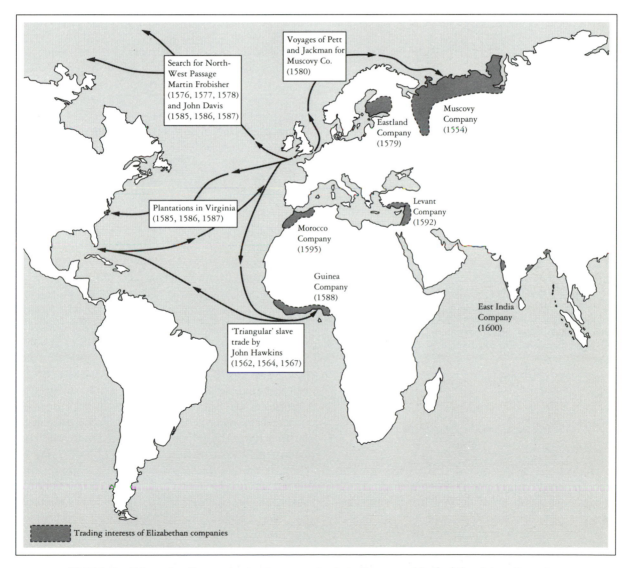

18.9(a) English exploration and extra-European trade in the second half of the sixteenth century

18.9(b) Elizabethan overseas trade and voyages of discovery

DAVIS, John (1543–1605). Commanded expedition seeking north-west passage to China (1585), reaching Greenland and Baffin Island. Discovered Falkland Islands (1593) and sailed to East Indies (1598).

DRAKE, Sir Francis (c.1543–96). Cousin of John Hawkins, whom he accompanied on slave-trading expeditions. Undertook voyages aimed at intercepting supplies of New World bullion to Spain (1570–1, 1572 and 1577–80). Knighted (1591). Queen's Admiral with permission to carry out attacks upon Spanish shipping (1585). Led attack on Cadiz which delayed the sailing of the Armada (1587). Served against the Armada (1588). Died on a further expedition with Hawkins against the Spaniards.

FROBISHER, Sir Martin (?1535–94). Participated in expedition to Guinea (1554) and later explored Greenland. Knighted for his service against the Armada (1588). Vice-Admiral of Hawkins's expedition in 1590.

GILBERT, Sir Humphrey (?1539–83). Educated at Oxford. Served in Ireland (1569). Knighted for services in Munster (1571). Founded colony of St John's, Newfoundland (1583). Lost in shipwreck off the Azores.

HAWKINS, Sir John (1532–95). Pioneer of the 'triangular' slave trade between Africa and the New World (1562–3, 1564–5, 1567–8). Attacked by Spanish forces at St Juan de Ulua (1568). MP for Plymouth (1571). Appointed Treasurer and Comptroller of the Navy (1577), and in these offices did much to prepare the navy to meet the Armada. Knighted during Armada campaign (1588). Died at sea accompanying Drake's final expedition.

RALEGH, Sir Walter (?1552–1618). Educated at Oxford. Prominent courtier, and rival to Earl of Essex. Commanded forces in Munster (1580). Lord Lieutenant of Cornwall (1583). MP for Devon (1584). Organised unsuccessful settlement of Virginia (1585–6). Led expedition to Manoa (1595). Played leading role in the attack on Cadiz (1596), and in expedition against the Azores (1597). Losing favour under James I, he was eventually executed as the result of court intrigues.

ELIZABETHAN IRELAND

In its dealings with Ireland, Elizabeth's government departed significantly from earlier Tudor policies. Instead of accepting that Ireland consisted of a series of border lordships, which could only be controlled indirectly and imperfectly, the English government now backed a policy of direct colonisation of Irish territory. In doing so, Elizabeth's government did not seek a solution to the 'Irish problem' so much as create problems that would persist for the next century or more.

English policy towards Ireland in the second half of the sixteenth century was dominated by the concept of 'plantation'. Based upon the assumption that Ireland would only be secure and peaceful if settled by a loyal English population, the policy directly challenged the authority of the Irish chieftains. The creation of 'Queen's County' and 'King's County' under Mary and Philip (1557) involved the confiscation of a large section of Leix and Offaly, to the west of the Pale, from its native lords and its allocation to English settlers. The material rewards offered by plantation ensured that Ireland would no longer be seen mainly as a troublesome, marginal concern. Instead, some of the most able administrators of the reign devoted their attentions to Irish affairs. A cyclical pattern arose whereby the process of plantation created confrontation with the existing holders of the land, which sometimes led to rebellion. The government responded with military expeditions, and where these were successful they created the perfect opportunity for further plantations, setting the process in motion once again.

Under Elizabeth the situation was complicated by two religious factors: the imposition in Ireland of an English, Protestant religious settlement, and the impact in Ireland of the Catholic Counter-Reformation. Much evidence has been uncovered of students from the more prosperous towns of Ireland travelling to study in Continental seminaries before returning to work against the Elizabethan settlement in Ireland. As English foreign policy veered towards hostility with Spain, Ireland once more assumed its role as England's 'Achilles' heel', where native hostility might be exploited by the enemies of the English crown.

The first major challenges to Elizabethan policy centred upon the remote regions of Ulster and the dominant personality of Shane O'Neill. By a combination of frustrating guerrilla warfare and skilful dealings with the English court, O'Neill thwarted the attempts of successive Lords Deputy, the Earl of Sussex and Sir Henry Sidney, to control him until 1567, when he was murdered in a clash with the rival O'Donnell clan. The second major disturbance, in Munster, owed more to the ruthless land-grabbing of an English West Country

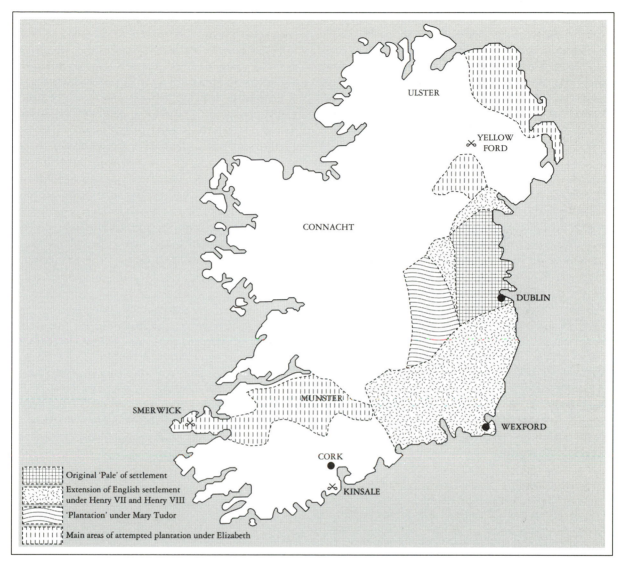

18.10 Tudor Ireland

adventurer, Sir Peter Carew, which threatened the traditional interests of the Butler and Desmond families. The 'Desmond Rebellion' (1569–83) was perhaps the last example of localised noble opposition to the authority of the Tudors, but it also comprised a religious element. A modest force provided by Pope Gregory XIII landed at Smerwick in 1580, where its brutal massacre illustrated very clearly the strategic danger that many Englishmen perceived in Irish affairs.

The failure of these rebellions provided a golden opportunity for Ulster and Munster to be 'planted'

by English settlers. The Earl of Essex encouraged settlement in Antrim (1573) and Sir Thomas Smith launched an unsuccessful project on the Ards peninsula (1572–3). Both elements in this 'enterprise of Ulster' were swept away by the Gaelic opposition that they provoked. In Munster, however, Sir John Perrot established a provincial administration, the Presidency of Munster (1570), on the same lines as the regional councils with which the earlier Tudors had tried to control the more remote areas of England. With the establishment of a similar presidency in Connacht it seemed that later generations of English administrators were achieving a veritable 'Tudor revolution in government' in Ireland.

This was not achieved, however, without one final, and extremely serious, challenge to English authority. The army with which Hugh O'Neill, Earl of Tyrone, launched the 'Ulster Rebellion' in 1598 was by far the largest and best-trained force that the Tudors had ever confronted in Ireland, and O'Neill had cultivated good relations with Spain. The 6,000 men Spain assigned to an Irish expedition in 1601 represented a threat to more than just English control of Ireland.

O'Neill's victory at the Battle of the Yellow Ford (August 1598) raised the possibility that English rule in Ireland might crumble, but the effect was to incite the English government to concentrate its resources as never before upon the pacification of Ireland. Some £2 million was spent upon the restoration of order in Ireland; and, although the initial decision to entrust the task to the Earl of Essex proved to be a disastrous mistake, his successor, Charles Blount, Lord Mountjoy, proved to be the most important influence upon Anglo-Irish politics for a century. He fought winter campaigns where his predecessors had never dared to do so, and he narrowed the base of O'Neill's support by burning and pillaging his territories.

When Mountjoy blockaded the Spanish interventionist force in Kinsale and defeated O'Neill's army in open battle (1601–2), the revolt was doomed, and O'Neill himself finally submitted (March 1603) six days after Elizabeth's death.

It is hard to exaggerate the extent of the sudden political success gained by England in Ireland. James I could realistically claim what no predecessor could, that he was the legitimate heir to the three crowns of England, Scotland and Ireland. Although the 'Irish problem' would re-emerge in later years in other forms, the problems with which the Tudor monarchs had grappled, the clash between English and Gaelic cultures and between royal authority and the privileges of Anglo-Irish magnates, had now been resolved.

Further reading

M.A.R. Graves (1987) *Elizabethan Parliaments, 1559–1601.* London and New York.

C. Haigh (1988) *Elizabeth I.* London and New York.

—— (ed.) (1984) *The Reign of Elizabeth I.* London.

N. Jones (1993) *The Birth of the Elizabethan Age.* Oxford.

D.M. Palliser (1983) *England under Elizabeth* (Social and Economic History of England Series). London and New York.

• CHAPTER NINETEEN •

The England of Elizabeth: The Realm in Danger

Elizabeth's inheritance

The questions of marriage and the succession

The marriage question in Parliament

The bases of Elizabethan foreign policy

Foreign policy

The threat of the Queen of Scots

The revolt of the Northern Earls

English Catholicism

The fall of the Queen of Scots

War with Spain

Conclusions

A classic solution to the problem of projecting an effective royal image for a female monarch. The Armada Portrait, painted c.1590, stylises the queen's physical appearance, but emphasises her authority by her dress, by the presence of the imperial crown, and by her hand resting upon the globe. The defeat and destruction of the Armada are portrayed in the top corners of the painting

Historical investigation of the Elizabethan period has traditionally followed two parallel but very different themes. Historians have found it easy to interpret the period as one in which constitutional and economic foundations were laid for future greatness and prosperity. On the other hand, the evident weakness of the state at the time of the queen's accession has created a theme which concentrates upon the slow establishment of national security over the next thirty years. This is the process with which this chapter is concerned.

19.1 Courtiers and statesmen

BURGHLEY, William Cecil, Lord (1520–98). Educated at Cambridge, served in household of Henry VIII and pursued successful legal career. Secretary to Somerset (1549). Secretary of State (1550–3). Knighted (1551). Secretary of State (1558–72). Master of Court of Wards (1561). Baron Burghley (1571). Lord Treasurer (1572–98). MP for Stamford (1549), Lincolnshire (1555 and 1559) and Northants (1562).

CECIL, Robert (1563–1612). Son of William Cecil, Lord Burghley. Served on major diplomatic missions to France (1584–7) and Spanish Netherlands (1588). Knighted (1591). Secretary of State (1596–1608), instrumental in accession of James I (1603). Earl of Salisbury (1605). MP for Westminster (1588, 1593, 1597 and 1601).

ESSEX, Robert Devereux, Earl of (1566–1601). Educated at Cambridge. Master of the Horse (1588). Knighted (1589). Commanded forces in support of Henry of Navarre (1591–2), against Spain at Cadiz (1596), and in Ireland (1599). Governor General of Ireland (1599). A fierce factional rival of Cecil, he abandoned his post in Ireland to return to court and was charged with dereliction of duty (1600). For leading a rising against the government, he was charged with treason and executed.

LEICESTER, Robert Dudley, Earl of (1532–88). Son of John Dudley, Duke of Northumberland. Implicated with his father in the proclamation of Jane Grey as queen (1553), but pardoned by Mary. Knighted by Elizabeth (1559) and appointed to Privy Council. Created Earl of Leicester (1564). Implicated in Revolt of the Northern Earls (1569) and temporarily lost the royal favour. Commander of English forces aiding the Dutch rebels (1585). Governor of the United Provinces (1586–8).

MILDMAY, Sir Walter (?1520–89). Lawyer educated at Cambridge. Surveyor-General of the Court of Augmentations (1545). Knighted (1547). Directed issue of new coinage (1560). Chancellor of the Exchequer (1566). Founded Emmanuel College, Cambridge, as a puritan institution (1585). Commissioner at trial of Mary Stuart (1586).

WALSINGHAM, Sir Francis (1532–90). Educated at Cambridge. In exile during Mary's reign, in Italy, Germany and Switzerland. Ambassador to France (1570–2). Secretary of State with responsibility for foreign affairs (1573–90). Advocated a Protestant foreign policy, and headed campaign against Mary Stuart. A leading figure in state security, he exposed the Ridolfi Plot (1568) and the Throckmorton Plot (1583).

ELIZABETH'S INHERITANCE

The new monarch faced a daunting range of dangers. Pessimism was widespread, as Armigail Waad summarised in *The Distresses of the Commonwealth*: 'The Queen poor, the realm exhausted, the nobility poor and decayed. All things dear. Divisions among ourselves. War with France and Scotland. The King of France bestriding the realm, having one foot in Calais and the other in Scotland.' Elizabeth had also to contend with severe public misgivings about the capacity of any female ruler to achieve stable and competent government. John Knox was at pains to explain that his *First Blast of the Trumpet against the Monstrous Regiment of Women* (1558) did not apply to Protestant queens, but its basic philosophy of male superiority reflected the accepted wisdom of the day: 'To promote a woman to bear rule, superiority, dominion or empire above any realm, nation or city is repugnant to nature.'

Elizabeth was extremely fortunate, however, in the upturn that coincided with her accession. The harvest of 1558 was a good one, and the epidemics that had marked the last years of Mary's reign were on the decline by 1560. Similarly, food prices which had doubled between 1540 and 1560 stabilised thereafter, and would rise only by a quarter over the next thirty years. There was no reason, however, to expect that religious problems would diminish. Delivering Queen Mary's funeral oration, Bishop White had warned that 'the wolves are coming out of Geneva and other places in Germany, and hath sent their books before, to infect the people'. The returning exiles certainly constituted a remarkable cross-section of English intellectual Protestantism. Ponet, Jewel, Coverdale, Grindal and Cox were among the past and future bishops in their ranks, while Knox and Foxe stood out among the preachers and publicists. The opposite religious 'corner' was equally distinguished. Mary's bench of bishops was as eminent as any inherited by an English monarch. If it had a weakness, it was in numbers, for at the time of Mary's death and that of the Cardinal-Archbishop of Canterbury a few hours later, five bishoprics were vacant, and death caused four more to be vacated by the end of the year. In addition, there was much evidence that religious conservatism dominated many parts of the realm outside the Home Counties, and the Spanish ambassador felt able to claim that the 'Catholic party is two thirds larger than the other'.

The Elizabethan 'golden age' was still at least a decade away. The immediate nature of the English political scene has been accurately summarised by Conrad Russell (*The Crisis of Parliaments*, 1971): 'In 1558 another mid-Tudor ruler was trying to make another mid-Tudor settlement with the aid of the same body of mid-Tudor councillors.'

THE QUESTIONS OF MARRIAGE AND THE SUCCESSION

Along with the religious settlement, the most pressing issue facing the new government was the settlement of the succession. The two issues were related, for the re-establishment of Protestantism would mean little if the next ruler were to favour Catholicism, and Elizabeth was the third monarch in the space of eleven years. The initial assumption was that, like Queen Mary, Elizabeth would acknowledge her feminine limitations and take a husband to relieve her of the burdens of government. There was much less agreement as to who that husband should be. Philip of Spain hinted that he might be willing to take on a second Tudor, while Henry II of France put forward a number of well-qualified French candidates. From the Protestant north came arguments in favour of King Eric of Sweden or the Scottish Earl of Arran. Some of these had undoubted personal disqualifications. Arran, for instance, was almost certainly teetering on the brink of insanity, while Eric of Sweden would have been wiser not to have sent Elizabeth his portrait. All candidates brought with them unwanted implications in international politics, and marriage in several cases would have meant a clear religious commitment at a time when Elizabeth wished her views to be as obscure as possible.

The implications of an English marriage were not much better. Attractive as Robert Dudley undoubtedly was to Elizabeth personally, she understood that she could not suddenly raise 'the most cordially hated man in the court' (Wallace MacCaffrey, *The Shaping of the Elizabethan Regime*, 1969) without causing great jealousy in domestic political circles. At the beginning of the reign, moreover, Dudley was already married, and the sudden death of his wife (September 1560) only increased the intense suspicions surrounding his political ambitions.

If Elizabeth did not marry at all, the rightful heir was clearly Mary Stuart, Queen of Scots, a direct descendant of Henry VII through his daughter's line. For some Englishmen, the fact that Mary was a Catholic and as closely connected to France as Mary Tudor had been to Spain was a cause for serious concern. Others preferred to note that the birth to Mary of the young Prince James (1566) meant that she had a male heir and thus provided some guarantee of long-term stability. A powerful faction at court, in which the Duke of Norfolk was prominent, saw Mary as the obvious and convenient successor if Elizabeth persisted in her refusal to marry.

Elizabeth's continued refusal to commit herself to a marriage alliance has produced much speculation from historians. Some have concluded that she always intended to remain celibate, and have explained this in terms of an emotional aversion to marriage, based upon the fate of her own mother. Others have seen Elizabeth's decision as a more pragmatic one, emerging slowly from her gradual realisation of political realities. Joel Hurstfield (*Elizabeth I and the Unity of England*, 1960) may be nearest the mark in writing: 'Elizabeth was a career woman. Marriage and motherhood would have deprived her temporarily – perhaps permanently – of the authority and power to rule.'

THE MARRIAGE QUESTION IN PARLIAMENT

Only with the benefit of hindsight can the queen's indecision be seen as calm and successful statesmanship. To contemporaries it must have appeared to be downright irresponsible. In the second Parliament of the reign (January 1563) the queen found herself under urgent pressure from the whole spectrum of the political nation. In their first session, the Commons petitioned Elizabeth to marry, but by the time financial necessity forced her to recall Parliament in September 1566 the situation was much more grave. Mary Stuart had entered into a Catholic marriage with Lord Darnley (July 1565), and that union had produced a son. In 1564, moreover, they had nearly lost their own queen through a severe attack of smallpox. This time, not only did the Commons make the grant of a subsidy conditional upon a satisfactory answer from Elizabeth, but the Lords also joined them in their stand. Despite the financial sacrifice involved, Elizabeth refused to give way. Berating her courtiers in private, she gave the Commons a more dignified answer. Reminding them of their place in the treatment of such lofty matters, she promised an answer in the near future, but forbade them to debate the succession any further.

THE BASES OF ELIZABETHAN FOREIGN POLICY

English foreign policy in the sixty years before Elizabeth's succession had a number of distinct and consistent themes. With rare exceptions, England was hostile to the crown of France and sought security in friendship with Spain and the Empire. Friendship with the Habsburg rulers of the Netherlands also ensured the safe conduct of much of England's foreign trade. In the course of Elizabeth's reign these traditional axes of foreign policy were largely reversed. Spain emerged as the most serious threat to English security, and England was to fight for much of the last decade of the century as the ally of the King of France.

Was this the result of policy or of a lack of policy? Elizabeth has been consistently charged with indecision and even panic in her conduct of foreign affairs. Such accusations were levelled by Charles Wilson (*Queen Elizabeth and the Revolt of the Netherlands*, 1970), who claimed that those who seek consistency in Elizabeth's policies are 'rationalising into policies what was, in reality, a succession of shifts and muddles into which the queen stumbled'. Elizabeth's shortcomings, Wilson added, made a significant contribution to the overall failure of English foreign policy, which left the realm no more secure at the end of the reign

than at the beginning. R.B. Wernham (*Before the Armada*, 1966), on the other hand, has argued that inconsistency arose primarily from lack of resources. The policy of a relatively weak state such as Elizabethan England, he argued, 'must turn and twist this way and that as an Elizabethan galleon had to tack back and forth in response to winds and tides'. Recent writers have also found virtue in the queen's limited aims, in her refusal to listen to the 'grand designs' of others. 'Her objectives', writes G.D. Ramsey (in *The Reign of Elizabeth I*, ed. C. Haigh, 1984), 'were prosaic and local, but practicable. Her success is to be measured by the survival of the cloth-export traffic to central Europe, and by the maintenance of the royal credit on bourses abroad, as well as by the defeat of the Armada in 1588.'

Nevertheless, the foreign policy of the reign was consistent in two respects. The queen's responses were highly predictable, and were based upon the experiences of her predecessors. From her father's experience she drew the conclusion that ambitious initiatives on the Continent were beyond the capacity of her small kingdom, and that policy must consist of pragmatic responses to the initiatives of others. From the reign of Queen Mary she learned that unconditional commitment to one ally usually brought greater benefit to the ally than to England. As a result, Elizabeth remained intensely jealous of her personal independence and intensely conservative. She showed no interest in the lordship of the Netherlands nor in dominion over Scotland, yet she retained a vague hankering after Calais, hers by right of inheritance and history. If pragmatism sometimes made her the ally of Dutch, Scottish or French rebels, it never made her their true friend. In her dealings with Mary Stuart, Philip of Spain and the kings of France, she never quite forgot the respect which she felt was due to members of the exclusive 'club' of anointed monarchs.

In a sense, Elizabeth's foreign policy was not 'foreign' at all. She defended her personal, royal authority against incursions by French or Spanish in the same way that she defended it against Catholic or puritan enthusiasts at home. While the mercantile horizons of the English expanded, the horizons of diplomacy remained where they had always been. They embraced Scotland, and the relations of that

19.2 A summary of Elizabethan diplomacy

July 1560	**Treaty of Edinburgh.** England and France undertook to remove their respective forces from Scotland. France undertook to prevent Mary Stuart from styling herself 'Queen of England'.
September 1562	**Treaty of Richmond.** Elizabeth agreed to give financial and military aid to the French Huguenots. In return England was to take possession of Le Havre, on the understanding that the port would be exchanged for Calais when that town had been captured.
April 1564	**Treaty of Troyes.** Elizabeth acknowledged the loss of Calais and forfeited two-thirds of the compensation that had been promised at Câteau-Cambrésis.
April 1572	**Treaty of Blois.** Elizabeth and Charles IX of France promised to aid each other against Spain, and undertook to seek the pacification of Scotland.
April 1573	**Treaty of Nymwegen.** England and Spain agreed to the restoration of English trade links with the Netherlands that had been ruptured by the confrontations of 1568–9. As a result, Elizabeth recalled all English volunteers from the Netherlands.
August 1585	**Treaty of Nonsuch.** Elizabeth agreed with the Estates-General of the Netherlands to send 6,000 troops to their assistance. She was to hold the ports of Flushing and The Brill as guarantees. The English force was to be commanded by an Englishman of great rank and prestige (Elizabeth chose to appoint the Earl of Leicester), who was to sit on the Dutch Council of State and share in the government of the United Provinces.
July 1586	**Treaty of Berwick.** Elizabeth and James VI of Scotland agreed upon the mutual defence of their realms. James received a pension of £4,000 per year from England.
May 1596	Treaty of alliance with Henry IV of France against Philip II. The United Provinces joined this alliance in October 1596.

state with France. They took in events in the Netherlands and in France, and especially their effects upon those areas of the Channel coastline from which a direct attack upon England could be launched.

FOREIGN POLICY

Scotland and France, 1558–64

The reign's first act of diplomacy put an end to the war with France. Although the peace terms of Câteau-Cambrésis provided relief for the English exchequer, they also involved the loss of Calais. By the treaty (April 1559) the port was ceded to France, on condition that France would pay 500,000 crowns in compensation within eight years or would hand Calais back. The condition, of course, was never fulfilled. Câteau-Cambrésis also appeared to threaten the security of the realm,

providing for a marriage between Philip II and a daughter of Henry II of France, and speaking vaguely of bringing 'all Christian Europe to a true accord'. While Cecil showed concern at the possibility of a Catholic League, however, Gresham reported from Antwerp that the crippled finances of both France and Spain ruled out any aggressive action in the foreseeable future.

Within two weeks of the conclusion of peace, the rebellion of the Protestant 'Lords of the Congregation' in Scotland against the rule of the French regent provided the English government with a great opportunity. Yet Elizabeth hesitated. To aid the rebels might hasten the expulsion of the French from Scotland and establish a government friendly to England. On the other hand, such action might invite French retaliation, and might set a dangerous precedent for rebellion against legitimate royal authority.

The beginnings of civil unrest in France reduced such misgivings, and after concluding a formal understanding with the rebel lords (the Treaty of Berwick) Cecil dispatched an army of 8,000 men to the north. Its appearance before Leith persuaded the garrison to conclude the Treaty of Edinburgh (July 1560). Although it remained unratified, the treaty was a remarkable diplomatic achievement. By rupturing the Franco-Scots alliance, it succeeded spectacularly where the long and costly campaigns of the 1540s had failed.

This success tempted the government into a second and much less successful intervention. When the Prince of Condé requested English aid for the Huguenot cause in the French civil wars, the two sides swiftly concluded the Treaty of Richmond (September 1562). This time, however, English troops intervened not as liberators, but with the express purpose of taking what all Frenchmen considered to be French territory. The failures of Condé's armies combined with siege, plague and French xenophobia to force the surrender of the Le Havre garrison (July 1563), and the subsequent Treaty of Troyes was even less advantageous than Câteau-Cambrésis. Elizabeth had undertaken an adventurous and aggressive policy and had been severely punished for it. In future she might extend furtive and indirect aid to foreign rebels, but would not undertake direct intervention again for twenty years, and then only as a last desperate remedy.

The 'Diplomatic Revolution'

The French threat to England's security declined considerably in the first six years of Elizabeth's reign, but was offset by the first stages in the degeneration of Anglo-Spanish relations. Although the 1560s witnessed some acrimony between Englishmen and Spaniards in the Caribbean, the true causes of diplomatic tension must be sought in the Netherlands. The troops which the Duke of Alva led into that region in 1568 were there simply to restore local order and obedience, but the English government could not ignore the theoretical dangers posed by such a force so close to its shores. There were many besides who viewed Alva's mission as part of a wider 'Catholic conspiracy' against Protestantism across Europe.

Elizabeth's hopes for the Netherlands remained clear throughout her reign. She wished to maintain their original status as a set of provinces under the legitimate rule of the King of Spain, free from French influence, but sustained in their traditional freedoms and privileges. In the contemporary definition of the Earl of Sussex, 'she wished neither to see the French possess nor the Spaniards tyrannise in the Low Countries'. In a situation that demanded tact on both sides, two curious incidents created confrontation. In November 1568, at the height of English concern at Alva's arrival, storms drove a fleet of ships into Plymouth carrying £85,000 from the bankers of Genoa to the paymasters of Alva's army. Elizabeth's decision to seize the money and to take on the loan herself left that army unpaid and mutinous. In retaliation, Alva ordered the arrest of all English merchants operating in the Netherlands, striking at English financial interests in a crucial economic zone. Was this therefore a telling blow at Spanish finances, or should we dismiss the action, in Charles Wilson's words (*Queen Elizabeth and the Revolt of the Netherlands*, 1970), as 'an escapade as costly as it was senseless'? The second incident revolved around the queen's decision (March 1572) to expel from English ports the 'Sea Beggars', Dutch Protestant pirates who had for some time harassed Alva's communications. What may have been a genuine attempt to improve Anglo-Spanish relations served in the event greatly to complicate Spain's position. The homeless Dutchmen crossed the Channel, established permanent bases on Dutch soil, and opened a new and more threatening phase in the conflict.

Ambiguous confrontation with Spain was paralleled by ambiguous friendship with France. With the apparent stabilisation of the French monarchy, Elizabeth turned her attention from the Huguenots to the legitimate rulers of France. A marriage alliance was first broached late in 1570, and Catherine de Medici formally proposed her son Henry, Duke of Alençon, the following year. Although Alençon's flexible Catholicism might still be objectionable to some Englishmen, the marriage offered a solution to the problem of the succession and would strengthen both states against Spain. Such was the basis upon which England and France concluded the Treaty of Blois in April 1572.

Was this truly a 'diplomatic revolution' as some contemporaries saw it, in which Elizabeth was

The Kingdom of Scotland, 1542–1603

(Continued from Chapter 11, p. 181).

For more than forty years after the Battle of Solway Moss, Scotland faced its traditional problems of internal disorder and international vulnerability without the advantages of an adult male monarch. The accession of James V's infant daughter Mary as Queen of Scots appeared to make it inevitable that the realm would lose its independence to one or other of the greater powers that had traditionally attempted to draw Scotland into its sphere of influence. The energetic English attempts to enforce the Treaty of Greenwich, betrothing Mary to the young Prince Edward, could only be resisted with substantial, and equally dangerous, French aid. Mary's eventual marriage to the French *dauphin*, Francis, was accompanied by diplomatic agreements that her realm would pass into French hands if she died without an heir. Such an unacceptable prospect formed the basis of the patriotic manifesto drawn up by rebellious noblemen, calling themselves the 'Lords of the Congregation', in 1559.

For all their emphasis upon patriotic rather than religious issues, the 'Lords of the Congregation' obviously represented an additional element in the political confusion facing the French Regent, Mary of Guise. The Reformation in Scotland was

not a rapid process, but it triumphed in two political paroxysms between 1559 and 1567. The country's first Protestant martyr, Patrick Hamilton, was burned in 1528, but it was not until the 1540s that the Scottish Church, led by the Archbishop of St Andrews, Cardinal Beaton, responded to the challenge with a mixture of aggression and attempted reform. On the one hand, Beaton secured the burning of George Wishart (1546), a notable Protestant scholar whose writings introduced Swiss religious teachings into Scotland, thereby provoking his own murder shortly afterwards. On the other, Provincial Councils (1549, 1552 and 1559) consistently sought to address such familiar issues as celibacy, pluralism and clerical ignorance, but without conspicuous success. The ending of decades of European political conflict in 1559 stimulated religious conflict in Scotland as it did in many other parts of Western Europe. The peace established at Câteau-Cambrésis appeared to give the pro-French Catholic faction respite to reimpose its authority, and the Protestants reacted with due urgency. The return from Geneva of the influential preacher John Knox coincided with outbursts of image-breaking and attacks on clerical property at Perth and St Andrews (May–June 1559). When the Regent, Mary of

Guise, responded by introducing French forces, superior to the 'Lords of the Congregation', she began a fateful process of escalation. The appeal of the Protestant lords to England provided an opportunity that English ministers could not ignore. By blockading the French garrison at Leith, English forces compelled them to accept the Treaty of Edinburgh, entailing their withdrawal from Scotland and confirming both the Protestant ascendancy and the orientation of Scottish policy towards England.

Widowed in France, Mary Stuart returned to her realm in 1561, her parentage, marriage and religion all setting her at odds with the main developments in Scotland over the previous two years. For several years, Mary appeared to deal with an extremely difficult situation with some tact, refusing to compromise in the exercise of her own religion, leaving the reformed Church (the Kirk) unmolested, and matching Knox in a famous series of 'interviews' on their doctrinal and political differences. Yet her remarriage, to the English Catholic nobleman Henry Stewart, Lord Darnley (July 1565), precipitated the second paroxysm. Whether the marriage emboldened Mary, or whether the blame lay primarily with Darnley's supposed arrogance and lack of judgement, the crown adopted a much more aggressive stance towards the Protestant lords. As the wounds of faction reopened, a series of scandalous mistakes undermined Mary's power-base. Her relations with Darnley were ruined by the latter's involvement in the murder of David Riccio (1566), the queen's Italian secretary and confidant. The subsequent murder of Darnley himself (February 1567) and Mary's hasty marriage to the prime suspect, the Earl of Bothwell, left the queen isolated and her personal credibility ruined. Forced to abdicate in favour of her infant son (July 1567), and unsuccessful in the brief civil war by which she sought to re-establish her authority, Mary fled into her lengthy English exile.

The fall of Mary Stuart completed the gravitation of her kingdom towards England. In the short term it also greatly complicated Scotland's political instability. The wounds of her brief reign continued to fester, and two of the regents who governed in the name of the young king (Moray 1567–70 and Lennox 1570–1) met violent deaths. Only under the fourth regent, the Earl of Morton (1572–8), was a degree of political order restored. Nevertheless, the young James VI faced two major challenges to his authority. One was presented by the Scottish Kirk. Under the leader-

ship of Andrew Melville, a Calvinist scholar appointed Principal of Glasgow University in 1574, factions in the Kirk restated its claims to moral superiority over the crown and its right to dictate to James on spiritual matters. The second challenge, of course, was mounted by a divided nobility. Indeed, James greatly complicated his own difficulties by his propensity to be influenced by favourites. The first of many courtiers to win his favour during his reigns in Scotland and in England was his cousin Esmé Stuart. As Earl of Lennox, he formed a powerful faction which maintained an ambiguous attitude towards the Catholic powers on the Continent. This, in turn, triggered a response from rival Protestant nobles led by the Earl of Gowrie, and in the so-called 'Ruthven raid' (August 1582) the young king suffered the humiliation of being kidnapped and forced to dismiss Lennox.

These, however, were the final twists in the complex story of Scottish factional struggles. The mid-1580s witnessed a substantial consolidation in James's political position. The eventual execution of his mother, after eighteen years of captivity in England, actually benefited him in several respects. First, it resolved the ambiguity of his own position in Scotland, for Mary had always claimed that she

remained the rightful monarch, even in her absence. More important, it left James as the clear, Protestant heir to the English throne, a prospect consolidated by the Treaty of Berwick (July 1586), which provided for the mutual defence of the two kingdoms and for an annual pension for James. The prospect of so prosperous a future did much to increase the prestige of the House of Stuart. In the seventeen years that remained before James took possession of his 'promised land', his authority was extended significantly over the Highlands, the Western Isles and the border regions, and effective action was taken against noble conspiracies headed by the earls of Huntly and Errol. Revenues were increased by the work of a selected government team (the 'Octavians'), and the crown steadily imposed its authority over the Kirk. The so-called 'Black Acts' (1584) of the Scottish Parliament named the king as head of the Kirk, and in the course of the 1590s the crown established its right to regulate the meetings of its General Assembly and to punish preachers for views expressed from the pulpit. By 1603, James had established something resembling the royal supremacy which pertained south of the border, together with a greater degree of monarchical authority than Scotland had known in the sixteenth century.

reversing the axioms of decades? Or was she, as R.B. Wernham has concluded, mainly concerned to help the stability of the French government, to keep the Guise dynasty in the shade, and to deter the French from any Dutch ventures? Whatever the motives behind the Anglo-French *rapprochement*, it lay in ruins within a few months. The Massacre of St Bartholomew (August 1572) plunged France into renewed civil war and made a French Catholic alliance intolerable to English Protestants. At least the adventure of the 'diplomatic revolution' had a satisfactory effect upon Spanish policy towards England. Between 1569 and 1572, Philip II refused the approaches of English and Irish rebels and forbade the publication within his territories of the papal bull excommunicating Elizabeth. Finally, in 1573, the states agreed to the renewal of trade links disrupted by the affair of the 'Genoese gold'.

The drift to war, 1573–85

For the rest of the 1570s England's status in Europe was as secure as at any time in Elizabeth's reign. Events in France ruled out any possibility of French interference in the Netherlands, and no practical cause existed for war between England and Spain. In the Netherlands, the withdrawal of Don John's troops (1577) and the the Pacification of Ghent seemed to give Elizabeth everything she sought there.

This national security was not evident to all. The neurotic belief in a 'Catholic conspiracy' persisted in many quarters of the English political nation, and the presence of the Queen of Scots, the papal bull of excommunication and the massacre of French Huguenots all fuelled fears that the present peace was merely a lull before the onslaught of the Counter-Reformation's forces. In 1577, indeed, in the Netherlands, Don John reversed his decision to withdraw Spanish troops and soundly defeated the Dutch at Gembloux (January 1578). In addition, the Spanish conquest of Portugal (1580) gave Philip access to the wealth of the Portuguese empire and to the Portuguese Atlantic war fleet. The outbreak of the seventh War of Religion (February 1580) reduced Spain's fears of French interference in the Netherlands, and the death of Alençon (May 1584), followed by the assassination

of William of Orange two months later, appeared to leave the Dutch rebels leaderless and in danger of collapse. A terrible year ended with the Treaty of Joinville between Philip and the French Catholic League (December 1584), which demonstrated that Philip was now ready to combat the international Protestant menace to his Dutch interests.

Although some on the Council, such as Leicester and Walsingham, called consistently for a policy of direct intervention, Elizabeth's first response was one of indirect pressure. She allowed 3,000 English volunteers to travel to the Low Countries under Sir John Norris (July 1577), while financing the further intervention of the Elector Palatine, John Casimir. By the early 1580s this had escalated into a policy of 'undeclared war', which might weaken Spain without precipitating a direct confrontation. She ostentatiously approved Francis Drake's anti-Spanish exploits, for instance, by knighting him upon his return from his circumnavigation of the globe (April 1581).

The events of 1584 pushed English policy beyond brinkmanship, and with the Duke of Parma recording unprecedented successes against the Dutch rebels Elizabeth undertook direct intervention, culminating in the Treaty of Nonsuch (August 1585). At the same time, Drake was ordered to undertake raids upon Spain's north-west coast. Whatever his plans may have been in the longer term, it was only in response to these direct acts of war that Philip ordered the preparation of an Armada to be sent against England.

THE THREAT OF THE QUEEN OF SCOTS

Mary Stuart, Queen of Scots, provided a consistent preoccupation throughout the first three decades of Elizabeth's reign. The threat she posed, or was believed to pose, to the political establishment of the realm increased, declined and transformed itself in the course of thirty years, but it remained based upon one immutable fact: as long as Elizabeth remained unmarried, Mary was the legitimate heir to the English crown. Apart from any direct, physical threat to Elizabeth's safety, this Catholic heir appeared to pose a constant threat to the Protestant vested interest of many of those who stood directly beneath the queen in the hierarchy of the realm.

Mary was at her most dangerous at the beginning of the reign, when she was Queen of France, wife of the young Francis II. As such, she was the very personification of the 'Auld Alliance' and potentially the mother of children who would have a direct claim to three kingdoms: Scotland, France and England. It was the greatest stroke of luck in a lucky reign that Francis's early death ended the marriage without offspring. Back in Scotland, however, Mary posed difficulties of a different kind. Religious civil war on England's borders was serious enough without the moral dilemma concerning aid to the Scottish rebels. In addition the English government faced the problem of Mary's remarriage, to Henry Stuart, Lord Darnley (July 1565). His English birth, his descent from English royalty and his Catholic faith all seemed to ensure that the children of the marriage – and Prince James was born in June 1566 – would inevitably become Catholic monarchs of England if Elizabeth retained her virginity.

In this case, too, Elizabeth's problems were resolved by circumstances beyond her control. Scottish domestic upheavals destroyed Darnley, drove Mary into renewed civil war and, ultimately, into her cousin's realm (1568) in search of asylum and aid. Her presence, however, presented Elizabeth with the most delicate of all the crises that she faced during her reign. In England, Mary would provide a natural focus for Catholic malcontents. On the other hand, Mary was undoubtedly the rightful Queen of Scots and there was a strong moral case for complying with her requests for help in regaining her throne. At the same time, Mary remained the only real claimant to the English succession. While many in the political nation tolerated Mary's continued presence as the inevitable consequence of her dynastic claim, committed Protestants in the country and at court were bound to see her as a fundamental threat.

There was also the awkward question of Mary's involvement in the violent death of Lord Darnley. While allowing Scots and English commissioners to meet at York (October 1568) and later at Westminster to consider the evidence against Mary, Elizabeth could scarcely side openly with Mary's enemies. As Knollys remarked at the time, 'one

that has a crown can scarcely persuade another to leave her crown because her subjects will not obey'. Mary's understandable refusal to abdicate destroyed any chance of a settlement agreeable to all parties in Scotland and ensured that for the time being – for two decades as it transpired – the Queen of Scots would remain a virtual prisoner on English soil.

THE REVOLT OF THE NORTHERN EARLS

Within a year of Mary's arrival in England a rebellion broke out in the north which typified the uncertainties of the first decade of the reign. The events of 1569 had their origins in a court intrigue centring upon Mary Stuart and the Duke of Norfolk. The idea of a marriage between them had an immediate appeal to conservative courtiers, regularising Mary's position in England and resolving the issue of the succession in a manner that would eliminate the dangers of foreign domination. Founded upon religious conservatism, the marriage would form the basis of better relations with France and Spain, and would strike a severe blow at the political dominance of Cecil. The plan was not strictly treasonable, yet it sought to regulate prerogative matters without reference to Elizabeth. Her anger when she learned of it was sufficient to panic Norfolk into flight, and he was subsequently arrested.

The acute disappointment of many northern nobles and gentry was one of the factors that precipitated rebellion. Another was the political decline of the great feudal families of the north in the face of increased central authority. The Earls of Northumberland and Westmorland both found themselves largely excluded from royal patronage by Cecil's ascendancy, and feudal stagnation was supplemented by religious conservatism. Some rebels were veterans of the Pilgrimage of Grace, and may thus be regarded as committed Catholics, but A.G. Dickens has stressed the role played in the rising by 'survivalism', a vaguer hankering after time-honoured traditions of religious practice.

Northumberland raised his tenants in November 1569, and the revolt continued with the rebels' great act of defiance in celebrating Mass in Durham cathedral. There was little more to it. The rebels marched south with 5,000 men, reached the limits of their leaders' feudal influence and, with the approach of 10,000 royal troops, broke and fled. The significance of the Revolt of the Northern Earls was largely negative. It was the last challenge of the territorial aristocracy to the centralised power of the monarchy. The execution of Northumberland (August 1572), the humilation of Norfolk and the passing of 700 death sentences upon the rank and file, all demonstrated to the northern commoner that his true lord was the Tudor and not the Percy or the Howard. The revolt's abject failure demonstrated the true strengths of the government's position, for subsequently the Elizabethan settlement in politics and religion was firmly established in all important respects. Yet the greatest triumph was Cecil's. He had survived all the conspiracies against him with his position and his policies intact. Only the problem of the Queen of Scots remained to be solved.

ENGLISH CATHOLICISM

The nature of the problem

The word 'Catholic' could be used in the early years of Elizabeth's reign to indicate two distinctly different religious positions. Those who specifically opposed the royal supremacy and upheld the authority of the Pope were thin on the ground, but there were many more Englishmen upon whom Protestantism had made little positive impact and who maintained a sentimental attachment to the old rites and ceremonies. While examples of outright recusancy were rare, examples abounded of the continuation, sometimes quite publicly, of Catholic practices. William Allen was probably close to the truth when he wrote that 'many laymen who believed the [Catholic] faith in their hearts and heard Mass when they could, frequented the schismatic church'. This broad 'Catholicism' was strengthened by an element of class distinction. Protestantism was still seen by many as a religion for 'basket makers and brewers', and in remoter areas Protestantism still appeared to be an outlandish innovation.

The laws that were formulated against English Catholics seem to leave little doubt as to the government's hostility. Refusal of the Oath of Supremacy meant automatic loss of office. Speaking in favour of the Pope led a man to the scaffold upon the third offence, and the penalty for saying Mass was death. Much to the distress of the Protestant enthusiasts in the House of Commons, however, the enforcement of this legislation was a very different matter. Archbishop Parker was directly instructed by the queen that the Oath of Supremacy should not be put to a man more than once, and no death penalty was imposed for saying Mass before 1577. The nobility, whose political opposition could have created the gravest difficulties, were specifically exempted from the punitive terms of the Act of Supremacy.

Was this a policy of leniency or of weakness? In areas where the power of the crown was uninhibited by distance, such as London, Essex and Oxfordshire, there were many prosecutions for such offences as administering the Roman sacraments. It seems fair to conclude that Elizabeth and some of her leading ministers remained highly dissatisfied with the level of Catholic non-conformity, yet realised their limited capacity to deal with the problem, and appreciated the risks to domestic and foreign policies of a more draconian approach.

Towards confrontation

For all this caution, events in the late 1560s and early 1570s drove the government towards confrontation. Under Pius V the papacy inclined towards force as the only means of winning England back to the fold. Misinterpreting the Revolt of the Northern Earls, Pius assumed that Elizabeth's throne was shaking, and that domestic pressure would bring it down. The result was the bull *Regnans in Excelsis* (February 1570), which excommunicated Elizabeth and threatened her Catholic subjects with the same fate if they did not withhold their allegiance from the heretic queen. The effects of the bull seem to have been negligible. There is some evidence of increased recusancy now that the Anglican Prayer Book had been formally condemned by the papacy, but no evidence of organised political opposition. The major effect was to heighten the Protestants' sense of danger. A series of statutes declared it high treason to bring papal bulls into the country, to publish *Regnans in Excelsis* or to defend its arguments.

Although Elizabeth continued to assure her Catholic subjects that it was not her intent 'to have any of them molested by any inquisition or examination of their consciences', government policy was clearly changed by the events of 1568–72. Parliament was firmly set in the ways of Protestant patriotism, and with the departure of Arundel and Norfolk the Privy Council lost any appearance of religious balance. This siege mentality increased over the next few years with the infiltration into the country of the first missionaries from the college founded at Douai (1568) by William Allen. The aims of these Catholic missionaries were treasonable by any definition. They hoped not merely to give aid to those wishing to practise their Catholic faith, but also to undermine the Anglican Church by forcing all Catholics into open recusancy. As the magnitude of their task dawned upon them, a number came to advocate foreign invasion as the only means of achieving their goals.

The mission took time to make its impact. In 1575 there were only eleven seminary priests at large in England, whereas by 1580 the number had risen to about 100. Their organisation also developed slowly, but the arrival of Robert Southwell and Henry Garnet (1586) put the mission on a more secure basis. Garnet could boast ten years later that 'many persons who saw a seminary priest hardly once a year now have one all the time and most eagerly welcome any others'. The lives of such priests remained dangerous and uncertain. Between 1581 and 1586 alone, thirty priests were executed and fifty more were imprisoned.

What was the overall effect of this mission? The argument of John Bossy (*The English Catholic Community, 1570–1850*, 1975) is that the mission transformed the native community, creating a degree of separation from the Anglican Church that had not previously existed. The number of detected recusants certainly rose in many parts of the country: from 60 to 700 in London and Middlesex (1587–1603), for instance, and from 534 to 3,500 in Lancashire (1590–1603); but it is unclear whether such figures represent increased Catholic

obstinacy or increased zeal on the part of the authorities. Bossy's view is challenged by Christopher Haigh (*The English Reformation Revised*, 1987), who views the Catholic community towards the end of Elizabeth's reign as 'a rump community, the residue of a process of failure and decline in which whole regions and social groups were neglected'. Haigh further claims that popular Catholicism declined as the years passed, and that the necessary reliance of the seminary priests upon the gentry and lesser nobility for shelter and funds largely limited active Catholicism to these élite strata of society.

The legislative assault

The Catholic mission clearly did not undermine the Tudor regime. The summoning of Parliament in 1581 marked the opening of a new anti-Catholic offensive with the dual aim of eliminating seminary priests as an overtly treasonable force and of persuading or bullying English recusants into Anglican conformity. The main product of the 1581 Parliament was the 'Act to retain the Queen's Majesty's subjects in their due obedience', which made it treason to persuade any subject from allegiance to the queen or from the established form of religion. In addition, the fine for convicted recusants was increased to the substantial sum of £20 per month.

The 1585 Parliament was less subtle in its legislation. It became treason to be a priest in England ordained by the Pope's authority, and a capital offence to 'receive, relieve, comfort or maintain' such priests. Of 146 Catholics executed between 1586 and 1603, 123 were convicted under these laws. In 1593 was passed an 'Act against Popish Recusants', commonly known as the 'Five Mile Act' because it limited the mobility of recusants to within five miles of their place of residence, making it harder to evade detection and conviction.

Did such legislation work? The evidence seems to suggest that the anti-recusant measures still failed where they were faced with local hostility. On the other hand, the real enemies of the Elizabethan supremacy, the seminary priests, seem to have been hunted with more zeal and success. The principal modern Catholic critic of Elizabeth's policy, Father Philip Hughes (*The Reformation in England*, 1950–4), has estimated that 'Queen Elizabeth put to death, solely because of their religion, between the years 1577–1603, 183 of her Catholic subjects'. He might have added that no such executions took place between 1558 and 1577, and that 125 took place in the atmosphere of national danger that prevailed in the years 1588–1603. The major success of government policy, perhaps, was that it achieved these results without goading a wide range of conservative subjects into open disobedience.

THE FALL OF THE QUEEN OF SCOTS

With the collapse of the hopes that she had placed in conservatives within the English establishment, Mary Stuart turned to conspiracy. She now placed her trust in foreign aid, making contact with the Spanish court through the ambassador, de Spes, and with the papacy. Nor could the Duke of Norfolk, his own hopes of semi-legitimate political gain frustrated, resist the temptation to become involved. The first major plot against Elizabeth is known as the Ridolfi Plot, after the Florentine banker who carried its messages.

The Ridolfi Plot set the pattern for the conspiracies that followed. Many of its agents were too careless; security at English ports was too tight; the work of Cecil, Walsingham and their agents at code-breaking and counter-espionage was too efficient. By the late summer of 1571 the government had enough evidence to arrest Norfolk and to expel de Spes. The Parliament that was summoned in May 1572 also demanded action against Mary, proposing measures which demonstrated fierce loyalty to Elizabeth but which went much further than the queen was willing to go. Unwilling to sacrifice a queen to the Commons, she fed them a duke instead. Rejecting their bill of attainder against Mary and a bill excluding her from the succession, Elizabeth allowed Norfolk to be executed for treason (June 1572).

The Ridolfi Plot transformed the status of the Queen of Scots. From being an honoured guest in 1568, sought out by men of influence, she was now isolated and unanimously condemned by the governing classes assembled in Parliament. Thus, Mary saw further conspiracy as her only hope. The failure of the Throckmorton Plot (1583) left Elizabeth equally unwilling to take direct action against her rival, and leading members of the governing class took a remarkable and unprecedented step. At the instance of the Council, a document known as the Bond of Association was drawn up and circulated in the localities. By subscribing to it, a gentleman undertook, in the event of an attempt upon the queen's life, to prevent the succession of the person on whose behalf the attempt had been made, and to bring about that person's death. Mary was not mentioned by name, but she scarcely needed to be. When Parliament next met (1585) the latter part of the Bond was enshrined in statute law.

In the course of 1586, Burghley and Walsingham discovered a new plot centring around a young Catholic gentleman named Anthony Babington. Infiltrating the conspirators' lines of communication, the government obtained clear evidence of Mary's specific approval of plans to murder Elizabeth. While Elizabeth still hesitated, Burghley took the initiative of dispatching Mary's death warrant to Fotheringhay Castle in Northamptonshire, where the Queen of Scots was beheaded on 8 February 1587.

Mary's death had no notable effect upon England's relations with her immediate neighbours. Both James VI and Henry III protested loudly, but left it at that. One had too much to gain by retaining his position as Elizabeth's obvious successor, while the other had too much to lose by cooperating with the Catholic League. The only truly negative effect of the execution lay in the greater liberty that it afforded Philip II at last to launch his 'Enterprise of England'.

WAR WITH SPAIN

Strategies

England's relations with Spain degenerated to the point of outright war in 1585 because of developments in the Netherlands, but also because of the renewed crisis in the affairs of France. The open rebellion of the French Catholic League against Henry III and the collapse of France into renewed civil war destroyed the balance of Continental power upon which English security traditionally depended. Unusually in the context of the sixteenth century, England fought, not over dynastic issues, but over urgent issues of national security.

England's prosecution of the war was based upon two distinct strategies. One was to weaken the Spanish war effort at long range by attacking her maritime communications. Some writers have viewed this as a 'silver blockade', a deliberate and coherent attempt to check the flow of precious metals upon which Philip II depended. Others, however, have seen English naval activity as a haphazard process of commerce-raiding, carried out as much for private profit as for reasons of patriotism. Either way, the strategy had little impact upon Spain's military potential. It failed to prevent the sailing either of the Great Armada in 1588 or of a string of subsequent, lesser Armadas.

The second theme of the war was that of direct military intervention in the Netherlands. The primary concern of Leicester's mission was to prevent Spanish control of the deep-water ports along the Channel coast which an Armada might use. In this Leicester might claim some modest success, for only Sluys fell into Parma's hands (July 1587). In all other respects Leicester's expeditions were disastrous. By accepting the office of Governor-General from the States-General (January 1586) he dragged Elizabeth deeper into Dutch politics than she had ever wished to go. At the same time he spent heavily: £160,000 in the first year of intervention instead of the estimated £126,000. In addition, Leicester alienated the Dutch in several respects, attempting to control their finances and to interfere with trade between the northern and southern provinces. The only real consolation when Leicester was finally recalled to England at the end of that year was that the vital port of Flushing had been kept out of Spanish hands.

After the Armada

The failure of the Armada represented the greatest blow struck against Spain in the course of the war, but it was not decisive. After 1588, naval operations continued to drain the profits of Spanish trade, but attempts to strike a decisive strategic blow invariably failed. The grandiose enterprise of Sir Francis Drake and Sir John Norris against Lisbon in 1589 degenerated into a confusion of conflicting aims, while Essex's expedition against Cadiz (1596) was thwarted by his companions' preference for plunder.

In the Continental theatre of war, Parma's army remained as great a threat as ever. Thus England remained committed for some years to direct intervention in Europe, only changing the geographical location of their intervention. The disputed succession of Henry IV to the French throne created a new imperative for English foreign policy. His defeat at the hands of his Catholic opponents would mean once more that a substantial part of the Channel coast would be controlled by England's enemies. Thus English troops came to the aid of French Protestants in 1591 for precisely the reasons that had led them to aid the Dutch six years earlier. The Earl of Essex besieged Rouen, but the campaign was handicapped by lack of cooperation on the part of England's allies. The conversion of Henry IV to Catholicism (1593) removed the motive and much of the enthusiasm for English intervention. By bringing peace and greater stability to France it also gave England less cause to fear the influence of Spain over that kingdom.

Even this decisive development, however, did not end the war with Spain. A 'war party', headed by the new royal favourite, the Earl of Essex, held the upper hand in the Council against the more pacific advice of Burghley's son, Robert Cecil. While Essex, like Leicester before him, had a vested political interest in a policy that offered him military command and the patronage that accompanied it, he also represented a new generation (b.1566) too young to remember the delicate balance that earlier Tudors had maintained between France and Spain. For this generation Spain was the natural enemy, and England could not rest until, in Walter Ralegh's graphic phrase, she had 'beaten that great Empire in pieces and made their kings kings of figs and oranges as in old times'. Thus the war dragged on throughout the final years of Elizabeth's life, until concluded by her successor in 1604, with volunteers fighting in the Netherlands and with commerce-raiding continuing at sea.

19.3 Social crisis in the 1590s

Source A. 1596: This year was such a dearth [i.e. shortage] of all sorts of grain in our land, that if the Lord in His mercy had not supplied our want with rye from Danzig, most miserable had been our case as well with rich as poor. To relieve the poor every alderman and worshipful man, and every burgess of this city that was of any worth, were appointed every day to find with victual [i.e. food] at his table so many poor people that wanted [i.e. lacked] work, whereby the poor of the city were kept from starving or rising.

From *Adam's Chronicle of Bristol*, published in 1623

Source B

	State of harvest	Grain prices	Other arable prices	Livestock	Food prices	Real wages
1589–90	Average	100	100	100	100	100
1590–1	Average	118	159	100	116	86
1591–2	Good	83	111	102	93	106
1592–3	Abundant	58	110	104	90	110
1593–4	Good	66	124	102	96	102
1594–5	Bad	117	141	116	130	76
1595–6	Bad	128	147	111	128	78
1596–7	Dearth	196	192	108	173	57
1597–8	Dearth	147	155	118	146	69
1598–9	Average	98	109	122	120	82
1599–1600	Average	105	124	118	115	86

An index of prices and wages, in which levels in the 1590s are expressed as a percentage of the levels pertaining in 1589–90. Figures calculated and adapted from D.M. Palliser, *The Age of Elizabeth, 1547–1603*, 1983

Source C. The dearth of all things maketh likewise many poor, and that cometh either by the excessive enhancement of the rents of lands, or by our immoderate use of foreign commodities. Lastly, the poor are exceedingly much multiplied because for the most part all the children of the poor be poor also, seeing that they are not taken from their wandering parents and brought up to honest labour for their living but, following their idle steps, so they do live and die, most shameless and shameful rogues and beggars.

From a speech by William Lambarde, a leading Justice of the Peace, 1594

Source D. I do not see how it is possible for the poor countryman to bear the burdens daily laid upon him. There be some that stick not to say boldly they must not starve, they will not starve. And this year there assembled eighty in a company and took a whole cartload of cheese from one driving it to a fair and dispersed

CONCLUSIONS

In the context of the immediate objectives which the government set itself, the war which occupied the last eighteen years of Elizabeth's reign was successful. With some assistance from other agencies, it kept the deep-water ports on the east coast of the 'English sea' out of Spanish hands, and prevented the military domination of the north-westerly part of Europe by forces hostile to English interests.

Yet the English monarchy paid a high price for such success. The crown, never rich since the death of Henry VIII, did not recover from the financial impact of these wars. Professor F.C. Dietz (*English Public Finance, 1485–1641*, 1964) estimated some years ago that, while the exchequer paid out only £149,000 in 1583, the figure had risen to £420,000 by 1588 and to £570,000 by 1599. The Armada

it among them, for which some of them have endured long imprisonment and fine. And when these lewd people are committed to the jail, the poor country that is robbed by them is enforced to feed them, which it grieves at. And this year there hath been disbursed to the relief of prisoners in the jail above £73.

From a letter to Lord Burghley from Edward Hext, Justice of the Peace in Somerset, September 1596

Source E

Yarnton. 6th December 1596.

Examinations before Sir William Spencer.

Roger Ibill of Hampton Gay, loader. Has heard divers [i.e. various] poor people say that there must be a rising soon, because of the high price of corn.

Peter Symonds, carpenter, of Hampton Gay. Was told by Steer that he need not work for his living this dear year, for there would be a merry world shortly. He tried to persuade Symonds to pull corn out of rich men's houses.

John Steer of Witney. Was told of the rising by his brother, who said that there would be 200 or 300 people from Woodstock, Bladon, Kirtlington, etc., and they would go from one rich man's house to another and take horses, arms and victuals.

From the investigation carried out by Sir William Spencer, Deputy Lieutenant of Oxfordshire, into an alleged rising in the county

Source F. And be it enacted that every person which is by this present Act declared to be a rogue, vagabond or sturdy beggar, taken begging, vagrant, wandering or misordering themselves in any part of this realm, shall upon their apprehension be stripped naked from the middle upwards and shall be whipped until his or her body be bloody and shall be forthwith sent from parish to parish by the officers of every the same the next straight way to the parish where he was born.

From the Act for the Punishment of Vagabonds. 1598

QUESTIONS

a. Compare the strengths and weaknesses of sources A, B and C as sources for the study of the economic problems of this period.

b. Compare the attitudes displayed in source A and in source C towards the problem of poverty in the 1590s.

c. What insight is provided by source D and source E into the problem of social disorder in late Elizabethan England?

d. In the light of the other sources above, how appropriate do the measures outlined in source F seem to be as a response to the economic problems of the 1590s?

campaign alone cost £161,000. The queen's ordinary income over this period varied between £200,000 and £250,000 per year, and there were limits to what could be gained by extra taxation or by borrowing. In the two crisis periods of 1590–1 and 1599–1601, Elizabeth was obliged to sell crown lands to the value of £645,000. Such a loss might be of relatively little significance when crown and people stood united in a common cause, but how would the crown maintain its position when domestic difficulties resurfaced?

Indeed, to a limited extent, the war contributed to such tensions resurfacing. The expedients to which Elizabeth had to resort for money caused bitterness and resentment. In 1593 the extraordinary request to Parliament for the granting of three subsidies led to three weeks of heated debate before the crown narrowly got its way; and even greater resentment was caused by the subsequent royal policy of raising money by the sale of trading monopolies. The conduct of the war also provoked increasing criticism, especially as it came to be associated with financial and other burdens for the citizen. There is too much hindsight in the view that draws direct links between Elizabeth's war and the fate of the monarchy under Charles I. Yet R.B. Wernham strikes a fair balance in his conclusion that 'the Elizabethan war with Spain and the long-drawn-out burdens that it imposed, did play a considerable part in changing sixteenth century Englishmen from a king-worshipping nation into a king-criticising nation'.

• CHAPTER TWENTY •

Henry IV and the Recovery of France

Re-establishing the traditional image of strong monarchy. This engraving, portraying Henry IV as a warrior-king, was executed in 1593, as he sought to rally a divided nation in war against Spain

THE HISTORICAL DEBATE

Few of the public images created by contemporary propaganda in the sixteenth century have survived as successfully as that of *Henri le Grand*. Most of the elements in this legend were well established by the time of the king's death. He was the 'Warrior King', the restorer of the monarchy, of peace, and of French greatness. He was the caring father of his people whose dearest wish was to see 'a chicken in every pot'.

In the course of the next two centuries, while the reputation of Francis I was adapted in the light of rationalism, revolution and republicanism, that of Henry IV possessed some elements which enabled it to endure. After the traumas of the French Revolution, supporters of both the Napoleonic Empire and the restored Bourbon monarchy could find a valuable model in Henry IV. For was he not the healer of deep national wounds, and the man who led France out of turmoil to stability and greatness? For Jules Michelet, the greatest and most critical French historian of the nineteenth century, Henry was a great romantic hero, 'the king singular and unique', who approached a tragic destiny for the good of the realm. As recently as the Second World War, the image of Henry as liberator and regenerator of France was sufficiently appealing to a defeated and oppressed nation to inspire such works as those of François Duhourcau (*Henri, libérateur et restaurateur de la France*, 1941) or Marcel Rheinard (*Henri, ou la France Sauvée*, 1943).

More recently, Henry's reign has been studied less for what it was than for what it led to. Brief though the period of domestic stability was at the end of Henry's life, it seemed to provide the foundations for the great age of French absolute monarchy typified by Louis XIV. R. Mousnier (*The Institutions of France under the Absolute Monarchy*, 1979), J.R. Major (*Representative Government in Early Modern France*, 1980) and D. Parker (*The Making of French Absolutism*, 1983) are among those who have studied the reign in this context in recent years. Many modern authorities, while acknowledging Henry's successful restoration of stability in France, still wish to stress the limits of his achievement. Recent work by British, French and American historians has also broadened the area of concern, concentrating upon the society and economy of France at the turn of the century. E. Le Roy Ladurie (*The French Peasantry, 1450–1660*, 1987) treats the political events of the age as only one set of factors among many which influenced the development of large areas of French society. J.H.M. Salmon (*Society in Crisis: France in the Sixteenth Century*, 1975) and M. Greengrass (*France in the Age of Henri IV: The Struggle for Stability*, 1984) have dwelt upon the transitional nature of the age. For them it was less the beginning of the age of Louis XIV than the end of an earlier age of religious turmoil and feudal rivalry. Henry's death in 1610 opened a new period of political uncertainty in France, and saw the recurrence of many of the familiar features of the civil wars. Similarly, it is now clear that Henry's solution to France's religious divisions was imperfect, and that, in the words of M. Prestwich (*International Calvinism, 1541–1715*, 1985), 'open war was replaced by cold war'.

THE FAILURE OF THE LEAGUE

Superficially, the Catholic League appeared to be a formidable obstacle in the path of Henry of Navarre as he sought to realise his claim to the French throne. By 1589, however, its strength was largely illusory, and Henry's success was in large part due to the divisions and weaknesses in the ranks of his opponents.

Above all, the Catholic cause was undermined by fundamental socio-political divisions. As the social radicalism of the 'Sixteen' increased in Paris, so did the mistrust and apprehension of Mayenne and other Catholic 'grandees'. The siege to which Paris was subjected by Henry (May–August 1590) caused great hardships and incited the extremists in the city's government to institute a virtual 'reign of terror' in order to root out those suspected of leaning towards Navarre. When the 'Sixteen' secured the execution of three prominent members of the Paris Parlement (November 1591) many suspected a systematic assault upon the powers and privileges of the established urban patricians. Mayenne was never more popular than when, in December, he entered Paris to execute or imprison the radical leaders. At a provincial level, religious and social radicalism caused similar concern to the League's leaders in Marseilles, Toulouse and Troyes.

The League also failed to produce a viable alternative monarch. Its official support for Henry's cousin Charles, Cardinal of Bourbon, was entirely unconvincing. Never known as a forceful character, he was now in his eighties, and unlikely by virtue of his age and his vocation ever to produce a Catholic heir. In any case, he died in May 1591. Some of the League's theorists fell back upon the idea of an elective monarchy. This merely created different problems, as political rivals canvassed the virtues of Mayenne, of the Duke of Savoy, or of Charles, the young son of the late Duke of Guise. To complicate the matter further, Philip II advertised the claims of the Infanta Isabella, his daughter by Elizabeth of Valois. Even more than at the time of the Treaty of Joinville, the policy of the League seemed to be exposing France to the familiar dangers of Spanish influence and control. The dangers of Spanish interference were certainly not lost upon the political realists within the Vatican. Thus, the League had to suffer the galling prospect of a Pope who looked with favour upon Navarre as a desirable corrective to the further spread of Spanish influence.

When Mayenne sought (1593) to convene a Catholic version of the Estates-General in Paris, the assembly was a sad anti-climax. Trapped between urban radicalism and ineffective noble leadership, the League's moderates saw more and more virtue in the political and social stability offered by Navarre. Before the end of April 1593, a group of them were already negotiating with his agents at Suresnes.

THE SUCCESS OF HENRY OF NAVARRE

Despite his traditional image as a 'warrior king', Henry's success owed most to the political skill with which he exploited the League's weaknesses. There were some notable military successes between his disputed succession and his entry into Paris in 1594. Henry's victory at Arques, near Dieppe (September 1589), secured his bases in Normandy, damaged the reputation of the defeated Mayenne, and encouraged English intervention on the side of the new king. His second victory, at Ivry

(March 1590), laid Paris open to its first siege, although Parma's Spanish forces were able to relieve both Paris (September 1590) and Rouen (January 1592). It was sheer luck that Parma sustained a wound in the course of his second campaign, which eventually led to his death in mid-1592. In the south, meanwhile, Damville won victories over the League's forces in Languedoc and forced a treaty upon them before the end of the year.

The decisive blow to the League came, however, from another quarter. It had long been known that Henry's religious beliefs were flexible in the extreme. Having already spent two periods of his life as a Catholic and two as a Huguenot, Henry had been suspected as early as 1584 of planning to secure his succession by reconversion to the Catholic Church. He held back from such a step because an announcement of his conversion at that time would have been transparent and would have alienated his Huguenot supporters. By 1593, however, with the League divided and many Catholic moderates eager for stability and for security from Spanish interference, the situation was perfect. In May the Archbishop of Bourges announced Henry's intention to prepare himself for acceptance into the Catholic Church, and his conversion received papal acknowledgement in September 1595. The will of the Parisians to resist their monarch was now severely undermined, and Henry entered his capital city in March 1594.

So who had won? The man who had led the Huguenot cause for twenty years sat on the throne of France. Yet the principal aim of the League had also been achieved, for he sat there as a Catholic. Above all, the principles of the *politique* cause seemed to have triumphed, for religious extremism seemed to have given way to stability and national consolidation.

In the course of the next two years, the remaining outposts of League resistance were mopped up by the most unglamorous methods. Having paid the governor of Paris nearly half a million *écus* to allow the royal entry into that city, Henry disbursed large sums to encourage Rouen, Lyon, Poitiers, Reims, Toulouse and Marseilles to open their gates to him. Further huge sums were paid to major captains of the League. A particularly complex agreement with Mayenne (January 1596) involved a complete pardon, the tenure of six garrisoned towns, the governorship of the Île-de-France and nearly a million *écus*.

The pacification of the realm: the Edict of Nantes

So great was the king's record of religious inconsistency that his accession was viewed by the Huguenot party with much reservation. Their suspicions were evident when a Huguenot assembly at La Rochelle (December 1588) demanded an oath to observe the confession of faith. Suspicions were increased by the king's promise (August 1589) to preserve Catholic officers in their posts, and there were moves in some quarters to find a new 'protector' for the reformed religion.

Henry's own priority was not to favour his fellow Protestants, but rather to avoid any move that might compromise his acceptance by the majority of his subjects. He revoked the anti-Protestant edicts

20.1 The Edict of Nantes

The following are extracts from the text of the Edict of Nantes. Say to what extent they support each or any of the following statements:

a. 'The Edict granted more to Catholics than to Protestants.'
b. 'Peace, rather than toleration, was the Edict's primary concern.'
c. 'Despite the Edict, French Protestants remained second-class citizens.'

1 That the memory of all things passed on the one part or the other since the beginning of March 1585 until our coming to the crown, and also all the other preceding troubles, shall remain extinguished and suppressed, as things that have never been.
2 We prohibit all our subjects of whatever state and condition they be, to renew the memory thereof, to attack, resent, injure or provoke one another by reproaches for what is past.
3 We ordain that the Catholic religion shall be restored and re-established in all places of this kingdom, and where the exercise of the said faith has been interrupted, to be there again, peaceably and freely exercised without any impediment.
6 We permit those of the reformed religion to live and dwell in all cities and places of our kingdom, without being inquired after, vexed, molested or compelled to do anything in religion contrary to their conscience.
9 We permit also to those of the said religion to hold, and continue its exercise in all cities and places under our obedience, where it has by them been established in 1586, and in 1597.
14 They will not exercise the said religion in our Court, nor in our City of Paris, nor within five leagues of the said city.
20 They [the Huguenots] shall also be obliged to keep and observe the festivals of the Catholic Church, and shall not on the same days work, sell or keep open shop.
21 Books concerning the said reformed religion shall not be printed or sold publicly, save in the cities and places where its public exercise is permitted.
22 We ordain that there shall not be made any difference or distinction on account of the said religion in receiving scholars to be instructed in the universities, colleges or schools.
25 We will and ordain that all those of the reformed religion shall be obliged to pay tithes to the ecclesiastics [of the Catholic Church].
27 We declare all those of the reformed religion to be capable of holding and exercising all estates, dignities, offices and public charges.
58 We declare all sentences, judgements, seizures and decrees made and given against those of the reformed religion, as well living as dead, henceforth cancelled, revoked and annulled.
82 All those of the said religion shall desist henceforth from all assemblies and councils established within the provinces to the prejudice of this present edict, prohibiting most expressly all our subjects to make henceforth any assessments or levies of money, fortifications and assemblies other than such as are permitted by our present edict, and without arms.

of 1585 and 1588, but when a new Huguenot assembly gathered at Mantes in 1593, the king's indifference to its requests for greater political liberty convinced the reformists that their struggle for religious security was not yet won. The years between 1594 and 1598 saw constant Huguenot pressure upon the king. At the same time as winkling out the last elements of League resistance and conducting the war with Spain, Henry had also to consider the prospect of major Huguenot assemblies at Saumur (1595), Loudun (1596) and Châtellerault (1597), growing both in size and in readiness to threaten their monarch. Their threats to withhold military assistance and to refuse payment of the *taille* at last had the desired effect. The result was the Edict of Nantes, signed in April 1598.

It is easy to overestimate the concessions granted by the Edict of Nantes. At the beginning of this century E. Lavisse (*Histoire de France*, 1901–11) claimed that it turned the Huguenot community into 'a state within a state'. One might prefer Mark Greengrass's conclusion that the Edict made the once rampant Huguenot party into 'an estate on the margins of traditional French society'. It was indeed a privileged position, but within little more than a century the revocation of the Edict by Louis XIV was to demonstrate how far the Huguenots were dependent upon the goodwill of the crown. This eventual revocation seems to justify Koenigsberger's dismissive phrase that the Edict 'was a temporary shelving of the problem of the co-existence of two religious faiths in one body politic'.

It is important, nevertheless, not to underestimate the novelty of such a religious settlement. In a century in which Germany had resolved its religious differences by the dubious principle of *cuius regio eius religio*, and in which the Netherlands had been forced to resort to religious partition, the Edict created for the first time in Western Europe a political system which accepted the existence of two different religious creeds in one state.

HENRY IV AND THE CATHOLIC CHURCH IN FRANCE

When the king converted to Catholicism he found the Church in France in a perilous position. Its hierarchy had been damaged terribly by the wars. In Protestant regions bishops had been driven out of their sees, but even in Catholic territories the Church had often been virtually annexed by the great noble families. As early as 1579 the Assembly of Clergy received the complaint that Montmorency had deliberately kept bishoprics vacant in Languedoc, or had put his own agents in control of them in order to be able to exploit their revenues. The assembly listed twenty-six bishoprics, nearly a quarter of the total, as vacant or usurped. The problem can only have been aggravated by subsequent years of civil war.

The political situation in the 1590s was far too delicate for the king to risk giving offence to prominent noble families. So far from challenging their control of Church appointments, therefore, Henry made new concessions in order to win political support. It is true that, once his domestic position was stabilised, he proceeded to fill existing vacancies. Eight new bishops were appointed in 1597, eleven in 1598, eighteen in 1599. On the other hand, the papacy consistently expressed its discontent at the standard of the bishops appointed.

With or without the active help of the king, the Catholic Church in France used the years of peace to put its house in order. It took advantage of the Edict of Nantes to re-establish itself in regions where its existence had been precarious during the wars, and there is much evidence that at least some of the bishops took their duties seriously. The number of episcopal visitations increased considerably, and twenty-four dioceses issued new sets of statutes during the reign. Yet much remained to be done. When the Estates-General met at last (1614) after Henry's death, 20 per cent of their grievances (*cahiers de doléances*) reflected complaints against the clergy or concerned other aspects of religious life in the localities.

FRENCH FOREIGN POLICY: WAR WITH SPAIN

In January 1595, Henry IV declared war on Spain. Coligny and Alençon before him had seen this traditional rivalry as the best means of healing domestic divisions, and Henry's motives, though similar, were even more pressing. Spanish military power represented for him the one element of the League's power that could not be bought off or scared off with the spectre of social revolution. Nor could he truly claim to be master of his realm while foreign troops occupied French soil, or while the King of Spain pressed the claims of his daughter to Henry's throne.

This war was one of the great triumphs of *politique* philosophy over religious zealotry, yet it soon appeared that a high price might have to be paid for it. Calais quickly fell to Spanish troops (April 1596), and the whole province of Picardy was threatened. With the Spanish seizure of Amiens (March 1597), that threat was extended to the region of Paris, and it took six months of expensive siege warfare to redeem the disaster. Meanwhile, a further Spanish thrust took invading forces deep into Burgundy.

It was less Henry's military prowess which brought about a negotiated peace than the accumulated pressure upon Spanish resources of decades of international conflict. Bankrupt again in 1596, Philip II accepted the mediation of the papacy in the Treaty of Vervins (May 1598). With the restoration to France of Calais, Amiens, Metz, Toul and Verdun, the settlement achieved at Câteau-Cambrésis in 1559 was virtually restored. Bellièvre's declaration that Vervins was 'the most advantageous treaty that France had concluded for five hundred years', sounds like an exaggeration, yet it echoed the relief of the French that the realm had been preserved in the face of a great foreign threat.

FINANCIAL CRISIS

Overcoming or buying off political opponents and fighting a great patriotic war had undoubtedly strengthened Henry IV's political position by 1598, but the vast expense of both policies greatly aggravated the enormous financial difficulties of the French crown. The financial legacy inherited from Henry III had, in any case, been little short of catastrophic. Mounting military costs and reduced income from taxation had created a capital debt of some 138 million *livres*. As late as 1596, some 20 per cent of royal revenue was still finding its way into the hands of the crown's political opponents in the localities, and the senior financial officers of the state were universally suspected of corruption.

The political and military urgency of Henry's position ruled out many elementary remedies. It was impossible, for instance, to write off international debts when further support from Germany, the Netherlands or England remained so important. In the interests of stability in the localities, it became necessary to cancel outstanding back-payments of the *taille* and of ecclesiastical taxes (1594). The repeated advice of Henry's Huguenot supporters to plunder the wealth of the Church had to be ignored when the political advantages of Catholic support remained so great. The king gained little by approaching the representative institutions of the realm with projects of financial reform or increased taxation, for the provincial estates were quick to plead their own poverty. In 1596 the Estates of Rouergue could provide barely half of the 396,000 *livres* that the king requested, while those of Quercy found only a quarter of their allotted 400,000 *livres*. When the fall of Amiens to the Spanish left the realm in a state of renewed crisis, Henry was still forced to meet the emergency by familiar, yet damaging measures, such as the sale of offices and of royal lands. The demand for financial stabilisation was urgent even by the standards of late-sixteenth-century France.

SOCIAL CRISIS AND RECOVERY

Continuing peasant unrest was another product of this economic turmoil. Disorders flared in Brittany in 1590, in the *Gaultiers* risings in Normandy (1589) and in those of the *Bonnets Rouges* in Burgundy in 1594. Most serious of all were the risings of the *Croquants* in 1593 in Périgord and Limousin. Their primary targets were the renegade captains who had preyed upon peasant livestock during the wars and the urban profiteers and financiers who had grown fat while the peasants suffered.

Widespread as the *Croquant* movement was, however, it provided further evidence of the essential strength of Henry's position. It was bitterly opposed to the economic and political chaos brought about by rebellious nobles and soldiers of fortune. It looked for leadership to the peasants' legitimate social superiors, and petitioned the king for the restoration of order and of just authority. Henry's inclination was indeed to disarm the revolt by kind words rather than by force. In May 1594 he accepted the major demands of the *Croquants*, and dispatched commissions to calm the localities and to spread the word of his good intentions. When a further failure of the harvest the following year led to renewed *Croquant* activity, the provincial gentry and nobility could no longer be restrained, and the movement petered out in skirmishes between peasants and those whose social pre-eminence was threatened. The rising of the *Croquants* represented the last major popular challenge faced by Henry's government. 'It advertised the fact that direct taxation had a clear limit beyond which it became unendurable. It indicated how important genuine peace and recovery were to preserve traditional French society' (Mark Greengrass).

The latter years of Henry's reign undoubtedly witnessed a degree of social and economic recovery in rural France. Localised research in many parts of France, in Languedoc, in Anjou and in the region around Paris, reveals similar trends in population figures. A fall in the number of baptisms by around 25 per cent in the last quarter of the sixteenth century gave way to a steady increase in the first quarter of the new century. Paris itself experienced a rise in population from a probable 275,000 (*c.*1580) to an estimated 415,000 in 1637. After the food shortages of the 1590s, France was free of major crop failures and famines until 1630.

We should beware, nevertheless, of regarding the last decade of Henry's reign as a 'golden age' for the French peasant. The English ambassador, Sir George Carew, writing in 1609, described the peasants as 'so infinitely oppressed, as they have their mouths filled with imprecations and bitter complaints; exclaiming that their king seeketh not to be *Roi des Français*, but *des Gueux* [King of the Beggars]'. This view is partly supported by local research showing a significant fall in the amount of land directly owned by smallholders. This also shows that in the southern part of France, at least, improved harvests and markets were offset by rising rents.

SULLY AND RECOVERY

With France enjoying her greatest degree of domestic stability for forty years, the conditions were right for the crown's financial decline to be arrested. This was also made possible by the emergence of an energetic minister. The background of Maximilian de Béthune, baron Sully, was an unusual one for a great minister of France. He was a soldier rather than a legal specialist, and he was a Protestant. Sully's main recommendation for high office was that he had been the king's faithful follower for nearly twenty years.

Sully's approach to financial matters always remained that of the soldier. It was already evident at the Assembly of Notables in 1596 that, while more traditional ministers such as Bellièvre sought to solve the crown's problems by compromise and caution, Sully advocated direct and ruthless action. When he was commissioned to seek out financial mismanagement and corruption in the localities (1595–6), at least four *receveurs* were arrested and about 300,000 *écus* were rescued for the royal coffers. In 1598 he was made Superintendent of Finances, and a year later he assumed control of France's communications system and of its fortifications and artillery. From 1600 he was the most prominent member of the king's inner cabinet.

Sully was never an original or imaginative financier. Instead, he accepted the need to rectify the royal deficit by the ruthless exploitation and rationalisation of existing resources. The *taille*, the most important direct tax, was lowered as it had been before the civil wars, but a greater profit was secured from the *gabelle*, both by increasing the price of salt and by raising the quantity that each individual was bound to buy. Fraud was pursued and prosecuted with unparalleled vigour, and substantial sums were secured for the crown by forcing those convicted of corruption to part with their ill-gotten gains. Similarly, titles to exemption from payment of the *taille* were closely examined, and up to 40,000 false claims detected. Finally, the contracts of many tax-farmers were cancelled and renegotiated on terms more favourable to the crown.

The single true innovation of Sully's financial career confirms this theme of placing convenience ahead of long-term planning. The *paulette*, introduced in 1604, was an annual tax on the value of offices. Its payment permitted the holder of the office to regard his post as hereditary and to pass it on to his descendants. Bitterly opposed by Bellièvre and other ministers, the new tax benefited the crown in two short-term respects – by bringing in revenue and by making the king the great patron of office-holders, when great nobles might otherwise have patronised and influenced them. In the longer term, of course, it multiplied and made more permanent the already well-established evils of venality of office.

The advent of peace after 1598 gave Sully the opportunity to reduce royal expenditure by a dramatic decrease in the armed forces. In Champagne the annual sum raised for the payment of troops, which reached 600,000 *livres* per year at the height of the wars, fell to 266,000 *livres* in 1599, while Brittany experienced an even more dramatic drop, from 1.9 million *livres* in 1597 to 100,000 in 1599.

Sully also achieved a dramatic reduction in the crown's debts. Henry's international debts, which stood in 1598 at more than 40 million *livres*, were reduced by a series of deals that varied from the skilful to the highly dubious. The Duke of Tuscany was persuaded (1600) to write off Henry's debts to him as part of the dowry of Marie de Medici on her marriage to the French king. The English were persuaded (1603) to view a 3-million-*livres* subsidy paid by France to the Netherlands as repayment of part of France's debt to England. Domestic debts posed an even more extensive problem, with some 40 million *livres* owed in arrears on *rentes* payments by the turn of the century. The crown's attempts to abandon interest payments on these debts were hugely unpopular, but could not effectively be resisted.

Sully's achievement was spectacular, although limited in its long-term impact. From a position of abject bankruptcy in 1589, Henry was estimated by Sully to be worth about 32.5 million *livres* in 1608. Between one-quarter and one-fifth of this sum was made up of the vast store of treasure kept in the Bastille as ready cash 'to provide for the security of the state'. This solvency, however, was the result of extraordinary expedients rather than of any fundamental innovation in the financing of the state's activities. A renewal of heavy state expenditure could easily renew the financial problems of earlier decades, and so it was to prove.

20.2 Key figures

BELLIÈVRE, Pomponne de (1529–1607). Active in diplomatic relations with Swiss cantons (1564–71). Councillor to Henry III and *surintendant des finances* (1575). Chancellor of France (1599–1605). Opposed Sully over the introduction of the *paulette* tax, and retired in semi-disgrace (1605).

LAFFÉMAS, Barthélemy de (1545–1612). Protestant economist, and a long-term servant of Henry of Navarre. Controller General of Commerce (1602). A leading advocate of mercantilist economic theories and of industrial development in France.

MAYENNE, Charles, Duke of (1554–1611). Second son of Francis, Duke of Guise. Succeeded his brother Henry at the head of the Catholic League (1588). Declared 'Lieutenant-General of France' by the Parlement of Paris (1589). Collaborated with Spanish troops against Henry IV, but made his peace with the king in 1595.

SULLY, Maximilien de Béthune, baron (1560–1641). Offspring of minor Huguenot nobility. Survivor of St Bartholomew massacre (1572). Fought in the army of Henry of Navarre, including the battles of Arques (1589) and Ivry (1590), and subsequently became Henry's leading minister. Member of Council of State (1594). *Surintendant des finances* (1598). Superintendent of Buildings (1600). Governor of the Bastille (1602). Governor of Poitou (1603). Duc de Sully (1606). Marshal of France (1634).

COMMERCIAL RECOVERY

Henry IV's conquest of his kingdom and the war with Spain further crippled French commercial activity. This final round of hostilities hit the northern regions of France with unprecedented severity and, similarly, studies of prices in Paris, Lyon and as far south as Toulouse show a steady rise during the 1590s. By the time peace was established in 1598, the list of economic casualties was long and harrowing. Lyon was never to recover its pre-eminence in European banking; Marseilles and other Mediterranean ports had been severely harmed, both by war in their hinterland and by Spanish interference at sea; textile exports from Amiens and Brittany had been wrecked; the coinage had degenerated into a proliferation of local varieties that threatened the realm with commercial chaos. In addition, famine and plague, caused both by military activity and by natural factors, repeatedly struck French towns.

Impossible as it was to restore all this in a decade of stability, a remarkable degree of recovery was achieved once the wars came to an end. Much of that recovery, too, was due to the direct action of Henry's government. Two men bear a large degree of responsibility for this government intervention. One of them was Sully, his competence extended by the variety of offices he held. As *Grand Voyer de France* from 1599, all roads, bridges and canals in the realm came under his supervision. In addition, he was responsible for the supply of all military materials. Important new bridges were built at Péronne, Amiens, Abbeville and in Paris itself. Reims, Troyes and Dijon were all connected to the sea by new canals. Important revisions were made in the system of internal tolls and duties, reducing the cost of transporting goods within the realm.

Sully's hand can also be seen in the body of government legislation concerning national commerce. The laws concerning bankruptcy were revised, the nobility were offered inducements to participate in trade, and trading companies were established to deal with the East Indies (1604) and 'New France' (1605). The interests of foreign trade were also served by a treaty with England (1606) and the threat of retaliatory trade sanctions against Spain (1604), which protected French commerce in those quarters.

The second prominent contribution was made by Barthélemy de Laffémas. In his capacity as Controller of Commerce from 1602, it was his task to direct the newly established Council of Commerce in its consideration of various schemes of re-establishment and innovation. In general, he followed mercantilist lines, forbidding the export of French raw materials and discouraging the import of finished goods from abroad. Perhaps his most spectacular success was the growth of the French silk industry, which by the mid-century constituted the main commercial activity in Lyon, Nîmes, Tours and Montpellier. The establishment of the Gobelins tapestry works in Paris was another monument to his work.

THE RECOVERY OF ROYAL AUTHORITY

A monarchy based upon the purchased loyalty of former enemies and upon the grudging acquiescence of a religious minority could not be satisfactory to Henry IV in the long run. French *politiques* had never ceased to stress the divine mystique and the practical authority of the monarchy, and Henry remained faithful to that tradition.

Henry's administration identified two main challenges to the authority of the crown. The first of these came from the representative institutions of the realm. To a large extent, these had regained their earlier legal and fiscal roles, on both a national and a local level, during the years of national instability, and the government was quick to reverse that trend. The Estates-General were never summoned in Henry's reign, and significant attacks were launched upon the powers of the provincial estates. Above all, notably in Guyenne, the role played by the estates in the levying of taxation was taken over by the administrative courts, known as *élections*. Evidence exists to suggest that Sully hoped in the long run to establish *élections* in all of the *Pays d'État*.

Sully encountered a greater degree of obstruction from the nobility who, in their roles as provincial governors, resented incursions into their own areas of patronage. It was thus of the greatest importance to the government to find an alternative to the administrative influence of the great warrior nobles of France, the *noblesse d'épée*. Consistently, therefore, it sought to establish and to promote the *noblesse de robe*, whose nobility depended upon service to the crown in legal and political administration. With the exceptions of Damville and of Sully himself, all the most prominent members of Henry's council, men such as Villeroy, Jeannin, Bellièvre and Brulart de Sillery, were 'men of the gown'.

Inevitably, such measures provoked opposition amongst the greater nobility. The largest revolt, that of the Marshal of Biron in 1600, involved the Montmorency and Montpensier families, and received support from Spain and Savoy. Biron's execution, however, seemed to prove that the heyday of provincial noble rebellion was past. The agitation of Bouillon in Limousin and around Sedan in 1606 was controlled by equally prompt, if less draconian, military action. It was also necessary to counteract the influence of noble patronage at a lower administrative level. It is far from coincidental, therefore, that the only truly novel element in Sully's financial policy was a measure that involved the direct obligation of office-holders to the crown. The *paulette* tax was proposed only four months after the execution of Biron.

Few monarchs of the age understood better than Henry the importance of re-establishing the mystique, the public image and impact of royalty. The new king, despite the restraints upon his financial resources, returned eagerly to the conspicuous display practised by the Valois monarchy at its peak. In particular he returned to the architectural traditions of Francis I and Henry II. Of the major royal residences that survive in France today, the Louvre, Saint-Germain-en-Laye and Fontainebleau clearly show the impact of Henry's reign, and further ambitious projects were undertaken at Vincennes and Blois. Overall, according to Sully's calculations as *surintendant des bâtiments* from 1602, the king spent some 6 million *livres* on building works between 1594 and 1607.

For all this, many Frenchmen never forgave what they saw as Henry's earlier heresies and betrayals, and it is estimated that he had survived twenty-three assassination attempts before, on 14 May 1610, he was stabbed to death by François Ravaillac while his carriage was stuck in a Paris traffic jam. Whereas the assassin of Henry III had been treated in some circles as a popular hero, Henry IV's killer bore the full weight of public hatred and condemnation. His public execution lasted an hour and a half, during which time Ravaillac was scalded with molten lead, torn with red-hot pincers, and ripped limb from limb by wild horses. Once he was dead, 'the entire populace hurled themselves upon the body with their swords, knives, sticks and anything else to hand and began beating, hacking and tearing at it'. The dreadful scene provided a favourable posthumous verdict upon Henry's success in restoring the charisma and the popularity of the French monarchy.

FRENCH FOREIGN POLICY: *PAX GALLICANA*, 1598–1610

In his memoirs, Sully created the myth that the foreign policy of Henry IV in the years after the Treaty of Vervins constituted a 'Grand Design'. His claim was that the French king dedicated himself to the removal of Spanish influence from all parts of Europe north of the Pyrenees. In reality, although it lacked the consistency and coherence of a 'Grand Design', French policy was indeed guided by an acute awareness of the dangers of Habsburg power.

In particular, the focus of French attention was upon the 'Spanish Road', the land route by which Spain maintained communications with the Netherlands. With the western sea routes to the Low Countries effectively closed by a combination of Dutch, English and French hostility, this eastern land route became the key to all Spanish initiatives in the Netherlands. All major political developments in these eastern regions were matters of great interest to the French crown.

The financial and political state of his own realm, on the other hand, made it important for Henry to avoid outright war with Spain. This became clear during France's confrontation with Savoy in 1600. Unable to cajole Charles Emmanuel of Savoy into returning the disputed territory of Saluzzo, seized in 1588, Henry judged the matter worthy of military intervention. Despite initial success, however, Henry appeared to take fright at the prospect of Spanish intervention on the side of Savoy, and agreed to a relatively unsatisfactory settlement. By the Treaty of Lyon (January 1601), France gained Bresse, Bugey and Gex, French-speaking territories to the west of the Rhône, while Saluzzo remained in the possession of Savoy. These new territories rendered Spain's communications highly vulnerable to French pressure in wartime.

For most of the next decade French foreign policy assumed a distinctly defensive air. Substantial sums were spent on modern fortifications, as at Metz and Rocroi, to confine the Spaniards to their own sphere of influence. Diplomatically, the basis of French policy seems to have been to repair and consolidate traditional friendships rather than to construct any grand anti-Spanish coalition. Relations with the Protestant cantons of Switzerland were restored by an agreement at Soleure in October 1601, and substantial subsidies to the Dutch were renewed in 1603. Yet Henry showed no desire to commit himself more positively to an anti-Spanish course, ignoring opportunities in the Netherlands during the siege of Ostend (1601–4) and in Germany during the Spanish invasion of Cleves-Jülich in 1598.

Nevertheless, the affairs of Cleves-Jülich came closest to ending France's decade of peace. In 1609 the duchy was occupied by Spanish forces acting on behalf of the Emperor Rudolf II. Such an increase in Habsburg influence in so sensitive an area could not be ignored by France. Henry issued an ultimatum to the Emperor (October 1609) and, mobilising in conjunction with the German Protestant princes, had raised an army of 50,000 men by May 1610. Henry's sudden death leaves historians uncertain whether his preparations should be seen as a piece of diplomatic brinkmanship or whether he really felt ready to open a new phase of European conflict. What can be stated with confidence is that the foreign policy of Henry IV, like his restoration of financial and political stability, remained incomplete and vulnerable in 1610.

Further reading

D.J. Buisseret (1984) *Henry IV, King of France*. London.

M. Greengrass (1984) *France in the Age of Henri IV: The Struggle for Stability*. London. (2nd edn 1996.)

J.H.M. Salmon (1975) *Society in Crisis: France in the Sixteenth Century*. London.

• APPENDIX •

Comparative Questions

1 Compare the problems that faced the Catholic Monarchs upon their accession in Castile with those that faced Henry VII in England. By what methods and with what comparative success were these problems confronted? (Consult Chapters Seven and Eight.)

2 Compare the methods and success of Thomas Wolsey and Thomas Cromwell in their domestic administration. (Consult Chapters Ten and Eleven.)

3 Compare the foreign aspirations of the kings of France between 1490 and 1530 with those of the kings of England at the same time. (Consult Chapters Eight, Nine and Ten.)

4 In what respects was royal authority greater at the death of Henry VIII than at the death of his father? (Consult Chapters Eight, Ten and Eleven.)

5 Compare the control exercised by Henry VIII over the Church within his realm in 1540 with that exercised at the same time by (a) the King of France, and (b) the King of Castile. (Consult Chapters Seven, Eleven and Twelve.)

6 Compare the governmental systems of Castile and France in the first half of the sixteenth century. (Consult Chapters Seven and Twelve.)

7 Were the wars that Francis I fought in Italy a major factor in weakening the French monarchy? (Consult Chapters Nine and Twelve.)

8 How similar were the motives of the German Protestant princes in the period 1520–40 to those of French Huguenots later in the century? (Consult Chapters Four, Thirteen and Fifteen.)

9 Compare the impact of Calvinism in France and in the British Isles. (Consult Chapters Five, Fifteen, Eighteen and Nineteen.)

10 Why did Charles V find it harder to govern Germany in partnership with the nobility than to govern Spain in that way? (Consult Chapters Seven and Thirteen.)

11 Was Elizabeth's government more stable in the 1560s than the governments of Edward and Mary had been? (Consult Chapters Fourteen, Eighteen and Nineteen.)

12 What similarities were there between the Schmalkaldic League in Germany and the Catholic League in France? (Consult Chapters Thirteen and Fifteen.)

13 In what ways was the religious dissent faced by the French crown in the second half of the sixteenth century more serious than that faced by the English crown at the same time? (Consult Chapters Fifteen, Eighteen and Nineteen.)

14 Compare the problems faced by Philip II in the Netherlands with those faced by his father in Germany. (Consult Chapters Thirteen and Seventeen.)

15 Compare the methods by which Elizabeth of England and Philip of Spain governed their realms. (Consult Chapters Sixteen, Seventeen, Eighteen and Nineteen.)

16 How different were the methods by which various kings of France tried to govern their realm between 1515 and 1610? Why were some more successful than others? (Consult Chapters Twelve, Fifteen and Twenty.)

17 In what respects, if any, was Spain a stronger and more prosperous country in the later sixteenth century as a result of her settlement of the New World? (Consult Chapters Three, Seven and Seventeen.)

18 Did the movement for reform within the Catholic Church have more impact in the New World than in the old? (Consult Chapters Three and Six.)

19 In what respects did Luther and Zwingli take criticism of the Church beyond the limits established by Erasmus? (Consult Chapters Two and Four.)

20 What elements were there in the religious revolt in Germany above and beyond those contributed by Luther? (Consult Chapters Four and Thirteen.)

21 Compare the impact of the Catholic Counter-Reformation on (a) the papacy, (b) Spain, and (c) England. (Consult Chapters Six, Seventeen and Nineteen.)

22 Compare the religious priorities of Ignatius Loyola with those of (a) Erasmus and (b) Calvin. (Consult Chapters Two, Five and Six.)

• INDEX •

Note: a page number in **bold** type indicates that a definition of the term may be found on that page.